National Intelligencer Newspaper Abstracts 1860

Joan M. Dixon

HERITAGE BOOKS
2009

HERITAGE BOOKS
AN IMPRINT OF HERITAGE BOOKS, INC.

Books, CDs, and more—Worldwide

For our listing of thousands of titles see our website at
www.HeritageBooks.com

Published 2009 by
HERITAGE BOOKS, INC.
Publishing Division
100 Railroad Ave. #104
Westminster, Maryland 21157

Copyright © 2009 Joan M. Dixon

All rights reserved. No part of this book may be reproduced or transmitted in any form or by any means, electronic or mechanical, including photocopying, recording or by any information storage and retrieval system without written permission from the author, except for the inclusion of brief quotations in a review.

International Standard Book Numbers
Paperbound: 978-0-7884-4791-4
Clothbound: 978-0-7884-8065-2

NATIONAL INTELLIGENCER NEWSPAPER
WASHINGTON, D C
1860

TABLE OF CONTENTS

Daily National Intelligencer, Washington, D C, 1860: pg 1

Acts passed in the 1st Session of the 36th Congress: 193-194
Alexandria City election: 81
Army Chaplains: 245
Alexandria [Va] city election: 84
Americans at Buckingham Palace Ball: 207
Annals of England: 60
Appointments by the President: 139; 177; 264; 272
Appropriations made during the 1st Session of the 36th Congress: 234-239
Baltimore Methodist Episcopal Conference: 83
Bids for laying water pipe in Washington City: 108
Bids for building new Center Market-house, Washington: 90
Bronze doors for the Capitol: 168
Cadets appointed by the President at West Point: 102
Columbia Engine Co: 8

Commencements: Gtwn College: 207
                      Medical Dept of Gtwn College: 79
                      Nat'l Medical College: 73
                      St Mary's Institute, Chas Co, Md: 227
                      Visitation Academy, Gtwn: 210; 211-212

Death of Jerome Bonaparte: 204-205
Death of Francis Otway Byrd: 143
Death of Mrs Elizabeth Crockett: 92
Death of Cmdor David Geisinger: 82
Death of David Hearmand: 32
Death of John Hewson: 6
Death of Maj Gen Thos Sidney Jesup: 177
Death of Miss Eliza Louis Matthews [Sr Mary Stanislaus]: 286
Death of Maj Gen Duncan McDonald: 320
Death of Col Michael Nourse: 317
Death of Benj S Pope: 10
Death of Capt Horace B Sawyer: 54

Death of Mr Edwin Sheriff; 90
Death of Cmdor Chas Wm Skinner: 281-282
Death of Col Joseph Tuley: 189
Death of John M Wyse: 91

Ellicott's Mills, Md: 15
English family of Geo Washington: 324-325
Gtwn, D C, tax sale: 71
Indian massacres-Texas: 329
Indian tribes in Massachusetts: 16
Jury-Washington City: 78; 187; 315
Ladies Washington Nat'l Monument Society: 252
Land Warrants-reissued: 259
Marquis of Bute: 289
Methodist Protestant Conference-Balt, Md: 101
Midshipmen: 186
Missionaries: 205
Mount Olivet Cemetery: 167; 171
Occupation of Fort Sumter by Maj Anderson, U S Army: 338
Officers of the Savannah: 304
Officers of the Corp of Washington City: 55-58
Police for Washington's Birthday: 62-64
Putnam Phalanx: 316
Railroad accident in Florida: 160
Redemption of Virginia certificates: 266-268
San Francisco-murdered by the Indians: 169
Speech of Mr Lincoln: 308

Steamer Lady Elgin disaster: See Index
Steamer H R W Hill disaster: 294; 297
Steamer Hungarian disaster: 70; 96
Steamer Ben Lewis disaster: 197
Steamer Pacific disaster: 309
Steamer R F Sass disaster: 154

Survivors of the steamer Walker: 192; 195
U S Consuls: 14
Washington City tax sale: 39-49
Water Board of Gtwn, D C: 61
Will of Henry D Gilpin: 36
Will of John Rose: 69

Index: pg 339

PREFACE
Daily National Intelligencer Newspaper Abstracts
1860
Joan M Dixon

The National Intelligencer & Washington Advertiser is hereafter the Daily National Intelligencer. It was the first newspaper printed in Washington, D C; Samuel H Smith, the originator. The same was transferred to Jos Gales, jr on Aug 31, 1810; on Nov 1, 1812, the paper was under the firm of Jos Gales, sr, & Wm W Seaton. The Library of Congress has microfilm of the paper from the first issue of Oct 31, 1800 thru Jan 8, 1870, the final paper. The Evening Star Newspaper of Jan 10, 1870 reports: The Intelligencer is discontinued: the proprietor, Mr Alex Delmar, says that having lost several thousand dollars, & being in poor health, he has resolved to discontinue its publication.

Included in the abstracts are advertisements; appointments by the President; Hse o/Rep petitions; passed Acts; legal notices; marriages; deaths; mscl notices; social events; military promotions; court cases; deaths by accident; & maritime information-officers-crews. Items or events which might be a clue as to the location, age or relationship of an individual are copied.

No attempt has been made to correct the spelling. Due to the length of some articles, it was necessary to present only the highlights of same. Chancery and Equity records are copied as written.

The index contains all surnames and *tracts of lands/places*. **Maritime vessels** are found under barge, boat, brig, frig, schn'r, ship, sloop, steamboat, tugboat, yacht or vessel.

ABBREVIATIONS:

AA CO	ANNE ARUNDEL COUNTY
CMDER	COMMANDER
CMDOR	COMMODOR
ELIZ	ELIZABETH
ELIZA	ELIZA
MONTG CO	MONTGOMERY COUNTY
PG CO	PRINCE GEORGE'S CO
WASH, D C	WASHINGTON, DISTRICT OF COLUMBIA

BOOKS IN THE NATIONAL INTELLIGENCER NEWSPAPER SERIES: 1800-1805/1806-1810/1811-1813/1814-1817/1818-1820/1821-1823/1824-1826/1827-1829/1830-1831/1832-1833/1834-1835/1836-1837/1838-1839/1840/1841/1842/1843/1844/1845/1846/1847/ 1848/1849/ 1850/1851/1852/1853/1854/1855/1856/1857/1858/1859/1860.
SPECIAL: CIVIL WAR 2 VOLS, 1861-1865

Dedicated to my cousin:
Audrey Neff
Born 1920, Wash, D C
Died: 1997, Chesapeake, Va
Married: 1943, Wash, D C
Arthur Clarence [Ace] Mullen
Born 1919, Montana

DAILY NATIONAL INTELLIGENCER NEWSPAPER
WASHINGTON, D C
1860

MON JAN 2, 1860
Trustee's sale of valuable farm in Montg Co, Md, containing 233¼ acres, more or less, at auction, on Jan 12, on the premises, formerly a part of the *Gaither estate*, known as *Exchange*; adjoins the land of a certain Jas Lee; per survey made by Wm Smith on Jun 27, 1803; *Culver's Chance*-on a boundary; with improvements thereon. The property is near the road leading from *Gettings' Cross Roads*, on the *Colvesville* or *Burnt Mill Road*, & the *Cross Roads* on the Brookville Turnpike, adjoining the farms of the late Jas Lee & Dr Mackle. –Asbury Lloyd, trustee -A Green auct

Obit-died: on Dec 31, in Wash City, Hon Isaac Blackford, senior Judge of the Court of Claims. He was appointed to his honorable & important trust by Pres Pierce in 1853; was a resident of the State of Indiana, at the time of his appointment.

Died: on Wed, at his residence in Jersey City, in his 64th year, Hon Jas S Nevius, formerly Judge of the Supreme Court of N J. He presided as Judge until impaired health incapacitated him for professional duties.

Died: on Dec 19, at Richmond, Texas, suddenly of apoplexy, Hon Mirabeau B Lamar, late U S Minister to Central America. The deceased played a prominent part in the struggle of the Texas colonists for independence of the Mexican Gov't, & was the second Pres of the Republic of Texas.

At the village of Eauclaire, Wisc, on Dec 23, Mr N B Boyden, receiver of public money for the Chippewa land district, was gagged & bound hand & foot, & the Gov't safe robbed of $5,360. He was in his office at the time. –Free Press

Fatal affray in the bar-room of the St Chas, at New Orleans, on Dec 20, between Edw L Israel & Geo Ross, two well known sporting men of that city. Israel shot Ross, who died soon after being removed to the Charity Hospital. They both had been drinking freely.

Mrd: on Dec 29, by Rev Fr O'Toole, Mr Chas W Schell to Miss Mary F Irving, all of Wash City.

Mrd: on Dec 27, 1859, at Falkland, Pitt Co, N C, by Rev Henry Pettz, Rev Needham Cobb, of Greenville, N C, to Miss M Louisa Cobb, of the former place.

Died: on Sat, at his residence in Wash, Hon Isaac Blackford, Presiding Judge of the Court of Claims, aged 73 years. His funeral will take place this afternoon at 3 o'clock, from Mrs Carter's, Capitol Hill.

Circuit Court of Wash Co, D C-in Chancery. Judson Mitchell & John Davidson vs Jos Davidson, Eliz E Davidson, Jos Thornton, Lawrence G Colineau. The bill of cmplnt states that John Davidson, Judson Mitchell, John Kurtz, Otho M Linthicum, John Pickrell, Jos Myers, Wm Jewell, Jos Smoot, & Clement Cox, were appointed trustees, & authorized to sell the estate, real & personal of the late Farmers' & Mechanics' Bank of Gtwn; that under the power thus given a contract was entered into with Jos *Davison* on Oct 11, 1848, for the by said trustees for the sale to him of lots 5 thru 8 in square 4, with the Brewery bldgs, erected thereon by the late Wm Hayman; that the terms of said sale were $1,000 cash, & $6,000 on Jan 1, 1850, with interest; that the said Jos *Davison* paid the cash instalment, & took possession of the premises, which he has held to this day & now holds; that at various times he paid several sums of money on account, & there is now due the sum of $3,000 with interest from Dec 31, 1857, which he refuses to pay; that the trustees gave him no deed, but a bond convenanting to convey upon full payment by him of what was due; that the said John Davidson & Judson Mitchell are the sole surviving trustees. The bill further alleges that the said Jos *Davison* has conveyed his equitable title in said premises to one Jos Thornton & his heirs upon certain trusts, for the benefit of Eliz E, the wife of the said Jos *Davison*; & further, that the said Jos Davison & wife have entered into an agreement with one Lawrence G Colineau to sell to him the said premises & to have executed to him a lease, with a covenant therein to sell & convey the same on payment of the purchase money. The object of the bill is to compel the said Jos *Davison* to pay the said sum of $3,000, with interest from Dec 31, 1857, by a day to be appointed by the Court, or else to have the said premises sold by a decree of the Court, for the purpose of paying the said debt & interest & costs of suit. It appears to his Hon Jas S Morsell, one of the Judges of the said Court, that Jos Thornton & Lawrence G Colineau are non-residents of this District, & out of the jurisdiction of the said Court. They are warned to appear in Court, by atty or in person, on or before the said first Monday in May next. –Jas S Morsell, Asst Judge -Marbury & Marbury for cmplnts. –Jno A Smith, clerk [Note: Davidson/Davison, copied as written.]

Miner's [Pottsville, Pa] Journal: Mrs Valentine Frantz, 5 children, & an elder daughter & her husband were moving to St Clair, when the driver had to leave them on a mountain to go home & have his horses' shoes sharpened. Cold & fatigue overcame the family. Mrs Frantz will recover, the babe is well, the boy first taken home has died, & the recovery of the other children is doubtful.

Died: on Dec 30, Dr Henry Dawes Appleton, in his 34th year. His funeral will take place on Jan 2 at 2 o'clock P M, from his late residence on C st, opposite Trinity Church.

Circuit Court of Wash Co, D C-in Chancery. John J Barnard, cmplnt, vs John Ball, David L Shoemaker, Richd P Jackson, & John Febrey, cmplnts. The bill of cmplnt in this case states that one Saml H Howell recovered against John Ball, at the Jan term, 1859, of said court, 2 judgments, one for $166.44, with interest from Feb 3, 1858, till paid, & costs of suit; & the other for $281.85, with interest from Mar 3, 1858, till paid & costs of suit; that writs of fieri facias were issued on both of said judgments & returned nulla bona; that since the return of these, the said John J Barnard has become, by transfer, possessed of both said judgments, copies of which said judgments & transfer are filed with said bill, & the cmplnt avers that the same are still subsisting & unpaid. The bill avers that, at the time of the rendition of said judgment & the issuing of said writs, the said John Ball was possessed of an equity of redemption in lots 9 & 8, in John Tayloe's subdivision of square 518, he having transferred his legal title to the same to Richd P Jackson to secure debts due to the said David L Shoemaker. The bill further alleges that, since the rendition of the said judgments & the return of said writs, the said John Ball sold all his estate & title in said lots to one John Febrey, who is a non resident of this District, & who had full knowledge of the aforesaid judgments; that said Febrey received a deed therefore, which he has not put upon record. The object of this bill is to procure a sale of said lots for the purpose of paying the debts to Shoemaker & the judgments & costs of suit aforesaid. John Febrey is a non-resident of this District: he is warned to appear in court, in person or by atty, on or before the first Monday in May next. –John A Smith, clerk
-J Carter Marbury, for cmplnt -Jas S Morsell, Asst Judge

WED JAN 4, 1860
Senate: 1-Ptn from Nathan Clark, asking compensation for services in preventing certain cannon falling into the hands of the enemy during the war of 1812: referred. 2-Ptn from John S Livermore, asking that the pay of invalid pensioners may commence from the day of disability: referred. 3-Ptn from Edw D Tippett, complaining of the decision of the Court of Claims, & also from Lt John L Worden, of the navy, making a like complaint: referred. 4-Ptn from John H Wickizer, asking compensation for services & expenses incurred in taking the census of Calif in 1850: referred. 5-Ptn from Nancy M Gunsally, formerly the widow of Lyman M Redmond, asking a renewal of her pension: referred. 6-Bill for the relief of Arthur Edwards & his associates: referred. 7-Bill for the relief of Theresa Dardenne, widow of Abraham Dardenne, deceased, & their children: referred.

The Richmond Enquirer of Jan 2 mentions the death, whilst on a visit to the South, of Gen John H Cocke, of Fluvanna Co, an efficient ofcr in the war of 1812. [No death date given-current item.]

Died: on Fri last, in Wash City, Dr Henry Dawes Appleton, aged 34 years. He had been a resident of Wash City about 5 years. In his domestic relations Dr Appleton was a most devoted kind, & affectionate husband, son, father, & brother.

Formula for egg-nogg. Take the yolks of 16 eggs & 12 table spoonsful of pulverized loaf sugar & beat them to the consistence of cream; to this add two-thirds of a nutmeg grated & beat well together; then mix in half a pint of good brandy or rum & 2 wine glasses of Madeira wine. Have ready the whites of the eggs beaten to a stiff froth & beat them into the above mixture. When this is all done stir in 6 pints of milk. There is no heat used. Egg-nogg made in this manner is digestible, &, if taken in moderation, will not cause head-ache. It makes an excellent drink for debilitated persons & a nourishing diet for consumptives.
–Balt Sun

Criminal Court-Wash-Tue. 1-Edw Johnson was acquitted on a charge of stealing boots & shoes. 2-Saml Spalding, Jos Parris, Dennis Magee, & W Delaway were found guilty of riot, & resisting polices ofcrs on Oct 10, in Gtwn. 3-Christopher Bohlayer was convicted on 3 indictments, assault & resisting ofcr Scarf; similar conduct against ofcr Irwin, & a third for assault & battery with intent to kill ofcr Thos Holden. The Court sentenced Bohlayer to one day's imprisonment in the county jail in each of the 2 cases of assault on Scarf & Irwin, & 8 years' imprisonment in the penitentiary in the case for assaulting & shooting ofcr Holden.

The U S sloop-of-war **Vandalia**, Cmder Arthur Sinclair, arrived at N Y on Sunday from Velapraiso, making the passage in 81 days.

Died: on Jan 2, in Wash City, Jas O'Brien, in his 41st year. He was a native of Ireland, but a resident of Wash City for 20 years. May he rest in peace! His funeral will take place from his late residence, 434 6th st, this afternoon at 2 o'clock.

THU JAN 5, 1860
Commodious first-class residence on First st, Gtwn, at Public Auction, on Jan 6: in front of the premises, 72 First st, recently occupied by Robt Ould.
–Barnard + Buckey, aucts

Senate; 1-Ptn from E R Merrill, asking relief on account of injuries received while at work for the Gov't on Bangs' Island, in Portland harbor, Maine: referred. 2-Ptn from Cromwell P Smith, an ordnance sergeant in the army, asking the reimbursement of an amount expended in the transportation of himself & family while traveling under orders, & for performing the duties of assist commissary of subsistence: referred. 3-Ptn from Pesy & Arliffe, asking indemnity for carrying the mails from Little Rock to Wash, Ark: referred. 4-Memorials from H B Sommerville & others, & from Oliver Moor & others, asking that Israel L Clark may be indemnified for depredations committed by Indians in Oregon: referred. 5-Bill for the relief of Chas McCormick, assist surgeon in the U S Navy: referred. 6-Bill for the relief of Simon de Visser & Jose Villarubia, of New Orleans: referred. 7-Bill for the relief of J E Martin: referred. 8-Bill for the relief of Susan E Rhea, late the widow of Dr J Burrows Gardiner, deceased: referred.

Death of the Mother Abbess of the Nuns: Mary Agnes O'Conor, of the <u>Order of Mercy</u>, died on Tue last, after a long & severe illness, & was buried yesterday, the service being performed at the Convent Chapel, in Houston st, by Archbishop Hughes, assisted by Rt Rev Mr Starrs, Vicar Genr'l. The coffin was deposited in the burial vault of the Order. -N Y Tribune, Dec 23.

Fire on Tues in the bldg at 203½, Division st, N Y, took the life of Marks Nathensham, after rescuing his wife & two children. Mrs Christiana Schosser, the keeper of a store, gave the alarm & got her children out of the house quickly.

Triple marriage: about 18 miles from Andalusia, on Oct 16, were married, at the residence of B B Bass, by G A Snowden, Judge of Probate, Jas Teel to Nancy Bass, Wm Teel to Mary Bass, Wilson Bass to Jane Teel. Jas, Wm, & Jane Teel are all sons & daughters of John & Anna Teel. Wilson, Nancy, & Mary Bass are all daughters & son of N B & Eliz Bass, all of Covington Co, Ala. The above connubial attachments were all formed, & but one ceremony delivered, a nuptial phenomenon perhaps unequalled in this State or the South. –Alabama Baptist

Criminal Court-Wash-Wed. 1-Thos Shaughnessy was tried & found guilty of petty larceny, & sentenced to ten months in the county jail. 2-Pink Coakley, colored, was convicted of grand larceny & sentenced to one year in the Penitentiary. 3-Frank Davis was acquitted of assaulting & beating a police ofcr.

Died: on Jan 4, in Gtwn, Edmund Miller, the youngest child of Rev B F Bittinger, in his 3rd year. His funeral will be today at 2 o'clock P M, from the residence of his grandfather, Jos Libbey, No 46 1st st.

Died: on Dec 30, at **Mount Prospect**, his residence, in Bedford Co, Va, in his 66th year, of his age, Hon Robt Allen, for many years a subscriber of this paper.

FRI JAN 6, 1860
Senate: 1-Ptn from Jacob Bigelow, adm of Francis Cazeau, asking that an amount inadvertently paid at the U S Treasury to an importer may be reappropriated for the use of the heirs of said Cazeau: referred. 2-Ptn from Jas C McFarland, postmaster at Meadville, & other citizens of Pa, asking that John Wightman may be compensated for transporting the mail from Pittsburg to Erie, in that State: referred. 3-Ptn from Mrs Ann W Angus, widow of Capt Saml Angus, of the navy, asking the allowance of certain pay: referred. 4-Bill for the relief of the heirs & legal reps of Mark Elisha: referred. 5-Bill for the relief of Solomon Wadsworth: referred.

On Dec 26 an interesting little daughter of Mr Zindorf, residing in Waynesboro, Md, was accidentally burnt to death. Her little brother, who was in the room with his sister, lighted a strip of paper, which he held in his hands until it burnt his fingers, when he let it drop on his sister's lap, catching her dress on fire instantly.

John Hewson, a soldier of the Revolution, died at his residence in Kensington yesterday; born in London in 1767; emigrated to the U S at an early age; joined the patriot army when the Revolutionary war broke out, & served during the war. He was at the battles of Monmouth, Trenton, Princeton, Germantown, & perhaps others; was at Valley Forge, & was also, at one time, captured by the British. Mr Hewson was a calico printer, & the first, it is said, to come to America; & received the first gold medal for manufacturing calico ever given in this country. He amassed considerable money, but he lost it during the financial troubles of 1837. He wrote an interesting memoir of his early recollections, which was published some years since.
-Phil Bulletin, Jan 2

Criminal Court-Wash-Thu. 1-Dennis Mohoney was found guilty for an assault & battery on Chas Wyse, in Gtwn. 2-Philip Parker, colored, found guilty of an assault on a woman, also colored. 3-Patrick Gormley, police ofcr, was tried for an assault & battery on Rudolph Buckley on Dec 26 last. A large number of witnesses were examined on both sides. The jury found Gormley guilty as indicted.

SAT JAN 7, 1860
Phillip Lynch, who killed Geo Coulter, at Bordentown, N J, about 3 months since, has been found guilty & sentenced to be hung at Mount Holly on Mar 23 next.

Rt Rev John N Neumann, D D, Roman Catholic Bishop of Phil died suddenly on Thu. When walking upon the sidewalk in Vine st, near 13th, he fell suddenly dead. Am eminent physician said that the cause of his death was apoplexy. Bishop Neumann was born in Bohemia on Mar 28, 1811; came to America about 1834; ordained a priest by Bishop Dubois, of N Y, on Jun 25, 1836; was the 4th Bishop of Phil. –Phil Press

Mr Peck, the Treasurer of the State of Maine is said to be a defaulter to a large amount. He has held the office of Treasurer since 1856.

Mrd: on Jan 5, by Rev Andrew G Carothers, Mr Fred'k A Stier to Miss Anna E Dorsey, both of Wash City.

Mrd: on Jan 3, at the residence of the bride's father, in Wash City, by Rev Dabney Ball, Mr Jesse B Haw to Miss Annie Edwards.

Mrd: on Jan 5, at Wesley Chapel, by Rev D Ball, Mr Orrin S Morrill to Miss Sarah J Hicks, all of Wash City.

Died: on Jan 6, Colmore Bean, aged 70 years, 3 months & 6 days, formerly of PG Co, Md. His funeral will be on Sunday at 2:30 P M, from his late residence, corner of 3rd & D sts east.

Died: on Jan 4, Otis Gouldin, infant son of John V & M Eliz Smith, aged 10 months & 27 days.

Died: on Jan 4, William R Nicholls, only son of W S Nicholls, of Gtwn, D C. His funeral will be from his father's residence on Gtwn Heights, Jan 7 at 1 o'clock P M.

Died: Miss Hannah Jones Waller, on Dec 26. Death was truly gain to our beloved sister, for she died in Christ. –H

Orphans Court of Wash Co, D C. In the case of Reuben Collins, adm of Mary A Campbell, deceased, the administrator & Court have appointed Jan 28th next, for the final settlement of the personal estate of the deceased, with the assets in hand. -Ed N Roach, Reg/o wills

Mrs Pfeifer, living on Pa ave, between 21st & 22nd sts, a few evenings ago, was severely burnt when her dress took fire. Her life is considerably imperiled.

Criminal Court-Wash-Fri. 1-Patick Gormley, police ofcr, convicted of an assault & battery on Mr Rudolph Buchly, was fined $30. 2-Wm O'Brien convicted of an assault & battery on David Brown, in Gtwn, & fined $5. 3-Dennis Mahoney, convicted of an assault & battery, was fined $6. 4-Cesarino Cesalto, an Italian, was convicted of stealing a horse, buggy, & harness, worth $150, from Mr Ira Hopkins, on Sep 13 last. Counsel prayed for a new trial. 5-Margaret Strother was acquitted on the charge of stealing mousseline-de-laine, valued at $1.50, from Mr Nathan A Schloss, in Gtwn.

Disastrous fire yesterday destroyed the premises of Mr John Walter, cabinet maker, on E st, between 10th & 11th sts; the adjoining dwlg occupied by Mr John Waters, market master; & the shoe store & dwlg of Mr Geo Einolf.

Circuit Court of Fred'k Co, Va, in Chancery. Mary Bush's adm, cmplnt, vs Mary Bush's distributes, dfndnts. Decree Jun 15, 1859. Parties interested in this cause are to appear at my ofc in Winchester, Fred'k Co, Va, on Mar 15, 1860.
–John W Page, Com'r C C F C

MON JAN 9, 1860
From Calif: 1-An application has been made by Judge Terry for a mandamus to compel the County Clerk to transfer the indictment against him for killing Senator Broderick to the Fourth District Court. 2-Col Fremont had obtained possession of all mines adjudged to him by the decision of the courts without any violent collision with the adverse claimants.

Died: on Jan 8, in Wash City, after a long & painful illness, Mrs Eleanor C Bulley, in her 62nd year. Her funeral is on Jan 10, at 2 o'clock, from her late residence, Va ave, near 8th st east.

Com'rs sale of real & personal estate, in pursuance of a decree of the Circuit Court of Fauquier Co, pronounced on Sep 14, 1859, in the chancery cause of Armistead vs Armistead's adm: public auction in Upperville, the tract of land belonging to the widow & devisees of Gen Walker K Armistead, deceased, known as **Ben Lomond**, containing about 350 acres, & a valuable slave named Henry. Apply to Thos N Latham, at Upperville, Va. –Thos N Lathan, Jas V Brooke, Com'rs of sale.

Criminal Court-Wash-Sat. 1-Patrick Keating was convicted for stealing a quantity of wood the property of Hon Amos Kendall: sentenced to 8 months in jail. 2-Buck Sweigart was convicted of assault & battery & sentenced to 6 months in jail. 3-Thos Sweeney was arrested on a bench warrant on a charge of perjury in court. He was one of the principal witnesses for the defence in Christopher Bohlayer's case.

Died: on Jan 7, Henry C Sanford, son of the late Chas H Sanford, of Westmoreland Co, Va, aged 15 years. For the last 15 months he has been the faithful & attentive assistant at the rooms of the Young Men's Christian Association. His funeral is today at 3 o'clock, at the 7th St Presbyterian Church.

Judge Jos Barker, said to be the oldest white native of Ohio, died at his residence at Newport, above Marietta, on Friday morning.

Died: on Jan 3, at Chattanooga, Tenn, Dr Saml M Edwards, aged 30 years, 6th son of Gen Saml M Edwards, of Wash City. The friends of the family are respectfully requested, without further notice, to attend his burial from the Chapel at *Oak Hill Cemetery*, Gtwn, this day, the 9th, at 12 o'clock M.

TUE JAN 10, 1860
First Ward Assoc for the Relief of the Poor meeting at the residence of J C Fearson, 434 19th st, Tue, 7 o'clock. –Jas P Tustin, sec

Meeting of the Columbia Engine Co No 1, on Fri: the following ofcrs were elected: Pres, Jas H Tait; Vice Pres, Jas A Brown; Sec, Jas McDermott; Treasurer, Jos M Adams; Corr Sec, Geo W Hitz; Librarian, P J Ennis; Marshal, Thos H Robinson; Capt of the Engine, Thos Marche; 1st assist, P Roach; 2nd assist, D Barnes; 3rd assist, S Wailes; Capt of the Hose Division, Jacob Dyser; 1st assist, Geo W Thompson; 2nd assist, John S Bootes; 3rd assist, Chas Campbell; Library Cmte, P J Ennis, John S Bootes, A McDermott, P Ferrel, & S Wailes; Election Cmte, Geo W Thompson, C Campbell, P J Ennis, C Kaufman, & Jas Barry.

Two brothers hung. On Dec 16th Jesse [23] & John Lewis [21] were executed in Jacksboro, Campbell Co, Ten, for the murder of S D Queener, sheriff, & Travis Gibson.

Mrd: on Jan 5, at Elmira, Chemung Co, N Y, by Rev David Murdoch, D D, Mr Wm W Cooper, of Wash, D C, to Miss Eleanor J, daughter of Nathan Reynolds, of Elmira.

Mrd: on Jan 9, in Wash City, B D Hyam, of San Francisco, Calif, to Margaret Catharine, youngest daughter of the late F Masi.

Died: Jan 8th, in Wash City, suddenly, of congestion of the brain, Rosanna Hassan, wife of the late Henry Howard, in her 52nd year. Her funeral is on Jan 11th at 10 o'clock, from her late residence, 336 5th st, between I & K sts.

Senate: 1-Ptn from F E Hassler, asking compensation for losses & expenses incurred by his father while Superintendent of the Coast Survey & works for the construction of standards of weights & measures: referred. 2-Ptn from Thos W Brown & others, urging upon Congress the passage of a law granting pensions to the surviving soldiers of the war of 1812, & to the widows of those who were deceased: referred. 3-Ptn from Chas G Ridgely, of the U S Navy, asking remuneration for various expenses necessarily incurred by him as commanding ofcr of the naval force on the South American station in 1820: referred. 4-Ptn from Paul Dillingham & others, asking a change in the time of service of the U S Courts of Vt: referred. 5-Ptn from Zopher B Holcomb & others, asking that land may be granted to the heirs of those who served in the Indian wars, & of 1812: referred. 6-Ptn from Mary Featherson, asking to be allowed a pension: referred. 7-Ptn from A H Phelps & others of Michigan, asking that the survivors of the war of 1812 be placed upon the pension roll: referred. 8-Ptn from the adm of Mrs Ann Peterson, asking to be allowed the pension due her under the act of 1838: referred. 9-Ptn from Jos Kirwin, an inmate of the Soldiers' Home, for an increase of pension: referred. 10-Ptn from Annie D Reeves, widow of Capt Reeves, formerly of the army, for a pension: referred. 11-Ptn of Jas A Peden, asking to be allowed an outfit as Minister Resident near the Gov't of the Argentine Confederation: referred. 12-Ptn from Wm H Crabbe & other clerks of the navy yard at Phil, asking to be placed on a footing with other yards in regard to pay: referred. 13-Ptn from the exec of the late Mrs Jane McClure, asking that the pension to which she was entitled under the act of Jul, 1838, may be allowed to her children: referred. 14-Cmte on Military Affairs: asked to be discharged from the consideration of the following memorials: Hodges & Landsdale, for indemnity for property destroyed by the British in the war of 1812; John Bronson, for goods destroyed on the Niagara frontier; Alex Miler, for property destroyed in the same war; Marie Gerrard, sole heir of John Hudry, for money expended by said Hudry for the U S in 1814-1815; Wm L S Dearing, for expenses for raising a company of volunteers for service in Fla, & that they be referred to the Cmte of Claims: which was agreed to. Same cmte: asked to be discharged from the consideration of the case of L W Boggs, asking an appropriation for his salary as alcalde & judge under the military gov't of Calif, & that it be referred to the Cmte on the Judiciary: which was agreed to.

John Campbell, son of Hon Lewis D Campbell, late member of Congress, was killed at Hamilton, Ohio, last week, by falling from a freight train. He was in the employ of the Cincinnati, Hamilton, & Dayton railroad.

Criminal Court-Wash-Mon: 1-Edw Ridaway was fined $3 & costs, for assault & resistance to ofcr King in the discharge of his duty. 2-Jas O'Connor was placed on trial for an assault & battery upon Andrew J Kimmel, in Dec last: acquitted.

Died: on Jan 8, in Alexandria, Va, Wm Fowle, in his 77th year. His funeral is today at 3 o'clcok, from his late residence on Prince st.

Died: on Jan 6, in Wash City, of croup, Minnie Hill, infant daughter of Ira A & Olive A Hopkins, aged 2 months & 24 days.

Orphans Court of Wash Co, D C. Letters of administration on the personal estate of Wm A Wilson, late of Wash Co, deceased. –Mary S Wilson, admx

WED JAN 11, 1860
Criminal Court-Wash-Tue. 1-Wm Tobin & Danl Rady were acquitted on the charge of riot. 2-Danl Rady found guilty of an assault & resistance of an ofcr: sentenced to 2 weeks in jail. 3-Clinton Smith, colored, convicted of stealing a coat from a store was sentenced to 15 months in the penitentiary. 4-*John Frere, one of the Auxiliary Guard, was tried for assaulting John & Jas Bligh during an arrest he was making of Jas Bligh: the Jury were out at the adjournment of the Court. 5-Danl Rady, John Leary, Patrick Myers, & David Boyle were indicted for riot, for assaulting & resisting an ofcr: guilty. The first 3 were fined $8, & the last, Boyle, was fined $9. 6-Geo T Allen was admitted to practice at the bar of this Court. 7-A habeas corpus having been obtained for the purpose, Danl Keenan, held by the Marshal of D C on a warrant charging him with murder in Balt, was brought before Judge Merrick, of the Circuit Court, sitting in chambers. The case for Keenan was argued by Chas Lee Jones, & for the U S, in comity to the State of Md, by the District Atty, of D C. Some 10 or 12 witnesses were examined & an alibi satisfactorily proven, the Judge therefore discharged Keenan. [*Jan 12th newspaper: John Frere was acquitted of the assault on Jas Bligh, but convicted of that on John Bligh: fined $20 & costs.]

Died: on Dec 27, Benj S Pope, of Madison Co, Ala, aged 77 years. Mr Pope was a native of Delaware, & in early youth engaged in commercial pursuits in Savannah, Ga; removed to Madison Co in 1815, where he remained a planter until his death. During 12 years of this time he was Register of the Land Ofc for the Hunstville district. He died away from home, but not among strangers. At the residence of his son, Dr Chas A Pope, of St Louis, he breathed his last, & the hands of wife & children smoothed his dying pillow.

Admx's sale of choice wines, on Jan 13, by order of the Orphans Court of Wash Co, D C, belonging to the estate of the late John H Buthman. –A E Buthman, admx -J C McGuire & Co, aucts

On Dec 3- Mr Jacob Diehl, residing near Middleburg, Carroll Co, Md, while gunning, & crossing the Beaver Dam creek on a log, his foot slipped, & falling he struck the cock of his gun against the log, which discharged, the contents entering under his chin & passing entirely through his head, his body falling to the water a corpse.

Boston, Jan 9, 1860. Mr Wm Sawyer & wife were found dead in their bed yesterday at their residence, Haverhill, Mass. Their death was caused by the coal gas escaping from the flue. Mr Sawyer was a member of the firm of Messrs Cheney, Averill & Co, expressmen, of this city. [Jan 12th newspaper: An invalid daughter who slept below stairs, experienced no problem; 3 sons in the attic had severe headaches.]

Died: on Jan 7, in Balt, in her 47th year, Mrs Adela S Graham, wife of Andrew Graham, & daughter of the late Fred'k D Tschiffely, of Wash City.

Died: on Jan 7, in Charlestown, Va, Britannia America, eldest daughter of the late Jabez Rooker, of Wash City.

Senate: 1-Ptn from John Reeves, asking that the U S Minister at Constantinople may be instructed to submit to the Sultan his claim for services while employed & detained in Turkey to construct vessels of war for that Gov't: referred. 2-Ptn from Catharine Hagie, asking a pension for the services of her husband as a volunteer with Gen Lafayette in the war of the Revolution: referred. 3-Ptn from R S Coxe, adm of Anna Gibson, widow of Col Geo Gibson, of the army, asking payment of an amount of money claimed to be due her: referred. 4-Ptn from Nathl Rye, a soldier of the war of 1812, asking to be allowed a pension: referred. 5-Ptn from J W A L & W W Dyer, asking that an amount of tonnage duties exacted from the ship **Corinthian** may be refunded: referred. 6-Ptn from Danl Davis & other citizens of Franklin Co, Maine, & soldiers of the war of 1812, asking that pensions may be granted to the surviving soldiers of that war: referred. 7-Ptn from Henry Hobbs, asking the passage of a law to enable him to locate a land warrant: referred. 8-Ptn from Anna Mitchell, widow of a Revolutionary soldier, asking a pension: referred. 8-Ptn from John H Wheeler, late Minister to Nicaragua, asking compensation for services, losses, & expenses incident to said mission: referred. 9-Bill for the relief of Jas Maccaboy: referred. 10-Bill for the relief of Jeremiah Pendergast: referred. 11-We were led into an error in characterizing the papers presented from Col Wm Gates. They have no reference to a pension, but ask indemnity for property lost by the wreck of the steamer **San Francisco**, whilst conveying U S troops to Calif, in 1853.

Mrd: on Jan 9, in Wash City, by Rev Fr Lynch, Benj D Hyam, of Calif, to Margaret C, youngest daughter of the late Francis Masi, of Wash City.

Died: on Jan 10, in Wash City, of consumption, in his 21st year, Addison Crossfield, son of the late W E Crossfield. His funeral is today at 3 o'clock, from his mother's residence, on 9th st, above N Y ave.

Died: on Tue, in Wash City, after a painful illness, of membrane croup, Georgianna, aged 3 years, 4 months & 28 days, eldest child of Robt & Malinda Downing, & grand-daughter of Thos Foster, late of Winchester, Va.

THU JAN 12, 1860

Senate: 1-Ptn from Edwin Green & others, citizens of Wash, asking the grant of a charter to an association for making passenger railway from the Navy Yard to Gtwn, D C: referred. 2-Ptn from Mary J Maltby, asking to be allowed a pension as widow of the late Lt Jas West, of the army. 3-Cmte on Naval Affairs: bill for the relief of David D Porter; of Richd W Meade; of Gen B Bacon, late acting purser of the sloop-of-war **Portsmouth**; of Saml A West, Geo McCullough, Hiram McCullough, & Chas Pendergrast. 4-Cmte on Indian Affairs: memorial of Tilman Leak, asking that certain money paid by him for land which had been previously sold & patented by the U S to certain persons may be refunded, submitted a report accompanied by a bill for his relief. 5-Cmte on Naval Affairs: bill for the relief of Mrs Ann Scott, widow of Wm B Scott, deceased.

The Phil papers announce the death in that city, on Jan 7, of Peter A Browne, an eminent lawyer, in his 78th year. Reference is made to the many enterprises of interest to Phil projected & carried out by Mr Browne's influence & energy.

Gen John B Plauche, a veteran soldier of the war of 1812, died at New Orleans on Jan 2, in his 75th year. He was an efficient ofcr under Gen Jackson in the defence of that city in 1814-1815.

Bangor Whig: Mrs Polly Spencer, of Lincoln, Maine, now in her 78th year, spun 40 skeins of woolen yarn, each skein containing 7 knots, in 5 successive days in Dec, in addition to doing the house work for a family of 6 persons.

On Christmas day, Mr W P Dulin, residing near Easton, Md, had a loaded revolver lying on a bed in the room where himself & his little child, wife, & another lady were, & in a playful manner he pointed it at the ladies, then the ball taking effect in the cheek below the brain. Mr Dulin was frantic with distress. The wound was at first supposed to be mortal, but it is now hoped Mrs Dulin will recover.

Ex-Pres Pierce & Mrs Pierce were to have sailed from N Y, on Sat, for Nassau.

Dr Wm R Palmer, who was arrested in Memphis, Tenn, some weeks ago, on account of supposed complicity in the schemes of John Brown, died at the Planter's Hotel, in Memphis, on Dec 31, of consumption. He had been held to bail to await a requisition from Govn'r Wise.

Criminal Court-Wash-Wed. 1-Henry Williams was found guilty for assault & battery with attempt to kill Edw Entwisle, on Capitol Hill, in Mar, 1858. He was sentenced to 8 years in the Penitentiary to commence after the expiration of the term he is now serving out.

FRI JAN 13. 1860
Senate: 1-Bills for the relief of Mariano G Vallejo; of Lydia Frazer, admx of John Frazer; of Augustus H Evans; of Jas Crooks, surviving partner of Jas & Wm Crooks; of Wm Geiger; & of Thos L Edwards, adm of Thos R Gedney.
2-Ptn from Wm Appleton & other merchants of the city of Boston, asking that a drawback may be allowed on Manilla cordage: referred. 3-Ptn from Catharine B Turner, asking remuneration for expenses incurred by her late husband in entertaining while in command of the naval force on a foreign station: referred.
4-Cmte on the District of Columbia: bill for the relief of Michl Nash, of D C.
5-Cmte of Claims: bill for the relief of Mrs Jane McCrabb, widow of the late Capt John W McCrabb, assist quartermaster of the U S army.

Mr John C Miles, of N Y, while attempting to fix his gas metre, which had become frozen up, brought a light too near it, producing an explosion, & very near a conflagration.

Household & kitchen furniture at auction on: Jan 23, by order of the execs, at 440 11th st, between G & H sts, all the personal effects of the late G C Grammer, consisting of general household effects. –Christopher C Grammer, Julius E Grammer, excs. –A Green, auct

$100 reward for runaway negro man Isaac Galloway. He has a sister in Gtwn, D C, belonging to Dr Grafton Tyler, of that place. –Absalom A Hall, Millersville, P O Anne Arundel Co, Md.

Wm Fowle, one of the oldest & most respected citizens of Alexandria, died on Sunday last. He was for many years an active merchant, & engaged largely in foreign & domestic trade. At different periods he filled the offices of Pres of the Alexandria Canal Co & Pres of the Bank of the Old Dominion.

The young man, Chas Polkinhorn, who was present at the time the violence was committed on C W Raborg, deceased, at the Salutation House, by John Essex, surrendered himself on Wed to Marshal Selden. To this course he was undoubtedly advised by his friends. He is now in jail.

SAT JAN 14, 1860
Chief Justice Taney is convalescing & the expected to resume his seat in Court very shortly. His attack was a severe catarrh of pneumonic form.

The Phil papers announce the death at that place on Jan 12, after a brief illness, Rev Jas Ryder, a distinguished clergyman of the Catholic Church. He was in his 60th year. He was eminent as a pulpit orator & as the head of Gtwn College during some of the most prosperous periods of its history.

Execution: Patrick Maude, who was sentenced to death on Oct 24 for the murder of his sister in May last, was executed in the jail bldg at Newark, N J, on Thu last.

The Senate has made the following confirmations. U S Consuls: W L Patterson, of Miss, to Genoa; P Moran, to Valentia; R S Newbold, of Pa, to the Island of Trinidad; J Winston, of Kansas, to Kingston, Jamaica; W G Webb, of Mass, to Zanizibar; W M Smith, of Miss, Consul Gen at Constantinople; R Runnells, of Texas, to San Juan del Sur; J W Maggill, of Ill, to Savilla; L Dent, of Calif, to Guaymas; L W Talbot, of N Y, to Dublin; F B Wells, of N Y, to Bermuda; T H Persse, of N Y, to Galway; J W Quiggle, of Pa, to Antwerp; C H Morgan, of Ky, to Messina; E L Mix, of N Y, to Lambazeque; H Martin, of Delaware, to Matanzas; T W Fox, to Plymouth, England; G H Leavenworth, of N Y, to Bay Islands; J Cunningham, to Seville, Spain; J J Springer, of Pa, to Dresden; L Gulls, to Santander, Spain; J J Barclay, of Va, to Cyprus; S L Gouverneur, of Md, to Foochoo; W Wright, of Md, to Santos. <u>Also the following</u>: A B Greenwood, Com'r of Indian Affairs; E R Geary, Superintendent of Indian Affairs in Oregon & Wash Territory; B S Schoonover, of Pa, Indian agent Upper Missouri Agency; S F Kendrick, of Miss, Indian Agent for New Mexico; D Newcomb, Indian Agent for Oregon; W E Moore, Indian Agent for the Omaha Agency. -Star

Hon Wm F Boone, Judge of the U S District Court for the Territory of New Mexico, died at his residence in Phil on Wed. He had just returned from New Mexico on a short visit to his family, after an absence of a couple of years in the discharge of his duties. He spent 3 years in the public service upon the Isthmus, & in 1858 was appointed by Mr Buchanan Judge of the U S District Court of New Mexico, the duties of which he discharged with ability.

Died: on Jan 13, in Wash City, Victoria Alberta, infant daughter of Edw & Maria Louisa Swann, aged 15 months & 2 days. Her funeral will take place from the residence of her father, on Louisiana ave, Jan 14 at 1 o'clock P M.

Died: on Fri, in Wash City, Danl P Barry, youngest son of the late Jas D Barry & Juliana Barry. His funeral will take place from the residence of his mother, 584 N J ave, Capitol Hill, on Sunday, at 3 o'clock P M.

Died: on Dec 7, in San Francisco, Calif, an infant son of Maj Wm W Mackall, of the U S Army. And, on Dec 10th, Henry C, another son of Maj Mackall, aged 2 years. Maj Mackall has been peculiarly unfortunate. A very short time ago before he sailed for Calif, a few years ago, two of his young children died on the same day within a few hours of each other, both of scarlet fever; & now two children, born to him in Calif, have been taken from him of the same disease.

MON JAN 16, 1860
Died: on Jan 14, at the residence of her mother, in Wash City, Bettie, the wife of Dr Logan Brandt, of Culpeper Co, Va, & eldest daughter of the late Mrs Jas M Selden. Her funeral will take place at 3 o'clock P M this day, from the residence of her mother, N Y ave, near 10th st.

Two lads of 12 years, one a son of Mr Morse & another a son of Mrs Dunbar, while skating at Plymouth, Conn, on Tue, fell through the ice & were drowned.

Lawrence, Mass, Jan 14. The Pemberton Cotton Mills, the scene of the catastrophe, is on Canal st, built some 6 years ago, in Lawrence, Mass. The mill employs 400 to 500 hands. It is supposed that over 200 persons were killed instantly. The fire caught from a lantern of burning fluid, which was accidentally dropped. The remains of Mary Barrett, aged 26, & Catherine Sweeney, aged 22, were discovered in the ruins today, both bodies nearly consumed by fire. The 10 year old daughter of Jas Banner, was also lost. Maurice Palmer, an overseer, perished. John Ward, one of the operatives in the carding room, & his wife, who worked near him, were saved. Miss Olive Bridges seized the hoisting chain of the elevator & went down 5 stories safely. Many others perished but their names have not been published. [Jan 12th newspaper & Jan 13th newspaper coverage contained in the above.]

Died: on Jan 14, Jas McClery, for many years a clerk in the Treasury Dept. His funeral will be on Jan 17, at 2 o'clock, from his late residence, 218 F st. [Jan 27th newspaper: Jas McClery was a native of Ireland, & when a mere boy emigrated with his father to this country; in 1803 he was appointed to a clerkship in the Treasury Dept, wherein he faithfully served for 56 years. He was an active & efficient volunteer in the war of 1812. He died at a ripe old age, leaving an estimable widow & numerous descendants. During the greater part of his life he was a devoted member of the Presbyterian Church.]

TUE JAN 17, 1860
Ellicott's Mills. The citizens of this thriving village are about to take measures to have it incorporated as a city, with a change of name. *Patapso City* is one of the names proposed. Hon John P Kennedy, Col Carroll, R H Archer, Andrew McLaughlin, H R Hazlehurst, & other property owners have called a town meeting to be held there with the view of securing the proposed charter.

Senate: 1-Ptn from Geo H Derby, Lt of the Topographical Engineers, asking the enactment of a law providing for the retirement of ofcrs who have become disabled: referred. 2-Ptn from Oliver R Guild & 260 others, asking that the militia of the Indian wars & that of 1812 may be placed on the same footing in regard to bounty land as those who served in the war with Mexico: referred. From the same, asking that pensions may be allowed to the militia of the war of 1812, & widows of those deceased: referred. 3-Ptn from Peter Joseph, for an increase of pension: referred. 4-Ptn from Asa Marsh, asking that the militia who served in the Indian wars of 1812 may be placed on the same footing in regard to bounty land; &, asking that pensions may be allowed to the militia of the war of 1812: referred. 5-Ptn from F W Pelton & others, asking that the militia of the Indian wars & those of 1812 may be placed on the same footing, in regard to bounty land, as those who served in the war with Mexico: referred. 6-Ptn from Wm Maxwell Wood, surgeon in the navy, asking compensation for services performed by him under the orders of flag ofcr Jas Armstrong: referred. 7-Ptn from the adm of Ruth Murphy, asking for arrears of pension, & from the adm of Wm White, deceased, asking for the same: referred. 8-Cmte on Indian Affairs: bills for the relief of Livingston, Kinkead & Co; & of Geo Stealey. 9-Bill granting a pension to Mrs Macomb, widow of Maj Gen Alex Macomb. 10-Bill to authorize & direct the settlement of the accounts of Ross Wilkins, Jas Witherell, & Solomon Sibley.

The last relics of the Indian tribes in Massachusetts, few & feeble, still make their annual appearance before the people in the reports of their appointed guardians. The Natick tribe seems to have dwindled to Patience Blodgett & Patty Jefferson & her family, living in East Douglas, for whom the guardian expended $77 last year, including $27 of the guardian's expenses. There are about 70 of the Troy Indians, of whom 50 live on their lands in Fall River. The amount expended for the support of their poor was $373. The Dudley tribe numbers 70, of whom only 13 live on their lands at Webster, for whose comfort the State expended $740 last year, besides the salary of their guardian. The expenditures for the Marshpee Indians were $2,398, & for the Herring Pond tribe $1,122.

Died, in Twinsburgh, Summit Co, Ohio, Jan 4, 1860, Mrs Molly Post, widow of Joshua Post, deceased. Mr Post came with his family from Saybrook, Conn, to Northfield, in Summit [then Portage] Co in 1820 & died in 1822, leaving Mrs Post on a new & but little improved farm, with 13 children, 2 sons & 11 daughters, in quite moderate circumstances as to property; but her energy, industry, & good economy overcame all pecuniary difficulties, so that she not only cared well for her own household, but gave liberally to her less fortunate neighbors. All of her children were respectably married in early life, & each one of the 13 raised a family of children, ten of which families have resided in Twinsburgh. Her posterity now living is 11 children, 75 grandchildren, [only 3 of her grandchildren have ever died, except a few infants,] 57 great-grandchildren-in all, of the 3 generations, the total comes to 143.

WED JAN 18, 1860
Senate: 1-Ptn from Ferdinand Coxe, asking an allowance of outfit due him as Charge d'Affaires ad interim at the Court of Brazil: referred. 2-Cmte on Finance: memorial of Ed N Kent, asking compensation for the use of his invention for separating gold from foreign substances, submitted a report, with a bill for his relief. 3-Cmte on Commerce: memorial of Richd Chenery, of San Francisco, Calif, & of Tench Tilghman, for losses sustained in consequence of his consulate, having been abolished by the Spanish Govt while he was on his way to take charge of the same, & of Francis Huttman, asking return of tonnage of light duties exacted & paid by him on Peruvian, Danish, & German vessels, severally reported bills for their relief. 4-Bill to authorize an increase of pension to Jos Verbiski: referred. 5-Bill for relief of Mrs Anne M Smith, widow of the late Brvt Maj Gen Persifer F Smith: referred. 6-Bill for relief of Jeremiah Moors: referred. 7-Bill for the relief of Mrs Eliz M Cocke, widow of Maj Jas H Cocke, late marshal of the district of Texas: referred.

A new gold vein has been found in Meriwether Co, Ga, 4 miles east of the Atlanta & West Point railroad, on the lands of Mr Allen Post. This vein had been penetrated to the depth of about 26 feet, & found at the depth to be about 8 feet thick, & has the appearance of being very rich. A pounding mill is being put up to crush the ore. Lead ore had been found in the neighborhood.

Orphans Court of Wash Co, D C. Letters of administration, with the will annexed, on the personal estate of Harrison P Lewis, late of Wash Co, deceased.
–H S Bowen, adm, w a

Europe: Lord Macaulay died at his residence in London, of disease of the heart, on Dec 28, after 2 weeks' illness. In 1852 he had a serious protracted illness, from declared disease of the heart. He was never married, & his title dies with him. Thos Barington Macaulay was born in 1800, the son of a wealthy merchant, & studied at Trinity College, Cambridge, winning some of the highest honors of the Univ. His War of the League & his Lays of Ancient Rome, have given him a reputation as a poet, but it is in the field of critical & historical writing that he had gained the widest reputation. [Jan 30th newspaper: The funeral of Lord Macaulay took place at Westminster Abbey on Jan 9th & the remains were interred in the Poet's Corner, in the midst of many of England's most distinguished authors. Among the pall-bearers were the Lord Chancellor, the Speaker of the House of Commons, Lord John Russell, & Earl Carlisle.]

Orphans Court of Wash Co, D C. In the case of Annia E Taylor, excx of Vincent J Taylor, deceased, the excx & Court have appointed Feb 18, for the final settlement of the personal estate of said dec'd, of the assets in hand.
-Ed N Roach, Reg/o wills

Mrd: on Jan 9, by Rev Mr Boyle, Mr Matthew O'Brien, of Balt, Md, to Miss Ella V Scott, of Wash.

Died: on Jan 17, Jas G Berret, infant son of J J & Isabella Geiger. His funeral will take place on Thu at 3 o'clock P M.

The remains of the late Rev Jas Ryder will reach Wash, on Thu next, by the first train of cars from Balt, & be conveyed immediately to Gtwn. At 10 o'clock of the same day the funeral services will take place in Holy Trinity Church.
–John Early, Pres, per P Duddy, Treas [Jan 20th newspaper: The remains of Rev Jas Ryder, D D, will be interred in the new cemetery of Gtwn College. The Philodemic Society, of which the deceased was the founder, made affectionate ceremony in his honor. A eulogy of the deceased, was pronounced by J F McLaughlin, a member.]

Health Report: monthly report of deaths in Wash City, for Dec, 1859: 52.
-Chas F Force, Com'r of Health

New Orleans, Jan 17. B R Webb, the Sec of State of Mississippi, is dead.
[No death date given-current item.]

THU JAN 19, 1860
Senate: 1-Ptn from the heirs of Henry Brockholst Livingston, a lt-col in the Continental army, asking to be allowed half-pay & arrears of pay: referred. 2-Ptn from Henry J Rodgers, author of the American code of signals, asking that the same may be adopted by Congress & distributed to all merchant vessels owned by U S citizens: referred. 3-Ptn from the members of the Legislature of Oregon, asking that pensions may be granted to H H Howard: referred. 4-Cmte on the Judiciary: adverse report on the resolution of the Legislature of Fla relative to the claim of Isaac Welch & other citizens of Fla to reimbursement of expenses incurred as witnesses of the U S, summoned by the marshal. 5-Cmte on Naval Affairs: bill for the relief of Wm D Moseley. Same cmte: bill for the relief of the legal reps of Jas H Frost & Eliza A Johnson.

Orphans Court of Wash Co, D C. Letters of administration, with the will annexed, on the personal estate of Emma A C Goddard, late of Wash Co, deceased. -Margaret E Eckloff, admx, w a

Died: on Jan 18, in Wash City, after a short illness, John Jacob Seufferle, in his 75th year, a native of Wurtemburg, Germany, a resident of the U S for 43 years, & of Wash for the last 25 years. His funeral will be from his late residence, 592 7th st, between D & E sts, [Island,] tomorrow at 3 o'clock.

Criminal Court-Wash-Tue. 1-Selby B Scaggs guilty for an assault on John Lighter: fined $15 & costs. 2-Geo Goldsmith found guilty of assault: fined $1 & costs. 3-Jas Chesley, colored, convicted of larceny.

FRI JAN 20, 1860
Senate: 1-Ptn from M C Dennier, asking remuneration for injuries received & losses sustained in consequence of destruction by fire of a dredging machine in which he was employed as sub-agent of the U S in charge of the St Mary's river improvement: referred. 2-Ptn from Danl Abbott, a soldier of the war of 1812, asking a pension: referred. 3-Ptn from the legal reps of C G Treikel & others, deceased, late clerks in the custom-house at Phil, asking that the compensation due the said clerks may be allowed: referred. 4-Cmte on Commerce: bill for the relief of Eliz M Cocke, widow of the late Maj Jas H Cocke, late Marshal of the District of Texas: report in its favor. 5-Cmte on Territories: asked to be discharged from the consideration of the memorial of David H Burr, surveyor General of Utah, & that it be referred to the Cmte on Public Lands: agreed to. 6-Cmte on Naval Affairs: bill for the relief of Henry Etting, purser of the navy, asking to be credited with the amount paid by him to Lt Rich as judge, & disallowed on the settlement of his accounts. 7-Cmte on Commerce: bill for the relief of Jeremiah Moors. 8-Cmte on Indian Affairs: asked to be discharged from the consideration of the ptn of John Shaw, & that it be referred to the Cmte on Military Affairs: agreed to. 9-Bill for the relief of Eliz Montgomey, heir of Hugh Montgomery: referred. 10-Bill for the relief of Saml V Niles: referred. 11-Bill to authorize the courts to adjudicate the claim of the legal reps of Sieur de Bonne & Chevalier de Repentigny to certain land at Sant de Marine, in the State of Michigan: referred.

Household & kitchen furniture at auction on: Feb 6, by order of the Orphans Court of Wash Co, D C., at the residence of the late G B Scott, deceased, on M st, between 13th & 14th sts, Navy Yard. –Marion M Taylor, adm de bonus non of Geo B Scott, deceased. -A Green auct

Bills have reported in the Va House of Reps granting a pension to Mrs Burley, whose husband was killed at Harper's Ferry, & a pension to Edw McCabe, wounded at Harper's Ferry. It is said the whole expense of the State at the Harper's Ferry affair will not exceed $100,000.

Gen Cass has given to the Board of Education of Detroit a lot of land, valued at $15,000 for a union school house.

In San Francisco, on Dec 5, Fred'k Elmore playfully caught hold of Mr Frank Hussey, a minstrel, & Thos Raleigh Mahan, another minstrel, interfered in behalf of his friend Hussey. A melee ensued. Hussey shot at Elmore, but the ball went through the heart of Mahan, instantly killing him. Mahan was widely known & highly esteemed. He was a native of Phil.

Obit-died: on Jan 15, at his late residence in Fred'k Co, Va, Hon Richd W Barton, formerly a Rep in Congress from the Fred'k district in Va.

Hon John Nelson, an eminent lawyer of Balt, died in Balt Wed, in his 71st year.

Mrd: on Jan 17, at Accokeek Church, St John's Parish, PG Co, Md, by Rev J Chipchase, Edw W Belt to Eleanor Douglas, only daughter of John H Hardesty.

Albany, Jan 19. The illness of Hon Clark B Cochrane has terminated in insanity. He has been taken to Utica Asylum, where it is hoped skillful treatment will restore his reason.

SAT JAN 21, 1860
Dr Livingstone in Africa is thought to have thoroughly seen the elephant. He writes to a London society that somewhere, upon some river, about 800 of these noble animals burst upon his astonished vision, naturally making quite a noise.

The loss of the Balt ship **Flora Temple**, Capt Chas Johnson, has been announced; she sailed from Macao for Havana on Oct 8, 1859, having on board a crew of 50, all told, & 850 coolies; on Oct 14 she struck upon one of the numerous reefs not marked on the charts, which rendered the navigation of the China Sea dangerous. She could not be extricated. The boats were sufficient for the ofcrs & crew, & were taken possession of by them, leaving the vessel & the coolies to their fate. A steamer of war was sent to the reef & scarcely a relic of the ship remained, & in all probability she went to pieces & all on board perished. 18 of the crew in one of the boats, are also supposed to be lost.

Railroad accident on Wed on the Hudson River railroad resulted in the death of Mrs Anna Field, [late Miss Anna Tuttle, who was just married that morning.] Her husband, Mr Thos W Field, of Brooklyn, who was not injured. They were on their way to Wash & the Southern States for a bridal tour. Some of the injured were left at Tarrytown, others at the Getty House, Yonkers, & others were taken to N Y.

Orphans Court of Wash Co, D C. Letters of administration on the personal estate of Hortence Kehrmann, late of Wash Co, deceased. –Henry Sievers, adm

Mrd: on Jan 4, 1860, in Buchanan, at the residence of Jordan Anthony, the bride's uncle, by Rev T M Ambler, Mr P Gilmer Breckenridge to Miss Julia M Anthony, all of Botetourt, Va.

Died: on Jan 20, Mrs Mary A Potts, widow of the late Saml J Potts, in her 64th year. Her funeral will take place on Jan 23, at 11 o'clock, from 497 17th st.

MON JAN 23, 1860
Utica, Jan 20. Dr Gray, Superintendent of the State Asylum, declares that Hon Clark B Cochrane is not in the least insane. He was overtasked by his Congressional & professional duties, & became prostrated & depressed in mind.

On Dec 8, Thos de Quincey died at Edinburgh, near which city he had resided for the past 16 years. For nearly 50 years he has been more or less of an invalid. He has left 20 or more volumes of his interesting life. He was the first man in Europe to appreciate Wordsworth, a fact which speaks volumes for the purity & moral elevation of his tastes. —Journal of Commerce

Trustee's sale of valuable dwlg house & lot, by decree of the Circuit Court of D C, passed in a cause of Isherwood against Barnsley & Duley; auction on Feb 17, of part of lots 150 & 151, in Beatty & Hawkins' addition to Gtwn, with 2 story brick dwlg house & other improvements, being at the s e corner of Market & 3rd sts, now in the occupation of B Clements. —W Redin, trustee -Barnard & Buckey, aucts

Mrd: on Dec 19, at Paris, in the Spanish Embassy, Lydia, youngest daughter of the late Wm Inglis, Edinburgh, Scotland, to M le Chevalier de Llorente, Attache to her Catholic Majesty's Legation in Naples. His Excellency Don A Calderon de la Barca, late Minister of Foreign Affairs in Madrid, gave away the bride. —Gallignani's Messenger

TUE JAN 24, 1860
Rev Mr Marshall, another priest in Phil, died on Jan 4, in 15 days. Rev Fr Vespre, formerly of Gtwn College & the Wash College, is now lying very ill in Phil.

Mr Chas S Jones, Assist Doorkeeper of the Senate, returned to Wash City on Thu last from his trip to Texas, having in his custody Mr Richd Realf, old Brown's Secretary of State, who has already been before the Senate's cmte charged with the investigation of Brown's raid at Harper's Ferry.

Senate: 1-Ptn from Wm Hammond, asking to be allowed an amount of pay which he claims to be due him as clerk of the navy yard at Kittery, Maine: referred. 2-Ptn from the inhabitants of Gtwn, D C, urging the enactment of a law granting the right of way to the Metropolitan Railroad Co: referred. 3-Ptn from Leslie Combs, asking to be allowed a pension for a total disability incurred during the war of 1812, to commence from the said date of said disability: referred. 4-Ptn from Cornelius Hughes, of Hawkins Co, Tenn asking the pension he now received may be increased: referred. 5-Cmte of Claims: bills for the relief of Miles Devine; of Saml H Taylor; & of Thos Crown. 6-Cmte on Pensions: adverse reports on the ptns of Abby S Chaplin & of Mary Everetts; also on the ptn of Wm Allen & John Pickett. Same cmte: bill for the relief of Mrs Ann M Smith, widow of the late brevet Maj Gen Persifer F Smith: recommended its passage. 7-Cmte of Claims: joint resolution relative to the claim of Geo Fisher, late of Fla, deceased. 8-Cmte on Pensions: bill for the relief of Abner Merrill, of the State of Maine. 9-Cmte on Patents & the Patent Ofc: bill for the relief of Jeremiah Pendergast. 10-Bill for the relief of Olivia W Cannon, widow of Jos S Cannon, late a midshipman in the U S Navy.

The New Orleans papers bring us accounts of murders committed in that city within one week: on Jan 8 Thos Purfield died from kicks received in a fight with a man named Pat Cross. Auguste Drose was killed by his step-son, Hermogene Perry, by stabbing him with a dirk-knife. The papers state that Perry's mother, the wife of the murdered man, instigated him to do the deed. This happened on Jan 8. On Jan 11, in the rotunda of the St Chas Hotel, Col W H Peck, of Madison parish, killed Mr Chas N Harris, of Carroll parish, La, who received revolver & bowie-knife wounds.

Rev John Finlay Crowe, founder of Hanover College, near Madison, Indiana, where he has been engaged for 37 years either as pastor, teacher, or professor, died on Tuesday last of ossification of the heart.

Mr Jas Barry, Clerk of the District Court for the Second Judicial District of New Mexico, & Mr E T Davis, formerly a printer at Santa Fe, were lately frozen to death on the road between Taos & Mora.

Circuit Court of Co, D C-in Equity, No 1,527. The Corp of Gtwn against Eliz Jewell, Thos Jewell, & others, excs, devisees, & heirs-at-law of Wm Jewell, deceased. Above parties & creditors of said Wm Jewell are to meet in my ofc, in City Hall, Wash, for a statement of the personal estate of said Jewell.
–W Redin, auditor

Fire in Gtwn yesterday consumed the premises of Mr Cruit, green grocer, corner of Bridge & Wash sts, Gtwn, his family barely escaping, & saving none of their property. The fire extended to the adjoining bldg, occupied by Mr Nixon, watchmaker. The third dwlg, occupied by Mr John Carroll, was considerably injured; also the small frame, inhabited by Wm Williams, on Wash st. The property occupied by Mr Cruit belonged to the estate of the late Mr Bowyer.

Orphans Court of Wash Co, D C. Letters testamentary on the personal estate of Geo Beckert, late of Wash Co, deceased. –Teresa Beckert, excx

Died: on Sunday, in Wash City, Mrs Margaret Ann Elgar Sherman, wife of Chas E Sherman. Her funeral will be from Trinity Church, on 3rd st, today at 2 o'clock. Mrs Sherman was for many years a member of the 4½ Presbyterian Church.

Died: on Dec 22, after a long & painful sickness, Mrs Alice Malihan. Her funeral is today at 10 o'clock A M, from her residence on 7th st, between L & M sts.

To rent-the large & commodious dwlg house belonging to the estate of the late W H Winter, situated on N J ave, near the Canal Bridge. –Alex'r Provest, exc

WED JAN 25, 1860
Prof Espy, the distinguished meteorologist, was attacked with paralysis on Tue last at the house of a relative in Cincinnati. He is about 75 years of age, & it is feared that he will not long survive this attack.

Handsome collection of stuffed birds at our Auction Rooms, on Jan 25, native & South American Stuffed Birds, prepared by A Galbraith, of Phil. The Birds are mounted on single stands or ranged in groups & glass shades. Terms cash. -J C McGuire & Co, aucts

Senate: 1-Additional papers relating to the claim of the widow of Com Matthew C Perry to a pension: submitted. Also, from Jonas P Levy, in relation to his claim against Mexico. 2-Ptn from Alfred Dunham & others, in favor of pensioning the militia who served in the war of 1812, & the widows of those who have died: referred. 3-Ptn from Henry Luce & others, asking that the militia of the Indian wars & that of 1812 may be placed on the same footing as those who served in the war with Mexico: referred. 4-Ptn from Rev B H Mitchell, chaplain in the army, asking that chaplains may be allowed service rations & a servant like commissioned ofcrs: referred. 5-Ptn from the widow of Capt Geo Shepherd, a soldier of the war of the Revolution, asking to be allowed a pension: referred. 6-Ptn from Peter Van Buskirk, asking to be allowed a pension in consideration of his services as commissary during the war of the Revolution: referred. 7-Ptn from Thos H Newell, asking to be allowed the same rate of damages for the detention of money due him as was exacted & paid by him to the U S under similar circumstances: referred. 8-Ptn from Keziah Pritchett, asking to be allowed a pension: referred. 9-Ptn from Capt Florian Kern, asking to be reimbursed the expenses incurred in raising a company of volunteers for the Mexican war: referred. 10-Ptn from Henry Carroll & other citizens of Minnesota, asking the establishment of a mail route from New Ulm, via Leavenworth, to **Fort Ridgely**, in that State: referred. 11-Ptn from Chas McClosky, asking that a pension which he now receives may be increased: referred. 12-Ptn from Alice Hunt, widow of Capt Francis Hunt, asking to be allowed a pension: referred. 13-Ptn from Amherst Crane & others, asking that pensions may be allowed to the militia of the war of 1812 & to the widows of those who have died: referred. 14-Ptn from Laura Humber, widow of Capt Chas H Humber, asking to be allowed a pension: referred.

Mr P T Barnum was nearly suffocated a night or two since in consequence of having neglected to turn off the register in his sleeping-room, the house being heated by a furnace. Mr Barnum found himself unable to walk on awakening in the morning, & although now moving about he is not yet entirely recovered from the effects of his negligence. –N Y Post

Mr Henry Farren, the lessee of the St Louis theatre, died in that city on Jan 8 of a pulmonary complaint.

Gen Robt Butler, Assist Adj Gen to Gen Jackson at the battle of New Orleans, died at his residence at Lake Jackson, near Tallahassee, Fla, on Jan 12. He had been in infirm health for a year or more. Only 3 of Gen Jackson's prominent ofcrs at that battle now survive, viz: Gen Wm O Butler, of Ky; Maj Shotard, of Miss; & Col A P Hayne, of S C.

Mrd: on Jan 2, at the residence of the bride's father, **Cedar Grove**, Mason Co, Ky, by Rev J A Shackelford, Mr Philip T Kaighn, of Leesburg, Va, to Miss Anna E Kirk.

Public sale, by an order of the Orphans' Court of Fred'k Co, Md, the subscriber, as excx of the last will & testament of John Noonan, deceased, will sell at public sale, at City Hotel, in Fred'k City, Md, the following real estate, the highly valuable farm, known as **Richlands**, 2 miles n e of Fred'k City, containing 352 acres; with a 2 story dwlg 50 feet front, with a two-story back bldg of 60 feet; with numerous out bldgs. On Mar 6 will be sold on the premises the entire stock of horses, cows, hogs, sheep, & all the farming implements. –Catharine A Noonan, excx -Jos J Noonan, Hugh McAleer, Agents.

Died: on Jan 24, Jas A Black, in his 38th year, a native of the State of Maine, but for the last 11 years a resident of Wash City. His funeral will take place on Jan 26 at 2 o'clock, from his late residence on I st east, between B & C sts north.

Criminal Court-Wash-Mon: 1-Celia Jenifer, charged with causing the death of her infant child: acquitted. 2-Michl Pfeiffer was tried for bigamy in having married a woman in Gtwn in Nov last, his wife still living in Balt: verdict guilty. 3-John Heineman & wife were convicted for harboring certain slaves, the property of Mr Jas J Fowler, of Wash City. They were convicted on two of the counts of the indictment, but acquitted on the other & found to have harbored the two negroes 18 hours. [Jan 28th newspaper: Mr Heinemann was fined $1.66 for every hour the jury found the negroes were harbored, which fine was therefore $30.]

THU JAN 26, 1860
Household & kitchen furniture at auction on: Jan 30, at the late residence of Geo H Fulmer, deceased, on 461 I, between 4th & 5th sts east. -A Green auct

Senate: 1-Ptn from Geo G Barnard, assignee of Hon David C Broderick, asking that a special act may be passed directing the Treasury of the U S to pay him the amount to which the said Broderick was entitled as Senator at the time of his decease: referred. 2-Ptn from Jas Birdsong, adm of Sallie Ellis, asking to be allowed a pension at the same rate that her husband received from the time of his death to that of her death: referred.

Died: on Tue last, Miss Catherine H Clements, in her 22nd year. Her funeral will be from her mother's residence, on 5th st, between I & K sts, this morning at a quarter before 10 o'clock.

Died: on Jan 25, in Wash City, infant son of Albert G & Carrie C Hall, aged 2 weeks. [No name given for the infant son.]

Died: in Oct last, at Port Townsend, Wash Territory, Oregon, after a very brief illness from disease of the heart, John E Vinson, in his 36th year. The deceased was born in Wash City, where there is still living many classmates who doubtless bear in memory his generous & noble aspirations of heart.

Died: at Dedham, Mass, of consumption, at the residence of her father, Hon W S Damrell, Kate K, wife of John E Gowland, resident of Washington. [No death date given-current item.]

Died: on Jan 24, in Wash City, Alex'r McIntire, in his 68th year. His funeral will be on Jan 26 at 2:30 o'clock, from his residence, 347 K st, opposite Franklin Row. He was the faithful Sec of the Firemen's Ins Co; a native of Delaware, & his father having emigrated to this city in 1798, he consequently was one of our very oldest inhabitants. In the war of 1812 he was a cavalry volunteer, & bravely faced the brunt of battle.
+
Members of the Assoc of the Soldiers of the war of 1812 are requested to attend the funeral of their deceased brother member, Alex'r McIntire.
—Jas Laurenson, sec

Adm's sale: by order of the Orphans' Court of PG Co, Md, the subscriber, as adm of Thos P Ryon, late of said county, deceased, will offer the late residence of said deceased, near **Long Old Fields**, on Feb 8, 3 valuable negro men & one woman, the wife of one of the men. Horses, cows, oxen, etc, wagon & carriage, implements, & household & kitchen furniture at auction, also. —Richd J Ryon, Adm of Thos P Ryon, corner of 9th & D sts, Wash, D C. -A Green auct

Geo Bomford, son of the late Col Bomford, U S Army, died in Florence, Italy, on Dec 17.

Hiram Powers, the sculptor, is reported to be loud in expressions of sympathy for John Brown among the literati at Florence. [This report has been emphatically contradicted.]

FRI JAN 27, 1860
Senate: 1-Cmte on Foreign Relations, to which was referred the bill for the relief of Francis Dainese, recommended its passage. 2-Cmte on the Judiciary: adverse report on the bill to authorize & settle the accounts of Ross Wilkins, Jas Wetherell, & Solomon Sibley. 3-Cmte on Public Lands: bill for the relief of Theresa Dardenne, widow of Abraham Dardenne, deceased, & their children: recommended its passage.

A clerk in the Chicago post ofc, Dennis McCarthy, has been detected in abstracting & opening money letters while he was distributing the mails. He was arrested & committed to jail. The evidence against him is positive.

The Mississippi papers give an account of the killing of Dr Shepherd, of Columbus, Miss, by Jas Blair. Dr S was the nephew of Thompson Shepherd, a most estimable gentleman, residing near Orange Court-house, Va. He formerly resided in Texas, & held the position of Sec of the Navy under Gen Houston, in the time of the Texas Republic.

It is a remarkable fact that nearly all of the candidates for the Vice Presidency in the Democratic Nat'l Convention at Cincinnati June, 1856, have since died. Lynn Boyd, of Ky; J C Dobbin, of N C; Gen Quitman, of Miss; Gen Rusk, of Texas; Aaron V Brown, of Tenn. Gen Quitman was nominated by the eloquent Harris, of Ill, who is also deceased. –Wheeling Union

Telegraphic dispatch from Cincinnati announces the death, by paralysis, of Prof Jas P Espy, of the Nat'l Observatory at Wash. This event was not unexpected.

Valuable red land farm at auction: called *Alma*, containing 524 acres & 28 perches, more or less, in Loudoun Co, Va, binding on the turnpike road leading from Leesburg to Wash City & Alexander, about 25 miles from either city; with a commodious new 2 story dwlg house & needed outbldgs. –Wm B Randolph, A McLean, trustees

Mrd: on Jan 24, by Rev Edw A Colburn, John W Bell to Eliz A Burford, both of Montg Co, Md.

Died: on Jan 25, in Wash City, of consumption, Robert James, eldest son of Robert & Martha A Clarke, aged 18 years, 8 months & 12 days. His funeral will be on Jan 28 at 3 o'clock, from the residence of his parents, on K st, between 8th & 9th sts.

Orphans Court of Wash Co, D C. In the case of Johanna E Ruppart, [late Thoma,] admx, with the will annexed, of Chas Thoma, deceased, the admx & Court have appointed Feb 18 next for the final settlement of the personal estate of said deceased, of the assets in hand. -Ed N Roach, Reg/o wills

Orphans Court of Wash Co, D C. Letters of administration on the personal estate of Alex'r Lee, late of Wash Co, deceased. –Henrietta Lee, admx [All claims, when passed by the Orphans Court of D C., may be left at the ofc of H M Morfit, 4½ st.]

SAT JAN 28, 1860
Two children on Monday, Mary O'Brien, 3, & Mary Ann Curtis, 6, fell into a cistern at N Y, & were drowned before assistance could be rendered.

The <u>Historical Society of New Mexico</u> was organized at Santa Fe, Dec 26, 1859. Ofcrs for the present year are: Col J B Grayson, U S Army, Pres; Wm A Street, Vice Pres; Wm J Sloan, Surgeon U S Army, Corr Sec; D V Whiting, Rec Sec & Treasurer; & W J Howard, Curator & Librarian.

Rev Dr O C Comstock died at the residence of his son in Marshall, Mich, a week since, aged 76 years. He was a physician in what is now Tompkins Co, N Y, & soon represented what was then Seneca Co in the Legislature during 1810 & 1812; elected to Congress in 1813-served until 1819; in about 1819 he abandoned politics, & served at intervals through 3 sessions as chaplain to Congress.
–Albany Journal

Orphans Court of Wash Co, D C. In the case of Josephine *Lewis, admx of Benj *Lews, deceased, the admx & Court have appointed Feb 18 next for the final settlement of the personal estate of the deceased, of the assets in hand.
-Ed N Roach, Reg/o wills [*Names copied as written.]

Died: on Jan 25, Henry Brewer, aged 49 years. His funeral is this afternoon at 3½ o'clock, from his late residence, on West st, Gtwn, D C.

Died: on Jan 27, of chronic croup, Sallie, daughter of C W & Martha D Schuermann, aged 7 years, 3 months & 22 days. Her funeral will be this afternoon at 2½ o'clock, from the residence of her parents, 402 16th st.

MON JAN 30, 1860
Mrd: on Jan 17, in Springfield, Mass, at Christ Church, Mr W Harvey Wheeler, of Grafton, to Miss Ellen P Washburn, of Springfield, Mass.

Circuit Court of D C-Wed. Plntf Mrs Cassandra L Cannon, dfndnt Patrick Dailey. In the declaration: on Jan 31, 1859, the plntf was carelessly driven against by dfndt, who is a hackdriver, so as to cause her to suffer the fracture of an arm & other injuries. The damages were laid at $1,000, but the Jury gave plntf a verdict of $500. For plntf, Robt A Scott.

Died; on Jan 29, in Wash City, after a long & painful illness, Mrs Emily Dalton, wife of Wm Dalton, & daughter of the late Wm Newton Croggon, in her 43rd year. Her funeral is this afternoon at 3 o'clock.

Died: on Jan 29, at **Cole Brook**, E D Addison, eldest daughter of the late John Addison, of Prince Geo Co, Md. Her funeral will be on Tue next at 11 o'clock.

Orphans Court of Wash Co, D C. Letters of administration on the personal estate of Jas A Black, late of Wash Co, deceased. –Saml Hoover, adm

Charleston, Jan 29. Francis Mitchel, late a porter of the steamship **Marion**, was yesterday sentenced to be hung on Mar 2 for assisting a slave in an attempt to leave the State on that steamer.

Phil, Jan 29. Henry D Gilpin, a U S District Atty, under Pres Van Buren, & ex-Mayor of this city, died here this morning.

Orphans Court of Wash Co, D C. In the case of Virginia S Oldfield, admx of Granville S Oldfield, jr, the adms & Court have appointed Feb 21 next, for the final settlement of the personal estate of said deceased, of the assets in hand. -Ed N Roach, Reg/o wills

Orphans Court of Wash Co, D C. Letters of administration on the personal estate of Henry D Appleton, late of Wash Co, deceased. –Catharine M Appleton, admx

TUE JAN 31, 1860
Thos Faulkner, of Halifax Co, Va, who, while intoxicated, had a habit of amusing himself by frightening his wife, carried his joke a little too far a few days since. He tied a rope around the joist, & then around his neck, & stepped from a box, elevating himself so he could easily reach the floor. This time he tied the rope too short & instead of reaching the floor, broke his neck.

Senate: 1-Ptn from John H Riley, adm of Maj Wm Riley, asking the half-pay of capt in the Md line during the war of the Revolution: referred. 2-Ptn from Nicholas Underhill, a soldier of the war of 1812, asking a pension: referred. 3-Additional papers in support of the claim of Brenton Boggs: submitted-referred. 4-Ptn from the widow of Thos Lee Brent, late a capt in the army, asking to be allowed a pension: referred. 5-Additional papers in support of the claim of Jno D Edmesnil: submitted-referred. 6-Cmte of Claims: bill for the relief of Aaron Haight Palmer, for compensation for collecting valuable information & statistics in relation to the trade, commerce, & resources, of the independent Oriental nations, submitted a written report. Same cmte: bill for the relief of W MacPherson for compensation for fitting & furnishing rooms for the U S District Court at San Francisco. Same cmte: bill for the relief of John Hastings. 7-Cmte on Pensions: bill for the relief of the widow of Brig Gen Childs. Same cmte: adverse report on the memorial of Mary Walbach, widow of the late Brig Gen Walbach, for a pension. 8-Cmte on Pensions: adverse reports on the following ptns: of Mrs Eliza J Vandeventer, widow of the late Maj E Vandeventer, asking Congress to provide for a back pension due her husband while holding a commission in the army; of Nathl Rye, a soldier of the war of 1812; of Jos Kerwin, for an increase of pension; & of Jno T Livermore, a soldier of the war of 1812, asking that pay of invalid pensioners may commence from date of disability.

Died: Jan 29, in Gtwn, D C, Mrs Ann Cammack, wife of Edmund Cammack. Her funeral is today at 2:30 PM, from her late residence, Bridge & Market sts.

Jas Young, an expert detective policeman of long experience, died in Phil on Fri last, aged 65 years. He commenced life as a policeman in 1833, at which time Mayor Swift was in power. He died of gout in the stomach, after a few hours' illness.

WED FEB 1, 1860

Vicksburg Whig of the 18th ult: Col Wm D Roy killed in that city by Mr J D Sheppard, which occurred in our streets yesterday. Sheppard stepped up & deliberately shot Sheppard. He is lodged in jail.

Senate: 1-Ptn from A W Von Schmidt & others, deputy surveyors in Calif, asking to be allowed the per centage deducted in the settlement of their accounts: referred. 2-Ptn from the widow of Jos Stout, of the army of the Revolution, asking to be allowed a pension: referred. 3-Ptn from Saml T Hensley, asking compensation for supplies furnished to Indians on the Gov't reserves in Calif, under contract with Indian Com'r: referred. 4-Cmte of Claims: bill for the relief of Eli W Goff, relative to compensation for property rescued while Inspector of Customs. Same cmte: memorial of Alex'r J Atocha, reported a bill further to carry out the provisions of the 15th section of the treaty between the U S & Mexico, concluded on Feb 2, 1848.

Fires in Kent Co, Md: 1-The barn & corn-house of Geo Spry, on Howell's Point, burnt on Thu. 2-On Jan 22, the barn of Abel J Rees, on the Mitchell farm, near the Chesapeake Bay, was burnt, with 8 head of horses, 2 mules, corn cribs, & over 400 bushels of corn. Four negroes have been arrested on suspicion of being incendiaries.

Renewal of copartnership, under the firm of W M Shuster & Co, will continue in the Dry Goods business. –W M Shuster, W H Clagett

Criminal Court-Wash-Mon: 1-Jos Donogue was convicted of a violent assault on John Dunn, in Gtwn, in dragging him from his bed & rolling him in the snow: not yet sentenced. 2-Wm McGee convicted of selling what are called "lottery public tickets." He was fined $100 & 6 months in the county jail. 3-Michl Pfeiffer, convicted of bigamy, sentenced to 4 years in the penitentiary.

Died: on Jan 30, in his 13th year, Archie W Graham, only son of John A Graham, recently of Coosa Co, Ala. His funeral services will take place at 11 o'clock today, at the residence of Mrs Hoyle, 58 Missouri ave, to which the Congressional delegation & the citizens of Alabama resident in Wash City, together with all other friends of Mr Graham, are invited without further notice. He was deprived at an early age of his mother & clung to his remaining parent.

Mrd: on Jan 30, in Wash City, by Rev Mr Nadal, Mr Ebenezer Hallock to Miss Sarah Jane Homan, of Long Island.

THU FEB 2, 1860
Senate: 1-Ptn from Edw D Tippett, a soldier of the war of 1812, asking to be allowed bounty land: referred. 2-Cmte on Military Affairs: bill for the relief of R F Blocker, E J Gurley, & J F Davis. 3-Bill granting to Jas M Hughes & John J Mudd the right of way through the public lands, to construct a line of telegraph from Missouri, Ark, or Texas, to Los Angeles, Calif: referred to the Cmte on Public Lands.

Hon Ely Moore died at Lecompton, Kansas, on Jan 26. He was a native of N J, a printer by trade. He represented N Y C in Congress from 1835 to 1839.

The daughter of Mr John Carhart, of Hickory Grove township, Iowa, aged 12 years, was bit on the arm in Nov last. Last week she complained of pain in her back & general indisposition. Sunday morning last she went into convulsions & died on Monday evening. –Davenport Gaz

The Alexandria [Va] papers announce the decease of John H Higdon. He served through the Mexican war, having left with the volunteers from Alexandria, holding the position of orderly sgt, & was afterwards promoted to adj in the regt of Va volunteers, under Col Hamtramck. At the time of his death he held the commission of adj in the 175th regt. He was at Charlestown during the troubles there. [No death date given-current item.]

The dwlg of John A Rogers, near the village of Indiana, Haldiman Co, Canada West, was destroyed by fire on Jan 20, & a little son, age 5 years, & a daughter, age 3 years, were consumed in the bldg.

Orphans Court of Wash Co, D C. In the case of Ellen A Brown, admx of Saml L Brown, the administratrix & Court have appointed Feb 21 next, for the final settlement of the personal estate of the deceased, of the assets in hand.
-Ed N Roach, Reg/o wills

Rev Jos Addison Alexander, D D, one of the learned faculty of the Princeton Theological Seminary, died on Sat last at his late residence in Princeton. Only a short time ago we announced the decease of his elder brother, Rev Jas Waddel Alexander, D D, who was scarcely less eminent as a divine. Rev Jos A Alexander was the 3rd son of the late Rev Archibald Alexander, D D, & was born in Phil, Apr 24, 1809; 1826 graduate of Princeton. –Phil Journal

Hon Henry D Gilpin, who died in Phil on Sunday last, was born in that city in 1801; took his degree from the Univ of Pa in 1819; appointed Atty of the U S for Pa in 1832; Solicitor of the Treasury of the U S in 1837; & in 1840 Atty Gen of the Confederacy. From 1826 to 1832 he edited entirely or in part the Atlantic Souvenir, the first literary annual published in America.

Trustee's sale by deed of trust, executed to the subscriber by Jas H Besant & Co, trading under the firm of Jas H Besant & Jos G Waters, at the Point of Rocks, & Jos G Waters & Co, at Gtwn, D C, sale on the premises, at the Point of Rocks, on or before Feb 24, the warehouse & all connected with the firm, many articles too tedious to mention. –Lloyd T Duvall, trustee -Wm B Tabler, auct

Mrd: on Jan 31, in Grace Church, Balt, by Rev Robt Sutton, Mr John F Gray, of Wash Co, to Miss Laura E Claggett, of Fred'k Co, Md.

Died: on Feb 1, in Wash City, Mrs Sylvia Brintnall, wife of S Brintnall, formerly of Watertown, Jefferson Co, N Y. Her funeral will take place at the Church of the Epiphany, on Friday next, at 12 o'clock.

Died: on Jan 31, suddenly, in Gtwn, Mrs Alcinda B, wife of Mr David English. Her funeral is this morning at 11 o'clock, from her late residence, 29 First st.

Died: on Jan 31, after a period of much suffering, Mrs Achsah Robb, consort of Rev John Robb. Her remains will be conveyed to Balt tomorrow morning for interment in *Mount Olivet Cemetery*.

Died: on Wed last, in Gtwn, Henry G Wilson, in his 68th year. His funeral will take place from his late residence, 101 Bridge st, at 3 o'clock.

FRI FEB 3, 1860
On Wed, at the Navy Yard, a young man, Wm Thorn, a machinist in the yard, was so seriously injured as to make it necessary to amputate his right leg yesterday at the Infirmary. The accident was caused by the falling of the piston of the steamer **Pensacola**, which was temporarily removed from its cylinder & imperfectly sustained by the temporary blocking, as to strike the body of Mr Thorn. He is from Wilmington, Dela.

Senate: 1-Additional papers in relation to the claim of Robt Harris: submitted-referred. 2-Ptn from Hugh Wiley, a soldier in the war of 1812, asking to be allowed a pension. 3-Ptn from Kate D Taylor, widow of Lt Capt H P Taylor, asking an increase of pension: referred. 4-Ptn from the heirs of Thos Van Buskirk, asking compensation for supplies furnished the army during the Revolutionary war. 5-Cmte on the Post Ofc & the Post Roads: asked to be discharged from the consideration of the memorial of Jas Myer, & that it be referred to the Cmte of Claims. Same cmte: bill for the relief of Sheldon McKnight; & bill for the relief of Arthur Edwards & his associates. 6-Cmte on Public Lands: bill for the relief of Lee Deatherage & John Deatherage, or their legal reps: recommended its passage.

Orphans Court of Wash Co, D C. Letters testamentary on the personal estate of Henry L Harvey, last of Wash Co, deceased. –Nancy W Harvey, excx

Died: on Feb 1, in Wash City, in his 39th year, after a lingering illness, Mr Jas O'Neill, book-binder, a native of Wash City, & the second son of the late Jas & Mary A M O'Neill. His funeral will take place on Sat at 10 o'clock, from the residence of Mrs Stoops, on 10th st, near C st.

Died: on Feb 1, Ellinor Galligan, in her 75th year, at the residence of her son, Thos Galligan, 11th st east, corner of C st north. Her funeral will be on Friday at 3 o'clock.

Died: on Wed last, in Gtwn, Henry G Wilson, in his 68th year. His funeral will take place from his late residence, 101 Bridge st, at 3 o'clock this afternoon.

SAT FEB 4, 1860
Mrs Eliza Lee Follen, widow of Prof C Follen, of Boston, died on Thu last, of typhus fever. For several years she edited The Child's Friend, & published Selections from Fenelon, & a work entitled the Well-Spent Hour. Her husband was professor of history in Harvard Univ, & was lost by the burning of the steamer **Lexington**, on Long Island Sound.

On Tue the corn-house, stable, & carriage-house belonging to Mr Philip Hill, jr, near **Long Old Fields**, PG Co, Md, together with about 50 barrels of corn, a carriage & farming implements, were consumed by fire. On Jan 21 the dwlg on the farm of Thos W Robinson, near Brandywine, same county, & occupied by Jas J N Edelen, was consumed, with most of the furniture.

David Hearmand, the famous centenarian of Montmartre, recently died in his 109th year. He served under Louis XV & Louis XVI, during the American war, & was in the first campaigns of the French Revolution. Up to the last moment he fully enjoyed his intellectual faculties. Pierre Dumont, a volunteer of 1792, died lately at Berthecourt, near Noailles, aged 91. He was in all the battles of the North & on the Rhine, & only quitted the public service when covered with wounds. The Bishop of Chalons, M de Prilly, is also of the recent dead. He was born at Avignon on Oct 14, 1775, & was the oldest member of the French Episcopacy. He was consecrated Bishop Jan 18, 1824.

Last week, in the Supreme Court at Lockport, a verdict of $3,500 was given against the N Y Central railroad, in favor of Mr Jesse H Warren, for the loss of an arm, owing to an accident on the road.

Hon J M Leach, of N C, has been called home by the alarming illness of a member of his family.

Jas Stephens, convicted of poisoning his wife, was executed at N Y yesterday.

House of Reps: 1-Bills for the relief of Shade Calloway; for the relief of Wm Lyon; & for the relief of Rev Jas Lacey.

On Jan 27, the house of Mr Luther Briggs, Delaware Co, N Y, was consumed by fire & 5 of his children perished: the oldest a daughter age 17, & the youngest age 3 years. One boy age 15 was burnt severely in the face, but they think not fatally. The parents went to spend the evening at a neighbor's about half a mile off, taking with them an infant child, leaving 6 children at home.

Wash City Corp-Jan 30. 1-Ptn of Jas Bligh; of W H Taylor; of Chas Frierick & others, for the remission of a fine: referred to the Cmte of Claims. 2-Ptn of Dr Cornelius Boyle, praying to be refunded certain money paid the Corp by him for paving tax assessed upon lot 10 in square 40, & lot 1 square 26: referred to the Cmte of Claims.

Mrd: on Feb 2, at Balt, by Rev Dr Coxe, Cmder Danl B Ridgely, U S Navy, to Eliz D Rogers, both of that city.

Died: on Jan 9th last, at Los Angeles, Calif, Maj Edw H Fitzgerald, of the 1st regt of dragoons, aged about 40 years. He was an accomplished ofcr & a very estimable gentleman.

Charleston, Feb 3. The Govn'r pardoned Francis Mitchell, who was sentenced to be hung today for assisting a slave to escape from this State on the steamship **Marion**.

MON FEB 6, 1860
Trustee's sale of valuable improved real estate, by decree of the Circuit Court of D C, passed in a cause in which Otis J Preston & others are cmplnts & Thos Welch is dfndnt: public auction of the west part of lot 29 in square 517, Wash City, fronting 24 feet on Mass ave, between 4th & 5th sts, with a frame dwlg house.
-C Ingle, trustee -Jas C McGuire & Co, aucts

Hon Joel Jones, ex-Mayor of Phil, died there on Fri. He was born Oct 25, 1795, in Conn; graduated at Yale College; practiced law in Easton, Pa; held the ofc of Judge of the District Court of Phil under the appointment of Govn'r Wolf, & was Presiding Judge of that Court. He was the first president of Girard College, & held that office 4 years. In 1849 he was elected Mayor of Phil, serving one year, & retired to the practice of the law. He was much beloved & his memory is held in high veneration.

Circuit Court of Wash Co, D C. Jardin et al vs Favier et al. Trustee reported he sold part of lot 2 in square 118 to Henry Emmert, on Jun 29, 1858, for $650; & that he has complied with the terms of the sale. –Jno A Smith, clerk

Orphans Court of Wash Co, D C. Letters of administration on the personal estate of Alex'r McIntire, late of Wash Co, deceased. –Mary M McIntire, admx

Orphans Court of Wash Co, D C. Feb 4, 1860. In the case of Jos Trimble & Jas Adams, adms of Matthew Trimble, deceased, the administrators & Court have appointed Feb 28 next, for the final settlement of the personal estate of said deceased, of the assets in hand. -Ed N Roach, Reg/o wills

Criminal Court-Wash-Sat: 1-Jos Donoghue was sentenced to pay $10 & costs for an assault on John Dunn, in Gtwn.

Mrd: on Feb 1, at Otterbourn, Fred'k Co, Md, by Rev R B Sutton, Wm G Busey, of Gtwn, D C, to Lizzie, daughter of Col Henry Dunlop.

Mrd: at **Mount Air**, PG Co, by Rev Fr Lenegham, John B Semmes, of Wash City, to Eddie Edelin. [No marriage date given. Current item.]

Died: on Jan 29th, at **Prospect Hill**, PG Co, Md, Henry Clay Duvall, in his 26th year.

Meeting of the Journeymen Bookbinders' Society, held on Feb 2, announced the death of Jas O'Neale, one of the members of highest standing in the association. -Jos Mattingly, Theodore Walmsly, Jas Harrison, cmte

Brookland School, at Greenwood Depot, Albemarle Co, Va. A few places have become vacant, which pupils may obtain upon application to the Principal. -Wm Dinwiddie, M A

TUE FEB 7, 1860
Senate: 1-Ptn from Sheldon Johnson & 75 others, asking that the militia of the war of 1812 be placed on the same footing in regard to bounty land as those that served in the war with Mexico: referred. 2-Ptn from W P Bowkay, asking compensation for his services & for certain inventions adopted by the Gov't in ship-bldg: referred. 3-Ptn from Lt T G Corbin, asking the difference of pay between what he received & that of Master during the time he acted in that capacity: referred. 4-Ptn from Wm B Shubrick, asking to be released on the books of the Treasury Dept for liability for a certain sum of money expended by him for the public service as cmder-in-chief of the naval forces in the Pacific: referred. 5-Ptn from Saml S Burton, asking to be allowed the pay & rations while he acted as musician in the war of 1812: referred. 6-Ptn from G R Barrett, asking the payment of a balance due him for revising & codifying the revenue laws of the U S: referred. 7-Cmte of Claims: bill for the relief of David Myerle; of Santiago E Arguello; of John Peebles; of Michl Nourse; of John Robb; of Moses Noble; of Asbury Dickens; of Richd Fitzpatrick; of Charner F Scaife, adm of Gilbert Stalker; & of John Ericsson. Same cmte: asked to be discharged from the consideration of the memorial of Wm Nason & other legal reps of John Lord, & that it be referred to the Cmte on Revolutionary Claims: agreed to. Same cmte: asked to be discharged from the consideration of the memorial of Adolphus G Glawecke & W H De Groot, & that they be referred to the Court of Claims:

agreed to. 8-Cmte on Commerce: adverse to the memorial of Leonard Grant, asking remuneration for the loss of a vessel in consequence of the discontinuance of one of the lights at Cape Elizabeth without giving notice. 9-Cmte on Pensions: adverse report on the bill granting a pension to Mrs McComb, widow of Maj Gen Alex'r McComb. 10-Cmte of Claims: adverse report on the memorial of H G Gallaher. 11-Cmte on Pensions: bill for the relief of Wm Wallace, of Ill, a soldier of the war of 1812. Same cmte: bill for the relief of Nancy H Gunsally; also a bill for the relief of Eliz Spear.

Mr W H Boyd has just issued, in handsome style, his Wash & Gtwn Directory for 1860, a book too convenient & useful for any body to do without, & too well known to need puffing.

Circuit Court of D C-in Equity, No 1,557. Patrick Sweeney against Robt A Hawke. Statement of the trustee's account on Mar 1st next, in my ofc, in City Hall, Wash. —W Redin, auditor

WED FEB 8, 1860

Executor's sale of soap, candles, horses, carriage, buggy, wagon, iron safe-by order of the Orphans Court of D C, sale of the estate of the late Timothy O'Donnoghue: public sale on Feb 14, on the premises, at First & Lingan sts, Wash, D C, all the stock in trade of the firm of T O'Donnoghue & Son. —Sarah O'Donnoghue, Jas O'Donnoghue, Peter O'Donnoghue, excs Thos Dowling, auct

Senate: 1-Additional papers in relation to the claim of Mary T Guthrie, widow of the late Capt Presley N Guthrie, of the army, for a pension: submitted. 2-Ptn from Drayton la Venture, asking that patents may be granted for reservations to half breeds of the Kansas tribe of Indians under the 6th article of the treaty of 1825: referred. 3-Cmte on Naval Affairs: bill for the relief of Cmder H J Hartstene, U S Navy: passed. Same cmte: resolution giving the consent of Congress to Capt Wm B Shubrick to accept a sword presented to him by Capt Genevre & Pres Urquiza, of the Argentine Confederation, & asked its immediate consideration: bill was passed.
4-Cmte on Pensions: adverse report to the ptn of Anna H Allen, a widow of an ofcr of the militia in the war of 1812. Same cmte: bill for the relief of Jas Smith. 5-Cmte of Claims: to be considered: bills for the relief of Nathan Ward; of Thos Fillebrown; of Ernest Fridler; of H & F W Meyer; of Jas Beatty's personal reps; of Cornelius Boyle, adm of John Boyle, deceased; & of Egleston & Battell.

The household of Mr Michl Fitzgerald, of Fairfield, Vt, consisted of father, mother, & 5 children. On Friday all were well; on Sunday following 4 of the children died of scarlet fever; on Tue following the 4 committed to one grave, the remaining child became sick with the same disease & died. —Burlington Sentinel of Feb 3.

The will of Henry D Gilpin: we hear he has bequeathed the whole of his property to his widow during her lifetime; at her decease she may dispose of $100,000 by will as she pleases. The remainder is to be applied to various public uses. His large & valuable library, Mr Gilpin bequeaths at the death of his wife, in whose possession it is to remain until that event takes place, to the Historical Society, & makes provision also for a bldg, in which it is to be properly preserved. He also leaves a handsome bequest to the academy of Fine Arts in this city, & to a public library in Chicago. The executors named by Mr Gilpin are his widow, Mr Chas Macalester, & Chas Gilpin, the former Mayor.
–Phil North American of Feb 2

Orphans Court of Wash Co, D C. Letters of administration on the personal estate of Pollard Webb, late of Wash Co, deceased. –J C Walker, adm

Circuit Court of Wash Co, D C-in Chancery, No 1,576. French S Evans & Susan P Evans, his wife, vs Geo Atkinson & Wm Atkinson. Object of this suit is to procure the conveyance of the legal title to lot 4 in square 368, in Wash City. The bill of cmplnt, in substance, states that said dfndnts, Geo & Wm Atkinson, claiming to be the owners in fee simple as tenants in common of lot 4 of square 368, in Wash City, by an instrument of writing under seal duly made & executed on Feb 8, 1836, authorized & empowered one David A Hall to sell certain property in said city, including said lot 4, at public or private sale, for cash or on credit, & to give full receipts & discharged for the purchase money, & to convey the same to the purchaser thereof by a good & sufficient title. That said Hall, acting as atty for & in the name of said Geo & Wm Atkinson, on Jun 1, 1842, sold lot 4 to one Chas Hibbs, for a full consideration in money & its market value at the time, & on the same day executed & delivered a deed to said Hibbs for the same, containing a covenant of general warranty; & said purchase money was duly paid to said Hall, as atty as aforesaid; that said Hibbs, afterwards, to wit, on Jul 1, 1843, conveyed to your oratrix, your orator's said wife, in fee simple, all of lot 4 in square 368, in Wash City. Geo & Wm Atkinson do not reside in D C, & they are to appear on the first Monday of Jul, 1860, at the ofc of the Clerk of said Court. –Jno A Smith, clerk

Mrd: on Feb 7, by Rev Byron Sunderland, Mr Snowden W Robinson to Miss Elvira E, daughter of Mr Geo B Smith, of Wash.

Died: on Feb 7, after a long & painful illness of 2 years, Mrs Julia F Draper, in her 27th year, wife of N C Draper. Her funeral will take place today at 11 o'clock, from the residence of her husband on 12th st, between B & C, Island.

Augusta, Geo, Feb 7. John W Walker, an overseer, shot Mr John Owens, a merchant, at Waynesborough on Monday, the latter dying of his wounds. The sheriff & his posse, in attempting to arrest Walker, met with resistance. Walker was shot dead, but, unfortunately, in resorting to this necessity his wife & children were fatally wounded.

THU FEB 9, 1860
Household & kitchen furniture at auction on: Feb 13, at the late residence of Henry Brewer, deceased, on West st, between Green & Montgomery sts, Gtwn. –Barnard& Buckey, aucts, Gtwn

Great catalogue sale of books, comprising the collections of the late Mr Templeman & late S G Deeth, of Gtwn, D C. –Joshua Ritchie, adm -J C McGuire & Co, aucts

Mr David P Heap, of Wash City, son of the late Dr S D Heap, who was for years U S Consul for the Regency of Tunis, Barbary, has been appointed British Vice Consul for the port of Pensacola.

At Marblehead, on Wed, a son of Chas Bartlett, 2½ years old, set fire to his clothes playing with matches, & was so severely burned that he died 2 hours after.

Senate: 1-Ptn from Mrs Ann E Smoot, widow of the late Capt Smoot, of the navy, asking the benefit of the 6th section of the act to amend an act to promote the efficiency of the navy: referred. 2-Ordered that the papers on file in the case of Leonard Rose for property destroyed by the Indians be taken from the files & referred to the Cmte on Indian Affairs.

Orphans Court of Wash Co, D C. Letters of administration on the personal estate of Jas McClery, late of Wash Co, deceased. –Christiana McClery, admx

Hawesville, Ky, Feb 7. H A Davidson went into the store of Messrs Duncan yesterday, with a lighted bomb in a basket of eggs. The bomb exploded, blowing the store to pieces, & wounding Hon Wm *Sterrett, C B Duncan, J J C Duncan, Jos Reading, & Wm Berrett, some of them mortally. Davidson, the incendiary, was mortally wounded. It is supposed that the object of the attempt was to kill *Sterrett for his course in regard to the late Lowe tragedy.
*[Two spellings of Sterritt/Sterrett.]

New Haven, Feb 8. Judge Chas A Ingersoll, who was last night reported in a dying state from rheumatism in the stomach, died this morning.

FRI FEB 10, 1860
Accident on Lake George on Wed last. Mr Albert Rand, with his wife & 3 small children, were driving up the lake, when suddenly horse & sleigh went through a crack in the ice. Mr Rand succeeded saving his wife & one child, carrying them to Mr Wheeler's residence. The bodies of the 2 children that were drowned were recovered.

Adm's sale of household & kitchen furniture at auction on: Feb 15, by order of the Orphans Court of D C., at the residence of the late Jas A Black, deceased, on C. st, between Dela ave & 1st st east. –Saml Hoover, adm -A Green auct

Senate: 1-Ptn from Marie, of Griedsburg, Colorado Co, Texas, widow of Oscar Gates, of the 2nd regt of dragoons, asking to be allowed a pension: referred. 2-Ptn from E R V Wright, & 105 others, citizens of N J, asking that the public lands may be laid out in farms for the free & exclusive use of actual settlers: referred. 3-Cmte on Naval Affairs: bill for the relief of Otway H Berry. 4-Cmte on Commerce: bill authorizing the Sec of the Treasury to grant a register to the owners of the barque **Helen Blood** & the barque **Sarah Bond**. Same cmte: bill for the relief of Francis Huttmann in relation to losses in consequence of illegal proceedings on the part of the collector of customs at San Francisco. 5-Cmte on Pensions: bill for the relief of Jeremiah Pendergast, of D C, for an increase of pension. Same cmte: adverse report on the ptn of Mary J Maltby for a pension, as widow of the late Jas West.

Capt Harrison, the well known cmder of the ship **Great Eastern**, lost his life by the upsetting of a boat near Southampton. He was crossing the Solent from his residence at Hythe to Southampton on Jan 21, in his own gig, in company with Dr Watson, the surgeon of the **Great Eastern**, Capt Lay, the chief purser, & a son of the latter. The boat was manned by 6 picked men, including Ogden, the coxswain of the **Great Eastern**. The weather was very squally & a heavy gust of wind capsized the boat. Capt Harrison clung to the boat, but fell into the waves. He was picked up but to restore animation was fruitless. Ogden, the coxswain, & Capt Jay's son also fell victims to the disaster. The event created a painful sensation throughout England.

Dissolution, Jan 9, of the copartnership existing under the firm of Young, Simpson & Co, by mutual consent. Jno B Young & Aldridge Young have sold their interest to Thos P Simpson, who is fully authorized to receive & receipt all claims against said firm. –Jno B Young, Thos P Simpson, Aldridge Young
+
The undersigned have this day entered into copartnership, in the Gen Wine & Liquor businesss, under the firm of Thos P Simpson & Co, 525 7th st, under the Avenue House. –Thos P Simpson, Aldridge Young

A daughter of Owen Relch, of Easton, Penn, aged about 2 years, died the other day from having eaten the tops of two or three matches. –Harrisburg Union

Obit-died: Chas A Ingersoll, Judge of the U S Court for the district of Conn, [says the New Haven Journal,] died at his residence in this city on Tue, at age 63. He has been suffering for several weeks from a complication of disorders, which have baffled the skill of the most accomplished physicians. He has, since the death of Andrew T Judson, filled the Judgeship of the U S Court for this district with distinguished ability, & also presided in the U S Court for the southern district of N Y during the whole term of his ofc. The complaint of which he died was gout or rheumatism in the stomach.

Balt, Feb 9. Edw Dowling, the former clerk of the Supreme Court, shot himself today, & died instantly.

On Sat night at the Volka Garden, N Y, Mrs Josephine Herskell, having concluded her performance on the tight-rope, leaped from it to the stage & came in contact with the foot-lights, which set fire to her dress, & in an instant she was enveloped in flames. Her husband was in the orchestra, & with others sprang to her assistance. She was frightfully burnt about the body & was conveyed to her residence, where she died the next morning. Her stage name was Louisette. She was about 22 years of age; & has a mother, & a little brother & sister, depending upon her for support, her father being dead.

City Property to be sold for taxes: Collector's ofc, City Hall, Feb 10, 1860. Public auction at City Hall, Wash City, May 8, for taxes due 1858 & 1859. –Jas F Haliday, collector [Earlier dates are noted along with the 1858 & 1859.]

Allen, Albert G
Anderson, Ann [1856]
Armitage, Benj
Alexander, Columbus
Ashton, C H B
Ashford, Craven
Arden, Danl D
Appleby, Geo W
Andrus, Horatio N
Acker, John F
Athey, John
Alexander, Maria, colored
Anderson, Saml J
Armistead, Saml
Adams, Thos N
Avery, Thos
Anderson, Wm, colored
Blakemore, Araminta E
Borland, Alex'r
Bohlayer, A J
Berry, Augustus F, trustee for J F Kidwell
Blanchard, Ann
Beall, Benj [1855]
Baylis, Buckner
Bennett, Clement W
Brooks, Chas
Barrett, Dennis
Biddleman, Danl
Bryant, Edw
Beale, Eliza A & Richd J
Brady, Edw
Brooke, Ellen M
Ballenger, Francis
Bryant, Geo, colored
Bomford, Geo
Brown, Geo, colored
Butler, Geo W
Bittinger, Henry
Bateman, Henry E
Butler, Henry, colored
Bond, Hugh L
Bell, Henry
Barnes, Hanson
Bond, Ignatius
Bush, Jas, colored
Butler, Jas, colored
Brereton, John
Boyle, John
Boss, Jas H
Beaseley, Jos
Bohlayer, John
Burche, John C, in trust for Catharine Burche
Beall, John W
Boyle, Junius J
Barron, Jas
Beck, Jos W
Barry, Julianna
Brickley, John
Bonini, John
Baker, John H

Bronaugh, John C
Butcher, Jas
Bourke, John
Birch, Jacob W
Baker, Mary & Lucy
Brosnahan, Michl
Brooks, Mary
Bosse, Martin
Brown, Michl
Brady, Nathl
Brady, Nathl, in trust for E McGil_on
Byrne, Patrick
Bradley, Phineas J
Briscoe, Palmer, colored
Browning, P W [1855]
Bradley, Phineas
Briscoe, Palmer & Wm Cragg, trustee
Barker, Quinton
Bridget, Richd B
Buckly, Rudolph
Beall, Richd J
Barry, Richd
Brent, R Y, surviving exc, etc [1854-55]
Byington, Saml
Brereton, Saml Bowen, Sayles J
Bowen, Sayles J
Beatley, Sophia M
Burche, Saml
Burley, Thos
Bell, Thos P, colored
Benton, Thos H
Barrett, Thos J
Bicksler, Thos J
Bayne, Thos
Carlisle, Jas M, Geo S Gideon & Walter D Davidge, in trust [1854]
Conroy, Jas
Coombs, J J
Coumbe, John T
Clark, John D
Cudmore, John
Clarke, Jos S & R G Briscoe
Clarke, Jas T
Callan, Jas N

Barnes, Thos
Blanchard, Wm
Barr, Wm
Birch, Wm Henry
Bagman, Wm
Branson, Wm
Bates, Wm
Burns, Wm
Bradley, Wm A
Bush, Wm
Brereton, Wm & Saml
Ball, Wm H
Burdine, Wm
Bradley, Wm
Boone, Wm
Bird, Wm, jr
Browning, Wm A, in trust
Baldwin, Wm T
Cheshire, Archibald
Cazenove, A C
Crown, Ann R, in trust
Chambers, Benj
Chubb, Chas St John
Coddington, Camilia
Church, Chas B
Calvert, Chas, in trust
Carroll, David & others, in trust
Conray, Dominic
Chapman, Eliz
Calvert, Edw
Costigan, Eliza
Coombe, Griffith
Chittenden, H A & H C Bowen [1857]
Chism, John
Clarke, Jos S
Coleman, Jas
Casparis, Jas
Coombe, Jas G
Crutchet, Jas
Carter, John P
Cushley, John
Costigan, John

Cull, Jas
Coombs, Jos J & John Welch
Coyle, Leonidas, & others, in trust
Cragin, Mary F & C H [due for 1858 in the name of H Foxall]
Chandler, Mgt, & W S, for 1857
Cluskey, Michl W
Childs, Mary
Callan, Nicholas, in trust for Jane Lynch
Callan, Nicholas, in trust
Crawford, R R
Clarke, Ruth Ann
Closkey, Robt B
Clarke, Richd H, in trust for E Hassler
Craven, Roady
Coxe, Richd S
Connelly, Robt J
Cochran, Robt
Clements, Rachel & Mary F
Crawford, Rachel Ann
Coakley, Sarah, colored
Clarke, Saml Cassin, Stephen
Chilton, Saml, in trust [1856]
Clarke, Stephen
Cook, Saml
Corcoran, Thos & W W
Corcoran, Thos
Connelly, Thos of John
Chandler, Walter S
Collins, Wm
Cox, Walter S
Chase, Wm H
Cripps, Wm M
Choppin, Wm
Campbell, Wm W
Chafee, Wm E
Cocking, Wm
Clarke, Wm T
Clements, Wm A
Clarke, Wm [1857]
Cox, Washington F
Carrico, Wm H
Cranch, Wm G & A O Dayton [1855]
Dulaney, Adam, colored

Cook, Leonard O
Carbery, Lewis, in trust
Davis, Alex's McD
DeSelding, Chas
Dodge, Chas
Davis, Catharine
Dulaney, Caleb, colored
Davis, Eliz
Deter, Eleanor
Dyer, Edw
Duvall, Edmund B
Dainese, Francis
Dowling, Hugh
Douglas, John
Dobson, Jos
Daley, John
Dixon, Jas
Dixon, Jas & H Naylor [1855]
Deasey, Jeremiah
Downing, Jos
Dalton, Joh
Downs, John & Wm
Daley, Jas [1855]
Devillers, L P
Douglas, Mary Ann
Davidson, Mgt
Dick, Mgt
Donoho, Moses
Donoho, Morgan
Donn, Orlando H
Dick, Robt
Davis, Richd, colored
Douglas, Saml E
Douglas, Stephen A
Drury, Saml T
Decatur, Susan
Donn, Thos C
Donn, Thos C, in trust
Dewey, Timothy
Dutton, Thos
Doniphan, Thornton A
Dove, Wm T [1855]
Dant, Wm E
Durr, Wm

Devers, Wm
Dewees, Wm
Donelan, Wm C
Doniphan, Wm T
Denham, Z W
Ecklof, Edw C
Elliott, Edw C
Elliott, Bernard
Evans, Estwick
Ewell, Fenton M
Emmerson, Geo W
Ennis, Gregory
Easby, John W
Evans, Jos T [1857]
Edelin, Jos
Elvans, John R & G R Thompson
Elvans, John R
Edwards, Lewis
Easby, Wm, in trust for E Denham
Edes, Wm H
Easby, Wm
Finch, David
Fisher, David, [colored]
Farquhar, Edw Y, in trust
Frere, Eliz, & others [1854]
Foy & Ennis [1854]
French, Geo E
Fisher, Geo J & R S Patterson
Felsom, Henry
Farrell, Harriet
Fischer, Harriet & T Gunton
Fischer, Harriet [1855]
Fearson, Jos N [1857]
Fowler, Henderson
Faber, John C
Freeman, John jr, & others
Fuss, John G & L Bart
Fugitt, Jos
Fenno, J Brooks [1857]
Fry, Jas
Fry, Jas T
Ferguson, Jos
Fitzgerald, Jas [1856]
Fraser, Jas, Jr
Fowke, Lucy B
Foy, Mgt & Sarah

Fulmer, Mgt A
Fagan, Mary Ann
Fowke, Mary
Foley, Rebecca
Fearson, Saml S
Franzonie, Virginia & Julia
Frazier, Simon
Ferguson, Wm, colored
Fletcher, Wm
Forrest, Wm H
Gladman, Addison B
Gibson, Amy, colored
Gerecks, Augustus
Graves, Banner
Green, Benj E
Gooch, Chas
Gallant, Edw
Godfrey, Francis
Gunnell, Francis M
Guest, Francis
Garner, Geo W, in trust
Grammer, G C
Gordon, Geo
Gillis, Groenvelt, & others
Garrett, Geo W
Gelston, Hugh
Gray, John A, colored
Greeves, John, in trust
Gadsby, John
Gray, J W D
Galligan, Jas
Goheens, John T
Gardner, Jacob B [1856]
Galligan, Jas & Son [1857]
Greenleaf, Jas
Gerecke, J P
Green, John
Groff, Michl
Gibbons, Mary Ann [1855]
Gallant, Peter
Greenan, Patrick
Grymes, Peyton, in trust
Greeves, Sarah A
Gedney, Thos R
Galligan, Thos
Gadsby, Wm & A Newton

Gunnell, Wm H
Greenwell, Wm E
Goddard, Wm C
Gallant, Wm
Gunton, Wm [1854]
Hyde, Anthony
Hager, Ann
Hetzel, A B
Hamilton, Ann M & others
Humes, Alex'r
Henderson, Archibald
Hicks, Chas, in trust
Haslup, Chas G
Hall, David A [1857]
Holland, Edw
Handy, E G
Hollidge, Eliz
Hoffman, Eliz R B
Haw, Eliza F
Higbee, Frances L & others
Hanna, Francis
Hines, Fred'k
Houzam, Fred'k
Howard, Flodoardo
Hall, Fred'k
Hill, Geo
Hill, Gustavus
Hanson, G D, in trust
Henning, Geo C & Geogianna Thompson
Hinton, Geo W
Horseman, Geo
Haney, Hugh
Heiskell, Henry L
Hoban, Henry
Hunt, H, & B O Tayloe
Hatton, Henry
Humphries, Hezekiah, colored
Herrell, John E
Hollingshead, John S
Hicks, Josiah
Henry, Jas
Hopkins, Ira A
Howard, Jos
Herity, Jas [1857]
Haggerty, Patrick

Hannay, Peter
Hogan, Philip
Harper, Phena
Harrison, Richd
Hollohan, Rose
Hawke, Robt A
Howe, Richd, & Ignatius, jr [1853]
Hobbie, Selah R
Hicks, Sarah Jane
Havenner, Thos
Hickey, Thornton [1855]
Hughes, Thos [1857]
Herbert, W W, in trust for Amelia J
Haggerty, Wm
Herbert, Wm J & T S
Heine, Wm
Hutchinson, Wm
Harper, Wm M
Ingle, Christoper, in trust
Isaacs, Jos C
Ingle, John P
Indermauer, Jeremiah
Iardella, E C, L A, & N M
Jones, Catesby Ap R
Jenes, David, colored
Jones, David, & B Minor
Johnson, Dearborn
Judson, E & wife, & Ann Bailey
Judson, E & Ann Bailey
Jenkins, Ann
Johnson, Josiah, & others
Jewell, Jas G
Johnson, John H
Johnston, Jas D
Jones, Isaac, & J Mazeen
Jordan, Lewis
Johnson, P C
Johnson, Richd W
Johnson, Robt W
Jackson, Thos
Jewell, Wm
Johnson, Wm, colored
Johnson, Wm, of Peter
Jacobi, Wm
Johnston, Wm P
Jones, W W

Kerr, Ann McK
Knox, Charlotte F
Kiernan, Danl
King, Edwin H
Kingman, Eliab
Koones, Fred'k
Keating, Geo
Key, Henry S
Klopfer, Henry A [1856]
Keiser, Henry
Knapp, J Newcomb
King, John H
Kurtz, John & others [1857]
Kelly, Jas
Kedglie, John
Kennedy, Jas [colored]
Kozel, John
Kay, Jas
Keefe, John P
King, Joshua, in trust
Lansdale, H N, in trust for Mrs Ladd
Lansdale, N H, in trust for Martha A Watkins
Lansdale, Henry N, in trust for Sarah P Mickum
Landsdale, Henry N
Lindsley, Harvey
Lenman, John T & Geo B
Lockwood, John A
Lewis, Jos S, use of assignees of John Frye
Lynch, Jas [due for 1858, in Geo Follanabee's name.]
Little, John E
Lafontaine, Jos D
Lane, Jonathan H
Lincoln, Martha A C
Lloyd, R B
Lunt, Sarah, & Peter Daggey
Lomax, Saml F
Lane, Thos H
Lumpkin, Thos
Law, Thos
Luce, Vinal
Lower, Wm S & Geo Barron
Mitchell, A C, in trust for C Goldsborough
Moore, Ann
Macomb, Alex'r
McIntire, Alex'r

Kendall, John E
Kidwell, John H
Kibbey, John B
Kinny, Mary
Knowles, Mary D
Kellar, Michl
King, Martin [1856]
King, Nathan g
Kearen, Robt
Kane, Stephen
Kiernan, Wm
Kibbey, Wm B
Lindsay, Adam
Little, Barbara & others
Lemon, Chas
Linkins, Danl
Lewis, Esther M
Lycett, Edw
Lowry, Geo & others, trustees
Loughborough, Hamilton

Lovejoy, John N & J Y Donn
Lynch, Jeremiah
Lomax, John
Lewis, John [colored]

Markland, A H
Myers, Ann M
McNamara, Anastasiz
McLeod, Alex'r
Moxley, B F
Middleton, B F
Myers, Benj B
Mullin, Basil, colored
Milburn, Benedict
Maniz, Casper
Munck, C H [1857]
McCorkle, Christiana
Miller, Christian
Myers, Chas colored
McDonald, Danl
Mitchell, Dennis & Rebecca
McCarthy, Eugene

Miller, Francis
Mohler, Fred'k
Miller, Francis
Mohun, Francis [1857]
McKnight, Geo B [1857]
Miller, Geo M
Markell, Geo H
Marryman, Horatio R
Marryman, H R, in trust
McCormick, Hugh
Magee, Jas S
Mason, Jas M
Moran, Jas T
Mason, Jos
Mason, John
Mickum, John T
McKnight, John L
McGinnis, John, use of E Hammond, colored
Miller, Jos
Mulloy, John J
Mankin, Jas
McGrann, Jas
Magill, John B
Mount, Jas
Mills, John E & Susan
Murphy, Jeremiah
McGraw, Jas & Eliza A
McWilliams, Jos L
Middleton, L J
Maynard, Lafayette
Martin, L J & M J
Machen, L H
McDowell, Mary B
Morton, Marion & others
Meade, Mgt C
Maxwell, Mary L
Martin, Mary Julia
Milburn, Mgt, in trust
Mitchell, Perry A, colored
Miller, Robt [1855]
McPiers, Sarah
Middleton, Saml colored [1857]
Masoletti, Sarah M [1857]
McNancy, Thos
Mosher, Theodore
Miller, Thos W

McDonald, Jas
McKenny, John S
McGill, John
Melvin, Josiah
Merman, Jane
Morgan, John B [1856]
Miller, John A
Marlow, John W
McCarty, Jas
Marr, Jas D
Meredith, John H
McGinnis, John, jr
McGuire, Jas C
Madigan, John
McCalla, John M
Macnamara, John

Maxcy, Virgil
Maud, Wm
Morton, Wm
McBee, Wilson
Maughlin, Wm W
Marshall, Wm [1857]
Mohun, Wm P
Nailor, Allison
Newton, A, in trust for J Gadsby, jr
Newton, Augustine
Nicholson, A A
Nailor, Dickerson, in trust for A C Nailor
Naylor, Henry, in trust
Naylor, Henry, in trust for E G Beall
Naylor, Henry
Naylor, Joshua S
Nelson, Madison
Newell, Mose
Norris, Wm B
Noyes, Wm
O'Rourke, Bridget
Osborne, E, & children [1856]
Oyster, Geo
Owner, Jas
Osborne, Mgt
O'Donnoghue, Timothy & Peter
O'Donnoghue, Timothy

O'Donnell, Wm & Michl
Price, Cicero
Pairo, Chas W
Phillips, Catharine
Price, Chandler, & S J Bowen
Phelps, Chas H
Peugh, David L
Peter, Geo
Parker, Geo
Page, Geo, & Geo Mattingly
Page, Geo
Parry, Henry
Potts, John
Polk, Jas
Pierce, Jos B
Plant, Jas K
Parke, John
Phillips, Jas B
Phillips, Jas B [another]
Purdy, John
Power, Jas A
Peake, Jas T
Pumphrey, Jackson h [1857]
Preston, Mary, in trust
Pearl, Mary, colored
Prout, Mary
Peters, Mary [1856]
Prather, O J [1856]
Prout, Robt
Posey, Richd
Pollard, Richd J
Pleasonton, Stephen
Proctor, Saml
Petit, Smith [1856]
Phillips, Saml
Peugh, Saml A
Pumphrey, Saml
Platt, S H
Phillips, Thos J
Purcell, Thos
Parker, Thos, & others
Plumsell, Thos
Pitcher, Thos J
Pumphrey, Thos B, & others
Parker, Wm H
Powell, W C & G W Uttermehle

Palmer, Wm G
Preston, Wainwright
Preston, Wm
Philip, Wm H
Pegg, Wm
Quirke, Edw
Quinn, Jas
Queen, John F, in trust
Queen, Maria A
Queen, Wm
Reed, Armistead
Richards, A & T A
Railey, Benedict J L
Rapley, Charity S
Ritchie, Catharine
Reese, Danl M
Ross, Danl, colored
Riley, E O
Reilly, Edmund
Ridgeley, Eliz M & Sophia Prather
Riggs, Geo W
Ryder, Geo F
Ritchie, Hiram
Roberts, John
Ray, Jas
Ricar, J C P
Ree, Jas, in trust [1857]
Ross, Jemima, colored
Rodgers, Johnson K
Rives, John C, in trust
Robinson, John G
Robinson, John G & Jas Friend [1856]
Ready, Jas
Reidy, John
Reeside, John E
Ragan, Jas
Robinson, John
Ricker, Lawrence
Ricker, Lawrence & Mary
Rodgers, Lloyd N
Reardon, Michl
Rannahan, Michl
Rodier, P L
Riley, Philander C [1855]
Rush, Richd

Ridgway, Robt O
Rose, Robt
Ringold, Susan B
Roberts, Sarah
Redfern, Saml
Rollin, Sarah E
Rin, Thos
Ruggles, Wm
Sheppard, Alex'r
Scott, Alfred V
Stoughten, A B
Shucking, Alfred
Sutherland, Ann D
Smith, Archer B
Strother, Benj H
Sands, B F [1856]
Shekell, B O & H N Henning
Shanchesney, Bridget
Sengstack, C P [1856]
Schussler, Chas
Sherman, Chas
Serrin, Danl
Smith, Danl T
Schwinghamer, Eugene
Slater, Eliz [1857]
Selden, E A & E L Knapp
Sommer, Edw
Swan, Edw [1857]
Short, Edw
Saeger, Eli J
Saeger, Eli J & Geo Mathiot
Stelle, Edw B
Shorter, Fanny, colored
Stinzing, Fred'k
Scalla, Francis M
Seitz, Geo [1857]
Semmes, Geo
Smallwood, Geo F
Steers, H, & H C
Suter, John
Sunby, Jas, colored
Schwartz, Jos
Smith, Jas H
Smith, Jas D
Smith, John Geo [1857]
Sims, Ignatius, colored

Sharretts, John F
Sharretts, John F & M A E
Saunders, Jane
Shreeve, Jas H, in trust
Surratt, John H
Scott, Jas W [1857]
Schureman, J H A
Springman, John M
Smitson, John H
Speake, Mary Ann
Scholfield, Mary E
Shinnors, Mary Ann
Sweetzer, Mary E
Simms, Mary C
Speddin, Matilda
Snyder, Nicholas
Sims, P H [1856]
Stacey, Richd
Sewall, Robt
Stettinius, Saml
Shoemaker, Saml M
Schureman, Sarah
Scott, Saml
Smitson, Sarah
Sugrue, Timothy
Sylvester, Thos
Sullivan, Thos
Smith, Thos L & A T
Swann, Wm T
Stewart, Wm & others
Stiger, Wm T
Stewart, Wm
Slade, Wm, colored
Smith, Wm S
Smith, Wm J, in trust
Stonestreet, Wm, colored
Stewart, Wm E
Tayloe, B Ogle
Thomas, Benj F, in trust for Anne E Bryan
Turner, Danl
Thomas, Edw M
Thomas, Edw A
Tull, Eliza Ann
Tilghman, Frisby
Thompson, Geo C

Todsen, Geo P [1857]
Thomas, Geo, in trust
Taylor, Geo
Timms, Henry [1857]
Thomas, Henry
Turton, John B
Turton, Jas E
Toll, Isaac D [1856]
Taggart, Jane L
Tayloe, John
Thompson, Michl, in trust for Mary Peters
Thorn, Mary Jane, in trust for M J & H T Thorn
Towers, Mary M
Taylor, Marion M
Towson, Nathan
Tompkins, Richd, colored
Travers, Sidney V
Turner, Thos
Thomas, Wm H
Turton, Wm
Todd, Wm B
Todd, Wm B & W H Philip
Upshaw, John H
Usher, John W & J Gibson
Van Patten, Chas H
Vass, Douglas
Woodward, C J, M Maguire, & C Miller [1857]
Whelan, Catharine Ann [185]
Wood, Chas F
Wallach, Chas S
Wiltberger, Chas H [1856]
Wilkes, Chas
Weaver, Cyrus M, & others
Waters, David S
Woody, Edw
Worthington, Eliz M
Wheeler, Ephraim, in trust
White, Geo W
Waterston, Geo W
West, Helen M
Whalen, John
Wilson, John
Watson, John J
Wise, John H
Winder, John H
Walters, Jas, & Thos

Towers, John T
Tobin, John
Tretler, John
Towers, John T & Lamue
Tough, John S
Trook, John N
Tucker, John H
Tucker, John W
Towers, Lemuel
Turner, Mary Ann

Varnell, Geo H
Vernon, Henry T
Van Ness, John P
Voss, Lisette J
Van Cortlandt, Philip
Voss, Wm [heirs of]
Venable, Wm P
Venable, Wm S [1855]
Wylie, Andrew
Williams, Anna
Wallingsford, Alfred
Wiltberger & Burche & R W Burche
Williams, Chas, colored
Winder, Chas H

Wood, John
Wroe, Jerome R [1854]
Wise, Jas
Williams, John S
Walker, Jonathan T, in trust
Waring, Jas J
Withers, John
Wise, John H
Williams, Jos [1856]
Wonderlick, John
Weed, J C & N S
Wail, John [1857]
Ward, Jos D
Wilson, John H
Wilson, Jacob
Williams, Lemuel
Wadsworth, Louisa J
Watkins, Martha A
White, Martha R & others

Wilson, Norval
Wagner, Philip F
Wilson, Patrick
Waters, R A
Williams, Sarah B
Wroe, Saml C
Williamson, Thos & Saml Rhodes
Welsh, Thos
Webb, Wm B, in trust for Mary Mechlin
White, Wm G, W, & Jas L [1857]
Wormley, Wm, colored
Willis, Wm B R
Wroe, Wm
Ward, Wm H
Walker, Wm, colored
Wayne, Wm
Wilson, Wm
Walker, Wm B
Weaver, Wm A
Worthington, Wm

Walter, Thos
Weeks, Rachel
Waters, Robt
Wantland, Thos
Ward, Ulysses
West, Virginia O
Ward, Wm J
Whitlock, Wm D

Worrell, Wm
Whitmore, Wm
Young, Alex'r H
Young, Amanda [1856]
Young, John M
Yates, Jas W
Young, Nicholas & others
Young, Noble
Young, Notley [heirs of]
Yeaton, Wm C & wife
Young, Wm L

SAT FEB 11, 1860

Hon S A Smith has resigned the position of Com'r of the Gen Land Ofc at Wash.

Among the passengers lost by the wreck of the steamer **Northerner**, off Cape Mendocino, on Jan 6th, were Mr Bloomfield, a son of the Bishop of London, & Mr French, son of Capt T W French, of the 42nd regt, British Army.

A woman named Deitrich, wife of a German doctor, died at Hagerstown, Md, on Monday, from injuries received by her clothes taking fire. She wore hoops.

The grand jury at Charlestown, Va, have found bills of indictment against Owen Brown, Francis J Merriam, & Jeremiah Anderson, charging them with conspiring with slaves to create insurrection. The persons named are a portion of John Brown's men who have thus far escaped arrest.

Mrd: on Feb 9, by Rev C H Stonestreet, J Fendall Cain to Edwardanna, youngest daughter of the late Edw J Hamilton, of Chas Co, Md.

Died: on Feb 10, in Wash City, after a short & painful illness, Martha Ellen, wife of Thos W Howard, in her 37th year. Her funeral will take place on Sunday at 3 o'clock, from the residence of her husband, near the corner of 9th & I sts.

Died: on Feb 10, Virginia, infant daughter of Wm H & Virginia A Nalley, aged 11 months & 18 days. Her funeral will take place on Sunday next at 2:30 P M, from the residence of her parents, H st, between 4th & 5th sts.

Phil, Feb 10. The gale this morning blew down the new house of the city gas works in the First ward, killing Jas Hart & Wm McLane.

MON FEB 13, 1860
Positive sale of a very valuable farm in PG Co, Md, on Feb 23, on the premises, part of **Greenwood Park Enlarged**, the residence of P Hill, jr, situated on the old Marlborough road, near **Old Long Fields**, containing about 211 3/8th acres; with a spacious dwlg house & out-bldgs. –Wall & Barnard, aucts

The N Y papers announce the death, at his residence, in that city, on Friday last, of Mr Wm E Burton, the popular theatrical manager & comedian, in his 57th year, having been born in London in 1804. –Phil American

Died: on Feb 9, at the Old Mansion, Caroline Co, Va, after a well-spent life, in his 76th year, Wm G Maury, beloved & lamented by all who knew him.

Trustee's sale of valuable farm, by deed of trust dated Nov 8, 1851, duly recorded in Liber J A S No 32, folios 140 thru 145, of the land records of Wash Co, D C, & Liber O N, No 1, folios 312 thru 315, of the land records for PG Co, Md: sale on Apr 23, 1860, on the premises, the farm on the river road leading from the Navy Yard Bridge, about 1 mile beyond the U S Insane Asylum, being parts of 2 certain tracts of land known as **Prevention Enlarged** & **Giesborough Manor**, in Wash Co & PG Co, being the place formerly owned by the late Dr Chas B Hamilton, containing about 365 acres, more or less. Improvements consist of a large & well arranged frame dwlg house & nearly new out-bldgs. –N M McGregor, trustee
-Jas C McGuire & Co, aucts

Circuit Court for St Mary's Co, Md, sitting as a Court of Equity-Nov Term, 1859. Jas L Foxwell vs W J Heard, Com of Lunacy, T S Griffin, Chas Medley, & others. The object of this suit is to obtain a deed for land sold. The bill states that 2 tracts of land, **Beckwith's Lodge**, & **Saturday Chance**, containing 232½ acres, more or less, in said count, were sold to Chas Medley, in a case in equity of John W Bennett, Com'r of Lunacy, against Thos S Griffin; that afterwards the said land was sold by Chas Medley to one John T Moore, who died without paying the said Chas Medley, & by ptn in equity upon the part of the said Chas Medley against the heirs of the sale, John Moore, G Fred Maddox, & Chas Medley were appointed, by a decree in said case, trustees for the sale of the real estate mentioned, at which said sale one Noah Schlosser became the purchaser & paid said purchase money to the trustees; that the said Jas L Foxwell purchased of the said Noah Schlosser & S C Schlosser, his wife, all their interest in said tracts of land; that he has since paid the whole purchase money, & now desires a deed from all the parties, as no title has yet passed; & that the Noah Schlosser & S C Schlosser, his wife, reside out of the State of Md.
-Peter W Crain, Jas T Blakistone, clerk

Information wanted of Thos Englesby, a native of England, laborer, about 42 years of age, who left Phil for Wash on Jun 10th last. He is about 5 feet 11 inches high, & stout built. Address Mrs P Farmer, 744 South 11th st, Phil.

House of Reps: 1-Memorial of Hugh M Solomon, for indemnification for advances of money by his father during the Revolutionary war: referred. 2-Memorial of Wm Johnson, of Phil, for increase of pension, having been entirely disabled in the service of his country, & is now unable to earn a livelihood: referred. 3-Joint resolutions of the Legislature of Iowa for the relief of Jas P Thomas & family: referred. 4-Memorial of John Daly, praying for relief for injuries sustained & loss of property occasioned by attacks of the Mohave Indians: referred.

Died: on Jan 11, in Winchester, Va, after an illness of a few days, Jas Madison Hite, in his 67th year. He was the only surviving child of Mrs Madison Hite, a sister of the late Pres Madison, & a grandson of Joist Hite, the first settler of the Shenandoah Valley.

Died: on Feb 7, at his residence, in Charlestown, Va, in his 31st year, Dr Henry Pendleton Cooke, son of the late John R Cooke, & son-in-law of the late Andrew Kennedy, of Jefferson Co.

TUE FEB 14, 1860
The Easton [Md] Gaz of Sat last announces the death of Saml Stevens, ex-Govn'r of Md. He was a native of Talbot Co, where he died on Feb 7, in his 82nd year. He was a man of the strictest integrity, with kind & generous impulses, held in high esteem by all who knew him. –Balt Exchange

A Newbern paper says that Mrs Alice Day, of that city, was lately delivered of four sturdy boys. We know not what a Day may bring forth.

Valuable Md farm for sale: lies on the Potomac river, 4 miles from Alexandria; contains between 600 & 800 acres; improvements are 3 large barns, granary built in 1856, a new overseer's house, & quarters sufficient for a large number of servants. Apply to Dr P R Edelen, Piscataway, PG Co, Md, or Wm S Holliday & Pinkney Brook, Wash City.

WED FEB 15, 1860
John J Bowen was executed in the jail yard at Newcastle, Del, on Fri, for the murder of John W Dewlin, in Aug last. The wretched man confessed his guilt, but professed to have repented. He alleged he was drunk when he committed the crime.

Mrd: on Feb 14, in Wash City, in Trinity Church, by Rev C M Butler, D D, Mr Saml J Cockerville to Miss Herila R Dufair, both of Wash.

Died: on Feb 14th, in Wash City, Mrs Adeline S Colvin, one of the oldest residents of Washington. Her funeral will take place this day at 12 o'clock, from 272 F st.

Died: on Feb 14, suddenly, Ada, infant daughter of Wm A & Fannie Brown, aged 5 months & 19 days. Her funeral is tomorrow at 2 o'clock, from her father's residence, 300 G st, between 13th & 14th sts.

Senate: 1-Bill relating to marriages in the District of Columbia: this bill provides that all marriages hereafter made & celebrated in Wash Co, D C, between a man & his niece, or a woman & her nephew, are confirmed & made valid in law from the time of such marriages respectively: referred. 2-Ptn from R L Dorr, asking that the Sec of State may be authorized to demand of the British Gov't indemnity for a violation by its subjects of the rights of Saml G Dorr, under a patent for an improved method of shearing cloth, issued by the U S Patent Ofc on Oct 20, 1792: referred. 3-Ptn from John Bingham, formerly employed in collecting the revenue in the district of Boston & Charlestown, for himself & others, urging the enactment of a law to create a retired list of certain clerks employed in the collection of the revenue: referred. 4-Cmte on the Judiciary: discharged from further consideration of the memorial of Jas & Theodore Walters: referred to the Cmte on the District of Columbia. Same cmte: discharged from the memorial of L W Boggs: referred to the Cmte on Military Affairs. 5-Cmte on Pensions: adverse report on the bill to increase pension of Jos Verbiski; & on the ptn of Harrison Sargent. 6-Cmte of Claims: bills received from the Court of Claims with the opinion of that Court in their favor, viz-relief-of Stanwood & Reid, merchants of Boston; of John Mitchell, merchant of N Y C; of Geo W Wales, merchant of Boston; T B Wales & Co, merchants of Boston; of Udolpho Wolfe, merchant, of N Y C; of J D & M Williams, merchants, of Boston; of Atkinson, Rotteris & Co, merchants, of Boston; of Saml A Way, merchant, of Boston; & of Alfred Atkins, merchant, of Boston. 7-Cmte on Patents: bill for the relief of Randall Pegg. 8-Cmte on Pensions: bill for the relief of Eleanor Ricker. Same cmte: adverse reports on the ptns of Wm R West, Emily L Slaughter, & Peter Joseph. Same cmte: adverse report on the ptn of Ann E T Partridge, widow of the late Capt Allen Partridge, formerly superintendent of the Military Academy at West Point. 9-Bill for the relief of Madison Sweester: referred.

THU FEB 16, 1860
About 12 3/4th acres of valuable land, near Wash City, at auction; by deed of trust, executed by Jesse B Haw, recorded in Liber J A S, 169, folios 190 thru 192, of the land records of Wash Co, D C: sale on Mar 19, at the Auction House of A Green, 7th & D sts, Wash City, all that piece of ground & premises lying on 7th st plank road, being the property purchased by the late Jesse Brown, & which the said Haw inherited. –F A Tucker, trustee -A Green auct

At Charlestown, Va, on Tue last, Aaron D Stevens & Albert Hazlett, the remaining Harper's Ferry conspirators under arrest, were sentenced to be hung on Mar 10th next.

Senate: 1-Ptn from Jos Cunningham & others, citizens of Green Co, Ky, asking for an alteration of the mail route from Glasgow to Greensburg, & the establishment of a post ofc at Oceola, Ky: referred. 2-Ptn from Danl B Marten, asking compensation for the use by the Gov't of his patent vertical tubular boiler: referred. 3-Additional papers in relation to the claim of F Woodruff; & additional papers in relation to the claim of Wm B Herrick: referred. 4-Cmte of Claims: bills for the relief: of Geo Phelps; of Wm Money; of R W Clarke; & of Jno R Nourse & others. Same cmte: asked to be discharged from the consideration of the memorial of Catharine L McLeod, & that it be referred to the Cmte on Revolutionary Claims: which was agreed to. 5-Cmte on Military Affairs: bill for the relief of A M Mitchell, late a colonel of Ohio volunteers in the Mexican war.

Orphans Court of Wash Co, D C. Letters of administration on the personal estate of Rufus Dawes, late of Wash Co, deceased. –Wm G Cranch, adm

House of Reps: 1-Cmte on Commerce: bill for the relief of Chas Knap. 2-Cmte on Invalid Pensions: bill increasing the pension of A W W Bayard, an invalid soldier of the war of 1812. 2-Cmte on Private Land Claims: bill to authorize the claimants in right of John Huertes to enter certain lands at any land ofc in the U S, being supplemental to the act of May 23, 1859. 3-Ptn of T W Turly & 38 others, praying for an invalid pension for Thos Glasgow, a soldier of the war of 1812: referred.
4-Ptn of John Maddox, praying for an invalid pension: referred. 5-Mr Florence, of Pa, asked leave to withdraw from the files of the House, the memorial & accompanying papers of Gregory Patti, to be referred to the Cmte on Invalid Pensions: referred. 6-Memorial & accompanying papers of Mrs Mary Bird, to be referred to the Cmte on Revolutionary Claims.

Departure of the Missionaires, on Monday, on board the barque **Smyrniote**, at Boston: Rev Amherst L Thompson & wife; Rev Wm F Arms & wife; Rev A B Goodale, M D, & wife; Rev Zenas Goss, Miss Aura J Beach, Miss Harriet W Crawford, Miss Adelaide L Mason, Mr & Mrs Thompson, with Misses Beach & Crawford, go to the Nestorian mission; Mr & Mrs Arms are expecting to join the North Armenian mission; Mr & Mrs Goodale & Mr Goss are destined to the South Armenian mission; Miss Mason is to be connected with the female boarding school in Syria. The services were conducted by Rev Mr Arms, of Norwich, Ct, father of the missionaries.

A charming book on Cuba! "A Trip to Cuba," by Mrs Julia Ward Howe, author of Passion Flowers, 1 vol, 16 mo, cloth, elegant, 75 cents. Published by Ticknor & Fields, Boston. For sale by the principal Booksellers in Wash City.

Mrd: on Feb 14, in N Y, at St Clement's Church, by Rev Dr J A Eaton, Venerando Pulizzi, of Wash City, to Irene E, daughter of Ira Goodnow, of the former place.

Died: on Feb 14, in Wash City, Capt Horace B Sawyer, U S Navy, in his 62nd year. His funeral is today at 1 o'clock at the Lafayette House, after which the remains will be conveyed to the cars to be removed to Burlington, Vt.

Died: at his residence, on the Navy Yard, in Wash City, John Cosgrove, a native of Ireland, aged about 65 years. His funeral is this afternoon at 2 o'clock.
[No death date given-or funeral place: current item.]

Died: on Feb 15, Chas Fremont, third son of C S & Rebecca E Jones, in his 11th year. His funeral is tomorrow at 10 o'clock, from 442 north H st.

Died: on Jan 10, at his residence, in Warren Co, Ky, Edmund Duncan, in his 72nd year-a Virginian by birth, but had been a resident of that county near half a century. He was emphatically one of God's noble-men.

Boarding: Mrs Jane Taylor, 411 Third st, between C & Pa ave. [Ad]

FRI FEB 17, 1860
Hon Benj Rush Floyd, of Wytheville, Wythe Co, Va, a brother of Hon John B Floyd, Sec of War, died suddenly on Wed night of disease of the heart, at the Lafayette House, on F, between 13th & 14th sts. He was engaged at the time in packing his luggage, for Richmond, to be present at the Democratic Convention. He complained of pain in the region of the heart & in less than 5 minutes expired.
[Feb 22nd newspaper: On Sunday Rev Fr Maguire, pastor of St Aloysius Church, [Catholic Church,] in his sermon alluded to the sudden death of Hon B Rush Floyd, who had been a consistent & practical Christian in that communion.
—Constitution]

Senate: 1-Ptn from Jonathan Ely, legal rep of Ed Ely, asking that the accounts of said Ed Ely as U S Consul at Bombay may be settled on principles of equity & justice: referred. 2-Ptn from Jno H Rountree, asking the return of rents illegally exacted by agents of the U S: referred. 3-Ptn from Jno R Gage & others, asking that the heirs of the militia of the Indian wars & that of war of 1812 may be placed on the same footing in regard to bounty land as those who served in the late war with Mexico: referred. 4-Cmte on Military Affairs: memorial of Theodore Eckerson, military storekeeper at Benicia Arsenal, Calf, submitted an adverse report on the same.

Died: on Feb 15, Mr Jos Butler, in his 69th year. He spent his early life in Richmond, Va, his native State, & was the founder of that sterling paper, the Richmond Whig. He was a man of unblemished reputation. His funeral is this afternoon at 3 o'clock, corner of N Y ave & Third st.

House of Reps: 1-Bill for the relief of the heirs of Wm York: referred. 2-Bill for the relief of Mrs Mary Ann Henry, of Pa: referred. 3-Bill for the relief of Danl Lookingdill: referred. 4-Bill granting a pension to John Jackson, an invalid soldier: referred. 5-Bill granting an invalid pension to Henry Miller: referred. 6-Bill for the relief of Lt Jona F Meredith: referred. 7-Bill for the relief of Jas Henderson, of Tenn: referred. 8-Bill for the relief of R K Depau: referred. 9-Bill for the relief of Wm Lennoy, late U S agent at Knoxville, Tenn: referred. 10-Bill for the relief of Shade Calloway: referred. 11-Bill for the relief of Saml Gwinn, only surviving child of Gen Luther Gwinn, a Revolutionary ofcr: referred. 12-Bill for the relief of Benj Sayers: referred. 13-Bill for the relief of Giles P Pierce: referred. 14-Bill granting a pension to John Pearce: referred. 15-Bill granting 160 acres of land to John Jackson: referred. 16-Bill for the relief of Jos W Hilton: referred. 17-Bill for the relief of the legal reps of David C Bates: referred. 18-Bill for the relief of Mrs Ferguson Smith: referred. 19-Bill for the relief of John S Greenbarth: referred.

Mrd: on Feb 14, by Rev N P Tillinghast, Julius H Von Schmidt, of San Francisco, Calif, to Eliz C, daughter of Saml M Bootes, of Gtwn, D C.

Mrd: on Feb 14, in Wash City, in Trinity Church, by Rev C M Butler, D D, Dr Saml J Cockerille to Miss Hevila Ruter Dufour, only daughter of Oliver Dufour, of In

Obit-died: on Feb 14, Mrs Adeline S Colvin, a member of the Episcopal Church, a sincere & pious Christian. Her distant connexions will deeply feel their bereavement. -R

Ofcrs of the Corp of the City of Wash:
Mayor-Jas G Berret
Register-Wm Morgan
Corp Atty-Jas M Carlisle
Tax Clerk- Wm J Donohoo
Book-keeper-Edwin J Klopfer

Surveyor-Wm Forsyth
Collector-Jas F Haliday
Clerks-Reuben Cleary & Wm H Williams
Messenger-Wm Q Locke

Board of Aldermen:
Wm T Dove, Pres
W B Magruder
Thos Donoho
Jos F Brown
Wm F Bayly
Thos J Fisher
Wm W Moore
Sec to the Board-Richd H Laskey
Messenger-Jacob Kleiber

Wm H Ward
Wm F Price
C W C Dunnington
Francis McNerhany
Aaron W Miller
E M Clarke
Peter M Pearson

Board of Common Council:
Chas Abert, President
John B Turton
Thos P Morgan
Wm Orme
Grafton Powell
Chas S Jones
P M Martin
Lambert Tree
Theodore Sheckels
W J C Duhamel
Elijah Edmonston
Wm P Mohun
Wm A Mulley
Wm F Wallace
T Van Reswick
Jas Boisseau
Franklin S Ober
John H Russell
D B Clarke
J T Given
J T Cassel

Sec-Wm A Kennedy; Messenger-Wm Q Locke

Members of the Board of Health:
Dr P C Davis
J B H Smith
Dr R K Stone
Jas E Dunnawin
Dr W G Palmer
Saml Cole
Dr W P Johnson
Richd Barry
Dr G McCoy
J P Ingle
Dr F S Walsh
John D Brandt
Dr J E Morgan
Henry A Clarke

Assessors:
S S Parker
John T Stewart
Zephaniah Jones
T W Burch
Geo F Smallwood
L A Tuell
John H Bird

Clerks of Markets:
John Waters
Jos Lyons, assist
Sylvester F Gates
Wm Walker
Geo D Spencer

Com'rs of Markets:
W E Spalding
Woodville Latham
B L Jackson
Wm H Walker
Wm Brown
Jas T Devine
John Dowling
W H Keilholtz
Lawrence A Tuel

Com'rs of Improvements:
Jos E Rawlings
R B Owens
Stephen Coster
Saml S Taylor

Apothecaries to Furnish Medicine to the Poor:
David G Ridgeley
S C Ford
Valentine Harbaugh
Jas N Callan
J B Gardiner
Jas D O'Donnell
Chas Allen

Physicians to the Poor:
Philip C Davis, M D
J W H Lovejoy, M D
Geo M Dale, M D
J M Toner, M D

J M Grymes, M D
J M Roberts, M D
J E Willett, M C

Com'r of Health: Chas F Force, M D

Board of Trustees of the Public Schools:
Wm B Randolph
Roger B Ironside
A B Stoughton
Mitchel H Miller
Saml Cole
Wm S Fort

Francis S Walsh
Geo A Bohrer
Z W McKnew
J E Willett
Fred'k Whyte
Robt Geddes

Inspectors & Measurers:
Inspector of Flour & Salted Provisions-Jos Lyons
Gauger & Inspector-Florian Hitz
Sealer of Weights & Measures-Hiram Richey
Inspector of Fire Apparatus-John W Martin

Inspectors & Measurers of Lumber:
Peter Gallant
Wm Douglass
Saml R Beer

John Faherty
Benj Bean
S F Gates

Measurers of Grain, Bran, etc-John Wilson & J Z Williams

Wood & Coal Measurers:
Jos Z Williams
Wm Riggles
Richd Wimsatt

John Cumberland
Wm P Drury

Police Magistrates:
Saml Drury
Thos J Williams
John D Clark
Wm Thompson

Thos C Donn
Patrick McKenna
Jas Cull
Wm Cooper

Police Dept:
Chief of Police-John H Goddard

Lts of Police-Noble J Thomas & Edw McHenry

Police Ofcrs: John McDermott; Wm Daw

Wm D Serrin	J F Carter
Jas F Edwards	H C Harrover
Wm H Fanning	C W Arnold
Jos Williamson	Jacob Ash
Chas G Eckloff	Geo Donaldson
Jas Ginnaty	Reuben Collins
Jas H Suit	Francis S Edelin
Patrick Gormly	Jas S Smith
Wm L Ross	John M Lloyd
Jacob F King	Jos A Gill
B T Watson	S N Chipley
H W Haskell	Josiah Beizell
Henry Yeatman	

SAT FEB 18, 1860
Trustee's sale of real estate by decree of the Circuit Court of D C, in Chancery, case No 1,514, wherein Antonio Figaro was cmplnt & Wm McGinnis & others were dfndnts: sale on Mar 16 next, on the premises, lot 3 in square 583, in Wash City, with bldgs thereon. —E C Morgan, trustee -Jas C McGuire & Co, aucts

Mr Jas Clark, an aged & retired merchant, while in the Hall of Reps at Boston, on Tue, listening to a debate then in progress, suddenly fell & expired of apoplexy.

Trustee's sale by decree of the Circuit Court of D C, in a cause of Anastasia & Thos Donoho against Michl, Jas, Margaret, & Sarah McNamara, & Bridget, & David O Shea, No 1,377, in equity: auction on Mar 13, in front of the premises, of part of lot 15 in square 677, in Wash City, with the frame tenement thereon. —Wm R Woodward, trustee -A Green auct

House of Reps: 1-Bill for the relief of Chas W Brooks, of N Y: referred to the Cmte on Invalid Pensions. 2-Bill for the relief of Wm W Compton: referred to the Cmte on Military Affairs. 3-Bill for the relief of Cmder H J Hartstene, of the U S Navy, was taken up & placed on the private calendar. 4-Consent of Congress to Capt Wm B Shubrick to accept a sword presented to him by Capt-Gen & Pres Urquiza, of the Argentine Confederation: passed.

Circuit Court of D C, in Equity, No 1,507. John W Thompson & others against Margaret F Lindsey & Beverly G Walter, Margaret J & Ann Lindsey, widow, admx, & heirs of Geo F Lindsey. Meeting on Mar 15 next at my ofc in City Hall, Wash, for a statement of the trustee's account. —W Redin, auditor

Died: on Feb 17, at Pittston, Maine, Clarkson P Hale, brother of Hon John P Hale, U S Senator from N H, aged 48 years.

Died: on Thu last, Mary, infant daughter of Job W & Antoinette Angus.

Obit-died: on Feb 14, Capt Horace B Sawyer; his remains left this city on Thu by the Northern train of cars for final burial at Burlington, Vt, the native town & the family residence of the deceased. They were accompanied by Cmder Emmerson, of the navy, a cousin of Capt Sawyer, & the afflicted family. Capt Sawyer entered the navy as midshipman in Jun, 1812; first service was on Lake Champlain, on board the ship **Growler** or **Eagle**, when those vessels were captured in Jun, 1813, & he was among the ofcrs sent as prisoners first to Quebec & afterwards to Halifax. He was attached to the ship **Constitution**, & in the action of that ship with the ship **Cyane** & ship **Levant** in 1815. The deceased had for many years lived in this city. His fatal illness was sudden. God alone can give consolation to the heart of the mother & her children.

Maj E H Fitzgerald, U S Army, died in Calif on Jan 9. He was a native of Pa, served in the Seminole war, & under Gens Scott, Wool, & Worth in the Mexican war. He was one of the first ofcrs of the invading army who stepped on shore at Vera Cruz. He was in every battle on Gen Scott's line, from the surrender of Vera Cruz to the fall of the city of Mexico. For conspicuous gallantry at the storming of Chapultepec, he received his commission as brevet major in the army. For several years past he has been serving in New Mexico & Calif.

Hon Benj Rush Floyd, of Va, died suddenly on Feb 15, in Wash City, while here on business in connexion with a prominent railroad. He was just preparing to leave the residence of his brother, Sec Floyd, when he was seized with a severe pain. He died in a little more than an hour. He was the son of the late Govn'r John Floyd, of Va, & was only 48 years of age. As a Christian gentleman, husband, father, & friend, his character shone the brightest. Tears of thousands will be mingled with those of his bereaved wife & children as his remains are laid in the soil of his nativity, whither they were yesterday conveyed. –G

Circuit Court of Wash Co, D C-in Chancery, No 1,440. Christiana McClery et al vs L W James et al. Gilbert Rodman, trustee, reported that on Jul 8, 1859, he made sale of the real estate in the proceedings mentioned to Jos C Willard, for $2,855, & the purchaser has complied with the terms of sale. –Jno A Smith, clerk

Circuit Court of D C-in Chancery, No 1,507. J W Thompson et al vs Margaret F Lindsay et al. The trustee reported he sold to Wm F Bailey lot 7, & part of lot 8, in Davidson's subdivision of square 248, in Wash City, for $4,100, & the purchaser has complied with the terms of sale. –Jno A Smith, clerk

MON FEB 20, 1860
Died: on Feb 15, Mrs Maria Washington, aged 65 years, wife of Fayette Washington, of Fred'k Co, Va, & daughter of the last Matthew Frame, of Jefferson Co.

Association of the Surviving Soldiers of the War of 1812 of D C: to assemble on Wed next, the Anniversary of Washington's Birthday. –Jas Lawrenson, sec

John Rogers & his children. A correspondent in Lawrence sent the following extract copied from a work published in London, in 1630, entitled "Annals of England, containing the reigns of Henry VIII, Edward VI, & Queen Mary." Written in Latin by Rt Hon & Rt Rev Fr in God, Francis, Lord Bishop of Hereford. Thus Englished, corrected, & enlarged with the author's consent, by Morgan Godwyn. It corroborates the conclusion that John Rogers had 10 children, according to the New England Primmer. On Feb 4, John Rogers, the Protomartyr of those times, was burned at London. He was Tindall's companion, after whose death, fearing persecution, went with his wife to Wirtemberg.where, having attained to the Germane tongue, he undertook the care of a certain Church there, until, under King Edw, he was recalled from exile by Ridley, Bishop of London, made a Prebend of Pauls, & Lecturer there. Queen Mary having attained to the Crowne, the Papists endeavored to affright him; & so to have once more forced him to a voluntary exile, commanding him not so much as to peep into the streets; & in this manner he lived a year, until at last, refusing to fly, he was imprisoned & condemned to fire, which cruel death [notwithstanding that he was to leave a wife & 10 children] he did most constantly undergo. –Boston Journal

Circuit Court of D C, in Equity, No 698. Jas Williams & Wm W Kennedy against Jas Williams, Thos H Havenner, John C McKelden, H Naylor, Jno H Jamison, Lemuel Williams, J C Harkness, M Delany, Robt Cruit, J W Maury & others, Thos Purcell, Emily Beale, & others. Creditors of Jas Williams are notified that at my ofc, on Mar 15 next, I shall state the trustee's account with the trust fund in his hands, & the claims of the creditors of said Jas Williams, who have liens on the property sold by the trustee, part of lot 9 in square 457, with improvements. –W Redin, auditor

Died: on Feb 17, at her residence, in Wash City, in her 76th year, Mrs Susan Graham, widow of Hon John Graham. Her funeral will take place at St Matthew's Church this morning at 10 o'clock.

Died: on Feb 18, Virginia Fletcher, wife of Maj W W Russell, Paymaster U S Marine Corps, in her 33rd year. Her funeral will take place from 252 I st, between 18th & 19th sts, this afternoon at 3 o'clock.

Died: on Feb 11, at her residence, *Roscoe*, PG Co, Md, in her 65th year, Eliza, wife of B D Mullikin, & eldest daughter of the late Thos McEldery, of Balt.

Died: on Feb 10, at *Montrose*, the residence of his grandmother, in St Louis Co, Mo, John Graham, 2nd son of John & Fanny G Wickham, aged 4 years & 3 months.

Died: on Feb 17, at New Lisbon, Ohio, Mrs Susan Key Wood, widow of Mr Wm Wood, of Wash City. Mrs Wood has of late years made her home with her daughter, Mrs Robt Whitacre, of New Lisbon.

Obit-died: on Feb 3, in New Orleans, very suddenly, of apoplexy, Hon Geo W Watterston, a past member of the Senate of Louisiana, & more recently, & for several years, Judge of the Circuit court of that State. He was a native of Wash City, & the eldest son of the late Geo Watterston. Judge Watterston was a graduate of Gtwn College, & received the degree of Dr of Laws there; he emigrated early in life to Louisiana & commenced practice. He married & was extensively engaged as a planter till the time of his death. He has left 4 children to mourn his loss. –J T A

Capt Meigs has presented to the <u>Water Board of Gtwn</u> his final report upon the distribution of water throughout that city. The work has been substantially completed, the last water pipe having been laid down on Dec 7 last. In all 7.81 miles of pipe have been laid, a, a portion of the Wash aqueduct mains having been used in the distribution, there are 8.78 miles of distributing pipe now in use in that city. The work of distribution water through the city has been done under the direction of the Water Board, Messrs Henry Addison, Jno T Bangs, & Jas A Magruder, by Capt M C Meigs & Mr E T D Myers, C E.

Mrd: on Feb 9, at Oakham, by Rev O A Kinsolving, Mr A K Phillips, of Fredericksburg, Va, to Miss Anna D Rogers, daughter of Col Ham Rogers, of Loudoun Co, Va.

TUE FEB 21, 1860

A fifteen miles skating match came off at Portsmouth, N H, on Thu last: Jas Ayres made the distance in 47 minutes; Geo W Marston in 47 minutes 6 seconds; Jacob Haddock in 50 minutes. Ayres & Marston each skated one mile in 2 minutes 20 seconds, which is within one-fourth of a second of Flora Temple's best time.

A boy, Henry D Kunkle, a telegraph operator, at Monroeville, Ohio, has been arrested, & confessed having robbed the mail at that place almost every day during the past year. Nearly a bushel of letters were found in an out-house rifled of their contents. S H Brown has been arrest in Louisville, Ky, on a charge of robbing the mail. He was a clerk in the Toledo post ofc, but was discharged last winter. -Cleveland [O] Herald

Senate: 1-Ptn from A Boschke, asking an appropriation to defray his expenses in making a munite & accurate survey of the District of Columbia, engraving the map, & furnishing the Gov't with 1,000 copies: referred. 2-Ptn from Jno L Hayes, in behalf of the citizens of the U S, asking the adoption of measures for securing international reciprocity in the rights of patentees: referred. 3-Addition papers in support of the claim of F R Stevens, Pres of the Calif Stage Co: referred. 4-Ptn from Isaac E Morse, asking additional compensation for his services as special com'r to New Granada: referred. 5-Addition papers in the case of H R de La Reintrie: referred. 6-Ptn from Barbara Glover, asking to be allowed a pension: referred. 7-Ptn from Micajah Hawks, assist surgeon in the navy in the war of

1812, asking a pension: referred. 8-Ptn from Jno Jordan, asking his pension may commence from the date of his discharge: referred. 9-Cmte of Claims: bill for the relief of Franklin Peale. 10-Cmte of Claims: referred the memorial of Geo M Western, submitted a report, accompanied by a bill to provide for the quieting certain land titles in the late disputed territory in the State of Maine, & for other purposes. 11-Cmte of Claims: bills for the relief: of Mrs Ann P Derrick, widow of Wm S Derrick, deceased; of Jas Maccaboy; & of Mills Judson, surety on the official bond of the late purser Andrew D Crosby. Same cmte: asked to be discharged from the consideration of the memorials of D Merriwether, superintendent of Indian Affairs in New Mexico, & of the heirs of Jabez B Rooker: which was agreed to. 12-Cmte on Revolutionary Claims: bill for the relief of Henry G Carson, adm of Curtis Grubb, deceased. Same cmte: bill for the relief of the surviving grandchildren of Col Wm Thompson, of the Revolutionary army of S C. 13-Cmte on Public Lands: adverse reports on the ptns, viz: of Edw D Tippett, a soldier of the war of 1812; of Jos Whitcomb, & of Benj Ward, a privateersman in the war of 1812, for bounty land to those imprisoned at Dartmoor; of A Edwards, late register of the land ofc at Kalamazoo, Mich, & of that of Allen Gaylord & other citizens of Ohio, asking that land may be granted to the heirs of those who served in the Indian wars & that of 1812. 14-Cmte on Pensions: adverse reports on the ptns of Jos Walcomb, of the war of 1812 for an invalid pension; of Danl Abbott, & of Hugh Wiley, of the war of 1812, to be allowed a pension; & to be discharged from the ptn of Jonas P Levy, & that it be referred to the Cmte on Public Lands: which was agreed to. 15-Cmte on Public Lands: adverse report on the ptn of Thos Jones & others, for bounty land for services in the war of 1812. 16-Cmte on Pension: adverse report on the ptn of Elias Carpenter, asking that his pension may date from the time of disability. Same cmte: ptn of Nicholas Underhill, a soldier of the war of 1812, asking a pension, & the ptn of Cornelius Hughes, asking an increase, submitted bills for their relief. Same cmte: bill for the relief of Rebecca A Connell; also, bill for the relief of Olivia W Cannon.

Foreign Obituaries: Our French journals announce the death of Count Serrurier, Grand Ofc of the Legation of Honor, former peer of France, & at one time French Minister for the U S. Mme Wilhelmine Schroeder-Devrient, one of the most celebrated actresses of Germany, died at Coburg, Jan 26, aged 54. She retired from the stage in 1849. Rudio, one of th accomplices of Orsini in the attempt on the life of Napoleon III, died lately in Brazil, to which country he had escaped from the penal colony of Cayenne.

Special police for Feb 22nd, celebration of Geo Washington's Birthday, & dedication of the Equestrian Statue of Gen Geo Washington on that day:

Fred'k Hager	D H Lakeman	M Holtzman
Geo Adamson	Saml Tinkler	Wm Hagerty
Jas Moran	F N Holtzman	Jas Chapman
Jas Crown	Saml Spadding	Danl Myers
Wm Nash	E Piggott	Geo W Edwards

Patrick Hagerty	Ignacius Reynolds	John Connody
Wm Tinkler	Thos White	Dennis Gleason
Wm Walker	Chas Balhuff	John Connel
Otho Yauger	Thos F Pendell	Jas Redmond
Geo W Meekum	Robt Warren	Wm Smith
Patrick O'Callahan	Wm Sullivan	Wm Blake
John McGuire	Jas T Slatford	A Shaffer
Danl Cahill	H Smith	Edw Brisk
Solomon Fowler	C Reichter	Jas McGrann
Jas Biggs	J Rous	Henry Gaughran
Francis Miller	Francis Straub	Chas Brannan
Wm Elwood	Jas Noland	H T L Wilson
R B Bridget	Eugene McCarty	J P Weller
Edw J Wilson	L Noland	Nicholas Keys
Solomon Goddard	Saml Taylor	Jas Shanahan
J T Stanley	Andrew Roth	Jos O Walling
Danl Vemeyer	Walter Grant	Paul Kraft
Jas Hilbus	Wm McCloskey	John Conaway
A S Dant	W Sauter	John Collins
John Hodgson	Adolph Landie	Thos J Kelly
D West	Benj Hillyard	Jacob Valentine
August Voss	A Columbus	Danl Donalson
Henry Fridley	A J Williams	John Dooley
J Toomey	David Harrover	Richd Lee
Jas Sinclair	John Dove	Geo Long
E E Barnes	Jas Larcombe	Patrick Barry
Wm Simmons	Dennis McNamara	Wm H Mullen
Wm A Barnes	John T Barret	Wm T McCuen
J H.Sessford	John Hough	Wm H Burdine
Thos May	John Murphey	Chas Muller
John T Coombs	John Robey	Hanson Brown
J Shackleford	Wm Shreve	Thos Dwyer
I J Newman	John Hurlehy	Henry Konig
G M Grubb	Jas Blakely	Wm Clemens
Wm Palmer	Danl Murphey	J F Fulmer
John Miller	Geo Miles	John Deal
John Moore	Danl McRae	Wm Hoofnagle
S C Davidson	Wm Becker	John Volk
J A Sullivan	Fred'k Rupp	Lewis Place
L C Robinson	Geo Donohoo	Chas Coleman
L Keeley	Jeremiah Connor	Thos Brown
Wm M Warren	Danl Luney	Thos De Coursey
Dennis O'Callaghan	Chas Schaffer	Thos McCafray
John Cunningham	Powel Heiss	Jos T Morgan
Kensey Brewer	Marcus Flaherty	Geo Thompson
John W Brewer	Danl Ready	Jas R Dobbin

Jno Collins	Wm Connor	Jos A Burch
G L Baldwin	J R Pettet	Saml Lomax
Jno Thompson	Stephen Gill	Saml C Espy
Jno Simmons	W C Harvey	John L Brooks
Jas Hutchinson	John F Clements	Thos Cassady
John Kreemer	Antone Smedley	John G Stafford
Jno McWilliams	Andrew Ferguson	John Buckley
Robt Devroux	John Mansfield	L McVerry
Andrew Norton	John F Gill	John Dwyer
David Potts	John Pearce	Dennis Griffin
Jas T Nally	J T Kidwell	Wm T McCain
Thos Williamson	Andrew Archer	Jas W Watson
A F Berry	J W W Wells	Richd Earl
John Fleming	Thos Brorick	Michl Kelly
Thos A Lomax	Wm Whalen	Jeremiah Reardon
Silas Tucker	J M Martin	
Wm Whalan	Clement Weeden	

Died: on Feb 19, in Wash City, Henry Forrest, in his 54th year. His funeral will be from his late residence, 337 21st st, today at half-past one o'clock.

Died: on Feb 9, at his residence, near Warrenton, Fauquier Co, Va, John Penn Philips, in his 58th year. He was one of the most prominent members of the bar of the circuit in which he practiced. His death was unexpected. His sorrowing household mourns his death. –B

Orphans Court of Wash Co, D C. In the case of Marion M Taylor, adm d b n of Geo B Scott, deceased, the administrator & Court have appointed Mar 13 next, for the final settlement of the personal estate of said deceased, of the assets in hand. -Ed N Roach, Reg/o wills

N Y, Feb 20. Five of the Calif steamships were sold today, under protest from one of the trustees of the owners. They were knocked off as follows:
The steamship **Illinois**, $106,000, to E H Cheever
The steamship **Moses Taylor**, $102,000, to E H Cheever
The steamship **Star of the West**, $15,000, to Moses Taylor.
The steamship **Philadelphia**, $5,000, to Francis Morris.
The steamship **Empire City**, $10,000, to Moses Taylor.

Circuit Court of Wash Co, D C-in Chancery. Eliza J Burke et al vs Walter L Burke et al. The trustee sold the real estate in this case to Owen O'Hara, for $650, on Jan 9, 1860. –Jno A Smith, clerk

WED FEB 22, 1860
Mrd: on Feb 14, by Rev J Spencer Kennard, Mr Geo W Harvey to Miss Mary A Evans, both of Wash.

Senate: 1-Ptn from Jane B Evans, widow, executrix of Cadwallader Evans, asking for a renewal of a patent granted to her husband for an invention to prevent the explosion of steam boilers: referred. 2-Ptn from Jas L Williams, of Ky volunteers, asking an increase of pension: referred. 3-Ptn from Thos P Dudley, asking to be allowed an increase of pension: referred. 4-Ptn from Geo P Ihrie, asking compensation for services on the boundary survey between the U S & Mexico, & allowance for transportation to his house: referred. 5-Ptn from John Brannan, employe in the Dept of State, asking compensation for extra services: referred. 6-Cmte on Revolutionary Claims: bill for the relief of the legal reps of Chas Porterfield. Same cmte: bill for the relief of the legal reps of Jas Bell, deceased. 7-Cmte of Claims: adverse report on the memorial of the legal reps of Geo Mayo, for services in the Post Ofc Dept. 8-Cmte of Claims: adverse report on the memorial of John H Wickizer, for compensation for taking the census of the counties of Monterey & Santa Cruz, in Calif. Same cmte: adverse report on the memorial of Wm L Downing for compensation for raising a company of volunteers in Fla.

Fire in Boston on Sat in the curled-hair & feather establishment of Messrs Manning, Glover & Co: Capt Chas E Dunton, of Washington Hose Co, & Chas Carter, of Warren Hook & Ladder Co, were killed, being crushed by a beam. Frank B Leach, Geo Dalno, & W Prescott, were severally bruised & cut. Mr Carter was about 40 years old & Mr Dutton about 35. Each leaves a wife & 3 children.

Mrd: on Feb 21, by Rev Dr Pinckney, at the Church of the Ascension, Mr Jas J Neagle, of Omaha City, Nebraska Territory, to Miss Virginia, 2nd daughter of J P Keller, of Wash City.

Died: on Dec 30, 1859, in San Francisco, Calif, in his 42nd year. Mr John Dobson, a native of Sanquhan, Dumfrieshire, Scotland. Mr Dobson was well known in Wash City by a large circle of friends, who now mourn his loss.

Circuit Court of D C-in Chancery. John F Coyle vs Franklin Philp. The receiver reported that he has sold the stock of F Philp on hand on Jul 27 last, with the lease & fixtures, to Messrs B & P Lawrence, of N Y, for $8,544.95, & the parties have complied with the terms of sale. –John A Smith, clerk

Circuit Court of Wash Co, D C-in Equity. Williams & Kennedy vs Jas Williams, et al. The trustee reported he has sold the northern part of lot 9 in square 457, fronting on 7th st, to Jas C McGuire, for $8,400, & he has complied with the terms of sale. -Jno A Smith, clerk

FRI FEB 24, 1860
Mrd: Feb 13th, at Abingdon Church, in Gloucester Co, Va, by Rev Mr Mann, Col Jas M Goggin, of Memphis, Tenn, to Miss Bettie Nelson Page, of Gloucester Co.

Died: on Feb 22, Susannah, wife of Jas A Ingram, in her 23rd year. Her funeral will from her late residence on north A st, Capitol Hill, today, at 1 o'clock P M.

The Equestrian Statue of Geo Washington, which was first thrown open to the public eye on Feb 22, the 128th anniversary of the birthday of that ever-to-be-honored Hero, Patriot, & Sage, was order by a resolution of the Congress of the U S to be fashioned & cast in bronze by Clark Mills, a native of N Y, & a citizen of S C, & the artist of the equestran statue of Gen Andrew Jackson, which stands in Lafayette Square, immediately in front of the Executive Mansion in Wash City. The statue was moulded & founded at the establishment of Mr Mills, near Bladensburg, Md, & has consumed the greater part of 5 years in its preparation & completion.

Wash Corp-Feb 20. 1-Ptn of Chas Frierick; of Geo M Miller; of Wm G Deale; & of Danl Connolly; for remission of a fine: referred to the Cmte of Claims. [Frierick's ptn was discharged from further consideration.] 2-Ptn of Christopher Hemmerdinger; & ptn of G Kahelrt: praying remission of fines: referred to the Cmte of Claims.

SAT FEB 25, 1860
Senate: 1-Ptn from Geo M Willing, delegate to Congress from the proposed Territory of Jefferson, urging the speedy orgainzation of a Territorial gov't. therefor. This memorial sets forth that the present population of the Territory is larger than that of Nebraska, & that its natural resources in the precious metals & agriculture cannot be surpassed. 2-Ptn from Jas E Linscott, a soldier of the war of 1812, for an invalid pension: referred. 3-Ptn from Horace E Dimock, asking remuneration for improvements by him in artillery: referred. 4-Ptn from Carlos Butterfield, asking that the Postmaster Gen be authorized to contract with him for the transportation of the U S mails from certain ports in the U S to certain ports in the Gulf of Mexico: referred. 5-Cmte on Naval Affairs: memorial of Lt John C Carter, of the navy, submitted a report, with a joint resolution for his relief. Same cmte: bill for the relief of F M Gunnell. 6-Cmte of Claims reported the following bills with the opinions of the Court of Claims thereon, viz: relief of O H Berryman & others; of Emilie G Jones, excx of Thos P Jones, deceased; of Jas L Edwards, adm of Thos T Gedney, deceased; of Nancy M Johnson, admx of Walter R Johnson, deceased; of Geo Ashley, adm of Saml Holgate, deceased; of Lydia Frazer, widow & admx of John Frazer, late of N Y C; of Thos Allen, of Augustus H Evans; of Wm Geiger; of Jas Crooks; of Mariano G Vallejo. 7-Joint resolution authorizing Capt Wm L Hudson & Joshua R Sands to accept certain testimonials awarded to them by the Gov't of Great Britain: referred.

Died: Feb 23rd, Evelyn, daughter of Owen & Margaret E Thorn, aged 6 months & 4 days. Her funeral is today at 3 o'clock, from 383 6th st, between G & H sts.

Died: on Feb 18, in Phil, Joseph, aged 4 years; on the same day, Francis, aged 1 year, both youngest children of Francis Hanna, formerly of Wash City.

Died: on Feb 23, Georgiana Sophia, aged 3 years & 2 months, oldest child of Geo & Helen M Perrie.

House of Reps: 1-Memorial of John L Kissick, who was a gunner's mate on board the U S ship **Princeton**, praying Congress for relief for injuries sustained on board of said vessel by the explosion of the large gun called the Peacemaker: referred to the Cmte on Invalid Pensions. 2-Leave to withdraw from the file of the House the ptns of Mrs Phoebe Ann Shockley, Mrs Abigail Paxon, & that of the heirs of Robt Bigby, to be referred to the Cmte on Invalid Pensions. 3-Cmte on Indian Affairs: bill for the relief of Anson Dart: committed. 4-Bills introduced & referred: relief of Arthur Edwards & his associates; of Saml F Harrison; of Wm McCormick; of W Y Hansell & others; & of Eben S Hanscomb. 5-Hon Levi M Waterson, of Tenn, was nominated for printer. Mr Tomkpins nominated Edw Ball, of Ohio. Resolved: that W W Seaton, of the firm of Gales & Seaton, be & he is hereby appointed printer of the House of Reps for the 36th Congress.

Circuit Court of Wash Co, D C-in Chancery. David Gordon & Susan E Gordon, his wife, vs Wm Chauncey Langdon & the heirs of Pollard Webb, deceased. The object of this suit is to procure the appointment of a Trustee in the place of Pollard Webb, deceased, to carry out the purposes of the deeds of trust hereinafter mentioned. The bill states that on Feb 23, 1858, Wm Chauncey Langdon, by deed of that date, sold & conveyed to Pollard Webb parts of lot 1 & 14 in square 531, in Wash City, described in said bill & exhibits, in trust for the benefit of said Susan E Gordon & for other purposes. The bill further states that on Mar 15, 1855, said cmplnt sold & conveyed to the said Webb certain slaves & articles of household & kitchen furniture, in trust for the benefit of said Susan F Gordon, & subject to her direction & appointment, & for the other purposes recited therein, to which reference is made, that the said Pollard Webb, trustee, departed this life intestate & leaving heirs to cmplnts unknown, although due efforts have been made to discover them; that by reason of the death of said Webb said cmplnts are without a trustee, & that they are without a remedy in a court of law, &, further, that the said Langdon is a non-resident. The bill prays the appointment of some fit person as trustee in place of Webb, deceased. Absent heirs of said Webb, deceased, & also to the said Wm Chauncery Langdon, are to appear in this Court, on or before the said first Mon of Jul next. -Wm M Merrick, A J -Jno A Smith, clerk

Mrd: on Feb 23, by Rev Dabney Ball, Mr Benj F Howard to Miss Annie E Martin.

Obit-died: Mrs Virginia Fletcher Russell, wife of Maj W W Russell, of the Marine Corps. Pneumonia attacked her on Feb 7, the day previous to the birth of her infant, & she died on Sat week, Feb 18, the skill of her physicians being insufficient to arrest or check the disease. Six little children, the oldest but 8 years, are left to the care of her grief-stricken husband.

Circuit Court for Dorchester Co, Md, Feb 14, 1860, in Equity. Thos M Flint & Sarah his wife, vs Thos Vickers, Jas Vickers, Harrison L Monroe & Margaret his wife. To the Honorable Thos A Spence, Judge of the Circuit Court of Dorchester Co, Md. The ptn of the cmplnts represent that they heretofore filed their bill in this Court stating that one Jas Vickers, by his last will & testament, devised certain lands in Dorchester Co, particularly named in said bill, to Thos Vickers, by his paying within 3 years from the death of the testator & his wife, or survivor of them, to the cmplnt, Sarah & Jas & Margaret Vickers, each $1,000 with interest till after the 3 years aforesaid. That the testator died, in 1855, & his wife previously, & more than 3 years has elapsed since the death of the survivor. That Thos Vickers has neglected & refused to pay said legacy to the cmplnts, or either of them, but has sold a part of said land to the dfndnt, Harrison L Monroe, who resides in Alexandria, Va, & who had notice & knew before & at the time of his purchase of the lien of said legacies & has neglected & refused to pay the same, & the cmplnts pray a decree against the said Thos & Harrison L, to pay said legacy, or in default that the said land or so much as is necessary be sold to pay said legacy. They now pray this Court will pass an order of publication, warning the said Harrison L to pay said legacy, or in default that the said land or so much as is necessary be sold to pay said legacy. They now pray this Court will pass an order of publication warning the said Harrison L Monroe & Margaret, his wife, to be & appear in this Court on or before a certain day, or be named in said order, to answer the said bill. Elias Griswold, Cmplnts' Solicitor
-Francis I Henry, clerk

Valuable Md farm for sale: lies on the Potomac river, about 4 miles below Alexandria, containing between six & eight hunderd acres. Apply to Dr P R Edelin, Piscataway, PG Co, Md, or Wm S Holliday & Pinkney Brook, Wash, D C.

Circuit Court of Wash Co, D C-in Equity, No 1,555. Edw Dolan & wife & Erasmus Booze & wife, against Thos J Fisher & Edw C Dyer, excs, & Geo W Maher & Jas Maher, jr, heirs of Jas Maher. Statement of the accounts of the excs of said Jas Maher, deceased, on Apr 14 next, at my ofc, in City Hall, Wash.
–W Redin, auditor

MON FEB 27, 1860
A telegraphic note was received by a Southern Rep on Friday last, announcing that Mr Keitt, of Pilatka, Fla, brother of Hon Mr Keitt, of S C, had been murdered in his bed by some of his servants. The simple fact was stated, without any other particulars. Hon Keitt set out for the South on Friday. [Feb 28th newspaper: The Ocala [Fla] Companion of Feb 21 reported the murder, on the Sunday previous, of Dr Wm J Keitt, a Senator of the Fla Legislature. He resided alone on a plantation near Ocala, & had been in ill health for some time. His throat was cut from ear to ear. The servants suspected of the crime have been lodged in jail.] [Mar 2nd newspaper: Dr Keitt moved to Fla about 6 years ago.]

The Supreme Court of Ohio is now occupied with a case involving interests to the amount of $1,000,000. It is the case of Geo S Coe, trustee, against the Columbus, Piqua, & Indiana Railroad Co, being an endeavor to foreclose certain mortgages. It excites considerable attention.

The will of Mr John Rose, a retired merchant of N Y C, whose decease was announced some weeks ago, makes a conditional bequest of $300,000 to the N Y C for the education in agriculture of indigent white children. The condition is that a corresponding sum should be appropriated by the city, or raised by charitable contributions, for the purchase & support of a farm in the neighborhood of N Y. If this is not carried out then the money goes to the American Colonization Society for the deportation & support of freed blacks in Liberia. The decedent was a bachelor, & a bachelor brother of large wealth is constituted his sole executor, with the remainder of his estate, about $550,000, placed in charge for benevolent & charitable distribution. The only personal bequests are a gift of $20,000 to his executor & $12,000 to another brother, now advanced in years. The whole value of the estate, principally in productive stocks, is reckoned at $880,000.

Extensive sale of fine new furniture, carpets, & oilcloths, on Feb 29, at the store of T H Brown, 360 7th st. –Wm Marshall, auct

Died: on Feb 25, in Wash City, Jesse, aged 8 months & 3 days, twin son of John W & Eliza S Glover. His funeral is today at 3 o'clock, from the residence of his parents, 537 11th st.

Died: on Feb 26, at Cumberland, after a short illness, Hazel S Butt.

Circuit Court of Wash Co, D C-in Equity, No 1,445. A McBlair, by etc, vs W Gadsby et al. Saml Chilton & A B Magruder, trustees, reported on Dec 15, 1859, they sold at auction, to John C Ten Eyck, lot 37 in square 167, Wash City, near H & Lafayette st, fronting on Jackson place 35 feet & 5 inches, at the price of $5,412.57, & the purchaser hath complied with the terms of sale.
–Jno A Smith, clerk

Circuit Court of D C-in Equity, No 232. Martha Isherwood, survivor, etc, against, Jonathan Barnsley & Jonathan Duley. W Redin, trustee, reported that on Feb 17 he sold at auction to Thos Knowles part of lots 150 & 151, in Beatty & Hawkins addition to Gtwn, with the 2 story brick dwlg-house & improvements, at the s e corner of Market & 3rd sts, at the price of $3,300; & the purchaser had complied with the terms of sale. –Jno A Smith, clerk

Circuit Court of D C-in Equity, No 1,435. Miller & wife & others, against Mason & others, heirs of Alex'r Macomb. I shall state the trustee's account on Mar 22 next. -W Redin, auditor

TUE FEB 28, 1860
The Nashville [Tenn] papers announce the death, on Feb 21, of Bishop Miles, Catholic Bishop of that diocese, from paralysis. He was born in PG Co, Md, in 1790, & at age 5 years removed to Ky; ordained a priest in 1816; removed to Nashville in 1838, since which time he has been a permanent resident.

Trustee's sale of frame house & lot on the Island, by deed in trust from Jas Butcher & wife, dated Aug 2, 18_4, recorded in Liber J A S, No 82, folios 334 et seq, sale on Thu, of the west half of lot 7 in square 389, fronting on south G st, with a 2 story frame dwlg-house. –Chas S Wallach, trustee
-Jas C McGuire & Co, aucts

The American Hotel in Denton, Md, kept by Mrs Millington, was entirely destroyed by fire on Feb 19th, supposedly from some defect in a chimney. Most of the furniture was consumed. The bldg was erected by the late Capt Jos Richardson, at the cost of about $7,000, & was owned by his widow, who resides in Cecil Co.

Charleston, S C, Feb 27. 1-Col J H Irby, formerly a Congressman from S C, died last week of apoplexy. 2-Yesterday the Connonsboro Rice Mill, the oldest mill in the city, was consumed, & the residence of Edw Lucas was much damaged by the flames. The property was insured.

Senate: 1-Ptn from Jose Morin, in behalf of Platte Co, Mo, for the purpose of securing the island opposite Leavenworth: referred. 2-Ptn from A L H Cranshaw & others, urging the establishment of mail routes to the gold fields of Western Kansas: referred. 3-Ptn from Gen Danl Morgan, asking to be allowed the amount of depreciation on the commutation received by his ancestor: referred. 4-Ptn from Mary B Hook, widow of the late Col Jas H Hook, asking a pension of Congress for services rendered by her husband to the Gov't: referred. 4-Cmte on Revolutionary Claims: bill for the relief of the heirs at law of the late Abijail Nason, sister & devisee of John Lord, deceased. 5-Cmte on Pensions: bill for the relief of Mary Featherston, widow of John Featherston. Same cmte: adverse report on the ptn of Jno W Eastman for a pension on account of disease contracted in the naval service. Same cmte: ptn of the widow of Capt J S R Reeves, of the army, for a pension, submitted a report, accompanied by a bill for the relief of Annie D Reeves. Same cmte: adverse report in the case of Jane C Perry, widow of Cmdor M C Perry. 6-Cmte of Claims: bill for the relief of J J Lints, for compensation for services as custodian of the public property, connected with the improvements of the harbor at Erie.

Halifax, Feb 27. There are no further tidings from the steamer **Hungarian**, the cutter **Daring** not having as yet reached the spot. Divers have gone there. A hat-box marked Wm Boulterhouse, Sackville, had been washed ashore.

Montgomery, Feb 27. Gen C M Jackson, ex-Speaker of the House of Reps, died at Autauga on Sunday.

Public sale on Mar 2, the following in Gtwn, D C, for taxes due the Corp of D C.
Jas Clagett's heirs: lot 29: 1856 thru 1858.
Eliz Dunlop's heirs: lot 65: 1858.
Jos Mason's heirs: part of 127: 1858.
Wm Queen: part of lot 66: 1857 & 1858.
Conrad Schwartz: part of lot 261; & part of lot 262; lot 274: 1858.
John H Waters: parts of lots 74 & 75: 1857 & 1858.
Hannah Bargy & others: part of lot 41: 1858.
-C F Shekell, Collector for 1856 thru 1858. Gtwn, D C, Dec 15, 1860.

WED FEB 29, 1860
Mrd: in Wash City, by Rev Stephen P Hill, Rev Addison Jones, of Ga, to Jane Briggs, of Wash City. [No marriage date given-current item.]

Mrd: on Feb 26, in Wash City, by Rev Stephen P Hill, Ephraim K Knowles to Letetia Leonard, all of Wash City.

Prof Chauncey A Goodrich, of Yale College, died at New Haven on Sat last, in his 70th year. He has long been widely known as a scholar, a writer, & an instructor.

Senate: 1-Ptn from Eunice Church, widow of Joshua Lambert, a seaman in the naval service, who died of wounds received in battle, asking to be allowed a pension: referred. 2-Cmte of Claims: bill for Robt Harrison, Letitia Humphreys, & memorial of Letitia Humphreys, admx of Andrew Atkinson, deceased, declaratory of the acts for carrying into effect the 9th article of the treaty between the U S & Spain. 3-Cmte on Revolutionary Claims: bill for the relief of Eliz Montgomery, heir of Hugh Montgomery: passed. 4-Cmte on Pensions: bill for the relief of Laura C Humber, widow of Chas H Humber; & a bill for the relief of Valentine Wehrheim. 5-Cmte on Indian Affairs: bill for the relief of Madison Sweetser. 6-Cmte on Pensions: bill for the relief of Angelina C Bowman, widow of Francis L Bowman, late Capt U S Army: to be remunerated the expense of conveying home the remains of her husband & to be allowed a pension. 7-Cmte on Revolutionary Claims: bill to refund the State of Georgia certain moneys paid by said State to Peter Trezvant, the legal rep of Robt Farquhar. 8-Cmte of Claims: adverse report on the memorial of Eliza E Ogden, asking for an equitable allowance of per centage on certain disbursements made by her late husband, Maj Edw A Ogden, for the suppression of Indian hostilities.

THU MAR 1, 1860
Obit-died: on Feb 20, 1860, at the residence of his brother, Col Thos Brown, in Westmoreland Co, Va, after a painful illness of nearly 2 years' duration, Arthur Brown, aged 34 years.

Senate: 1-Ptn from L A Gobright & others, in behalf of the Grand Lodge of the Independent Order of Odd Fellows of D C, asking an act of incorporation: referred. 2-Ptn from John Cradlebaugh, one of the Associate Judges of the Supreme Court of the Territory of Utah, asking the payment of the expenses of transporting the books, papers, etc, of the Judicial Court of that Territory: referred. 3-Cmte on Military Affairs: memorial of Florian Kern, asking reimbursement of the expenses incurred in raising a company of volunteers for the Mexican war, submitted an adverse report on the same. 4-Cmte on Pensions: bill for the relief of F L Colclaser, a soldier in the army; & a bill for the relief of Alice Hunt, widow of Thos Hunt. Same cmte: adverse report on the ptn of Thos O'Sullivan for a pension.

Wash Corp-Feb 27. 1-Ptn from Geo P Wells, praying the remission of a fine: referred to the Cmte of Claims. 2-Cmte on Improvement: bill for the relief of Jacob Gideon: passed. 3-Cmte of Claims: bills for the relief of J R Worster; & of Christopher Hollohan: both for the remission of a fine: passed.

Died: Rev John Barker, D D, suddenly, at Meadville, Pa, was formerly Vice President & Prof in Trannsylvania [Ky] University, & for the past 12 or 13 years Pres of Allegheny College, Pa. He was distinguished for his scholastic attainments. [No death date given-current item.]

Died: on Feb 28, at Phil, aged 12 years, Augusta Yorke, daughter of S Yorke AtLee, of Wash City.

Circuit Court of Wash Co, D C-in Equity, No 1,516. John F Lee against Eliz A B Upshur & Jas N Ringgold. By an order of the Court I am directed to ascertain & report what debts, if any, of the late Abel P Upshur & of his late daughter, Susan B Ringgold, remain unpaid & in what manner the same should be discharged. Meeting at my ofc, in City Hall, on Mar 28 next, at 10 o'clock. –W Redin, auditor

FRI MAR 2, 1860
Senate: 1-Court of Claims: adverse reports on the following claims: of Sarah D Webber, admx of John A Webber; of Joshua Eddy, Chas A Dubois de Luchet, & of John H Merrill. 2-Ptn from J Heudebert, asking to be allowed a salary for the period of his service as Consul at Lyons, in France: referred. 3-Ptn from L D Benedict & others, asking that the militia of the war of 1812 & of the Indian wars may be placed on the same footing in regard to bounty land as those who served in the war with Mexico: referred. 4-Additional papers relating to the claim of Mary Loyd for balance due on a contract with her late husband for carrying the mails: referredto the Cmte on the Post Ofc & Post Roads. 5-Memorial of Mary Chase Barney, sole daughter & survivor of Saml Chase, of Md, asking to be allowed a pension, was taken from the files & again referred to the Cmte on Pensions. 6-Cmte on Indian Affairs: bill for the relief of W A Gorman, as special

agent to investigate the charges against A Ramsey, late Superintendent of Indian Affairs in Minn.

House of Reps: 1-Cmte of Claims: adverse report on the ptn of Benj Gregg: laid on the table. Same cmte: bill for the relief of Lydia Frazee, widow & admx of John Frazee, deceased: committed. Same cmte: adverse on the ptns of Chauncey Smith & Jemima Christian: laid on the table. Same cmte: bill for the relief of Mariano G Vallejo: committed. Same cmte: bill for the relief of Wm Geiger: committed. 2-Bill for the relief of Shade Calloway: committed. 3-Cmte on Commerce: bill for the relief of Chas Knapp: committed. Same cmte: bill for the relief of Isaac S Smith, of Syracuse, N Y: committed. Same cmte: adverse on the ptn of Geo R Jackson: laid on the table. Same cmte: Senate bill to authorize the Sec of the Treasury to isue registers to the schnr **Helen Blood** & the schnr **Sarah Bond**: passed.

Nat'l Medical College annual commencement took place last evening in the hall of the Smithsonian Institution. Prayer by Rev Dr Samson, Pres of Columbian College. Dr J G Holston rose & stated that the hand of sickness having been laid on Prof Lincoln, who was to address the class, it had devolved to himself to supply his place. The graduating class was called by Dr Jno C Riley, the Dean of the Faculty. The degree of Dr in Medicine was conferred upon Lee M Alexander, Missouri; Saml Wm Bogan, D C; Jas W Brown, Va; M Van Congdon, Vt; J F Culpeper, S C; L M Dinsmoor, N H; Thos H Elder, Ohio; C Hurley Foreman, Mo; H P Fricker, Ohio; *Jno E Rowland, Mass; Chas W Harper, Ky; Jeffin M Harbison, Tenn; E B Holland, N C; Jno S Hougland, Ind; Sam H Jackson, S C; Edwin W Latimer, Va; Nath M Lawrence, N C; C E Lippett, Va; Chas W Lewis, Va; Edw W Mayo, Maine; L C Osmun, Va; L M Osmun, Va; J M Pettigrew, Pa; Wm O Slade, jr, Va; Thos Smith, D C; Isaac Holden Stearne, Mass; David B Sturgeon, Pa; R G Syme, Va; Dowe Danl Talman, N Y. Honorary degree of M D was also conferred on John Thompson Mason, surgeon U S Navy, & Wm Stimpson, of Mass. [Mar 3rd newspaper correction: the name of Mr *Jno E Rowland, of Mass, should have been John E Gowland. It was the fault of the manuscript, & not of the compositor.]

Mrd: on Mar 1, in Wash City, by Rev Mr Butler, Alfred B Welby, of Louisville, Ky, to Miss Hester R Wrightson, of Talbot Co, Md.

Tragedy in Henry Co, Va: a grand-daughter of Vincent Witcher, of Pittsylvania Co, Miss Smith, married a gentleman from Henry Co, named Clemmens. After 18 months of marriage Mr Clemmens desired a separation from his wife & instituted proceedings for divorce, at the same time impeaching her honor as the grounds for his course. Last Sat was set apart for the taking of depositions, & the parties met at a magisterial precinct in Henry Co. Mr Witcher appeared to defend the suit & honor of his grand-daughter. Mr Witcher asked a question, which greatly exasperated the husband, Mr Clemmens. He drew a pistol & fired at Mr Witcher; Mr Witcher drew a pistol & fire at Mr Clemmens striking him in the forehead & killing him instantly. A nephew of Mr Witcher, & a Mr Smith, brother of Mrs Clemmens, fired into the room; a brother of Mr Clemmens fired at a nephew of Mr Witcher, producing a fatal wound. Upon seeing his nephew shot, Mr Vincent Witcher again fired, striking Clemmens No 2, & killing him instantly. Mr Smith, a brother of Mrs Clemmens, drew a bowie-knife & was fired upon by a second brother of Clemmens, the ball producing a painful wound. Mr Smith rushed his antagonist & thrust his knife, completely disembowling Clemmens No 3, who died on the spot. Three dead & 3 wounded. Vincent Witcher, the chief actor in this truly terrible affair, is widely known throughout Va. The whole matter will undergo a judicial investigation, until which we forbear further comment.

Died: on Mar 1, after a short & painful illness, Mrs Catharine Rheem, in her 60th year. She was formerly a resident in Alexandria, Va, but for the last 17 years a resident of Wash City. Her funeral will take place from the residence of her son, Mr Benj Reese, 267 G st, between 14th & 15th sts, on Mar 2 at 3 o'clock P M.

Europe: Sir Wm Napier is dead.

SAT MAR 3, 1860
Senate: 1-Ptn from Augustus Steele, asking for payment of an amount claimed to be due for salary & expenses while inspector of the customs at Tampa Bay: referred. 2-Ptn from Jos B Walker, asking indemnity for losses of money in its transmission by mail: referred. 3-Cmte on the Judiciary: bill for the relief of McFarland & Downey. Same cmte: adverse reports on the cases of Geo G Barnard, assignee of Hon David C Broderick, asking the enactment of a law authorizing him to receive the amount due said Broderick for salary & mileage at the time of his death. 4-Cmte of Claims: bill for the relief of Thos Brown for balance due him as Sec of the Senate of the Territory of Fla: passed. Same cmte: bill for the relief of Saml V Niles for compensation for services performed as a temporary clerk in the Genr'l Land Ofc. 5-Cmte on Military Affairs: asked to be discharged from further consideration of the memorial of L W Boggs, asking to be allowed compensation as alcalde under the military gov't of Calif, & it was referred to the Court of Claims. Same cmte: adverse report on the memorial of Horace E Dimick for renumeration for improvements made by him in artillery. 6-Cmte on Commerce: memorial asking that certain tonnage duties exacted from the ship Corinthian might be refunded, submitted a report, accompanied by a bill for the relief of J W Dyer, A L Dyer, & W W Dyer. 7-Cmte on Private Land Claims: bill for the relief of the heirs & legal reps of Mark Elisha, & recommended its passage. Same cmte: bill to confirm the title of Benj E Edwards to a certain tract of land in the Territory in New Mexico. 8-Cmte on Naval

On Thu of last week Thos Monks, aged about 21 years, & residing about 3 miles from Bel Air, Md, whilst engaged in felling trees was instantly killed by coming in contact with the limb of a falling tree.

Affairs: bill for the relief of Lt A McCraven. 9-Bill for the relief of the legal reps of Chas Pearson, deceased: referred. 10-Bill for the relief of M C Gritzner: referred. 11-The following bills were passed-relief of: Mrs Jane M McCrabb, widow of the late Capt John W McCrabb, Assist Quartermaster U S Army; of Livingston, Kinkhead & Co; of Geo Stealey; of Edw N Kent; of Richd Chenery; of Simon de Visser & Jose Villarubia, of New Orleans; of Francis <u>Hittmann</u>; of Tench Tilghman; of the legal reps of John A Frost, deceased; of Wm D Moseley; of Henry Etting; of Eliz M Cocke, widow of Maj Jas H Cocke, late marshal of the district of Texas; of Jeremiah Moors; of John Scott, Hill W House, & Saml O House; of Arnold Harris & Saml F Butterworth; of Richd W Meade; of David D Porter; of Geo B Bacon, late acting purser of the sloop-of-war **Portsmouth**; of Saml A West, Geo McCullough, Hiram McCullough, & Chas Pendergrast; & of Mrs Ann Scott; of Michl Nash, of D C. The bill for the relief of Mrs Anne M Smith, widow of the late brevet Maj Gen Persifer F Smith, led to quite a discussion. Mr Iverson moved to amend the bill by adding the name of Mrs Gen McComb, a case he considered quite as meritorious as the one before them. Mr Seward moved to amend the amendment by adding the name of Mrs Gen Riley, but, without taking any questions. The Senate adjourned.

Hon Geo W Rowles has declined the appointment of U S Treasurer, tendered him by Pres Buchanan.

Wm Woehler, an old citizen of Bethlehim, Pa, was suffocated on Feb 21st by the gas escaping from a coal stove in a room adjoining his bed-room, the door of which was open. He was at the time confined to his bed by illness. His wife & daughter were affected but got up making preparations for breakfast, unconscious it was evening when they awoke. They found Mr Woehler in his room dead.

The Lynchburg Republican of Wed says that Mr Vincent Witcher & his grandson, who killed Messrs *Clements, in Franklin Co, Va, on Sat, surrendered themselves to the authorities, & were promptly acquitted, on the ground of self-defence. [Mar 2nd newspaper: note- *Clemmens was used in the first article/Clements in this one.]

Died: on Mar 2, Jas Thecker, in his 58th year. His funeral will take place on Sunday at 2 o'clock P M, from his late residence, Cherry st, Gtwn, D C. The service will take place at Trinity Church.

Died: on Feb 27, at sea, Capt G Porter Adams, a native of Alexandria, Va, but for a number of years past a citizen of Charleston, S C.

Died: on Mar 2, in Wash City, after a short but painful illness, Peter Alex'r Hutchins, in his 44th year. His funeral will take place from his brother-in-law's residence on 10th st, today at 2 o'clock.

In Chancery-Dec 27, 1859. Tilghman Nuttle, vs Hannah McCartee, Levin Henry Wooters, Sarah Catharine Wooters, Jos Smith Wooters, & Chas Wooters. The object of this suit is to procure a decree for the sale of the real estate of which Levin Wooters, sr, died seized & possessed, lying in Caroline Co, Md, to pay off his creditors, who remain unpaid because of the insufficiency of his personal estate. About 1857, the said Levin Wooters, sr, departed this life, being indebted unto Tilghman Nuttle, on 2 judgments obtained in the Circuit Court for Caroline Co, Md, at the Oct term, in 1856; the said Levin Wooters, sr, was largely indebted unto other parties besides himself, & that there have been letters of administration granted by the Orphans' Court of Caroline Co to one Sarah Wooters, who has exhausted the personal estate in due course of administration, & it is found to be insufficient to pay off the creditors of the said Levin Wooters, & that the said Levin Wooters left as his heirs at law Nancy Hignutt, Sarah Beachamp, Cecelia Colescott, Geo W & Wm Wooters, Francis & Wm H Wooters, Sarah Beachamp, & Edw & Pratt Wooters, all of the State of Md, Caroline Co, & Hannah McCartee, wife of Jas McCartee, of the State of Indiana, & Lewis Henry Wooters, Sarah Catharine Wooters, Jos Smith Wooters, & Chas Wooters, all children of Jas T Wooters, who was one of the main or principal heiars of said Levin Wooters, sr, deceased, & who was also a resident of the State of Indiana & now resident of the State of Md. Absent dfndnts are to appear in this Court, in person or by solicitor, on or before the first Mon of Jul, 1860. -Robt J Jump, Clerk Ciruit Court for Caroline Co.

House of Reps: 1-Bills committed to the Cmte of the Whole on the private calendar: relief of: the heirs of Lot Hall; of Thos Atkinson, of Ind; of John Dixon; of Robt Johnston; of Geo F Brott; of Eben S Hanscomb; of Cassius M Clay; of Charner T Scaife, adm of Gilbert Stalker; of Moses Noble; of legal reps of Robt H Morris, late postmaster of N Y C; of legal reps of Chas Porterfield, deceased; of heirs of Dr Geo Yates; of heirs of Maj John Ripley; of Maryett Von Buskirk; of legal reps of Lt Francis Chandonet; of legal reps of Brig Gen Wm Thompson; of orphan children of Col Philip Johnston; of legal reps of Capt Lewis Marnay; of heirs of Clement Gosselin; of children of Basil Mignault; of heirs of Capt Saml Miller; of heirs & descendants of Capt Jas Baptiste Laborite; of legal reps of Lt Thos Williams; of legal reps of Capt Pierre Ayott; of heirs of Nehemiah Stokely; of heirs of Capt Jos Traverse; of orphan children of Jos Jewett; of Chas Oliver Du Closel, of Louisiana; of R K Doebler; of Valery Landry, of Louisiana; of heirs or legal reps of Francois Guillory; of W Y Hansell & others; of John Johnstone, of Ohio; of Chas Stillman; of Fred'k Stephens; of Brevet Lt Col Martin Buke & Capt Chas S Winder, U S Army; of Mrs Anne W Augus; of children of the late Martha Swilling, widow of Geo Swilling; of Micajah Hawkes; of Timothy Cravan, an invalid pensioner; of children of Lt Nathl Smith, dec'd; & of Mrs Hannah McDowell. Also, granting a pension to Jas Lacy, of Tenn; to John Madden, of Tenn; to Cyrenus C Bluckman, of Louisiana; & to Adelaide Adams, widow of Cmder Geo Adams, U S Navy. 2-Mr Lovejoy, of Ill, reported a bill for the relief of Anthony Schandler, & asked that it be put on its passage. 3-Adverse reports on the ptns of Danl Wright & Jos P Eaton: laid on the table.

MON MAR 5, 1860
N Y, Mar 3, 1860. Mr Gerrit Smith, on his recovery from lunacy, has ordered suits for libel against Messrs Watts Sherman, Royal Phelps, & J M Bailou, of this city, $50,000 damages in each case, for their publication, as members of the N Y Democraic Vigilant Association, identifying him with the bloody & horrible purposes of a certain Central Association, & the work of John Brown. His son-in-law, Dr Chas D Miller, who writes for him, says Mr Smith never before had heard of that association, or of the Provisional Gov't adopted by the Convention at Chatham, Canada West.

Maj Gaines, Paymaster of the Army, died at **Fort Smith** on Feb 18 from being thrown from a buggy 8 weeks previously.

Sir Wm Napier, the great historian of the memorable Peninsular war died on Feb 12, in his 74th year. He was born in Castletown, Ireland, in 1785. During the latter part of his life he was devoted to his brother, Sir Chas Napier. Sir Wm, after his brother's death, defended his memory during the Indian debates with much ardor. -N Y Evening Post

Died: on Mar 3, George A, aged 16 years & 9 months, eldest son of George W & Catharine J Hinton. His funeral will be this afternoon at 3 o'clock, from 493 Md ave, between 4½ & 6th sts.

Died: on Mar 4, in Wash City, Isaac K Hanson, in his 71st year. His funeral will take place from his late residence, 517 17th st, this day, at 3 o'clock. [Mar 7th newspaper: Isaac K Hanson: he was always associated with the memory of his 3 gallant sons, who, in all the pride & bloom of manhood, offered themselves on the altar of their country, with the last breath commending their beloved parent to the care of that Covenant-God who is better than sons or daughters. They died gloriously; their deeds speak for them. To their family they leave in sacred keeping their memory, & their country's legacy, even the trusty swords they wielded gallantly to the death.]

Died: on Feb 25, at Louisville, Ky, in her 68th year, Mrs Mary M Gilliss, relict of the late Geo Gilliss, for many years residents of Wash City.

Died: Feb 26, at Carlisle Barracks, Robt E Jackson, of Athens, Ga, in his 24th year.

Died: on Feb 25, in Jersey City, N J, Alfred, youngest child of Jas & Josephine Morss, aged 2 years, 10 months & 9 days.

TUE MAR 6, 1860
Capt Shannon, of the steamer **Africa**, states that the passengers in the ill-fated ship **Hungarian** numbered about 140, & these with the crew amounted to 214 persons, none of whom have been saved to tell the said story of wreck & suffering

The President appointed Wm D Chapman U S Dist Judge for Connecticut, in place of Judge Ingersoll, deceased.

Harpers Ferry expenses: total amount audited & reported: $185,667.63.

Died: Mar 4, in Gtwn, Jas Henry, son of Dr Ashton Miles, aged 9 years. His funeral will be from the residence of his grandfather, 91 Fayette st, Mar 6 at 3:30 P M.

Criminal Court-Wash-Mon.
1-Jos Goldsmith convicted for robbery of the house of Emmanuel Kaufman, in Gtwn, of a sum of money.

Grand Jury:

John M Broadhead	John P Ingle
Joshua Pierce	Chas L Coltman
Geo A Bohrer	Francis Mohun
John Van Reswick	Benj F Middleton
Stephen D Castleman	Benj O Tayloe
Geo W Young	Wm B Todd
Wm J Stone, sr	Danl English
Robt S Patterson	Robt White
Bushrod W Reed	Jonathan Prout
Eleazer Lindsly	Thos J Fisher
Chas Wilson	Wm G Flood
Richd R Crawford	Geo W Beall

Petit Jury:

John F Bridget	Saml Lewis
Geo E Jillard	Edmond Brooks
John Crowley	Raymond B Hall
Bendict Milburn	David Jackson
Wm Shanks	Jos S Smith
Sam R Sylvester	Theodore Sheckels
David A Gardiner	Orlando H Donn
J Owens Berry	Lewis Wright
Chas W Drury	Norvell W Burchell
Wm E Spaulding	Francis Lamb
Danl Lightfoot	Francis Miller
Geo Taylor	Thos F Herbert
Benj C King	Henry Barron
Thos E Clark	Henry M Hurdle
Thos Thornley	Theodore F Boucher

Senate: 1-Ptn from Lockey Simpson, asking an increase of pension: referred. 2-Ptn from A Armstrong & others, asking the establishment of a weekly mail from Rockford, Iowa, to Albert Lea, Minn: referred. 3-Ptn from Chas M Smith, asking compensation for defending, at the request of the Superintendent of Indian

Affairs in Utah, 2 Indian boys who were indicted for a grave criminal offence in the 2nd judicial district of that Territory: referred. 4-Cmte on Revolutionary Claims: adverse report on the memorial of Burnet M Dole. 5-Ptn from citizens of Phil, asking that Congress grant a pension to John J Kissick, a quartermaster in the navy, who was wounded by the bursting of a cannon on board the U S steamship **Princeton**: referred.

WED MAR 7, 1860
The Ocala Companion says: the slave Lewis, having been proved guilty of the murder of Dr W J Keitt, was examined on Wed, was immediately sentenced & hung.

Medical Dept of Gtwn College will hold its annual commencement tomorrow, at the Smithsonian Institution. The graduates will be: John W Davis, of Ind; Richd C Croggon, of D C; Van-Deusen Naylor, Md; A G Browning, Ky; David R Lindsay, Ala; A Zappone, Italy; Leroy M Taylor, Mich; John C Harrison, Va; Fred J McNulty, Conn; & Jas H Peabody, D C.

Executor's sale of Rosewood Piano, & household & kitchen furniture at auction on Mar 15, at the residence of the late Jas Galligan, deceased, C & 1st sts east, Capitol Hill. –Thos Galligan, exc -Wall & Barnard, auct.

Senate: 1-Ptn from Jas Flemming, of Portsmouth, Va, asking to be remunerated for the use by Gov't of a pile-cutting machine: referred. 2-Ptn from Thos Kirkman, of Ala, asking indemnity for losses caused by the failure & refusal of the U S Gov't to convey a title to a section of land purchased by him: referred. 3-Ptn from Lt A C Rind, a lt in the navy, who was dropped by the naval board but since restored to active service, asking to be placed on the same footing as other ofcrs restored to service: referred. 4-Ptn from Geo W Greene, asking the aid of Congress in publishing the life & letters of his grandfather: referred. 5-Ptn from Mr Pitachaca, asking to be allowed to locate other lands in lieu of a grant made to his mother by treaty with the Delaware Indians, in Ohio, in 1818: referred. 6-Cmte on Pensions: adverse report on the ptn of Lemuel Worster for a pension on account of disability incurred while acting as waiter to a militia ofcr in the U S service during the war of 1812. 7-Cmte on Pensions: bill for the relief of Mary E Castor. 8-Cmte on the Judiciary: resolution in relation to the contract made with Mrs Adeline Sergeant for binding certain reserved documents. 8-Cmte on Pensions: bill for the relief of Kate D Taylor, widow of the late Brvt Capt Oliver H P Taylor. 9-Cmte on Indian Affairs: bill for the relief of Saml J Hensley. 10-Cmte on Revolutionary Claims: adverse report on the ptn of Catharine Lydia McLeod, daughter of a Canadian refugee, for compensation for the suffering of her father in aiding the cause of the American Revolution. 11-Bill for the relief of John B Rittenhouse: referred.

House of Reps: 1-Cmte on Revolutionary Claims: bill for the relief of the heirs of John Paulding, David Williams, Isaac Van Wert, & Sergeant John Champe: committed. 2-Rev Thos H Stockton, of Phil, elected chaplain of the House.

Died: on Mar 5, in her 13th year, Laura, the youngest daughter of Francis Mohun. Her funeral will take place this afternoon at 3 o'clock, from the residence of her father, 446 6th st.

Died: yesterday, in Wash City, Capt John Reese, in his 37th year. His funeral will take place tomorrow at 3 o'clock, from his late residence, on Missouri ave, between 4½ & 6th st.

Easton, Pa, Mar 6. A new steamboat, built here, when about starting on her first trip, at noon, burst her boiler. She is a complete wreck. Killed were Richd Holcomb, Jos Weaver, Geo Smith, Judge Sharp, Wm Sharp, jr, Valentine Schooley, Jos Labarre, & Geo Schaef. Injured: John Smith, Solomon McIntyre, badly; Andrew Mebek, &
B M Yonnells.

THU MAR 8, 1860
Senate: 1-Ptn from Jos Pattee, a sergeant in the war of 1812, asking to be allowed a pension: referred. 2-Ptn from C T Alexander, in relation to his rank in the medical corps of the army: referred. 3-Ptn from Richd Stout, asking compensation for carrying the mail from Easton, Pa, via New Brunswick, to N Y: referred. 4-Cmte on Claims: adverse reports on the following memorials, viz: Wm G Ridgely, of D C, for indeminty for tobacco destroyed by the British in the war of 1812; of John G Mackall, for indemnty for a house destroyed during the war with Great Britain; & of Hodges & Lansdale, for property destroyed in the same war. 5-Cmte for D C: adverse reports on the memorials of Jas & Theodore Walters, asking that certain lots in Wash City be conveyed to them. Same cmte: memorial of L A Gobright & others, reported a bill to incorporate the Grand Lodge of the Independent Order of Odd Fellows of D C. 6-Cmte on Indian Affairs: bill for the relief of the legal reps of Wetonsaw, son of Jas Conner. 7-Bill for the relief of Lewis W Chatfield: referred. 8-Bill for the relief of John V Dobbin, a purser in the U S Navy: referred. 9-Bill for the relief of Nancy Bukey, widow of John Bukey: referred. 10-Bill for the relief of Jacob Amman: referred. 11-Bill granting a pension to John Jackson, an invalid soldier: referred. 12-Bill for the relief of John W Taylor, & certain assignees of pre-emption land locations: committed.

The Woonsocket Patriot says that John Kelley, of North Blackstone, now in his 84th year, had tended the same grist-mill for 70 years, & still delights in his old occupation. Mr Kelley was never in a railroad car or steamboat in his life, & never 100 miles from home.

Trustee's sale of highly valuable farm on the Turnpike, near the Village of Baldensburg, on Apr 10th, on the premises, by deed of trust, dated Apr 4, 1859, recorded in Liber C S M, No 3, folios 72, of the land records for PG Co, & Liber J A S, No 172, folios 1, of the land records for Wash Co, D C: sale of all that tract or part of a tract of land called **Brothers' Fifth Part**, adjoining the farms of Chas B Calvert, containing 87¼ acres, more or less; with a two story double framed dwlg house, with necessary out-bldgs. –Thos J Fisher, trustee -Jas C McGuire & Co, aucts

Criminal Court-Wash-Wed. 1-Danl Barry, an old soldier, formerly at the Military Asylum, was found guilty for setting fire to an old unoccpied dwlg-house on 7th st, near Park, the property of Mrs Emily Boscoe, on Feb 9: he was sentenced to 3 years in the penitentiary. 2-John Barron was found guilty of assault on Thos Young as a private individual. [Ofcr Young is a member of the Auxiliary Guard.] 3-Jas Ford, a youth, was found guilty of stealing a gun, valued at $10, the property of John W Sothoron, of Gtwn: sentenced to 1 year in the penitentiary. The same prisoner, was found guilty of stealing a pair of pantaloons, the property of John S Shackelford, of Gtwn, was sentenced to 2 weeks in the county jail.

Died: on Mar 5, at Alexandria, Va, Dr Horatio Nelson Lloyd, after prolonged sufferings.

Died: on Mar 6, at his father's residence, near Sandy Spring, Md, Albert G Palmer, late of the firm of Nairn & Palmer, late of Wash City, in his 31st year.

City election in Alexandria on Tue: elected, as follows: <u>Mayor</u>, Wm B Price. <u>Aldermen</u>: D Kinzer, Henry L Simpson, Geo Bryan, & Geo L Cazenove. Councilmen: Lewis McKenzie, Edgar Snowden, jr, Geo H Markle, W A Harper, Geo T Whittington, Jas S Hallowell, Chas Alexander, A W Eastlack; W J Boothe; H C Dorsey; Andrew Jaloson; J H McVeigh; J W Atkinson, J B Smoot, W D Massey, F W Ashby. <u>Collectors of Taxes</u>: John A Field, W Avery, Corp Atty, David L Smoot. Assessors, P E Henderson, Wm Davis. Auditor, Thos McCormick. City Surveyor, Wm G Atkinson. Superintendent of Gas, T W Smith. Superintendent of Market, Thos Whittington. Chief Engineer Fire Dept, Jas Javins. Superintendent of Police, Geo Davis. Measurers of Lumber, Wm H McKnight, Wm R Howard. Measurer of Wood & Bark, Jas P Colman. Guager, S R Shinn.

Chicago, Mar 5. While 4 men were crossing in a batteau the Big Vermillion river, near Ottawa, it capsized, & 3 of the men drowned: Porsser, Domber, & Bell.

FRI MAR 9, 1860
Washington & New Orleans <u>Telegraph Co</u>, Wash, Mar 8, 1860. Board of Directors meeting at the Nat'l Hotel, Wash, on Mar 14, at 11 o'clock.
–Amos Kendall, Pres

Obit-died: on Monday, at his residence in Phil, aged 70 years, Cmdor David Geisinger, of the U S Navy. He was born in the State of Md, & became a midshipman in 1809, & in the second war with Great Britain was in the sloop-of-war Wasp in her famous cruise on the English coast in 1814. When the ship **Wasp** captured the British brig **Atlanta**, & sent her to Charleston as a prize, Mr Geisinger was put in command of her-a lucky thing for him, as the **Wasp** was never again heard of. His commission as capt dates from May 24, 1838, 29 years after he entered the service. He was for many years stationed at the naval asylum in Phil, where he made many friends. He was 7th among the capts on the reserved list.

Senate: 1-Ptn from Carroll Spence, late Minister to Turkey, asking compensation for negotiating a treaty with Persia: referred. 2-Ptn from Capt Hiram Paulding, asking remuneration for expenses incurred in defending a suit brought against him in consequence of having caused Wm Walker & his followers to leave San Juan, Nicaragua: referred. 3-Cmte on Military Affairs: bill for the relief of Mrs Agatha O'Brien, widow of Brvt Maj J P J O'Brien, late of the U S Army: passed. 4-Cmte on Commerce: adverse report on the memorial of F E Hassler, adm of the late superintendent of the coast survey & of the construction of standard weights & measures. 5-Cmte on Public Lands: bill for the relief of Elias Yulee, late receiver of public moneys in Wash Territory. 6-Cmte on Private Land Claims: bill for the relief of Thos L Disharoon. Same cmte: adverse report on memorial of Wm Petchaka, asking to be allowed to locate land under a granr made by a treaty with the Delaware Indians. 7-Cmte on Foreign Relations: bill for the relief of Wm R Jennings & others, legal reps of Wm Bean, asking compensation out of the fund provided by the treaty of Ghent for negroes carried off by the British troops in the war of 1812. 8-Cmte on Patents: asked to be discharged from further consideration of the memorial of Jas Flemming, & that it be referred to the Cmte on Naval Affairs. 9-Cmte on Naval Affairs: asked to be discharged from further consideration of the memorial of Danl B Martin for the use by the Gov't of his patent tubular boiler: which was agreed to.

Mrd: on Feb 20, in PG Co, Md, by Rev Mr Martin, Edward L Smoot, of Chas Co, to Carrie M Ward, of the former place.

Criminal Court-Wash-Thu. 1-John W Wade was acquitted of larceny in stealing one pair of boots. 2-Thos Brett was convicted of stealing a watch: sentenced to 18 months in the penitentiary. 3-John Sullivan was convicted for an asault & battery with intent to kill Margaret Sullivan, his wife: sentenced to 2 years in the penitentiary. 4-Richd Ellis, colored, was convicted of grand larceny in having stolen a lot of chickens valued at $6, the property of Timothy Maher: sentenced to 18 months in the penitentiary. 5-John Cockerill was convicted of stealing 12 chickens, valued at $4.50: sentenced to 6 months in jail. 6-Jos Goldsmith convicted of stealing money from the bedroom of Emmanuel Kaufman, in Gtwn, sentenced to 1 year in the penitentiary, to commence on Monday next.

Obit-died: on Jan 9, at Los Angeles, Calif, at age 41, Maj Edw Harold Fitzgerald, U S Army, capt in the 1st dragoons. He was born in Norristown, Pa, & in 1839 was appointed a 2nd lt in the 6th regt U S Infty. He served in the Seminole war from the date of his appointment until 1841. From 1841 to 1846 he served in the Cherokee Nation. He served gallantly in the Mexican war, & was in every battle on Gen Scott's line, from the surrender of Vera Curz to the fall of the City of Mexico. For conspicuous gallantry at the storming of Chapultepec he received his commission as brevet major in the army.

SAT MAR 10, 1860

House of Reps: 1-Bills referred to the Cmte of the Whole: relief of the children of Eliz M Cocke, widow of Maj Jas H Cocke, late U S Marshal of Texas; of Mrs Mary Ann Henry; of Emma Wood, widow of Maj G W F Wood, U S Army; of Elmira White, widow of Capt Thos R White; of Smith Hunt, of Toledo, Ohio; of Andrew E Marshall; & of Rev Jas Craige, deceased. Also, pension to John Sandles & to Abraham Crum.

Marlboro [Md] Advocate: the dwlg of Mr Marsham Warring was entirely destroyed by fire, with all the furniture & $3,000 in money, recently.

Senate: 1-Ptn from Wm H Vesey, U S Consul at Havre, asking to have refunded the money paid by him on account of the default of certain bankers in Paris with whom he had deposited the funds of the Gov't: referred. 2-Ptn from Thatcher Perkins & Wm McMahon, asking an extension of their patent for an improvement in the wheels of locomotive engines: referred. 3-Ptn from Loomis L Langdon, a lt in the army, asking remuneration for baggage carried off by the Mexicans under Cortina: referred. 4-Ptn from Mira M Alexander, asking to be allowed a pension on account of the services of her father, Geo Madison, in the war of the Revolutin & of Indian wars: referred. 5-Ptn from Theron Hamilton, asking Congress to have printed & bound, in pocket form, 5,000 copies of the Declaration of Independence & Washington's Farewell Address, with a steel-plate engraving of Washington on the title page, & reserve a copy for each ofcr of the Gov't & each member of Congress: referred. 6-Cmte on Revolutionary Claims: memorial of Haym M Soloman, asking indemnity for moneys advanced & losses sustained by his father during the war of the Revolution, submitted an elaborate report, with a bill for his relief. 7-Bill for the relief of Mrs Anne M Smith, widow of the late Brvt Maj Gen Persifer F Smith; & Mrs Harriet B Macomb, widow of the late Maj Gen Macomb; & Mrs Arabella Riley, widow of Brvt Maj Gen Bennet Riley: pay them pensions at the rate of $50 per month, from the date of the approval of the act: yeas 33: nays 15.

Farming implements, live stock, & household & kitchen furniture at auction on Mar 21, at the farm of Ruel Keith, on Rockville Turnpike.
–Barnard & Buckey, aucts, Gtwn, D C

Balt Methodist Episcopal Annual Conference at Winchester, Va, ended on Thu. Cmte: Ministers: John Bear, Saml Register, John Lanahan, S Samuel Roszel, Jas N Davis, A Burhman, Jas S Gardner. Laymen: John S Berry, Robt Ricketts, W P Conway, J S Carson, P Herring, A L Pitzer, Henry Stewart. Wash & Alexandria district appointments for the ensuing year:

Wash District: L F Morgan, P E.
Foundry, W B Edwards
Wesley Chapel, J A McCauley.
Waugh Chapel, J R Effinger
McKendree Chapel, W Hamilton
East Washington, W M D Ryan
Ryland Chapel, J H Cooms
Gorsuch Chapel, J H M Lemon
Union Chapel, H C Westwood
Fletcher & Province Chapel, H N Sipes
Asbury, Mount Zion, & Ebenezer, J M Grandin
Rockville, T A Morgan & J A Williams
Howard, S V Leach
Bladensburg, F S Cassaday & G E Kramer
Patapsco Station, C A Reid
Patapsco Circuit, W Prettyman
Woodville, H C McDaniel
Patuxent, J N Davis & J H Swope
Metropolitan, S S Roszel

Alexandria District:
B N Brown, P E
Alexandria, J Lanahan & S M Dickson
Gtwn, N J B Morgan
West Gtwn & Tennalytown, J H Ryland
Fairfax, W G Coe & G H Zimmerman
East Fairfax, W E Magruder
Chas, C Parkison & E H Jones.
St Mary's, J W Start & H McNemar
Fredericksburg, S Rogers
Stafford, C B Young
Brentsville, C F Linthicum
Montgomery, J L Gilbert & A B Dolley
Leesburg, John Landstreet
Loudoun, D Thomas, S Cornelius, & W V Tudor
Rehoboth, J P Etchison
Warrenton, E D Owen

Died: on Mar 8, in Wash City, Mr S H Young, in his 29th year. His funeral will take place this afternoon at 3 o'clock, from the residence of his father-in-law, J C McKelden, 416 F st. [Mar 13th newspaper: Saml H Young-here he was born, lived, & died; a member of the Methodist Church. -W J R.]

Died: on Feb 24, in Gatesville, N C, Mrs Sarah Ann Nixon, consort of Rev Robt T Nixon, of the Va Annual Conference. Precious in the sight of the Lord is the death of his saints.

Criminal Court-Wash-Fri. 1-John Myer was convicted of stealing a coat of the value of $10 from Richd H Laskey: sentenced to 18 months in the penitentiary. 2-Margaret Russell was convicted of stealing articles of female dress valued at $4.75: sentenced to 3 months in the county jail. 3-Sarah Jane Norton, colored, was found guilty of stealing $1.05 in silver coin, from Nina Netita, & sentenced to 1 month imprisonment in the county jail & fined $1. She was acquitted of stealing bed & other clothing from Edw Leipziger.

Chancery sale of improved property: by deed of the Circuit Court of D C, in Chancery, dated Oct 26, 1859, passed in a cause therein depending between John Foller, cmplnt, & Andreas Fischer, dfndnt, [No 1,477, Chancery,] I shall offer at public auction, on Apr 3, property on L st north, between 6th & 7th sts west, part of lot 4 in square 449, in Wash City, with the bldgs & improvements thereon, consisting of 2 frame houses. –Asbury Lloyd, trustee -A Green, aucts

MON MAR 12, 1860
Died: on Mar 10, in Wash City, A M Willie, 2nd son of Wm & Jessie McDermott, in his 10th year. His funeral is today at 4 o'clock P M, at 229 I st.

On Fri last the stable of Ezra M Sayers, of Waynesburg, Pa, was burnt to the ground, & two of his children, one 5 & the other 2 years old, perished in the flames. It is supposed that the children accidentally set it on fire with matches. Their sad fate was not known until their little bones were found among the smouldering ruins.

The Cmte of the Legislature of Maine, charged with the examination of the case of Benj D Peck, the defaulting Treasurer of the State, have ascertained the amount of the deficit to be a little upwards of $94,000. Mr Peck has made a written confession to the cmte.

A daughter of Capt Henry Smith, of Vinalhaven, Main, was instantly killed last Sat by the accidental discharge of a pistol in the hands of a young man, Henry Berwin, of Rockland. She was about 18 years old.

Com'rs sale of valuable real estate, by decree of the Circuit Court of Wash D C, dated Feb 15, 1860, on the ptn of John G Adams & others for a division of the real estate of Saml H Adams, deceased, [No 170, petition docket,] public auction on Mar 20 of lot 14 & parts of lot 12, 13, & 15 in square 847, in Wash City, with a frame dwlg. -J Russell Barr, Nathl Wells, Eustice E O'Brien, Walter C Johnson, John W Simms, Com'rs -A Green, aucts

Trustee's sale of valuable real estate, by decree of the Circuit Court of Wash D C, passed in chancery No 1,517, wherein Edw Tohuler & others are cmplnts & Thos H Garner & others are dfndnts, we, as trustees will sell on Apr 6, lots 19 thru 22 in square 117, with improvements thereon. –E C Morgan, Walter S Cox, trustees -Jas C McGuire & Co, aucts

Mrd: on Feb 21, in the Church of the Holy Trinity, by Rt Rev Saml Bowman, D D, E Bowman Miner, M D, of Wilkesbarre, Pa, & Jerusha Lindsley, of Lindsley Town, Steuben Co, N Y.

Died: on Mar 10, in Wash City, in her 69th year, Rachel Klopper, a native of Harford Co, Md, but for 34 years past a resident of Wash City. Her funeral will take place from the residence of her husband, 456 7th st, tomorrow at 4 o'clock.

Died: on Mar 10, in Wash City, in her 27th year, after a brief illness of only 48 hours, Mrs Mary Ann Keys, wife of C M Keys, & daughter of the late Rev Dennis Maulden, of Fred'k, Md. Her funeral will take place from her late residence at 3½ o'clock today.

Balt, Mar 11. The police yesterday arrested Wm K Bagby on telegraphic information from Savannah, who was charged with having obtained $21,000 by fraudulent means from the State Bank of Savannah. He was committed to await a requisition from the Govn'r of Georgia.

Orphans Court of Wash Co, D C. Letters of administration on the personal estate of Geo R West, late U S Consul, deceased. –Beckwith West, adm

TUE MAR 13, 1860
John Shed, one of the very few surviving soldiers of the Revolution, died in Fairfax Co, Va, a few miles above the county seat, on Friday last, at the age of 102 years. The last of the noble band will soon be gone.

Trustee's sale, by decree of the Orphans Court of Wash Co, D C., made in the case of the heirs of the late Saml Leishear, deceased: public auction on Mar 15 of that desirable property on south side of First st, Gtwn, D C, fronting on said st 426-12 feet, runing back 85 feet, with a 3 story frame house, suitable for a large family. -S T Brown, Atty for the heirs. –Barnard & Buckey, aucts

Senate: 1-Ptn from David E Boies & others, asking that the surviving soldiers of the Indian wars & that of the war of 1812 may be placed on the same footing as those serving in the war with Mexico: referred. 2-Ptn from J H Merrill, asking that his claim, which has been decided against by the Court of Claims, may be considered on its merits: referred. 3-Ptn from Deborah S Witham, asking the enactment of a law authorizing the issue of a warrant for bounty land due for the services of her husband in the war of 1812, upon the surrender of a certificate of right to locate the same: referred. 4-Additional papers in relation to the claim of Geo W Bounin: referred. 5-Ptn from Maj S Russell, asking indemnification for losses & damages & for the payment for transportation of military stores & supplies in 1857: referred. 6-Ptn from citizens of Black Hawk Co, Iowa, asking that Jno Morgan may be placed on the pension roll on account of his military service: referred.

Very valuable farm on the Rockville Turnpike at auction on Mar 21, being the residence of Ruel Keith; improved a few years ago by John C McKelden: contains 116 acres; dwlg house is plain but comfortable; with out-bldgs.
-Barnard & Buckey, Gtwn, aucts

House of Reps: 1-Cmte on Foreign Affairs: to inquire into the expediency of increasing the salary of Isaac N Diller, U S Consul at Bremen. 2-Bill for the relief of the legal reps of Chas Pearson, deceased: passed.

Died: on Mar 11, in Wash City, in his 35th year, Chas E Davis, son of Rev Chas A Davis, Chaplain U S Navy, & son-in-law of Rev Dr Finckel. His funeral will take place from Union Chapel, 20th st, near Pa, this evening at 3:30 P M.

Died: on Mar 12, in Wash City, in his 68th year, Horatio C Scott, formerly of Upper Marlboro, Md. His funeral will be on Mar 14 at 10 o'clock, from his late residence, 466 6th st, between D & E sts.

Died: on Mar 5, at his residence in Montg Co, Md, Mr Saml Blunt, in his 71st year.

WED MAR 14, 1860
Senate: 1-Cmte on Foreign Relations: bill for the relief of John H Wheeler, late U S Minister to Nicaragua. Same cmte: bill for the relief of John P Brown, principal interpreter of the Turkish language to the U S Legation at Constantinople. Same cmte: bill for the relief of Chas E Anderson, Sec of Legation to France, asking to be allowed additional compensation during the time he acted as Charge d'Affaires at that Court. Same cmte: bill for the relief of Townsend Harris, for compensation for diplomatic services in negotiating a treaty with the Kingdon of Siam, while Consul General at Japan. 2-Cmte on Pensions: bill for the relief of Assist Surgeon Micajah Hawks in the naval service of the U S in the war of 1812. Same cmte: adverse report on the ptn of Adam Sener, a soldier of the war of 1812, for a pension. 3-Cmte on Revolutionary Claims: to which were referred the papers relating to the claim of the administrator of Le Caze & Mallet, bill for the relief of Fred'k Vincent, adm of Jas Le Caze, surviving partner of Le Case & Mallet. 4-Cmte on Pensions: bill for the relief of Peter Van Buskirk to be allowed a pension as commissary in the war of the Revolutionary. 5-Cmte on Indian Affairs: adverse report on the memorial of the children of Stephen Krebs, a Choctaw Indian. Same cmte: asked to be discharged from further consideration of memorial of John Rogers, & that it be referred to the Cmte of Claims: agreed to. Same cmte: adverse report on the claim of the heirs of Sour John. 6-Cmte on Claims: bill for the relief of Isaac Varn, sr. Same cmte: bill for the relief of Thos M Newell. 7-Cmte on Naval Affairs: bill for the relief of D G Farragut.

Household & kitchen furniture at auction on Mar 15, at the residence of Rev Isaac Cole, 441 12th st. -J C McGuire & Co, aucts

The great breach of promise case is again in course of trial at St Louis between dfndnt, Henry Shaw, aged between 50 & 60 years of age, wealth estimated between $1,500,000 & $2,000,000. Plntf, Miss Effie Catharine Carztang, a little over 30 years of age. The first trial gave the plntf $100,000. She has been living in comparative obscurity on 5th st, in St Louis, with Mrs Seaman, her sister. Her acquaintance with Mr Shaw commenced during 1856, & the promise to marry is alleged to have been given in 1856. The testimony is said to be of a vast amount.

Orphans Court of Wash Co, D C. Mar 13, 1860. Decision regarding the unsigned & undated will of Alex'r McIntire, deceased. Alex'r McIntire, deceased, was an intelligent man; he understood perfectly well the formalities necessary to make his will effective as to his estate, & it cannot be presumed that he intended this unfinished paper to operate as his will. This paper, therefore, cannot be admitted to probate, & the motion is over-ruled. –Wm F Purcell

Orphans Court of Wash Co, D C. Letters of administration on the personal estate of Saml H Young, late of Wash Co, deceased. –J C McKelden, adm

Died: on Mar 3, at Aiken, S C, in his 30th year, Jas Monroe, son of Gouverneur S Bibby, & brother of Edw A Bibby, of N Y C, & son-in-law of Saml L Gouverneur, of Md.

THU MAR 15, 1860
Wash Corp, Mar 12, 1860. 1-Ptn from Patrick Scanlon & others for the erection of a bridge on G st, between North Capitol st & First st east: referred to the Cmte on Improvements. 2-Ptn from Redmund Burk, asking to be remunerated for certain work done for the Corp: referred to the Cmte on Improvements. 3-Ptn from Jas Ginnaty & others, praying to have curbstone set & footway laid on the west front of square 214: referred to the Cmte on Improvements. 4-Ptn from Darius Clagett & others for cleaning Pa ave: referred to the Cmte on Police. 5-Act for the relief of C Borreman; act for the relief of Ignatius Hass: both referred to the Cmte of Claims.

Criminal Court-Wash-Wed. 1-Jas Walsh, [or Wallis,] the curtain thief, was put on trial on a further indictment for burglariously entering into & stealing a curtain, valued at $20, from the dwlg-house of Mr Hugh C McLaughlin, on Feb 26: guilty.

Sale of valuable real estate: pursuant to a decree of the County Court of Alexandria Co, Va, on Jun 6, in the suit of Kincheloe & Bruin, plntfs, against Thos Coyle & others, dfndnts: a tract of land in Prince Wm Co, Va, near Bull Run, containing about 227 acres & 22 poles, being the same tract of land which was conveyed by Wilmer McLean & others to Geo D Fowle, & the the latter conveyed to said Coyle. There is on there a commodious barn & stable, nearly new. –S Ferguson Beach, com'r

Senate: 1-Ptn from Jas Harrington, a laborer on the public grounds, asking to have the benefit of the joint resolution of Aug, 1858: referred. 2-Ptn from Danl Brown, asking compensation for extra services as clerk in the Patent Ofc: referred. 3-Ptn from Chas A Robinson, asking that his pension may commence from the time of the injury for which it was granted: referred. 4-Ptn from Hetty G Dorr, daughter of a postmaster at the headquarters of the American army during the Revolution, asking that the law relating to the relief of the ofcrs & soldiers, or their widow & orphans, may be construed as to include the heir of said postmaster: referred. 5-Ptn from Chas Hare, asking that the schnr **Emma**, a foreign vessel, may be registered & enrolled: referred. 6-Ptn from H T A Rainals, asking compensation for his services as U S consul at Elsinore, Denmark: referred. 7-Ptn from F B Rittenhouse, of the ofc of the Treasurer, asking compensation for preparing the estimates for appropriations: referred. 8-Cmte on Military Affairs: adverse report on the memorial of Geo P Ihrie, for compensation on the boundary survey between the U S & Mexico, & for transportation from said survey to his home. Same cmte: bill for the relief of F W Landes. 9-Cmte on Naval Affairs: bill for the relief of Eliphalet Brown, jr. 10-Cmte on Patents & the Patent Ofc: bill for the relief of M C Gritzner, & recommended its passage. Same cmte: asked to be discharged from further consideration of the resolution of Mr Sumner in relation to so amending the patent laws as to abolish discrimination between citizens & foreigners in the fees for issuing patents, & also from the memorial of R L Dorr: which was agreed to. 11-Cmte of Claims: bill for the relief of John Brannan.

Sale of valuable farm in Fairfax Co, Va, on Mar 24, on the premises, a tract of land containing about 50 acres, in said county, on the Leesburg turnpike. The bldgs on the place consist of a comfortable cottage, a large barn, stables, & smoke houses. -Amelia T Young, S Ferguson Beach, trustees

Died: on Mar 14, in Poolesville, Montg Co, Md, Fannie, in her 18th year, a lovely & most interesting daughter of Mr & Mrs Fred'k S Poole, of the above place.

FRI MAR 16, 1860
Mrs Allibone, the oldest sister of Geo W Turner, who was slain at *Harper's Ferry*, by John Brown & his associates, was buried at Charlestown on Friday last by the side of her brother. She died at Mount Hope lunatic asylum, whither she was taken shortly after her brother's death. She never rallied after his murder, but continued to sink until her broken spirit burst its eartly bonds & returned to its Maker.

Died: on Mar 14, in Gtwn, Mrs Mary Shaaf, widow of the late Dr John Thos Shaaff, of Gtwn. Her funeral will be on Mar 17, at 11 o'clock, from her late residence, 26 First st, Gtwn.

Hon Lewis C Levin, formerly a member of Congress from Phil, died in that city on Wed.

Senate: 1-Ptn from Cols E B Alexander, H K Craig, & P St George Cooke, of the army, complaining that injustice has been done them by the promotion of Lt Col J E Johnston, their inferior in rank, to superiority in rank over them, as announced by general order of Mar 6, 1860, wherein he has been assigned to the position of acting inspector general of the army. They say they believe the act unsupported by law & against law, & they feel injured & aggrieved, & therefore ask the Senate to consider the matter & do them justice: referred. 2-Additional papers in relation to the claim of Maj W Williams for remuneration for expenses incurred in fitting out & equipping men for the protection of the frontier before the commencement of depredations at Spirit Lake: referred. 3-Ptn from A A Nicholson & others, asking that pensions may be granted to the surviving militia of the same war: referred. 4-Ptn from the marine underwriters of N Y C, asking that the results of surveys made by Capt Ringgold, of the navy, may be published: referred. 5-Resolved that there be paid out of the contingent fund of the Senate to the widow of Thos Clarke, late a messenger in the service of the Senate, $150 for the funeral expenses & 3 months' pay of the deceased from the time of his death. 6-Bill for the relief of Mary E Castor: passed.

Hon Lewis C Levin, formerly a member of Congress from Phil, died in that city on Wed.

<u>Local Matter: Bids for building the new Centre Market-house:</u>
John B Williamson, [Jan 1, 1862, 2 years] $256.000.
J N Easby, [18 months] $246,360.
Richd J Dobbins, [12 months] $217,000.
Entwisle, Barron & Co, [Nov 1, 1861] $198,460.
W H Baldwin & S J Digges, [1 year & 8 months] $197,490.
E Bird & Bro, [2 years] $193,300.
Wm Henderson: $190,700.
W H Clampitt & John W Maxwell & Co, [18 months] $189,000.
J W Osgood, [2 years] $184,369.
Lewis & Angus: $175,000.
Gilbert Cameron, [2 years] $174,500.

Mrd: on Mar 14, in Christ Church, Alexandria, Va, by Rev C Dana, Wm Silvey, U S Army, to Isabella A Heileman, daughter of Col Julius F Heileman, late U S Army.

Died: on Dec 8, 1859, in Fulton, Callaway Co, Mo, Mr Edwin Sheriff. He was born in Bladensburg, Md, May 3, 1803, & removed with his family to Ohio in 1834; from thence he removed to St Louis in 1840. Since 1850 he resided in Fulton, Callaway Co, Mo, & was at the time of his death Mayor of the city. He joined the Methodist Episcopal Church in 1828, in Wash City, D C. His illness was protracted.

SAT MAR 17, 1860

St Louis, Mar 16. Mr Hartnell, Sec of State for the Territory of Utah, died here last night.

Senate: 1-Papers in relation to the claim of Capt Wm L Hudson, U S Navy, for reimbursement of certain expenditures made by him while in command of the ship **Niagara** engaged in laying the Atlantic cable: referred. 2-Addition papers relating to the claim of Barrow, Porter, & Crenshaw, for carrying the mail from Kansas City, Mo, to Stockton, Calif, for mules stolen & wagons destroyed: referred. 3-Ptn from Eli Goss, a soldier in the Aroostook expendtion, asking to be allowed bounty land: referred. 4-Cmte of Claims: adverse report on the memorial of Geo G Durham, asking compensation for services as clerk in the Indian Bureau. 5-Cmte on Pensions: adverse report on the ptn of Lemuel Wooster: recommitted to the Cmte on Pensions. 6-Bills passed-relief of: Jeremiah Pendergast; of Abner Merrill, of the State of Maine; of Miles Divine; of Saml H Taylor; & of Thos Crown. Also passed: right of pre-emption to a certain tract of land in the State of Missouri to the heirs & legal reps of Thos Maddin, deceased. 7-Joint resolution relating to the claim of Geo Fisher, late of Fla, deceased, was postponed.

Hon David A Bokee, who had been boarding since Dec 1st at Willards' Hotel, in Wash City, was found dead yesterday in his chamber in that hotel. Verdict: his death probably occurred on Thu, of congestion of the brain. He was about 55 years of age, & was a member of Congress from a N Y district some 10 or 12 years ago.

It has been the concern among the friends of Mr John M Wyse, whose death occurred on Nov 27th, 1859, that no notice of this event has yet appeared in public print. Mr Wyse, although a native & resident of Balt Co, Md, spent the greater part of his manhood in Wash City, employed in the adjustment of foreign claims, sometimes under the appointment of Gov't, & often privately, on account of his familiarity with the French & Spanish languages. Mr Wyse was born in 1795, being descended from a very distinguished Waterford family of that name, one of whom, Mr Thos Wyse, in our day, occupied a conspicuous rank in the British Parliament, & in the councils of the British Gov't. He was educated at St Mary's College, Balt, Md, where he was among the brightest students of his time. While a young man he was selected, with Mr Jas Hood, as Federal candidate for elector of the Md State Senate under the consitution. In 1834 he was chosen a member of the Gen Assembly of Md; in 1851 he was again a member of the Legislature. In private life Mr Wyse was one of the kindest men, prominet for his singular devotion to his family. As a Christian Mr Wyse entertained a profound respect for the Catholic Church. His ancestors in Ireland were conspicuous for their advocacy of Catholic rights.

Died: on Mar 16, in his 58th year, Wm M Mann, a native of Pa, but for the last 10 years a resident of Wash City. His funeral will be from the residence of Mr J G Schott, 362 north B st, Capitol Hill, on Mar 18 at 3 o'clock.

Died: on Thu, after a brief illness, Willie T Thomas, eldest son of Wm & Jane Thomas, in his 13th year. His funeral is this morning at 10 o'clock.

Charlestown, Va, Mar 16. Stevens & Hazlitt were hung at noon. Stevens died very hard, but Hazlitt died without a struggle. Both bodies were forwarded to Marcus Spring, of South Amboy, N J.

MON MAR 19, 1860
Extensive sale of groceries & liquors at auction, on Mar 21, at the store of H M B McPherson, 413 7th st, near H st. -A Green, aucts

Explosion of the steamer **J M Manning**, for Hawkinsville, on the Ocmulgee river, upward bound, on Monday night. All of her crew are missing except Capt Taylor. Eight negroes & 5 whites were lost, & others wounded. White passengers known to have been killed are Jos Williams, John Harrell, & Jacob Parker, all citizens of Telfair Co. All the heavy freights were lost.
–Savannah Republican

Criminal Court-Wash-Sat. 1-Andrew Kidwell & John Larner, alias John Maher, were convicted for stealing from Mr Wm R Edes, of Gtwn, a buffalo robe & other articles of a value making the crime grand larceny: sentenced to 18 months each in the penitentiary. 2-John Dougherty, John Hickman, & Eberling were sentenced to 10 years in the penitentiary for their heinous crime spree in Gtwn. Patrick Keenan, their hack driver, was also sentenced to 10 years in the penitentiary.

Died: on Mar 14, in Nashville, Tenn, Jas E Brown, son of the late John & Eliz Brown. His funeral is today at 2 o'clock, from the residence of Mr A J Duvall, 421 5th st.

Orphans Court of Wash Co, D C. In the case of Fred'k W Jones, exc of Mary A Miler, deceased, the executor & Court have appointed Apr 10th next, for the final settlement of the personal estate of the deceased, of the assets in hand.
-Ed Roach, Reg/o wills

TUE MAR 20, 1860
The dwlg of Humphrey Owens, a few miles north of Salem, Ohio, was destroyed by fire on Tue, & 5 children perished in the flames.

Mrs Eliz Crockett, widow of Davy Crockett, member of Congress from Tenn, & the hero of the Alamo, died on Mar 2 of apoplexy, in her 74th year. Mrs Crockett had lived for several years in Johnson Co, Texas, & was a most estimable & amiable woman.

Senate: 1-Ptn from Robt A Matthews, asking the confirmation of a tract of land in the Sioux city upon certain conditions: referred. 2-Ptn from Susan & other daughters of Chas Rhind, deceased, asking the compensation due their father for negotiating a treaty with the Ottoman Porte: referred. 3-Ptn from the citizens of the State of N Y in favor of the freedom of the public lands, & papers in relation to the claim of John Reed for a pension for services in the war of 1812: referred. 4-Ptn from John M & Geo O Foot, asking the right to locate certain land scrip: referred. 5-Cmte on Naval Affairs: memorial of Capt Wm B Shubrick, asking to be released on the books of the Treasury from liability for a certain sum of money expended in the public service while cmder of the naval squadron in the Pacific, passed a bill for his relief. 6-Cmte on Military Affairs: bill for the relief of Wm Vance & Brothers. 7-Cmte on Patents & the Patent Ofc: asked to be discharged from further consideration of the memorial of John L Hayes, in behalf of citizens of the U S, on the ground the the case was provided for in a bill just reported. 8-Cmte on Indian Affairs: bill to compensate Israel Johnson, for supplies furnished the Miami & Pottawatomie Indians. 9-Bill for the relief of Mary Preston, widow of Geo Preston: referred.

House of Reps: 1-Bills committed-relief of: Chas Jas Lanman; of Moses Mecker; of Jas Phelan; of Edw Jarvis; of the legal reps of Sylvester Day, late surgeon in the U S Army; of Thos Fillebrown; of David Myerle; of P P Hall, deceased; of Oliver Harris; of Hannibal Graham; of Peter Rogerson & Son, of St John's, Newfoundland; of Tench Tilghman; of Francis Huttmann; of Arthur Edwards & others; of Allen F Porter; of John Scott, Hall W Howe, & Saml P House; of Jas Hooten; of Thos R Livingston; of J C Ferry, for conveying the mail for one quarter from Pittsburgh to Franklin; of Alex'r Albertson, of Platte Co, Nebraska Territory; of Wm H De Groot; of Michl Nash, of D C; of the creditors of Danl B Vondersmith; of Stephen O Gibbs; of John Kelly; of the legal reps of John Moshier; of the children of Mrs Harriet de la Palm Baker, deceased, daughter & legal heir of the late Lt Col Fred H Wisenfels, of the army of the Revolution; of the legal reps of Capt Saml Jones, of the Va continental line during the Revolutionary war; of the surviving children of Israel Frishie, a Revolutionary soldier; of the heirs of Capt John A Hopper; of Josiah Atkinson, of Ohio; of Wm Packwood; of Braxton Bragg & R L Gibson; of Tilman Leak; of Geo Stealey; of Livingston Kincaid; of Michl T Summons; of Israel Johnson; of Jos B Eaton; of John C McFerran, of the U S army; of Wm Hutchinson; of Mrs Jane M McCrabb, widow of the late Capt John W McCrabb, assist quartermaster in the U S Army; of Richd W Meade; of the legal reps of John A Frost, deceased; of Henry Etting; of David D Porter; of Hiram Paulding; of David V Whiting; of the legal reps of the estate of Chas H Mason; of Reuben & Rhoda H Champion; of the children of Tousant Savarnway; of the surviving children of John Forrester, a soldier of the Revolution; of Jas Saxton, a soldier of the Revolution; of Sylvanus Burnham; of Chas W Brooks, of N Y; of Zena Williams; of Saml Goodrich, jr; of Stephen Bunnell; of Henry Taylor; of Mary J Madden; of Chauncey W Fuller; of Lt Michl R Clark; of Jas Floyd; of the legal reps of Gustavus B Horner, deceased; & of

Mary Bennett. 2-Bills also committed: Pension to Susannah Scott, widow of Wm Scott; invalid pension to Sutton M Young; invalid pension to Beriah Wright, of N Y; granting a deficiency & increase of pension to Isaac Carpenter; invalid pension to Adam Farlock; invalid pension to John Piper; invalid pension to Nathl Randall; continuance of pension to Ann G Barker; pension to Sarah Blackwell; pension to Adeline Caddis; increased pension to Richd Brazier; invalid pension to Michl Hanson; increase pension to Jos Files; pension to Phebe Ann Shockley; & invalid pension to Ezekiel Jones.

The steamer **Judge Porter**, Capt Shields, from Montg Ala, bound to New Orleans, took fire on Mar 13th. The second engineer, the steward, the second cook, & Mr Farrar, the second clerk, are missing. Of the 15 passengers, one is known to have been saved.

From the Rio Grande. Correspondence of the New Orleans Delta. Brownsville, Mar 8, 1860. The Ranger under the command of Capt Ford, are still encamped at Rosario. Capt Littleton has gone into the interior of the State, to recruit his company up to the number authorized, 83 men. There are now at this post about 320 effective regulars, including Capt Stoneman's company of 2nd Cavalry, which is encamped a few miles above on the river. Yesterday an additional company of the 2nd Cavalry arrived, numbering 70 men. The ofcrs at this post now are as follows: Maj Heintzleman, 1st Infty; Capt Dawson, 1st Artl; Capts A Lee & Jordan, 8th Infty; Lts Gillium, Langdon, & Graham, 1st Artl; Lt Thomas, 1st Infty; Lts Hortz & Read, 8th Infty; Lt Kimmell, 2nd Cavalry. Brvt Lt Col Brown, Inspector of Artl, is also here temporarily.

On Feb 24 Queen Victoria held a levee, at which Capt McClintock, the cmder of the steamboat **Fox** in the last Arctic expedition, received the honor of knighthood.

Robt Ferguson, an elderly farmer living near Utica, N Y, died a few days ago. His physician afforded him no hope in surviving his severe illness. Mr Ferguson made his will, gave directions in regard to his funeral, wished his body to be interred in the grave-yard at New Hartford, some 5 miles distant, enjoined upon his wife & daughter, who were weeping over him, to have the funeral procession leave the house for the grave-yard at an early hour in the morning, in order that they might get home in season to milk the cows before dark.

Circuit Court of Wash Co, D C. Alex'r Close et al vs Baruch Hall et al. Special Auditor to state the account of Baruch Hall & Bro on Apr 4, in Wash, at 11 o'clock. -Walter S Cox, special auditor

Circuit Court of Wash Co, D C. In Chancery: Otis J Preston et al vs Martha Winter et al. Trustee reported that he sold real estate to David G Day for $1,375 on Mar 7, 1860. –John A Smith, clerk

Orphans Court of Wash Co, D C, Mar 17, 1860. In the case of John Costigan, adm of Mary A Perkins, deceased, the administrator & Court have appointed Apr 10 next, for the final settlement of the personal estate of said deceased, of the assets in hand. -Ed Roach, Reg/o wills

Died: on Mar 19, in Wash City, Francis A Harry, in his 51st year. His funeral will take place from 213 Pa ave, between 14th & 15th sts, this afternoon, at 2 o'clock.

Died: on Mar 18, in Wash City, Thos Baldwin, in his 6th year, son of T B & Laura E Brown. His funeral will be this morning at 10 o'clock, from the residence of the family, on I st, near 6th.

WED MAR 21, 1860
Senate: 1-Ptn from Hannah M King, widow of a soldier of the war of 1812, asking a pension: referred.

On Sat last, at Jefferson City, Mo, Mr Jas Hughes, deputy warden of the prison, & Mr Dozier, who was formerly a guard, had a personal difficulty. In the firing of some 8 or 10 shots, both men died in less than 5 minutes. Both leave families.

A fire at Mobile on Tue consumed the theatre, which belonged to the heirs of the late Hope H Slater, formerly of Balt. It was under the management of Mr Duffield.

On Mar 12, shortly after the family of Mr Wm Rhoads, a farmer residing in Knox township, Pa, had retired to rest, the dwlg was discovered to be on fire. Mr Rhoads was absent at the time, & his wife, rushed out of the house & called her children, who slept upstairs. They could not be aroused. Four sons, one of them almost of age, perished in the flames. Five smaller children slept in the first story & were saved.

Furniture & effects of the Steamboat Hotel kept by Mr Gust Wren, on 7th st near Pa ave, at auction: on Mar 27, the entire effects. –Wall & Barnard, aucts

Chancery sale: by decree of the Circuit Court of D C & Circuit Court for PG Co, Md, passed in a cause wherein Sewell & others are cmplnts, & the widow, heirs at law, & adms of John Brereton are dfndnts: auction on May 2 next, on the premises, part of the tract called **Granby**, near Bladensburg, containing 77 acres, 1 rood 27 perchess, with the dwlg house & other improvements thereon.
–W Redin, turstee

Died: on May 19, Dr Albert Dorman, in his 89th year, a native of the city of Paris, but for the last 25 years a resident of Wash City. His funeral will take place from the residence of Mr Keller, 469 13th st, this day, at 4 o'clock P M.

Died: Mar 19, in Wash City, after a long illness, Miss Margaret R Novell, in her 32nd year. Her funeral is this morning at 10 o'clock, from St Dominic's Church, Island.

Died: on Mar 20, in Wash City, Dominic Conroy, in his 79th year. His funeral will be from his late residence, 195 N J ave, at 8 o'clock, on Thu. Mass will be said for him at 9 o'clock in the Church of St Aloysius.

Died: on Mar 20, in Gtwn, Jas C Wilson, in his 17th year. His funeral will be this afternoon at 4½ o'clock, from his late residence, on First st.

Obit-died: Horatio C Scott, who died at his residence in Wash City on Mar 12, had been for many years an esteemed citizen of Upper Marlborough, & removed to this place about 2 years since. He was temperate & simple in his habits, a consistent Christian. –C M B

Orphans Court of Wash Co, D C. In the case of Priscilla L Adams, admx with the will annexed of Alex'r Adams, deceased, the Court & administratrix have appointed Apr 14 next for the final settlement of the personal estate of said deceased, with the assets in hand. -Ed Roach, Reg/o wills

N Y, Mar 20. The agent of the steamer **Hungarian** gives the following as the number of souls on board when she sailed for Portland. The cabin passengers from Liverpool were 30 in number, viz: J E Wilson, Mrs Woods, W R Crocker, Dr & Mrs Saminego, Mr Wyatt, Mrs Delaus & child, Mr & Mrs Balmer, Mr & Mrs E Evan, J W Crocker, ____ Barry, Mr Boultenhouse, Dr Barret, Rev Jas Stuart, Allen Cameron, Mr Leslie, A B Cortin, Mr Boulton, & C J Nash, ofcr in charge of the mails. The steerage passengers from Liverpool were 40, viz: Hugh McCaffrey, John Richardson, Fred'k Child, Richd Madden, Geo Shank, John Delaney, Michadal Lucy, Miss Ellen Sheehan, Abram Tagg, Henry Richardson, Mrs T Child, Robt Martin, Geo McDermott, Wm Kerley, [or Kepley] Martin Downes, Patrick McGuerin, Wm Coyle, T Allen, Bell Morrison, E A Bartlett, John Daly, Wm Wright, Francis Richardson. The crew consisted of 80 persons in all.

THU MAR 22, 1860
House of Reps: 1-Cmte on Military Affairs: bill for the relief of Danl Redinger's heirs & others: referred.

Trustee's sale of a tract of land containing 62 acres & 13 perches of land, by deed of trust, dated Jan 12, 1857, executed by Saml F Burrows & John H Burrows, recorded in Liber J A S No 128, folios 41, et seq, of the land records for Wash Co, D C: sale on Apr 5 next, at the auction rooms, a tract of land adjoining Tenally Town, in Wash Co, D C, being part of a tract of land called *Friendship* & the tract of land conveyed to Saml F & John H Burrows by Wm D C Murdock.
–W L Childs, trustee -Jas C McGuire & Co, aucts

Very valuable farm of 100 acres, near Benning's Bridge, for sale at auction, on Apr 5, with a dwlg house, & numerous out bldgs, now occupied by R Frisby, jr. -Jas C McGuire & Co, aucts

Senate: 1-Ptn from Geo W Torrence, asking to be remunerated for moneys expended & losses sustained while in the U S military service during the war with Mexico: referred. 2-Additional papers presented relating to the claim of Jas H Matte & Ann Mathieson: referred. 3-Ptn from Caleb Swayze & numerous citizens of Warren Co, N J, urging the passage of a homestead bill similar to that passed by the House of Reps, which they consider a wise & beneficent bill: referred. 4-Ptn from the adms of Wm Wood & others, asking indemnity for depredations committed by a band of Sioux in Minnesota in the spring of 1857: referred. 5-Ptn from Jas K Hatwood, asking to be allowed compensation for extra services performed as purser during the expedition to Paraguay: referred.

Great catalogue sale of books belonging to the estate of the late Sylvanus G Deeth, comprising, nearly 150,000 volumes. -J C McGuire & Co, aucts

Obit-died: Mr Jas C Wilson, a clerk in the Bureau of Engineers, died at his residence, [**Smith's Row**,] Gtwn, on Tue. He was the only ofcr in D C who was attached to the volunteer artl companies of Balt [three in number] which were stationed in **Fort McHenry** during the bombardment of Sep, 1814. Mr Wilson has long been looked upon as one of the most competent & efficient ofcrs of his bureau, or the whole clerical corps of the Gov't.

The Marshal of the District of Columbia yesterday received from the Executive pardons for the 5 Germans who were 2 years ago convicted & sentenced of a heinous offence against a German woman whom they met on the turnpike between Wash & Bladensburg. They were of a party of 10 or 12 who had returned from the Potomac Fisheries, & were on their way to Balt. The facts in the case were all proven, & from all that appeared on the trial there was nothing left for the jury & judge but to do as they did, namely, to convict & pass the sentence of the law, which is not less than 10 nor more than 30 years in the penitentiary in each case. Judge Crawford sentenced 4 of the men to 12 years each & 1 to 15 years.

Life of George M Troup, by Edw J Harden, 1 volume, $3-. For sale at the Wash Bookstore, Taylor & Maury, 334 Pa ave.

Orphans Court of Wash Co, D C. Letters testamentary on the personal estate of Thos Clarke, late of Wash Co, deceased. –Chas S Clarke, exc

Mrd: on Feb 14, 1860, in Grace Church, San Francisco, Calif, by Rev F C Ewer, J Frank Miller, Deputy Collector & Auditor, formerly of Wash City, to Miss Eliz Dickinson, formerly of Staten Island, N Y.

Died: on Mar 20, in Gtwn, D C, after a brief illness, Francis, the 2nd son of Francis & Mary Harper, aged 2 years & 8 months. His funeral is this afternoon at 4 o'clock, from the residence of his father, 2nd & Fred'k sts.

Died: on Mar 20, in Balt, Berwick B Smith, M D, eldest son of Prof N R Smith.

Died: on Mar 9, at the residence of Col Wm L Wynn, Assumption Parish, La, Edw Edelin Garner, formerly of Va, & the youngest son of the late Capt H Garner, U S Army, in his 22nd year.

Richmond, Mar 21. Judge John B Clopton, of the Henrico district, & one of the ablest jurists of the State, died yesterday.

FRI MAR 23, 1860
Springfield, Mar 21. The funeral ceremonies of Hon W H Bissell, late Govn'r of Illinois, took place today. The remains were interred with the services of the Roman Catholic Church. Lt Gov Wood was formally inaugurated Govn'r this afternoon.

Senate: 1-Ptn from Richd B Jones, Consul-General of the U S at Alexandria, Egypt, asking compensation for judicial services under the act of Congress of Aug 11, 1848: referred. 2-Ptn from Frances M Webster, widow of Brvt Lt Col Lucien B Webster, & Mrs Araballa Riley, widow of Maj Gen Riley, for a pension: referred. 3-Ptn from J W Zacharie, in relation to the proposals of Spearing & Co to transfer the U S mails semi-monthly between New Orleans & Vera Cruz: referred. 4-Ptn from Wm J Young, of N Y, asking the passage of the homestead bill bankrupt bills: referred. 5-Ptn from Alpheus T Palmer, a lt in the navy, asking an increase of pension: referred. 6-Cmte on the Post Ofc & Post Roads: asked to be discharged from further consideration of the following memorials, viz: of C T Smead, in favor of increased mail facilities in the State of Iowa; & of Jos B Walker, to be indemnified for money lost in its transmission by mail. 7-Bill for the relief of Alex'r Cross: laid on the table. 8-Mr Foot moved to recommit the memorial of Eliza A Ogden, on which an adverse report had been made, to the Cmte of Claims: which was agreed to.

From Paris: our distinguished countryman, John Lathrop Motley, of Boston, author of the History of the Rise of the Dutch Republic, has been chosen Corresponding Member of the French Institute, in the dept known as the Academie des Sciences Morales et Politiques, & in the place made vacant by the lamented death of Mr Prescott.

Died: on Mar 21, in Wash City, after a long & painful illness, Mrs Martha P McGregor, consort of Mr Alaric McGregor, of PG Co, Md. Her funeral will take place this morning at 10 o'clock, from the boarding house of Mrs Dwyer, on Capitol Hill, Carroll Place.

Died: on Mar 22, in Wash City, Rebecca Eliz Moise, 2nd daughter of Aaron & Eliz C Moise, aged 3 years & 2 months. Her funeral service will take place at her parents' residence, 434 G st, between 7th & 8th sts, at 4 o'clock.

Obit-died: Purser Saml Forrest, of the U S Navy, at Staunton, Va, on Mar 15. The sickness that preceded his death was short; but the ill health from which he suffered more or less during the last few years of his life was the result of disease contracted while performing his duties as purser on board of one of our large vessels. His death is mourned not only by his wife & children & an aged mother, but by a number of relatives who loved him. So well known in Wash City, his many friends will hear that his death was tranquil. He was a member of the Episcopal Church; buried in Lexington, Va, by the side of a little daughter recently dead; & near the parents of his wife, Dr Thos Henderson, of the U S Army, & Mrs Henderson; they, like himself, for a long time residents of Washington.

SAT MAR 24, 1860
London Era: M Jullian the celebrated chef d'orchestre, attempted suicide in Paris last week by stabbing. He has been placed under restraint.

Senate: 1-Ptn from Sylvester Gray, a free man of color, asking that a patent may be isued to him for land settled under the pre-emption laws of 1841: referred. 2-Ptn from Thos B Davis & other citizens of Vinton Co, Ohio, in favor of the establishment of a post route from McArthur, in that county, to Vinton Station, on the Marietta & Cincinnati railroad: referred. 3-Additional papers presented in the case of John Carter, for a pension: referred. 4-Ptn from J W Rea & Anne Matthieson, asking the right to purchase the lands settled by Jas H Matlock & Robt Matthieson, who were murdered by the Indians at Spirit Lake, Iowa: referred. 5-Cmte on Indian Affairs: bill for the relief of Seth Eastman. 6-Cmte on Private Land Claims: asked to be discharged from further consideration of the memorial of John M & Geo O Foot: which was agreed to. 7-Cmte on Naval Affairs: memorial of Chas J Sweet for compensation as purser, during the time he acted as such on board the ship **San Jacinto**: bill for his relief. 8-Joint resolution relating to the claim of Geo Fisher, late of Fla, deceased: passed. 9-Passed: bill for the relief of Theresa Dardenne, widow of Abraham Dardenne, deceased, & their children; relief of Francis Dainese; & relief of Mrs A E Childs. Also, a bill authorizing the courts to adjudicate the claim of the legal reps of the Sieur de Bonne & Chevalier de Repentigny to certain lands at Saut Ste Marie, Michigan: passed. 10-Bill for the relief of A W McPherson: passed. 11-Bill to authorize & direct the settlement of the accounts of Ross Wilkins, Jas Wetherell, & Solomon Sibley: passed. 12-Bill for the relief of John Hastings, collector of the port of Pittsburg: passed.

The wife of Mr Henry L Pope, of Louisville, Ky, came to her death on Saturday, when she inhaled chloroform to alleviate the pain of a headache. Her little children were at dancing school when she died.

House of Reps: 1-**Bills referred to the Cmte of the Whole on the private calendar**: relief of Edw N Kent; of Joel M Smith; of Wm Lyon, late pension agent at Knoxville, Tenn; of the sureties of Chas W Cutter; of Jethro Bonney, of N Y; of Jas Henderson; of Philip D Homes & Wm Pedrick; of John Y Sewell; of the heirs of Jonathan Skinner; of the children of Henry Brockholst Livingston; of Kerr, Brierly & Co; & of the heirs of Barnt de Klyn, deceased. Also, relief of John F Sanford, adm; of Mrs Eliza A Merchant, widow of the late 1st Lt & brvt Capt Chas G Merchant, U S Army; of Geo B Bacon, late acting Purser of the sloop-of-war **Portsmouth**; of Benj Tyson, legal rep of Wm B Draper; of Eliphalet Brown, jr; of Ann Scott; of Saml A West, Geo McCullough, Hiram McCullough, & Chas Pendergrast; of the heirs of Wm York; of Nancy Weeks, of Ga; of the children of Elnathan Sears, an officer of the Revolution; of the children of Danl Cois; of the surviving children of David Richardson & his widow, Sarah Richardson, deceased; of the surviving children of the late John Moore & his widow, Mary Moore; of Erastus Hutchins; of Harriet R F Verison; of Eunice Cobb; of Thos Berry; of Wm Bullock; of Mrs Rachel McMillan; of Lt Robt Cunningham; of Henry Fedler; of A W Flemming; of Wm Pierey; & of Jane B Evans. Also referred to the Cmte of the Whole: Invalid pension to Esther P Fox, widow of Augustus C Fox; to Wm Burns, of Ohio; to Anselm Clarkson, of Mo; to Chauncy Hoyt, of Chenango Co, N Y; to Wm Eddy; to Chas Appleton; to Hugh Baker; to Saml Hamilton; to Thos Glasgow; & to Eliza Reeves. Also, pension to Mary Shircliff, widow of John Shircliff; to Jas Alexander, an invalid soldier of the war of 1812; to Asa Wells; to Andrew Templeton; to Jas Alexander, an invalid soldier of the war of 1812; & increase pension to Jas Dunning. 2-**Adverse reports on the following cases-relief of**: Thos Brown; legal reps of Jacob Weed; of Luke Hilton; of Eliz McCormick; of Benj S Pope; of Larnet Hall; of M M Roberts; of John Ferguson & John H Wickizer; of Nahum Ward; of Jas B Wood; of Chas D Arfroedson; of Geo Ashley, adm; of Zenas King; of Wm F Bowden; of Fulsom & Gardner; of Oliver Bowley; of Chas Brewster; of agents of schnr **Coquette**, for fishing bounty; of agents of schnr **Metamora**; of John Bingham & others, of Mass, for a civil retired list; of Clark Jolley; of Wm McCormick; of Absalom Anchison, of Albany, N Y; of John D Colmesnil; of Pacificus Ord, for compensation for services rendered to the U S; of John Palmer; of John M L Gardner; of Mary Cutter, John L D Cutter, & others; of heirs of John De Treville; of Timothy Emerson; of J F Tracy; of Chas J J Leopole; of Oribino Perez; of Frank Madison; of Hayden & Atwill; of Hill & McGunnigle; of J M Miller; of Moses J Gale, for an appropriation for testing an invention for percussion bombshells; of Edw Willard & others; of widow & heirs of Thos Bird; of T C Lysle, adm; of Salem Larned; of T A Cheney; of Jos T Frisbee, for a pension; & of Thos Crawford. 3-**Private Calendar: bills to which there was no objection**: relief of Cmder H J Hartstene, U S Navy; of Wm Brown; of Lydia Frazee, widow & admx of John Frazee, late of N Y C; of Mariano G Vallejo [amended;] of Shade Calloway; of Chas Knap; of Isaac S Smith, of Syracuse, N Y; of Wm Geiger; of the heirs of Lott Hall [amended;] of John Dixon; of Geo F Brott; of Charner T Scaife, adm of Gilbert Stalker; of Moses Noble; of the legal reps of Robt H Morris, late postmaster of the city of N Y; of the legal reps of Chas

Porterfield, deceased; of Mangett Van Buskirk, hier of Thos Van Buskrik; of the heirs of Maj John Ripley; of the legal reps o Brig Gen Wm Thompson. The cmte then rose & reported the various bills agreed upon to the House. All the bills were passed except those for the legal reps of Chas Porterfield; the heirs of Maj John Ripley; & the legal reps of Francis Chaudonet. 4-Memorial of J L Harper, praying for an increase of pension: referred to the Cmte on Invalid Pensions.

Methodist Protestant Church Annual Conference on Wed in Balt. Appointments for the ensuing year: Stations: Alexandria: J T Ward; East Balt, D A Shermer; West Balt, David Wilson; South Balt, B F Benson; Cumberland, J Clay; Gtwn, Washington Roby; First M P Church, Phil, J Thos Murray; Salem, Dr F Swentzell; Twentieth st, Phil, Danl Bowers; Ninth st, Washington, P Light Wilson; Harper's Ferry, W W Reese. Missions: East Wash, W T Dumm; East & North Balt, J Shreeve, O Cox; Charleston, S B Southerland; Fred'k, W M Strayer, assistant. Superannuated: Eli Henkle, Josiah Varden, R T Boyd, John Morgan, T L McLane, Alfred Baker, T M Wilson, & N S Greenway.

Loss of a Portugeuese Brig of war. The ship **Uriel**, Capt Walker, from Calcutta, bound to Boston, on Jan 22, observed a vessel astern, showing signals of distress. It was the Portuguese brig of war **Mondeigo**. Nine ofcrs & 55 of the crew, including two women, were saved, but the number lost is not given. The **Uriel** carried those she had saved to Port Louis, Isle of France, & landed them there. Capt Walker is entitled to high praise for his gallant & perservering conduct in saving so many lives.

Some evil-hearted person or persons have poisoned & killed two fine cows, the principal support of a poor widow woman, Mrs Carr, living on N st, near 12th. These cows were kept by Mrs Carr for the milk they furnished, & which she sold to her neighbors. No human passion or desire could be gratified by it.

Mrd: on Mar 22, in Wash City, by Rev J C Smith, Mr Jas E Turton to Miss Mary E, daughter of Mr Wm B Wilson, all of Wash City.

MON MAR 26, 1860
Died lately in London, Gen John Devereux, aged 82. He raised the Irish legion which, under Bolivar, engaged in the successful struggle for independence in Columbia.

Andrew Buchanan, formerly Attache to the British Legation at Wash, & at present British Minister to Spain, has been raised to the dignity of K C B.

The last military forces at Charlestown, Va, the company of Capt J W Rowan, which has been on duty since Oct 17, was dismissed from service on Friday last.

Orphans Court of Wash Co, D C. Letters testamentary on the personal estate of Francis A Harry, late of Wash Co, deceased. –Chas S Wallach, exc

A very serious case of mutiny occurred on board the ship **Norway**, of N Y, Capt Major, on her recent passage from Macao to Havana, which very nearly proved disastrous to the ofcrs, passengers & crew. The **Norway** sailed from Macao Nov 26 with about 1,000 coolies on board; five days out a mutiny broke, who set fire to the ship in two places, & endeavored to force the hatches. Mr Stimpson, of Boston, one of the mates, rushed to the hatch; the Surgeon, an English gentleman, drew his pistol & threatened to shoot the first man of the crew who dared to leave the ship; the crew rallied & assisted in fighting the coolies. Thirty of the coolies were killed & more than 90 wounded. The mutineers soon came to terms. Capt Major had his wife & 2 daughters with him, & also a lady passenger & child, but during the night the lady died of fright, & in the morning the child also died.

Cadets recently appointed by the Pres to the military school at West Point: Chas C Moore, Jos L S Kirby, Alex'r Sanford Clark, Francis W Foote, Wm Waller, Jas W Fetter, Jas Wayne Culver, Edw W Anderson, Walter Abbot, & Burdet E Terret.

Orphans Court of Wash Co, D C. In the case of Mary M Brown, admx, with the will annexed of Maria Brown, deceased, the admx & Court have appointed Apr 17 next for the final settlement of the personal estate of the deceased, of the assets in hand. -Ed Roach, Reg/o wills

TUE MAR 27, 1860
Senate: 1-Ptn from Rice, Baird & Heebner, contractors for furnishing marble for the Capitol extension, asking Congress to prevent a threatened reduction of their contract by the Sec of War: referred. [The Sec of War intends procuring the columns from other parties, while they have a contract with the U S to deliver said columns.] 2-Ptn from J M Price & other citizens of N Y, urging the passage of the homestead bill: referred. 3-Ptn from Edw Learned, of N Y, submitted a method for building a railroad to connect the Atlantic & Pacific coasts of the U S by the present railroad companies of the U S: referred. 4-Document presented in relation to the Houmas grant: referred. 5-Cmte of Claims: memorial of Col Wm Gates, of the army, asking indemnity for losses sustained by the destruction of his property on board the steamer **San Francisco**, submitted a report, accompanied by a bill for the relief of the ofcrs & soldiers who sustained loss by the disaster to the steamer **San Francisco**. 6-Cmte on Pensions: bill for the relief of Mary J Maltby. Same cmte: asked to be discharged from further consideration of the ptns of C Champ & others, asking a grant of land to the heirs of those who, if living, would be entitled to bounty land, & that it be referred to the Cmte on Public Lands.

House of Reps: 1-Bill for the relief of Wm McCormick was recommitted to the Post Ofce Cmte. 2-Bill for the relief of Capt John Hall, of the State of Missouri. 3-Bill for the relief of Reuben J Champion, only child of Reuben & Rhoda Champion, deceased. 3-Adverse report of the Court of Claims in the case of Willie Benefield, for reference to the Cmte on Public Lands, was objected to & laid over.

Groceries, wines & liquors at auction on Mar 29, at the store of J T C Clark, K & 7th sts, his entire stock. -J C McGuire & Co, aucts

Ex-Pres Franklin Pierce delivered an eloquent speech recently at Nassau, N P, the occasion was a complimentary dinner to Hon C R Nesbitt, Colonial Sec of New Providence, promoted to be Lt Govn'r of the Island of St Vincent. Over 700 guests were present.

Philip Lynch, the murderer of Geo Coulter, of Bordentown, in Sep last, was executed in the jail yard at Mount Holly, N J, on Friday. He declared his innocence.

Died: Mar 26, in Alexandria Co, Va, of disease of the lungs, Mrs Caroline H Shuster, consort of Saml P Shuster, in her 60th year. Her funeral will take place from the residence of her son, Wm M Shuster, H st, between 6th & 7th sts, today at 2 o'clock.

Norfolk, Mar 26. Hon Francis Mallory, formerly a member of Congress from this district, died this morning.

Trustee's sale of valuable property; by decree of Hon Madison Nelson, Judge of the Circuit Court for Fred'k Co, in Equity: public sale at Weverton, Md, on Apr 13, all that part of the real estate of the *Weverton Mfgr Co* not heretofore disposed of by said company, lying in Fred'k Co, Md. –Wm P Maulsby, trustee

WED MAR 28, 1860
Jas A McCorkle, cashier, embezzled $15,000 of the funds of the People's Bank, Richmond, Indiana, & was convicted & sentenced to pay a fine of $500, be disfranchised for 5 years, & imprisoned 4 years in the State prison. After committing the crime, McCorkle fled to Texas, but was followed & captured.

Sale of groceries & liquors at auction on Apr 2, at the store of Theodore Jones, 10th & N Y ave. -A Green, aucts

Senate: 1-Ptn from O Evans Woods, of Phil, in relation to a plan for increasing the revenue of the Post Ofc Dept of the U S: referred. 2-Ptn from Dr Thos Goodsell, asking a pension for services as a surgeon during the war of 1812: referred. 3-Ptn from Emmanuel Cronkright, a soldier of the war of 1812, for a pension: referred. 4-Ptn from Wm G Easton & others, citizens of Michigan, urging the passage of a uniform bankrupt law: referred. 5-Ptn from Ed D Tippett, in relation to his discharge from the U S army, & the report of the Court of Claims made upon the subject: referred. 6-Ptn from the adm of Jas Mitchell, asking to be reimbursed for the loss of a horse while employed by said Mitchell in the war of 1812: referred. 7-Ptn from Thos W Tansell, asking that the amount of money advanced by him as quartermaster & commissary for the commission to run & mark the boundary between the U S & Mexico may be refunded: referred.

8-Ptn from Margaret Ann Marble, asking to be allowed to enter a certain tract of land improved by her husband, who was murdered at Spirit Lake, Iowa, by the Indians: referred. 9-Ptn from Jas Harriot, making a like request for land improved by his son, who was murdered at the same place: referred. 10-Ptn from Ford Barnes, asking compensation for the services of his father during the war of the Revolution: referred. 11-Cmte on Foreign Relations: asked to be discharged from further consideration of the memorial of John Reeves, asking the intervention of Gov't in behalf of his claims against the Sultan of Turkey: which was agreed to.

Attention, Knights Templar. This Wed at 7 o'clock a sword, ordered by the Grand Encampment, will be presented to M E B B French, Grand Master of Knights Templar, by Sir Albert Pike.

Wm M Cook, a prominent lawyer of Roanoke Co, Va, was drowned on Monday last, while on his way to Craig Co Court. Together with another gentleman, he attempted to cross Morris' Creek in a buggy, but the stream being very much swollen at the time, Mr Cook & his companion were washed from the buggy. Mr Cook was unable to help himself & was drowned almost instantly. His companion saved himself.

Notice to Augustus N Y Howle. Peter C Howle & others, heirs of Joanna Howle, deceased, having filed in the Circuit Court of D C a ptn praying for a division of the real estate of which the said Joanna Howle died seized, situated in Wash, D C, amongst those entitled by law, & a commission having issued from the said Court to the undersigned, commanding them to make such division of the lots of land & improvements thereon mentioned, & the undersigned having appointed Jun 27th next ensuing, to go upon the respective lots aforesaid to make division thereof, you are hereby notified & requested to attend & be present with the undersigned & other parties interested on the said Jun 27, & thenceforward from day to day until said division shall be completed. –John Henderson, Geo E Kirk, Henry A Clark, Cornelius A Dougherty, John G Robinson, Com'rs, Wash, D C, Mar 27, 1860.
+
Notice to Augustus N Y Howle. Peter C Howle & others, heirs of the late Park G Howle, deceased, having filed in the Circuit Court of D C a ptn praying for a division of the real estate of which the said Park G Howle died seized, situated in Wash, D C, amongst those entitled by law, & a commission having issued from the said Court to the undersigned, commanding them to make such division of the lots of land & improvements thereon mentioned, & the undersigned having appointed Jun 27th next ensuing, to go upon the respective lots aforesaid to make division thereof, you are hereby notified & requested to attend & be present with the undersigned & other parties interested on the said Jun 27, & thenceforward from day to day until said division shall be completed. –John Henderson, Geo E Kirk, Henry A Clark, Cornelius A Dougherty, John G Robinson, Com'rs, Wash, D C, Mar 27, 1860.

On Mar 12 the house of Mr Humphey Owens, in Goshen township, Mahoning Co, Ohio, was destroyed by fire, & with it 5 of his children. One daughter, a young woman, & 6 boys slept above. Mr Owen, his wife, & 8 day old child slept below. The daughter was able to save only the 2 year old boy.

Orphans Court of Wash Co, D C-Mar 21, 1860. In the case of Mary M Browne, admx with the will annexed of Maria Browne, deceased, the admx & Court have appointed Apr 17 next for the final settlement of the personal estate of the deceased, of the assets in hand. -Ed Roach, Reg/o wills

Died: on Mar 27, in Wash City, after a short but painful illness, Mr John McK Clokey, in his 57th year. His funeral will take place from the residence of his wife, Mrs M A Clokey, 280 N Y ave, between 6th & 7th sts, on Mar 29 at 3½ o'clock P M.

Died: on Mar 24, after a painful illness, Mrs Jane W Hodson, in her 38th year, wife of Wm Hodson, of PG Co, Md.

Obit-died: Hon L C Levin, who was seriously ill for more than a year, terminating in an apoplexy, which caused his death at Phil, on Mar 11. He had a thorough acquaintance with the classics & belles lettres. His greatest enjoyment was ever to be surrounded by his lovely family. -G

THU MAR 29, 1860
Household & kitchen furniture at auction on Apr 4, at the residence of N Walter, 430 north side of I st, between 9th & 10th sts. -A Green, aucts

Senate: 1-Ptn from Capt Jas Glynn, of the navy, asking remuneration for expenses & loss incurred while performing the duties of purser in addition to those of commanding ofcr: referred. 2-Ptn from Cornelius Wendell, asking Congress to establish a Gov't printing ofc in Wash: referred. 3-Ptn from Danl Jones & 100 other citizens of Watertown, Wisc, urging upon Congress the enactment of a uniform bankrupt law: referred. 4-Additional papers relating to the claim of Catharine Wilkey for compensation for services rendered by her father in the war of the Revolution: referred. 5-Ptn from E Steele, containing valuable suggestion for the better management of the Indians in Calif: referred. 6-Ptn from H P Leslie, of the navy, asking a pension for injuries received in the line of his duty: referred. 7-Ptn from Francis B Schaffer, a military storekeeper, asking to be allowed the same extra pay as was given to other ofcrs of the same grade serving in Calif & Oregon: referred. 8-Ptn from Henry Wells & others, asking the establishment of a weekly mail from Crown Point to Dyer's Station, in Indiana: referred. 9-Additional papers in relation to the claim of M K Simons, a soldier in the late war with Mexico: referred. 10-Ptn from Zephaniah Knapp, a soldier of the war of 1812, for a pension: referred. 11-Ptn from Patrick Quigley, asking compensation for services as U S Depositary of public money: referred. 12-Cmte on Foreign Relations: bill for the relief of I Hosford Smith, late U S Consul at

Beirut, Syria, asking an increase of compensation for his services as consul, & compensation for judicial services: referred. Same cmte: bill for the relief of Isaac E Morse, asking additional compensation as special commissioner to New Granada: referred. 13-Cmte on Public Lands: asked to be discharged from further consideration of the memorial of David H Burr, late Surveyor Genr'l of Utah, asking to be allowed the salary pertaining to that ofc until he was relieved of the responsibilities of the same, & that it be referred to the Cmte of Claims.

Household & kitchen furniture at auction on Mar 30, at the Ryland Chapel Parsonage, 10th & C sts, Island. —Wall & Barnard, aucts

Mr Wm Euston, of Charleston, S C, died on Friday last of disease of the heart. His wealth is variously estimated at from three to five millions of dollars. He leaves all the income of his estate, real & personal, to his widow, [having no heirs,] charged, however, with the payment of certain bequests & annuities to relatives.

Orphans Court of Wash Co, D C, Mar 27, 1860. In the case of Margaret Lyon, admx of Eliz Braden, deceased, the admx & Court have appointed Apr 29 next, for the final settlement of the personal estate of the said deceased, of the assets in hand. -Ed Roach, Reg/o wills

Mrd: on Thu last, at the residence of the bride's mother, in Winchester, by Rev C C Walker, J Smith Gilkeson to Miss Virginia Lee Cabell, all of Winchester.

Mrd: on Mar 21, at Carlton, near Charlottesville, by Rev R K Mead, Prof M Schele Devere, of the Univ of Va, to Miss Lucy B, daughter of Alex Rives.

Died: on Mar 27, in Wash City, of consumption, Jeremiah McKnew, aged 29 years, after a lingering illness. As husband & father he had few equals.

Died: on Mar 21, in New Orleans, Mrs Eliz Key Johnson, excellent wife of Ex-Govn'r Henry Johnson. She was suddenly laid aside by illness & her spirit returned to God who gave it.

Died: on Mar 26, Willie Lawrence, aged 1 year & 23 days, only child of J M & Amanda A Witherow, of Wash City.

Died; on Mar 27, in Gtwn, Edmund Kirby, son of Capt Henry & Martha Kirby, aged 11 months. His funeral will take place from the residence of his grandfather, Mr Edmund Cammack, Bridge & Market sts, this morning at 10:30 o'clock A M.

Died: on Mar 2, at Kingston Place, Glasgow, Scotland, in her 88th year, Mrs Isabella, relict of the late Andrew Smith, of Wash City, & daughter of Mrs Isabella Graham, formerly of N Y.

N Y, Mar 28. A dwlg was destroyed by fire this morning in 45th st, in which 10 persons perished, viz. The wife & 4 children of Andrew Wheeler & the wife & 4 children of Mr Burnett.

FRI MAR 30, 1860
Died: Mar 27th, in Wash City, John E Foulkes, in his 67th year, a native of Glamorganshire, South Wales, but for the last 40 years a resident of Wash City. His funeral is this morning at 10 o'clock, from his late residence, E & 11th sts.

Senate: 1-Ptn from Mary Towson, widow of a soldier in the war of 1812, asking for bounty land: referred. 2-Ptn from Louisa T Whiting, widow of the late Maj Fabius Whiting, of the army, asking to be allowed a pension: referred. 3-Additional papers in relation to the claim of Henry R Schoolcraft: referred. 4-Cmte on Commerce: to which was referred the memorial of Henry J Rogers, American editor of the commercial code of signals for the use of all nations, asking that the same may be adopted by Congress & distributed to all merchant vessels of the U S, submitted a report, accompanied by a bill to provide for the general introduction of an international code of marine signals. 5-Cmte on Private Land Claims: bill for the relief of Robt A Matthews. 6-Cmte on the Post Ofc & Post Roads: bill for the relief of the legal reps of Robt H Morris, late postmaster of N Y C. 7-Cmte of Claims: reported the following bills from the Court of Claims: relief of Melinda Durkee, of the State of Ga; of Polly Booth, of Madison Co, N Y; of Mary Robbins, of Westmoreland Co, Pa, of Margaret Taylor, of Putnam Co, Tenn; of Mary Burt, of Scioto Co, Ohio; of Ann Clark, of Madison Co, Tenn; of Tempy Connelly, of Johnson Co, Tenn; of Mercy Armstrong, of Gloucester Co, R I; of Esther Stevens, of Van Buren Co, Mich; of Anna Weaver, of Wayne Co, Pa; of Anna Parrott, of Clinton Co, Ohio; of Nancy Madison, of Fairfield Co, Ohio; of Rosamond Robbinson, of Belknap Co, N H; of Lavinia Tipton, of White Co, Tenn; of Mary Grant, of the State of S C; & of Mary Ann Hooper, of Va. 8-Cmte on Pensions: adverse report on the ptn of Barbary Glover, widow of a soldier of the Revolution. 9-Bill for the relief of the heirs at law of the late Abigail Nason, sister & devisee of John Lord, deceased, which elicited some discussion: postponed.

Jos E Monroe & Wm Howard fought on Mar 8th, when Howard was severely beaten. Coroner's jury verdict: that Jos E Monroe came to his death by a ball from a pistol in the hands of W Howard, which was used in self-defence. Howard was discharged on the rendition of this verdict. -Alex Gaz

Fairfax land for sale: execs of Dr Danl Janney, deceased, offer at private sale 2 farms, adjoining each other, one contains 315 acres, the other 275 acres, 7 miles west of the Court House. Inquire of Henry Janney, 348 Pa ave, Wash, or H S Janney, Chantilly, Fauquier Co, Va.

Bidders for supplying the Washington Corp with materials for the distribution of water & for the laying the water pipes in Washington City during 1860:
L H & G C Schneider: Corp stops
Peter Mack: laying mains
Dennis Mack: laying mains
Jno McClelland, stop valves, hydrants & fire-plugs
Edgar Z Stover: Corp stops
Chas F Thomas: Corp stops
Warren Foundry & Machine Co: water pipes
C W Cunningham: laying mains
Myers & McGhan: laying mains
W B Dyer: laying mains
Richd A Hill: laying mains
Asabel Sylvester: stop valves, hydrants, & fire-plugs
P & J P Crowley: laying mains
Wm Johnson: Corp stops
Jno Heffern: laying mains
Colwell & Co: water pipes
Celadon Snyder: laying mains
Jno E Buckingham: laying mains
R D Wood & Co: water pipes
Wm M Ellis & Bro: stop valves, hydrants, & fire-plugs
McRee Swift: furnishing & laying patent sheet iron & cement pipe
Regester & Webb: Corp stops
Wm M Ellis & Brother: fire-plugs & service hydrants

Obit-died: on Mar 17, at **Woodley**, the seat of her husband, in the parish of Pointe Coupe Louisiana, Mrs Eliz R Key, wife of Govn'r Henry Johnson, after a protracted illness of nearly 2 years, occasioned by an attack of paralysis. Her remains were interred in the family vault at her residence. Mrs Johnson was born in Md about 1796, & had long resided in Gtwn, D C. Her father, Philip B Key, formerly a member of Congress, ranked among the eminent lawyers of the U S. She was cousin of Francis S Key, author of the Star Spangled Banner. She continued to live in Wash City after her marriage to Gov Johnson, then a member of the U S Senate. A beautiful tribute to her worth has been placed on record by the biographer of Mr John Randolph. Mrs Johnson has long been a member of the Episcopal Church. She had made liberal bequests to her relations, & also charitable institutions, besides one to the Rt Rev Bishop Polk for the poor of Trinity Church, New Orleans. -Picayune

SAT MAR 31, 1860
The death of Judge John B Clopton, of Va, was prematurely announced last week. A despatch from the Richmond Whig states that he died on Wednesday last.

A woman, Mrs Bilansky, was hung at St Paul, Minnesota, on Mar 22, for poisoning her husband. She denied her guilt to the last.

Geo Acker was hung at Morristown, N J, on Fri, for the murder of Isaac H Gordon, on Oct 18 last. The prisoner had previously made a confession.

Senate: 1-Additional papers in relation to the claim of John Dixon: referred. 2-Cmte of Claims: memorial of Jos K Boyd, submitted a report, accompanied by a bill for the relief of the captors of the frig **Philadelphia**. 3-Bill for the relief of the heirs-at-law of Abigail Nason, sister & devisee of John Lord deceased: passed. 4-Bills passed-relief: of R F Blocker, E J Gurley, & J F Davis; of Sheldon McKnight; of Arthur Edwards & his associates; & of A T Spencer & Gurdon S Hubbard.

House of Reps: 1-Cmte of the Whole: bill for the relief of the legal reps of Chas Porterfield, deceased. Same cmte: bill for the relief of the heirs of Maj John Ripley. Same cmte: bill for the relief of the legal reps of Francis Chandonet. 2-Cmte on the Whole: bill for the relief of Mrs Jane B Evans, was placed on a private calendar. 3-Senate bill for the relief of Eliz M Cocke, widow of Maj Jas H Cocke, late Marshal of Texas: passed. 4-Bills referred to the Cmte of the Whole on the private calendar-relief: of Hall Neilson; of Jos C G Kennedy; of Guadalupe Estudillo de Arguello, widow of Santiago E Arguello; of Hockaday & Luggett; of Saml O Green; of A T Spencer & Gurdon S Hubbard; of Geo F Means; of Robt Douglass, survivor of Douglass & Beman; of Harry Allen, of Wisc; & a bill authorizing the Postmaster Gen to reopen & adjust the accounts of Saml H Woodson. 5-Cmte of the Whole: bill to incorporate the Metropolitan Gas Light Co in D C. Same cmte: relief of J R Camp; of the heirs of Lt Jas Taylor, of the Va State line; of Geo G Dunham; of Julius Martin; of Mrs Agatha O'Brien, widow of Brvt Maj O'Brien, late of the U S army; of Beda Hays; of Abner Merville; of Aaron Quigly, an invalid seamen; of Catharine K Russell; of Mary F Parker; of Effisia C De May, widow of Chas F V De May, late a surgeon in the U S army; of Margaret Whitehead; of Edw Rumery; of the heirs of Mary Bullock; of the surviving children of Geo Walker, deceased; & of Chas E Anderson. 6-Cmte of the Whole: pension to Richd M Hayden; to Adrienne Rich; to John P Smith; to Wm H Rogers; to Chas Lee; to Jonathan W Swift, U S Navy; to Chas Goodspeed, a soldier of the war of 1812; to Rufus Call, jr, a soldier of the war of 1812; to Gregory Patti; to Hester Sergeant Barton; to the children of Mrs Ferguson Smith; to John Jackson, an invalid soldier. Also, invalid pension to Richd M Hayden; & to Martha Sanderson. 7-Adverse reports made in the following cases, which were laid on the table: ptn of Henry Miller & Co; of Hiram Humphreys; of Saml B Elliott; of Saml S Wood & others; of Jas Denny; of Jacob W Morse; of Warren Tebbs; of Conrad Duvall; of Jacob W Hall; of Jos Perkins; of Henry Brewer; of Peter D Ankenny; of the heirs of Don Carlos de Villamont; of Mrs Jane Venable, of Tenn; of Solomon Whipple, of Albany, N Y; & of Maria Bunnell, widow of Isaiah Bunnell. Also, bill to authorize the settlement of the accounts of Ross Wilkins & others. 8-Bills reported favorably to the House-relief: of Anson Dart; of Thos Atkinson, of Parke Co, Ind; of Robt Johnson; & of Eben S Hanscomb. Adverse reports from the Court of Claims-laid aside: in the cases of Robt Harrison, David Myerle, & heirs of Dr Geo Yates.

Also, adverse report in the cases of the ofcrs & owners of the brig **Gen Armstrong**, Dennis Cronans, Lydia R Shreve & others, & Richd W Meade: referred.

Circuit Court of Wash Co, D C-in Equity. John R Woods vs Jos S Clark, Richd G Briscoe's heirs & adms & others. The above cause is referred to me as special auditor to state the amount due on the judgment of the cmplnt & on all the judgments & debts of all other creditors of said Richd G Briscoe & of the firm of Briscoe & Clark, & to take an account of the personal estate of said Briscoe. Appear at my ofc, in Wash, on Apr 24, at 11 o'clock.
–Walter S Cox, Special Auditor

MON APR 2, 1860
Trustee's sale of valuable improved real estate, by decree of the Circuit Court of D C, passed in a cause in which Otis J Preston & others are cmplnts & Thos Welsh is dfndnt: public auction on May 2 next, of west part of lot 29, in square 517, in Wash City, fronting 24 feet on Mass ave. –C Ingle, trustee
-Jas C McGuire & Co, aucts

Trustee's sale of farm near Bladensburg, Md, on May 3, by deed of trust from Robt Strong, dated Jul 25, 1856, recorded in Liber J A S, No 117, folios 6, of the land records for Wash Co, D C, & in Liber C S M, No ___, folios 321, of the land records for PG Co, Md: sale on May 3 next, all that parcel of land partly in D C & in PG Co, called *Chillon Castle Manor*. Also as appurtenant to the land hereinbefore granted a perpetual right of way through, over, & along the adjoining land of W Scott, from the land hereby granted to the public road, as the said right of way granted by said Scott to said Strong & his heirs & assignees, & his & their household, family, servants, carriages, horses, wagons, carts, cattle, flocks, & herds, & to & for all persons going to & returning from said land.
–Thos J Fisher, trustee -Jas C McGuire & Co, aucts

Senate: 1-Ptn from Philp & Solomon, Thos A Clark, L Oppenheimer, I Kidinski, Geo F Scott, & Geo Kloman, asking to be allowed to construct a double track railway for the transportation of passengers along Pa ave, & expressing their willingness to embrace other streets also, on such rates of fare & on such terms & conditions as Congress may prescribe: referred. 2-Ptn from Danl Whitney, asking that patents may be issued for certain land at Green Bay to the parties to whom said land was confirmed under the act of Feb 21, 1823, by com'rs appointed under said act: referred. 3-Ptn from Saml Colt, asking an extension of his patent for an improvement in fire-arms: referred. 4-Ptn from Saml A Clark, & other residents of Prairie du Chien, remonstrating against the grant of certain lands lying west of farm lots 1 thru 3, & between them & the Mississippi river, to H L Dousman & others: referred. 5-Bill for the relief of Alice Hunt, widow of Thos Hunt: passed. 6-Bill for the relief of Kate K Taylor, widow of the late Brvt Capt Oliver H P Taylor: passed.

Emperor Napoleon has conferred a pension of $6,000 on Capt Delvigne, the first inventor of the percussion locks. The invention has been worth a great deal to France.

Household & kitchen furniture at auction on Apr 5, at the Restaurant & Boarding House of Jas Gordon, 277, south side of Pa ave, between 10th & 11th sts, all the goods & chattels in said house. –A Green, aucts

The trial of Wm T Talbert for the murder of John A Goldsborough was concluded at Ellicott's Mills, yesterday, the jury returning a verdict of guilty of murder in the 2nd degree. The murder was committed in PG Co, & was removed to Howard Co for trial, the deceased having been killed by a shot from a pistol in the hands of the accused. A plea of insanity was not sustained by the testimony.

Late from Europe: Death of Marshal Reille, one of the few remaining ofcrs who served under the first Napoleon, in the wars of the first Empire. He was born on Sep 1, 1775, in Atibes, in the depts of Var, in southern France, & entered the army when 17 years old as a 2nd Lt. [No death date given-current item.]

John Cummings was executed at the city prison in N Y on Friday. He acknowledged the commission of the crime, but stated that he did not intend to kill McHenry.

John E Taylor, a native of Phil, a skillful shipmaster, died Jan 27 last, in the 53rd year of his age, at Sierra Leone, west coast of Africa, where he was acting in capacity of American Consul.

Orphans Court of Wash Co, D C. Letters testamentary on the personal estate of Jos M Adams, late of Wash Co, deceased. –Jas A Adams, exc

Orphans Court of Wash Co, D C. Letters of administration on personal estate of Peter Casanave, late of Wash Co, deceased. –Wm Henry Daingerfield, adm, w a

Mrd: on Mar 22, in Nansemond Co, Va, by Rev Geo T Williams, Henry Macrae, Engineer Tarboro & Rocky Mount [N C] Railroad, to Miss Eliz S Cowling, of Nansemond Co, Va.

Died: on Apr 1, in Gtwn, D C, Mrs Margaret Chandler, relict of the late Walter S Chandler, in her 77th year. Her funeral will be from the residence of Mrs Fenwick, Fayette & 4th sts, on Apr 3 at 11 o'clock.

Died: in Nov, 1859, in Beirut, Syria, Margaret Holt Johnson, daughter of J Augustus Johnson, U S Consul at Beirut.

St Louis, Mar 31. Maj F N Page, of U S army, died at **Fort Smith**, Ark, on Mar 25th.

Nashville, Mar 31. P P Trevitt, of Sparta, Tenn, killed Dr Carrow at the Commercial Hotel yesterday while the latter was writing a prescription. The act is attributed to mania a potu.

TUE APR 3, 1860
Senate: 1-Ptn from Francis Miller, asking compensation for services while assistant keeper of the D C Penitentiary: referred. 2-Ptn from Sarah G Bryant, widow of Chas Bryant, a commissary of subsistence to a company of rangers called into service by the Govn'r of Texas, asked a pension & arrears of pay: referred. 3-Additional papers in relation to the claim of Jas Pool to compensation for corn furnished the Seneca & Shawnee Indians: referred. 4-Cmte on Pensions: bill for the relief of Mary J Walbach, widow of Brvt Brig Gen Walbach. Same cmte: ptn of Mary Chase Barney, sole daughter of & survivor of Saml Chase, one of the signers of the Declaration of Independence, made an adverse report thereon, & the cmte were unanimously of opinion that her prayer ought not to be granted. Same cmte: adverse on the ptn of Geo W Bonnin for increase of pension. 5-Cmte on Pensions: bill for the relief of Jos Pattee. Same cmte: asked to be discharged from further consideration of the ptn of of Adam Huter, & that it be referred to the Cmte on Public Lands. Also, the ptn of Catherine Wilkie: referred to the Cmte on Revolutionary Claims. Same cmte: adverse report on the ptn of Jno Jordan. 6-Cmte of Claims: following bills received from the Court of Claims-relief: of Ann B Johnson, of Henrico Co, Va; of Eliz King, of Va; of Lydia Clapp, of Wash Co, N Y; of Hannah Menzies, of Ky; of Nancy Ittig, of Herkimer Co, N Y; of Eliz Morgan, of Rennselaer Co, N Y; of Anna Hill, of Munroe Co, N Y; of Sarah Eaton, of Worcester Co, Mass; of Almira Renniff, of Pa; of Phebe Polly, of Otsego Co, N Y; of Jane Martin, of Harrison Co, Va; of Mary Pierce, of Cortland Co, N Y; of Temperance Childress, of Va; of Sarah Weed, of Albany Co, N Y; of Sarah Loomis, of New London Co, Conn; of Rebecca P Nourse, of Ky; & of Jane Smith, of Clermont Co, Ohio. 7-Cmte on Pensions: adverse report on the ptn of the citizens of West Point, Ky, asking that the pension allowed to Franklin W Armstrong may be increased; & of the ptn of Philetus Bircle, asking a pension from the time of his discharge until his name was placed on the pension roll. Same cmte: bill for the relief of Stewart W MacGowan, recommended its passage.

House of Reps: 1-Cmte on Commerce: bill for the relief of Jeremiah Moors. 2-Cmte on Revolutionary Claims: bill for the relief of the heirs of John Hopper, deceased. 3-Cmte on Private Land Claims: bill for the relief of Francis Lavonture & Pierre Grignon. 4-Cmte on Invalid Pensions: bill for the relief of Valentine Wehrheim; of Phineas G Pearson; & of Thos W Phelps. Also, granting an invalid pension to John Purcell; & a pension to Harriet S Wyman. 5-Cmte on Indian Affairs: bill for the relief of O F D Fairbanks, Fred'k Dodge, & the Pacific Mail Steamship Co. Also, a bill for the relief of Chauncey A Horr, of Nebraska.

Wm Seymour, an eminent lawyer of Hardy Co, formerly a member of the Legislature of Va, died on Mar 30.

Capt Danl Searles, Doorkeeper of the Louisiana House of Delegates, committed suicide at Baton Rouge, La, on Mar 21, by blowing out his brains. For years he had kept his coffin & winding sheet in his house, & he already had his tombstone in the cemetery, with his name inscribed.

Wm Roberts, a worthy citizen of Carroll Co, Md, & formerly a State Senator, committed suicide on Thursday last, at his residence, near Uniontown, in that county. It appears he partook of his dinner as usual, & informed his wife that he intended to visit his brother. He was later discovered in his carriage-house suspended by the neck, & life extinct.

Abel Potter, a farmer in easy circumstances, about 70 years of age, residing in Greenfield, Mass, was shot by his son, Philander F Potter, on Thu, receiving wounds which it was thought must shortly terminate his life. There had been a long standing dispute between the parties, the son claiming a large sum for labor upon his father's farm.

In Equity, No 1,066. Agnes M Easby against Horatio N Easby, John W Easby, et al. Horatio N Easby, John W Easby, & Agnes M Easby reported they sold to Richd Wallach lots 1 thru 3 in square east of square 708, for $280.50; & to the same party lot 1 in square 705, for $82.26. The purchaser has paid the purchase money in full with interest. –Jno A Smith, clerk

In Equity, No 1,066. Agnes M Easby against Horatio N Easby, John W Easby, et al. Wm B Webb, Richd H Clarke, & Jos H Bradley, jr, trustees, sold on May 20, 1857, lot 10 in square 1,111, to Andrew Rothwell, for $95.41. On May 4, 1858, lot 6 in square 578, to Wm F Bayly, for $121.21. Lot 20 in square 702, to John B Kibbey, for $27. Lot 2 in square 12, to W B Bayly, who has substituted John W Easby, for $35.87½. Lot 9 in square 708, to John W Easby, for $2. Lot 20 in square 743, for $25. On May 6, 1858: lot 1 in square 925 to John Bayne, for $219.24. Lot 2 in square 925, to John Bayne, for $258.54. Lot 6 in square 925, to Philip V R Van Wyck, for $304.48. Lot 3 in square 925 to J Esputa, for $282.06. Lot 8 in square 925, to Horatio N Easby, for $38.25. –Jno A Smith, clerk

On Sat, as Benj Traphagen was standing on the stoop of Mr Cross' store, at Shokan, Ulster Co, N Y, leaning upon the muzzle of a loaded gun engaged in conversation, the butt of the gun slipped & the load went off, lodging in Mr Traphagen's body. His wife arrived in time to see him die, which was only about 2 hours after the accident.

Died: on Mar 29, at Boston, of desease of the heart, Mrs Mary Anne Appleton, wife of Hon Wm Appleton, aged 68 years. She resided in Wash City for several years during her respected husband's service in Congress, & won general esteem.

Died: on Apr 2, in Wash City, at the residence of his brother-in-law, Stanislaus Murray, 441 5th st, after a brief illness, Saml Hamilton, in his 33rd year. His funeral is this evening at 3:30 o'clock P M.

Died: on Mar 31, in Wash City, suddenly, J Wm B Garner, in his 36th year, leaving a wife & 3 children to mourn their loss.

WED APR 4, 1860
Senate: 1-Ptn from the heirs of Chas Webber, a lt in the army of the Revolution, asking to be allowed a pension, or bounty land, or any arrearages that said Webber or his widow was entitled to: referred. 2-Ptn from Maj Alvord, paymaster in the army, asking that the accounting ofcrs of the Treasury be authorized to credit him with $14,000 of the public funds lost by the shipwreck of the steamship **Northerner** on Jan 5, 1860: referred. 3-Cmte on the District of Columbia: adverse report on the memorial of Francis Miller for compensation for extra services while assistant keeper of the penitentiary. 4-Cmte on Foreign Relations: bill for the relief of the legal heirs of the late John Forsyth, [Minister at Madrid.] 5-Cmte on Patents: bill for the relief of Fred'k E Sickels. 6-Cmte on Military Affairs: to inquire into the propriety of providing for the payment of the claim of David Waldo for damages sustained by him on account of the non-fulfilment on the part of the Gov't of a contract made with him by the War Dept on May 20, 1850

The U S sloop-of-war **Vincennes**, Cmder Totten, from the west coast of Africa, Feb 4th, arrived at Boston on Sat. The **Vincennes** brought as prisoners Thos Morgan, Capt; Byron Chamberlain 1st ofcr, & Wm Dunning 2nd ofcr of the slave barque **Orion**, of N Y, captured off the coast of Africa. She also brought as passengers from the African squadron M E Wandell, acting master's mate, & W B Hall, midshipman. She left U S ships **Constitution** & the **Marion**, & the U S steamers **Mystic** & **Sumter**. The **Vincennes** has been absent 30 months. The **Orion** was seized by the British ship **Pluto**, Lt Le Roy, some months since, with eight or ten hundred negroes on board, & taken into the port of St Helena. From thence Capt Morgan & his 2 ofcrs were taken by the **Pluto** to Loando, & transferred to the flag-shipof the squadron, where they were placed on prison diet & kept in irons. They remained on the flag-ship until the sailing of the **Vincennes**. The prisoners were delivered into the custody of the U S Marshal at Boston.

Public sale of valuable lots on the Island, on 6th st west, by virtue of the last will & testament of Hanson Barnes, deceased, & an order of the Orphans Court of Wash Co, D C: sale on Apr 24, of lot 19, in W B Todd & W H Gunnell's subdivision of square 465, on 6th st, between D & E sts. Title indisputable. –Josiah Simpson, adm -A Green, aucts

Coal & Wood for sale, the subscriber having purchased the Wood & Coal Yard of the late S H Young. –Geo Bogus, 9th st, between D & E sts.

Circuit Court of Wash Co, D C-in Equity. John R Woods et al vs Richd G Briscoe's heirs & adm, Jas S Clarke, & others. Statement of the Trustee's account of said Richd G Briscoe & Briscoe & Clarke, & distribution of the funds raised by the sales made by the trustees. Appear at my ofc in Wash on Apr 27.
–Walter S Cox, special auditor

Died: on Mar 26, in Petersburg, Va, at the residence of her grandmother, Mrs J F May, in her 21st year, Annie Bayly, eldest daughter of the late Hon Thos H Bayly, of Accomac.

THU APR 5, 1860

Large & handsome private residence in Gtwn at auction, in front of the premises, on Apr 11, the residence of the late Col Humphrey, on Gay st, near Green st, fronting 56 feet, & running back 220, through to Olive st, on which street it fronts 60 feet. It a brick dwlg in good repair, with a large brick stable attached & a smokehouse. The title is perfect. –Barnard & Buckey, aucts, Gtwn, D C

Trustee's sale of bldg lot in the First Ward at auction, by deed of trust, dated Oct 17, 1855, by heirs of Henry Bryant, lot 21 in square 172, in Wash City.
–H Loughborough, trustee -A Green, aucts

Comrs' sale of frame house & 2 lots, by order of the Circuit Court of D C, decreed Jan 25, 1860, sale on Apr 12 of lots 19 & 20 in square 172, with improvements, of which Edmund Bryant died seized. –H Loughborough, A H Loughborough, Nicholas Callan, Jas Nourse, Wm W Davis, Com'rs
-A Green, aucts

Senate: 1-Ptn from Anthony F Navarre & Wm M Rice, agents of the Pottawatamie nation of Indians, asking that the Com'r of Indian Affairs be required to furnish them with a statement of the condition of their affairs: referred. 2-Ptn from Gen Duff Green, in relation to the Pacific Railroad, which he asked to have printed, as it contained much valuable information: referred. 3-Memorial of Philp & Solomons, & their associates, relative to constructing a double-track on Pa ave: referred to the Cmte on D C. 4-Cmte on Commerce: adverse report on the memorial of Chas Hare to have the name of the schnr **Emma**, a foreign vessel, changed, & for her enrollment. 5-Cmte on Military Affairs: adverse report on the memorial of Geo W Torrence, asking remuneration for moneys expended & losses sustained while in the military service of the U S during the war with Mexico. 6-Bill finally passed for the relief of the legal reps of Robt H Morris, late postmaster of N Y C. 7-Bill for the relief of Saml J Hensley: passed.

Walter S Land's trial for the murder of Mr Flanagan, in Princess Ann Co, Va, closed last Sat, with a verdict of guilty of murder in the 2nd degree, & affixing his punishment at 18 years in the penitentiary.

Mrd: on Apr 3, at the Ninth st Methodist Protestant Church, by Rev L W Bates, Chas R Waters, of Wash City, to Julia E, daughter of the late Chas R Simpson, of Howard Co, Md.

Died: on Mar 24, in Phil, in her 75th year, Mrs Lucy Lee Carter, relict of the late B Moore Carter, of Va, & daughter of the late Maj-Gen Henry Lee, of the army of the Revolution.

FRI APR 6, 1860
Senate: 1-Ptn from Lt A F Warley, asking relief from the consequences of a sentence of a court martial: referred. 2-Ptn from the excs of Saml B Richardson, asking payment for certain number of days' service in the Senate of the Legislature Council of Fla: referred. 3-Cmte on Patents: adverse report on the memorial of Bancroft Woodcock, in relation to the extension of his patent for an improvement in the construction of the plough: referred. 4-Cmte of Claims: bill for the relief of Wm P Bowkay, asking compensation for certain inventions in ship-bldg, adopted by the Gov't. Same cmte: bill for the relief of Eliza E Ogden. 5-Cmte on Military Affairs: bill for the relief of Maj Alvord, to be credited for $14,000 public money lost by the shipwreck of the steamer **Northerner**. 6-Bill for the relief of Gotleib Scheerer: referred. 7-Joint resolution for the relief of Rev R R Richards: referred. 8-Bill for the relief of Angelina C Bowman, widow of Francis L Bowman, late capt U S army: which was agreed to. 9-Bill for the relief of Wm B Shubrick: passed.

The dwlg-house, barn, & shed of Asa Warren, in Naples, Maine, with furniture, 3 horses, 3 carriages, cow, hog, hay & grain, & farming utensils, were destroyed by fire on Monday, & Mr Warren & his son, about 8 years old, perished in the flames. It was the work of an incendiary. It was discovered by a daughter of Mr Warren, who aroused her parents. Mr Warren got his wife & daughter & an infant child to the door & went back to save his son. Mrs Warren with the infant & the daughter escaped in their night clothing.

Geo Yanner, private watchman, was shot at Market & Third sts, Louisville, on Friday night, & instantly killed. He was shot in self-defence by Chas Junot, an ex-policeman. Some 16 years ago at the White Mansion Talbott Oldham killed Wm Benham. In the same house, a few days later, Henry Driehaus, the proprietor of the White Mansion, was cruelly murdered by Wm Howard, who was convicted, sentenced to be hung, & made his escape from the jail at Lagrange. A few months since Jas White fatally stabbed John Bosley, & he died the next day.

Correspondent of the Newark Advertiser writes from New Orleans, under date of Mar 25: an affair of honor came off in this city a few days since between a native of your city, Mr S W Plume, & a Mr Isaac Stone, which took place back of the Metairie race track. In the second fire Mr Stone was shot dead.

For sale: elegant country seat, **Dumbarton**, on the west side of the York Turnpike Road, 5½ miles north of the city of Balt: contains 180 acres of land; with a Mansion House-an elegant double brick dwlg with wings, 2 stories, containing 16 chambers, etc. Improvements are extensive. –Robt A Taylor

J W Colley & Co, fancy Dress Goods, 523 7th st, above Pa ave. [Ad]

Orphans Court of Wash Co, D C. In the case of Wm A Maury, adm of Philip B Key, deceased, the adm & Court have appointed Apr 28 next, for the final settlement of the personal estate of the said deceased, of the assets in hand. -Ed Roach, Reg/o wills

Died: on Apr 4, Sarah Eveleth, infant daughter of Kate Eveleth & Causten Browne.

SAT APR 7, 1860

Trustee's sale of valuable lot of ground, containing between 5 & 6 acres, in Wash Co, near Wash City, at auction, on May 8, on the premises, by deed of trust from Mary A Hamilton, recorded in Liber J A S, No 175, folios 375 thru 379, of the land records for Wash Co, D C, being **Peters' Mill Seat**, with all improvements thereon. -Lewis L Brunett, trustee -A Green, aucts

Hon Jas Kirke Paulding died at Hyde Park on Wed. A native of Dutchess Co, he was born Aug 22, 1779. In early manhood came to this city, where he resided most of the time. In 1807 he was connected with Washington Irving in the publication of Salmagundi. Lately he has withdrawn from the public eye & has been living quietly at his home on the Hudson. –N Y Commercial Adv

Josephus Barbee, of N C, has received a verdict for $2,200 against the Wilmington & Weldon Railroad Co for injuries sustained by the breaking of the axle of one of the cars a year or two since.

Orphans Court of Wash Co, D C. Letters testamentary on the personal estate of Susan Graham, late of Wash Co, deceased. –Geo W Graham, exc

Orphans Court of Wash Co, D C. Mar 24, 1860. In the case of Richd H Henderson, adm with the will annexed of Archibald Henderson, deceased, the adm & Court have appointed May 1 next, for the final settlement of the personal estate of the said deceased, of the assets in hand. -Ed Roach, Reg/o wills

Dr Henry Carow, a well-known physician & surgeon of Nashville, was shot & instantly killed on Sat last by P P Trewitt, Postmaster at Sparta, Tenn. It is presumed he was laboring under a fit of delerium tremens. –Nashville Gaz of Apr 1.

Mrd: on Thu, by Rev John C Smith, Mr Wm Reed to Miss Anna Woods, all of Wash City.

The municipal election at Annapolis on Monday last resulted in the success of the American candidates, viz: John R Magruder for Mayor; Thos J Wilson for Recorder; John Ridout, jr, Solomon Phillips, Joshua Brown, Jas Monroe, & Geo E Franklin, for Aldermen.

Died: on Apr 5, Mrs Rhoda O'Neal, aged 89 years. Her funeral will take place from the Union Chapel M E Church, 20th st, near the avenue, on Apr 8 at 3 o'clock P M.

Died: on Mar 25, in Dorchester, Mass, at the house of his father, John H Robinson, jr, aged 19 years.

Senate: 1-Ptn from Jos Wilson, a surgeon in the navy, asking that the surgeons of the navy may be allowed an increase of pay: referred. 2-Ptn from Wm Fairfield, a soldier in the war of 1812, asking to be allowed a pension: referred. 3-Cmte of Claims: asked to be discharged from further consideration of the memorial of J T Adams, late Clerk of the U S Court for the Territory of Minnesota, & that it be referred to the Cmte on the Judiciary: agreed to. Same cmte: asked to be discharged from further consideration of the House bill for the relief of Anson Dart, & that it be referred to the Cmte on Indian Affairs: which was agreed to. 4-Cmte on Revolutionary Claims: bill for the relief of the legal reps of Chas Porterfield, deceased: passed. 5-Bill for the relief of Wm P Bowhay: amount was increased from five to eight hundred dollars & passed. 6-Bill for the relief of Mrs Olivia W Cannon, widow of Jos S Cannon, late a midshipman in the U S Navy: passed. 7-Bill for the relief of F W Lander: laid over. 8-Bill for the relief of John R Nourse & others: passed. 9-Bills passed-relief: of Eli W Goff; of Lee Deatherage & John Deatherage, or their legal reps; of Wm Wallace, of Ill; of Eliz Spear; of Nancy M Gunsally; of Michl Nourse; of John Robb; of Asbury Dickens; of Moses Noble; of Richd Fitzpatrick; of Chas T Scaife, adm of Gilbert Stalker; of Cornelius Boyle, adm of John Boyle, deceased; of Thos Fillebrown; of Francis Huttmann; of Jeremiah Pendergast, of D C; of Otway H Berryman; of Ebenezer Ricker; of Randall Pegg; of Elijah R Merrill; of H H Howard; of A M Mitchell, late colonel of the Ohio volunteers in the Mexican war; of Wm Money; of Geo Phelps; of R W Clarke; of Nicholas Underhill; of Cornelius Hughes; of Rebecca A Correll; of Mrs Ann P Derrick, widow of W S Derrick, deceased; of Jas Maccaboy; of Mills Judson, surety on the official bond of the late Purser Andrew D Crosby; of Henry G Carson, adm of Curtis Grubb, deceased; of the surviving grandchildren of Col Wm Thompson, of the Revolutionary army, of S C; of Franklin Peale; of the legal reps of Jas Bell, deceased; of Lt John C Carter; of F M Gunnell, a passed assistant surgeon U S Navy; of O H Berryman & others; of Emilie G Jones, exc of Thos P Jones, deceased-this bill was amended to include Nancy M Johnson, admx of Walter R Johnson, deceased; of Jas L Edwards, adm of Thos R Gedney, deceased; of Thos Allen; & of Augustus H Evans.

10-Bills passed-relief: of Moses Noble; of Chas T Scaife, adm of Gilbert Stalker; of Mariano G Vallejo; of Lydia Frazee, admx of John Frazee, late of N Y C; & of Wm Geiger.

Three days from Europe. Mrs Jameson, the authoress, is dead. Florence Nightingale is seriously ill, & prayers had been offered for her recovery in the garrison chapels.

House of Reps: 1-Bills referred to the appropriate cmtes-relief of: Alex'r Thompson, late Consul at Maranham, Brazil; of Sarah Murphy; & of Peter & Alexis Navarre. 2-Bill for the relief of Margaret Whitehead: passed. 3-Bills committed-relief: of Saml H Taylor; of Messrs Cole & Barr; of Theresa Dardenne, widow of Abraham Dardenne, & their children; of Wm Y Strong; of Thos F Bowler, of New Mexico; of John Monty; of the legal reps of Jas Bell, late of Lower Canada, deceased; of the legal reps of Lt Francis Ware; of the heirs & legal reps of Jean B d'Antrive; of Jacob Hall; of the legal reps of Fred'k F Brose, deceased; of Geo P Marsh; of Anthon L C Portman; of Saml N Elliott & others, children of Arthur Elliott; of Rebecca Davis, widow of Jesse Davis; of the children of Wm Humphrey, a soldier of the Revolution; of Alice Hunt, widow of Capt Thos Hunt-[passed;] of Kate D Taylor, widow of Brvt Capt Oliver H P Taylor; of Caroline E Clark; of Henry Sanford; of Judith Nott, widow of John Nott, late of the U S Navy; of Jas Van Pelt; & of the children & heirs of Alex'r Montgomery-passed; of Sheldon McKnight. Also, pension to Moses Young; to Archibald Merryman; to Danl Lucus; to Leopold Snyder; to Robt Purchase, a soldier of the Revolutionary war; invalid pension to Henry F Bowers; & increase pension to Wm W Diehl. 4-<u>Adverse reports on the following cases</u>, laid on the table-ptn: of Adolphus Glavesveck; of Susannah A Sawyer; of Wm Hicks; of Jos D Green; of Wm Morse; of Wm McCormick; of John Winslow; of Saml M Hockie; of John Randall, of Warren Co, Tenn; of Saml M Puckett; of Sarah Brashear; of Wm Hayes; of Catherine Compton; of Jas H Bradford; of Hector St John Beatles; of Henry Miller; of Henry S Moore; of C Mellville Reeves; of Silas Stevens; of Jas S Rowland; of Saml January; of Isaac Allen; of Thos Coward; of Ed Hardesty; of Antoine Robideau; of Thos Satterlee; of Nathl Wilbur; of Charlotte Butler, widow of John Butler; of John R Tucker; of Danl Doland; of Edw Mayo; of John Perry; of Andrew J Tark; of Ebenezer Hitchcock; of Wm Walton; of Catherine Welding; of Ellen Bowie; of Wm A Johnson; & of J L Harper. 5-<u>Bills favorably reported to the House</u>-relief: of R K Doebler; the legal reps of Francois Guillory, deceased; of W Y Hansell, the heirs of W H Underwood, & the reps of Saml Rockwell; of Chas Stillman; of Fred'k Stephens; of Brvt Lt Col Martin Burke & Capt Chas S Winder, of the U S army; of Mrs A W Angus, widow of the late Capt Saml Angus, U S Navy; of Micajah Hawkes; of Mrs Hannah McDowell; of Webster S Steele; & of John W Taylor, & other assignees of pre-emption land location. Also, pension to Jas Lacey, of Tenn; to John Madden, of Tenn; to Cyrenus C Blackman, of Louisiana; & to Adelaide Adams, widow of Cmder Geo Adams, U S Navy.

MON APR 9, 1860
Trustee's sale of valuable improved property on north L, between 6th & 7th sts, at auction, on May 1, 1860, by deed of trust from Wilson McBee, dated Jan 19, 1859, recorded in Liber J A S, No 168, folios 63 thru 66, of the land records for Wash Co, D C: part of lot 3 in square 449, with a spacious brick bldg thereon. –Chas H Utermehle, trustee –A Green, aucts

Orlan, Richland Co, Wisc: the house in that village oocupied by a family named Reagan was destroyed by fire last Tuesday, & 6 children perished in the flames, the eldest of whom was 16 years old.

Mr Alfred Moss, recently elected Delegate to Charleston by the Warrenton Convention, died at Fairfax Court-house on the Friday following. [Apr 11th newspaper: the report of the death of Mr Albert Moss, of Fairfax, Va, turns out to be unfounded. He had been ill, but has recovered.]

Chancery sale of improved property on 11th st, between F & G sts, by decree of the Circuit Court of D C, in chancery, passed on Feb 2, 1860, in a cause wherein Jas E Morgan & Jas F Slater are cmplnts & Chas Slater & Saml A Peugh are dfndnts, No 1,436, chancery: sale on May 3 of part of lot 5 in sqaure 346, with the bldg & improvements thereon, a small brick house. –Edw Swann, trustee C W Boteler & Sons, aucts

Senate: 1-Bill for the relief of the heirs & legal reps of Olivier Landry, of the State of Louisiana: referred. 2-Bill for the relief of Mary Walbach, widow of Brvt Brig Gen Walbach: passed. 3-Cmte of Claims: bill for the relief of Jas Myer for compensation for services rendered & losses sustained as quartermaster to the Mexican boundary line commission.

House of Reps: 1-Cmte of the Whole-bill with no objection-relief: of Emma A Wood, widow of the late Brvt Maj Geo W F Wood, of the U S Army; of Andrew E Marshall; of Rev Jas Craig, deceased; of Jas Phelan; of the legal reps of Sylvester Day, late a surgeon in the U S army; of Thos Fillebrown; of the legal reps of P P Hull, deceased; of Peter Rogerson & Son, of St John's, Newfoundland, owners of the British brig **Jessie**; of Francis Hutman; & of Tench Tilghman: all bills were passed.

Died: on Apr 6, in Wash City, Thomas Coombs, infant son of Thomas & Ellen Lucas, aged 5 weeks & 3 days.

New Orleans, Apr 7. The Knights of Golden Circle here met yesterday & expelled Gen Bickley from the order, & appointed Col Greenhow the cmder-in-chief of the organization.

TUE APR 10, 1860
Guns, pistols, & fishing tackle at auction, on Apr 10, at the Hardware Store of Messrs Tucker & Co, 7th & E sts. -A Green, aucts

Bailiff's sale of stock of fine liquors, wines, & cordials, at auction, on Apr 12, by order from the bailiff in a distrain for rent, at the store of J P Levy, Pa ave, between 1st & 2nd sts. —Jas H Hilton, Bailiff -Wall & Barnard, aucts

Senate: 1-Ptn from Amory L Babcock & others, of Sherborn, Mass, & also from Noah Fairfield & others, citizens of Weymouth, Mass, asking the repeal of the fugitive slave law, the abolition of slavery in D C & in the Territories, the prohibition of the inter-slave trade, the passage of a resolution pledging Congress against the admission of any slave State into the Union, & the employment of slaves by an agent, ofcr, or contractor of the Federal Gov't: referred. 2-Ptn from G Campbell, asking to be allowed to enter land in the Greenville land district in Alabama: referred. 3-Testimonials in favor of Capt Geo C Stouffer, of ship **Antartic**, for his gallant conduct in rescuing the ofcrs & soldiers of the army & other passengers from the sinking ship **San Francisco**: referred. 4-Ptn from the members of the Senate of Pa, asking that a pension be granted to Mrs Mary Burnett, widow of an ofcr of the revenue service: referred. 5-Ptn from Jas A Gallaway & Lewis Rent, asking that pensions be may granted to the surviving soldiers of the war of 1812: referred. 6-Cmte on Indian Affairs: bill for the relief of Anson Dart, reported without amendment. 7-Cmte on Pensions: bill for the relief of Micajah Hawkes: passed. Same cmte: adverse report upon the ptn of Nancy Stout, widow of a soldier of the Revolution. 8-Cmte on Pension: adverse report on the claim of Stephen Bunnel, of the war of 1812, for a pension. 9-Cmte of Claims:memorial of John R Bartlett, late Com'r of the U S: passed. 10-Bill for the relief of M C Gritzner: passed. 11-Bill for the relief of Jos Pratte: passed. 12-Bill for the relief of Mary Walbach, widow of the late Brvt Brig Gen John B Walbach: passed.

Capt Wm Beatie, the oldest man perhaps in Southwestern Va, departed this life at the residence of his son, Madison Beatie, near Glade Spring, in this county, on Wed last. Capt Beatie was about 100 years old, & was the last survivor of the King's Mountain veterans from Va. He was an honest, upright, kind-hearted, Christian gentleman. He had been blind for many years, & for that reason had lived very retired. -Abingdon Virginian

Saml G Ogden, well known old shipping merchant, died at his residence, in Astoria, on Thu, at the advanced age of 81 years. He was the father of Mrs Anna Cora Mowatt Ritchie, the authoress & actress. He will be remembered as being the chief agent in fitting out the Miranda Expedition, from this port in 1806.

Died: on Apr 9, in Wash City, Mr Jas Little, in his 68th year. His funeral will be from his late residence, near the **Congressional Burial Ground**, at 3:30 P M, today.

At Randolph Superior Court last week in Asheborough, Rev Danl Worth was tried for circulating a book of an incendiary character, known as Helper's Impending Crisis. Verdict rendered: guilty. He was sentenced to 1 year imprisonment. -Fayetteville [N C] Courier

House of Reps: 1-Bill confirming a claim of the heirs & legal reps, & assigns of Simon Gonor to a tract of land: referred. 2-Bill confirming the claim of the heirs, legal reps, & assigns of Jean Florentine Poiret, F P C, to a tract of land: referred. 3-Bill for the relief of Chas Radcliff: referred. 4-Bill granting a pension to Michl S Bailey: referred. 5-Bill to change the name of the steamboat **Antelope**: referred. 6-Cmte of the Whole: discharged from further consideration of the bill for the relief of Arthur Edwards & his associates.

In Equity, No 1,221. John Van Reswick against Mary A Ayton, Mary V, Adeline C, Ellen S, Abram C, & Richd P Ayton, admx & heirs of Richd Ayton. On May 2, at my ofc, in City Hall, Wash, I shall state the account of the trustee, & distribute the fund in his hands. –W Redin, auditor

WED APR 11, 1860
Circuit Court of Wash Co, D C. Geo Schley & Mary H Schley his wife, & Jas M Schley & Ellen N Schley his wife, vs Wm Henry Schley & Buchanan Schley. This suit is to procure a decree for a sale of certain real estate in Wash City, lot 6 in square 103, that a certain Fred'k A Schley, late of Fred'k Co, Md, was seized & possessed of, on Feb 5, 1858, when he departed this life intestate, leaving the parties to this suit, Geo Schley, Jas M Schley, Wm Henry Schley, & Buchanan Schley, his only children & heirs at law. That the said Wm Henry Schley is a lunatic, & incapable of managing his estate, & that the said Buchanan Schley is an infant, under the age of 21 years, & that both the lunatic & infant reside in the State of Md; that it will be for the benefit of said lunatic & infant, & of all other parties concerned, that said lot or piece of land be sold, & the proceeds of sale be divided amongst the parties according to their respective rights. Wm Henry Schley is to appear in the Court on or before the first Monday of Sep next.
–Wm M Merrick, A J -Jno A Smith, clerk

House of Reps: 1-Cmte on Indian Affairs: Senate bill for the relief of Saml J Hensley: committed.

Henry T Pearson, son of the late Mr Amos Pearson, died suddenly at the Gymnasium, Newburyport, Mass, on Friday. He was only 16 years of age, & his first experiment at lifting was to raise 400 pounds dead weight. We hear he had been subject to palpitation of the heart.

Orphans Court of Wash Co, D C. In the case of Eleanora Knott, admx of Geo Knott, deceased, the admx & Court have appointed May 12th next, for the final settlement of the personal estate of the said deceased, of the assets in hand.
-Ed Roach, Reg/o wills

Senate: 1-Ptn from Jos D Greene, asking increased compensation for the performance of duties as post clerk of the Gen Post Ofc Dept: referred. 2-Additional papers relating to the claims of Miriam Hungerford & others to indemnity for Indian depredations in Utah: referred. 3-Ptn from Maj Alloshan Edwards, of Kalamazoo, Mich, a captain in the war of 1812, asking for a pension: referred. 4-Ptn from Wm C Morris, & other reps of Jos Morris, of the war of the Revolution, asking to be allowed commutation pay: referred. 5-Ptn from T T Grant, of St Louis, relative to the judiciary act of 1789, & in favor of changing the time allowed for taking the appeals & writs of error to the U S Supreme Court: referred. 6-Ptn from Tucpenhocken, Pa, urging that Michl Lauck, a soldier of the war of 1812, may be placed on the pension roll: referred. 7-Ptn from Miriam Davis, widow of Lot Davis, who died of wounds received in Dartmoor prison, asking to be allowed a pension: referred. 8-Cmte of Claims: bill for the relief of Jos C G Kennedy, for a repeal of the joint resolution relative to the salary of the sec of the Census Board, & that for indemnification for damage to bldgs belonging to him while used by Gov't, submitted reports & bills for his relief in each case. 9-Cmte on Pension: bill for the relief of Hester Stoll, widow of Urban Stoll. 10-Cmte on Revolutionary Claims: adverse report on the memorial of Catharine Wilkie, asking relief on account of the military services & sufferings of her father during the war of the Revolution. 11-Cmte on Revolutionary Claims: adverse report on the memorial of Hetty G Dorr, daughter of a postmaster at the headquarters of the army of the Revolution, asking that the laws passed for the relief of the ofcrs & soldiers of that war might be so construed as to include the heirs of B P Muster.

Died: on Apr 8, in N Y C, at the residence of her brother-in-law, John Priestley, after a short illness, Miss Mary Priestley Heaton, aged 55 years, formerly of this District.

THU APR 12, 1860

We understand that Robt Dowling, U S Consul at Cork, in a recent letter to a friend in this city, says he is overwhelmed with verbal & written inquiries from numerous relatives of the late Senator Broderick in that vicinity as to the nature of his alleged will, the disposition made of his property, & as to the proceedings necessary to be had, under our laws, to enable them to establish their heirship.

By virtue of 7 writs of fieri facias, issued by Jas Cull, a justice of the peace, against the goods & chattels, lands & tenements, rights, & credits of Jas Little & John Little, at the suits of A G David & F Columbus, Dr J Costigan, Mary A Mason, John L Fowler, Richd Brooks, & Nimrod Garretson, & to me directed; sale on May 10 of lot 13 in square 919, on 9th st. –Thos Plumsill, bailiff

Darnestown Parochial School will commence on Apr 16. Address Rev D Motzen, Darnestown, Montg Co, Md; or inquire of Rev Dr Cocock, Gtwn; Rev Dr Gurley, Rev Mr Bittinger or F A Tschiffely, Wash.

Senate: 1-Ptn from G T St John & other citizens of Ashtabula Co, Ohio, in favor of a judicious bankrupt law: referred. 2-Ptn from E D Tippett, urging an examination of a plan of ship-bldg: referred. 3-Ptn from Jeremiah Greenleaf & other ofcrs & soldiers of the war of 1812, asking that pensions be granted them the same as were allowed to the ofcrs & soldiers of the Revolution: referred. 4-Ptn from John A Winslow, a Cmder in the navy, asking the passage of a supplementary act regulating the pay of ofcrs of the navy promoted in consequence of the action of the retiring board: referred. 5-Ptn from John Butterfield & other contractors for carrying overland mail from St Louis & Memphis to San Francisco, remonstrating against the enactment of any law which would change or annul their contract: referred. 6-Cmte on the Judiciary: asked to be discharged from further consideration of the communication from T G Grant, of St Louis, Mo, in favor of changing the time allowed for taking appeals & writs of error to the Supreme Court: which was agreed to. 7-Cmte on Naval Affairs: referred testimonials in favor of Capt Geo C Stouffer for gallant service in rescuing the ofcrs & soldiers from the steamer **San Francisco** in 1854: to be referred to the Cmte on Military Affairs. Same cmte: bill for the relief of Lt T G Corbin; also, a bill for the relief of Lt Saml R Franklin. 8-Cmte on Pensions: ptn of Alpheus T Palmer, of Maine, for an increase of pension, submitted an adverse report thereon. Same cmte: bill for the relief of Lemuel Worster for a pension for disabilities incurred while employed as a waiter to a militia ofcr during the war of 1812. 9-Cmte on Indian Affairs: memorial of J B Williams, asking a grant to the heirs of Jos Biggs the amount paid by him for boarding, nursing, & medical attendance, on account of being wounded in the Indian war of 1788, asked to be discharged from further consideration, & that it be referred to the Cmte on Revolutionary Claims: which was agreed to. 10-Cmte on Revolutionary Claims: adverse report on the memorial of the heirs of Henry Brockholst Livingston, a lt col of the Continental army for arrears of pay.

Died: on Apr 2, at New Orleans, Mrs Mary W P Handy, formerly of Wash City.

Died: on Mar 2 last, in Tacua, Peru, Geo W Taylor, commission merchant of Arica, Peru, aged about 65 years, leaving a wife & a large circle of friends. He was a native of Braddockfield, near Pittsburgh; &, having joined the South American patriots during their struggle for independence, he has ever since, with the exception of a recent 3 months' visit to his native place, resided in South America, but principally in Peru. He was agent for the British line of steamers at Arica, & was well known to all commercial men visiting the South Pacific.

FRI APR 13, 1860
The trial of Wm H Burkley, in King & Queen Co, Va, came off before an Examining Court on Fri last, upon the charge of shooting Jos Broach. The charge was admitted, & justified upon the plea that Broach had wilfully & maliciously slandered his daughter, a young lady in her teens at school. The Court, after hearing the evidence, discharged the prisoner.

Senate: 1-Ptn from Abby S Chaplin, widow of Col J Snelling, asking a pension: referred. 2-Ptn from Michl S Martin, of Tenn, for a pension: referred. 3-Cmte on Naval Affairs: bill for the relief of Mrs A W Angus, widow of the late Capt Saml Angus, U S Navy: recommended its passage. 4-Cmte on Patents & the Patent Ofc: bill for the relief of Thatcher Perkins & Wm McMahon, asking the extension of a patent for an improvement in the wheels of locomotive engines. Same cmte: bill for the relief of Jane B Evans, a widow & excx of Cadwallader Evans, asking a renewal of a patent granted to her late husband. 5-Cmte on Commerce: bill for the relief of Chas Knap: passed.

Mrd: on Apr 11, at Trinity Church, by Rev Dr Butler, Chas T Jones, of Indiana, to Olivia, eldest daughter of Saml Bacon, of Wash City.

Died: Wed, Eliz Fisher, widow of Saml Fishr, in her 77th year. Her funeral will be from the residence of her son, Ellwood Fisher, 3rd & C sts, today at 11 o'clock A M.

Died: on Apr 12, Mr Michl Sardo, in his 84th year. The deceased was a native of Catania, in Sicily. He emigrated to this country in 1805, & has since that time, for a period of 55 years, living a much respected citizen of Wash, a consistent Christian, & amiable in all the relations of a well spent life. His funeral will take place on Sat, at 10 o'clock A M, from his late residence, 317 G st, between 12th & 13th sts.

Died: on Apr 12, in Gtwn, D C, in her 3rd year, Mary Threlkeld, the eldest daughter of John P & Ellen M McElderry.

SAT APR 14, 1860
Senate: 1-Additional papers to the memorial of F B Sanborn to redress for outrages committed against him by the ofcr executing the precept of the U S Senate: referred. 2-Additional papers in relation to the claim of Peter Campan for arrearages of pay for taking care of the U S dredge boat belonging to the St Clair flats improvement: referred. 3-Ptn from Edw Satey, asking compensation for his services as servant to the staff of Gen Bankhead in the war with Mexico: referred. 4-Cmte of Claims: asked to be discharged from further consideration of the memorial of Saml S Burton for pay & rations as musicians in the war of 1812: which was agreed to. Same cmte: bill for the relief of Capt John B Montgomery. 5-Joint resolution authorizing the accounting ofcrs of the Treasury to revise & adjust the accounts of John Randolph Clay, U S Minister to Peru: referred. 6-Bill for the relief of Mary L Lear. 7-Bill for the relief of David Myerle: amount reduced from $44,400 to $30,000. 8-Bills passed-relief of Lambell Wooster; & A M Fridley, late agent of the Winnebago Indians.

House of Reps: 1-Bills committed-relief: of Wm Cowing; of Hull & Cozzens; of John Naylor & Co; of Margaret Taylor; of Augustus H Evans; of Benj Sayre; of Capt Alex V Fraser; of Stephen F Willis; of Richd Cheney; of Simon de Visser &

Jose Villarubia, of New Orleans; of J W Nyer; of the heirs of Nathl Heard; of the heirs of Wm P McCully; of the heirs of Mark Elisha; of Chas Triche & Edw Rodrigue; of Erastus S Joslyn; of M M Marmaduke; of the heirs of Abraham Livingstone; of Maurice K Simons, of Jackson Co, Texas; of the surviving children of John McDaniel, a soldier of the Revolution; of Sarah Howard, widow of Jas Howard; of the children of Nathl Emnson; of Mary Hopper; of Nicholas Underhill; & of Mrs A E Childs. Pension to Nathan Whitman; to Herman J Ehle; to Thos Booth; to Prentis Champlain. 2-Bills passed-relief: of Hocaday & Liggit; of the widow & other heirs of Wm Higgins; of John T Robertson, of Va; of Wendell Trout; of Angelina C Bowman, widow of Francis L Bowman, late a capt in the U S army; & of Mary J Harris, widow of Col Thos L Harris, deceased. 3-Bill for compensation to Rev R R Richards, late Chaplain of the U S penitentiary in D C: passed. 4-Adverse reports in the following cases-pention to: Josiah Foster & others; to Jas M Stocker; to Jas Harrington; to Mary Helmer; to Luke Putnam; to Geo Parkhurst, a soldier of the Revolution; to David Sayre; to Hugh Ferguson; to Geo Hall; to Alphonse Barbot; to Eliza M Archer; to Saml Remick; to Abigail Huntley & others; to the heirs of Obediah Hodesty; to the children of Danl Starr; & to Esther Cole. Also, for the relief of Lewis W Chalfield; of Jacob Cummin; & of Nancy Bukey, widow of John Bukey.

Circuit Court of Wash Co, D C-in Equity. Walter Butler, Mary Ann Butler his wife, & Ann Butler, cmplnts, vs Amelia Butler, Betsey Butler, Jane Queen, Richd Butler, Jane Butler, Alfred Savage & Adeline Savage his wife, Edmund Butler, & Harriet Ann Butler, widow & heirs at law of Jas Butler, deceased, dfndnts. Jas Butler died intestate & seized & possessed of certain real estate in Wash City, being lots 3 & 4 in square 216, with bldgs, leaving the cmplnts & dfndnts, his widow & heirs at law; that said real estate is not susceptible of division & that a sale will be equally for the benefit of said cmplnts & dfndnts, & that said Amelia Butler is non compos mentis, & incapable of managing her estate or making a sale or conveyance thereof, & all other dfndnts reside out of D C. Non-resident dfndnts to appear in this Court on the first Monday of Sep next.
–Wm M Merrick, A J -Jno A Smith, clerk

Household & kitchen furniture at auction by order of the Orphans Court of D C., at the late residence of Alex'r McIntyre, deceased, 347 K st, between 12th & 13th sts, all of the furniture & other personal effects. –Mary M McIntyre, admx
-C W Boteler & Sons, aucts

Died: on Apr 12, in Wash City, Mary Philomena, daughter of the late Richd B & Mary Ann Nalley, in her 17th year. Her funeral will be on Sunday at 2 o'clock, from the residence of her grandfather, Chas Keenan, 519 I st, between 6th & 7th st, proceeding to St Patrick's Church, F st.

MON APR 16, 1860
Vestrymen of the Church of the Ephipany: Wm Maynadier, Geo M Davis, Jas M Gillis, Geo C Ames, Gilbert Rodman, Thos M Smith, Saml Cole, & L J Middleton.

Fatal accident. In Wilmington, N C, on Apr 7, Jos S Canady, a young mechanic, who had just purchased a dirk, while jesting with a companion, playfully struck his own breast with the knife, crying 'Lay on Macduff." It was supposed he intended to strike himself with the handle.

Died: on Apr 15, in Wash City, Francis McGrann, son of Jas & Mary McGrann, in his 4th year. His funeral will be from his father's residence, 291 B st, between 2nd & 3rd sts, this evening at 5 o'clock.

Died: on Apr 15, after a long & painful illness, Frank Pierce, son of Jas F & H Eliz Divine, aged 7 years, 6 months & 5 days. His funeral will take place at his parent's residence, L st, between 7th & 8th sts, this afternoon at 5 o'clock.

Died: on Apr 7, at Memphis, Alexander Wadswroth Baylor, son of C G & Louisa W Baylor, aged 1 year.

TUE APR 17, 1860
Senate: 1-Ptn from Wm T Kendall, asking indemnity for property seized & confiscated by the alleged authority of the British Gov't, & for the value of guano on an island claimed under the act of Aug 18, 1856: referred. 2-Ptn from Mary A Berault, heir & legal rep of the late Jos Wheaton, of the Revolutionary army, asking to be allowed the half-pay provided by Congress to those who should serve to the end of the war: referred. 3-Ptn from Jno L Kissick, a gunner's mate, injured by an explosion on board the U S frig **Princeton** in 1844, asking to be allowed a pension: referred. 4-Ptn from Henry Durkee, asking indemnity for losses sustained in fulfilling a contract for supplying the U S troops at Plattsburg with fresh beef in 1839: referred. 5-Cmte on Revolutionary Claims: memorial of Eliz Lansdale & Maria M Fox, sole heirs of Gen Stephen Moylan, of the army of the Revolution, asking that his accounts might be settled on the basis indicated as just by the late Mr Hagner, Third Auditor of the Treasury: bill for the relief of the heirs of Gen Stephen Moylan. 6-Cmte on Pensions: bill granting a pension to Jas Lacey, of Grainger Co Tenn, & recommended its passage. Same cmte: bill for the relief of Mary B Hook, widow of the late Col Jas Hook, & that it be referred to the Cmte of Claims. Same cmte: bill for the relief of Webster S Steele. 7-Cmte on Indian Affairs: bill for the relief of W Y Hansell, the heirs of Wm H Underwood, & the reps of Saml Rookwell: recommended its passage. Same cmte: asked to be discharged from further consideration of the House bill for the relief of the heirs of Alex'r Montgomery, & that it be referred to the Come on Revolutionary Claims. Same cmte: adverse report on the ptn of citizens of Upper Tulpehocken, Pa, asking that a pension may be granted to Michl Lauck, a soldier of the war of 1812. 8-Cmte on Pensions: bill for the relief of Andrew F Marshall:

recommended its passage. 9-Cmte on Revolutionary Claims: adverse on the memorial of the heirs of Chas Webber, of the Revolutionary army, asking to be allowed a pension or bounty land.

Married in Campbellton, Fla, on Mar 21, by Jas Hall, Master Robt Cherry, aged 16 years, to Miss Josephie Gregory, aged 12 years.

Died: on Apr 15, at his lodgings in Wash City, after a lingering illness, Hon Wm Cost Johnson, of Md, aged about 53 years. He represented his native district of Fred'k in Congress during several sessions, from 1833. His remains were conveyed in the morning train yesterday to his home in Fred'k Co for interment.

Died: on Apr 14, after a brief but painful illness, Mrs Maria Norris, in her 54th year. Her funeral will be from the residence of her son-in-law, W P Parke, 269 4th st, between Mass ave & I st, today at 1 o'clock.

WED APR 18, 1860
Senate: 1-Ptn from the heirs of Thos Brody, a soldier of the war of the Revolution, asking to be allowed bounty land: referred. 2-Ptn from Jno B Miller, for a pension on account of injuries received while a teamster in the war with Mexico: referred. 3-Papers in relation to the claim of Thos Kirkpatrick for a balance due for keeping U S convicts: referred. 4-Cmte on D C: bill to incorporate the ***Prospect Hill Cemetery***, & recommended its passage. 5-Cmte of Claims: bill for the relief of Geo D Durham, asking compensation for services as a clerk in the Indian Bureau. Same cmte; adverse report on the memorial of A B Thompson & other citizens of Calif for remuneration for horses, mules, & other property taken by the ofcrs of the army & navy in the conquest of Calif, under a promise of payment by the same. 6-Cmte on Pensions: bill for the relief of Keziah Pritchett, formerly widow of David Moore. 7-Cmte on Foreign Relations: bill for the relief of Edw Ely, U S Consul at Bombay, to have his accounts settled. 8-Cmte on Indian Affairs: asked to be discharged from further consideration of the papers relating to the claim of Jas Pool for corn furnished the Seneca & Shawnee Indians, & that it be referred to the Cmte of Claims. 9-Bill for the relief of John M Brooke, & making an appropriation for the use of his deep-sea soundings: referred.

A verdict of acquittal has been rendered by the jury in the case of J B Brownlow, on trial last week at Abingdon, Va, for the killing of Jas W Reese, [both students at Emory & Henry College,] on Feb 24 last. The jury was absent but a few minutes.

Trustee's sale of an extensive collection of superior houseold furniture, being the effects of the Union Hotel, Gtwn: by 2 deeds of trust, dated Nov 11, 1859, & Jan 7, 1860, executed by E R Abbott to the undersigned, recorded in Liber J A S, No 186, folios 104 to 110; & the other in Liber J A S, No 190, folios 22 to 26, in the land records for Wash Co, D C. –Jno A Linton, trustee -Thos Dowling, auct

Two little girls, aged 3 & 5 years, children of Mr Jas McCoy, residing in Wmsburgh, N Y, were burnt to death by setting their clothes on fire with matches, with which they were playing. They were locked in a room during the temporary absence of their mother. They died a few hours afterwards.

An entire family, named Henry, numbering 6 persons, living on Deep Run, Belmont Co, Ohio, were swept away by the water on Tue last, & 5 of them drowned. The sixth one clung to drift wood during the night & was rescued the next morning.

Cottage residence for sale in Warrenton, Fauquier Co, Va; with 8 acres, built within the last 5 years; with numerous out-bldgs. If desired the furniture, most of which is new, will also be disposed of. –Wm N Bispham, Warrenton, Fauquier Co, Va.

Orphans Court of Wash Co, D C, Apr 14, 1860. In the case of Alex'r Provest, exc of Wm H Winter, deceased, the executor & Court have appointed May 12 next, for the final settlement of the personal estate of the said deceased, of the assets in hand. -Ed Roach, Reg/o wills

THU APR 19, 1860
Senate: 1-Ptn from Caleb E Parker, asking to be allowed a pension on account of injuries received in the military service during the war of 1812: referred. 2-Ptn from Yelland Foreman, asking an appropriation to enable him to construct an apparatus for enabling vessels to pass over bars, with a view to test the feasibility of his invention: referred. 3-Ptn from Wm T Sherrod, asking compensation for his services as assist surgeon during the war with Mexico: referred. 4-Cmte on the Judiciary: bill for the relief of Judge Cradlebaugh, of the Supreme Court of the Territory of Utah, for payment of expenses in transporting books & papers of the judicial court of that Territory. Same cmte: adverse report on the memorial of Jeffrey T Adams, late clerk of the U S Court for the Territory of Minnesota. 5-Cmte on Pensions: bill for the relief of Mary Preston, widow of Geo Preston, reported it without amendment. 6-Cmte on Revolutionary Claims: bill for the relief of Maryett Van Buskirk: recommended its passage.

House of Reps: 1-Cmte of Claims: bill for the relief of Sarah S Stafford: committed.

The Grand Jury of Nashville has found a true bill for murder against Pinkney P Trewitt, for the killing of Dr Carew, at a time when Trewitt was under the influence of delirium tremens. He was bailed in the sum of $10,000.

Died: on Apr 17, in Wash City, Stephen Duncan, senior. His funeral will be from his late residence, 21 Indiana ave, today at 11 o'clock A M.

FRI APR 20, 1860
Senate: 1-Ptn from Henry G Rogers, asking the allowance of salary & other expenses due as charge d'affaires to Sardinia: referred. 2-Ptn from D D Addison, asking that an appropiration be made to pay him for an index made to the Wash papers purchased of him by the Sec of State: referred.

Trustee's sale of valuable real estate, by decree of the Circuit Court of D C, passed in chancery cause No 1,517, wherein Edw Wheeler & others are cmplnts & Thos H Garner & others are dfndnts; sale on May 14 next, lot 19 thru 22, in square 117, with improvements thereon, in Wash, D C.
—E C Morgan, Walter S Cox, trustees -Jas C McGuire & Co, aucts

Mrd: on Apr 17, at Trinity Church, by Rev Dr Butler, H C Loving, of Va, to Marion R, daughter of Wm H Gunnell, of Wash City.

Mrd: on Apr 17, by Rev Stephen P Hill, Edw R Taylor, of Va, to Mary F Jefferies, of Tenn.

SAT APR 21, 1860
House of Reps: 1-**Referred to the Cmte of the Whole**-pension to: Saml Gibbs; Margaret Watts; Fred'k Schaum; Mrs Adelia C Place, widow of Lt Chas W Place, late of the U S Navy; Wm M S Riley; & Sparhawk Parsons. Increase pension to Wm G Bernard, late a soldier in the U S Army; & to Mary Perrigo, widow of Fred'k Perrigo. Relief of Wm Sutton; of Edwin W Jones; of Jos Pike; of Wm C Greitzner; of Wm P Bowtray; of Aaron H Palmer; of Franklin Peale; of Ephraim Hunt; of Eli W Goff; of Saml Perry; of Richd Fitzpatrick; of Thos Allen; of Gottleib Scheerer-passed; & of Stewart McGowan-passed. Also, authorize the Postmaster Gen to settle the accounts of Capt J H Estes. 2-**Adverse reports in the following petitions**: of Maurice R Simmons; of Mich S Bailey; of Danl Reynolds; of Randolph J Shoemaker; of Sarah Post; of Abraham Richards; of Abel M Bryant; of John S Livermore; of Asa Pratt; of Margaret Doug; of Enoch Moore; of Jas Young; of Lizur B Canfield; of the heirs of Wm Hodges; of Louis Blodgett, heir of Arba Blodgett, deceased; of Nathl Enos; of John McGarvey; of Stephen P Lamb; & of Jos Bindon, jr. Also, joint resolution for the relief of Wm Hazard Wigg. 3-Bill for the relief of Cassius M Clay: laid aside to be reported to the House.

Newstead Abbey is to be sold at auction on Jun 13 next. This Abbey was founded by Henry II. In a latter period, it became, by royal grant, the property of the Byron family. It descended to the poet Byron, but was ultimately purchased by Col Thos Wildman, in 1818. Its present sale is consequent upon the death of that gentleman. All the relics of the past centuries have been sacredly preserved. Among them are the tomb of Boatswain, & the twin elms bearing Byron's own name, which he cut there in the bark years ago.

Died: on Apr 20, in Wash City, of disease of the heart, James C Barry, son of Juliana & the late James D Barry. His funeral will take place from the residence of his mother, 584 N J ave, Capitol Hill, tomorrow at 3 o'clock P M.

Among the distinguished gentlemen in Wash City at present is Ex-Govn'r Wise, of Va, who is on a visit to his son-in-law, Dr A Y Garnett, 9th st.

Mr Geo H Glenville, who lives in West st, was on his way home from a ball. His wife was with him. They were going through Canal st, when suddenly Mr Glenville was knocked down & his gold watch taken. The robber ran & was out of sight. A policeman heard a cry for police, & observed a boy running away. His supposition proved to be correct. The boy turned out to be Thos Lloyd, & the watch was recovered. Lloyd is only 17 years of age. –N Y paper

MON APR 23, 1860
Trustee's sale of valuable bldg lot, at auction, on May 2, by deed of trust from Robt Adams, dated May 5, 1857: part of lot 12 in square 401 on 8th st, between L & M sts. –C Ingle, trustee -Wall & Barnard, aucts

Com'r sale of valuable real estate improved, by decree of the Circuit Court of D C, dated Dec 13, 1859, passed in the case of Richd Frere for a division of the estate of Jas B Frere, deceased, public auction on May 8, on the premises, the following real estate & improvements, subject to the dower interests of the widow of said Jas B Frere, deceased, being one-third of the rents & profits of the said estate during her life, as prescribed & determined by said order & decree, namely: lot of ground 10 in square 86, in Wash City, with a 2 story frame house with basement & one two story brick house. –Geo T McGlue, John Henderson, Wm T Smithson, Thos C Donn, Chas Walter, Com'rs -Wall & Barnard, aucts

Circuit Court of Wash Co, D C-in Equity, No 1,558. Jos C Walsh vs Geo Page. The trustee reported that on Apr 13, 1860, he sold the premises mention in the proceedings to Reuben B Clark, for $723.04, & purchaser had complied with the terms of sale. –Jno A Smith, clerk

The barn of Hon Wm H Seward, at Auburn, N Y, was destroyed by fire last week.

In the suit of Mary E Cloyes against the Boston & Worcester Railroad Co for $20,000 damages for personal injuries on the road, the jury of the Supreme Court at Boston on Friday awarded the plntf $10,000 damages.

Died: on Apr 21, in Wash City, Mrs Catherine McNamee, aged 70 years, a native of Ireland, County Tyrone, for the last 42 years a resident of Wash City. Her funeral will take place at 3 o'clock, from her residence in 6th st & Pa av.

Died: on Apr 21, at his residence, in Upper Marlborough, PG Co, Md, Danl C Digges, in his 47th year.

Died: on Apr 21, Mrs Deborah Tilley, aged 70 years. She had been for about 40 years a consistent & pious member of the Methodist Episcopal Church, & was prepared for the time of her departure. Her funeral is Oct 23 at 3 o'clock, from the residence of Mr Jas Anthony, her son-in-law, 268 C st north.

Died: on Apr 17, at the Family Mansion, in Canandaigua, N Y, in her 90th year, Mrs Mindwell P Granger, relict of Gideon Granger, & mother of Hon Francis A Granger & Gen John A Granger.

Died: on Apr 21st, in Gtwn, Mrs Ellen Carter, widow of the late Hon John Carter, formerly of S C, & daughter of the late Capt Wm Marbury. Her funeral is this morning at 11 A M, from her her late residence, corner of West & Congress sts.

TUE APR 24, 1860
For sale, a large dwlg house on the corner of E & 9th sts. Public auction, under the will of the late Mrs Eliz H Newman, on May 15 next, of lot 1 & parts of lots 2 & 24, in square 377, in Wash City, with the dwlg-house thereon. This property fronts 83 feet, more or less, on 9th st, & on E st, 91 feet 7½ inches, more or less. -Chas B King, Benj F Larned, trustees -A Green, aucts

Senate: 1-Ptn from Hiram Corum & others, claimants of portions of the Delaware trust lands, asking that their rights may be placed in the position of those claiming under Fred'k Samuel: referred. 2-Ptn from J S & Geo Douglass & others, asking that certain land patents heretofore issued be cancelled, & the issuing of others in lieu thereof: referred. 3-Ptn from Wm M Armstrong, a capt in the U S Navy, asking the amount due him while on the reserved list: referred. 4-Cmte on Military Affairs: bill for the relief of Brvt Lt Col Martin Burke & Capt Chas S Winder, U S Army: recommended its passage. Same cmte: asked to be discharged from further consideration of the memorial of Alex'r Randall, exc of Danl Randall, asking payment of a balance of compensation for collecting & disbursing moneys during the late war with Mexico: referred to the Cmte of Claims: which was agreed to. 4-Bill to authorize the issuance of patents in the name of J S Douglass upon certain land entries made at Chocchuma: referred to the Cmte on Public Lands.

On Apr 14 an old lady, 82 years of age, Miss Mary Weary, of Nanscoe, Wadebridge, died. She was known to possess a considerable amount of property, part of which came to her as the survivor of 2 sisters, from her brother, the old Squire John Weary, who was well known for eccentricity throughout Cornwall. After Miss Weary's death, her room, which no one had been allowed to enter for 10 years before, was searched & about L9,000 was found in the room Some of the land will pass to the heir-at-law, Mr Thos Cleave, but the remaining landed property will pass, with the other property, to 16 nieces & grand-nephews & nieces, who will probably made a better use of it than keeping it idle.
–Plymouth [Eng] Journal

Criminal Court-Wash-Mon: 1-John H Frizzel charged with 2 cases of assault was acquitted in one case & convicted in the other: fined $20 & costs.

Capt Wm Mure, of Caldwell, one of the first classical scholars of the British Empire, is dead. [No death date given-current item.]

Mrd: on Apr 12, at Christ Church, Alexandria, Va, by Rev Mr Dana, D McCarty Chichester, of Fairfax Co, to Miss Julia Sully, of Alexandria.

Died: on Apr 20, at *Oak Hill*, Montg Co, Md, Mrs Henrietta Maria Brooke, in her 75th year.

WED APR 25, 1860

Sale of 2 brick dwlg houses, on May 4, at auction, the 3 story brick house on First st adjoining the residence of Mr John H Smoot. This property is on the handsomest st in Gtwn. The 2 story brick house on Bridge st, below Montg st, occupied by Capt Mitchel. –Barnard & Buckey, aucts, Gtwn, D C.

Admx sale of household & kitchen furniture, horse, wagons, carryall & harness at auction on Apr 30, at Piney Grove Tavern, 7th st road. –Mrs C Moreland, admx -Barnard & Buckley, aucts, Gtwn, D C

Trustee's sale of superior & nearly new furniture & effects, being the entire effects of the Vernon House, by deed of trust dated Mar 2, 1860, executed by Henry F Johns, recorded in the land records of Wash Co, D C: sale on May 10, at the Vernon House, Mo ave & 3rd st. –Wm A Browning, trustee
-Jas C McGuire & Co, aucts

St Louis, Apr 24. A collision occurred yesterday near Jefferson Barracks, on the Iron Mountain railroad, between a construction train & a special train conveying a portion of the St Louis Board of Health. Dr Klein, clerk of the board, John Simonds, treasurer of the railroad company, a brakesman, & a boy were killed. [Apr 27th newspaper: John Simonds died in a short time; Mr Geo Klier, clerk of the Board of Health; Jas Murray, about 15; & Geo Pilcher were crushed. Klier was killed & Murray died soon after. Pilcher, brakesman, will probably die before morning.]

Died: on Apr 24, in Wash City, from the effects of a malignant carbuncle, David Lynch, of Pittsburgh, Pa, in his 67th year. His funeral will take place from the Wash Infirmary this day, at 3;30 o'clock P M, & proceed to *Mount Olivet Cemetery*.

THU APR 26, 1860

Mrd: on Apr 17, at *Windsor Place*, Lancaster Co, Pa, by Rev Alfred Nevin, D D, assisted by Rev Prof Leaman, of Lafayette College, Jas S L Cummins, of N Y C, to Kate C, daughter of the late P Wager Reigart.

Lately decided in the Court of Sessions at Edinburgh, Scotland, Mrs Catharine Leslie, entered a suit to have it declared that she was the wife of the late Rev Cathcart Leslie. It was proved they became engaged in 1822, & in 1827 they formally accepted of each other as man & wife, without any other ceremony or witnesses, agreeing to keep it secret until he was rich enough to support her. They lived apart for 30 years, continually corresponding until his death in 1857. The Scotch judges decided in favor of Mrs Leslie, in accordance with the <u>law of Scotland</u>, which, in order to make a marriage legal, requires no form or ceremony, civil or religious, but merely the consent of the parties, whether living together or not.

Died: on Apr 13, at Sandy Springs, Md, Mahlon Kirk, in his 77th year.

Died: on Apr 24, in Balt, Mrs Catherine Wise, widow of the late Geo Stewart Wise, of the U S Navy.

FRI APR 27, 1860
English paper: Miss Victoire Balfe, daughter of the English composer, & herself an artiste of great merit, has just been married at St Petersburgh to Sir John Fiennes T Crampton, Bart, her Majesty's Minister at the Court of Russia. Sir John is in his 53rd year. Mr Crampton was for many years attached to the British Legation in this city.

Senate: 1-Two memorials from Col Johnson & other ofcrs of the army in Utah, urging that Milton Carpenter, Buren D Hungerford, Mira Hungerford, Jacob Paulin, & the family of Abel L Root & other parties be indemnified for losses & sufferings occasioned by an attack of the Indians while on the route from Iowa to Calif on Aug 20, 1859: referred. 2-Ptn from Chas M Anderson & others interested in the welfare of seamen, urging that the spirit ration may be abolished in the navy: referred. 3-Ptn from W H Granger, asking to be allowed the right of pre-emption to a certain quarter section of land settled upon by his mother, who was afterwards murdered by the Sioux Indians: referred. 4-Ptn from A Wegener & other heirs & reps of certain settlers on the public lands at Spirit Lake, Iowa, who were massacred by a band of Sioux Indians at their settlement, asking to be allowed the right of pre-emption to those lands: referred. 5-Cmte on Pirvate Land Claims: bills for the relief of the heirs or legal reps of Francois Guillory, & for the relief of R K Doebles: recommended their passage. Same cmte: bill for the relief of the heirs & legal reps of Olivier Landry, of the State of Louisiana: recommended its passage. 6-Cmte on Public Lands: bill for the relief of Solomon Wadsworth: recommended its passage. 7-Bill for the relief of the heirs & legal reps of Pierre Dolet, of the State of Louisiana: referred. 8-Bill confirming certain land titles to Andrew Ormond, of Ala: referred. 9-Bill confirming titles to certain lands to John Fryer, of Ala: referred. 10-Bill confirming the title of certain lands to Wm E Carter: referred.

Died: on Tue, in Richmond, Va, after a protracted illness, Mrs Julia Mayo Cabell, wife of Dr R H Cabell. She was the daughter of Mrs Abigail Mayo, of Bellville, & sister of Mrs Winfield Scott. Mrs Cabell had acquired some literary reputation, & was known for her numerous charities.

Mrd: on Apr 18, at Pensacola, Fla, by Rt Rev Bishop Quinlan, of the Diocese of Mobile, Maggie, daughter of Hon S R Mallory, to Henry Bishop, of Bridgeport, Ct.

Mrd: on Apr 16, in N Y, by Rev T Gallaudet, Rector of St Ann's Church, Mr Clarence Morfit to Miss Annie E Laverty, both of that city.

Died: on Apr 24, in Boston, Anna Wroe, wife of Hon Benj R Curtis, aged 43 years.

SAT APR 28, 1860

Deputy U S Marshal Cable, of Ohio, arrested, on Wed last, Jos L Ball, of Newburg, Jefferson Co, Ohio, on the charge of counterfeiting. Ball is an old man of 60 years, & is very wealthy. The evidence is positive.

A little 5 year old girl, named Patten, was killed at Mansfield, Ohio, a few days ago, when he playfully put her head through two rails, when one broke loose & struck her on the neck, breaking her neck, & causing almost instant death.

Mr Arms, a Deputy U S Marshal, was shot dead at Topeka, Kansas, by Ritchie, whom he was attempting to arrest on an old charge of robbing the post ofc.
[No death date given-current item.]

Mr Macready, the actor, now in his 68th year, has just married Miss Cecile L F Spencer, who is only in her 23rd year. Macready has left his home at Sherbourne to take up his residence elsewhere.

Mrd: on Apr 26, in Fred'k, Md, at All Saints Church, by Rev Chas Seymour, John L Edwards, of Wash, D C, to Mary E, youngest daughter of the late Danl Coolidge, of Poughkeepsie, N Y.

Died: Apr 24, in Memphis, Tenn, Maria H Dabney, wife of Virginius Dabney, of Memphis, Tenn, & daughter of Jas E Heath, of Richmond, Va.

Died: Apr 25, at Phil, after a short illness, Mrs Hannah B Soulard, in her 60th year.

MON APR 30, 1860

Jas Morgan, some week or two ago, in Cheatham Co, Tenn, fell asleep reading in his bed, & was so badly burnt that he died in a day or two afterwards. He had some $3,000 in his room, the greater part in gold, some of which was recovered in a damaged condition, but the paper money was entirely lost.

Obit-died: Apr 25, at Mills House, Hon John S Robinson, delegate at large from Vt. He had an apopletic stroke & died immediately. He was about 55 years of age; member of one of the oldest & most influential families in Vt, a family distinguished with the Allens & Crittendens of that State.
—Charleston Mercury of 26th.

Private sale of valuable property, the fine residence belonging to the late Andrew Hoover, & now known as *Rosslyn*, in Alexandria Co, Va, on the height overlooking Gtwn, adjoining the Aqueduct. This property extends to about 140 acres. Apply on the premises to the manager, Alex Cassels, or to Jas Roach, *Prospect Hill*, Va.

Sale of valuable farm in Fairfax Co, Va, on May 5, by deed of trust from Amelia T Young, dated Jul 1,1856, of record in the Fairfax Co, Va, I will sell at public auction, a tract of land now occupied by Mrs Young, containing about 50 acres, on the Leesburg Turnpike; bldgs on the place consist of a comfortable Cottage, barn, stables, & smoke-house. —S Ferguson Beach, trustee

Died: on Apr 29, Maria Ann Bacon, daughter of Washington & Sarah R Bacon, in her 19th year, after a brief illness. Her funeral is today at 4 o'clock P M, from the residence of her parents, 317 6th st, between K & N Y ave.

Died: on Apr 29, in Wash City, Mrs Jane Donohoo, in her 30th year. Her funeral will take place from her residence on L st, between 12th & 13th sts, on Tue, at 9 o'clock.

Died: on Apr 27, at New Brunswick, N J, Nancy, only daughter of C L Hardenbergh, & grand-daughter of the late John G Warren, of N Y.

Died: on Mar 22, at *Sandy Hill*, Wash Co, N Y, Hon Henry C Martindale, a member of the House of Reps from 1823 to 1831, & from 1833 to 1835.

Died: on Apr 28, in Gtwn, Catharine, beloved infant daughter of Hobart Catharine Berrian. Her funeral will be this morning at 10 o'clock, from the residence of her parents.

Criminal Court-Wash-Sat. 1-Henry Weasner was convicted of stealing a horse valued at $75 from John Jones: sentenced to 3 years in the penitentiary. 2-Wm Johnson was acquitted of a charge of assault on Jas Fletcher. 3-The case of Justice Henry Reaver, of Gtwn, indicted for charging an illegal fee in his capacity as magistrate: guilty, with a recommendation to the mercy of the Court. 4-Richd Lee, charged with an assault on Ann Johnson, submitted his case, & the Court sentenced him to 2 months in jail & pay a fine of $20. Prayed in commitment till the fine was paid.

Lawrence Johnson, the well known type founder & stereotyper of Phil, died of paralysis on Thus morning. He was taken ill while attending a city passenger railway meeting, was taken home & died. He was in his 60th year; born in England, but emigrated to this country when quite a young man.

Circuit Court of Wash Co, D C-in Chancery. Catherine Madison vs John A Bailey, Frank Moore & Laura M his wife, Alex'r C Washburn & Ellen his wife, & David A Hall. Object of this bill is to procure a conveyance for lots 21 & 22 in square 569, in Wash City, D C. The bill states that the dfndnts, John A Bailey, Alex'r C Washburn & Ellen M his wife, & Laura M Baily, [since married to the dfndnt, Frank Moore,] by instrument of writing appointed the said Hall their agent to sell certain property claimed to be owned by them; that in pursuance of said authority said Hall, by writing on Jul 1, 1850, contracted with the cmplnt to sell her lot 21 in square 569, for $110.11, & on Jun 21, 1851, by like writing, contracted to sell to her said lot 22 for $187.50; that she paid in full to said Hall both said prices; that the dfndnts, Baily & Frank Moore, or one of them admitted to her that dfndnt, Hall, had authority to sell said lots; that on Mar 28, 1851, the dfndnts, John A Bailey, Alex'r C Washburn & Ellen M his wife, & Laura M Bailey, [now Moore,] did execute deeds to her for lot 21, but the acknowledgments to the same were defective; that all of said dfndnts, except said Hall, reside out of D C. Non-resident dfndnts are to appear in this Court on or before the first Monday of Oct next. –Jno A Smith, clerk
-W Y Fendall, Solicitor for cmplnt

Orphans Court of Wash Co, D C. Letters of administration on the personal estate of Saml Hamilton, late of Wash Co, deceased. –John C C Hamilton, adm

TUE MAY 1, 1860
Senate: 1-Ptn from G C Johnston, asking the payment of a balance of an amount which the Sec of War was authorized to pay him out of the annuity of the Shawnee Indians: referred. 2-Ptn from Solomon Whipple, asking extension of his patent for a machine for cutting files: referred. 3-Additional papers in relation to the claim of Sallie Moor, widow of Elisha Moor, to a pension: referred. 4-Cmte on Revolutionary Claims: asked to be discharged from further consideration of the memorial of J B Williams, & that it be referred to the Cmte of Claims: which was agreed to. 5-Cmte on the Judiciary: adverse report on the memorial of Geo G B Barnard, assignee of Hon David C Broderick.

From Europe: Col Wm Mure, well know to the scholars in this country & throughout the literary world for his attainments as a Helenist, & his contributions to the histroy of Grecian Literature, died. [No death date given-current item.]

Criminal Court-Wash-Mon. 1-Florence Donoghue & Dennis Cady were found not guilty of an assault & battery on Dennis Driscoll. 2-Jas Grant, Peter Hyde, Benj King, Robt Hepburn, & Jos Lavender were found guilty for riot at the house of one Burckhardt. Each was fined $20 & sentenced to 2 months in jail.

Died: on Apr 30, in his 64th year, Rev Levin I Gilliss, formerly Rector of the Church of the Ascension in Wash City, & for more than 40 years a Minister to the Protestant Episcopal Church. His funeral will be on Wed next at 11 o'clock A M, from the Church of the Epiphany.

Died: on Apr 23, in Bedford, Pa, in prospect of a blissful immortality, Mrs Caroline M Anderson, wife of Dr Geo W Anderson, & daughter of Saml Morsell, of PG Co, Md.

WED MAY 2, 1860
Household & kitchen furniture at auction on May 8, at the residence of Mrs Bechtel, G st, between 13th & 14th sts. -Jas C McGuire & Co, aucts

Annual exhibition of the Junior Class of Columbian College was held on Monday at the Smithsonian Institution. List of the orators: Townsend McVeigh, jr, of Va; John M Roane, of Va; John Y Bryant, jr, of N C; John Wheeler, of N C; Chas P Harmon, of Va; Elliott Cones, of N H; Wm A Gordon, jr, of D C; S K Sorsby, of Miss; Otis T Mason, of Va; T Edwin Brown, of D C.

Fifteen descendents of Roger Williams, & nearly as many citizens, met in Providence on Thu, resolved that Roger's memory deserves a monument, & appointed a cmte of 15 to see about it.

THU MAY 3, 1860
Senate: 1-Court of Claims: made in pursuance of law, in favor of the claims of Richd S Coxe; the claim of Alex'r M Jackson, adm of John Gorman; the claim of Nehemiah Garrison, assignee of Moses Perkins; & the claim of Danford Mott. Adverse reports to the claims of Edw Sangeter, adm of Hugh West; of Danl Nippes; & of John P Norton: all referred to the Cmte of Claims. 2-Ptn from C S Drew, late adj of the 2nd regt of Oregon mounted volunteers, giving a detailed account of the origin & prosecution of the Indian war in that country: referred. 3-Ptn from J Alexis Port, asking indemnity for losses sustained by being forcibly dispossessed of certain tobacco purchased by him at a sale by an ofcr of the U S army at Puebla, Mexico, during the late war: referred. 4-Ptn from Seth Driggs, a citizen of the U S residing at Caraccas, Venezuela, complaining of the delays & expenes attending the prosecution of business by citizens of the U S with the Ministers of their Gov't in foreign countries, praying that Congress will regulate by law the powers & duties of its ofcrs: referred. 5-Cmte on Revolutionary Claims: bill for the relief of the heirs of Rev Jas Craig, deceased: reported the bill ought not to pass.

I have this day associated with me Mr J B Dawson in the Coal, Wood, Lime, & Sand business, under the title of Sheriff & Dawson. –G L Sheriff

Wash Corp-Apr 30. 1-Ptns from S C Veirs, jr; of Philip Hogan; & of Jas Cantwill; for the remission of fines: referred to the Cmte of Claims. 2-Ptn from

Antoin Heitmiller, asking a return of taxes erroneously paid: referred to the Cmte of Claims. 3-Bills referred to the Cmte of Claims-relief: of Wm M Ellis & Brother; of Margaret Fleet; of Geo W Cochran; of Thos Hagerty; & of E C Sterling.

Diplomatic appointments: Mr J S Lumley, [formerly British Sec of Legation at Wash,] now Sec at St Petersburgh, is appointed Sec at Constantinople in the room of Mr Alison, appointed to succeed Sir Henry Rawlinson as Minister at the Persian Court. Mr Erskine, [lately attache at Wash,] now at Stockholm, is appointed Sec of Legation at St Petersurgh. Mr Edwin Corbett, [formerly attache at Wash,] now at Florence, succeeds Mr Erskine at Stockholm.

The steamer **A T Lacey** left St Louis on Apr 24, with 800 tons of freight & 40 or 50 passengers, about 25 in the cabin & balance on deck. On Thu fire was discovered by the watch on the forward deck, & the alarm was immediately given by Capt Taylor, cmder of the boat, who with others rushed to the spot & found an open bale of hay in flames. The flames spread rapidly. The boat was run ashore. The number of persons said to be lost is 17, 3 or 4 having been burnt to death in their berths. 116 cattle on board were roasted alive.

Criminal Court-Wash-Tue. 1-JohnWalker, charged with assault & battery with intent to kill Michl Keating: verdict not guilty. 2-Edw Humphreys was tried & convicted of an assault on Teresa Eberling: verdict not guilty. 3-Isaac Contee & Lemuel Harris, colored, were convicted of stealing a coat valued at $6: each sentenced to 18 months in the penitentiary.

FRI MAY 4, 1860
Trustee's sale of a small tract of land near Wash City at public auction, by deed of trust dated Aug 31, 1855, recorded in Liber J A S No 113, folios 5 thru 8, of the land records of Wash Co, D C: public auction on Jun 7, of a tract of land near Piney Branch Road, in Wash Co, D C, adjoining the lands of Enoch Moreland, Chas Stuart, Wilson, & Belvey Butler, containing by survey, made by Lewis Carbery, 11 acres of land, with a small house thereon. –Edw Swann, trustee -C W Boteler & Sons, aucts

House of Reps: 1-Cmte on Military Affairs: bill for the relief of Harriet F Fisher, admx of M W Fisher, deceased, & Richd M Bouton: committed.

Norfolk, May 3. Capt Brayley, of the British schnr **Alice Rogers**, was found guilty today in the U S Circuit Court of selling 2 free negroes, & was sentenced to 3 years in the penitentiary.

By order of the Orphans Court of D C., on May 7, I shall sell, at the late residence of Jos Owens, deceased, on D st, between 3rd & 4th sts, all personal effects of the deceased, including household & kitchen furniture. –Jas Owens, adm -A Green, aucts

Died: on May 2, after a short illness, Andrew J Humes, in his 27th year. His funeral is today at 3 o'clock, from the residence of his mother, on 5th st, between G & H sts.

Died: on Apr 21, at his residence, in Upper Marlborough, Md, after a severe & lingering illness, Danl Carroll Digges, in his 47th year. The deceased was a native of
PG Co, Md, & was descended from the ancient & distinguished family of Digges, of Chilham Castle, county Kent, England, & of the patriotic family of Carrolls, of Md. He graduated with the highest honors at Gtwn College, D C, & soon after commenced the study of law with Judge Magruder, of Annapolis. He was admitted to the bar & located in Anne Arundel Co, where he was engaged in a large & lucrative practice up to the period of his death. In his domestic relations he was a kind & affectionate husband, a most devoted & indulgent father, a dutiful son, & an affectionate brother.

SAT MAY 5, 1860
On Sat last Danl C Kenyon, the defaulting Cashier of the Rhode Island Exchange Bank, was sentenced to 8 years in the State Prison by the Court of Common Pleas, Judge Shearman. He remains in the custody in the custody of the Sheriff of Kent Co, in Greenwich jail, where his confinement has been shared by his wife ever since his incarceration in Feb last. –Providence Post

Senate: 1-Ptn from the widow of E A Ogden, late quartermaster in the army, asking to be allowed a pension: referred. 2-Additional papers on the claim of Wm Welsh, a soldier in the last war with Great Britain & subsequent Indian wars, for a pension: referred. 3-Cmte on Private Land Claims: bill for the relief of the heirs & legal reps of Pierre Dolet, of the State of Louisiana, reported it back with an amendment. 4-Cmte on the Public Lands: bill for the relief of John W Taylor & certain other assignees of pre-emption land locations: recommended its passage. Same Cmte: bill for the relief of the widow & other heirs of Wm Higgins, deceased: recommended its passage. Same cmte: bill for the relief of Ashton S H White. Same cmte: bill to authorize the issuance of patents to Jas S Douglas upon certain land entries made at Chochuma, Miss: passed. 5-Cmte on Pensions: adverse report on the ptn of Thos P Dudley, asking an increase of his pension. 6-Bill for the relief of Evelina Porter, widow of the late Cmdor Porter: referred to the Cmte on Pensions. 7-Bills passed-relief: of Mary Featherston, widow of John Featherston; of J J Lints; of Annie D Rheves; of Laura C Humber, widow of Chas H Humber; of Eliz Montgomery, heir of Hugh Montgomery; of Fred'l L Colclaser; of Willis A Gorman; of J W Dyer, A L Dyer, & W W Dye; of McFarland & Downey; of T A M Craven; of Sweeny, Rittenhouse, Fant & Co; of the legal reps of Wetonsaw, son of Jas Connor; of Elias Yulee, late Receiver of Public Money at Olympia, in Wash Territory; of Mary K Guthrie, widow of Presley N Guthrie; of John P Brown; & of the legal reps of J E Martin. Also, to confirm the title of Benj E Edwards to a certain tract of land in the Territory of

New Mexico. 6-Bills postponed until tomorrow-relief: of John Erickson; of John H Wheeler; of O H Berryman & others; & of Chas E Anderson.

Comrs' sale of valuable real estate, by decree of the Circuit Court of D C, in the matter of the heirs of Fred'k Mohler, deceased, made on Apr 13, 1857, at public auction, on May 23, all of square 271 in Wash City. –Saml E Douglass, E C Carrington, Thos E Lloyd, Chas Walter, Geo Theo McGlue, Com'rs -A Green, aucts

Obit-died: suddenly, while out deer hunting, Hon Geo S Yerger, of the State of Mississippi. As a patriot he was devoted to the whole country, & his judicial talents known throughout all the States. The High Court of Appeals was informed of his death, on Apr 21. [No death date given-current item.]

House of Reps: 1-Bills referred to the Cmte of the Whole-relief: of Mrs Eliz Bliss Wolf; of Randall Pegg; of John R Nourse & others; of Moses Meeker; of the legal reps of David G Bates; of the heirs of Capt Thos Hazzard, deceased; of the heirs of Lt Geo Walton; of the heirs of Capt Andrew Russell, deceased, of the Va line; of the legal reps of Jas Bell, deceased; of the surviving grandchildren of Col Wm Thompson, of S C; of Albert Elfe & others; of Madison Sweetzer-passed; of Richd C Martin; of A M Fridley, late agent of the Winnebago Indians; of Antone Robidoux; of Eliz Smith, of Tenn; of A M Mitchell, late colonel of Ohio volunteers in the Mexican war-passed; of Arsenath M Elliott; of Harriet Brent & others; of F M Gunnell, passed assist surgeon in the U S Navy; of Wm Maxwell Wood, a surgeon in the U S Navy; & of Ralph King 2-Adverse report on the ptns of: the surviving children of John White; of the heirs of Stephen Damon; of the children of John Thomas; of the heirs of Saml Crossman; of Mary Bird; of Jonathan Willard; of the heirs of Geo Dearman; of Henry E Marble & others, owners of the sloop **Harvard**; of the excs of Jas Diliard; of Jas Monroe; of Jas W Brent; of Mason Ratley; of Jacob Warner; of Harriet B Howe; of Saml F Harrison; of Nancy M Trowbridge; & of the widow & son of Thos P Anderson, late of the Texan navy. 3-Bill to authorize the issuing of patents in the name of Jas S Douglass, upon certain land entries in Mississippi: passed. 4-Bills passed-relief: of Chas Jas Lanman; of Thos P Livingston; of Jas Hooten; of Alex'r Albertson, of Platte Co, Nebraska; of the heirs of Capt John A Hopper; of Josiah Atkins, of Ohio; of Tilman Leak; of Geo Stealey; of Israel Johnson; of Jos B Eaton; & of Braxton Bragg & Randall L Gibson.

Coroner's inquest was made yesterday on Mr G D Noble, of N Y C, at Peters Emerich's European Hotel, on 11th st & Pa ave. He came to Wash on Apr 6 & took up residence under the name of Davis, in a room where a man or boy slept to take care of him. The verdict of the jury was that deceased had come to his death by reason of an excessive use of opiates taken as medicine. There is no idea of suicide. The body will be received by his relatives, some of whom will arrive here today.

Rev Jacob S Harden, a minister of the Methodist Episcopal Church, has been convicted at Belvidere, N J, of murder in the first degree. He courted Miss Dorland, a young lady in his parish, about 2 years ago, & their courtship cannot be commended for prudence. She eventually insisted upon immediate marriage. Harden declared he had no means to support a family, that Miss Dorland was too ignorant for a minister's wife, & such a marriage would ruin him. The girl & her parents signed a paper releasing him from all obligations to marry her, & he on the same day signed an instrument binding him to marry her in the course of the year. He was compelled to marry her, which he did with reluctance. He never removed her from the father's house, but visited her there occassionally as her husband. A few months after the marriage Mrs Hardn died, after a brief illness, thought to be consumption. Evidence of poisoning & arsenic was found in her body. Harden made his escape, going first to Canada, & then to Va, under an assumed name, was was tracked by the ofcrs, arrested, brought to trial, & convicted. He was sentenced to be hung on Jun 8 next.

Trauter's Double Trigger & Safety Revolver, an English article of very superior workmanship. Also, Adam's, Colt's, & Sharp's Revolvers, the Derringer Pistol. A large assortment just received. -M W Galt & Bro, Jewellers, 354 Pa ave, Wash.

Mrd: on May 1, by Rev Dr Butler, Hon J E Bouligny, of Lousiana, to Miss Mary E, 2nd daughter of Geo Parker, of Wash City.

Mrd: on Apr 26, in Wash City, by Rev J L Bartlett, Mr Harrison S Bowen to Miss Mary J Prettyman, all of Wash City.

Died: on May 3, in Wash City, at the residence of her parents, of consumption, Mrs Mary A S Tate, in her 31st year, relict of the late Capt Jos B Tate, & eldest child of John & Mary A Mills. Her funeral will take place this afternoon from her parents' residence, 504 Pa ave. [No time given.]

MON MAY 7, 1860
Late news from Europe: Gen Ortega, having been duly sentenced, was shot at Madrid on Apr 18, for conspiracy against the Crown of Spain. The Queen, who only had power of pardoning him, refused to exercise that power, & poor Ortega was shot for high treason. –N Y Post

House of Reps: 1-Bills passed-relief: of Wm Hutchinson; of David V Whiting; of Chas W Brooks, of N Y; & of Sylvanus Burnham. Also, a bill granting an invalid pension to Beriah Wright, of N Y, amended.

Greensburg [Pa] Herald: died on Apr 11, in New Derry, of scarlet fever, Lavinia K, aged 4 years; on the same day, Alzinas Herman, aged 10 years; on Apr 16, Sarah Eliz, aged 2 years; & on Apr 19, Melissa C, aged 15 years, children of Jacob & Amy Bear. In the brief space of 8 days, from a circle of 5 lovely children, 4 have been removed by death.

Francis Otway Byrd died in Balt on Tue last, in his 70th year. He was the grandson of Col Wm Byrd, of Westover, Va. In 1805 Col [then Capt] Byrd served in the war with Tripoli & distinguished himself under Gen Eaton at the battle of Derne. In the last war with Great Britain he was in the regular army, & was engaged in the battle of Tippecanoe, on Nov 7, 1811, where he was conspicuous for his gallantry & courage. He was also present at the battle of Bridgewater, or Lundy's Lane, on Jul 25, 1814, where he served under the orders of Gen Scott. He received from the Legislature of Va, his native State, a vote of thanks, & was also presented with a sword, in testimony of the high estimation in which his services were held. In 1855 Col Byrd removed from ClarkCo, Va, to the city in which he died.

The will of Mr John G Boker, a German merchant of N Y, whose name obtained notoriety some 2 or 3 years ago by the indiscretion of his daughter, Mary Ann, who ran off & married her coachman, was admitted to probate last week. In this will Mr Boker directs that his remains be conveyed to his native place, Dusseldorf, Germany, &, by a codicil to the will, Mary Ann is entirely disinherited of all property formerly bequeathed to her, & her name is obliterated from among the other members of the family of the deceased in the distribution of his estates. His property consists of real estate in N Y C & Westchester Co, & is valued at $1,800,000.

Fatal accident or suicide. Mr John W Browne, a lawyer of Boston, took the Fall River train to go to Middleboro to attend the Probate Court. On the way he appears to have changed his mind, & got from the train at the East & West Bridgewater station. He took the next train of cars for Boston, but when the train was coming from Braintree to Quincy, & going at 35 miles an hour, he suddenly jumped from the cars, upon which he was standing. Conductor Dimon soon stopped the train, but Browne never breathed after they got there. The deceased was a native of Salem, & his age was about 50 years. He was educated at Harvard, & was in comfortable circumstances. He was in rather poor health, having overworked himself in his profession.

New Orleans Delta: Last Sat a dispute arose between Danl Cunningham & Jas Weyman. Cunningham hauled off to strike him, when Weyman pulled out a pistol & fired at him. Cunningham died soon afterwards. Weyman made good his escape.

For sale: the property of the late Mrs Richd W Meade, 167 F st, Wash, D C. The house was built by day's work in the best & most substantial manner, containing 14 rooms, besides a bath-room & a rear brick bldg for servants, with wood & coal houses. Apply to R K Scott, 497 12th st.

Died: on May 5, in Wash City, Mrs Sarah C L Martin, in her 29th year, the eldest daughter of Thos C Donn.

Died: on May 3, in Brooklyn, N Y, Emily May, youngest daughter of the late Geo Willis, of Portland, Maine, aged 20 years.

Died: on Feb 17 last, at Shanghai, China, Francis Thos Shankland, of N Y C, aged 22 years. Under the advice of physicians he sailed for the Celestial Empire, with the hope of being benefited by a sea voyage, but the Great Physician only understood his case, adopting as his patient & treating him successfully for immortality & glory hereafter; healing all his diseases, relieving all his pains, & transferring him from the Celestial Empire of China to the celestial regions of bliss, where sickness & suffering are never known. -L

Orphans Court of Wash Co, D C. Letters of administration on the personal estate of Saml Malvin, late of Wash Co, deceased. –W Y Fendall, adm

TUE MAY 8, 1860
Senate: 1-Ptn from Wm Hoard & others, remonstrating against the abolition of the right of appeal from adverse decisions of the Com'r of Patents: referred. 2-Ptn from Jas M Bucklin, asking that an appropriation may be made to test his improved gear for military service: referred. 3-Ptn from John Cook, jr, & associates, proposing to establish a line of steamships from New Orleans to Vera Cruz, & asking the aid of Gov't to sustain the same, on the ground that a service could not be kept up without it: referred. 4-Ptn from Mrs S D Page, widow of Francis N Page, Brvt Maj & Assist Adj Gen of the army, asking to be allowed a pension: referred. 5-Ptn from Mrs E B Mills, widow of Robt Mills, an architect, asking to be allowed $500, to which her husband was entitled for his professional service: referred. 6-Ptn from Jos W Knife, asking an increase of his pension: referred. 7-Cmte on Pensions: bill granting a pension to Abraham Crum: recommended its passage. Same cmte: bill granting a pension to Adelaide Adams, widow of Cmder Geo Adams, U S Navy, & to Cyrenus C Blackman, of St Helena parish, La: recommended that they do not pass. 8-Cmte on Pensions: bill granting a pension to Maj John F Hunter: recommended its passage. Same cmte: bill for the relief of Margaret Whitehead: reported back the same without an amendment. 9-Cmte on Revolutionary Claims: adverse report on the memorial of the heirs of Nathan Weeks. Same cmte: adverse report on the claim of Wm C Morris & others. 10-Cmte on Pensions: adverse report on the ptn of Catharine Shepherd, widow of Geo Shepherd, a soldier in the war of the Revolution.

House of Reps: 1-Ptn of H H Dillard, John Taylor, & others, asking for a new post route.

Walter C Whiteman, dealer in fine groceries, 17th & Arch sts, Phil. [Ad]

Among the visiters in Wash City is Hon John Minor Botts, of Va, who, we learn, has been called to Washington by the alarming illness of his brother, at present sojourning here.

We announce the sudden death of Mr Marcus R Southwell, an English gentleman, from injuries received from a fall while returning from hunting on Monday last. The mare he was riding, unused to leaping, stumbled over a small fence, falling on her head & rolling completely over, crushing the unfortunate gentleman beneath her. He received some severe internal injury. –Montreal Adv of May 3.

Executor's sale of rare & beautiful Green House Plants, at public auction, on May 8, at *Forrest Hall*, Gtwn, belonging to the estate of the late Mrs Col Jno Carter, deceased. –John Marbury, exc -Barnard & Buckley, aucts, Gtwn, D C

Obit-died: Hon Thos Sergeant expired at his residence in Phil on Sat at age 79 years. He was half brother of the late Hon John Sergeant. He belonged to the old school of Phil lawyers, & was an ornament to the bar.

The venerable Littleton Waller Tazewell, formerly a U S Senator & ex-Govn'r of Va, died at Norfolk on Sunday last, at age 85 years.

Orphans Court of Wash Co, D C. In the case of Asa W Wait, adm of Harding S Wait, deceased, the administrator & Court have appointed May 29th next, for the final settlement of the personal estate of the said deceased, of the assets in hand. -Ed Roach, Reg/o wills

Orphans Court of Wash Co, D C. Letters testamentary on the personal estate of Ellen Carter, late of Wash Co, deceased. –Jno Marbury, exc

Orphans Court of Wash Co, D C. Letters of administration on the personal estate of Michl O'Brien, late of Wash Co, deceased. –Rodey O'Brien, adm

Mrd: on Apr 26, at Lancaster, Pa, by Rt Rev Bishop Bowman, Edw Reilly to Anna R Heiner, daughter of Henry Rogers, of Wash City.

Mrd: on May 3, by Rev Fr Walter, at St Patrick's Church, Jas T Keleher to Mary M Collins, both of Wash City.

Died: on Apr 26, at White Marsh, his residence in Gloucester Co, Va, John Tabb, in his 76th year.

Augusta, May 7. Twenty-nine girls & boys, composing a picnic & fishing party, were drowned in Boykin's mill-pond, 9 miles from Camden, S C, on Sat. The flat boat in which they were is said to have sunk. The families of the youths drowned reside in Camden. Their names are Messrs Alexander, Howell, Crosby, Robinson, McGagen, Kelly, Young, McCowns, Jenkins, Nettles, Oakes, Hacatts, Richbourg, Legrand, McLeod, & Huggins. Twelve of the victims were buried at Camden yesterday. The others have not yet been recovered.

Died: on Apr 28, at Randolph, Mass, Ellen Montgomery, wife of Mr Seth Turner, of Randolph, & only child of Capt Jos Manahan, of Wash City, aged 26 years & 9 months. Mrs Turner was a lovely woman, & her death has brought sorrow to a large circle of relatives & the friends of her childhood & youth in this city. She leaves a bereaved husband & sorrowing father.

Valuable property for sale: the undersigned offers at private sale her valuable property in the village of Brookville, Montg Co, Md. The house has been built for & occupied as a Seminary for Females, with all necessary out bldgs, large yard & garden. Apply to the subscriber at Rockville, Montg Co, Md; Wm H Stabler, Sandy Spring, Md; or G H Reese & Bro, Balt, Md. –Mary E Porter

WED MAY 9, 1860
Senate: 1-Ptn from C E Spangler, & others, of Phil, against the abolition of the right of appeal from adverse decisions of the Com'r of Patents: referred. 2-Ptn from Chas R Webster, late U S Consul for the Isthmus of Tehuantepec, asking compensation for his services & remuneration for baggage lost: referred. 3-Cmte on Pensions: adverse report on the bill for the relief of Eveline Porter, widow of the late Cmdor Porter. 4-Same cmte: adverse reports on the ptns of Mrs Jane W Brent, widow of Thos Lee Brent, of Mrs Anna Mitchell, widow of Darius Mitchell, & of Mrs Catharine Hagie, widow of John Hagie, a volunteer under Gen Lafayette. Same cmte: bill for the relief of Reuben Clough. 5-Cmte of Claims: bill for the relief of C L West & others. Same cmte: bill for the relief of Chandler S Emory, sole surviving administrator of Calvin Read, of Duval Co, Fla.

The Marietta [O] Intelligencer announces the death of Geo I Slocomb, of that city. A few weeks since, in Big Run, Athens Co, while he was sitting at the instrument in his office, during a heavy storm, lightning ran in upon the wires & completely stunned him. A few days developed the horrible fact that his limbs were paralyzed, & his muscles deprived of action. The paralysis extended over the body until death ended his affliction.

Obit-died: the N Y papers announce the death at Utica, on Sunday, of Hon Saml Beardsley, after an illness of several days. He was a State Senator in 1823; Rep in Congress from 1831 to 1835; appointed Judge of the Supreme Court of N Y in 1844; in 1847 he was Chief Justice, with Messrs Whittlesey & McKissock, as associates.

The venerable Geo Griffin, one of the oldest lawyers in the country, who occupied a leading position at the N Y bar in the last generation, died in that city on Sunday, aged 83 years. He was a learned & an eloquent advocate.

Mrd: on Apr 26, at St Anne's Church, Annapolis, by Rev J R Davenport, Hollins McKim, of Balt, to Eliza F, daughter of Cmdor Voorhees, of Annapolis.

Breach of promise case: Supreme Judicial Court, Lowell, Mass, before J Bigelow. Sarah H Travis vs Abel Pond; both parties reside at Holliston, Mass; plntf is about 25 years of age, the daughter of a wealthy farmer of that place. The dfndnt, at the time his alleged attentions to the plntf were paid, was a widower, aged 51, who had long resided at Holliston. His first wife had been dead less than a year. She said he visited her and made proposals of marriage. She began making preparations for the marriage, & he gave her a wedding ring & gold watch, & was having a new house built to live in. He had a change of mind & wished her to release him. Eight months later he married & took another wife to his new house. The jury returned a verdict for the plntf, damages $3,000.

The Austin [Texas] Intelligencer of Apr 25, says that John Taney, who had been arrested, was being tried at the court-house on suspicion of having killed John Edwards, whose assassination was reported 2 weeks since, while he was in the custody of the Sheriff of Travis Co. Jesse Graham came up to Taney & jerked him from Sheriff Blackwell, & the men with him discharged a volley of shot at Taney, killing him. The Sheriff, assisted by Messrs Cullen, Norton, Hancock, & other citizens, arrested Parson Milton T Caperton & his son Reuben, & put them in jail. Taney was a young man who had become, from force of circumstances, desperate & abandoned.

Orphans Court of Wash Co, D C. Letters of administration, with the will annexed, on the personal estate of Jos Owens, late of Wash Co, deceased.
–Jas Owens, adm

Obit-from the Vicksburg [Miss] Citizen of Apr 30. John S Byrne, long in failing health from the ravages of a disease for which medicine had no curative power, died yesterday, at the residence of R O Edwards, in Hind Co. Mr Byrne was a native of Wash, D C, & born, we believe, in 1825, & was in his 35th year. After an excellent education, he settled in our beautiful city in 1847. Retiring from the Mayoralty of the city he commenced the practice of the law. In his last illness he had the care of kind friends, & all the consolation of the Catholic religion.

THU MAY 10, 1860
Senate: 1-Cmte on Military Affairs: bill for the relief of Wm Hutchinson: recommended that it do not pass. Same cmte: adverse report on the memorial of C T Alexander, in relation to his rank in the medical corps of the army. Same cmte: discharged from the further consideration of the memorial of Jas M Bucklin for an appropriation to test him improved gun. Same cmte: memorial of Jos Hill & sons, asking compensation for horses & mules stolen by the Indians in Calif, asked to be discharged from further consideration, & that it be referred to the Cmte of Claims, on the ground that it had been before the cmte in the years 1851, 1852, & 1857. 2-Cmte on the Judiciary: joint resolution from the House of Reps for the relief of Francis C Ware: recommended its passage. Same cmte: joint resolution from the House of Reps for the relief of John T Robertson, of Va, & a bill for the relief of Gottleib Scheener: recommended their passage. 3-Cmte on

Pensions: bill for the relief of Mira M Alexander, asking remuneration for the services & sacrifices of her father while in the army of the U S. 4-Bill referred: relief of Elias Hall.

Two counterfeiters, Geo B Graham & Phineas M Finch, have been arrested at Elmira, N Y, for circulated counterfeit tens on the Farmers & Mfgrs' Bank of Poughkeepsie.

Dorsey's Self-raking Reaper & Mower, greatly improved for 1860. Busey & Barnard, aucts, Agents for Wash, Gtwn, & Alexandria. [Ad]

Circuit Court of Wash Co, D C-in Equity. Jane E Gray & als against Mary D Dudley & als. Allan B Magruder, trustee, reported that he sold two lots, with dwlgs, late the property of Mrs Ann Simms, at 11th & Md ave, in square 353, for $1,355 to John A Stephenson, & that he has complied with the terms of sale. –Jno A Smith, clerk

Died: on May 9, in Gtwn, after a brief illness, in his 48th year, John W Ott, son of the late Dr John Ott, of Gtwn. His funeral will be today at 10 o'clock, from Trinity Church, Gtwn.

Savannah, May 8. In the U S Circuit Court the Grand Jury have found true bills against C A Lamar, C W Stiles, J M Middleton, & Wm Stone, the rescuers of Capt Farnum, of the yacht **Wanderer**, from the county jail.

FRI MAY 11, 1860
Senate: 1-Ptn from H A Klopfer, messenger in the ofc of the Atty Gen, asking to be allowed an increase of compensation: referred. 2-Cmte on Pensions: bill for the relief of Ruth Ellen Greenland, widow of John H Greenland, deceased. 3-Cmte on Military Affairs: bill for the relief of Fred'k Stephens: recommended that it do not pass. 4-Cmte on Commerce: bill for the relief of Slade Calloway: recommended its passage.

Executor's sale of very superior rosewood parlor furniture, on May 15, at the residence of the late Mrs Col Carter, deceased, Congress & West sts, Gtwn. -John Marbury, exc -Barnard & Buckley, aucts, Gtwn, D C

We are glad to see among us our old friend, Hon Lewis Condict, of N J, who is enjoying a green old age in his 87th year, loved & revered by all who know him. He was first elected in the House of Reps in 1811. He is staying here with his friend, Dr Lindsley.

Mrd: in Wash City, at the Church of the Ascension, by Rev A F Norville Rolfe, Rector of St Andrew's Church, Balt, Leroy C Bishop, of N C, to Miss Eliza E Williams, of this place. [No marriage date given-current item.]

Died: on May 10, in Wash City, Geo W Taylor, in his 29th year. His funeral will be tomorrow at 2 o'clock, from the residence of A Cooley, 576 M st.

Died: on May 7, at Schenectady, N Y, Mrs Margaret G Mechlin, wife of A H Mechlin, of Wash City.

SAT MAY 12, 1860
Senate: 1-Ptn from David Brister & other citizens of Texas, asking compensation for property taken by the Camanche & other tribes of Indians: referred. 2-Additional papers in relation to the claim of Herman D Stratton, a soldier in the late war with Mexico: referred. 3-Cmte of Claims: asked to be discharged from further consideration of the memorial of Ford Barnes, asking compensation for the services of his father in the war of the Revolution, & that it be referred to the Cmte on Revolutionary Claims. Same cmte: asked to be discharged from further consideration of the House bill for the relief of Lot Hall, & that it be referred to the Cmte on Revolutionary Claims. Same cmte: asked to be discharged from further consideration of the memorial of the widow of Col Jas Hook, U S Army, & that it be referred to the Cmte on Pensions. Same cmte: to which was referred the memorial of Marie Genand, sole heir of John Hudry, reported a bill for the relief of the heirs & legal reps of Jean Hudry, & asked its immediate consideration. 4-Bill for the relief of Arthur Edwards & his associates: referred to the Cmte on the Post Ofc & Post Roads. 5-Bills passed: relief of Townsend Harris or his legal reps; of D G Farragut; & of John Brannan.

N Y, May 11. Augustus M Connor attempted to make a balloon ascension last evening from Palace Garden. The balloon collapsed & he was precipitated upon the roof of a bldg. He expired at 11 o'clock today. [May 14th newspaper: Mrs Connor, wife of the aeronaut, fainted & fell helpless to the ground.]

Died: on Apr 21, in Dayton, Ohio, in his 78th year, Peter Fenelow, a native of the parish of Myshall, county Carlow, Ireland. He was never known to lose a friend or make an enemy in the circle of his family & acquaintance. –R J P

MON MAY 14, 1860
Fauquier White Sulphur Springs for sale on May 17 next, consisting of 400 acres of land with commodious brick bldgs, covered with slate & built of the best materials, well arranged for conducting a first class watering establishment; will accommodate at least 600 visiters. Also for sale, a parcel of land adjoining containing 293 acres, called *Withers*. –Robt Bowling, Bowling Green, Va Apr 26, 1860 ad. Same ad in the newspaper of May 14 ended: for any desired information address Robt Hudgin, Bowling Green, Va.

Orphans Court of Wash Co, D C. Letters of administration on the personal estate of Edw Brooks, late of Wash Co, deceased. –Letitia J Brooks, admx

Circuit Court of D C, in Equity, No 1,595. Fred'k W Shellhausen against Wm H Clementson & Henrietta his wife, Chas Mades & Wilhelmina his wife, Geo C Schad & Henry R Schad, exc & heirs of Bonaventura Schad, deceased. The parties named & the creditors of said Bonaventura Schad are notified that on May 29, in my ofc, in City Hall, Wash, I shall state an account of the personal estate of B Schad. -W Redin, auditor

Orphans Court of Wash Co, D C. In the case of Adam Raab, adm of Ferdinand Greentrup, deceased, the administrator & Court have appointed Jun 5 next, for the final settlement of the personal estate of the said deceased, of the assets in hand. -Ed Roach, Reg/o wills

Orphans Court of Wash Co, D C. Letters of administration on the personal estate of Edw Brooks, late of Wash Co, deceased. –Letitia J Brooks, admx

TUE MAY 15, 1860
Fatal tragedy in Lebanon, Tenn, on May 4, resulting in the mortal wounding of one of the students of the law dept of Cumberland Univ, Jas Cahal, by a fellow-student, Spot McClung. Cahal struck at McClung, with a stick, over a trivial matter, when McClung drew a pistol & shot Cahal the ball entering the brain. Although alive on May 5 no hopes were entertained of his recovery. McClung was put under $15,000 bail. Jas Cahal was the son of the late Judge Cahal, of Tenn, & McClung is a son of Col McClung, of Huntsville, Ala, & a nephew of the late Col McClung, of Mississippi.

Country residence for rent: the new Berne Brick Cottage, now elegantly furnished, containing large airy parlors & rooms, on Piney Branch road, within half an hour's drive from the Pres' Mansion. Apply to B Jost, 181 Pa ave, near 17th st.

Orphans Court of Wash Co, D C. Letters of administration on the personal estate of Levin I Gillis, late of Wash Co, deceased. –John C Kennedy, adm

Orphans Court of Wash Co, D C, May 12, 1860. In the case of Timothy J O'Toole, adm of Peter Slevin, deceased, the administrator & Court have appointed Jun 5 next, for the final settlement of the personal estate of the said deceased, of the assets in hand. -Ed Roach, Reg/o wills

Died: on Apr 25, suddenly, at Brookeville, Albemarle Co, Va, [the residence of G A Farrow] Mrs Virginia L Hansbrough, wife of David Hansbrough, in her 33rd year. She was the daughter of Gen J D Learned, formerly of St Louis, Mo. She was a member of the Presbyterian Church, having joined Dr Pott's Church, of St Louis, in her 13th year, & at the time of her death was a member of Lebanon Church, Albemarle. She leaves a husband & 4 little daughters to grieve her departure.

Died: on May 12, Mary L, daughter of John C & Mary McKelden, in her 16th year.

Died: on May 10, at *Needwood*, Fred'k Co, Md, the residence of her grandfather, Saml L Gouverneur, aged 11 months, Eliz Monroe, infant & only daughter of Eliz K & the late Jas Monroe Bibby, of Balt.

Died: on May 14, in her 8th year, at the residence of Mr Woodville Latham, in Wash City, Sally, the eldest child of Jos & Judith E Settle, of Culpeper Co, Va. Her remains will be taken home for interment.

Local Matters. Wash City Council yesterday. 1-Mr Donoho presented the protest of Thos Lewis & Job Angus against the award of the contract for bldg the Centre market-house to Gilbert Cameron. 2-The following were elected Com'rs for conducting the coming municipal election:

Saml Duvall	Jas H Towers	Clarence Baker
Geo W Emerson	Jas S Holland	Isaac Bartlett
Jas Kelly	B E Gittings	H N Ober
A W Denham	C W Boteler, Jr	John D Brandt
Jesse Mann	John Dowling	Jos Tucker
Wm H Perkins	Benedict Milburn	Lemuel Gaddis
Geo Jillard	Andrew Rothwell	Valentine Conner
G W Stewart	H G Fant	Wm S Venale
Saml W Owen	J E Kendall	Geo W Hinton
Saml Lewis	A McD Davis	Wm H Hope
E C Dyer	Philip J Ennis	T H Barron
Wm P Shedd	Jacob Fleischell	Wm G Flood
C S O'Hare	S C Wailes	Henry Knight
H L Chapin	Thos Hutchinson	Danl Rowland

Obit-died: Dr Chas Kraitsir, the distinguished philogist, suddenly at his residence in Morrisania, N Y, on Monday last. He was afflicted with disease of the heart, & was 56 years old. He was a native of Hungary, educated in the Univ of Peath; participated in the Polish revolution, & at its close came to this country in 1833. In 1842 he was appointed Prof of Modern Languages in the Univ of Va.

Obit-died: Mr S G Goodrich, ["Peter Parley"] on Wed at his residence in N Y C, in his 67th year. On Tue he came in from the country, where all his family save one son were, & on the following day, feeling unwell, summoned his family physician, who visited him 3 times during the day, but without suspecting that he was dangerously unwell. Just before 4 o'clock his disease assumed a severe form, & in 20 minutes he was dead. His death was painless & peaceful.

Mrd: on May 2, at Dedham, Mass, by Rev Dr Lamson, Fred'k M French, of Phil, to Isabella F, daughter of Jonathan H Cobb, of Dedham.

WED MAY 16, 1860
Valuable lots for sale in squares 108 & 185, part of the property of the late Purser Fitzgerald: public auction on May 14. The title to al this ground is perect.
-Thos Carbery, trustee -Jas C McGuire & Co, aucts

Superior trotting horse, buggy, & harness, at public sale, on May 11, in front of the Auction Rooms, the celebrated Trotting Horse, Snow Storm, said to be the fastest in the city, recently the property of Col Landers. The owner has no further use for him. -Jas C McGuire & Co, aucts

Senate: 1-Ptn from Jethro S Smith, asking to be allowed his pension from the time of his discharge to that upon which his pension commenced: referred. 2-Cmte on Indian Affairs: adverse report on the memorial of G C Johnson for payment of a balance of an amount which the Sec of War was authorized to pay him out of the annuity of the Shawnee Indian. 3-Cmte on Pensions: bill for the relief of Mrs Louisa T Whiting, widow of Maj Fabius Whiting. Same cmte: adverse report on the ptn of Dr Thos Goodsell for a pension for services during the war of 1812.

Supreme Judicial Court, Worcester, Mass. Friday: Geo W Ela et al, excx, vs Thos Edwards. This was an appeal from the decree of the Judge of Probate & Insolvency, disallowing the will of Susan S Edwards, wife of Thos Edwards, artist, of this city. Mrs Edwards was killed about a year since, at Westborough, while attempting to cross the railroad in a chaise. She was possessed of a considerable amount of property. Soon after marriage, in Apr, 1855, she wrote the will in question, by herself, on 7½ sheets of paper, numbered, & signed by her, & the names of 3 persons were subscribed to the paper nearly opposite to her own. The contestant, her husband of the deceased, contended that there was no proof that she signed the will before the witnesses. The appellants, who were the executors & trustees, contended there was sufficient evidence on these points. The Court disallowed the will, on the ground of the insufficiency of the evidence, but would report the case for the consideration of the full Court.

N Y Evening Post: heavy defalcation in the N Y Post Ofc-$150,000 gone. The deficiency is on the part of Isaac V Fowler, postmaster of N Y C. The deficit amount may be found to be much larger.

Robt McDonald, of Mobile, who killed Vrginia Stewart in front of the Brandreth House, in Broadway, N Y, last July, committed sucide in the Tombs on Monday by taking poison. His trial was expected soon to take place.

Circuit Court of D C. John F Coyle against Franklin Philp. Statement of the partnership account between the said parties, shall be executed at my ofc, in City, Hall, Wash, on Jun 7, at 10 o'clock. –W Redin, auditor

Died: on Apr 30, at **Meadow Grove**, her residence, in Fauquier Co, Va, Miss Sally S Scott, in her 70th year. She had been a communicant in the Episcopal Church for 46 years, & in her life & character she illustrated her profession.

Balt, May 15. The venerable Thos Murphy, formerly & for 40 years one of the proprietors of the Balt American, [from which he retired about 7 years ago,] died at his residence in this city this morning in his 81st year. He was connected with the first paper published in Balt, was widely known & highly respected & esteemed.

[May 17th newspaper: Thos Murphy was born in Ireland in 1780, & came to this country in his infancy. He assisted in the establishment of the Balt Telegraph, the first daily newspaper published in Balt. In 1809, in connexion with the late Geo Dobbin, he became one of the proprietors of the Balt American.]

THU MAY 17, 1860

Senate: 1-Memorial from Capt J W Davidson, U S Army, asking to be reimbursed an amount deducted from his pay on account of public moneys stolen while in his keeping as Acting Commissary of Subsistence: referred. 2-Cmte on Pensions: bill for the relief of Mrs Hannah McDowell: recommended that it do not pass. 3-The papers of Wm H Wigg, referred to the Cmte on Revolutionary Claims, to be returned.

Henry H Leeds, Auctioneer, Sale Room, 23 Nassau st, N Y. [Ad]

Mrd: on May 15, by Rev Mr Finkel, Mr John C Joachim to Miss Sophia Kaufman, both of Wash City.

Died: on May 15, in Wash City, Alex'r L Botts, aged 61 years, brother of Hon John Minor Botts. His funeral is this morning at 11 o'clock, from Mrs Campbell's boarding house, 4½ sts, between C & Pa ave.

Obit-died: on Apr 30, 1860, Rev Levin I Gillis, after a brief illness of suffering patiently borne, in his 64th year of his age & 42nd of his ministry. He was ordained by Bishop Kemp, of Md, when but 22 years of age. Obit-died: on May 1, at **Mount Pleasant**, near Upper Marlboro, Md, Mrs Grace H Clagett, relict of the late Dr Richd H Clagett. Had she one care to delay her dissolution it was the melancholy parting of a mother. She wished only to live for a son, to inbue him still better with those characteristics of herself. She died as she had lived, a true believer in the Holy Catholic Church. –Wash, May 10, 1860

FRI MAY 18, 1860

Yesterday at Hammack's restaurnat, on Pa ave, near 15th st, Thos Freeman, of Phil, who appeared to be very ill, died in a very few moments. He had disease of the heart. His body has been taken possession of by the officers of Wash City until the friends of the deceased in Phil can be heard from.

Obit-died: on May 1, at ***Mount Pleasant***, near Upper Marlboro, Md, Mrs Grace H Clagett, relict of the late Dr Richd H Clagett. Had she one care to delay her dissolution it was the melancholy parting of a mother. She wished only to live for a son, to inbue him still better with those characteristics of herself. She died as she had lived, a true believer in the Holy Catholic Church.

Mississippi Bulletin of May 12. The steamer **R F Sass**, Capt W B Philips, bound from New Orleans to Cincinnati with a full cargo & about 150 cabin & deck passengers, struck a snag when opposite Clark's Bar, on Thu night, & immediately settled down in deep water. The deck passengers generally escaped, & the ofcrs & deck crew were all saved. Capt Montford, her clerk, had barely time to open the safe & grasp one bag of specie, when he found himself knee-deep in water. The steamer **Edward Walsh**, Capt Burke, arrived at the scene about an hour later. Mr Frank Graham, his wife & child, of Cincinnati, were found clinging to a small piece of plank, 4 miles below the scene of the disaster, & taken on board the **Walsh**. List of those known to be lost or missing: Mrs Jas V Lindsay, New Orleans; Mrs Kate Whittier & son, 15, Lafayette Indiana; Mrs H C Neal & daughter, 4, Parkersburg, Va; Mrs Wm Harris, do; John Pankey, Ill; O Klingaman, Iowa; Wm Wilson, Cincinnati; Chas Allendale, Syracuse, Ohio; Francis Eavitt & Wm Eavitt, one 12 & the other 9; daughter & son of Mrs Cavanah, of Louisiana, going to Indiana; Wm Henry Dewitt, colored fireman, Cincinnati; Goff, Porter of the boat, Cincinnati; two servants of Dr Robertson, of Nashville; & Rose, servant of Mrs Corey, New Orleans.

SAT MAY 19, 1860
Senate: 1-Ptn from Wm H Bell & Francis H Bell, asking Gov't to purchase for the use of the army & navy a patent improved primer: referred. 2-Ptn from Capt E A F Lavalette, of the Mediterranean squadron, asking that certain moneys charged to his account may be refunded: referred. 3-Ptn from Jos D Greene, a clerk in the Post Ofc Dept, asking compensation for performing the duties of a clerk while paid as a laborer: referred. 4-Ptn from Wm A Bradley, asking Gov't to purchase ***Analostan Island*** as a site for the penitentiary & jail in D C, & setting forth that no location comparing in eligibility with said island can be found: referred. 5-Additional papers in relation to the claim of Mary J Maultby: referred. 6-Cmte of Claims: bills for the relief of Jas Phelan & for the relief of Chas J Lanman: recommended that they do not pass. Same cmte: asked to be discharged from further consideration of the memorial of the heirs of Alex'r Miller, a soldier during the last war with Great Britain, & the memorial of John Bronsen for payment for goods destroyed on the Niagara frontier during the last war with Great Britain, & that they be referred to the Court of Claims. Same cmte: adverse report on the bill for the relief of Wm Brown. 7-Cmte on Pensions: adverse report on the memorial of Francis M & Henreitta L Green, children of the late Lt Col Green, asking to be allowed pensions. 8-Cmte of Claims: bill for the relief of the legal reps of Sylvester Day, & recommended its passage. 9-Bill for the relief of Solomon Wadsworth: passed. 9-Bills committed-relief: of Wm Money; of David Myerle; of Emilie G Jones, excx of Thos P Jones & Nancy M Johnson & Walter

R Johnson, deceased; of Jas L Edwards; of Thos Young & Geo Young, owners of the schnr **Mary Elizabeth**; of Harris & Hodge, of Mo; of Arnold Harris & Saml F Butterworth; of Sampson Stanfill; of the heirs at law of the late Abigail Nason, sister & devisee of John Lord, deceased; of Reuben J Champion, only child & heir of Reuben & Rhoda Champion; of A H Jones & M H C Brown; of Geo D Darsman; of John Van Cott & Saml Malin, of Utah; of Wm B Dodd & others; of Chas E Roberts, of Wash Territory; of Mrs Ann E Smoot; of Henry Etting; of Sarah Whitney & Mary Huggeford; of the heirs of John L Mersereau, a Revolutionary soldier; of the surviving children of Catharine Heanna; of Wm Dudley, of Ky; of H H Howard; of Jas Smith; of Rebecca A Correll; of Eliz Spear; of Jeremiah Pendergast, of D C; of Ebenezer Kicker; of Jos Pattee; of Cornelius Hughes; of Wm Wallace, of Ill; of Nancy M Gunsally; of the surviving children of Margaret Reynolds, deceased; of the legal reps of John & Sarah Mandeville, deceased. Also, granting a pension to Mrs M Cavard, widow of Thos Cavard; to Abigail A Bingham; to Jas S Williams; increase pension to Jane W McKee, widow of Col Wm R McKee, of the Indian Regt Ky Volunteers; & half pay for 5 years to Louisa Sweetman, widow of Jas Sweetman.

10-<u>Adverse reports on the following cases, laid on the table</u>. Memorial of Saml B Elliott; of Danl Cannon; of Jas Johnson; of Maj E H Fitzgerald; of Larkin Snow & Zenas Snow; of A Delmas; of the heirs of Jas McDaniel; of John Daly; of Horace E Dimmick; of Geo Durant & others, for a wagon road across the Cascade Mountains; of C J Cook & A D Lockwood; of Eliza M Evans; of E R Potts; of John T Smith; of C C Penniston; of the reps of the late Purser Jas H Causten; of Wm P Rathbone; of Joel Williams; & of Caleb Warner.

Mrd: on May 18, by Rev J C Smith, Evander J Jackson to Miss Virgin W Omohundro, both of Va.

Mrd: on May 15, at the residence of J A Kennedy, by Rev Thos H Stockton, Mr John Wagner, of Wash City, to Miss Franck E Joyce, of Balt.

Mrd: on May 15, in the Methodist Protestant Church, Cumberland, Md, by Rev P Light Wilson, Geo H B White, of Wash City, to Fannie V, second daughter of A L Withers, of the former place.

Boston, May 18. Hon W S Damrell, an ex-member of Congress from this State, died here yesterday.

MON MAY 21, 1860
Adm's sale of valuable books, on May 30, belonging to the estate of the late Sylvanus G Deeth, in the auction rooms. –Joshua A Ritchie adm
-Jas C McGuire & Co, aucts

Died: on May 18, in Wash City, D O'Hare, aged 49 years.

Died: on May 20, Alfred Pearce, eldest son of F Louis & Cornelia A Grammer, aged 2 years, 3 months & 22 days.

It is stated that Gen La Vega, recently taken prisoner at San Luis Potosi by the Liberaliste has been shot. It will be remembered that he was captured by Capt May at Ressea de la Palma, & subsequently at Cerro Gordo. All the prisoners taken with Gen La Vega were shot.

Senate: 1-Ptn from John F Coyle & other holders of property fronting on Missouri ave, between 3rd & 6th sts, Wash City, asking to have a sidewalk on the south side of that avenue paved: referred. 2-Ptn from Capt F Martin of the revenue cutter service, in favor of an amendment of the act to organize an institution for the insane of the army & navy, to include the revenue cutter service: referred. 3-Cmte on Public Lands: bill for the relief of Geo F Brott: passed. Same cmte: bill for the relief of Ellen S Hanscomb, reported it back with an amendment. Same cmte: adverse report on the bill for the relief of John Dixon. 4-Bill for the relief of Mary Towson, widow of Joshua Towson, a soldier of the war of 1812. 5-Bill for the relief of Sylvester Gray.

House of Reps: 1-Bill for the relief of Alfred C Murphy & Hiram Burlingham: referred. 2-Bill for the relief of the legal reps of Francis Chaudenet: postponed. 3-Cmte of the Whole-no objections, laid aside to be reported favorably to the House: invalid pension to Nathan Randall, to Michl Hanson, & to Ezekiel Jones. Pension to Sarah Blackwell; & to Adaline Caddis. Relief of Mary J Maddux; of Chauncey W Fuller; of Lt Michl R Clark; of Jas Floyd; of Mary Bennett; of the legal reps of Danl Bedinger, deceased; of Edw N Kent; of Joel M Smith; of Wm Lyon, late pension agent at Knoxville, Tenn; of Jethro Bonney, of the State of N Y; of Jas Henderson; of John Y Sewell; of Sweeney Rittenhouse, Fant & Co; of John F Sanford, adm de bonis non of the estate of Robt Sanford, deceased; of Eliza A Merchant, widow of the late 1st Lt & Brvt Capt Chas G Merchant, U S Army; of Geo B Bacon, late acting purser of the sloop-of-war **Portsmouth**; of Ann Scott; of Saml A West, Geo McCullough, Hiram McCullough, & Chas Pendergrast; of Nancy Weeks, of Ga; of Mary Bennett; & of Wm H De Grost [passed.]

Pittsburgh, May 19. Sylvester Langdon, convicted of uttering forged paper for the purpose of buying stock in the Monongahela bank at McKeesport, has been fined $500, & to serve an imprisonment of 3 years in the penitentiary.

TUE MAY 22, 1860
Nine valuable bldg lots on the Heights of Gtwn at Public Auction, on Jun 5, owned by & in the present occupancy of Col B S Roberts, bounded by Fred'k, 8th & High sts, divided into 9 lots, two fronting on 8th st, opposite the property of Mrs John Robinson. -Barnard & Buckley, aucts, Gtwn, D C

Senate: 1-Cmte on Pensions: bill for the relief of John B Miller, for a pension. Same cmte: bill for the relief of Emanuel Croukright, a soldier of the war of 1812, for a pension. Same cmte: bill to grant a pension to Mary J Harris, widow of Col Thos L Harris: recommended its passage. 2-Cmte of Claims: adverse report on the memorial of Richd Mackall, asking indemnity for property destroyed by the enemy during the war of 1812. 3-Cmte of Claims: bill for the relief of Cassius M Clay, without an amendment. Same cmte: asked to be discharged from further consideration of the ptn of the widow of David Delk, a soldier in the Creek war, & that it be referred to the Cmte on Pensions. 4-Cmte on Revolutionary Claims: asked to be discharged from further consideration of the ptn of Wm H Wigg: which was agreed to. 5-Bill for the relief of Thos T Page: referred. 6-Bill for the legal reps of Stephen Pleasanton: referred. 7-Bill for the relief of Cmder Thos J Page, U S Navy, referred.

House of Reps: 1-Bill granting an invalid pension to Jacob Yates: referred. 2-Bill making compensation to J N Miller for services in the war of 1812: referred. 3-Bill for the relief of John F McRae; of the heirs of Anna Taylor; & of the legal reps of Wm Austin, deceased: referred. 4-Bill for the relief of A M Fridley, late agent of the Winnebago Indians: passed. 5-Bill for the relief of Asenath M Elliott, widow of Capt Edw G Elliott: passed.

Mrd: on May 15, at Albany, N Y, by Rev Dr Halley, Fanning Barnard to Linda, youngest daughter of Francis Harvey.

WED MAY 23, 1860
Lt A W Habersham has resigned from the navy, & is now living in Yokohama, being engaged in mercantile business, in partnership with Mr Stearne, a gentleman from Hong Kong.

Senate: 1-Ptn from Logan Hunton, late U S Atty for the eastern district of Louisiana, asking compensation for prosecuting suits against Narcisso Lopez, John Henderson, & others, for violation of the neutrality laws. 2-Bill for the relief of John S Waite, late deputy postmaster at Los Angeles, Calif: referred. 3-Joint resolution for the restoration of Lt Augustus S Baldwin to the active list from the leave of absence list of the navy: referred.

Circuit Court-Wash-Tue. Breach of promise of marriage, in which suit was made by Catharine Young against Geo Schnell for alleged failure to comply with the promise aforesaid. Verdict for dfndnt.

In the recent disaster to the steamer **R F Lass**, the mate, Mr H C Neal, whose wife & 2 children were on board, hastened to place the children in the life-boat, & then turned to his wife Molly, as he believed, & placed her in safety. He found that the woman was Mrs Loney, of New Orleans, La, while his own partner had sunk with the rest. Mr Neal, his wife & child, had 2 years since, made a narrow escape from the steamer **Homer**, which was sunk in the Red River.

Orphans Court of Wash Co, D C. Letters testamentary on the personal estate of Aaron Leggett, late of N Y, deceased. –Wm H Macy, Wm L Jenkins, excs

Died: on May 21, at the Washington Infirmary, John E Keech, of PG Co, Md. His funeral is this afternoon at 5 o'clock.

THU MAY 24, 1860
Senate: 1-Ptn from Wm Applegarth & Son, & other merchants of Balt, asking that an appropriation may be made for the removal of a snag & sunken wreck at the head of Chesapeake Bay: referred. 2-Additional papers in relation to the claim of Wm W Coxe: referred. 3-Cmte on Naval Affairs: bill for the relief of Cmder Thos J Page, of the U S Navy, & for the relief of Thos J Page: recommended their passage. 4-Cmte on Military Affairs: adverse report on the House bill for the relief of Jos B Eaton. Same cmte: bill for the relief of Aseneath M Elliot, widow of Capt Edw G Elliot, one of peculiar hardship: passed. 5-Cmte on Foreign Relations: bill for the relief of Wm H Vesey, U S Consul at Havre. 6-Cmte on Revolutionary Claims: adverse report on the memorial of Jemima Watson, daughter of Israel Honeyville, for property destroyed during the Revolutionary war.

Naval Affairs: 1-Capt Jos R Jarvis, now in command of the *frig **Savannah**, at Vera Cruz, appointed a flag ofcr of the Home Squadron, vice McCluney, detached. 2-Capt Chas H Bell, now in command of the Norfolk navy yard, has received preparatory orders for the command of the Mediterranean Squadron, & the new steam sloop-of-war **Richmond**, now fitting out at Norfolk, has been designated as his flag ship. 3-The ship **Dacotah**, now nearly ready for sea at Norfolk has been designated for the East India Squadron; the ship **Seminole**, also at Norfolk, for the Brazil Squadron, & the ship **Pawnee**, at Phil, for the Home Squadron. The ship **St Louis**, now at San Juan del Notre, has been ordered on a cruise. The U S steamer **Mohawk**, Lt Cmder F A M Craven, sailed from Key West on May 12, on a cruise. The *sloop-of-war **Savannah**, Capt Jarvis, sailed from Pensacola on May 8 for Vera Cruz. [*Copied as written: frig/sloop of war.]

Com'rs sale of a valuable tract of land in Alexandria Co, Va, by decree of the Circuit Court of Alexandria Co, in the suit of Hooe, guardian, vs Hardin & others, public auction of 240 acres, on the road leading from Falls Church to the Little Falls, with a good 2 story brick dwlg house. –J Louis Kinzer, Com'r

Albert W Hicks, alias Johnson, charged with piracy & the murder of the capt & two of the seamen of the oyster sloop **E A Johnson**, below N Y, not long since, has been tried & found guilty.

Mrd: on May 1, at Albany, N Y, by Rev E P Rogers, D D, Rev Cornelius Gates, of Montague, N J, to Mrs Matilda A Sacia, daughter of the late Nicholas Marselis, of Schenectady.

Died: yesterday, of summer complaint, Mary Ann Virginia, infant daughter of Fannie L & T W Johnson. Her funeral is this afternoon at 6 o'clock, from the residence of her father, 487 6th st.

Died: on May 23, Mary C, wife of Peter Lammond, in her 39th year. Her funeral will be on May 25 at 10 o'clock A M, from the residence of her husband, L st, between 15th & 16th sts.

Augusta, May 23. Hon Wm C Preston died at Columbia, S C, yesterday.

FRI MAY 25, 1860
Senate: 1-Ptn from Jas & A H Porter, asking indemnity for losses in consequence of the stopping their trains engaged in transporting goods to Salt Lake City to the cmder of the U S army: referred. 2-Ptn from Wm Ellis, a soldier in the Ky militia during the war of 1812, asking to be allowed a pension: referred. 3-Ptn from Young Williams, asking compensation for his own services & use of his vessel **Dolphin**, pressed into service by Gen Jackson during the war of 1812: referred. 4-Cmte on the District of Columbia: joint resolution from the House of Reps for the relief of Wm H De Groot, asking its immediate consideration, as it was a case involving some hardships: referred. 5-Bill for the relief of Anthony Gale: referred.

Mr Geo Brubaker, a citizen of Lancaster Co, Pa, reached St Joseph, Mo, last Wed, on his way home. He was captured by a band of Camanches while on his way to Calif in 1847, 13 years ago, & has just escaped from them. He was made a medicine man, & converted 200 to the Christian religion. It was only after the most solemn promises that he would return that they allowed him to depart, & he will go back as soon as he has seen his family, who have mourned him for years as dead.

At auction, on Jun 1, the beautiful country seat, *Glen May*, on 7th st, adjoining the property of J C Lewis & W G White, in the immediate neighborhod of Dr Page & Mr Lindsey, improved by a dwlg 40 feet front. Title indisputable.
-A Green, aucts

SAT MAY 26, 1860
Auction on May 29, of a family declining housekeeping, at the residence of C M Koones, 456 D st north, between 2nd & 3rd sts, his entire household effects.
-Ward & Barnard, aucts, Gtwn, D C

The elopement & marriage of Miss Queen A Rose of Ala, at Phil, with Mr Bogart, a Southern medical student, was recently chronicled in the papers. Buoyant with happiness, they departed for the South. On Monday, in the North American, intelligence reached Phil from Mr Bogart announcing the sudden death of his young wife. She had been married scarcely a month & was only 18 years of age.

House of Reps: 1-Bills committed-relief: of J J Sents; of Van Camp Chapin, & others; of M V Jones, late collector of customs for the district of Wilimington, N C; of Harriet Beard, widow of Jas Beard, deceased; of Jas Talbott, late register of the land ofc at Indianapolis, Ind; of Lee Deatherage & John Deatherage, or their legal reps; of Thos L Disharoon, of St Louis Co, Mo; of the heirs of Benj Moore, deceased; of R F Blocker, E J Gurley, & J F Davis; of the legal reps of Wetonsaw, son of Jas Connor-passed; of D G Farrigut; of Miles Judson, surety on the official bond of the late Purser Andrew D Crosby; of Wm Haynie, adm of Ann Haynie; of Eliz Cole, widow of Levi Cole; of the children of Eliz Yancey, widow of John Yancey; of Catharine Ansart; of Molly W Hobbs, widow of Josiah Hobbs, of N H; of the surviving child or children of Mary Harkins, deceased; of Mowry Bates, of Rhode Island; of Nancy G Van Rensselaer widow of Lt Col Henry K Van Rensselaer, of N Y; of Sarah Hildreth; of Elias Wilson & other surviving children of the late Lt John Wilson, an ofcr of the Revolution; & of the heirs of Eliz Hickman. Also, invalid pension to Levi Parks; granting a pension to Ethelred Stafford, of Louisiana; & an increase of pension to Wm Roberts. 2-<u>Adverse reports made in the following cases</u>, which were severally laid on the table-petition: of Adolph Renard; of the heirs of Jas Elliott; of the heirs of Francis Martin; of the heirs of Mrs Eliz Martin; of Ann Eliza Knight; of Wm Hutchinson; of the children of Adam Swart; of Gersham Van Verst; & of Rufus Phelps. Also, Senate bill for the relief of Wm B Shubrick. 3-No objection to the following bills-relief: of Harriet R F Vinson; of Eunice Cobb; of Thos Berry; of Mrs Rachel McMillan; of Geo F Means; & of Wm P Bowhay. Granting a pension to Asa Wells; Andrew Templeton; Jas Alexander, an invalid soldier of the war of 1812; & to Mary Shircliff, widow of John Shircliff. Increase of pension to Jas Dunning. Invalid pension to Esther P Fox, widow of Augustus C Fox; to Anselm Clarkson, of Mo; to Chauncey Hoyt, of Chenango Co, N Y; to Wm Eddy; to Chas Appleton; of Hugh Baker; to Saml Hamilton; & to Thos Glasgow.

Railroad accident in Fla: the down train from Lake City to Jacksonville, on May 16th, when within about 7 miles of Jacksonville, encountered a number of cattle on the track. The engineer was able to miss all except the last one which was thrown under the forward wheels of the tender, which instantly disconnected from the engine & thrown from the track. Persons killed were Geo L Bryant, cashier of the Bank of St John's, in this city; Anthony Mott, brakeman, a resident of this place, & Stephen Martin, of St Johns Co, Fla, formerly of Newbern, N C. Thos Roberts, of Hamilton Co, formerly agent of the road at Baldwin, was seriously injured, his left arm being so badly mutilated as to render amputation at the should necessary. He is yet in a critical situation. Col John G Haddock, of this county, had his leg broken near the thigh. His other wounds are not dangerous. J C Folson, of St John's Co, had his left should dislocated, besides sustaining serious internal injuries. He is doing well, however. Saml E Hope & wife, at Brooksville, Hernando Co, were considerably bruised. E L Bill, conductor, Messrs H W Gower, Dr A M Sabal, & David Stratton, were somewhat bruised. The wounded were taken to Jacksonville.

The following constitute the Board of Visiters to the Naval Academy to assemble Jun 1st: Cmdor Lavalette, Capts Wilke, Glendy, Price, & W R Taylor.

Orphans Court of Wash Co, D C. Letters of administration on the personal estate of Dennis O'Hare, late of Wash Co, deceased. –Thos R Lovett, adm

Died: on May 24, in Wash City, after a long & painful illness, Miss Lucia Berry. Her funeral will take place this afternoon at 4 o'clock, from the residence of Robt Beale, Capitol Hill.

MON MAY 28, 1860
House of Reps: 1-Bills committed-relief: of Geo W Mundy, adm of Maj Gen Ebenezer W Ripley; & of Anna M Rolas Y Robaldo. 2-Bills considered & passed-relief: of Anson L C Portman; of Wm Y Strong; of Jeremiah Pendergast; of Richd C Martin; of Mrs Jane M McCrabb, widow of the late John W McCrabb, Assist Quartermaster U S Army; & of Erastus Hutchinson. Granting a pension to Martha Sanderson, widow of Maj Winslow F Sanderson-amended. Also, Senate bill to grant the right of pre-emption to a certain tract of land in the State of Missouri to the heirs & legal reps of Thos Maddin, deceased. 3-No objection to the following bills-relief: of J R Crump; of Julius Martin; of Beda Hayes, widow of Dudley Hayes, of Granby, Hartford Co, Conn-amended; to Effisia C De May, widow of Chas F V De May, late a dragoon in the army of the U S; & of Aaron Quigley. Granting a pension to Edw Lee; to Jane Yates; to Richd M Haden; of Adriene Rich, of Habersham Co, Ga; to John P Smith, of Habersham Co, Ga; to John Jackson, an invalid soldier; to Rufus Call, jr, a soldier in the late war with Great Britain-amended; & to Gregory Patti.

Ofc *Oak Hill Cemetery* Co, Gtwn, D C, May 25, 1860. Election Notice. Holders of lots containing not less than 300 square feet in *Oak Hill Cemetery* are notified that an election will be held at the Cemetery on Jun 4, at 5 P M, for four managers to manage the affairs of the company for the ensuing year.
–Henry King, sec

Wm C Preston who died on May 22, 1860, was born Dec 27, 1794, in Phil, while his father was attending Congress at that place as a member from Va. His maternal grandmother was a sister of Patrick Henry. He was an 1812 graduate at the Univ of S C & returned to Va, where he studied law in the ofc of Wm Wirt, at Richmond. In 1816 he went to Europe, & after visiting France, England, & Switzerland, resided for some time in Edinburgh, where he attended the lectures of Hope, Playfair, & Brown. In 1819 he returned to the U S, & being admitted to the bar in 1822 he removed to Columbia, S C, where he continued to practice his profession. In 1832 he was elected to the U S Senate; in 1842 he became the Pres of the Univ of S C, which ofc he held until he was forced to resign because of ill-health & live in retirement.

Died: on May 25, Mrs Mary Eliz Peyton, wife of Jas M Torbert, in her 46th year. She was an affectinate wife, devoted mother, dutiful daughter, true friend, & kind neighbor. Her death is an irreparable loss to her immediate family & relatives.

Mrd: on May 23, at Cedar Grove, King Geo Co, Va, by Rev Hugh Roy Scott, Julia Calvert, daughter of Dr R H Stuart, to Dr E Lee Jones, of N Y C.

Senate: 1-Bill for the relief of A H Jones & H M Brown: referred to the Cmte on Indian Affairs.

Circuit Court-Wash. 1-The Court was engaged the last week in the case of Margaret Lyons, admx of Eliz Braiden, against Agnes R Hazard, Oliver E P Hazard, & others. This was a suit originally in chancery, but as the Judges deemed it best to obtain the verdict of a jury on matters of fact involved in the case, it was placed upon the trial docket of the Circuit Court. The gist of the contest laid in the proof or disproof of the geniuneness of a certain paper purporting to be a receipt for $5,850, the purchase money of some real estate sold by the since deceased to one of the dfndnts, which receipt it was stated by the defence was presented by the deceased to Mrs Hazard as a gratuity. The verdict was for the plaintiff. 2-A suit was then disposed of whereto Miss Filley Brink was plntf & Wm Forrest dfndnt. This was for defamation of character, the dfndnt having called in question the honesty of plntf by ascribing to her agency the loss of some property which was missed at the time she left his house, where she had been an inmate. Damages were laid at $6,000; the jury gave a verdict for plntf, damages $50; which the Court, however, immediately set aside as not in conformity with the evidence.

Circuit Court of Wash Co, D C-in Equity. Benedict Jost & others vs Wm Redin, adm de bonis non of Michl Miller, Gotlieb Rupert & Margaret Rupert his wife. Statement of the trustee's account, of Michl Miller, late of Gtwn, deceased, on Jun 18 next, at the ofc of Walter S Cox, Special Auditor, Wash.

Died: on May 25, in Wash City, in her 29th year, Mrs Altona Cameron, the excellent wife of John W Cameron, of N C, & youngest daughter of the late Weston R Gales, of Raleigh.

TUE MAY 29, 1860
Senate: 1-Cmte on Indian Affairs: bill for the relief of Thos J Henley. 2-Cmte on Public Lands: bill for the relief of H C Dousman in behalf of himself & other owners of land at Prairie du Chien, for the relief of certain claimants to farm lots at Prairie du Chien, Wisconsin: passed. 3-Cmte on Pensions: bill granting an invalid pension to Nathan Randall: recommended its passage. Same cmte: bill for the relief of Chauncey W Fuller, with an amendment. 4-Cmte on the District of Columbia: adverse report on the memorial of C B Baker, asking to be allowed expenses for subsistence while in the employ of the Coast Survey Ofc in the Gulf of Mexico.

Circuit Court of Wash Co, D C-in Chancery, No 1,377. Thos & Anastasia Donoho vs Michl, Jas, Margaret, & Sarah McNamara & David & Bridget O'Shea. The trustee reported that a sale was made by him on Mar 13, 1860, & David O'Shea became the purchaser of part of lot 15, in Cabot's subdivision of square 677, in Wash, fronting 12 feet 6 inches on G st by 87 feet 6 inches in depth, for $300, & hath complied with the terms of sale. –John A Smith, clerk

Died: on May 28, 1860, in Wash City, Ellen B, wife of David H Bevans, & daughter of the late Thos Hunter. Her funeral will take place from her late residence, 35 C st, tomorrow at 4 o'clock.

Died: on May 14, at Salem High School, in Greene Co, Miss, Colin McRae, son & only surviving child of Hon John J & Mary A McRae, of Wayne Co, Miss, in his 19th year.

Orphans Court of Wash Co, D C. Letters of administration on the personal estate of John W B Garner late of Wash Co, deceased. –Wm Dixon, adm

WED MAY 30, 1860

Mrd: on May 29, at Waugh Chapel, by Rev John P Effinger, John J Peabody to Miss Mary J, eldest daughter of J T Ball, of Alexandria Co, Va.

Died: on May 10, near Charlestown, Jefferson Co, Va, Mrs Euphemia Manning, relict of the late Nathl Manning, of Loudoun Co, aged 74 years. Mrs Manning was a resident of Wash City for a number of years. While on a visit to her friends in Jefferson Co, she was suddenly called to her rest. She was a woman of great energy, & well did she perform the duties of mother towards a large family. Her beneficent life will long be remembered by all who knew her.

Died: on May 27, at the Wood Yard, PG Co, Md, Ann Hays, aged 15 months, daughter of Capt J W T & A E Gardener.

Senate: 1-Ptn from Henry Rice, asking that the amount of two bonds given by him for the payment of duties on goods imported into Castine while in possession of the British army during the war of 1812, & subsequently paid, may be refunded: referred. 2-Papers in relation to the claim of Annie W Angus: referred. 3-Ptn from Jas Baldwin & others, citizens of N Y, asking that pensions may be granted to the surviving soldiers of the war of 1812 & the widows of those deceased: referred. 3-Cmte on Pensions: bill for the relief of Mary G Maddox: passed. 4-Cmte of Claims: bill for the relief of Jethro Bonney, of the State of N Y: recommended its passage. Same cmte: bill for the relief of Geo W Flood. 5-Cmte of Claims: bill to provide for the payment of the claim of J W Nye, assignee of Peter Bargy, jr, & Hugh Stewart. 6-Cmte on Territories: bill for the relief of the legal reps of the estate of Chas H Mason: asked it immediate consideration; but objection was made.

Died: on May 26, at Dover, Dela, Mrs Mary Schee, wife of Hon Arnold Naudain, M C, of that place, aged 72 years & 6 months.

Two Misses Achin, of Velvet Ridge, Tenn, while fleeing from a house to escape an approaching tornado, were overtaken by the tornado, & dreadfully mangled & killed. Other members of the family were injured.

Chancery Sale: by decree of the Circuit Court of D C, made in the cause of the Mayor, Recorder, Alderman, & Common Council of Gtwn vs W Jewell's excs & devisees, No 1,527, in Equity, dated Feb 18, 1860, we will offer at auction, on Jun 20 next, on the premises, for the Wash City property, & for the following property in Gtwn, the following real estate: all that part of lot 12 in square 117 in Wash. Also, part of lot 2 in the Slip, & of 28, in Beall's addition to Gtwn, fronting 57 feet on Gay st, by 120 feet deep. –Hugh Caperton, Walter S Cox, trustees -Thos Dowling, auct

Trustee's sale of valuable improved property on L, between 6th & 7th sts, at auction, on Jun 20 next, by deed of trust from Wilson McBee, dated Jan 19, 1859, recorded in Liber J A S No 168, folios 63 thru 66, of the land records for Wash Co, D C: part of lot 3 in square 449, with a spacious brick bldg thereon. –Chas H Utermehle, trustee -A Green, aucts

Circuit Court of D C-Wash, Mon. 1-Alfred H Marlow vs Thos J Magruder was tried, & yesterday the jury rendered a verdict for dfndnt. 2-The naturalizations in this Court are now very numerous. More than 100 persons have been naturalized during the present term.

Hygeia Hotel, Old Point Comfort, Va: the famed Seaboard Watering-place will be ready for the reception of visiters on Jun 1. –Jos Segar, C C Willard, proprietors

Circuit Court of D C, No 1,606, in Equity. Danl Chandler & others against John F Broome & others. The bill states that the late Walter S Chandler died intestate & seized in fee of lots 18 thru 24, & another lot north of the above, in Gtwn, at the n w intersection of West & Congress sts, with the dwlg house thereon, & other real property, all of which, except the above, have been divided among his heirs; that the above lots were assigned to his widow Margaret Chandler, for her dower, that she hath recently departed this life; that the dfndnt, John F Broome, above named, is one of the parties interested in the estate of the late Walter S Chandler, & resides out of this District; & the object of the bill is to obtain a partition or sale for the purpose of division of said lots & premises among the heirs of said Walter S Chandler, some of whom are minors as mentioned in the bill. John F Broome is to appear in person or by solicitor on the first Monday of Oct next.
–Jno A Smith, clerk

Circuit Court of D C, No 1,559, in Equity. Ernst Laeffler against Adam Raab, adm, Thos Blagden, Jos Fugett, & the heirs [unknown] of Ferdinand Greentrup, deceased. The parties above & the creditors of said Ferdinance Greentrup, deceased, are to appear at my ofc on Jun 21 next, for a statement of the account of the personal estate of said F Greentrup. –W Redin, auditor

Circuit Court of D C, No 1,445, in Equity. McBlair & others vs Gadsby & others. Report of sale of lot 31 in square 167 to Levin M Powell for $4,157.05, on Mar 29, 1860. –Jno A Smith, clerk

Wilmington, N C, May 29. The steamer **Kate McLaurin**, hence for Fayetteville, burst her boiler this morning, 8 miles below Elizabethtown, killing Capt Evans, 2 deck hands, & scalding the fireman.

THU MAY 31, 1860
A monument to the Virginians who were slaughtered at Wood's Barn, Roxborough, Pa, in 1777, was dedicated at that place on Monday with much parade & ceremony. Inscription: "This monument is designed to perpetuate the memory of Virginia troopers, taken by surprise and killed at Wood's Barn, in the winter of 1777-"78, by a company of British cavalry. Erected by the Pennsylvania Dragoons in 1860. Honor to the brave. The Constitution and the Union, esto perpetua." Horatio Gates Jones delivered the oration, addresses by Hon Wm B Reed & Chas J Biddle.

Mrd: on May 29, at St John's Church, by Rev Dr Norwood, Capt Douglas Scott, of the British Indian army, to Hariette, widow of A De Bodisco, late Russian Minister.

Died: on May 30, Lemuel Middleton, infant son of Alex'r & Kate M Henderson, aged 11 months. His funeral will take place this afternoon at 4 o'clock, from the residence of his grandfather, L J Middleton, corner of F & 12th sts.

Died: yesterday, Ernest, second son of Hudson & Christiana Taylor, aged 10 years. His funeral will take place this afternoon at 4 o'clock, corner 9th & D sts.

Senate: 1-Ptn from the adm of Wm A Linn, late collector of the customs at St Louis, Mo, asking payment of the claims of Thos C Reynolds, late U S Atty, for compensation for defending suits brought against said Linn for acts done in his official capacity: referred. 2-Additional papers in support of the claim of Adelaide Adams to a pension: referred. 3-Cmte on Naval Affairs: to which were referred papers relating to the claim of John B Rittenhouse, purser in the navy, for losses sustained while purser of the U S steamship **Susquehannah** during the prevalence of yellow fever on board that vessel; & also a bill for the relief of Jno B Rittenhouse, submitted an adverse report on the same. Same cmte: adverse report on the memorial of Lt T H Patterson, asking to be allowed pay due him for service as an ofcr of the astronomical expedition to Chili. Same cmte: adverse report on the memorial of A C Rhind, dropped by the navy board & since restored to active service, to be placed on the same footing with other ofcrs restored. Same cmte: adverse report on the memorial of Capt Wm L Hudson, of the navy, asking remuneration for certain expeditures made while in command of the steamship **Niagara** engaged in laying the cable. Same cmte: adverse report on the memorial of John Sample, asking to have his invention tested with a view to its adoption in the public service to protect tiller ropes from fire. Same cmte: asked to be discharged from further consideration of the memorial of Eunice Church, widow of a seaman who died of wounds received in battle, & that it be referred to the Cmte on Pensions. 4-Cmte on Revolutionary Claims: memorial of Virginia Rose & other heirs of Capt Alex'r Rose, of the Revolutionary war, submitted a report, with a bill for the relief of the heirs of Capt Alex'r Rose. 5-Cmte of Claims: bill for the relief of Isaac S Smith, of Syracuse, N Y: recommended its passage. 6-Bill from the House granting a pension to Adelaide Adams, widow of Cmder Geo Adams, U S Navy, & reported on adversely by the Cmte on Pensions, back to the same cmte; which was agreed to.

FRI JUN 1, 1860
The English papers announce the death, on May 16, at Regent's Park, London, of Anne Isabella, Baroness Noel Byron, widow of the late Lord Byron. She was born in 1794, the only daughter & heir of Sir Ralph Milbanke Noel, Bart, by the sister & co-heir of the second Viscount & ninth Baron Wentworth. On the death of the other co-heir, Lord Scarsdale, in 1856, she succeeded to the barony of Wentworth by writ, the viscounty becoming extinct. She was married to the great poet in 1815, but the union, as is well known, was a most unhappy one for both the husband & wife. The only child, Ada, was married to Earl Lovelace, & died in 1852.

Senate: 1-Ptn from Maria W Sanders, widow of the late Brvt Maj John Sanders, of the Engineer Corps, asking to be allowed a pension: referred. 2-Ptn from S A Wood, M F Conway, & other citizens of Kansas Territory, asking the establishment of certain mail routes in that Territory: referred. 3-Cmte of Private Land Claims: bill for the relief of Braxton Bragg & Randall L Gibson: passed. 4-Cmte on Naval Affairs: joint resolution for the restoration of Lt Augustus S Baldwin to the active list from the leave of absence list of the navy, reported it back without amendment, accompanied by a report. 5-Cmte on Revolutionary Claims: adverse report on the memorial of Ford Barnes, asking compensation for the services of his father in the war of the Revolution. 6-Cmte on Pensions: bill for the relief of Frances M Webster for a pension. 7-Cmte of Claims: bill for the relief of Richd S Coxe; of Danford Mott, adm of John Gorman, deceased; of Alex'r M Jackson; & of Nehemiah Garrison, assignee of Moses Perkins.
8-Cmte on the Judiciary: bill for the relief of Logan Hunton for compensation for prosecuting suits against Narcisso Lopez, & other violations of the neutrality laws.

Died: on May 31, Mrs Eliz Eliot Dawes, widow of the late Rufus Dawes, aged 55 years. Her funeral will take place on Sat next, at 4 o'clock P M, from the residence of her brother, Wm G Cranch, 2nd st east & D st north.

Shocking affair on board a Mississippi steamboat on May 19. A deformed madman, B L Sheath, walked up to a table where Mr F G Jernigan, a passenger, was sitting, & seizing him by the head attempted to cut his throat with a sharp Bowie knife, inflicting a terrible wound. Two other passengers, Mr C M Fort & J R Lyle, of Nashville, Tenn, rushed from their state rooms on hearing the outcry, & were both met & stabbed in the heart by the maniac. Both died instantly, & Sheath was secured.

Mount Olivet Cemetery. The Young Catholic's Friend Society, having been invited by The Board of Managers of ***Mount Olivet Cemetery*** to be present at the blessing, Sunday next, will assemble at the school room of the Washington Seminary, on Sunday afternoon, at 2 o'clock. A full attendance of the members is earnestly requested. Appropriate badges will be provided for the designation of the members. -F McNerhany, Pres -P J McHenry, Sec

Richmond, May 31. Judge Peter V Daniel, of the Supreme Court of the U S, died here today.

SAT JUN 2, 1860
Sale of superior carriages, saddle horses, harness, stable furniture, on Jun 6, at 10 o'clock, at the Livery & Sale stables kept by Mr Lakemeyer, on G st, between 17th & 18th sts. -Jas C McGuire & Co, aucts

Senate: 1-Ptn from Geo W Earhart, asking to be allowed the amount paid by him for transportation while employed as agent in the Quartermaster's dept: referred.
2-Ptn from Thos H Burley, asking that the right to use a machine invented & patented by him for dove-tailing wood may be purchased by the U S: referred.
3-Cmte on Pensions: bill for the relief of Harriet Crocker, to be allowed a pension.

Mrs Maria Post, widow of Capt Post, an ofcr in the Continental army, expired on Sunday last at her residence in Aquackanock township, Passaic Co, N J. She had reached the age of 106 years, having been born in 1754. At the breaking out of the Revolution she married, & lived with her husband until 1847, when the latter died at the age of 97 years. Forty of her descendants, including several great-great-grandchildren, & a daughter 81 years old, attended her funeral.

The ***Loretto Springs***, Cambria Co, Pa, will be opened for visiters on Jun 20, under the management of Maj John Brady, well known as the highly competent landlord, for many years of the Brady House, Harrisburg, Pa.
–F A Gibbons, jr, sec

Died: on May 26, in Upperville, Fauquier Co, Va, Mrs Ann Washington Rose, relict of the late Dr Henry Rose, of Alexandria, in her 82nd year.

Died: on May 27, at Piscataway, Md, after a protracted illness, Mary E Harbin, in her 25th year. She leaves a husband & child to mourn their untimely loss.

Died: on Jun 1, in Wash City, Franck, youngest son of Augustus E & Mary Jane Perry, aged 19 months & 16 days. His funeral is this afternoon at 4 o'clock, from the residence of his parents, F st, between 6th & 7th sts.

Died: on May 27, at the residence of his father, in Fairfax Co, Va, R T Paine, infant son of Cmder W T Muse, U S Navy.

Alexandria, Jun 1. Dr M M Lewis, of this city, shot his brother-in-law, Courtney Brent, an hour since, in self-defence, some 3 or 4 balls striking his person. Brent is badly wounded. Great excitement prevails.

Farms for sale: due to declining health requires the influence of a more Southern climate. Farm in the Piedmont region of Va, Culpeper Co, at private sale; the home place, **Stillmore**, lately the residence of Hon J Morton, contains 956 acres; dwlg is a good one, with 4 rooms on the first floor & 4 rooms on the second floor. The other farm, **Garvey**, in Culpeper Co, contains 600 acres of land; the dwlg is small & the bldgs are all new. –John Taylor
-Stevensburg, P O, Culpeper Co, Va.

MON JUN 4, 1860
St Mary's Co, Md. John B Long, Oscar Miles, Geo H Morgan, L W B Hutchins, & Uriah Tippett, of Md, obtained warrants from the land ofc at Annapolis for 200,000 acres of land under the waters immediately surrounding St Mary's Co, & that Benj Tippett was engaged in making surveys for the company. The survey, it appears, would divert from public to individual uses the oyster bars & other water privileges in Chesapeake bay, & Patuxent, & Potomac rivers & their tributaries. The gentlemen referred to above, to quiet public feelings, have determined not to exercise any further right, & will not execute the warrants from the land ofc. -Sun

The celebrated bronze doors for the Capitol modelled by Rodger, & cast in Munich, Bavaria, have arrived at N Y. They have cost some $40,000, & have excited general admiration abroad.

Dissolution, May 21 last, of co-partnership, by mutual consent, under the firm of Sullivan & Stewart, plasters, John A Stewart having sold & disposed of all his interest to John J Sullivan. –John J Sullivan, John A Stewart

Rev C R Martin & wife, of the Methodist Episcopal Church, & Rev M T Yates & wife, of the Southern Baptist Church, arrived at Shanghai on Mar 7. Mr Martin joins his mission at Fuh Chow.

San Francisco, May 18. Several Americans murdered by the Indians while asleep at Miller's station, on Carson river, some 30 miles from the settlements of Carson Valley. Volunteers united in one body, under command of Maj Ormsby, mounted & numbering 165 men. On May 12 they came upon the Indians at the bend of the Quichie river. The Indians were in ambush at a narrow pass through which Maj Ormsby's party was proceeding & opened fire upon the troops from their safe hiding place. Maj Ormsby ordered a charge, which lasted about 2 hours, when Ormsby's ammunition gave out. The Indian then closed upon our men, pouring in volley after volley, killing many on the spot, the balance retreated. Among the slain are Maj Ormsby, Henry Meredith, a distinguished Calif lawyer; Mr S Speer, Richd Snowden, Mr Arsington, Dr Jader, Chas Dersus, Jas Lee, T Johnson, Chas McLeod, John Sileming, Andrew Schealled, M Kuezorwitch, Jno Garmbo, A K Elliott, W Hawkins, Geo Jones, Wm Macintosh, O McNaughton.

House of Reps: 1-<u>Bills with no objections-relief</u>: of Guadalupe Estudillo de Aguello, widow of Santiago E Aguello-amended; relief of John C McFerran, of the U S army; of the heirs of John Hopper; of Francis Lavonture & Pierre Grignon; of Phineas G Pearson-amended; of Thos W Phelps-amended; of Coale & Barr; of Eliz Smith, of Coffee Co, Tenn. Also, a bill for the relief of the survivors of the <u>Sublette Cut-off</u> massacre of Jul 24, 1859, & for the payment of expenses incurred in sending said destitute survivors to their homes-amended by a substitute.

Died: Sunday, at the residence of her uncle, Mr J L Clubb, Mary Frances, second daughter of Mr R B Owens, in her 20th year. Her funeral will take place on Jun 5 at 10 o'clock, from the residenc of Mr Clubb, 524 I st, between 6th & 7th sts.

Died: on May 29, at his residence, near Fairfax Court-house, Va, Dr Elcon Jones, only son of Raphael Jones, of Wash City.

TUE JUN 5, 1860
Medina, N Y, Jun 4. Hon Silas M Burroughs, member of Congress from the 31st district of N Y, died at his residence in Medina on Jun 3.

Senate: 1-Ptn from Anna Rogers, widow of John Rogers, late of the navy, asking to be allowed a pension: referred. 2-Ptn from Lemuel Spooner, asking to be allowed a pension for military services in the war of 1812: referred. 3-Additional papers in relation to the claim of Henry Rice: referred. 4-Additional papers in relation to the claim of Chas Grampp to date his pension from the time of his discharge: referred. 5-Cmte on Pensions: bill for the relief of Chas W Brooks, of N Y: recommended its passage. Same cmte: adverse report on the bill for the relief of Lt Michl R Clark. Same cmte: adverse report on the ptn of Sallie Moore for a pension. Same cmte: bill for the relief of Valentine Wehrheim, asked its immediate consideration, but it was objected to. 6-Cmte on Revolutionary Claims: bill for the relief of the heirs of Capt Jno A Hopper, & recommended its passage. Same cmte: bill for the relief of the children & heirs of Alex'r

Montgomery: recommended its passage. 7-Cmte on Pensions: bill granting an invalid pension to Ezekiel Jones: recommeded its passage. 7-Cmte on Public Bldgs & Grounds: bill for the relief of Eliza B Mills, widow of Robt Mills, architect. 8-Cmte on Patents & Patent Ofc: bill for the relief of Fred'k E Sickles: recommended its passage. 9-Cmte on Revolutionary Claims: adverse report on the memorial of the reps of Richd Taliaferro, deceased, for the commutation pay due the deceased for Revolutionary services.

House of Reps: 1-Cmte on Commerce: bill for the relief of J W Dyer, A L Dyer, & W W Dyer: committed. Same cmte: bill for the relief of Francis Huttman: committed. 2-Cmte of Claims: bill for the relief of Alex'r Cross: committed. Same cmte: bill for the relief of Isaac Lilly: committed. 3-Cmte on the Post Ofc: bill for the relief of A Bledsoe, Wm C Scott, Wm Doty, & others: committed. Same cmte: bill for the relief of John I Barron, Jas Porter, & Aaron A H Crenshaw: committed. Same cmte: bill to authorize the Postmaster Genr'l to open & readjust the accounts of L J Sawyer & John Frink & Co, mail contractors: committed. 4-Cmte on the Judiciary: bill for the relief of Wm A Linn's estate: committed. Same cmte: adverse on the ptn of H M Hoxie & others: which was laid on the table. 5-Bill for the relief of Saml J Hensley: passed. 6-Bill for the relief of the surviving grandchildren of Col Wm Thompson, of the Revolutionary army, of South Carolina: passed. 7-Bill for the relief of Philip B Holmes & Wm Pedrick: passed. 8-Bill for the relief of M C Gritzner: passed. 9-Bill for the relief of Mrs Ferguson Smith: passed. 10-Bill for the relief of Geo P Marsh: passed.

A little daughter of Mr Wm Baird, a farmer, residing a short distance west of Sing Sing, N Y, hung herself in her father's wood-house on Monday. She was swinging by a rope & her head got caught in the noose at the loose end. The family was in an adjacent field at the time, the mother being the first to return, when she found the child in the last agonies of death. She was a bright girl of four summers.

Died: on Jun 2, John Edward, youngest child of Stanislaus & Mary H Murray.

U S Court for the N Y District held yesterday. Albert W Hicks was convicted of robbery & piracy on board an oyster sloop, killing the capt & his 2 sons & robbing the vessel. The three victims were his companions & had broke bread with them just a few hours before. He was sentenced to be hung at Bedlow's Island on Jul 13.

The Arabia brings intelligence of the death of Sir Chas Barry, the architect of the new Houses of Parliament in London, at the age of 65 years. He was born in May, 1795, apprenticed as an architect in London, & upon attaining his majority spent several years in travel upon the Continent. In 1834 the old Houses of Parliament were burnt down & the Gov't made liberal offers for designs. That of Mr Barry was deemed the best. Some two millions of pounds have been expended upon it, & it is now nearly completed.

Died: on Jun 2, at Alexandria, Va, Augusta Newton, wife of John C Whitwell. Her funeral will take place on Jun 6 at 11 o'clock, from the residence of her sister, Mrs Saml McCormick, 35 Cameron st, Alexandria.

Died: on Jun 4, in Wash City, Dearborn B Johnson, in his 47th year. His funeral will be from his late residence, on 13½ st, near Md ave, [Island] at 2 o'clock today.

WED JUN 6, 1860

Senate: 1-Memorial of Lewis Tappan, S W Green, & other citizens of the State of N Y, calling the attention of the Senate to the character of the imprisonment now being suffered by Thaddeus Hyatt, a citizen of N Y, & expressing the belief that such imprisonment is of such a nature, regarding the condition of the jail, the closeness of the restraint, as to endanger the health & life of the prisoner, especially in view of the summer heats & deleterious atmosphere of Wash, to which he is unaccustomed; that, not being imprisoned for any moral crime, but simply for conduct compelled by his differing in opinion with a majority of the Senate in regard to their constitutional power, they ask that if the imprisonment of Mr Hyatt is to be continued into the hot months of summer, that he be removed to a well ventilated residence: referred. 2-Ptn from F G Hungerford, jr, & others, in favor of the establishment of a mail route on the south side of the Kanawha river, from Brownstown to the Falls, Kanawha, Va: referred. 3-Ptn from A Hamilton Patterson, asking compensation for his services as a clerk & artist while attached to the U S expedition to Japan under Cmdor Perry: referred. 4-Ptn from Mary Bartholomew, widow of a soldier of the war of 1812, asking to be allowed a pension: referred. 5-Ptn from the heirs of B R Milam, asking the confirmation of their title to a tract of land granted by the Mexican Gov't to said Milam, & also land scrip for so much of said land as has been disposed of by the U S: referred. 6-Cmte of Claims: bill for the relief of Elias Hall: recommended its passage. Same cmte: bill for the relief of John H Rountree for the return of certain land rents illegally exacted by the agent of the U S. Same cmte: adverse report on the bill for the relief of John F Sanford, adm de bonis non of the estate of Robt Sanford, deceased. Same cmte: bill for the relief of Jno R Crump: recommended its passage. Same cmte: bill for the relief of the legal reps of P P Hall, deceased: recommended its passage. 7-Cmte on the District of Columbia: bill to incorporate the trustees of the New Jerusalem church of Wash City, & the bill to incorporate the ***Mount Olivet Cemetery*** of D C, reported them back with amendments.

Jas Thread, the mail contractor between Olney & Granville, Ill, was arrested on Sunday, at the instance of W D Gilmore, special agent of the Post Ofc Dept, charged with robbing the mail. The extent is not known, but supposed to be large.

Circuit Court of D C, in Equity, No 1,463. Jas C McGuire against the adm, widow, & heirs of Wm L Young. The trustee's account & the distribution of the funds will be stated at my ofc, City Hall, Wash, 11 o'clock, Jun 27.
–W Redin, auditor

Circuit Court of D C, in Equity, No 1,436. Slater & Morgan against the heir & adm of Eliz Slater. The trustee's account & the distribution of the funds will be stated at my ofc, City Hall, Wash, 10 o'clock, Jun 27. —W Redin, auditor

Died: on Jun 4, in Wash City, Ellen Douglas, only daughter of Stephen A & Adele Douglas, aged 8 months & 5 days. Her funeral will take place at the residence of Judge Douglas, corner of I & N J ave, today, at 12 o'clock M.

Died: on May 31, at the residence of A H Pickrell, in Gtwn, D C, Mary E, infant child of Robt H & Sarah E Watkins.

N Y, Jun 5. Wm R Hallett, Pres of the Bank of Mobile, died here today.

THU JUN 7, 1860
Chancery sale of valuable property in Wash City: the undersigned trustees, by a decree of the Circuit Court of D C passed on Jun 1, in a cause between John R Woods & others, cmplnts, & Richd G Briscoe's heirs-at-law, Jos S Clarke, & others, dfndnts, No 1,227 in equity, will sell on the premises, on Jun 29: parts of lots 1 & 2 in square 350; lot 5 in square 263; part of lot 2 in square 414; part of lot 15 in square 494; lot 6 in square 575, & lot 7 in reservation C. On Jul 2: west half of lot 2 in square 633; part of lot 10 in square 633; lots 3, 4, 9, 11, 16, & 17, in square 1,027. —Wm R Woodward, trustee -A Green, aucts

Mrd: on May 2, at the British Protestant Church, Ortakeui, by Rev H G O Dwight, Alexander, eldest son of Wm C Thompson, of N Y, & Vice-consul for the U S A at Constantinople, to Louisa Hannah, youngest daughter of Jos Phillips, of Ortakeui.

Senate: 1-Ptn from Henry Addison, the Mayor, Jos Libbey, & other citizens of Gtwn, urging the speedy appropriation of money sufficient to complete the Wash Aqueduct: referred. 2-Cmte on Military Affairs: asked to be discharged from further consideration of the bill for the relief of Eliz Smith, of Coffee Co, Tenn, & that it be referred to the Cmte of Pensions. Same cmte: bill for the relief of J W Davidson, a capt in the army, of the reimbursement of an amount deducted from his pay on account of public moneys stolen, while he was acting commissary of subsistence. 3-Cmte on Naval Affairs: asked to be discharged from further consideration of the memorial of Anna Rogers, widow of John Rogers, & that it be referred to the Cmte on Pensions: which was agreed to. 4-Cmte of Claims: bill for the relief of Augustus Steele, for salary & expenses while Inspector of Customs at Tampa Bay, Fla. 5-Cmte on Militay Affairs: bill for the relief of David Waldo, & asked its immediate consideration: passed. 6-Cmte on Foreign Relations: bill for the relief of Anton L C Portman: recommended its passage. 7-Cmte on Post Ofcs & Post Roads: House bill for the relief of Hockaday & Liggit: ordered to be printed. 8-Mr Bingham gave notice that he would tomorrow call up the bill for the relief of Arthur Edwards & his associates, returned by the Pres with his objections thereto.

Final judgment in the Forrest divorce case. The Court ordered that Mr Forrest should pay into the U S Trust Company in N Y, for the benefit of Mrs Forrest, the sum of $35,593, being the amount adjudged, & also $966.98 for costs, disbursements, etc. [Etc as written.]

House of Reps: 1-Cmte on Invalid Pensions: adverse reports in the cases of Danl Dailey, Anne Johnson, Saml Graves, & Luther Wingot: laid on the table. Same cmte: bill for the relief of Lt Geo W Malone, of Ga: committed. Same cmte: bill granting an invalid pension to Geo W Allen: committed. 2-Cmte on Patents: adverse report on the ptn of Hezekiah Haynes: laid on the table.

Circuit Court of Wash Co, D C-in Chancery, No 1,426. Branch Jordan vs Wm G Palmer & Wm Towers, adms, Eliza P Towers, widow, & Jos B Towers, & others, heirs at law of John T Towers, deceased. Chas S Wallach, trustee, reported on Apr 5, 1859, he sold the undivided half part of part of lot 12 in square 402, to Lemuel Towers, for $350; & on Jun 7, 1859, part of lot 5 in square 426, with bldgs, improvements, & appurtenances to Jas Towers, for $1,425; & on Feb 13, 1860, another part of lot 5 in square 426, with bldgs, improvements, & appurtenances, to said Jas Towers, for $1,490, who have since complied with the terms of sale. --Jno A Smith, clerk

Rencontre occurred at Warrenton on Monday, between Drs Selser & Bell & Col Wm DeGriffin, gentlemen of high standing, which resulted in the death of Dr Selser & Col DeGriffin. Dr Bell had been visiting Dr Selser's house quite often of late, & his visits became very disagreeable to Dr Selser's sister. Dr Selser notified him of this by a note. They met on Monday near the show-boat **Banjo**, where Dr Bell immediately drew a knife & inflicted 2 wounds on Dr Selser, from which he immediately died. Col DeGriffin caught Bell by the shoulder to separate them, when Bell stabbed him 3 times, lingering until the next afternoon, when he expired. Dr Bell was arrested by the citizens of Warrenton.
-Vicksburg Whig of May 30

Died: on Jun 4, at her home at ***Longwood***, Montg Co, Md, Maggie, youngest daughter of E J & Mary B Hall, aged 15 years & 1 month.

N Y, Jun 6. Hicks, the pirate of the sloop **E A Johnson**, has made a confession of the murder of Capt Burr & the brothers Watts of that vessel. He also acknowledged being implicated in the mutiny of the barque **Saladin** in 1844, when 8 of the crew were murdered.

FRI JUN 8, 1860
Senate: 1-Cmte on Pensions: recommending their passage: relief of Thos Berry & Erastus Hutchins. Invalid pension to Wm Eddy, Hugh Baker, & Anselm Clarkson, of Mo. Also, granting a pension to Adelaide Adams, widow of Cmder Geo Adams, U S Navy.

Trustee's sale of valuable improved real estate, near Gtwn, D C, by deed of trust from Jos Ehrmantrout, dated Dec 13, 1858, recorded amongst the land records of D C; public auction, on Jul 2 next, on the premises, a part or section of the Foundry property, lying west of Gtwn, recently purchased by John S Berry & Co from the estate of Gen John Mason, deceased, & conveyed, by Wm Selden, trustee, to said John S Berry & Co by deed, recorded in Liber J A S No 111, folio 300. –Hugh Caperton, trustee -Thos Dowling, auct, Gtwn

Amboy, Ill, Jun 4. The tornado reached about 8 miles in length. John Hubbell's farm-house, barn, fences, & stock were destroyed. Mr & Mrs Hubbell were dangerously injured, & Henry Hubbell's wife badly injured. Mr Moss' farm-house, barn, fences & stock are destroyed; Mrs Moss is killed; Mr Moss & daughter are dangerously injured, & 2 sons were slightly injured. J Rosebrugh's farm-house, fence, & stock destroyed; Mr Sackett badly injured; Mr Northway's farm-house & barn destroyed; Mr Northway's son badly injured; Bigsby's farm house & barn destroyed; Crombies farm-house, barn & stock destroyed, his child killed & another dangerously injured; Judge Wood's farm-house, barns, fences, & stock destroyed; Mr Wright's farm-house, barns, fences & stock destroyed; Mr Wright dangerously injured; Mr McEmmett's house, barn, fences & stock destroyed. Mr Maine's farm-house, barn, fences, & stock destroyed. Sterling, Ill, Jun 4. David Scott's house had the upper story taken off; Alonzo Golder's, torn in pieces, & his son seriously injured; Jas Wood's house was taken from its foundation; Wm Goodrich's house, entirely demolished, the family escaped injury by taking refuge in the cellar; house belonging to E D Cook, occupied by a family name Pike, was taken down; Mr Pike's wife died in a few hours, his son's leg & daughter's arm were broken; Mr McComber's house was moved from its foundation; Capt Doty's house was torn in pieces; his son & a hired man, Wm Yooward, were badly injured; Wm Kimball's house down, his wife badly hurt & child killed; Cyrus Scott's house & barn blown down; Jesse E Scott's house blown down & his family all dangerously injured; S Russell's house blown down; Mr Jennings & his mother were both killed.

Salt Water Bathing. **Marshall's Pavilion**, Moore's Landing, will be open for visiters on Jun 13. Persons wishing to address the proprietor will direct to Leonardtown, St Mary's Co, Md. –R J Marshall, Proprietor

Blantyre for sale: by decree of the Fauquier Circuit Court: public auction on Jul 17 next, of the desirable farm, on the Manassas Gap Railroad, 1 mile from Broad Run Station, containing 375 acres, with a comfortable dwlg house containing 7 rooms. -Jas K Skinner, Com'r, Broad Run Station, M G R

Mrd: on Jun 5, at Trinity Church, Gtwn, D C, by Rev Fr Maguire, Geo Forrest Green, of Rosedale, to Maria L Devereux, daughter of the late Wm Devereux, of Wash City.

Died: on Jun 6, suddenly, Mrs Susan Jack, relict of the late Jas Jack, aged 72 years. Her funeral will take place from her late residence, 41 4½ st, between Pa ave & Mo ave, this afternoon at 3 o'clock.

Died: on Jun 7, in Wash City, Jas Browne, youngest child of Martha E & Thos W Howard, in his 4th month. His funeral is this evening at 3 o'clock, from the residence of his father, 390 9th st.

Died: on May 31, at the Continental Hotel, Phil, Mrs Penelope Lavinia, wife of Col Robt T Paine, of Edenton, N C.

In Equity, No 1,463. McGuire vs Young et al. The trustee reported that he sold to John A Campbell, for the sum of $1,000, the property mentioned in the proceedings; that said purchaser subsequently assigned his purchase to Albert A Boschke, who subsequently assigned the same to E C Carrington & A Lloyd; that the trustees took the notes of said Campbell with said Boschke as security; & that having conveyed the said property to said Boschke as assignee, the deferred payments were further secured by deed of trust on the premises; & that the terms of the sale have been complied with. –Jno A Smith, clerk

SAT JUN 9, 1860
Senate: 1-Ptn from Robt Mayo, asking compensation for the services of Geo Mayo in the Post Ofc Dept in 1831 & 1832: referred. 2-Ptn from P Della Torre, asking compensation for his services while acting as U S Atty in the district of Calif in the management of certain land caes: referred. 3-Ptn from Waters Lathrop & others, of Jackson, Mich, manufacturers & dealers in steel, remonstrating against any increased duty on the same: referred. 4-Ptn from Andrew J Holmes, a soldier in the late war with Mexico, asking to be allowed a pension: referred. 5-Cmte on Claims: bill for the relief of Geo P Marsh: objection made. 6-Cmte on the Judiciary: asked to be discharged from further consideration of the bill for the relief of Gottleib Scheerer: which was agreed to. Same cmte: asked to be discharged from further consideration of the memorial of Geo C Durham, assignee of Hon David C Broderick, deceased, asking the passage of a law to enable him to receive the amount of salary & mileage due said deceased at the time of his death. 7-Cmte on Territories: bill for the relief of Danl V Whiting. Same cmte: discharged from the further consideration of the memorial of the execs of Saml B Richardson, for payment for 15 days' service as a member of the Legislature in Florida for 1845: which was agreed to. 8-Cmte on Indian Affairs: bill for the relief of Anson Dart. Same cmte: adverse report on the House bill for the relief of O F D Fairbanks, Fred'k Dodge & the Pacific Steamship Co. 9-Cmte of Claims: adverse report on the bill for the relief of Jas Henderson. 10-Cmte on Revolutionary Claims: bill for the relief of Beda Hayes, widow of Dudley Hayes, of Granby, Hartford Co, Conn, reported the same. 11-Cmte on Pensions: bill for the relief of Miriam Davis, wife of Lot Davis, who died of wounds received in Dartmoor prison. Same cmte: pension to Andrew Templeton; & bill for the relief of Mrs Rachel M Millan, & recommended its passage. 12-Bill for the relief of

Mark W Izard: referred to the Cmte on Military Affairs. 13-Bill for the relief of Lt Wm Winder, of the U S army: passed. 14-Bill for the relief of Sylvester Gray: passed. 15-Bills passed-relief: of Israel Johnson; of Anthony Schlander; of Andrew C Marshall; of Emma A Wood, widow of the late Brvt Maj Geo W F Wood, U S army; of W Y Hansell, the heirs of W H Underwood, & the reps of Saml Rockwell; of the widow & other heirs of Wm Higgins, deceased; of Maryett Van Buskirk; of the heirs or legal reps of Francois Guillory; of R K Doebler; of John T Robertson, of Va; of Gotlieb Scheerer; of Shade Calloway; of Jas Phelan; of Chas Jas Lanman; of the legal reps of Sylvester Day, late a Surgeon in the U S army; of Peter Rogerson & son, of St John's Newfoundland, owners of the British brig **Jessie**; of Henry Woods; of Chas W Brooks, of N Y; of the children & heirs of Alex'r Montgomery; of Webster S Steele; of John Dixon; & of Wm H De Groot. Also, pension to Jas Lacy, of Grainger Co, Tenn; pension to Abraham Crum; & pension to Adelaide Adams, widow of Cmder Geo Adams, U S Navy.

Orphans Court of Wash Co, D C. Letters of administration on the personal estate of Sarah Smith, late of Wash Co, deceased. –Thos P Morgan, adm

Mrd: on Jun 4, in Balt, by Rev Stephen P Hill, of Wash, D C, Wm Renshaw, jr, to Emma, 3rd daughter of Wm C Conine, of Balt.

Mrd: on Jun 4, at Pontiac, Mich, by Rev Mr Russell, Benj F French, of Wash City, to Miss Sarah A Parke, of Pontiac.

Mrd: on Jun 5, in N Y, at the residence of Hon Judge Woodruff, by Rev Henry Montgomery, Wm R Kibbey to Rose M Lincoln, all of that city.

Died: on Jun 2, in Leesburg, Va, Mary E, wife of J Edwin Young.

Died: on Jun 5, at his residence in N Y C, Col Wm R Hallett, late Pres of the Bank of Mobile. He arrived on Sunday in the ship **Cahawha**, exceedingly prostrated by a lingering illness. He leaves many & sincere friends to mourn his loss.

Died: on Jun 7, in Wash City, Martha Helen, youngest child of Martha S & F J Bartlett, aged 4 months & 5 days.

MON JUN 11, 1860
Col Jos Plympton, of the U S Army, died at Staten Island, on Jun 5. He was a Lt in the war of 1812, & since then has been employed in various frontier posts, & in Mexico, whither he went as Lt Col, & took an active part in the seige of Vera Cruz, & at the battle of Cerro Gordo. For his gallant & meritorious conduct on the latter occasion he received the brevet of colonel. His regt also performed desperate service at the battles of Contreras & Cherubusco.

Maj Gen Thos Sidney Jesup died in Wash City, yesterday, from paralysis. He was but a few days ago in the active personal discharge of his duties as Quartermaster Gen of the Army. He was born in Va in 1788, & entered the army in 1808 as 2nd lt of the 7th infty, & his subsequent military history is as follows: in 1812 he was Brig Major & Acting Adj Gen to Brig Gen Hull; in 1813 he was Major of the 19th infty; transferred in 1814 to 25th infty as Brvt Lt Col for distinguished service in the battle of Chippewa of Jul 5, 1814; in Nov, 1814, he was brevetted Col, for gallant conduct in the battle of Niagara, of Jul 25, 1814, in which he was severely wounded. On the reduction of the army in 1815 he was retained in the 1st infty, & in 1817 was Lt Col of the 3rd infty. In 1818 he was appointed Adj Gen, with the rank of Col & the same year Quartermaster Gen with the rank of Brig Gen; & was brevetted Maj Gen in May, 1828, for 10 years meritorious service. He was assigned to the command of the army in the Creek nation, Ala, in 1836, & succeeded Gen Call in Florida on Dec 8, 1836; was wounded in action with the Seminole Indians, near Jupiter Inlet, on Jan 24, 1838; & was succeeded by Col Z Taylor on May 15, 1838; whereupon he returned to the duties of his dept, which he managed with distinguished ability.

Chancery sale of valuable improved & unimproved property, by decree of the Circuit Court of D C, passed in the cause wherein Fred'k W Selhausen is cmplnt, & Chas Mades & others, excs & heirs at law & devisees of Bonaventura Schad, deceased, are dfndnts: public sale of the following in Wash City: lots 9 thru 12 in square 785, B & 3rd sts east; lot 9 in square 642, on Dela ave; the whole of square north of square 642, on Va ave; lots 1 thru 16 in square 894, comprising the whole square, fronting on D st; lot 8 thru 10 in square 584, fronting on south F st. Sales on Jul 10, Jul 12, Jul 13, & Jul 16, 1860. —Chas S Wallach, trustee
-J C McGuire & Co, aucts

Died: on Jun 3, Samuel, son of E E & Rebecca O'Brien, in his 21st year.

Appointments by the Pres:
John Appleton, of Maine, to be Envoy Extraordinary & Minister Plenipotentiary of the U S at St Petersburgh, vice Francis W Pickens, resigned.
Wm H Trescot, of S C, to be Assist Sec of State, vice John Appleton, resigned.
Julian A Mitchell, of S C, to be Sec of Legation at St Petersburgh, to fill a vacancy.
Cave Johnson, of Tenn, to be Com'r on the part of the U S under the convention with the Republic of Paraguay.
Saml Ward, of N Y, to be Sec & Interpreter to the Com'r on the part of the U S under the Convention with Paraguay.
Tilton E Doolittle, of Conn, to be Atty of the U S for the district of Connecticut, to fill a vacancy.
Richd A Edes, of Kansas, to be Consul of the U S at Pernambuco.
David N Carpenter to be Deputy Postmaster at Greenfield, Mass.

Sale of valuable real estate, by order of the Circuit Court of D C, passed on May 6, 1859, in the matter of the ptn of the heirs of J A M Duncanson, deceased: sale on Jul 5 next of part of lot 2 in square 374, with brick dwlg house; part of lot 2 in square 374; part of lot 7 in square 558; lots 34 & 7 in square 340; lots 13 thru 15 in square 327; & half of lot 5 in square 340. —Wm B Todd, Francis Mohun, Isaac Clark, com'rs -A Green, aucts

Trustee's sale of very valuable real estate on 7th & E sts, by decree of the Circuit Court of D C, passed in 2 causes in which Statham, Smithson & Co, & Austin Sherman, respectively, are cmplnts, & John F Callan & others are dfndnts, the undersigned will sell at public auction, on Jul 12, on the premises, lot 8 in square 456, in Wash City, with improvements. —C Ingle, A Austin Smith, trustees -Jas C McGuire & Co, aucts

Senate: 1-Ptn from Washington Goff, asking that the Postmaster Gen be authorized to contract with him & his associates to carry the U S mails between San Francisco & Japan in fast sailing vessels or steamships: referred. 2-Ptn from Lt W Nelson, of the U S Navy, asking that he may be allowed, in the settlement of his accounts, the value of certain naval stores which were stolen from him: referred. 2-Cmte on Naval Affairs: memorial of Lt Wm F Lovell & other ofcrs & seamen of the expedition in search of Dr Kane, reported a joint resolution authorizing the Sec of the Navy to pay to the ofcrs & seamen of the expedition the same rate of pay that was allowed the ofcrs & seamen of the expedition under Lt De Haven.

Explosion of a fire-works factory owned by J W Hatfield, in Middle Village, near Wmsburgh, on Friday. Mr Chas Hatfield & Mr Jacob Gresk were instantly killed, & Henry Hatfield, John Hertnee, & Robt Brundell, were severely injured. -Journal of Commerce

Mrd: on Jun 7, at the First Presbyterian Church, 4½ sts, by Rev Byron Sunderland, Mr W G Whittlesey, of Evansville, Indiana, to Miss Sallie H, daughter of Dr S Houston, of Wash City.

Died: on Jun 9, in Gtwn, D C, at the age of 48, Mrs Charlotte Sedgwick Stevens, wife of Gen H L Stevens, & daughter of the late Abraham W Sedgwick, of Rochester, N Y. Her grandfather was Gen Caleb Hyde, of Revolutionary memory. In the minds of her husband & children her memory will be blended with al this is best & loveliest.

Died: on Jun 10, John Thomas, infant son of Thomas M & Sallie A E Cassell, aged 2 months & 12 days. His funeral is this evening at 4 o'clock, from his parents' residence, 7th st, between E & F sts south.

Circuit Court of D C, in Chancery. Rachel Mason, in her own right, & as guardian & next friend of Thos R Neale, Jas Neale, Saml C Neale, & Joshua R Neale, vs Cynthia B Mason, Louisa Mason, Serena Mason, Helen Mason, Thos H Mason, Martha Ferguson, Martha Nugent, Richd Nugent, Mary Nugent, & Emma Nugent. The object of this bill is to procure a sale & distribution of the proceeds, thereof, under the direction of this Court, of the real estate of Jos Mason, deceased. Jos Mason, late of Wash Co, D C, died intestate, seized in fee simple of the land & premises in D C, described as follows: part of lot 127 in Beall's addition to Gtwn; lot 17 in square 77; lots 17 thru 20, & part of lot 5 in square 73; & left surviving him his wife, Cynthia B Mason, & 6 children, all of full age, viz: Rachel E Mason, Louisa Mason, Serena Mason, Helen Mason, Thos Mason, & Martha Ferguson, who intermarried with one Jas Ferguson, now deceased, & 8 grandchildren, all infants under the age of 21 years, viz: Thos R Neale, Jas Neale, Saml C Neale, & Joshua R Neale, children of Mary Neale, late Mason, whose father is also dead, & Martha Nugent, Richd Nugent, Mary Nugent, & Emma Nugent, children of Matilda Nugent, late Mason, widow of Eli Nugent, both of whom are dead, all born in lawful wedlock. That the personal estate left by said Jos Mason, intestate, was so small that no administration was ever had upon it, & the only improved parts of the above real estate are lot 18 in square 73, & part of lot 127, in Beall's addition to Gtwn; that the residue is entirely unproductive, & the whole of said real estate, excepting said part of lot 127, has been sold at least once for taxes, & although every effort has been made it has never been & will never be redeemed while it remains in its present unproductive condition. The bill further states that the estate is indebted to Fred'k & Wm Bates in the sum of 114.68, or thereabouts. That said Rachel Mason has been appointed guardian of said Thos R, Saml C, Jas, & Joshua R Neale, who are entitled by descent to their mother's share of said property, an undivided one-eighth part. None of the heirs of said Jos Mason are willing or able to pay the said taxes, & by reason of the infancy of some of them, & outstanding tax-titles to parts of said property, they cannnot sell it, & it is in danger of being lost. All the adult heirs desire to have it sold, & the cmplnt says a sale of part of it may & will release the whole of its burdens; that said infants, Richd Nugent & Mary Nugent, reside in Centre Co, Pa, & that it will be for the benefit of all the parties interested to sell the said property & distribute the proceeds of such sale under the direction of said Court. Richd & Mary Nugent are to appear in this Court on or before the 3rd Mon of Oct next. –Wm M Merrick –Jno A Smith, clerk

TUE JUN 12, 1860
Holston Springs for sale: the partnership being dissolved. Public auction on Feb 13 next. The property lies on Holston river, North Fork, in Scott Co, Va, 26 miles west of Bristol; consists of about 200 acres of river & upland; brick hotel, cottages & numerous out bldgs. Apply to Wm D Jones, *Holston Springs*, or to Thos B Bailey, Swannanoa, Buncombe Co, N C.

Stock & fixtures of Family Grocery Store at public auction on Jul 19, at the store of H H Voss, Pa ave & 10th sts. -Jas C McGuire & Co, aucts

The Cincinnati papers of Friday contain the particulars of the assassination of H S Crawley, Prof of Mount Auburn Female Seminary, by four rowdies. On Thu, with 2 young ladies, they were on their way from a concert to their residence at Mount Auburn. The young ladies were grossly insulted by a party of 4 men. Mr Crawley turned at the outrage & was stabbed to the heart. The deceased was 32 years of age & a resident of Cincinnati for 5 years. He was the assistant principal teacher there. His murderers escaped.

For sale: 5 acres of wood land, suitable for a country seat. The subscriber, as atty for Mr Chas C Callan, offers this beautiful site on Piney Branch road. If not disposed of by Jun 19th, it will be sold at public auction by J C McGuire & Co, aucts, at 6 o'clock P M. –Wm S Holliday, 324 Pa ave

The subscriber is desirous to employ a Governess in his family, a lady qualified to teach the usual English branches, French & Music. A lady attached to the Protestant Episcopal Church preferred. –M F Goldsborough, near Easton, Talbot Co, Md.

Circuit Court of D C–in Equity, No 1,426. Branch Jordan against Wm G Palmer & Wm Towers, adms, Eliza P Towers, widow, & Jos B Towers, Mary A Towers, Walter L Towers, Laura J Towers, & Wm P Towers, heirs of John T Towers. The trustee's acount & the distribution of the funds will be stated in my ofc, City Hall, Wash, on Jul 3. –W Redin, auditor

Senate: 1-Ptn from Mrs Eliza Plympton, widow of the late Col Jos Plympton, U S army, asking to be allowed a pension: referred. 2-Cmte on Public Lands: bill for the relief of Robt Johnston: recommended its passage. 3-Cmte on Private Land Claims: bill for the relief of Josiah Atkinson, of Ohio: recommended its passage. Same cmte: bill for the relief of Francis Laventure & Pierre Grignon: passed. 4-Cmte on Pensions: bill for the relief of Mrs Eliza Merchant, widow of the late 1st Lt & Brvt Capt Chas G Merchant, of the U S army, reported it with an amendment. Same cmte: asked to be discharged from further consideration of the House bill for the relief of Eliz Smith, of Coffee Co, Tenn, & that it be referred to the Cmte on Public Lands. Same cmte: adverse report on the ptn of Jethro S Smith, asking to be allowed a pension from the time of his discharge to that at which his pension commenced. 5-Cmte on Naval Affairs: adverse report on the memorial of Wm B Boggs, a purser in the navy, asking to be allowed additional pay during the time he was attached to the exploring expedition & survey of the China Seas. 6-Cmte on the Post Ofc & Post Roads: bill for the relief of John Y Sewell: recommended its passage. 7-Cmte on Pensions: recommended the passage of: pension to Sarah Blackwell; to Adriene Rich, of Habersham Co, Ga; to Asa Wells; invalid pension to Chas Appleton; & invalid pension to Jas C Myers. 8-Cmte on Finance: bill for the relief of Henry Rice. 9-Cmte on Naval Affairs: adverse report on the memorial of Surgeon Wm Maxwell Wood.

Died: on Jun 11, in Wash City, Wm Flaherty, aged 46 years. His funeral will take place from his late residence, G st, between 3rd & 4th sts, on Jun 13 at 4 P M.

Died: on Jun 11, George, youngest child of Surgeon George Clymer, U S Navy, aged 22 months. His funeral will take place from the residence of Cmdor Shubrick today at 5 o'clock.

WED JUN 13, 1860
The Northampton [Mass] Free Press reports a suit brought in the Superior Court by Lydia French against Lucius W Stone, for breach of promise of marriage, damages being laid at $10,000. The trial was last week. The parties became engaged 5 years ago. The engagement was broken off by a letter on the part of Mr Stone, in Jan, 1859, on the plea of financial difficulties & bodily infirmity. These did not prevent him from marrying another young lady in Sept of 1859. The jury returned a verdict of $1,800 damages for the plntf, which she afterwards compromised for $1,245.

Some years since Lewis Washington, a descendant of the General, presented to the State of Va the lot of land in Westmoreland Co on which stood the house in which the <u>Father of his Country</u> first saw the light of day. The spot was to have some suitable monument put there by the State. Last week the Govn'r & Sec of State visited the spot. It is proposed to have the ground, about an acre, enclosed, & a road-way made to it. A monument will be put up to designate the spot. A piece of hearthstone of the ancient edifice [perhaps the only remaining relic,] is now in the State Capitol at Richmond.

I will dispose of, at private sale, the celebrated stallion, Black Hawk, which has just completed a successful season. He, with his pedigree, can be seen at my stable at L st & 5th, near the Navy Yard. Being called to Europe, I offer this rare opportunity to any one who may want a first class stallion. –M J Pope

Senate: 1-Cmte on Pensions: bill for the relief of Effisia De May, late a dragoon in the U S army; & granting a pension to Mary Shirecliff, widow of John Shirecliff: recommened their passage. 2-Cmte on Revolutionary Pensions: asked to be discharged from further consideration of the memorial of Oliver Towles, asking the passage of an act providing for the payment of their claim to 7 years' half pay as heirs at law of Capt Oliver Towles, of the 3rd South Carolina Continental Regt: which was agreed to. 3-Cmte on the Post Ofc & Post Roads: bill for the relief of Thos R Livingston; & relief of Geo F Means: recommended their passage.

Desirable farm for sale or rent, containing 550 acres of land in PG Co, Md, on the Potomac river; improved by a fine new brick house & all necessary out-bldgs. Apply to Chas B or Frank W Rozer, Duffield Post Ofc, Chas Co, Md.

Preparations are being made for the funeral of the late Maj Gen Thos S Jesup, U S Army, from the Church of the Epiphany, on G st, at 2 o'clock P M, on Wednesday-today.

Mrd: on Jun 7, at St Paul's Lutheran Church, by Rev J G Butler, Henry Maddin, of Wisc, to Sallie A D Connell, of Wash City.

Mrd: on Jun 11, by Rev C M Butler, Mr John Wilson to Miss Mary Bell, both of Wash.

Mrd: on Jun 12, by Rev Alfred Holmead, Benj Strothier, of Ky, to Frances, youngest daughter of the late Wm McCauley, of Wash City.

Died: on Jun 12, Jas H Lewis, in his 27th year. His funeral is today at 4 o'clock, from the residence of his mother, I st, between 4th & 5th sts.

Died: on Dec 19 last, at Springfield, Ark, Mrs Jane Turner, wife of Col Wm Turner. An exemplary Christian, an affectionate wife, & devoted mother, she leaves her husband & an only son, Capt W S Walker, U S Army, to mourn her loss & cherish her memory.

THU JUN 14, 1860
Household & kitchen furniture at auction on Jun 18, at the residence of W R B Williss, 517 L st, between 9th & 10th sts. -J C McGuire & Co, aucts

The tallest man in the Chicago Convention was Mr Buskirk, of Indiana, measuring six feet & eleven inches.

House of Reps: 1-Cmte on Invalid Pensions: bill for the relief of Amanda Botts; granting an invalid pension to Asa Haskin; bill for the relief of Fred'k L Balcolm. 2-Senate bill for the relief of Mary Pendleton, widow of John Pendleton: & relief of Geo W Sampson: committed. 3-Bill for the relief of Edw Dashu: committed.

Senate: 1-Cmte on Naval Affairs: adverse report on the memorial of Capt Jas Glynn, of the navy, asking remuneration for losses incurred while performing the duties of purser, in addition to those of commanding ofcr. 2-Cmte on Military Affairs: bill for the relief of John C McFerran, U S Army: recommended its passage. 3-Cmte on pensions: bill for the relief of Jas Floyd & that granting a pension to Jane Gates: recommended their passage. Same cmte: adverse report on the memorial of citizens of Iowa, asking that a pension be allowed John Morgan. 4-Cmte of Claims: bill for the relief of Joel M Smith: recommended its passage. Same cmte: bill for the relief of Wm Lyon, late pension agent at Knoxville, Tenn, with an amendment. 5-Cmte on the Post Ofc & Post Roads: adverse report on the House bill for the relief of Jas Hooter.

Funeral services of the late Maj Gen Thos S Jesup were conducted yesterday. The body was conveyed from his late residence, on F st, to the Church of the Epiphany, on G st, the beautiful service of the Episcopal Church performed over by Rev Drs Pyne & Hall, & concluded about 3 o'clock. The Pres & his Cabinet, Diplomatic Corps, many members of Congress, a number of soldiers of the war of 1812 were present. The procession moved towards 15th st, with Gen Wool & aid-de-camp, Assist Adj Gen L Thomas, & Maj Brown, of the U S artl, at its head. About 40 carriages followed, conveying Lt Gen Winfield Scott, general-in-chief of the army, & other ofcrs. The body of the gallant & faithful deceasd ofcr was deposited in the ***Congressional burying ground***

For several years a difficulty has existed in the Capitol extension work in consequence of the supposition that monoliths could not be obtained from any of the marble quarries in the U S, & the law required that they should be of native material. Mr John F Connolly, of Balt, was awarded a contract by the Sec of War to furnish 100 monolithic columns, & he has begun the work at the Beaver Dam quarry, near Cockeyville, in Balt Co. Each column weighs 23 tons, or 46,000 pounds. A railroad has been constructed from the quarry to connect with the track of the Northern Central railway at Cockeysville, on which they will be transported. Thus far Mr Connolly has been successful in getting out the columns, but a considerable time will yet be required before the whole number will be completed. -Balt Sun

Died: on Jun 12, in Smyrna, Dela, Sarah Corbit, wife of Presley Spruance, aged 65 years.

FRI JUN 15, 1860
Senate: 1-Ptn from W W Richmond, asking compensation for his services as Sec of Legation at Brussels from 1853 to 1856. 2-Cmte on Pensions: bill granting a pension to Adeline Caddis, with an amendment. Same cmte: bills-recommended their passage-increase of pension to Jas Dunning; invalid pension to Saml Hamilton; pension to Richd M Haden; & bill for the relief of Eunic Cobb, with an amendment. Same cmte: recommendation that they do not pass: pention to John Jackson; invalid pension to Chauncey Hoyt, of Chenango Co, N Y; & invalid pension to Thos Glascow. 3-Cmte on Military Affairs: bill for the relief of Mark W Izard: recommending its passage. 4-Cmte on the Judiciary: asked to be discharged from further consideration of memorial of Mary E Whicker, admx of Stephen Whicker: which was agreed to. Same cmte: asked to be discharged from further consideration of the memorial of Isaac Lilly for remuneration for loss of a vessel unjustly seized & sold under the erroneous pretence that timber on board had been cut from lands belonging to the Gov't: which was agreed to. 5-Bill for the relief of Miss Charlotte Hays: referred to the Cmte on Pensions.

The Members of the Bar of Adams Co, Miss, announce the death of their venerable brother, Hon Edw Turner. –Jas Carson, jr, Chairman -Chas A Pipes, Sec [No death date given-current item.]

Dreadful fall. About 5 o'clock yesterday, Christopher Connor, an artisan employed on the iron work of the dome of the Capitol, accidentally fell from a part of the work to a distance of about 30 feet, thereby fracturing his skull in a shocking manner. He was taken to the Infirmary, but at 10 o'clock last night there were few hopes of his surviving. He is about 28 years of age, unmarried, & came here from New York.

Arrest of Swindler. Detective Hicks arrested Josiah Austin Gee, alias Austin Ghee, on Jun 10, who has been doing business in Charleston for about a month as the firm of Ghee, Willson & Co, or Wilson & Co, bankers & agents for loaning money on behalf of different British banks. He is unquestionably an accomplished cracksman. -Charleston Mercury

Orphans Court of Wash Co, D C, Jun 12, 1860. In the case of Seraphim Masi, adm of Bernard Brien, deceased, the administrator & Court have appointed Jul 7 next, for the final settlement of the personal estate of the said deceased, of the assets in hand. -Ed Roach, Reg/o wills

SAT JUN 16, 1860
Senate: 1-Bill for the relief of Mary Preston, widow of Geo Preston, & the bill was about to be passed, when Mr Toombs called for the reading of the report; which was read when Mr Toombs contended that the pension was in direct violation of law. Mr Davis knew the old Sgt well, the husband of the widow about to be placed on the pension roll, a meritorious & excellent, nay, a remarkable man, that had been 36 years in service, & he thought such length of faithful service should entitle his widow to the pension. There was no quorum voting & hence no business could be done. 2-House bills passed: relief of Benj Sayre; & of Joel M Smith. Pention to Martha Sanderson, widow of Winslow F Sanderson.

House of Reps: 1-Bills committed-relief: of Olivia W Cannon; of Laura C Humber; of Thos H Baird, adm; of John Hastings, collector of the port of Pittsburgh; of Asbury Dickins; of the heirs at law of the late Maj Wm S Henry.
2-Bills passed-relief: of John Brannan; of R W Clark; to change the name of the ship **Rockville** to the ship **Massachusetts**; & relief of Solomon Wadsworth.
3-Adverse report on the following cases: ptn of Wm D Latshaw; of Zachariah Jellison; of David Wood, John Michel, Atkinson, Rollins & Co; Aymar & Co; Wolfe & Co; Stanwood & Reed; Saml A Way; J D & M Williams; Udolpho Wolfe; Alfred Atkins; & Geo W Wales, T B Wales & Co. Ptns of Lemuel Balek & others for bounty lands. Ptns of Geo Hazlett, Abel M Butler, heirs of Robt Rigby, Cyrenus Glass, Mary M Davidson, heirs of Adam J Pichard, & Wm S Colquhoun. Senate bill for the relief of Elias Yulee, late receiver of public moneys at Olympia, Wash Territory.

Died: on Jun 15, in Wash City, Mrs Susanna Holmead, wife of Mr Jas B Holmead, in her 63rd year. Her funeral will be on Jun 17 at 3 o'clock P M, from the residence of her afflicted husband, 533 13th st, between B & C sts south, Island.

Murder committed 7 years ago. New Orleans Bee describes the arrest of Valleor Vallot, there, a few days since, for a murder committed in 1853. Among the many wealthy families engaged in rearing & dealing in cattle in the Attakapas district, Lafayette parish, those of Vallot & Ditrez held a prominent place, & for a long time were hostile with each other. On Jun 17, 1853, Sosthene Ditrez, age 20, having found in one of the Vallots, a boy of 16, a rival for the hand of a young lady, slapped him in the face. Valleor, 5 years older than his brother, hearing of the insult, met him in a coffee house & knocked him down with a cane, & the blow was instantly fatal. He fled to Cuba. His wife followed him. In 1859 he returned to the U S & he was arrested at Brookhaven & brought to New Orleans, where he is now in prison.

Tragedy on Friday, at the residence of Mr U G Flowers, of Warren Co, Miss. A few years ago Mr Lafayette Lee was married to Miss Hicks; Lee began to treat her unkindly; a separation took place; on Thu last Mrs Lee wanted to visit her mother. Mr Flowers, a relative, with whom they had been residing, informed her that his carraige was at her service. Lee said she should not go & threatened to kill her. On Friday Mrs Lee sat down to pay a game of chess with Mr Flowers, Mr Lee shot Mrs Lee twice & Mr Flower once. Mr Flowers drew a revolver from his pocket & fired 5 times over his shoulder at Lee. Lee fell & died immediately. Mrs Lee is in a critical condition. The jury of inquest acquitted Mr Flowers.
–Mississippi paper

MON JUN 18, 1860
Valuable farm containing 140 acres, more or less, in PG Co, Md, at auction, on Jun 23, it being the farm formerly belonging to the late Jos Owens, lying on the road leading from the Balt turnpike, between Scaggs' & Brown's White House, to the Point Chapel: improved by a frame dwlg, stable & barn. -A Green, aucts

The death of Maj McMicken, the American Consul at Acapulco, is announced. He served in the Mexican campaign, & was an active participant in most of the battles. He died of yellow fever, which is said to have carried off nearly all the Americans residing in the place. [No death date given-current item.]

Mrd: on Jun 14, in the Church of the Epiphany, by Rev Chas H Hall, John A Pickett, of Va, to Hallie I Randolph, daughter of Wm B Randolph, of Wash City.

Mrd: on Jun 12, in Trinity Church, Wash City, by Rev Harvey Stanley, Dr Richd G Mackubin, of Annapolis, to Miss Mary Virginia, daughter of Marsham Waring, of PG Co, Md.

Died: on Jun 15, Harmon Yerkes, in his 65th year.

Died: on Jun 16, Mrs Margaret Freeman, widow of the late Dr Freeman, of Tenn, in her 44th year. Her funeral will take place from the residence of H F Pritchard, 746 N J ave, today at half-past two o'clock.

Senate: 1-Cmte on Public Bldgs: asked to be discharged from further consideration of the memorial of Jas Harrington, asking to have the benefit of the joint resolution of Aug 18, 1856: which was agreed to. 2-Cmte on Foreign Relations: asked to be discharged from further consideration of the memorial of Wm I Kendall, asking indemnity for property seized & confiscated by the alleged authority of the British Govn't, & for the value of guano on an island claimed under the act of Aug 18, 1856: which was agreed to. Same cmte: in favor of printing 10,000 extra copies of the Report of Majors Mordecai & Delafield on the Crimean war: which was agreed to. 3-Bill granting a pension to Jas Alexander: passed. 4-Bill for the relief of Anton L C Portman: passed. 5-Bill for the relief of J R Crump: passed. 6-Passed-resolution for the restoration of Lt Augustus S Baldwin to the active list from the leave of absence list of the navy. 7-Bill for the relief of Thos R Livingston: passed.

Died: on Jun 17, in Wash City, Miss Mary J R Smith. Her funeral will take place this afternoon at 5 o'clock, from the residence of her brother, Mr B P Smith, near the Navy Yard.

Erie, Pa, Jun 15. Hon John Galbraith, ex-member of Congress, & Presiding Judge of the 6th judicial district of Pa, died suddenly at his residence in this city this morning.

TUE JUN 19, 1860
Orphans Court of Wash Co, D C, Jun 16, 1860. In the case of Jane Dowling, admx of Hugh Dowling, deceased, the admx & Court have appointed Jul 10 next, for the final settlement of the personal estate of the said deceased, of the assets in hand. -Ed Roach, Reg/o wills

List of newly appointed Midshipmen: late graduates at the Naval Academy, in order of merit, who received their warrants yesterday:

M S Stuyvesant	J L Tayloe	I L Harrison
A D Wharton	H B Robinson	J L Hoole
J D Maron	A R McNair	S B Paddock
J O Kane	W H Barton	F L Hoge
S P Gillett	F S Brown	S Casey
T L Swann	H H Manley	E G Read
S D Ames	W Whitehead	C W Read
T L Dornin	E A Walker	
J C Watson	W S Schley	

-Star

Trustee's sale by decree of the Circuit Court for Montg Co, in Equity, passed in the case of Emory M Beall & others vs Grafton Beall & others, the subscribers, as trustees for the sale of the real estate of Jas Beall, of Jas, late of Montg Co, deceased, will offer at public sale, on the premises of said deceased, near Old Monocacy Chapel, in said county, on Jul 25 next, all the real estate of which said Jas Beall, of Jas, died seized & possessed of in Montg Co. There is about 660 acres of land with a brick dwlg & all necessary out-bldgs. This farm lies in a beautiful valley on the road leading from Barnesvile to Poolesville.
--Richd H Jones, Lemuel L Beall, trustees -Wm B Tabler, auct

John S Hollingshead, Notary Public & Com'r of Deeds. I have for some time desired to resign my commission as justice of the peace, & have done so.

Senate: 1-Cmte on Naval Affairs: adverse report on the memorial of Sarah F Anderson, widow of the late Thos P Anderson, surgeon in the Texas navy, asking for relief. 2-Cmte on Revolutionary Claims: bill for the relief of the heirs of Lot Hall: recommended its passage. Same cmte:asked to be discharged from further consideration of the memorial of Richd S Coxe, adm of Anna Gibson, widow of Col Geo Gibson, for payment of an amount of money claimed to be due her. 3-Bill granting a pension to Ezekiel Jones: passed. 4-Bill for the relief of Alex'r H Randall: passed. 5-Bill for the relief of Henry Rice: passed. 6-Bill for the relief of Fred'k Vincent, adm of Jas Le Caze, surviving partner of Le Caze & Mallet: objection withdrawn: passed.

Criminal Court-Wash-Mon: Grand Jury:

Wm F Bayly, foreman	Jas E Morgan	Jos C Lewis
	Geo Mattingly	Wm W Moore
Wm Orme	Matthew W Galt	John Purdy
Lemuel J Middleton	Chauncey Bester	Thos H Parsons
Chas H Wiltberger	Stanislaus Murray	Nathl M McGregor
Henry M Sweeny	John L Kidwell	Robt C Brooke
Aaron W Miller	Jenkin Thomas	Robt Beale
Benj L Jackson	Adolphus H Pickrell	
Edw C Dyer	Wm Wall	

Petit Jury:

Richd Petit	Warren Lowe	John Scrivener
Jas S Holland	Jas McColgan	Abraham Butler
A Lewis Newton	Jas Espy	John J Joyce
Wm Albert King	John S Waugh	Chas F Wood
Wm H Flood	Columbus Lewis	Jos L Savage
Benj F Moxley	Wm Bond	Benj F Gray
Thos Orme	Terrence Drury	Thos D Larner
John B Turton	Harry W Blunt	A Boyd Brooks
Caleb Buckingham	Valentine Connor	John Messiner
Stewart Smith	John R Minor	Wm Cleary

1-Hugh Atwell, about 19, was convicted for stealing 6 pairs of boots & 1 pair of shoes from Matthias Nolti: sentenced to 2 years in the penitentiary. 2-Edw Johnson was acquitted on a charge of assault & battery on Timothy Connor.

Lost child. Archibald B Zimerman, who goes by the name of Benny, has strayed from the residence of his parents since Thu last, & no tidings of his whereabouts have yet been obtained. He is about 10 years of age, & was dressed when he left home in a cloth cap, white linen jacket, & dark pants. His parents are deeply distressed, & have exhausted every effort to find him. Any information concerning Benny will be most joyfully received by his father, at the firm of M M McGregor & Co, on 7th st, between Louisiana ave & D St, or at the ofc of Justice J H Johnson.

Died: on Jun 10, at the residence of Thos W Wood, in Albemarle Co, Va, Amanda Farrow, youngest daughter of David & Virginia Hansbrough, aged 5 months.

WED JUN 20, 1860
Senate: 1-Ptn from Francis M & Susan Mourks, asking that an appropriation be made to indemnify them for certain losses incurred by the U S bldg a free bridge by where they had established a ferry, under a grant from the Choctaw Council: referred. 2-Communication from Lt R W Meade, U S Navy, in relation to the claim of his father, R W Meade, deceased, setting forth that this claim has been urged upon the Gov't session after session for the last 40 years, originally by his father, who died in 1828, subsequently by heirs who died in 1853, & since by himself, & invoking the action of Congress upon the claim: referred. 3-Cmte on Indian Affaris: bill for the relief of Redich McRay. 4-Bill for the relief of Mary Heisinger de Waldegg, widow of the late Julius Heisinger de Waldegg: referred to the Cmte on Pensions. 5-Bill for the relief of Isaiah Atkins, of Ohio: passed. 6-Bill for the relief of Philip B Holmes & Wm Pedrick: passed. 7-Bill for the relief of Saml Hamilton: Mr Toombs objected.
8-Bill for the relief of Saml B Franklin: passed.

In 1867 a Catholic priest, living at New Orleans, was murdered under circumstance of peculiar atrocity. 12 persons were implicated in the murder, & all were convicted of the crime. Two of the murderers were executed, when the remaining 10 broke out of jail & escaped. Francisco Dominic Mayo, one of the parties convicted, was traced to Texas, eluded the ofcrs, & went to N Y. Capt Seaman, of the 4th precinct, arrested Mayo & the prisoner will be sent back to New Orleans. –N Y paper

As the New Braintree Base Ball Club was playing on Jun 9, one of the players, when about to bat the ball, threw the batstick back so far that he hit the catcher, Mr John Carney, jr, a very severe blow on the forehead. Mr Carney, jr, was carried home & died on Friday. He was a young man much liked.
–Worcester Transcript

Orphans Court of Wash Co, D C. Letters of administration on the personal estate of Margaret Freeman, late of Wash Co, deceased. –V Harbaugh, adm

Mrd: on Jun 19, at the Congress st Church, Gtwn, D C, by Rev David Wilson, Thos S King, [former editor of the San Francisco Bulletin] to Miss Hester Berry, eldest daughter of Peter Berry, of the former place.

Mrd: on Jun 19, by Rev Dr Pyne, Mr John McRoberts, of Chillicothe, Ohio, to Miss Alice R Fleury, of Wash City.

Mrd: on Jun 2, by Rev J Spencer Kennard, Mr Lewis H Young to Miss Fannie Louisa Stanhope, both of D C.

Mrd: on Jun 14, by Rev J Spencer Kennard, Mr Wm H Read to Miss Lydia Ellen Arnold, both of Va.

Died: on Jun 16, at his residence, near Millwood, Clarke Co, Va, Col Jos Tuley, aged about 60 years. His health had been failing for some time. He leaves a doting wife & a large number of relatives & friends to mourn his loss.

Died: on Jun 16, Mrs Lucy Boarman, aged 77 years, consort of the late Dr Geo Boarman, of Chas Co, Md.

THU JUN 21, 1860
Adm's sale, by order of the Orphans Court of D C, excellent household & kitchen furniture at auction on Jun 26, at the late residence of Sarah Smith, deceased, in the brick house, Nos 130 & 132 Pa ave, between 19th & 20th sts. –Thos B Morgan, adm -A Green, aucts

Senate: 1-Bill for the relief of Isaac C Smith, of Syracuse, N Y: reconsidered.

Executor's sale of valuable quarry & other lands on the Potomac river, between the Aqueduct & Little Falls Bridge. On Jun 13, the subscribers, as excs of the last will & testament of the late Wm Easby, will sell a body of valuable Quarry Lots, about 50 acres. –Agnes M Easby, Horatio N Easby, John W Easby, excs
-Jas C McGuire & Co, aucts

At New Orleans, on Friday last, the extreme penalty of the law was inflicted upon police ofcr Mathew Hughes, who shot Henry Hyams, in that city, on Nov 8 last, at the door-step of Hymans' boarding houese. Hughes, at the time of the murder, was laboring under liquor, & with Geo Wolfe, sought difficulty with Hyams. A quarrel occurred & as Hyams turned to run into his house, he was shot in the back by Hughes, & fell dead. He was a native of New Orleans, 27 years of age.

Died: on Jun 20, in Wash City, Mrs Sarah Alsten, in her 57th year. Her funeral is today at 12 o'clock, from the Wash Infirmary. Her friends, & those of her brother, Geo W Bray, are respectfully requested to attend.

Died: on Jun 20, in Wash City, William Joseph, aged 9 months, only son of Joseph A & Virginia Burch.

Obit-died: on Sat last, at his residence in Phil, in his 88th year, venerable John Binns. He was born on Dec 22, 1772, in the city of Dublin, Ireland, & sympathizing warmly with the liberal party of his native country & of England, he became connected with revolutionary movements which led to his arrest at Birmingham on the charge of high treason. He was confined for nearly 2 years. In 1801, soon after his release, he embarked at Liverpool for Balt, & proceeded to Northumberland, Pa, where in 1802 he commeced the publication of the Republican Argus. In 1807 he commenced the publication in Phil of the Democratic Press. In 1824 Mr Binns earnestly opposed the election of Gen Jackson to the Presidency, & supported John Quincy Adams. The popularity of the former was so great that many of the reader of the Democratic Press withdrew their patronage, & the prosperity of the journal rapidly dwindled away.
-Phil papers

FRI JUN 22, 1860
The Supreme Court of N Y on Monday last confirmed the judgment of the referee in the case of Agnes Kidder vs Walker Kidder, annulling the marriage of the parties upon the ground of fraud on the part of the dfndnt. The parties were married in July last, the girl was 14, & the dfndnt 21. She was the daughter of a wealthy ship owner, & the dfndnt a waiter in a dining saloon. He induced to perform the marriage ceremony after he had put a narcotic on a handkerchief, & told her it was cologne.

Mrs Martin, of Monroe, Green Co, Wis, was killed by lightning on Mon. The bolt entered through the window, breaking several panes of glass, & killing her instantly.

Executor's sale of improved & unimproved real estate. The undersigned, excs of the last will & testament of Wm Easby, deceased, in conformity with the directions in said will, under decree of the Circuit Court of D C, in Chancery, No 1,066, wherein Agnes M Easby is cmplnt, seeking an admeasurement of dower & other relief in equity, & Horatio N Easby, & John W Easby, Henry King & Marian, his wife, Cecilia J Hyde, Wm R Smith & Wilhelmina, his wife dfndnts, will proceed to sell at auction, on Jul 17, numerous parts of parcels of real estate in Wash City. -Horatio N Easby, John W Easby, Agnes M Easby, excs
-Jas C McGuire & Co, aucts

Hon John Schwartz, a Rep from Pa, died last night at age 67 years. The House will attend his funeral tomorrow morning at 6 o'clock.

House of Reps: 1-The House concurred in certain amendments of the Senate to sundry House bills, among them the following-relief: of Cassius M Clay; of the heirs & legal reps of Chas H Mason; of David Waldo; of Sylvester Gray, a free man of color, to confirm a pre-emption claim; relief of Lt Wm A Winder; of Arthur Edwards & his associates; of Mary Preston, widow of Geo Preston; of Wm Nelson; of E G Squires, of N Y-gives him about $9,000, or two outfits, as former Minister to Central America. Also: increase pension to Wm G Bernard, late a soldier in the army;

In all probability the breach of promise case between Miss Carstang & Mr Shaw has been brought to an end. Last Thu Judge Rebee overruled the motion for a new trial, & an appeal to the Supreme Court is the only course left for the plntf.

Criminal Court-Wash-Thu. 1-Jos Fugitt, about 16, was put on tiral on a charge of setting fire to the stable of Chas H Brown, on Mar 24 last. The evidence for the prosecution appearing to be insufficient, the District Atty entered a nol prosequi. 2-Henry Turner was charged with larceny in feloniously obtaining from A H Crozier, at one of out hotels, a $100 note of the Bank of Va under pretence of giving gold for it & then pretending the note was counterfeit. Trial postponed to Monday next.

Carlisle White Sulphur Springs, Cumberland Co, Pa, is now open for visiters. Mr F J Vischer, one of proprietors, will give information of the same at Brown's Hotel on Jun 21 & 22.

Information wanted of John Clark, an iron moulder & bricklayer by trade, about 26 years of age. He was in Phil 18 months ago at Mr Savory's Iron Foundry, near the Navy Yard. About 5 years ago he boarded with Mr Randall, an employee in Mr Savory's foundry. Any information respecting his present whereabouts will be thankfully received by his mother, Mrs Ann Clark, 573 L st, between 6th & 7th sts, Wash.

Mrd: on Jun 21, in Wash City, at the parsonage, by Rev Byron Sunderland, Jas F Bayly, of Balt, Md, to Miss Caroline Polkinhorn, of Wash City.

Mrd: on May 10, at St James Church, West River, Md, by Rev M M Dillon, Wm Wade Addison, of Balt, U S District Atty, to Maria, daughter of the late Henry Hall, of the former place.

Balt, Jun 21. A son of Josiah Randall this afternoon made an attack on Mr Montgomery, of Pa, at the corner of Gay & Fayette sts. He struck him in the face with his fist. Mr Montgomery knocked him down; some say he drew a rvolver. He was taken off by his friends; his face covered with blood. This affair has added to the prevalent excitement.

Died: on Jun 21, at his residence in Gtwn, D C, Lewis Carbery, in his 66th year. His funeral will take place from Trinity Church, on Sat, at 10 o'clock.

SAT JUN 23, 1860
House of Reps: 1-The House, under a suspension of the rules, passed numerous bills, among them authorizing the location of certain land warrants, an act for the relief of Wm B Shubrick, a bill for the relief of Wm Sutton, a bill granting an invalid pension to John Pursell, & a bill to confirm certain entries of land in the State of Missouri.

On Wed a fight took place between two intoxicated men on the track of the Hudson River Railroad, near Peekskill. Another person tried to pull the men apart when a train was coming around the curve. The engineer was unable to stop, & is entirely free from blame. Killed were: Henry W Hail, an American, aged 35; Thos Granger, an American, aged 28; & Geo Rawcliffe, an Englishman, aged 22. -N Y Post

Died: on Jun 18, at his residence, near Jeffersonton, Culpeper Co, Va, Dr Peter V Bowen, in his 74th year.

Phil, Jun 22. The steamship **Delaware**, from N Y via Cape May, arrived here with the survivors of the wreck of the steamer **Walker**. List of the missing:

Henry Bread	Robt Wilson	Jas Farren
Timothy Conner	Cornelius Crowe	Geo Price
Jeremian Cozzey	Chas Miller	N G Porter
John M Brown	Geo W Johnson	S J Hudson
Michl McGee	Saml Seger	E Smith
Marquis Boneviento	Peter Conway	John Englison
Jas Patterson	Danl Smith	Wm Taylor
Michl Allman	John Farren	
John Driscoll	Jos Batti	

The ofcrs & 43 men were saved in the boats.

Died: on Jun 22, Wm T Swann, at *Oakville*, near Alexandria, Va, the residence of his brother, Thos W Swann. The deceased was a son of the late W T Swann, a nephew of the late Thos Swann, formerly U S Atty for the District of Columbia, & a grandson of the late Chas Alexander, one of the founders & original proprietors of the city of Alexandria. He had resided for many years in Wash City, where he practiced law, until ill health drew him into retirement. His funeral will take place from the residence of his brother, near Alexandria, on Jun 24 at 2 o'clock.

MON JUN 25, 1860
Died: on Jun 19, at the residence of Dr Chas Duvall, Mary H, aged 28 years, youngest daughter of the late Geo W Duvall, of PG Co, Md.

House of Reps: 1- Bill for the increase of pension to Wm Burns, of Ohio: passed. 2-Bill for the relief of Lt Geo Walton: passed. 3-Bill for the relief of Wm A Linn's estate: passed. 4-Bill granting a pension to Harriet S Wyman, widow of capt Wyman, after debate was passed. 5-Bill for the relief of Eli W Goff: passed.

Died: on Friday last, in her 39th year, Mary Ann, beloved wife of H C McLaughlin. Her funeral will take place from the residence of her husband, 439 F st, between 6th & 7th sts, at 4 o'clock, this afternoon.

Died: on Jun 24, Wm H L Burch, in his 20th year. His funeral is this afternoon, at 4 o'clock, from the residence of his grandmother, 5th & H sts.

Lynchburg, Va, Jun 23. Street affray this afternoon between 2 brothers Hardwickes, of Lynchburg Republican, & Jos & Robt Button, of the Virginian. The Buttons were fired on by the Hardwickes. Jos Button has since died, & Robt is seriously wounded. The Hardwicke brothers are in jail, & the ofcs of both papers are closed.

TUE JUN 26, 1860
Acts passed at the First Session of the 31st Congress:
Relief of: John Dixon; of Anthony Schandler; of Geo F Brott; of the legal reps of Robt H Morris, late postmaster of N Y C; of the legl reps of Chas Porterfield, deceased; of Mary Ett Van Buskirk; of the heirs or legal reps of Francois Guillory; of Brvt Lt Col Martin Burke & Capt Chas S Winder, of the U S Army; of Micajah Hawkes; of Webster S Steele; of John W Taylor & certain other assignees of pre-emption land locations; of Emma A Wood, widow of Maj Geo W F Wood, U S Army; of Smith & Hunt, of Toledo, Ohio; of Andrew E Marshall; of Chas Jas Lanman; of Jas Phelan; of the legal reps of Sylvester Day, late a surgeon in the U S Army; of Peter Rogerson & son, of St John's, Newfoundland, owners of the British brig **Jessie**; of Braxton Bragg & Randall & Gibson; of Israel Johnson; of Mary J Maddox; of Erastus Hutchins; of Beda Hayes, widow of Dudley Hayes, of Granby, Hartford Co, Conn; of Francis Lavonture & Pierre Grignon; of the children & heirs of Alex'r Montgomery; of the widow & other heirs of Wm Higgins, deceased; of Wendell Trout; of Gotleibb Scheere; of Aseneath M Elliott, widow of Capt Edw G Elliott; of John Scott, Hill W House, & Saml O House; of Arthur Edwards & his associates [vetoed.] of the heirs & legal reps of Mark Elisha; of Jeremiah Pendergast; of Tilman Leak; of Richd W Meade; of David D Porter; of Geo B Bacon, late acting purser of the sloop-of-war **Portsmouth**; of Saml A West, Geo McCullough, Hiram McCullough, & Chas Pendergrast; of Ann Scott; of Mrs Jane M McCrabb, widow of the late Capt John W McCrabb, assist quartermaster U S Army; of Geo Stealey; of Mrs Anne M Smith, widow of the late Brvt Maj Gen Persifer F Smith; Mrs Harriet B Macomb, widow of Maj Gen Alex'r Macomb; Mrs Arabella Reilly, widow of Brvt Maj Gen

Bennet Reilly; of Edw N Kent; of Francis Huttman; of Tench Tilghman; of Eliz M Cocke, widow of Maj Jas H Cocke, late marshal of the district of Texas; of Guadalupe Estudillo de Arguello, widow of Santiago E Arguello; of A M Mitchell, late colonel of Ohio volunteers in the Mexican war; of Thos Fillebrown; of Madison Sweetzer; of the surviving grandchildren of Col Wm Thompson, of the Revolutionary army of S C; of Wm B Herrick; of Stewart McGowan; of Valentine Wehrheim; of Angelina C Bowman, widow of Francis L Bowman, late capt U S Army; of Alice Hunt, widow of Thos Hunt; of M C Gritzner; of the legal reps of Chas Pearson, deceased; of Sweeny, Rittenhouse, Fant, & Co; of Mary E Castor; of Saml J Hensley; of Kate D Taylor, widow of the late Brvt Capt Oliver H P Taylor; of the legal reps of Wetonsaw, son of Jas Conner; of Agatha O'Brien, widow of Brvt Maj J P J O'Brien, late of the U S Army; of Wm P Bowhay; of Benj Sayre; of Isaac S Smith, of Syracuse, N Y; of Thos R Livingston; of Joel M Smith; of J R Crump; of Anton L C Portman; of Francis Dainese; of Solomon Wadsworth; of David Myerle; of R W Clark; of John Brannan; of Josiah Atkins, of Ohio; of Chauncey W Fuller; of Eben S Hanscomb; of the legal reps of Chas H Mason; of Margaret Whitehead; of Cassius M Clay; of Hockaday & Liggit-no notice of its approval; of Peay & Ayliffe; of Mrs Anne W Angus, widow of the late Capt Saml Angus, U S Navy; of Saml H Taylor; of Emelie G Jones, excx of Thos P Jones, deceased, & Nancy M Johnson, admx of Walter R Johnson, deceased; of Sylvester Gray; of Sherlock & Shirley; of Wm Nelson; of Wm A Winder, U S Army; of Robt Johnston; of Mary Preston, widow of Geo Preston; of Sheldon McKnight; of Geo P Marsh; of Chas Knap; of R K Doebler; of Isaac S Smith, of Syracuse, N Y; of E Geo Squier, of N Y; of Wm B Shubrick; of Eli W Goff; of Wm A Linn's estate; of Eliz Smith, of Coffee Co, Tenn; of Chas W Brooks, of N Y; of Anson Dart;of Wm Y Hansell, the heirs of W H Underwood & the reps of Saml Rockwell; of Shade Calloway; claim of the legal reps of Sieur de Bonne & of Chavalier de Repentigny to certainland at the Saut Ste Marie, in the State of Michigan. 2-Also: pension to Jas Lacy, of Grainger Co, Ten; to Adelaide Adams, widow of Cmder Geo Adams, U S Navy; to Israel Johnson; to Mary I Harris, widow of Col Thos L Harris, deceased; to Maj John F Hunter; & invalid pension to Binah Wright, of N Y; invalid pension to Nathan Randall; invalid pension to Ezekiel Jones.
3-Resolutions for the relief of: Thos C Ware; of Wm H De Groot; of Henry Woods; of John T Robertson, of Va; of Geo Fisher, late of Fla, deceased; of Cmder H Y Hartstene, U S Navy; A M Fridley, late agent for the Winnebago Indians; & of Stewart McGowan-to correct a clerical error in the act approved May 4, 1860. 4-Restoration of Lt Augustus S Baldwin to the active list of the navy. 5-Compensation to Rev R R Richards, late chaplain to the U S penitentiary in D C. 6-Settlement of the accounts of John R Bartless, late Com'r of the U S to run & mark the boundary line between the U S & Mexico, & for other purposes. 7-Authorizing Capt Wm L Hudson & Joshua R Sands to accept certain testimonials awarded to them by the Gov't of Great Britain. 8-An act to authorize divorces in the District of Columbia & for other purposes.

Senate: 1-Ptn from Jas L Langdon, 2nd Lt in the 1st Artl, asking remuneration for losses incurred while defending Brownsville, in Dec, 1859: referred.

Teacher wanted: the Board of Trustees of Union Academy at Snow Hill, Worcester Co, Md, wish to employ a competent teacher, to fill the place of principal beginning on Sept 24 next. Salary $600. –Geo M Upshur, M D, sec

Loss of the U S steamer **Walker**, under the command of Lt J J Guthrie, had been absent for several months engaged in the work of the coast survey at the South, & was returning to N Y for repairs. She collided with an unknown schnr off Absecom on Monday, & twenty lives were lost. The steamer **Kennebec** arrived at N Y on Friday with 44 of the ofcrs & crew who were saved. The schnr **R G Johnson**, Capt Hudson, picked up the boats & rendered timely & important service.

Criminal Court-Wash-Mon: 1-Wm Hensley was convicted of assault & battery on a man named Walker. 2-Geo W Bray was found guilty for renting a house for disorderly purposes: motion for a new trial.

Mrd: on Jun 19, by Rev A G Carothers, J Seton Johns to Lucy, daughter of Wm S Darrell, of Wash.

Died: on Jun 23, Mrs Eliza Cissel, consort of Thos Cissel, in her 51st year. Her funeral will be from the residence of L F Clark, 418 H st, between 11th & 12th sts, this morning at 10 o'clock.

WED JUN 27, 1860
Extensive sale of fine liquors, wines, cigars, sauces, store fixtures, horse & wagon, on Jul 3, at the store of Hamilton & Leach, a few doors east of the Nat'l Hotel. -John E Leach, surviving partner -J C McGuire & Co, aucts

Hudson M Garland, jr, editor of the Blue Ridge Republican, [Culpeper Courthouse, Va,] died at his residence at that place on Wed last, after a protracted illness. He was a brother of Hon Jas Garland, of Lynchburg, & of Gen John Garland, U S Army. He had been connected with the press of Md & Va for 10 or 12 years, & was a polished & vigorous writer. –Richmond Enquirer

The celebration of the Pioneers of Northern Ohio occurred on Wed, at Newburgh. The Cleveland Plaindealer remarks: among the relics on exhibition is an English oak chest that came over in the ship **Mayflower** with the Pilgrims. This ancient chest is the property of Mrs Kellogg, & it has been in her family for many years. It is still in a good state of preservation.

Halifax, Jun 26. Three days later from Europe. G P R James, the novelist, is dead.

Ex-Mayor Chas M Waterman disappeared; his hat was found on the Second District ferry-boat, & other circumstances connected with his disappearance, leave no doubt that he drowned himself. Bodily suffering & pecuniary difficulties are supposed to have impelled him to commit the act.
-New Orleans Bulletin, 19th.

On Wed last Mr Benj G Fletcher, of Kittery, Me, aged 45, was drowned by falling from his boat. In sight of his home at Kittery Point he took the vessel's boat to visit home. His wife had just come out to meet him, & her eyes were upon him when he fell from the boat & was seen no more. She rushed into the water up to her neck to rescue him, but it was of no avail.

The subscriber has a beautiful farm near Wash for sale or rent: she desires to be absent for some time with her family, & offers the farm on which she now resides. It adjoins the farms of W W Corcoran & Conway Robinson, & the Soldiers' Home: improvement consist of a dwlg house, & numerous out-bldgs.
–Eliz Wood

Obit-from the Tallahassee Sentinel of Jun 18. Died, on Jun 14, in Tallahassee, at the residence of her father, Hon Thos Randall, Mrs Catharine Ann Giddings, the wife of Maj Luther Giddings, of Md. The loss of their mother in early childhood removed for the rest of that period Mrs Giddings & her sisters far away from the father's roof in Florida. Their mother was the daughter of the distinguished Wm Wirt. While still in youth Mrs Giddins was restored to the paternal home in Fla. Her marriage to Maj Giddings, who for several years has resided near Annapolis, Md, soon removed her from out society. Early in the last winter, which she spent with her father's family, symptons of decline excited the alarm of devoted relatives. She was destined to leave a family of lovely daughters motherless in early childhood. –C G E

Obit-died: on Jun 17, Col Jos Tuley, of a disease of the heart, at his residence, in Clark Co, Va. He had just reached home, from a winter's sojourn in Cuba, taking St Louis on his way, at which city he tarried a month with his relatives. Col Tuley had reached his 64th year. He was perhaps the foremost agriculturist of this country. His elegant mansion was enriched by his interesting & noble wife; his farm adjoined the ground of **Greenway Court**, the residence of Lord Fairfax. Born to wealth, he held up perpetually to the youth of Va, by his precepts & example, the dignity & nobility of labor. I write this from his mansion, now wrapped in mourning. –U W

Died: on Jun 23, at Natchez, Miss, Hon Edw Turner, long identified with the history of the State. Successively Atty Gen of the State, Judge of the Superior & Supreme Courts, Chancellor of the State, Judge of the High Court of Errors & Appeals, for a number of years in each station, he retired at age 65. He was subsequently prevailed on to become State Senator for the counties of Franklin & Jefferson, serving 4 years.

THU JUN 28, 1860
Superior rosewood piano-forte, household & kitchen furniture at auction on Jul 2, at the residence of Hon L J Gartrell, 420 F st, between 6th & 7th sts. –Jas C McGuire & Co, aucts

Orphans Court of Wash Co, D C. Letters of administration on the personal estate of Chas H Gordon, late of Wash Co, deceased. –Wm F Downing, adm

Wm H Lyons, son of Jas Lyons, has been elected Judge of the Hustings Court of the city of Richmond, Va, by a handsome plurality over 2 distinguished members of the bar of that city.

Died: on Jun 25, in Wash City, Mrs Eliza Brown, wife of Absalom Brown, in her 31st year. Her funeral will take place this evening at 3 o'clock, from her late residence, on 3rd st, between I & K sts.

Died: on Jun 25, in Wash City, after a lingering illness, Ebenezer S Rodbird, in his 58th year.

Died: on Jun 27, John Henry, infant son of Jacob C & Mary A Gibson, aged 3 months & 27 days. His funeral is this afternoon at 5 o'clock, from the residence of is parents, 6th st, between G & H sts.

Died: on Jun 10, at the residence of Thos W Wood, in Albemarle Co, Va, Amanda Farrow, youngest daughter of David & the late Virginia Hansbrough, aged 5 months.

Died: on Jun 20, in Shepherdstown, Va, of chronic gastritis, John H McEndree, aged 54 years & 3 months.

FRI JUN 29, 1860
Willards' Hotel will be closed on Jul 2 until further notice. –J C & H A Willard

St Louis Democrat of Jun 26. Explosion of the steamer **Ben Lewis**. Mr H H Harrison, of Lexington, Mo, took passage at Memphis for St Louis; on Monday the boat exploded her boiler; I saw the first clerk of the boat, Mr Marshall, coming out of the cabin, scalded & in a bad plight. He jumped overboard to escape the heat, got a hold of one of the stages, & held on until taken off by a skiff. My partner's name, Martin, was saved. Jas Banon, deck-hand, says the boat kept floating & burning for 1½ miles. Frank Neville, age 15, lived in Napoleon, Ark, & took passage at Memphis, to go up to friends in Iowa; the tow boat **Lake Erie** & the steamer **Sunnyside** came along & saved some. My mother saved herself by putting on a life preserver & jumping into the water. The **Ben Lewis** was built by Capt Brierly only 2 years ago at this port. Her value was $40,000, & there is an insurance on her here & in Pittsburgh of $25,000. About 20 are killed or missing, & as many wounded, some who cannot survive.

Geo Philip Rainforth James, novelist, who died recently, was born in Hanover Square, London, in 1801, & went to school to a French emigrant at Greenwich, from whom he early acquired a taste for French literature & history. His first novel, Richlieu, was written in 1827. His last work, published in 1859, is called the Cavaliers. Some 2 months since he was attacked with paralysis. –N Y Post

Criminal Court-Wash-Wed. 1-Richd Merryman was acquitted on a charge of burglariously entering the home of Edmund Riley, on Capitol Hill, in Sep last, & stealing 30 pairs of shoes, valued at $15. Marion Ward was convicted with the same burglary. He was found not guilty of breaking into the store of Maurice McConnel. Marion Ward was again put on trial of highway robbery near the tollgate upon the person of Saml Duley, on Dec 21 last, taking from him the carcasses of 2 hogs, valued at $20: not guilty. Richd Merryman was again brought to trial for burglariously breaking into the store of Mr Wm H Burdine: guilty of grand larceny. John Conner was found guilty of assault & battery on John Shea on Jun 5, by beating his head with a shovel.

Died: on Jun 28, Jas Middleton, in his 84th year. His funeral will take place from the residence of his son, E J Middleton, near this city, this afternoon at 4 o'clock.

Died: on Jun 28, in Wash City, Jas Caden, in his 82nd year. He was born Sep 29, 1778, in the county Monahan, Ireland. For over 40 years he has been a resident of the District of Columbia, chiefly of Wash City. His funeral will be on Jul 1, from his late residence on F st, above 12th, at 2:30 o'clock. The funeral to proceed to St Patrick's Church; from thence to **Mount Olivet Cemetery**.

Died: on Jun 26, at the Convent of the Visitation, Sister Mary Louise, daughter of S Masi, of Wash City.

Died: on Jun 17, at Cape Girardeau, Mo, in her 34th year, Mrs Sophronia Smith Caruthers, wife of Hon Saml Caruthers. She leaves a bereaved husband & children to mourn their loss.

Died: on Jun 25, at the residence of his uncle, W D Clagett, in PG Co, Md, Allen Thos Bowie, late of Maury Co, Tenn, in his 22nd year.

Died: on May 24 last, at Louisville, Ky, Col Henry Crawford, of that city, at an advanced age. The deceased left Jefferson Co, Va, some time in 1816 or 1817, &, after some years' residence in the interior of Ky, removed to Louisville. Col Crawford was a patriot soldier of the war of 1812; was in the campaign of 1812 at Norfolk, & in the battle of Crany Island as Adj of Col & late Gen A T Mason, & remained in service on that station until the close of the war under Col late Judge Richd E Parker, & afterwards under Col late Gen Chas F Mercer. Jefferson Co, Va, Jun 23, 1860

Chicago, Jun 27. The propeller **Kenosha**, of the Collingwood & Chicago line, exploded her boiler off Sheboygan yesterday, instantly killing Curtis Burton, of Cleveland, clerk, & Michl Carey, of Buffalo, 1st engineer. Three deck-hands & the chambermaid were dangerously injured.

SAT JUN 30, 1860
Sunstroke. F G Smith, one of the assist marshals employed in taking the census in the parish of Plaquemines, La, was killed a few days since by a "coup de soleil," while engaged in the discharge of his duties.

Coroner Schirmer held an inquest yesterday at 264 10th st, on the body of Dr Patrick McMenany, who died from burns accidentally received on Sunday last. Mr R W Stires, who occupied a room adjoining, stated that he heard the cry of fire. The engines soon arrived. The deceased was 44 years of age, & a native of Ireland. –N Y Commercial Advertiser

On Jun 27, in Manchester, N H, A L Richardson was instantly killed & Benj Whipple fatally injured by the premature explosion of a cannon.

On May 26, Capt Rufus Shepard, of Granger, Alleghany Co, N Y, in filling a lighted camphene lamp, an explosion occurred, setting his clothes on fire. His wife came to his rescue, got him out of the house, tore off his remaining clothing, & extinguished the flames. He lived only 6 hours after the accident. The house & all its contents were consumed.

Wm Dewall, a farmer, who lived about 3 miles from Lake Hill, in Woodstock, was killed on Thu last. He had been ploughing & when called to dinner by his wife unhitched his horse, threw the traces over its back, & mounted it to ride to the house. One of the traces slipped down, the chain end wound closely around his ankle. His horse became unmanageable & started at full speed, drawing him along on the ground. Mr Dewall's person was torn & crushed to pieces.
–Kingston [Canada] Journal, Jun 23

The terrible drama in the life of Rev Jacob S Harden, of N J, will draw to a close on Jul 6, after he suffers death on the scaffold. He administered poison to his wife on his return to Ramsey, & was giving it to her while sitting on his knee, even during the endearments of an apparently loving wife. He had spread an apple with arsenic for her, & she ate it.

Local News: yesterday John O'Day, Patrick Cooke, & Thos Herney, were engaged on Gtwn Heights, near the residence of Mrs Robinson, in removing a high bank of earth. A mass of earth fell upon them, which pinned them to the places where they stood. O'Day & Cooke received non-life threatening injuries; Herney lived but a short time. Herney bore the character of an honest, industrious man, & leaves a wife & 3 small children

Mrd: on Jun 28, by Rev J Spencer Kennard, Mr Wm T Padgett to Miss Mirantha A Frincks, both of Alexandria, Va.

MON JUL 2, 1860
Household & kitchen furniture at auction on Jul 5, at the residence of Hon Wm Bigler, 426 11th st, between H & I sts. -Jas C McGuire & Co, aucts

A young man called Eugene Pepe, convicted of murder at New Orleans & sentenced to be hung, committed suicide on May 21 by taking strychnine.

From letters recently received it would appear that Mr Erastus L DeForest, who so myseriously disappeared from N Y C on Jan 17, 1857, is still alive & residing in Melbourne, Australia. The letters received from him refer to his financial affairs, & authorizes the collection of the dividends on his stock, which have been regularly drawn, by his father, as administrator, as they fell due. What makes his disappearance the more mysterious is the fact that he left his trunks, containing valuable property, at the hotel.

Rev Timothy E O'Toole, Pastor of St Patrick's, in Wash City, has been appointed by Archbishop Hughes to the Church of the Nativity, in N Y C.

Criminal Court-Wash-Sat. 1-Jas Muntz was convicted of an assault on Wm C Newton: fined $5 & costs. 2-Martin King was found not guilty of stealing live chickens from Mr Wm A Kennedy. 3-Robt Costello was found guilty of assault & battery & fined $5 & costs. 4-John Connor, previously convicted of a violent assault on a man named Shea, was sentenced to 18 months in jail. 5-Wm Butler, colored, was acquitted of stealing several chickens from Bernard McGee, in Gtwn.

Orphans Court of Wash Co, D C. Letters testamentary, with will annexed, on the personal estate of Gen Thos S Jesup, late of U S Army, deceased.
–L Sitgreaves, adm

Mrd: on Jun 27, by Rev A M Randolph, Mr Fayette W Johnston, to Miss Gabriella Johnston, all of Fredericksburg.

Mrd: on Jun 27, in Middleburg, Va, by Rev O A Kinsolving, Geo Lee, of Nashville, Tenn, to Laura F, youngest daughter of Gen A Rogers, of Loudoun.

Died: on Jun 30, at ***Wood Cot***, the residence of her son, Col Wm Henry Daingerfield, in PG Co, Md, at a very advanced age, after a brief illness, Mrs Maria H Daingerfield. Her funeral will take place at 10 o'clock on Jun 2, at St Ignatius Church, 4 miles from Alexandria, on the Marlborough road.

Died: on May 30, Nathaniel Pope, son of N P & E M Causin, aged 2 years. The friends of the family are invited to attend the funeral services this [Monday] afternoon at 6½ o'clock, at the chapel of *Oak Hill Cemetery*, Gtwn.

Died: on Jul 1, in Wash City, after a lingering illness, Martha, wife of Peter Polishly, in her 67th year. Her funeral is Tue morning at 9 o'clock, from her late residence, 345 6th st, between H & I sts.

From Calif: Ex-Senator Haun died at San Francisco on Jun 6 of congestive chills.

TUE JUL 3, 1860
On Friday Nathl Harten expiated on the gallows, at Moundsville, Va, the crime of murdering Melissa Morris, to whom he confessed to have waylaid & thrown into the ravine, where her body was found. A very large crowd was in attendance, & an extra train was run by the Balt & Ohio railorad at that point.

Sale of valuable real estate by order of the Circuit Court of D C, by decree passed on Dec 8, 1859, in the matter of petition of Jacob Filius, late of Wash Co, deceased, on Jul 25: lot 23 in square 282, with improvements; part of lot 1 in square 416; & part of lot 2 in square 416. –Wm H Ward, Jas Y Davis, H B Sweeny, Francis Mohun

Orphans Court of Wash Co, D C. Letters of administration on the personal estate of Jas Thecker, late of Wash Co, deceased. –Mary Ann Thecker, admx

Criminal Court-Wash-Mon. 1-Bernard Donelly, a member of the night watch, convicted of an assault & battery on Danl Stewart: sentenced to 3 months in the county jail & fined $30 & costs. 2-Benj Mortimer, charged with an assault by throwing a stone, submitted his case: sentenced to 6 weeks in jail & fined $5.

Died: on Jun 30, Mrs Kate, wife of Marion Offutt, in her 20th year.

WED JUL 4, 1860
Double murder in N Y on Sat night. Killed while attempting to arrest the assassin, are Mr John Walton, a wealthy distiller, of the firm of Long & Walton, & Mr John Watts Mathews, a railroad contractor, lately residing at 31 Union Pl. Mr Walton resided over a store with his cousin, Mr Richd H Pascall, who acted as his clerk. Mr Walton was shot in the head after passing a man on the street, & died at Bellevue Hospital soon after. Mr Pascall, Mr John Watts Mathews, & others, pursued the murderer, who turned & shot Mathews, in the breast, & he soon died. Mr Walton's life has been repeatedly threatened by a son of his wife's by a prior marriage. From this lady Mr Walton was endeavoring to procure a divorce on the ground that she treated him cruelly & he was afraid to live with her. Her name was Ellen M Russell. Her two sons, by a previous marriage, Chas & Edwin Jefferds, threatened to take Mr Walton's life if he did not stop the suit. Warrants have been issued for the arrest of the two Jeffords. -Courier

Died: on Jul 3, after a long & painful illness, Mrs Laura M Tree, wife of Lambert Tree. Born on Jul 4, 1804, she lacked but one day of having completed 56 years. Her funeral is on Thu at 4 P M, from the residence of her husband, 497 9th st, between D & E sts north.

The copartnership of McGill & Witherow, in the Printing business, will be carried on after this date, Jul 4, 1860. –Thos McGill & J M Witherow

Orphans Court of Wash Co, D C. Letters of administration on the personal estate of Lewis Carbery, late of Wash Co, deceased. –Joshua A Ritchie, Jas L Carbery, adms

Mrd: on Jul 2, by Rev Andrew G Carothers, Mr Levi W McMullen, of Pa, to Miss Cansady W Taylor, of Va.

Died: on Jul 3, in Wash City, John Van Ness Throop, in his 63rd year, after a protracted illness. His funeral is on Jul 5 at 4 o'clock P M, from his late residence.

Died: on Jul 3, in Wash City, Willie L, only child of Henrietta W & Lt Thos Wilson, U S Army, aged 11 months & 21 days. His funeral is today at 11 A M, from the residence of his parents, 580 N J ave, Capitol Hill.

Died: on Jun 27, in Wash City, Melinda Robert, infant daughter of J L & M R Williams.

FRI JUL 6, 1860
Sale of valuable real estate, by order of the Circuit Court of D C, passed on May 6, 1859, in the matter of the petition of the heirs of J A M Duncanson, deceased, we will, on Jul 5 next, sell part of lot 2 in square 374, with a large brick dwlg house & out bldgs; part of lot 2 in square 374; east half of lot 5 in square 374; south half of lot 7 in square 558; half of lot 5 in square 340; & lots 13 thru 15 in square 327. -Wm B Todd, Francis Mohun, Isaac Clark, Jas Towles. Com'rs -A Green, aucts

Chas Jeffords, suspected of the murder of his step-father, Mr John Walton, was arrested on Tue & committed to the Tombs for trial. –N Y World

Chas Goodyear, inventor of the art of vulcanizing india-rubber, died at his residence in N Y on Jul 1. His disease is said to have originated in the severe privations he endured & the anxiety he suffered while trying to introduce his invention to the public. Mr Goodyear was born in New Haven, Conn, Dec 29, 1800. N Y Express

On Jun 28, Patrick Egan, indicted for the murder of his wife, who died on Jun 10, from a brutal beating, was convicted in the First District Court of New Orleans, La, of murder, without qualification.

At the close of the college regatta at New Haven, on Friday, two sail boats were upset by the high winds. Mrs Charlotte M Sperry, of Maine, was drowned. Her body was soon recovered.

The schnr **Andrew Stewart**, of N Y, Capt Abrams, which arrived at Alexandria on Tue, lost two of her crew coming up the river, during a squall. Drowned: Wm Hickman, mate, who came from Somerset Co, Md, & called N Y his home-a single man. The boy, his name unknown, hailed from Long Island.

Died: on Jul 5, in Wash City, after a short illness, John E Law, in his 65th year. His funeral is this morning at 9:30 o'clock, from his residence on E st, between 4½ & 6th sts, Island.

Died: on Jul 4, in Gtwn, Thomas Fisher, infant & beloved son of Thomas & Amanda E Dowling, aged 1 month.

SAT JUL 7, 1860

Any one wishing to possess a souvenir of our late Japanese visitors will find in the stores copies of a most admirable statuette of Prince Sagozaimon, one of the ambassadors, executed by Dr H Stone.

Dog Lost-$5 reward. Lost on Piney Branch rd, a Shepherd's Dog, of black & yellow color. –J Gideon, 468 7th st, opposite the Post Ofc.

Died: on Jul 5, at his residence in Wash City, Mr Rezin Beck, in his 63rd year. His funeral will be on Jul 8 at 3:30 P M, from the Wesley Chapel.

Died: on Jun 27, at his residence in Chillicothe, Ohio, Cadwallader Wallace, aged 70 years.

Died: on Jul 3, at Annapolic, after a painful & lingering illness, Mrs Jane E Hicks, wife of the Govn'r of Md, in her 40th year. [She was an estimable lady, & greatly beloved by all who knew her modest worth-Annapolis Gaz.]

Died: on Jun 26, in Courtney, Grimes Co, Texas, after a short but severe illness, Norman Windsor, M D, in his 26th year, youngest son of Richd Windsor, of Hayfield, Fairfax Co, Va. None knew him but to love him.

Died: on Jul 6, at Aquia Creek, Va, Chas Bingham, infant son of W H & Adele Clagett, aged 9 months & 25 days. His funeral will be on Jul 8 at 3 o'clock P M, from the residence of his parents, 530 H st.

Died: on Jul 4, Richard, infant son of Jas & Eliz M Colegate, aged 3 months.

Tribute of respect to the memory of Chas F Mathews, Gtwn College; we deeply sympathize with his parents. –Wm Beresford Carr, Robt Y Brown, Leon B Michel, John Domas, J Escobarr Y Amendariz; P Warfield Semmes, V Domingues, cmte. Gabriel A Fournet, Chariman -Lassaline P Briant, Sec
+
By the Philonomosian Society of Gtwn College: tribute of respect to the memory of Chas F Mathews. –Chas A Donegan, Oscar Aubert, Emile Tircuit, Cmte on Resoluting, Gtwn College, D C, Jul 1, 1860.

Tribute of respect to Mrs Margaret Freeman, late a Teacher in the Public Schools. The Board has heard with regret of the decease of Mrs Margaret Freeman, for the last 9 years an efficient Teacher in the Third District; what, while we bow with submission to the will of Divine Providence, we deplore her loss to our public schools, & heartily sympathize with her bereaved family & friends.
–Ro Ricketts, Sec of the Public Schools

Belividere, N J, Jul 6. Harden was executed today for the murder of his wife. He made no speech on the scaffold. He made a confession of the crime for which he was to suffer to his brother, which will probably be published.

MON JUL 9, 1860
Death of Jerome Bonaparte, the last of the Bonapartes of the same generation as the great founder of the dynasty; & although inferior to the other brothers in most respects, none of them, except his illustrious brother, has been regarded with such interest by the people of this country. It is to his American marriage & his disgraceful practical denial of it that Jerome Bonaparte owes his notoriety [we know no better word] in the U S. He was born at Ajaccio, Corsica, on Dec 15, 1784, & was 76 at the time of his death. He was 15 years younger than Napoleon I. In Balt he became acquainted with Miss Eliz Patterson, the daughter of a wealthy merchant of that place, & after a short courtship was married to her on Dec 24, Bishop Carroll officiating. The alliance created considerable talk at the time. Young Jerome was 20 years old at the time, & after a year he decided to return to France & inform his brother personally of the marriage. He embarked with his bride in an American ship for Lisbon, whence he hastened to Paris, leaving Madame Bonaparte on the vessel. Of course Napoleon had heard of the alliance, was highly indignant, & his reception of his young brother was anything but cordial. The Emperor issued a decree annulling the marriage, although the Pope, Pius VII, with conscientious heroism, refused to allow a divorce, notwithstanding the threats of the angry Napoleon. Jerome sacrificed his wife & the child she had given birth to in England. Such was the influence Napoleon exercised over the members of his family that at his demand the husband deserted his bride & the father disowned his child. Jerome re-entered the navy, & Madame Bonaparte returned to Balt. They never met again. She lived in dignified retirement in her native city. Her grandson, who graduated at West Point, & is

now an ofcr in the French army, has never been willing to disgrace himself by impeaching the legality of his grandmother's marriage, though tempted in various ways to an extent which no ordinary fortitude could resist. Jerome, after deserting her, married again on Aug 12, 1807, the Princess Frederica Catherina, daughter of the present King of Wurtemberg. His children by his second wife are Prince Napoleon, born in 1823, who married the Princess Clotilde of Sardinia, &, in case of the death of the Prince Imperial, is heir to the throne of France; & the Princess Mathilde, a lady now 41 years old, & the divorced wife of Prince Demidoff. Another son, Jerome Napoleon, born in 1814, died at Florence in 1846.
–N Y Post

Departure of Missionaries for Asia, from Boston, during the last week: Rev S A Rhea & wife, of Tenn; Rev Henry Cobb & wife, of N Y-destined for the mission among the Mountain Nestorians; Rev Benj Labaree, jr, of Middlebury, Vt, & wife, to the Armenian Mission in Persia; Dr Franklin N H Young, destined to the same place; Rev Henry N Cole & wife, & Rev L F Burbank, of N H, & wife, of N Y C, for Betlis, Turkey; Rev Mr Crane, wife, & 3 children, for Constantinople; & Rev Mr Livingston & wife, & Miss White, of Detroit, who return to fields of labor where they have been before.

Hon Henry P Haun, late U S Senator from Calif, died at the residence of his brother, near Marysville, Calif, on Jun 8. He was born in the State of Ky, on Jan 18, 1815; studied law in Lexington, & married in that State; emigrated to Iowa in 1845; & settled in Calif in 1849 in Yuba Co. –Calif paper

Suicide. The Carroll Co [Md] Democrat says that Perry Johnson hung himself in Freedom district last Tue 2 weeks. He became dissatisfied about a distribution of a legacy between him & his brothers, supposing partiality had been shown his younger brother. He had a key suspended on a belt, tied round his waist, which unlocked a chest that contained $3,000, which it seemed he was also troubled how to dispose of.

At the Jul 4th celebration at Pungoteague, Accomac Co, Va, Wm Garrison was killed by the premature discharge of a cannon, & Jas V Hall, Principal of the Seminary, was terribly injured, & is probably dead.

Mrd: on Jul 6, by Rev J Spencer Kennard, Mr Lawrence B White to Miss Eliza Taliaferro, both of Fredericksburg.

Fatal affray a few days ago, at the White Sulphur Springs, in Hamilton Co, Fla, between Col Richd Inge Wynne, a lawyer, who attempted to chastise Dr Curlee with a cane. Wynne died after a sword was run into his body, how many times is not known. –Southern paper

One of the oldest English language papers printed is about to be discontinued: the London Morning Chronicle. It was established in 1770, 18 years before the Times. -Boston Post

Fatal affray in Charleston, S C, on Tue last, between two gentlemen of standing in the community, Robt C Browne & Warren Andrews, over a misunderstanding. They fired at each other, but neither were dangerously wounded. -Courier

On Sat the bodies of Patrick Estrange & Chas Curran, were found lying together at the bottom of a hoistway on the Atlantic dock, Brooklyn. They appeared to have fallen to the bottom of the hoistway while intoxicated, & broke their necks.

Criminal Court-Wash-Sat. 1-Tobias Brown, a white boy, was found guilty of petty larceny with stealing butter & a tin can, valued in all at $4.50, the property of Dr Wm Gunton: sentenced to 1 year in the county jail. 2-The trial of Edmund French was set for today; he died of jaundice that morning; Maj French was a gentleman of middle age; Dr Thos Miller was with Mr French when he died. 3-Chas McVeigh, age 17 years, was convicted of participation in the theft of which Tobias Brown was convicted: sentenced to 1 year in the county jail. 4-Lucinda Bailey was convicted of keeping a disorderly house: sentenced to 1 year in jail.

Died: on Jul 8, in Wash City, Mrs Sophia B Bache, widow of the late Richd Bache, & daughter of the late Hon Alex'r Jas Dallas. Her funeral is on Tue next at 10 o'clock, from her residence.

Died: on Jul 7, at Newburgh, N Y, Mrs Edw A Pollard, aged 20 years, daughter of Geo W Barry, of Wash City. Her funeral is on Tue at 10 o'clock, from the Church of the Epiphany.

St Louis, Mo. Jul 7. A new 4 story bldg in that city, owned & occupied by Nooe, McCord & Co, wholesale grocers, fell yesterday, crushing a frame bldg adjoining, occupied by 3 families. Killed instantly were Mrs Boyce & 3 children, Mr & Mrs Cogswell, & 4 others, whose names are unknown. [Jul 13th newspaper: Mr Harburger, his wife, 2 children, & a servant girl were taken out dead; the family of Mr Boyce, 6 persons, were all, with the exception of Mr Boyce, & his son-in-law, Mr Cogswell, taken out of the ruins dead; Mr Boyce is seriously injured & not expected to live; Mr Cogswell is bruised. –The West]

TUE JUL 10, 1860
The vessel **Spring Hill** is now the vessel **United States**. Dr Hayes & his company of Artic explorers sailed from Boston on Sat, & the departure of his vessel, formerly called the **Spring Hill**, but now changed to the **United States**, was honored with a salute by order of Maj Lincoln. They had a farewell, with speeches by Gov Banks, Hon Edw Everett, Dr Hayes, Prof Felton, Prof Agassiz, & others.

Trustee's sale on Aug 13 next, of very valuable brick house & lot, corner of C & 3rd sts, at auction: by deed of trust to Andrew Wylie & Wm T Swann, dated Jul 7, 1857, recorded in the Clerk's ofc of the Circuit Court of D C in Liber J A S No 145, folios 393, etc: sale of lot 36 in reservation 10, in Wash City. Subject to the widow's dower in the same as reserved in the deed of trust aforesaid.
–Andrew Wylie, surviving trustee -A Green, aucts

Sale of two story frame house & lot at 4½ & G sts, Island, at auction, on Aug 2, 1860: part of lot 10 in square 539, with house. –Sarah M Anderson, devisee under the will of Jos T Evans. -A Green, aucts

Mrd: on Jul 2, at St Peter's Church, by Rev Fr Knight, Jas Beacham, of Balt, to Mrs Mary J Clements, eldest daughter of the late N L Adams, of Wash City.

Died: on Jul 7, Joseph Parker Norris, infant son of Dr P J & Caroline N Horwitz.

WED JUL 11, 1860

The Annual Commencement of **Gtwn College** took place yesterday: Addresses were by Henry L McCullough; Alphonse Rost; Robt C McRee; Henry W Clagett; Robt Y Brown; Jos P Orme; Jas H Dooley; Tallmadge A Lambert; John F Marion; Jas F Hoban; Augustine W Neale; & Henry Bawtree.

Degree of A B was conferred on:
- Rev Alphonsus Heimler, O S B, Pa
- Emile Rost, Louisiana
- Edmund P Zane, Va
- Wm A Choice, S C
- Jas D Dougherty, Pa
- Jas M McLeod, D C
- Michl W Baby, Canada
- Jeremiah Cleveland, S C
- Thos B King, D C
- Dr Reuben Cleary, D C
- Chas A Hoyt, N Y
- Nicholas S Hill, Md
- Wm I Hill, Md
- Wm Duncan, Ala
- John H Dooley, Va
- Robt Y Brown, Miss
- John Kidwell, D C
- Alphonse Rost, Louisiana
- Augustine W Neale, Md
- Jas F Hoban, D C
- J Escobar, Mexico
- Mich R Strong, Pa
- Augustus Wilson, Md
- Anatole Landry, Louisiana
- Henry W Clagett, Md
- Louis A Buard, Louisiana
- Placide Bossier, Louisiana
- Paul Bossier, Louisiana
- Jas F McLaughlin, Va
- P Warfield Semmes, D C.

The degree of A B was conferred on the following students of the College of the Holy Cross, Worcester, Mass: Raymond J Hill, Calif; Lawrence Kenny, Mass; & Wm A M Walker, S C.

Queen Victoria gave a State Ball at Buckingham Palace, on Jun 22. Among the Americans present were Mr Dallas, Mrs Dallas, & the Misses Dallas, Mr & Mrs John Bigelow, Miss Grinnell, Mr Robt C Winthrop, Mr Wm Everett, Mr Wm C Rives, jr, Maj S G Barnard, Mr Wm B Lawrence, Miss Lawrence, Miss Cornelia Lawrence, Mr & Mrs Butterfield, & Miss F Lyman.

Mr Edmond Armant, a gentleman of one of the oldest families in Louisiana, committed suicide this morning by cutting his throat with a pocket knife. He was a bachelor in affluent circumstances & had a great many friends. He had been suffering for some time past from ophthalmia, & was fast losing his sight.
–New Orleans Picayune, of Jul 3, 1860.

Two little daughters of Mr Abraham Crofts, of Cedar Hill, Dutchess Co, N Y, were drowned on Sat, when they ventured out too far in the water.

On Wed near Sandtuck, S C, Mr Busby was walking with his wife, when he was attacked & shot by a man named Jeter, & instantly killed. Jeter has not yet been captured. –Charleston paper

Orphans Court of Wash Co, D C. Letters of administration on the personal estate of Lucia R Berry, late of Wash Co, deceased. –Barbara E Hume, admx

Died: on Jul 10, at **Spring Vale**, Fairfax Co, Va, Frances Charlotte, aged 1 year & 9 months, only daughter of Emily M & Wm B Webb, of Wash City.

THU JUL 12, 1860
Adm's sale of household & kitchen furniture at auction on Jul 14, by order of the Orphans Court of D C., the personal effects of Margaret Freeman, deceased, in front of A Green's store, 526 7th st. –V Harbaugh, adm -A Green, aucts

Information wanted. The Gentleman [Dr Boyd by name,] who was on board the N Y & Phil train, on his way to Ky, on Oct 11, 1859, & who gave a prescription for abscess in the head to Rev T G Haughton, will please send his P O address to him, at Salisbury, N C, as the information will be of very great importance to him.

Valuable farm, **Happy Home**, near Beltsville, a private sale: contains 128 acres, 3 roods & 8 perches; with a comfortable brick dwlg & out-bldgs.
-Jas C McGuire & Co, aucts

Died: on Jul 10, in Wash City, Mrs Catharine S Waters, daughter of the late Raphael Jamison, of Chas Co, Md, & wife of Mr John Waters, of Wash City, in her 62nd year. She bore her lingering sickness with Christian fortitude. Her funeral is on Friday at 10 o'clock, from her late residence on E st, between 10th & 11th sts.

Died: on Jun 25, at the Rectory of All Saints' Parish, in Calvert Co, Md, Eliz Marshall, the beloved wife of Rev Wm Christian, & eldest daughter of Rev Alex M Marbury, M D. She died in the communion of the Catholic Church.

FRI JUL 13, 1860
At Gtwn, Brown Co, Ohio, on Jul 4, Homar Higgins & Robt Glaze were severely wounded by the premature discharge of a cannon. On Jul 7, at a large Douglas meeting at the same place, the same prematurely discharged, instantly killing N J Oussler, & severely wounding A J Baily.

Trustee's sale of part of a tract of land called *Peter's Mill Seat*, in Wash Co, on the Piney Branch Road, being part of the property known as the *Piney Branch Trotting Course*; by 2 deeds of trust, one dated Aug 9, 1858, recorded in Liber J A S, No 159 square 340, of the land records of Wash Co, D C, the other dated May 14, 1859, recorded in Liber J A S, No 177, folios 464: public auction on Aug 7, 1860 of *Peter's Mill Seat*, with spacious well built 2 story frame dwlg-house & out-houses. -R H Laskey, trustee -A Green, aucts

The steamer **Malabar**, Capt Grainger, wrecked on May 22 in Galle harbor, in a sudden squall. Permission granted, Mr Loch, Col Crealock, & others, have the boat ready for launching. Among those on the vessel were the English & French Ministers to China, Lord Elgin, & Baron Gros. The **Malabar** was an iron built ship of 1,080 tons, in 5 compartments.

At Milford, N H, on Tue, Saml Scripture was detected stealing from the ticket master's drawer at the Wilton Railroad depot. His wife, after hearing the news, was soon missing, her bonnet found upon the bank. Her body was recovered in about 20 minutes, but life was extinct. During the excitement Scripture escaped & is at large.

Mrs Senny, of Springfield, troubled with a drunken husband, pitched him into the Connecticut river. He swallowed a small quantity of water, & it acted as a mortal poison. The coroner's jury acquitted her at once of any criminal intent.
-Exchange paper

The New Orleans Delta of Jun 2 gives the particulars of a murder committed there the night before last, when Geo Schwagge was stabbed by John Renk, & died yesterday. Schwagge was setting with his wife, at his door, when Renk approached & exclaimed, "There's one of my wives," alluding to Mrs Schwagge. The husband leaped to his feet, utters an angry word, & slaps the ruffian in the face. Renk drew a bowie knife & plunged it into the side of Schwagge. He lingered some 15 hours & then expired.

Fairfield, Jul 5. Kephart, the murderer of Mrs Jane Willis & her two children, was taken from his cell by some 250 men, who took the feeble old man, black with guilt, from the jail. He is now on his way to his gallows & grave.

Died: on Jul 11, William Henry Wheat, son of Joseph Henry & Eliza J Wheat, in his 28th year. His funeral is today at 4 o'clock P M, at 12th & O sts.

Annual Distribution of Premiums at Gtwn Academy of the Visitation on Wed, in the Odeon. The presentation was by the hand of the Pres of the U S. Miss Lane graced the occasion with her presence. The highest honors in the Senior Circle were conferred on Miss Louisa Walker, of Louisiana; Miss Mary Soulard, of Mo; Miss Emily Warren, of N Y, & Miss Amanda Bush, of Louisiana. The second honors were conferred on: Miss Pauline Seymour, of D C; Miss Emma Malbon, of D C; Miss Mary Nicholson, of Tenn; Miss Isabella Seyfert, of Pa; Miss Marianna McLaughlin, of D C; Miss Nannie Bradley, of Ill; Miss Clara Craig, of Va; & Miss Mattie Cook, of Ga. In the Junior Circle honors were conferred on Miss Josephine Herron, of D C; Miss Lena Kisselstein, of S C; Miss Roberta Seymour, of D C; & Miss Mary Easby Smith, of Ala.

Criminal Court-Wash-Thu. 1-Jos W Whalen was convicted of an aggravated assault on his wife Nancy Whalen. 2-John Campbell was convicted of stealing a clock, valued at $25, from Mr Geo W Utermuehle. 3-Louisa Brown, colored, was found guilty of stealing a silk dress & a half dollar, in all valued at $6. 4-Constantine Edwards was convicted of an assault & battery.

SAT JUL 14, 1860
Trustee's sale of a country seat near Wash City, on Aug 1, by a deed of trust dated Mar 9, 1857, recorded in Liber J A S, No 129, folios 364, of the land records for Wash Co, D C: sale of lot 2 in Geo Taylor's subdivision of a part of a tract of land called *Pleasant Plains*, containing 5 acres, more or less, with a comfortable 2 story square cottage, & out bldgs. It is situated on 7th st. –W H Ward, W G Palmer, trustees -Jas C McGuire & Co, aucts

John Hughes, a wealthy citizen of Glouceser Co, Va, worth $100,000, one of the most honorable & estimable men in the county, committed suicide on Jun 28. It appears that about 2 weeks previous he lost his youngest son, which had a powerful influence on his mind, & he reminded those around him that he did not care to live.

Local Matter: this morning a neckcloth, hat & letter were found tied to the railing of the Long Bridge. The letter was signed with the initials C J B, saying he was weary of life, & had determined to commit suicide. Two gentlemen entered the ofc of Capt Goddard inquiring if he had heard anything of Chas J Burgess, who was missing from his home. Capt Goddard handed him the hat, which he instantly recognized, as having been the property of his son, he being the father of Mr Burgess. Mr Chas J Burgess was aid-de-camp to Gen Wool during the war with Mexico, & was a prisoner for some time, since which he has been laboring under this oppression of mind. His father went to the river in order to have search made for the body. -States
[Jul 16th newspaper: the body of Mr C J Burgess was found yesterday & was buried as soon as measures to that end could be taken.]

Criminal Court-Wash-Fri. 1-Thos Hardeman was found guilty of stealing a ham worth $2 from Mr Pfhegee, butcher: motion for arrest of judgment. 2-Mary Snyder, convicted of a violent assault with an axe on a feeble person, was sentenced to 18 months in jail. 3-Jos Whalen, for assault on his wife, sentenced to pay $7 & cost.

The death of Mr Thos Motley, after a long life of 76 years, is noticed under our death head. He was a native of England, though for many years a resident of the U S.
+
Died: on Jul 13, in The Wash Infirmary, Thos Motley, in his 76th year; born in Bristol, England; belonged to the Society of Friends; was a civil engineer & had given much attention to ship bldg. Gen Sir Chas Passey, late Inspector of Railways in England, pronounced the bridge he built at Bath, over the river Avon, the strongest in the world. His funeral will take place from the Infirmary at 10 o'clock this morning.

Died: on Jul 13, at his residence in PG Co, Md, after a short but painful illness, Mr Richd Young, in his 69th year. He was a native of Wash City, where he was well & favorably known to many of its oldest inhabitants, & had resided in PG for more than 35 years. His funeral is on Sunday next at 10 o'clock.

N Y C, Jul 13. Hicks, the murderer & pirate, was hung today. He died easy, but made no remarks on the scaffold, except to tell the marshal to hang him quick.

MON JUL 16, 1860
Annual distribution of premiums on Jul 11th at the **Academy of the Visitation**, B V M, Gtwn, D C. Distribution by the Pres of the U S assisted by Rev J Early, Pres of Gtwn College. Premiums awarded to:

Louisa Walker, La
Amanda Bush, La
Emily Warren, N Y
Mary Soulard, Mo
Josephine Walker, La
Harriet Butts, Texas
Josephine Hurdle, D C
Mary Forsyth, D C
Pauline Seymour, D C
Emma Malbon, D C
Ida Ryon, S C
Mary Nicholson, Tenn
Sallie Major, D C
Kate Irving, D C
Stella Clark, Ga
Mary Gormley, D C
Helen Clemens, Mo
Mary Kennedy, D C
Irene Chadwick, N J
Mary Kelly, Va
Eugenia Moore, D C
Isabella Seyfert, Pa
Clementine McWilliams, Md
Lucinda Clements, Md
Ella Bass, Miss
Theodora Patterson, Mo
Bettie Hurdle, D C
Clara Craig, Va
Mary Smith, Miss
Nannie Bradley, Ill
Mary Cleary, D C
Mary Leuber, D C
Mariana McLaughlin, D C
Eliz Montgomery, Ark

Mary Jane Cannon, D C
Emma Chapman, Va
Roberta Wright, D C
Jane Barbour, D C
Lena Kisselstein, S C
Lizzie Woolard, D C
Mary Rainey, D C
Mary Payne, D C
Louisa Bush, La
Carrie Kirkwood, D C
Mattie Cook, Ga
Fannie Jones, Miss
Fannie Petit, D C
Mary Keith, Ill
Eliz Cis, D C
Lelia Hassler, D C
Mary Conrad, D C
Mary May, D C
Emma Kidwell, D C
Amelia Ross, D C
Annie Davis, Va
Mary Stake, D C
Xariffa Smith, D C
Margaret Chadwick, N J
Regina Sewall, D C
Elvira Offutt, D C
Imogen Trunnell, D C
Mary Hines, D C
Lizzie Boucher, D C
Susan Jones, Miss
Rose Moran, D C
Mary Walsh, D C
Rachel Gants, D C
Virginia Williams, D C

Mary Guthrie, D C
Mary Boucher, D C
Pauline Rhodier, D C
Virginia Williams, D C
Sallie Batemen, D C
Mary Walsh, D C
Rose Moran, D C
F E Jones, D C
Rachel Gants, D C
Jeannette Clark, D C
Dora Tollman, D C
Annie Stake, D C
Marion Trunnell
Mary Easby Smith, Ala
Julia O'Neale, D C
Bessie Bellenger, S C
Mary Offutt, D C
Margaret Owens, Pa
Mary Waring, Md
Mary Moxley, D C
Virginia Seymour, D C
Margaret Dillon, Ga
Margaret Martin, Md
Agatha O'Neale, D C
Mary Cis, D C
Josephine Herron, D C
Fannie Long, La
Mary Waters, D C
Mary Gorin, Ala
Eugenia Bass, Miss
Ella Dickinson
Bessie Bellenger
Anna Le Comte

No clue has been found of Jos Fugitt who escaped on Friday from the bailiff in charge of him.

Died: on Jul 13, Saml Belden, youngest son of Wm B & Caroline M Chase, aged 16 months.

Died: on Jul 14, at *Cliffburne*, the residence of her mother, near Wash, of consumption, Julia Hobbie, wife of Chas A James, & daughter of the late Hon S R Hobbie, of Wash City.

Calamity at Lake Calhoun, Minn, on Thu, when the following persons drowned: Rev Mr Nichols, pastor of the Congregational Society of Minn, Nancy, his wife, & Henry, their son, aged 13, Mr A Cleveland, brother-in-law of Mr Nichols & Emerette, aged 13, & Ella, aged 11, daughters of Mr Cleveland. But one little boy, aged 2 years, is left of the Nicholas family, while the Cleveland family remaining consists of a bereaved sorrowing wife, & 2 interesting daughters of tender years. The families were visiting on the lake on a picnic excursion, when, owing to the abrupt descent of the water, some 20 feet, as they ventured out & were drowned. On Thu the bodies of Mr Nichols, wife, & son, Mr Cleveland & his 2 daughters, were in appropriate coffins in the parlor of the late residence of Mr Nichols.

Sad case of drowning. A gentleman named Harris & 2 young ladies, cousins of his, were boating on the lower Potomac, when the boat capsized. Mr Harris could have saved himself, but was sacrificed to his efforts to save his cousins. There was a fourth person, a man who had been hired to assist in managing her. He was saved. [Jul 17th newspaper: Mr Grant Harris resided near the shore & purchased a sail-boat in Balt for amusement of himself & friends. His family was visited by Mr Morgan Harris & his 2 sisters, Ursula & Nannie Harris, of Cincinnati, Ohio, all related by family ties. The boat capsized & Grant Harris clung to his niece Ursula, while Morgan Harris grasped his sister Nannie. Ursula, who was rather stout, released her hold on Grant & sunk. Grant & Nannie sunk. Morgan Harris alone remained clinging to the boat & was rescued. Grant Harris was 26, Ursula 21, Nannie 19. This melancholy occurrence spread a gloom over Chas Co such as has not been witnessed for many years.] [Jul 21st newspaper: The bodies of Mrs & the two Misses Harris were recently recovered.]

TUE JUL 17, 1860
London News, Beyroot, Jun 9, 1860. Massacre of Christians at Rashayia, a large Christian settlement at the foot of Mount Hermon: Rashayia had been for some days invested by Druses, & on Jun 5 increased greatly in numbers. A parley took place, & it was agreed on both sides not to fight on condition that the Christians of the place promised not to join the Zhalie Christians. After sunset the Druses changed their mind & assaulted the place. The Christians feld for refuge to the palace in which the regular Turkish soldiers were stationed. The latter shut the gates in their faces, & the Durses had it all their own way. The men were murdered, the women violated, & young children torn to pieces. Of the 2,000 inhabitants of the place, besides refugees from other villages, not twenty are left to tell the tale.

Died: on Jul 15, near York, Pa, Isabella Grace, only daughter of Alex'r & Grace Morrison. Her funeral is Tue afternoon at 4½ o'clock, from the family residence, 317 9th st.

Died: on Jul 16, Mrs Susan Maria Teleford. Her funeral is on Jul 18 at 5 o'clock P M, from the house of her father, Gen Totten, 203 G st.

Funeral services will be performed over the remains of Mr Chas J Burgess, at *Oak Hill Cemetery*, Gtwn, on Jul 17 at 5 o'clock. The friends of the deceased & those of the family are invited to be present.

Health report for Wash City for the month of Jun 1860. Whole number of deaths resported: 69. –Chas F Force, Com'r of Health

Criminal Court-Wash-Mon. 1-Danl Ratcliffe was administered the oath of ofc as Solicitor of the Court of Claims. 2-Asbury Scrivner was found guilty of stealing a watch valued at $50 from Mr Wm M Gouge. The prisoner was recommended to the mercy of the Court on account of his youth & previous good character.

At the recent Commencement of the Female Academy of the Visitation at Fredericktown, we see that a young lady of Wash, Miss Victoria Worster, received the gold medal for success in the senior class, embracing all the language, sciences, & other studies of the senior class in our Universities.

Obit-Died: on Jun 29, at *Greenwood*, John Cooke Green, in his 42nd year; model son of a widowed mother; he was the cherished adviser of talented brothers; as a husband & father his devotion was unequalled; as a legal adviser his many clients will attest his fidelity; a pious mother nourished & instructed him in infancy. On the death of an only sister, he addressed a letter to an absent brother full of religious feeling & conviction. He was a regular attendant upon the house of God, yet he never united himself to the Church. –J M

WED JUL 18, 1860
A monument to the memory of the Maid of Orleans, after the design of the Princess Marie of Orleans, is to be erected by order of the French Emperor near the old bridge of Compeigne, where Joan of Arc was taken prisoner by the English on May 23, 1430.

An article titled "Valuable Relic" is going the rounds of the public papers, describing a snuff-box, given by Charles Second to Sir Wm Pepperell, after the capture of Louisburg. Unfortunately for the story, Charles Second died before Sir Wm Pepperell was born, & at least 60 years before the capture of Louisburg.
–Boston Atlas

Among the late inventions is a clear white glass coffin by John R Cannon. It is made very cheaply, & may be ornamented to any extent. –Austin Gaz

Mrd: on Jul 12, at St Paul's Church, Balt, Md, by Rev Dr Wm Pinkney, of Wash, Wm T Magruder, U S Army, to Mary C, daughter of the late Wm Hamilton, of Balt.

Died: on Jul 17, in his 33rd year, James, son of T O'Donoghue. His funeral is this evening at 5 o'clock, from the residence of his mother, 99 First st, Gtwn, D C.

Died: on Jul 16, at the residence of his father, in Milroy, Mifflin Co, Pa, Mr Jas C Dellett, formerly a resident of Wash City.

Obit-died: on Jun 26, on board the U S ship **Iroquois**, in the Bay of Naples, Lt Thos Truxton Houston, son of John H Houston, of Wash City, in his 29th year. Lt Houston was born & raised in Wash; he was very determined to enter the profession of his grandfather, Cmdor Truxton, & in 1845 was appointed a midshipman in the navy. After a 3 years cruise he returned to the U S & attended the Naval School at Annapolis. Upon examination for promotion, he passed at the head of his class. His young wife & sister were on the way to Naples when they were met at Marseilles by information that he was no more.

THU JUL 19, 1860
Lt Edw F Beale & Fred'k E Kerlin left Chester on Wed last on their way to Calif by the overland route. They will probably go over the wagon-road on the 35th parallel, surveyed & completed by Mr B in order to examine throughly its practical advantages as an emigrant route. It is said to be the best & shortest road now in existence between *Fort Smith* & the Colorado. –Chester [Pa] Republican

Sale of horses, carts & wagons at the auction, on Jul 23, at the stable of John Fletcher, corner of 4th & I sts.

The Newark Mercury of Jul 16 says that on Sat, as Mr Wm Stevens was gunning on the meadows in the vicinity of the Kossuth woods, his dog strayed out into a marshy spot to the right of Oliver st, & commenced barking, causing Mr Stevens to follow him. He found the body of Wm Henry Findlay, who has been lost from his parents since Jul 5. His legs were firmly imbedded above his knees in the marsh & was unable to free himself. The child was 4½ years old & rather large for his age.

Criminal Court-Wash-Wed. 1-Wm Lowe, a youth, was convicted for an assault & battery on Jul 4 on Wm T Ferry, near 10th & L sts: fined $6 & costs.

The British Army List for the month of July records the death of several distinguished ofcrs, viz: Field Marshal-John, Earl of Stafford, G C B, G C H, Col Coldst Gds. Generals-Sir R J Harvey, C B, Col 2nd W I Regt. Lt Generals: Thos Dyneley, C B, Col, Comm Roy, Art; Sir Wm Chalmers, C B, K C H, Col 7th F.

Orphans Court of Wash Co, D C, Jul 17, 1860. In the case of Francis Ballinger, adm of Susan Ballinger, deceased, the administrator & Court have appointed Aug 11 next, for the final settlement of the personal estate of the said deceased, of the assets in hand. -Ed Roach, Reg/o wills

Orphans Court of Wash Co, D C. Letters of administration on the personal estate of Washington Brunner, late of Wash Co, deceased. –F C Brunner, adm

N Y, Jul 18. Six convicts attempted to escape from the Sing Sing prison today. One named John Rham was killed, & Christian Beckstein, the ringleader, who was serving his 7th term in prison, was knocked insensible.

Ogdensburgh, Jul 17, Mr Day, a law student of this place, was accidentally shot through the head by Mr Russell, of Derby, with whom he was in company on a hunting expedition.

FRI JUL 20, 1860
For 2 months past remittances sent to the post ofc at Stittsville, N Y, failed to come to hand. D M Bull, post ofc detective, suspected Wm Owens, the clerk in the ofc. Decoy letters were resorted to, & one containing $33.35 in silver, was found upon Owens when he was searched.

Circuit Court of D C-in Equity, No 1,639. The Pres & Dirs of Gtwn College vs Notley Young, Jos Howard & Sarah Ellen Howard, Washington Young, Louisa Young, Nicholas Young, & Sienna Young, Edw Hurtt, Maria H Hurtt, Eugenia E D Hurtt, Edgar D Hurtt, & Maria E Hurtt, & others. The bill states that Nicholas Young, deceased, in his life time, to wit, on Oct 30, 1809, sold &, by his deed duly recorded among the land records for Wash Co, in said District, attempted to convey the whole of square 438 to the Pres & Dirs of Gtwn College; that at the date of the said deed there was no corporation or body politic by the name of the Pres & Dirs of Gtwn College in whom by law the title to said square of ground could vest by virtue of said deed, & that the title to the same remained in the said Nicholas Young, & by virtue of the residuary clause in his will & testament passed to his residuary legatees, & that he said Notley Young, Jos Howard, Sarah Ellen Howard, Washington Young, Louisa Young, Nicholas Young, Sienna Young, Edw Hurtt, Maria H Hurtt, Eugenia E D Hurtt, Edw T Hurtt, Constantine Hurtt, Edw D Hurtt, & Maria E Hurtt are, by virtue of the said residuary clause in said last will & testament, interested in the said piece of groung, & reside out of D C, & that the said Maria H Hurtt, Eugenia E D Hurtt, Edw T Hurtt, & Constantine Hurtt are minors under the age of 21 years. The bill further states that since the date of the deed aforesaid the institution known as Gtwn College at the time said deed was made, & to which said Nicholas Young, by said deed, intended to convey said square of ground, has become incorporated & capable to take & hold real estate under & by virtue of an act of the Congress of the U S. The object of the bill is to obtain a decree appointing a trustee to convey, by a good & sufficient deed, the said square of ground to the said cmplnts. It is ordered that the above named parties appear in person or by solicitor, on the first Monday of Dec next. –Wm M Merrick, A J -R H Clarke, Solicitor for cmplnt -Jno A Smith, clerk of the Circuit Court

On Jul 11th Wm Chalmers, aged 14 years, residing in N Y, was fatally injured by a revolving circular saw that entered his skull. He died on Monday.

Wheeling Intelligencer of Monday: Alex'r Greenwood, jr, a painter who pursued his trade by boat coasting down the Ohio, was accidentally shot by his wife a few days since, near Gallipolis. She pulled the trigger on a gun that she thought was unloaded, sending the contencts through his heart, killing him instantly.

For sale in Gtwn, that large lot of ground on Bridge st, & adjoining the residence of Mr John Marbury, & opposite that of Mr Geo Poe. Apply to J Carter Marbury, Atty, Masonic Hall.

For rent, a brick house on L st north, No 350. It has 8 rooms, stable, carriage house, & a pump of good water in the yard. Possession given on Aug 1, by applying on the premises to Mr Harry or A Borland, next door.

N Y, Jul 19. The jury in the Walton murder case, before the coroner, returned a verdict that the death of Mr Walton occurred from a pistol shot fired by the hand of Chas Jeffords.

SAT JUL 21, 1860
Col John Johnson, of Cincinnati, now in his 86th year, is probably the oldest Free Mason in America; a member in good standing for 65 years, & sat in the lodge presided over by Washington. He has been a regular subscriber to the Nat'l Intelligencer for 59 years. -Editors

Criminal Court-Wash-Friday. 1-Richd Plummer, colored, was convicted of stealing a wheelbarrow, valued at $3, from Jas Harris: sentenced to 9 months in jail. 2-Mary F Brooks, colored, convicted of stealing a dress from Mrs Julius Baumgarten: sentenced to 10 months in jail.

MON JUL 23, 1860
Commencement Day at **Harvard College** on Wed last. Among the prominent gentlemen present were: Hon S A Douglas; Hon Solomon Parsons, Ill; Hon Mr Horton, Ohio; Dr Peter Parker, Ex-Com'r; Rev Nehemiah Adams, class of 1826; Hon S A Eliot, class of 1817; Rev R M Hodges, class of 1815; Hon Henry Wilson; Hon A H Rice; Hon Anson Burlingame; Rev Dr Newell, class of 1824; Geo Livermore; Rev Thos Worcester, of Boston, class of 1818; Lucius R Page; Hon Danl A White, of Salem, class of 1807; Col Thos Aspinwall, 1804; Dr Jacob Bigelow, 1806; Rev Andrew P Peabody, D D, of Portsmouth, 1826; Dr Nathl B Shurtleff, 1831; & many others in various walks of life. On Thu Cornelius C Felton was inaugurated Pres of Harvard College. Addresses by Gov Banks; Mr Felton; & Rev Dr Osgood, of N Y.

Mr Jos Gales died on Sat last, at *Eckington*, his late residence, near Wash City, in his 75th year. He has been in infirm health for some months past.

Three boys, 11, 10, & 8, sons of Mr McNaughton & Mr Cooney, residing near Stuyvesant, Columbia Co, were drowned in the creek near there on Sat. They had a holyday that afternoon, & went into the creek to bathe.

Died: on Jul 21, Mrs Susan Decatur, in her 84th year, relict of the late Cmdor Stephen Decatur. Her funeral will take place from her late residence, Third & Lincoln sts, this morning at 9:30 o'clock A M.

Died: on Sunday, Ida, only child of Geo A C & Eliza Smith, aged 19 months. Her funeral will take place this morning at 10:30 o'clock, from the residence of the parents, on M st, near Kendall Green.

Died: on Jul 18, Alice, aged 11 months & 18 days, youngest daughter of Jennie C & the late Saml H Young.

TUE JUL 24, 1860
Valuable improved & unimproved property on the Island at auction on Aug 2 next, the residence of the late Peter Cazanove, deceased, it being all of square 233, with a frame cottage dwlg house, & other out-bldgs; bounded by 14th st west, south D & Water sts. Also, lots 1, 7 thru 10 & 15, in square 265, on 13½ & 14th sts. –M E Dangerfield, Residuary Devisee. -A Green, aucts

Stock & fixtures of a Confectionary & Ice Cream Saloon at auction on Jul 27, at the establishment of C M Kugler, 518 Pa ave, between 2nd & 3rd sts.
–Wall & Barnard, aucts

The steamer **Pennsylvania** left Phil on Wed last & stopped at Norfolk & landed all her passengers except Mr Geo D Graham, Mrs Dietz & 4 children-[3 girls & 1 boy, the oldest being 11 years old & the youngest not quite 2 years old,] & Mrs McClung, of Richmond, who was returning from Phil, where she had been on a visit. On Thu the steamer left Norfolk & later Mr Graham heard the cry of fire. Mr Smack, the pilot, Mr Graham, Mrs Deitz's children, Mrs Deitz & Mrs McClung were lowered down on the companion way plank. When the ladies were getting on board, the raft tilted & 3 of the children & the 2 ladies went overboard. The captain jumped in & rescued the 2 ladies. The 3 children disappeared forever. Much credit is due to Capt Teal, of the **Pennsylvania**, & Capt Moore, of the vessel **Curtis Peck**, for their exertions in behalf of the women & children & the other sufferers by the disaster.

Patrick Miles is in confinement for the recent murder of Prof Crowley, an accomplished gentleman lately connected with a prominent literary institution in Cincinnati, who was brutally stabbed in the streets of that city while defending some ladies who were in his charge, at night.

Orphans Court of Wash Co, D C. Letters testamentary on the personal estate of Alfred V Scott, late of Wash Co, deceased. –Wm O Nixon, exc

The funeral of the late Jos Gales will take place at *Eckington* this afternoon at 4 o'clock. The funeral procession will proceed from there to the *Congressional Burying Ground*, where his remains will be interred. Carriages for the conveyance of the pall-bearers to *Eckington* will be in waiting at the door of Mr Seaton, in Wash City, at 3 o'clock.

Fine Culpeper Farm at auction: as excs of John Cook Green, we will sell at public auction, on Sep 20, *Greenwood*, the late residence of Mr Green, containing 900 acres; the dwlg is commodious with out-houses of the most substantial character. Also, 175 acres of a large tract of 507 acres in the *Flat Grounds*, a mile further off.
-Jas W Green, Culpeper C H, Va -Geo Morton, Raccoon Ford, Culpeper Co, Va.

Valuable residence in Prince Edw Co, Va, for sale. The undersigned, intending to remove his negroes to Texas, affers for sale his Plantation, *Poplar Hill*, containing 1,040 acres, situated on both side of Briery Creek. The dwlg is of brick with 9 convenient rooms. Mr Jos Robinson, will, in my absence, show the plantation. My post ofc address is Farmville, Va. [Note: The "undersigned" did not sign his name.]

Died: on Jul 21, at the Kirkwood House, Col Shelden McKnight, of Detroit, aged 53 years.

Died: on Jul 20, at Harmony, Pa, at the residence of his mother, John F Steele, Purser U S Navy, in his 43rd year.

Dissolution of the partnership between John F Gerecke & Wm Gerecke, at 381 Pa ave, by mutual consent-Jul 23, 1860. The business will be continued at the old stand by John F Gerecke. –John F Gerecke, Wm Gerecke

THU JUL 26, 1860
Nathl Harden was hung at Moundsville, Va, on Thu last, for the murder of Miss Melissa Morris. A large crowd witnessed the execution, & no sympathy was evinced for the culprit.

Trustee's sale of highly valuable Farm on the Turnpike, near the village of Bladensburg, on Aug 30, on the premises, by deed of trust dated Apr 4, 1860, recorded in Liber C S M No 3, folios 72, of the land records for PG Co, & Liber J A S, No172, folios 1, of the land records for Wash Co: sale of *Brothers' Fifth Part*, containing 87¼ acres, more or less, with a two story double frame dwlg-house, with necessary out-bldgs. –Thos J Fisher, trustee -Jas C McGuire & Co, aucts

The St Louis Republican mentions the death of Hon Saml Caruthers, formerly a member of Congress from the 7th district of Missouri. [No death date given-current item.]

A small brass cannon has been found at the botton of a deep well of the Castle de Clucy, in France, with the date of 1258 upon it. The date of the invention of the cannon has historically been assigned to the year 1324, 66 years later.

Fire in a dwlg-house on Sat on the extensive farm of Hon A B Conger, in Clarkstown, Rockland Co, N Y, burnt to death John Blackhurst, Thos Long, & 3 other farm hands, whose names are not ascertained.

Died: on Jul 23, in Wash City, Hannah M Hazard, wife of Joel Hines, aged 53 years.

Died: on Jul 13, at his late residence in PG Co, Md, in his 68th year, after a very short but severe illness, Mr Richd Young. He was a kind & indulgent father, affectionate husband, & a thoughtful master.

Died: on Jul 24, Florence, infant daughter of Henry C & Hattie R Windsor, aged 2 months. Her funeral will take place from the residence of her parents, 358 7th st, this evening at 5 o'clock P M.

Orphans Court of Wash Co, D C. Letters testamentary on the personal estate of Euphemia Manning, late of Wash Co, deceased. –Jacob H Manning, exc

Benj Smith, collector, has been appointed by the Orphans Court of Wash Co, D C agent to secure & collect the property of the late Jas O'Donnoghue, of Gtwn D C.

FRI JUL 27, 1860
Com'rs sale of valuable real estate improved: by order of the Circuit Court of D C, dated Dec 12, 1859, passed in the case of Richd Frere for a division of the estate of Jas B Frere, deceased, No 126, the undersigned will offer at public auction, on Aug 2 next, on the premises, the following real estate & improvements, subject to the dower interest of the widow of said Jas B Frere, deceased, being one-third of the rents & profits of the said estate during her life, as prescribed & determined by said order & decree, namely: lot 10 in square 86, of Wash City, with one two story frame house with basement & one two story brick house. The north house & premises will be sold at the cost & expense of the defaulting purchaser. The property fronts on the east side of 20th st, between I & K sts. Title deed to be retained until the whole of the purchase money is paid. –Geo T McGlue, John Henderson, Wm T Smithson, Thos C Donn, Chas Walter, Com'rs -Wall & Barnard, aucts [At the same time & place we will sell all the dower interest & estate of Eliz M Frere, the widow of Jas B Frere, deceased, thus affording at once an entire & absolute title.]

Tragedy in Boundbrook, N J, on Fri, when Coe Lewis, living near Chimney Rock, had an altercation with his wife, & on Sat he found her dead in bed. He had not intended to murder his wife, but was prompted by liquor. He then took his own life by cutting an artery in his arm.

On Jul 12, at the residence of Col John Pope, near Memphis, a melancholy accident occurred which resulted in the death of one of his sons, Leroy, aged about 17 years. Apprehending a visit from negro burglars, Leroy & his elder brother, Andrew, repaired, late at night to the garden with guns, separating shortly afterwards. The dogs made a noise & Andrew fired in the direction of the noise, accidentally shooting Leroy, who expired some time afterward.

I offer my Farm *Airley*, in Fauquier Co, Va, adjacent to Catlett's Station, for sale: contains 1,466 acres; improvements consist of a new convenient commodious dwlg, with the usual out-bldgs. Apply to my atty, Rice W Payne, Warrenton, Va. -C J Stovin, P O Catlett's Station, Fauquier Co, Va.

Local Matters. Rev Henry Clay Westwood, pastor, last Sabbath stated that a member of that Church, lately deceased, had left, among her dying requests, directions that a silver goblet, inlaid with gold, should be presented to that Church, to be used on Sacramental occasions. The pastor presented it to the ofcrs of the Church, whereupon Thos S Morgan, one of the oldest Stewards of the Church, came forward & received it on behalf of the Church. The deceased, Mrs Rhoda O'Neal was for many years a member of the Methodist Church & was one of the first of the Foundry Chapel, that, after the Union Chapel was erected, she removed her relation to the latter station. The inscription on the cup was: "From Rhoda O'Neal to the Union Chapel Church, 1860."

Criminal Court-Wed. 1-Ann Thomas, acquitted of stealing sundry articles from Sydney DeCamp. 2-John Peifer acquitted of malicious mischief. 3-Margaret Griffin acquitted of assault on Margaret Dunivan. 4-Michl Boucher acquitted of assault on Patrick Scanlin. 5-Wm Johnson guilty of assault & battery on Wesley W McNair: sentenced to 4 months in jail. 6-Wm Lomax not guilty of an assault on Ann Dougherty. 7-John Eliason, John Hatcher, & Jos Penny, guilty of an affray only.

Mrd: on Jul 26, in Wash City, at St Paul's Lutheran Parsonage, by Rev J G Butler, John W Brown, of Fairfax, Va, to Annie E O'Neal, of Wash City.

Obit-died: on Jul 23, at their family residence in Wash City, after a brief illness, Mrs Hannah M Hazard, wife of Joel Hinds, in her 53rd year. Mrs Hinds has left behind a heart-stricken family & a wide circle of devoted friends, who, throughout the country where she has at different time resided, will mourn her decease.

Balt, Jul 26. Jas Logan was arrested today charged with being the murderer of Geo Kyle on the last election day. The witnesses fully identified him. [Jul 28th newspaper: Jas Logan was charged with having killed Adam Barklie Kyle, jr, on Nov 2 last, near the 15th ward polls. Mrs Dochterman, to whose house Kyle ran for protection, identified the prisoner.]

Personal Information Wanted. If Jas Winn, of Va, whose sister married Jos Cooper, who resided in Petersburg, Va, & afterwards removed to Memphis, Tenn, where he died a few years since, will be so good as to let his present where-abouts be known he will greatly oblige his niece. –S C Carithers. Address, for the next 30 days, the above at Wash City. Virginia papers will please copy.

SAT JUL 28, 1860
Orphans Court of Wash Co, D C. Letters of administration on the personal estate of Jas W Stewart, late of Wash Co, deceased. –Eliz Stewart, admx

Rev Reuben Lowrie, missionary of the O S Presbyterian Board in China, & son of Rev Walter Lowrie, senior Sec of the Board, died Apr 16, at Shanghai. This is the second son whom the afflicted father has been called by Providence to sacrifice to the cause of Missions in China-the first, Rev Walter M Lowrie, having perished by the hands of pirates in the China Sea in 1847.

Rev Courtland C Van Rensselaer, D D, died at his residence in Burlington, N J, on Jul 24, after an illness of some months. The deceased belonged to the family of Van Rensselaer of Albany, & inherited a good fortune, which he was ever ready to use in good works. Many important enterprises of the Presbyterian [O S] Church owe much to the noble liberality of Dr Van Rensselaer.

Valuable farm at public auction, in compliance with the provisions of the last will & testament of Nicholas J Worthington, deceased, & by order of the Orphans' Court of Anne Arundel Co, the subscribers will offer at public sale, at the Court House door, on Sep 4, the farm, part of the estate known as *Wallace's*, on which the deceased for many years resided. It is on the South River & contains 291 acres; with a comfortable dwlg, tobacco house, & other necessary out-bldgs. Possession will be given on Jan 1 next. -Hester A Worthington, John Ridout, excs

Died: on Jul 26, at the residence of Dr Foley, in Salem, Fauquier Co, Va, Jennie Massie, infant daughter of Rev J C & Jennie M Granberry, aged 9 months & 19 days. Her funeral is this morning at 10 o'clock, from the residence of Mrs Massie, on N st north, between 13th & 14th sts.

MON JUL 30, 1860
Sale of Ladies, Misses, & Children's Boots & Shoes at T Clark & Co's, 16 Market Space, Pa ave, between 8th & 9th sts, on account of T Clark's failing health & to close business: public auction on Jul 31. –T Clark & Co -Jas C McGuire & Co, aucts

Lincoln [Ill] Herald. On Friday a little son of Thos Lindsey stood on his head near 5 minutes, & expired in a few hours, the blood rushing to his brain causing apoplexy.

Mr Victor Thompson, a wealthy druggist of Hagertown, Md, died on Jul 17, & devised [in addition to a large sum to his sisters,] the sum of $20,000 to four Boards of the Old School Presbyterian Church; $5,000 to the Board of Education; $5,000 to the Board of Publication; $5,000 to the Board of Foreign & $5,000 to the Presbyterian congregation of Hagerstown for the enlargement & improvement of its Church edifice; $1,000 to the Charity School of the town; $2,000 to the Mayor & Council of Hagerstown for the purchase of fuel for the poor; $1,000 to his colored servant woman, which at her death is to revert to the town, & be appropriated as the preceding legacy, & $500 for the purchase of *Miller's Spring* for use of the public.

John Dawson was appointed deputy postmaster at Columbus, Ohio, vice Thos Miller, removed.

Rev C W Stonestreet, S J, who has been pastor of St Aloysius Church, in Wash City, ever since its dedication, & Pres of Gonzaga College for some years, has been transferred to Gtwn College. The members of the choir assembled a few evenings ago at the residence of Mrs Cecilia Young, their accomplished leader, to express their high apprecation of the merits & labors of their late pastor. Rev Wm M Clark, formerly of St Ignatius Church, Balt, is assigned to the pastorate of St Aloysius.

Died: on Jul 29, Mrs Anna Cochrane, in her 81st year. Her funeral will be on Jul 31 at 4 o'clock in the afternoon, from her late residence, 250 F st.

Obit-died: on Jul 7, at his residence, near Knoxville, Tenn, Hon Wm B Reese, LL D. He was born in Nov, 1793, in adjoining Jefferson Co, & his whole life had been spent there & at Knoxville, to which place he removed about 1820. He was in his 67th year at the time of his death. His father, Hon Jas Reese, one of the earliest pioneers who settled this region of country, was a lawyer. The son adopted the father's profession. He died in communion with the Protestant Episcopal Church.

Watertown, N Y, Jul 28. A boat containing 5 persons, Mrs S B Priman & child, Mrs J J M Priman, Mrs Jansoleil, & Miss Louisa Beband, went over the Black River Falls at this place this afternoon & all the party were drowned. The body of one of the ladies can be seen hanging upon a rock below the falls. [Aug 4th newspaper: Northern [N Y] Journal of Jul 30: Mrs J J B Primeau, with her $\underline{4}$ year old boy; Mrs Jos J M Primeau, & her mother, Mrs Beasoleil; & Miss Louisa Bibeand, went over the Falls & were drowned. Mrs Jos J M Primeau was a bride of but 3 short weeks, age 17 years. Mrs Beausoleil was the wife of Anthony Beausoleil, & the mother of Mrs Jos J M Primeau, 35 years of age. The little boy was the son of J J B Primeau, & was $\underline{5}$ years of age. Mrs J J B Primeau was the daughter of Mr J Mailliard, of Juhelville, aged 24 years.]

On Tue night, at Portsmouth, N H, Miss Ann Maria Martin, daughter of Mr Thos Martin, died from the effects of a singular wound received on Sat, when a salute was fired from the yacht **Zinga**. The wad of waste cotton struck Miss Martin, broke several steel hoops in her skirt, & then cut a fearful gash across her body. She was taken home, to die with her mother.

TUE JUL 31, 1860
Groceries, liquors, & store-fixtures, at auction on Aug 1, at the Grocery Store of Mr Theodore Sheckles, 371 7th st, between I & K sts. –A Green, aucts

Mrd: on Jul 26, at Castle Point, by Rt Rev W H Odenheimer, Hon M R H Garnett, of Va, to Mary P, daughter of E A Stevens, of Hoboken.

Died: on Jul 30, in Wash City, Mrs Susan M Sears, in her 65th year. Her funeral will take place from the residence of her daughter, Mrs Charlotte O Clark, 215 Pa ave, between 14th & 15th sts, this afternoon at 3 o'clock.

Died: on Jul 22, Mrs Mary M White, wife of Saml H White, in her 68th year.

WED AUG 1, 1860
Orphans Court of Wash Co, D C. Letters of administration on the personal estate of Wm Flaherty, late of Wash Co, deceased. –Eliza Flaherty, admx

Mrd: on Jul 24, at the residence of the bride's father, near Clarksville, Ga, by Rev R C Ketchum, Mr Ben F Slocum, of Miss, to Miss Rosa W, daughter of Col John R & Mrs Cordelia St L Stanford.

Died: on Tue, after a painful illness, Mrs Susan C Robinson, aged 23 years, wife of Chas Robinson. Her funeral will take place on Thu at 3 o'clock, from the residence of Mr Jas Steele, on Mass ave, 3 doors from 7th st.

THU AUG 2, 1860
Pre-emptory sale of millinery & straw goods, embroideries, trimmings, laces, & perfumery, on Aug 4, at the store of R C Stevens, 339 Pa ave, between 9th & 10th sts. -J C McGuire & Co, aucts

Wash Corp-Jul 30, 1860. 1-Ptn of Danl Donovan for the remission of a fine: referred to the Cmte of Claims. 2-Ptn of John E Vanskiver for permission to erect a fish-house on Water st, between F & G sts south: referred to the Cmte on Improvements. 3-Cmte on Finance: ptn of S Rush Seibert: laid on the table. 4-Cmte on Police: confirmed the nomination of Saml Hoffman as superintendent of sweeps for the 7th Ward, vice W H Hook, rejected. 5-Cmte of Claims: bill for the relief of A Heitmiller: passed. Same cmte: ptn of Chas Klotz for the remission of a fine: passed. Same cmte: ptn of J M Cohen for the remission of a fine: passed. Same cmte: bill for the relief of Geo McNaughton: reported the same back with an amendment.

FRI AUG 3, 1860
English Nobility 500 years ago. In 1321, Hugh Spencer, head of one of the great families, for some political misbehavior was expelled from the realm, & his property confiscated. On taking inventory of the same, it was found that he possessed, in different parts of England, 59 manors.

The Boston papers announce the death, on Sunday last, in his 83rd year, of Hon Jonathan Phillips, who for nearly 60 years has been prominently & honorable identified with Boston. He was the oldest liiving descendant of Rev Geo Phillips, of Watertown, Mass, the first of the name in America, who came to New England with Govn'r Winthrop in the ship **Arabella**, in June, 1630.

Trustee's sale of improved property on 11th st, between Pa ave & E sts, by deed of trust from Francis Lombardi & wife, dated Mar 29, 1848, recorded in Liber W B No 142, folios 37 et seq, of the land records of Wash Co, D C, being part of lot 6 in square 348, with a 3 story brick house. –N Callan, trustee
-Jas C McGuire & Co, aucts

Dreadful accident yesterday on the farm of Mr Pettis, one mile s w of Tecumseh village, when Mr John Lowe, one of the proprietors of a threshing machine was there threshing wheat. Mr Lowe accidentally fell upon the feeding apron & his left leg was ground off above the knee, & his right foot taken off above the ankle. He died in the night. –Adrian [Mich] Watchtower

At the depot in Fred'k, Md, on Monday, a lad from Wash, about 12, who is on a visit to the family of Mr Geo Mehrling, fell from the platform & the train passed over his foot & ankle, crushing the bones so that amputation is thought to be unvoidable.

Chief Justice Shaw, of the Supreme Court of Mass, has resigned, to take effect from Sep 1st.

Henry Middleton, a young man, gunning in the fields north of Wash City, suffered the loss of 2 forefingers of the left hand, besides an injury to the 3rd finger, when the gun burst at the breech, close to the spot where it was grasped by his left hand.

Criminal Court-Wash-Thu. 1-Chas P Sengstack, jr, was convicted for an assault & battery on John Kane: fined $30 & costs. 2-John Riley was acquitted on a charge of picking the pocket of a man named Malone, from Miss, on Feb 22, but no identification was made of the money in Court.

Mrd: on Jul 30, at St Peter's Church, Peekskill, N Y, by Rev Edmund Roberts, W C Johnson, of Utica, N Y, to Mary C, daughter of the late Maj A A Nicholson, U S Marine Corps.

Concord, N H, Aug 1. Senator Douglas arrived here yesterday & was received with a salute, & a procession escorted him to the Senate House, where he made a speech.

SAT AUG 4, 1860
Hon John S Wells, formerly a Senator in Congress from N H, died at his late residence in Execter on Jul 1.

The copartnership existing under the firm of Elms & Bradley has this day been dissolved by mutual consent, Mr Elms withdrawing, & Mr Bradley assuming all the liabilities thereof. –Jas Elms, Wm A Bradley, jr, Jul 18, 1860.
+
John S Berry & Wm A Bradley, jr, have entered this day into a copartnership to carry on the milling business, at the same Aqueduct Mills, Water st, under the name of Berry & Bradley. -Gtwn, Jul 23, 1860.

Fire broke out yesterday in the stables of Mr Wm C Hazel, on Beale st, Gtwn, & extended to the adjoining stables of Mr Davis, & to the dwlg-house & hotel of Mr Hazel, consuming the whole. The fire is supposed to have originiated from a candle left by some of the negro hostlers who had been playing cards to a late hour.

MON AUG 6, 1860
Jesse Boorn, aged 76 years, was last Wed sentenced by the U S Court at Cleveland to 5 years in the penitentiay for counterfeiting.

Mr Sherman M Booth escaped on Wed last from his prison at Milwaukee, Wisc. He was found guilty of the rescue of a slave from the custody of the U S ofcrs. About 11 o'clock yesterday Brudder Booth was seen to issue from the custom-house, hanging upon the arm of his brother-in-law, T J Salsman, with the butt end of a six shooter occasionally showing. He departed in a carriage, driven rapidly out of the city. Two men, La Grange & Prof Daniels, tendered a fake card bearing the name of the Marshal, which granted them admittance to the room of Booth, & his escape.

A young man named Louis Maude was fatally shot at St Louis, on Monday, on the premises of Mr Albert Becker. Mrs Becker awoke her husband, saying there was a robber about the place. Mr Becker shot outside at a dark object & returned to bed. At daylight the corpse of Maude was found on the sidewalk with a handkerchief full of pears from Becker's trees. The coroner's jury found that the killing was justifiable under the circumstances.

Died: on Aug 4, at the residence of her mother, Mrs E Hall, Mrs Virginia Fellius, in her 20th year. Her funeral is tomorrow at 6 o'clock, at Christ Church, G st, between 7th & 8th sts.

N Y papers: Obit-died: Mrs Joanna Bethune, aged 93 years, the daughter of Dr & Mrs Graham, who was born at what is now called *Fort Niagara*, where he father was a surgeon in the British army, in 1768. After the death of her father in Antigua, in 1779, she returned with her mother to Scotland, & at the suggestion of the mother of Sir Walter Scott, Mrs Graham opened a young ladies' school in Edinburgh, her daughter acting as an assistant. After 10 years' success in her school, Mrs Graham removed to N Y, where in 1789 she re-opened her school under the patronage of Gen Washington, Bishop Moore, & Rev Drs Rodgers & Macon. In Jul, 1795, Joanna Graham was married to the late Rev Divie Bethune. She was the other of two daughters, who became the wives of Rev Drs McCartee & Duffield, & of one son, Rev Dr Geo W Bethune.

Mrd: on Aug 2, at St Aloysius Church, by Rev Fr Maguire, Peter Gallant, of Wash City, to Miss Mary E Murray, of PG Co, Md.

TUE AUG 7, 1860
The Winchester [Va] Republican, now in its 50th year, has changed proprietor & editor. Mr Geo E Senseney, who has conducted it with great ability for 10½ years, has disposed of the paper & good will to Mr John D Ridenour. Mr Senseney has retired. Mr Henry B Beall is the new editor.

Distribution of premiums at St Mary's Female Institute, near Bryanton, Chas Co, Md, Jul 26, 1860. Premiums awarded to:

Anna Surratt, PG Co, Md
Louisa McLean, Wash, D C
Mollie Queen, Chas Co, Md
Martha J Bridget, Wash, D C
Mary J Campbell, Chas Co, Md
Celestia Waring, Chas Co, Md
Lucy Higdon, Chas Co, Md
Martha Purcell, Wash, D C
Annie Berry, PG Co, Md
Estelle Gardiner, Chas Co, Md
Mittie Carrico, Chas Co, Md
Charlotte Reynolds, Wash, D C
Emelie Gartland, Wash, D C
Margaret Sothoron, St Mary's Co, Md
Sallie Keleher, Wash, D C
Ida Jameson, Chas Co, Md
Fannie Lloyd, Chas Co, Md
Fannie Morgan, St Mary's Co
Grace Morgan, St Mary's Co
Ellen Keleher, Wash, D C
Nannie Burch, Chas Co, Md

Orphans Court of Wash Co, D C, Aug 4, 1860. In the case of Francis S Walsh, exc of Susan Evans, deceased, the executor & Court have appointed Aug 28 next, for the final settlement of the personal estate of the said deceased, of the assets in hand. -Ed Roach, Reg/o wills

Criminal Court-Wash-Mon. 1-Jos Fugitt, convicted of horse-stealing, who escaped & was re-captured, was convicted & sentenced to 3 years' hard labor in the penitentiary. 2-John Krouse, of Gtwn, convicted for resisting Constable Donaldson when in the discharge of his duties: sentenced to 4 months in the county jail.

Died: on Aug 3, at Cape May, Eleanor Rozer, daughter of Henry & Henrietta DeC May, of Balt. [Note: DeC copied as written.]

Orphans Court of Wash Co, D C. Letters of administration on the personal estate of Michl Lee, late of Wash Co, deceased. –John Lee, adm

WED AUG 8, 1860
Moses S Beach, for 25 years connected with the N Y Sun, & for several years its principal conductor, has retired from that concern. Mr Wm C Church is the present proprietor.

Mr Obed Hussey, of Balt, the inventor of a successful reaping machine, came to his death on Sat last by falling from a railroad train at Exeter, whilst on his way from Boston to Portland, Maine. He had stepped into the depot to get some refreshments for his children, & when he came out the train had started. He attempted to get to the platform of the car & fell between the cars, the wheels passing over his chest, killing him instantly.

Columbian College, Wash, D C, will open on Sep 26, the Preparatory School on Sep 12. At the establishment of this College, Mr Monroe was the Pres of the U S. -Geo W Samson, D D, President

High School, at Eastwood, Staunton, Va. Mrs Saml Forrest proposes to open on Sep 17, a House School for Young Ladies, limited to 16 pupils. Board & English tuition $200 per annum. Music & French extra.

Orphans Court of Wash Co, D C. Letters testamentary on the personal estate of Dolly Mullen, late of Wash Co, deceased. –Basil Mullen, exc

Died: on Aug 5, Esther Emanuel, infant daughter of Alfred & Eliz A M Gregory.

THU AUG 9, 1860
Fred'k Follett has been appointed by the Pres, Marshal of the Western District of N Y, in place of S B Jewett, removed.

Four boys, two of them sons of Mr G W Blair, & two of them sons of Mr Mitchell, were drowned at Mosinee river, Wis, on Jul 26th, when they got beyond their depth.

Mrd: on Aug 2, in Wash City, by Rev Wm B Edwards, Geo S Roux, of Fernandina, Florida, to M Lizzie, daughter of Judson Mitchell, of Gtwn, D C.

Died: on Aug 5, in Wash City, Sophie M Whitney, wife of Dr H N Wadeworth, aged 35 years.

Died: on Aug 8, at his residence in Wash City, Wilson M C Fairfax, in his 62nd year. His funeral will take place at St Paul's [Episcopal] Church, Alexandria, on Aug 10 at 3 o'clock.

FRI AUG 10, 1860
Rev Wm Neill, D D, esteemed minister of the Presbyterian Church died on Wed last at his residence in Phil, in his 82nd year. He was formerly Pres of Dickinson College. Infirmities of age affected his physical frame, but left his pure & vigorous mind unimpaired. His death ws the natural result of his age, as he has suffered but little from disease. –Bulletin

Wash Corp-Aug 6. 1-Ptn from John M Flynn for the remission of a fine: referred to the Cmte of Claims. 2-Ptn of L L Brunett, of Wash Co, for permission to erect scales for the weighing of hay: referred to the Cmte on Police. 3-Ptn of Chas Newton: referred to the Cmte on Improvements. 4-Ptn from John Ott, praying to be refunded taxes twice paid: referred to the Cmte of Claims. 5-Ptn from Chas W Thielecke & 4 others against opening an alley in square 513: referred to the Cmte on Improvements.

Maplewood Young Ladies Institute, Pittsfield, Mass: next session opens Oct 4, 1860. -Rev C V Spear, Principal

Encyclopedia Britannica, 8th edition, now publishing in Edinburgh, to be completed. The 7th edition was issued in 1842. –Franck Taylor

Died: Aug 9, in Wash City, Ada Caroline Nourse, in her 17th year. Her funeral will be from the house of her father, Mr John R Nourse, 291 8th st, at 5 o'clock today.

Died: on Aug 9, in Gtwn, Jos H Gross, aged 37 years, from affection of the heart, to which he had been subject for the last 6 months. His funeral is this day at 5 o'clock, from his last residence, east side of Market Space, Gtwn, No 22.

The subscriber offers for sale 44 acres of land in the District, 3 miles from Wash, with a comfortable farm-house & stable. This land adjoins the farm of Mr R K Verettad & Dr Manning. This land is offered at $2,000, $1,000, to be paid in cash, the balance in 9 or 12 months. Inquire of R T Ryon, D & 9th sts, Wash, D C. -S B Scaggs

Died: on Aug 9, in Wash City, Robt Whiteley, infant son of Jas B & Henrietta W Dodson, aged 4 months & 6 days.

SAT AUG 11, 1860
Orphans Court of Wash Co, D C. Letters testamentary on the personal estate of Leonard Cash, late of Wash Co, deceased. –Wm Nourse, exc

Mrd: on Jul 31, at Wellington, Me, by Rev Mr Ferrell, Harry C Nicely to Miss Hattie L Shryock, both of Balt, Md.

Died: on Aug 8, in Washington, Pa, Mary Eliz, wife of Jas C Acheson, of that place, & daughter of Alex'r Mahon, late of Harrisburg, Pa.

Died: on Aug 10, James Hamilton, only child of Wm H & Mary Ann Goods, aged 9 months & 28 days. His funeral is tomorrow at 5 o'clock.

Died: on Aug 9, at Mount Holly Springs, near Carlisle, Pa, Sidney Taylor Skerrett, aged 3 months & 11 days, son of Jos S Skerrett, Lt U S Navy.

Female Academy, I st, between 18th & 19th sts, will commence on the first Monday in Sept. –Ellen E Janney, Principal

Mme. D'Ouville's French & English Boarding & Day School, 1411 Spruce st, Phil, will re-open on Sep 10th.

Miss Jeannette S Douglass, late Principal of Goshen Female Seminary, N Y, Preceptress of Newburg Seminary, head English teacher of Washington Female Institute the past year, has the pleasure of announcing that on the second Monday of Sept next she will open in Wash City an Institute for Young Ladies.

MON AUG 13, 1860
Hon Mr Greenwood, Com'r of Indian Affairs, accompanied by C H Rhett & Macon Thompson, son of Hon Jacob Thompson, Sec of the Interior, will leave Wash City on Wed next for Pike's Peak to settle some existing difficulties with the Indians. -Constitution

Fire in Salisbury, Somerset Co, Md, nearly consumed the town on Aug 8. It swept away the stores of Messrs Rider & Toadvine, of Wm Burkhead & C F Dashiells, Bush's Hotel, & the Episcopal Church, one of the oldest in the State. It is suspected to have been the work of an incendiary.

Groceries & household furniture at auction on Aug 16, at the store & residence of Thos Dwyer, corner of East Capitol & 3rd sts, Capitol Hill, all his stock of groceries. Immediately after the sale of groceries we will sell the household goods. -J C McGuire & Co, aucts

The Memphis papers announce the death of Mrs Augusta Walker, consort of J Knox Walker, former private secretary of Pres Polk. [No death date given-current item.]

Fire in Gtwn yesterday, the stable & barn of Mr Rittenhouse, near his residence on the heights of Gtwn,] formerly Mr Saml Whitehall's,] was found to be on fire. The barn was entirely consumed.

Circuit Court of D C-in Chancery. Wm W Corcoran & Geo W Riggs vs Henry C Matthews, Wm M Corcoran, W Alex'r Kirk, Martha E Kirk, John C Fremont, Wm Carey Jones, Eliza P C Jones, & others. The object of this suit is to procure the appointment of a trustee in the stead of Thos Corcoran deceased, to carry out the trusts of the deed hereinafter mentioned. The bill alleges that on Mar 14, 1845, the late Thos Hart Benton & wife conveyed to the said Thos Corcoran, his heirs & assigns, all that part of lot 28 in Reservation 10, in Wash City, on C st north, to secure the payment of a certain indebtment of $4,000 from said Thos Hart Benton to the said cmplnts, Wm W Corcoran & Geo W Riggs; that the said debt is past due & unpaid; that since the execution of the said deed the said Thos Corcoran hath departed this life, having first duly made his will, thereby devising all his real estate to Henry C Matthews, his heirs & assigns, in trust to sell & dispose of the same, & to divide the proceeds thereof among the heirs at law of him, the said Thos Corcoran; that the heirs at law of the said Thos Corcoran are as follows, to wit: Wm M Corcoran, Sarah C Corcoran, who hath intermarried with one Christopher M Thom, Emily Corcoran, Martha E Corcoran, who hath intermarried with one W Alex'r Kirk, & Jas W Corcoran; that since the making & delivery of the said deed the said Thos Hart Benton hath also departed this life, having first duly made his will, thereby giving & devising the said parcel of ground to Wm Carey Jones, John C Fremont, Richd Taylor Jacobs, Montgomery Blair, Saml Phillips Lee, & the survivor of them, his heirs & assigns, in trust for the sole & separate use of Eliza P C Jones, the wife of said Wm Carey Jones; that it is necessary that the said Court should appoint a new trustee in the place of said Thos Corcoran, deceased, to execute & carry out the trust in the said deed limited & set forth, & that the said Wm M Corcoran, W Alex'r Kirk, Martha E Kirk, John C Fremont, Richd Taylor Jacobs, Wm Carey Jones, & Eliza P C Jones are non-residents, living beyond the limits of this District. It appearing to the satisfaction of the Court that said Wm M Corcoran, W Alex'r Kirk, Martha E Kirk, John C Fremont, Richd Taylor Jacobs, Wm Carey Jones, & Eliza P C Jones, do not reside in the District of Columbia. Absent dfndnts are to appear in the ofc of the Clerk of this Court on the first Monday of Jan, 1861. –Wm M Merrick, A J
-Jno A Smith, clerk

Died: on Aug 5, at Queen Anne, Md, [where he had gone for the benefit of his health,] Saml Thos Davis, in his 24th year; a native of PG Co, Md; during the past 8 years has been a resident of Wash City, engaged in mercantile pursuits. He was left an orphan at tender years, & early learned self-reliance. I never knew a more honorable or amiable young gentleman.

Died: on Saturday, in Wash City, Mrs Eleanor M Melvin, in her 53rd year, wife of Josiah Melvin.

Died: on Aug 12, Mary Agnes, youngest child of John F & Mary Bridget, aged 8 months. Her funeral will be from the parents' residence, on D st, between 1st & 2nd sts, this afternoon at 5 o'clock.

Lafayette Institute will commence on Sep 10th, at the new Institute Bldg, 369 I st, adjoining Caroline Terrace. –L C Loomis

TUE AUG 14, 1860
Executor's sale of riding mare, carriage, harness, cows & calves, old wines & liquors, at auction, by order of the Orphans Court of D C, on Aug 29, a part of the effects of the late Maj Alfred V Scott, deceased. –W O Nixon, exc
-Wall & Barnard, aucts

On Sunday at Long Branch, N Y, among the bathers were Dr Edw O Dummer, of Jersey City, & Mr John Whittaker, of Trenton, & a party of ladies. The ladies got in danger & Dummer & Whittaker proceeded to their relief, when both became exhausted & drowned. Dr Dummer was taken ashore. Mr Whittaker, a large stout man, a brother of Mr Green, swam ashore. His wife & son, about 17, were with him at the time. There are 5 or 6 other sons & daughters left to mourn the unexpected & sudden loss of the two men.

Knighthood was conferred on an American Sea Captain. The ship **Uriel**, Capt Thos Walker, on her last voyage from Calcutta, fell in the Portuguese brig-of-war **Mondiego**, in a sinking condition, & rescued the 9 ofcrs & 55 of the remaining portion of the brig's company; 47 persons went down with the ship. The Portuguese Gov't has made Capt Walker a Knight of the Flower & Sword. The first & second mates, Thos H Griffin & Edw A Hall, received a splendid silver medal from the Govn't of Portugal.

Metropolitan Collegiate Institute, A Boarding & Day School for Young Ladies, 44 E st, between 6th & 7th sts, Wash, will commence on Sep 3rd.
–Mr & Mrs T H Havenner, principals

Kalorama Family School, Staunton, Va, will commence on Sep 26. This school, opened 15 years ago by Mrs Sheffey, relict of Danl Sheffey, at Kalorama, the family residence, & still offers to parents & guardians home education.

Orphans Court of Wash Co, D C-Aug 11, 1860. In the case of Morris S Miller, adm of John Mason, deceased, the administrator & Court have appointed Sep 18 next, for the final settlement of the personal estate of the said deceased, of the assets in hand. -Ed Roach, Reg/o wills

Mrd: on Aug 12, at the parsonage of St Patrick's Church, by Rev Fr Boyle, Lt Z Forrest, U S Revenue Service, to Miss Victoria A J, daughter of Dr J Rutherford Worster, of Wash.

Died: on Aug 13, at the Union Hotel, Gtwn, D C, Wm B Walworth, a clerk in the Gen Land Ofc, & a nephew of Chancellor Walworth, of N Y, aged about 44 years. His funeral will be from the Union Hotel this evening at 5 o'clock.

WED AUG 15, 1860
The Hannah More Academy, 8th & West sts, Wilmington, Del, Principals, Miss Charlotte & Isabella & A H Grimshaw, A M, M D. The next session will commence on the first Monday of Sept next.

Gtwn College, D C: studies will be resumed on the first Monday of Sept next.
-John Early, S J, President

Brookville Academy, Montg Co, Md, will commence on Sep 3.
-E B Prettyman, A M, Principal

John Howlett invites the public to his choice varieties of Ripe Grapes, for sale at his residence, 176, corner of N Y & N J aves.

Orphans Court of Wash Co, D C-Aug 14, 1860. In the case of Ellen Downs, admx of Timothy Downs, deceased, the administratrix & Court have appointed Sep 8 next, for the final settlement of the personal estate of the said deceased, of the assets in hand.
-Ed Roach, Reg/o wills

Orphans Court of Wash Co, D C. Letters testamentary on the personal estate of Elisha C Grant, late of Wash Co, deceased. --Palmer Briscoe, exc

THU AUG 16, 1860
Died: on Aug 13, at her residence on N st, Mrs Margaret O'Reily, daughter of Mr Jacob Colclazer, in her 36th year.

Died: on Aug 7, at his residence, in Nottingham district, PG Co, Md, Mr Saml B Fowler, in his 34th year. He was a good neighbor & a peaceful & quiet citizen.

Circuit Court of D C, in Equity, No 1,165. Statham, Smithson & Co vs John F Callan et al. In Equity, No 1,192. Austin Sherman vs John F Callan et al. The trustees reported that on Jul 12, 1860, they sold lot 8 in square 456, with improvements, in Wash City, to one Jas S Waring for $23,100, & purchaser has complied with the terms of sale. –Davidge & Ingle, A Austin Smith, for cmplnts.
-Jno A Smith, clerk

Orphans Court of Wash Co, D C. In Re, the ptn of Chas Walter, guardian of Adolph, Wm, & John Lipphardt. Sale of real estate: said guardian reported to the Court that he has, as trustee, on Dec 20, 1859, sold the east half of lot 23 in square 496, to Eberhard Anhaeuser for $92.61, & the purchaser had complied with the terms of sale. -Wm F Purcell, Judge of the Orphans Court
-Ed Roach, Reg/o wills

On Monday a row occurred at Delta Grove, N J, among some excursionists from Phil, in which a man, John Hockey, of the Hibernia Hose, was killed by one Keyser, a member of the U S Hose Co. Ill feeling existed between the rival fire companies.

Appropriations made during the First Session of the 36th Congress:
1-Act for the relief of Asenath M Elliott, widow of Capt Edw G Elliott: for compensation for private property applied to the payment of a balance erroneously appearing due from the said E G Elliott on the books of the Treasury Dept: $5,000.
2-Act for the relief of Jeremiah Pendergast: for the difference of pay allowed him as a watchman on the construction of the Patent Ofc extension & that allowed to other watchmen: $139.91
3-Act for the relief of Mrs Agatha O'Brien, widow of Brvt Maj J P J O'Brien, late of the U S Army: for such sums of money as may be found due to her late husband as capt of artl, from Dec 31, 1849, when he was last paid, to Mar 31, 1850, the day of his death, & that his accounts on the books of the Treasury be balanced: Indefinite.
4-Act for the relief of the legal reps of Wetonsaw, son of Jas Conner: for the amount secured to said Wetonsaw in schedule B of the treaty of Jan 14, 1837, with the Saginaw Chippewa Indians: $400.
5-Act for the relief of Wm P Bowhay: for severe personal injuries received by him whilst employed by the U S on board the frig **Congress**, & which rendered him a cripple for life: $800.
6-Act for the relief of Mrs Jane M McCrabb, widow of the late Capt John W McCrabb, assist quartermaster U S Army: for commissions for disbursements of special appropriations by her late husband, Capt John W McCrabb, prior to Sep 30, 1838: $5,293.96.
7-Act for the relief of M C Gritzner: for compensation & damages on account of the rescinding by the Govn't of a contract made with the Com'r of Patents on Mar 30, 1857, for the execution of descriptions & illustrations of the Patent Ofc report for that year before the work was completed: $379.77.
8-Resolution for the relief of A M Fridley, late agent for the Winnebago Indians: the amount of judgment paid by him on Mar 26, 1858, & which was obtained against him on Jan 15, 1856, in the U S district court for the 2nd district of Minnesota, in consequence of his having, under positive orders of the Com'r of Indian Affairs, disregarded an injunction obtained against him in said court in regard to the payment of certain moneys belonging to the Winnebago Indians, & which orders said Fridley was compelled to & did obey & carry out: Indefinite.

9-Resolution for the relief of Arthur Edwards & his associates: for carrying the through mails on their boats between Cleveland & Detroit, Sandusky & Detroit, & Toledo & Detroit, during the years 1849 & 53, & the intervening years: Indefinite.
10-Act for the relief of the surviving grandchildren of Col Wm Thompson, of the Revolutionary army of S C: for the half pay for life, to which their ancestor, the said Wm Thompson, was entitled, under the resolutions of Congress, for his services as colonel as aforesaid, throughout the war of the Revolution, the said Col Wm Thompson having elected not to take the commutation of 5 years' full pay: $7,388.82.
11-Act for the relief of Saml J Hensley: for 1,285 head of cattle by him actually delivered in May 1852, to the agents of the U S for the use of the Indians in Calif, as found by the Court of Claims; $96,375.
12-Act for the relief of Chas Jas Lawman: for his services & expenses while acting as a receiver of the U S land ofc at Monroe, Mich, from 1823 to 1831: $2,578.81.
13-Act for the relief of Guadalupe Estudillo de Arguello, widow of Santiago de Arguello: for losses of property sustained by him during the period of such service, & in consequence thereof: $14,888.
14-Act for the relief of Israel Johnson: to pay to Israel Johnson, of Cass Co, Ind, for expenses incurred by order of the com'rs to make a treaty with the Miami tribe of Indians, in 1833: $570.
15-Resolution authorizing the settlement of the accounts of John R Bartlett, late Com'r of the U S to run & mark the boundary line between the U S & Mexico, & for other purposes: Indefinite.
16-Joint resolution for the relief of Wm H De Groot: to settle the account of Wm H De Groot on principles of justice & equity, allowing to said De Groot the amount of money actually expended by him in & about the execution of the said contract, & also to indemnify him for such losses, liabilities, & damages, as, by virtue of the said joint resolution, he was entitled to receive: Indefinite.
17-Act for the relief of the legal reps of Chas Pearson, deceased: for the amount of money paid into the U S Patent Ofc by the said Pearson, whilst he was laboring under a state of insanity: $140.
18-Act for the relief of Thos Fillebrown: for salary as secretary of the board of com'rs of the navy hospital fund, from Feb 7 to May 16, 1827, & for commissions on the disbursement of said fund between 1825 & 1829: $430.
19-Act for the relief of Shade Galloway: for work done by him on the Tenn river, under his contract with Brvt Lt Col J McClelland, dated Sep 16, 1853, according to the account approved & certified by the agent place in charge of said work at the death of the said ofcr: $1,350.
20-Act for the relief of the legal reps of 5 deceased clerks in the Phil custom-house: to pay the legal reps of David Gibson, John B Shull, Eli Valette, Wm Bryant, & C G Treichel, deceased, late clerks in the Phil custom-house, the sums due them, respectively, for arrears of compensation, as per certified statement of said custom-house, payable out of the balance of the surplus emoluments of the collector, erroneously deposited & still remaining in the treasury, in like manner

as the other 8 surviving clerks in said custom-house were paid their arrears of compensation accruing during the same period, & under the same circumstances, as per report of the First Comptroller, dated Mar 7, 1846, approved by the Sec of the Treasury: $9,895.17.

21-Act for the relief of Lydia Frazee, widow & admx of John Frazee, late of N Y C: for the services of the said John Frazee, as architect & superintendent of the N Y custom-house, from Mar 3, 1841, to May 21, 1842: $2,868.

22-Act for the relief of Wm Geiger: for all claims against the U S by virtue of his contract made on Oct 18, 1854, at **Fort Smith** City, with Capt French, for lime, stone, & mason work, for & on the barracks at **Fort Washita**, in the Cherokee nation: $4,010.62.

23-Act for the relief of Moses Noble: to pay to Moses Noble, agent for the brig **Good Hope**, & the schnr **Delta**, schnr **Jasper**, schnr **Sardine**, schnr **Five Sisters**, schnr **Commonwealth**, & the schnr **Two Brothers**, for the benefit of the persons entitled thereto, for fishing bounties to which said vessels became entitled in the fishing season of the year 1852: $1,704.68.

24-Act for the relief of Charner T Scaife, adm of Gilbert Stalker: for the use & service of the steamboat **James Adams**, belonging to said Stalker, from Aug 1, 1841, to Jul 9, 1842: $5,645.16.

25-Act for the relief of Mariano G Vallego: for the occupation by the troops of the U S of a bldg on the square of Sonoma, Calif, from May 30, 1848, to Aug, 1853: $8,800.

26-Act for the relief of Tench Tilghman: for losses sustained by him in consequence of his appointment to a consulate, which was abolished by the Spanish Gov't while he was on his way to take charge of same: $1,000.

27-Act for the relief of A M Mitchell, late colonel of Ohio volunteers in the Mexican war: for transportation from Monterey to Cincinnati, & from Cincinnati to Monterey, in 1846, the trip not having been performed under orders, but by leave granted in consequence of temporary disability, caused by wounds received in action on Sep 21, 1846: Indefinite.

28-Act for the relief of Richd W Meade: for expenses incurred by him & his clerk for subsistence, while under orders of the Navy Dept & detained on shore at San Francisco, from Jul 15 to Sep 30, 1849, less the amount already received by them for commutation of their rations during the same period: $566.20.

29-Act for the relief of Geo Stealey: for services rendered & expenses incurred by him as agent, appointed by the Indian com'rs of the U S for the State of Calif to visit the northern tribes of Indians in said State: Indefinite.

30-Act for the relief of David D Porter: for certain extraordinary expenses incurred by him in the discharge of his duty, under the orders of the Navy Dept, on special service to the island of St Domingo: $743.

31-Act for the relief of Geo B Bacon, late acting purser of the sloop-of-war **Portsmouth**: for the amount properly payable to a purser, of a sloop-of-war, for his services as acting purser as aforesaid during the period he acted as purser, deducting therefrom the amount paid to said Bacon for the same period as cmder's clerk: Indefinite.

32-Act for the relief of Edw N Kent: for the perpetual use, in all the present & future minting establishments of the U S, of the apparatus for separating gold & other precious metals from foreign substances, of which the said Edw N Kent is the inventor & patentee: $20,000.

33-Act for the relief of W Y Hansell, the heirs of W H Underwood, & the reps of Saml Rockwell: to pay the balance of the sum of $60,000 reserved in the treaty between the U S & the Cherokee nation, [negotiated on Dec 29, 1835,] for the payment of said claims, & misapplied by the com'rs of the U S to the payment of other claims: $30,000.

34-Act for the relief of Jas Phelan: for his services in prosecuting ___ Craig, indicted before the district Federal court of the U S for the northern district of Miss, under the appointment of Hon Saml J Gholson, on a charge of robbing the U S mail: $250.

35-Act for the relief of the legal reps of Sylvester Day, late a surgeon in the U S Army: to pay to the legal reps of the late Sylvester Day, a surgeon in the U S Army, in reimbursement of that sum paid for medical services at Allegheny arsenal: $426.

36-Act for the relief of Peter Rogerson & Son, of St John's, Newfoundland, owners of the British brig **Jessie**: for losses incurred by reason of the rescuing of the passengers & crew of the American ship **Northumberland**, in Dec, 1857, when in a sinking condition, & conveying them to Cork, Ireland: $7,788.75.

37-Act for the relief of Maryett Van Buskirk: for forage, grain, cattle, & other supplies furnished to the American army by the late Thos Van Buskirk, deceased, of Bergen Co, N J, during the Revolutionary war: $20,367.

38-Act for the relief of Geo P Marsh: for all claims he may have on account of special services rendered by him in Greece in 1852 & 1853, under instructions from the State Dept: $9,000.

39-Act for the relief of Francis Dainese: for all claims & demands of said Francis Dainese upon the U S for his travelling, contingent, & other expenses, as well as for losses sustained by him in & connected with the consulate at Constantinople: $4,820.99.

40-Act for the relief of Anson Dart: to pay to Dart, late superintendent of Indian affairs in the Territory of Oregon, $4,000 per annum, deducting therefrom $2,500 per annum, already received for the time he served as such superintendent, being Jul 1, 1850, to May 4, 1853: Indefinite.

41-Act for the relief of John Brannan: for extra services as librarian in said dept from Sept 15, 1858, to Jan 15, 1859, being at the rate of $4.00 per day, after deducting the pay received by him as an employe during said time: $280.

42-Act for the relief of R W Clarke: for extra services performed by him in said ofc as clerk from Jan 1, 1851, to Oct 1, 1852: $225.

43-Act for the relief of David Myerle: for losses, sacrifices, & expenses incurred by him in testing & establishing the practicability & safety of the process of water-rotting hemp, under the direction of the Navy Dept: $30,000.

44-Act for the relief of J R Crump: for his expenses in returning from Santa Fe in 1859, & for services, subsequently, in aiding superintendent E F Beale in the preparation of the official report of his wagon road exploration: $750.

45-Act for the relief of Anton L C Portman: for his services as Dutch interpreter during the negotiation of the treaty between the U S & the Empire of Japan, from the preliminary preparations to the final completion of said negotiations: $3,000.

46-Act for the relief of Benj Sayre: for work & labor, under his contract with the U S dated Dec 8, 1832, in section 67 of the Cumberland road in Indiana, in the division east of Indianoplis: $2,043.

47-Act for the relief of Saml H Taylor: for extra service performed by him as messenger in the ofc of the Third Auditor of the Treasury from Jun, 1853, to Sep, 1855: $270.

48-Act for the relief of Cassius M Clay: for the amount of a judgment, costs, & interest, recovered against him by one Eliza Bowles for trespass in executing a military order of his superior ofcr in 1846, together with interest from Oct 1, 1848, the date of payment of said judgment, costs, & interest: $533.20.

49-Act for the relief of the heirs or legal reps of the estate of Chas H Mason: for the difference between the salary of the Govn'r of the Territory of Washington & the Sec during the time that the Govn'r of said Territory was absent from the Territory by permission of the Pres, & the duties of Govn'r were discharged by said Chas H Mason: Indefinite.

50-Act for the relief of Philip B Holmes & Wm Pelrick: for the invention of a machine for cutting raw hides into strips for making hide ropes for the use of the U S Navy: $3,000.

51-Act for the relief of Peay & Ayliffe: to enable the Postmaster Gen to adjust the accounts of Peay & Ayliffe, late contractors on mail route 7,503, in the State of Ark: Indefinite.

52-Act for the relief of Emilie G Jones, excx of Thos P Jones, deceased, & Nancy M Johnson, admx of Walter R Johnson, deceased: for the services of the said Thos P Jones, as a member of the board of examiners, appointed by the Sec of the Navy, to provide for the better security of the lives of passengers on board of vessels propelled in whole or in part by steam, approved Jul 7, 1838: $2,350. For the services of the said Walter R Johnson, as a member of the board of examiners, appointed by the Sec of the Navy, for the same: $4,250.

53-Act to authorize the settlement of the accounts of Edw Ely, deceased, late Consul of the U S at Bombay, on principles of justice & equity: & to pay to the legal reps of the said decedent whatsoever sum shall appear to be due upon the settlement of the said account: Indefinite.

54-Act for the relief of David Waldo: for the amount of damages awarded by the report of the Quaartermaster Gen of the U S army for the non-fulfilment on the part of the Gov't of a contract made with him in May 1850, for delivering corn at *Fort Laramie*, & the payment of which is recommended by the Sec of War: $9,936.

55-Act for the relief of Mrs A W Angus, widow of the late Capt Saml Angus, U S Navy: for the amount of pay which he would have received if he had remained in the navy, from the date of his dismissal to the date of his death, at the same rate he was drawing when dismissed: Indefinite.

56-Act for the relief of Shelden McKnight: for carrying the mail during the years 1849 to 1857, inclusive, deducting therefrom the amount heretofore paid: Indefinite.
57-Act for the relief of E Geo Squier, of N Y: for outfits to the Republics of Central American, & balance of salary due him as Minister of the U S to said Republics: $9,937.
58-Act for the relief of Isaac S Smith, of Syracuse, N Y: for his work & labor bestowed, for materials furnished, & for expenses incurred in atempting to build for the U S a lighthouse on the Horse-shoe reef, in the Niagara river, near *Fort Erie*, in the Province of Canada: $17,743,77.
59-Resolution for the relief of Cmder J H Hartstene, of the U S Navy: for extra expenses incurred by him in restoring the barque **Resolute**: $2,008.60.
60-Resolution for the compensation of Rev R R Richards, late chaplain to the U S Penitentiary in D C: for his half year's salary, ending Jul 30, 1857: $300.
61-Resolution for the relief of the legal reps of John A Frost, deceased: claim of John A Frost, acting boatswain of the U S brig **Porpoise**, in the late exploring expediition, from Jan 1, 1839, to Jul 7, 1842, & the amount due to him shall be paid to his legal reps: Indefinite.
62-Joint resolution for the relief of Thos C Ware: for services he rendered to the U S Gov't at the request of D O Morton, late district atty of the U S in the case of the U S vs Lyman Cole & others, indicted & tried in the Circuit Court of the U S: amount blank.

Yesterday the mortal remains of Mrs Holt, consort of the Postmaster Gen, were conveyed from the residence of her husband on Capitol Hill to the railroad depot, & thence to a car, enroute for the family homestead in Ky. Besides the Postmaster Gen himself, the father of the deceased, Gov Wickliffe, & near friends of the family went in the same train to pay their last tribute.

Mrs M E Kingsford's Seminary, 415 E st, Wash, will commence on Oct 1, 1860.

Greatest sale of the finest land ever sold in Va for the last 50 years. Also, 165 valuable negroes. In pursuance of a decree of the Circuit Court for Caroline Co, entered in the case of Corbin et al vs Corbin et al: public auction on Sep 25 next, at *Moss Neck*, the land, slaves, & perishable property in the proceedings in said suit mentioned. The land comprises about 4,000 acres on both side of the Rappahannock river; improvements consist of a large & elegant brick mansion, finished in 1856, containing 16 rooms; stabling for 60 horses; 16 negro cabins, lathed & plastered, with brick chimneys. *Farley Vale*, containing about 1,700 acres is opposite to *Moss Neck*, in King Geo Co, with frame dwlg house. Also will be sold at the same time & place, 165 slaves. Richd Corbin, residing at *Moss Neck*, & S Wellford Corbin at *Farley Vale*, will show the premises.
–T B Barton, W S Barton, Counsel & Com'rs of sale, Fredericksburg, Va, Aug 15, 1860.

FRI AUG 17, 1860
In a paper published in Pa, the Record of the Times, is an interesting article from the pen of Hon Chas Miner, a venerable citizen of that State, now more than 80 years old. He was a member of the House of Reps from 1825 to 1829.

Long Branch, N J, 3 fatal casualties to bathers on Sat last. At Long Branch, on Sat, Mr John Whittaker, a retired merchant of Trenton, & Dr E O Dummer, of Jersey City, lost their lives in an effort to rescue 2 ladies, Miss Zabriskie & Miss Parker, from drowning, when they were suddenly swept out by a strong undercurrent.
Yesterday two gentlemen drowned while bathing at Thompson's, a few miles from this place. Mr Gustavus Ratz & his wife were bathing, when Mr Ratz, an excellent swimmer, was carried down by the current. Mr R E Evans succeeded in bringing in the body of Mrs Ratz, who was insensible, but was restored by the proper remedies. Mr Ratz was 27 years old, & leaves a wife & one child. Efforts were made in the case of Edw Gardiner, a young gentleman, who too was carried under by the current. He was rescued by his companions, but not until he was quite dead.

At a meeting of the friends of Lincoln & Hamlin, held in Springfield, Ill, on Aug 8, Mr Lincoln was surprised into the delivery of a very brief speech. Mr Lincoln then retired from the grounds amidst the wildest enthusiasm, being seized upon & carried hither & thither by the immense crown, which filled the grounds to overflowing.

Andrew Jackson O'Bannon, Fourth Auditor of the Treasury, died at Capon Springs, Va, on Aug 14, stricken with paralysis a few days previous. He was a native of Jefferson Co, Va, a courteous & popular ofcr, & highly respected citizen.
+
Taliaferro Hunter, of Va, has been appointed Fourth Auditor of the Treasury, to fill the vacancy occasioned by the death of A J O'Bannon.

We notice in the window of O E Duffy, bookseller, a splendid painting of St Peter, in a sitting posture, painted by Prof Brinide for the new Church of St Peter, Rev Fr Laneghan pastor, Chas Co, Md.

Wash Corp, Aug 13, 1860. 1-Cmte of Claims: bills passed-relief of Wallis & Denhan; of J W Blake; & of John Pfleuger. Same cmte: discharged from further consideration of the bill for the relief of F Dainese.

Mrd: on Aug 1, at the residence of the bride's father, in Anderson village, S C, by Rev J M Carlyle, Mr Wm D Williams, of Greeneville, Tenn, to Miss Sarah Ann, 2nd daughter of Dr O R Broyles.

Died: on Aug 14, at Conshocken, Pa, at the residence of Theodore Trewendt, of acute hydrocephalus, Mary Chaplain, infant child of Dr H N & Sophia Whitney Wadsworth, aged 4 months & 22 days.

Died: on Aug 12, at **Walnut Hill**, Howard Co, Md, the residence of his parents, of cholera infantum, Ethan Allen, youngest son of Ethan A & Mary Virginia Edmonston, aged 17 months & 5 days.

SAT AUG 18, 1860
Miss Brooke's English & French Boarding & Day School for Young Ladies, Seven Bldgs, 138 Pa ave, Wash: will resume on Sep 10.

Mrd: on Aug 7, at the country residence of the bride's mother, Bay Saint Louis, Miss, by Rev Dr Leacock, Wm Grayson Mann, atty at law, New Orleans, to Miss Fannie Ogden, daughter of the late Judge Ogden, of Louisiana.

Died: on Aug 17, in Wash City, Mrs Jane Castleman, wife of Stephen D Castleman, & daughter of Thos Cookendorfer, in her 41st year. Her funeral is tomorrow at 5 o'clock P M, from the residence of her husband, corner of 26th & Pa ave.

Died: on Aug 17, in Wash City, Benedict, infant son of Benedict & Martha Milburn, aged 15 months & 25 days. His funeral will take place this afternoon at 4 o'clock, from the residence of his father, 535 north H st, between 6th & 7th sts.

Died: on Aug 15, at his residence in Jefferson Co, Va, Saml Strider, aged about 70 years. The deceased was one of the most respectable & enterprising citizens of that region of the State. In 1814, upon news of the invasion of Washington, Mr Strider, with three of his brothers volunteered in the company of Capt Geo W Humphreys, & was at the battle of the White House on Sep 5 of that year, displaying all the characteristics of a brave soldier. It may be mentioned here that only 10 members of the company of Capt Humphreys are now surviving.

Wanted, a situation as a Teacher in a family or school, by a young gentleman well qualified to teach the usual English branches, Latin, Greek, & Spanish.
–Jos W Weston, Princ Acad, Danville, Pa.

Obit-died: on Jul 5, at Sullivan's Island, near Charleston, S C, Mrs Sally Maria Martin, daughter of the late Judge Clement Dorsey, of Md, & widow of Judge D D Martin, of S C. Devoted in the sacred relationship of wife, daughter, mother, sister, mistress, & friend, she died, as she lived, universally beloved, trusted, & admired. She fell asleep in Jesus.

MON AUG 20, 1860
The Detroit Free Press of Aug 12 says that Cyrus Woodbury, the postmaster at White Pigeon, Mich, was arrested & conveyed to Detroit the day previous on a charge of robbing the mail.

Mr J D Hayden, a well-known telegraph operator, died at Phil on Sunday of consumption. For several years Mr Hayden was one of the principal operators on the Washington & New Orleans telegraph line, & for the last 2 years occupied the same position in New Orleans. His loss will be deeply felt. –Phil Bulletin

Mr Nathl Knight, of Falmouth, Maine, is now 89 years of age, in good health, & has this season mowed hay upon the same field where he had swung the scythe 78 summers before. A veteran farmer, truly.

The family of Rev Josiah W Brown, of Manchester, Vt, have lost 5 lovely children, all they had, fallen victims to that new & terrible scourge, diptheria, that is raging in many localities, & they all died within the space of 32 days.

An inquest was held on Sat on the dead body of a child of 5 years of age, named Mary McLean, whose parents live on Capitol Hill, near 1st st. A few hours before her death she had partaken of some liquid given her by the daughter of a man who keeps a liquor-store on East Capitol st. No other cause but this could be given for her decease, as insensibility was produced soon after the stuff was taken.

In virtue of an order of distrain from O M Pettit against Jos R Quinter, for rent due & in arrears of *Meridian Hill* estate, I have distrained goods & chattels of Mr Quinter for public sale, for cash, on Aug 25, in front of the Bank Washington, to satisfy said rent due & in arrears. –J A Wise, Constable & Bailiff

Died: on Aug 18, John Fred'k Gerecke, in his 58th year. His funeral will leave his residence, 13 Missouri ave, between 4½ & 6th sts, this afternoon at 2 o'clock.

Died: on Aug 11, at his residence, near Sandy Spring, Md, Thos S Stabler, formerly of Lynchburg, Va. He was distinguished for his noble qualities of head & heart.

Died: on Aug 6, at Decatur, Ill, of consumption, at the residence of her brother, J J Peddecord, Mrs Laura E Miller, a native of Wash City, & consort of John F Miller, aged 21 years.

Died: on Aug 1, at *Hill View*, St Mary's Co, Md, Wm H Hebb, in his 59th year.

Staunton, Aug 18. Last night the following straightout Douglas electoral ticket was chosen: Geo Blow, H L Hopkins, J B Stoveall, Jas Garland, Benj Randolph, J H Cox, J B Ailworth, G H Howe, G W Brent, Israel Robinson, J N Leggett, G P Hoge, G W Hopkins, C T Stuart, W G Brown.

Cincinnati, Aug 18. Last night Chas B Brown, the U S Marshal, was shot dead by Geo J Caldwell, of the firm of Alfred Wood & Co. The affray occurred at Caldwell's house, in consequence of Brown's having forced his way into Caldwell's chamber. The orginal cause grew out of bad feeling relative to the adjustment of a legal claim. Caldwell immediately surrendered himself to the authorities.

TUE AUG 21, 1860
Peter Force has been appointed Maj Gen & Col Hickey Brig Gen of the militia of the District of Columbia. –States

Judge Dewey, of Watertown, aged 90 years, is not only the oldest living graduate of Yale College, but the best rifle shot in his neighborhood. He walks easily & rapidly, & preserves his mental faculties to a remarkable extent, & can see with great distinctness.

Orphans Court of Wash Co, D C. Letters testamentary on the personal estate of Jas Caden, late of Wash Co, deceased. –Eleanor M Caden, excx

Orphans Court of Wash Co, D C. Letters of administration on the personal estate of Wm H Topping, late of Wash Co, deceased. –Geo Patten, adm

Died: on Aug 8, in Wash City, Miss Christy Ann Kurtz, formerly of Gtwn, D C, aged 72 years.

WED AUG 22, 1860
A fatal accident occurred in Hampden, Conn, on Thu. Mrs Jacob Gruner, a bride of only 2 months, was preparing dinner, & poured some camphene on the fire to make it burn more brightly. The flames caught the fluid & Mrs Gruner was at once enveloped in flames. She died on Thursday after suffering great agony.

Prof Henry Marix, 454 D st, between 2nd & 3rd sts, will form classes for young ladies & gentlemen at his residence, teaching French, German, & Russian languages.

Deaths by lightning: in Newark, Stephen McCune, age 22 years, a son of Jas McCune, residing at Broome & Kinney sts, was struck by lightning & instantly killed. Wm Corby, of Orange, in the meadow with his sons, was struck & instantly killed. He was about 50 years of age. The wife & child of the gardener of Mr Sandermeister, at Middleville, were also struck, & one-half of the person of each paralyzed. –Newark Mercury, Aug 20

Orphans Court of Wash Co, D C. Letters of administration, with the will annexed, on the personal estate of Jos Gales, late of Wash Co, deceased. –S J M Gales, admx w a

Orphans Court of Wash Co, D C. Letters testamentary on the personal estate of John F Gerecke, late of Wash Co, deceased. –Eliza Gerecke, Chas Walter, Augarty Gerecke, excs

Circuit Court of D C, No 1,436, in Equity. Jas E Morgan & Jas F Slater, vs Chas Slater & Saml A Peugh. Report of sale of part of lot 5 in square 346, made to Geo R Adams, for $581.25, on May 3, 1860, by trustee in this cause. –John A Smith, clerk.

Died: on Aug 20, in her 62nd year, Miss Anne Reed Dermott, a lady extensively known in Wash City. Her funeral will be this afternoon at 4 o'clock, at the Church of the Epiphany, G st, between 13th & 14th sts.

THU AUG 23, 1860
Condensed account from the Home Journal of the town & locality in Western Va. Staunton, the county town of Augusta, is 163 miles from Washington, & it has been the residence of several prominent characters, among whom may be mentioned the late Danl Sheffey, Gen Robt Porterfield, a gallant ofcr of the Revolution, Judge Archibald Stuart, father of Hon Alex'r H H Stuart, Sec of the Interior under Pres Fillmore's administration, who also resides here. The venerable widow of Mr Sheffey still occupies the beautiful spot, *Kalorama*, which was formerly the *Beverly Manor House*, where the Home School for Young Ladies has been conducted for 25 years, under the superintendence of Mrs Sheffey & her accomplished daughters. Mr Stuart, the widow of Judge Stuart, only died about a year ago, having lived to a great age. The bar here numbers some of the finest legal minds of Va: Thos J Michie, Alex H H Stuart, John B Baldwin, Hugh W Sheffey, a nephew of the distinguished statesman & jurist of the name, Gen W H Harman, & others.

Gtwn Female Seminary, [formerly Miss L S English's,] a Boarding & Day School, will be resumed on Sep 3 next. Miss M J Harrover, Gtwn, D C, Principal.

FRI AUG 24, 1860
Positive sale of valuable bldg lot in Gtwn at public auction on Aug 28, in front of the premises, the lot owned by John Cassin, on the n w corner of Prospect & Potomac sts, in Gtwn. –Barnard & Buckey, aucts

Mr Henry Bryan, a farmer of Queen Anne's Co, Md, was run over by his lime wagon, last week, at Centreville, & killed.

Miss Mary Bochman, a milliner, was burnt to death on Sat, in Jefferson, Tenn, when a lamp was accidentally overturned & the flames communicated to her dress. She expired in the greatest agony in a few hours.

New Carpets, New Oilcloths: at the New Carpet Rooms, Perry Bldg, Pa ave & 9th st. -Louis F Perry & Co [Ad]

Alex Rutherford: Pioneer Steam Marble & Brown Stone Works, Pa ave & 13th st, Wash, D C. [Ad]

Orphans Court of Wash Co, D C-Aug 21, 1860. In the case of Thos C Wilson, adm of Mathew Wilson, deceased, the administrator & Court have appointed Sep 15 next, for the final settlement of the personal estate of the said deceased, of the assets in hand. -Ed Roach, Reg/o wills

Died: on Jul 16, 1860, at the residence of her father, in Randolph Co, Va, in her 15th year, Miss Mary Truman Hillery, daughter of A Washington & Emiline Hillery. She had been ill 10 days, receiving the unremitting attention of her devoted father & mother.

Died: on Aug 23, Eva Ernestine, only child of Wm W & Maria V McCathran, aged 1 year & 10 months. Her funeral will take place from 424 G st south, between 6th & 7th sts, at 4 o'clock this afternoon.

Died: on Aug 23, in Wash City, Anna, infant daughter of Norval W & Sarah Frances Burchell. Her funeral is this afternoon at 5 o'clock, from the residence of her father.

Oswego, Aug 23. The steamer **Niagara** collided last night with an unknown vessel, receiving much damage. Mr John Adger, of S C, had both legs broken.

SAT AUG 25, 1860
List showing the places in which the present number of **army chaplains** are employed: name, church, locality
Mark L Cheevers, E, *Fort Monroe*, Va
John O'Brien, E, *Fort Mackinac*, Mich
John McCarty, E, *Fort Vancouver*, Wash Ter
Wm Vaux, E, *Fort Laramie*, Neb Ter
John McVicker, D D, E, *Fort Columbus*, N Y
Joshua Sweet, E, *Fort Ridgely*, Minn
Wm Stoddard, P, *Fort Union*, New Mexico
Tobias H Mitchell, E, *Fort Chadbourne*, Texas
John W French, E, Military Academy, W Point
Matthias Harris, E, *Fort Mountrie*, S C
John F Fish, E, Jefferson Barracks, Mo
Chas H Page, E, Newport Barracks, Ky
John Burke, E, *Fort Washita*, Cher Nation
H S Bishop, M, *Fort Fillmore*, New Mexico
Hiram Stone, E, *Fort Leavenworth*, Kansas
E G Gear, E, *Fort Ripley*, Minn
David Rendig, E, *Fort Steilacoom*, Wash Ter

Household & kitchen furniture at auction on Aug 29, at the residence of Mrs Massie, on N st, between 12th & 13th sts. -A Green, aucts

Mrs Ingersoll, wife of Hon John N Ingersoll, the editor of the Owosso American, & the Republican candidate for Senator in the Shiawassee district of Mich, met with a frightful death on Aug 18. She was in the act of filling a fluid lamp, when an explosion took place & she was so badly burnt that she died in a few hours.

Guy's Monument House, directly opposite the Battle Monument, Monument Square, Balt, Md: will comfortably accommodate 120 guests; guests can have their meals at any hour they wish. –Wm Guy & Co [Ad]

In the case of Ephraim Halleck, detained in jail to answer the charge of abducting & selling a slave from N C, the jailer of this District undertook to release the prisoner, the 3 weeks allowed the prosecutor to bring testimony from N C having expired. Halleck bent his way Northward, glad to escape the heavy penalty which the laws of N C inflict upon such a crime.

Pic-Nic & Fair will take place on Sep 12, on the farm of the late John Brookes, near the new Catholic Church of the Most Holy Rosary. The proceeds will go towards the erection of a dwlg-house on the church lot & the enclosing of the old grave yard at Boone's Chapel. The route to the place is the Nottingham road, by Woodyard Farm. Persons desiring to assist or contribute will please call next week on the pastor of St Dominic's Church, Island.

Died: on Aug 22, in Wash City, Wm H Starr, in his 56th year.

Died: on Aug 23, in Gtwn, after a short illness, Wm D Kerr, aged about 37 years. His funeral is this evening at 2 o'clock, from the residence of W H Thecker, No 8 Market st, Gtwn.

MON AUG 27, 1860
Wm C Bryant & Jas O Putnam are happily combined as the Senatorial [Presidential] Electors on the Lincoln ticket. Mr Bryant is our greatest living poet, & has been an editor for nearly 40 years, & was an oracle of Radical Democracy for more than 20 years. Jas O Putnam was a Whig of the school of Clay & Webster, united with the Americans, & was elected by them to the Senate. He zealously supported Milliard Fillmore in 1856. His is now heartily with the Republicans for Lincoln & Hamlin, as are most of the former Americans of West N Y.

Mr John B Gough, who is now in this country, having arrived at Boston on Wed in the ship **Arabia**, has been tendered a public reception by 480 clergymen of various denominations, to take place at Tremont Temple. During his last stay abroad he delivered 390 addresses to an aggregate of at least half a million hearers, nearly 12,000 of whom are said to have signed the temperance pledge.

Stock of retail grocery, paint, & ship stores, at auction, in Gtwn, D C, on Aug 30, at the Store of J C Johnson, 97 Water st. -Barnard & Buckley, aucts, Gtwn, D C

Extensive sale of Liquor Establishment at auction on Sep 3, at the store of John Fred'k Gerecke, 381 Pa ave, between 4½ & 6th sts, the whole of his stock & fixtures. -A Green, aucts

The steamer **Edinburgh** brought to N Y Rev Mr & Mrs Bird, of Deir-el-Komr, & Rev Mr & Mrs Eddy, of Sidon. These missionaries have been in the midst of the massacres in Syria. Rev Dwight W Marsh, of Mosul, arrived in the steamer **Etna**; in company with him was Mr Edw K Goodell, of Constantinople, who comes to this country to complete his education. Boston paper: Rev J E Frazer, wife & 2 children, arrived at that port in the steamer **Arabia**. Mr Frazer was an American missionary at Damascus, as a co-laborer with Rev Mr Graham, of the Irish Presbyterian Mission. Mr Frazer lost considerable property in Damascus. Letters from Constantinople: Rev Dr Hamlin was to leave that city about the middle of July for the U S.

Suicide denounced as murder. Concord, N H: Isaac H Russell came to his death by violently forcing himself into the water of Merrimack river, at or near Garvin's Falls, so called, between Aug 8 & Aug 11.

An estray Cow came to the subscribers. The owner is to prove property, pay charges, & take her away. –Matilda Young, near **Long Old Fields**, PG Co, Md.

The valuable farm of Dr P R Edelen at auction, on the premises, on Sep 5, on the Potomac river, 4 miles from Alexandria: contains between 700 & 800 acres. It has all necessary out-bldgs. –Wm S Holliday, 524 Pa ave, atty for the owner.

TUE AUG 28, 1860
Household & kitchen furniture at auction on Aug 30, at the residence of R B Norment, 22 north K st, between 7th & 8th sts. -Jas C McGuire & Co, aucts

Stanmore School, Sandy Spring, Montg Co, Md, will be resumed on Oct 1.
-Francis Miller, Proprietor & Principal

Gonzaga College will be resumed on the first Monday in Sept.
–W F Clarke, S J, President

St Matthew's Female Academy, 18th st & N Y ave, under the direction of the Sisters of Charity, will be opened for the reception of pupils on Sept 3. A Free-school for girls will also be conducted by the Sisters at the same place, but in a separate house.

Mrd: on Aug 16, in Spartanburg, S C, by Rev Edwin Cater, A T Cavis, of Spartanburg, to Miss L A Hamilton, formerly of Norfolk, Va.

Obit-died: on Aug 25, at the residence of Wm Clagett, in PG Co, Md, Miss Evelina Lyons, second daughter of Evan Lyons, Gtwn, D C. She was attacked by the typus fever, & but a few days ago was the centre of attraction to so many hearts.

Trustee's sale of a desirable farm, by decree of the Circuit Court of PG Co, Md, Court of Equity: public sale on Sep 19 next, the Farm on which Thos P Ryon, late of said county, deceased, resided, containing 135 acres, more or less; adjoins the farm of the late Thos B Crawford; it has on it a comfortable dwlg-house, tobacco-house, corn-house & stables. For further information inquire of the subscriber, 9th & D sts, Wash. –Rd J Ryon, trustee

Orphans Court of Wash Co, D C. Letters testamentary on the personal estate of Thos Motley, late of Wash Co, deceased. –Thos Champion, adm

WED AUG 29, 1860
The Manitowoc [Wis] Tribune of Aug 14 states that the house of Frank Sinnot, in the town of Schleiswig, in that county, caught fire on Aug 10, & was burnt to the ground, with all the contents. His 3 children, 1, 2, & 3 years of age, were alone in the house, & perished in the flames.

Nashville [Tenn] Gaz of Aug 24: On Thu of last week a duel fought in the Indian nation between Dr Mitchell & Dr Gantt, opposing candidates for Congress in the late election in Arkansas, Mr Gantt, the successful aspirant, was killed. The deceased was brother to Geo Gantt, a well known lawyer & politician of Columbia, Tenn.

Orphans Court of Wash Co, D C, Aug 28, 1860. In the case of Ellen Dorr, admx of Michl Murphy, deceased, the administratrix & Court have appointed Sep 22 next, for the final settlement of the personal estate of the said deceased, of the assets in hand. -Ed Roach, Reg/o wills

Mrd: on Aug 27, at Trinity Church, in Wash City, by Rev Dr Harrold, Felix Miklos De Nemegyei to Bettie G, daughter of Dr Noble Young, of Wash City.

Died: on Aug 27, Alice Stanley, infant daughter of Wm & Isabella B Nourse, aged 7 months. Her funeral is today at 11 o'clock A M.

Wytheville, Va, Aug 27. O Staite, editor of the Wytheville Telegraph, on Sat shot & killed W W Hanson, cashier of the Farmers' Bank of Wytheville. The wound was inflicted with a pistol, & proved fatal in a short time. The difficulty grew out of newspaper publications.

THU AUG 30, 1860
Capt Henry W Ogden, of the U S Navy, died in N Y on Sat night. He entered the navy in Sep, 1811. His last service as sea was in 1842.

Brown soap, tallow, ashes, cow & calf, at auction, on Sep 3, at the factory of the late Jas O'Donoghue, on 1st st, by order of the Orphans Court of Wash Co, D C. -Thos Dowling, auct

Household & kitchen furniture at auction on Sep 5, at the residence of Mrs Williams, 444 8th st, between D & La ave, all her effects.
—C W Boteler & Sons, aucts

Adm's sale of furniture, stock, growing crop, hay & oats, on Sep 5, by order of the Orphans Court of Wash Co, D C, at the late residence of Edmond French, deceased, on the west side of Rock Creek, on the road leading past *Adams' mill.* -Henry S Davis, adm -A Green, aucts

Prof Agassiz's School for Young Ladies, at Cambridge, Mass, will re-open on Sep 27. A course of Lectures on English Literature will be given by Prof J R Lowell.

FRI AUG 31, 1860
Mrd: on Aug 30, in Wash City, in the Fourth Presbyterian Church, by Rev John C Smith, Geo Ailer to Miss Sophia A Seitz, all of Wash City.

Mrd: on Aug 23, at the residence of T C Evans, near Hendersonville, N C, Gen H W Palfrey, of New Orleans, to Miss Laura Virginia, daughter of Gen R B Campbell, U S Consul at London.

Mrd: on Aug 30, in Wash City, by Rev Fr Boyle, Mr John McPherson to Mrs Ann McNeal, all of Wash City.

Mr Wm Greenough, one of the oldest printers in that part of the country, died at his residence in Boston on Monday, at age 88 years & 7 months. He was born in Wellfleet, Barnstable Co, Mass, Jan 6, 1772. He came to Boston in 1780, & in 1784 was placed as an apprentice in the ofc of Saml Hall, a noted printer & newspaper publisher of the period. In 1795 he was one of the publishers of the Federal Orrery. In 1799 he made the voyage around the world, as a seaman, engaged in the sealing trade, returned to Boston in 1801, & was engaged in publishing a newspaper in Haverhill & Worcester county. Subsequently for some years he resided in Washington, but the latter years of his life were spent in Boston.

SAT SEPT 1, 1860
Household & kitchen furniture at auction on Sep 6, at the residence of Dr T T Mann, Prospect st, Gtwn. -Jas C McGuire & Co, aucts

At Jacksonville, Fla, on Aug 22, G Parratt, while sitting with his wife at the tea table, was handling a loaded pistol, when it went off, the ball passed through her throat, causing her death in a short time.

On Wed, in an accident on the Nat'l Road, less than a mile of Wheeling, Mrs Steenrod, age over 70, mother of Hon Lewis Steenrod, was killed. Hon Lewis Steenrod, with his mother, & a small negro girl, were ascending a hill & drove near the precipice or embankment. Mr Steenrod's horse became frightened & jumped over the precipice. Mr Steenrod had 2 ribs broken, & so badly injured he may not recover. The negro girl was not seriously injured.

Died: on Aug 31, Wm Stirling, aged 50 years. His funeral will take place at his late residence, M st, near 7th, this afternoon at 1 o'clock.

MON SEP 3, 1860
The Northern Pa says that a resident of Susquehanna Depot, John England, died on Thu from the bite of a rattlesnake. On Wed he had the snake in a barrel with one head out for the purpose of exhibiting it. He died on Thu.

The newspapers speak of a great gathering of the Andrews family at Wallingford, Conn, on Wed. About 1,000, more or less, connected with the Andrews family, were present. They had a great banquest & lots of speeches.

Alexandria High School, Va. A Select Boarding School for Young Men & Youths. The Institution will be resumed on Sep 18. –Caleb S Hallowell

Died: on Sep 2, in Wash City, Michl R Shyne, a native of Limerick Co, Ireland, but a resident of Wash City since 1836. His funeral will take place on Tue, at 10 o'clock, from his late residence, 341 F st, between 9th & 10th sts. May he rest in peace.

Died: on Friday last, in Wash City, Mr Henry B Sage, in his 31st year.

Died: on Aug 28, at Chelsea, Mass, Dr Saml R Addison, Surgeon U S Navy.

New Orleans, Sep 1. Capt Jas McIntosh, a native of Georgia, Commandant of the U S Navy Yard at Pensacola, died there this morning. [Sep 5th newspaper: Capt McIntosh received his appointment in 1811; he was an ofcr for 49 years, of which 20 were spent at sea; his last commission bears date Sep 5, 1850.]

TUE SEP 4, 1860
Miss De Boye has resumed giving lessons in Music, at her residence, 352 D st, between 9th & 10th sts.

Died: on Aug 30, at Leesburg, Va, Marie Cooper Chandler, daughter of Catharine & Wm Chandler, Cmder U S Navy, aged 23 months & 1 day.

Died: on Sunday, at 10 o'clock, Jas W Coombs, in his 34th year. His funeral will be from his late residence on F st, between 17th & 18th sts, this morning at 9 o'clock.

The partnership between Thos Thompson & Danl Hannan, under the firm of Thompson & Hannan, was dissolved by mutual consent on Sep 3, 1860. Thos Thompson will continue the business at the old stand, 367 Pa ave.
–Thos Thompson, Danl Hannan, Wash.

WED SEP 5, 1860
Trustee's sale by decree of the Circuit Court of Wash Co, D C, passed in a cause of Cropley against Jas & Mary Thecker & others: auction on Sep 27, all that part of lot 72 in old Gtwn, with the bldgs thereon. –W Redin, trustee
-Barnard & Buckley, aucts

Austin, Aug 18, 1860. I withdraw my name from the list of candidates for the Presidency. Very respectfully, Sam Houston

Govane Female Institute, Govanstown, Md. Mrs C M & MissE P Ricers Principals. References: Rev R C Galbraith, Govanstown, Md; Rev Geo W Musgrave, D D, Phil; Rev John P Carter, Oxford, Pa; John S Tyson, Ellicott's Mills, Md; Rev C Huntington, do; Rev M B Grier, Wilmington, N C.

Orphans Court of Wash Co, D C. Letters of administration on the personal estate of John Q Sauter, late of Wash Co, deceased. –Wm Sauter, adm

Mrd: on Tue, in Wash City, by Rev John C Smith, Alex'r S Steuart to Miss Emma Josepha, daughter of Wm Nourse, all of Wash City.

Died: on Sep 3, in Wash City, after a short but painful illness, Grace Annie, aged 2 years & 6 months, daughter of John & Ann Bury. Her funeral will take place from the residence of her parents, on L st, between 18th & 19th sts, in the evening on Sep 5.

Died: on Aug 26, after a lingering illness of consumption, Judge Robt Baldwin Sherrard, of Marysville, Calif-son of Jos H Sherrard, of Winchester, Va, aged 33 years. Mr Sherrard returned to his native place, a few weeks since, in consequence of declining health, & closed his earthly career under the paternal roof. Thrice have the esteemed parents, within a brief space of time, been called to mourn a similar affliction.

Died: on Sep 4, Richard, only child of Edw A & the late Adelaide M Pollard, aged 5 months & 10 days.

Died: on Aug 30, in Hogansburgh, N Y, after a long & painful illness, Wm Brisband, formerly of Charleston, S C.

THU SEP 6, 1860
Saml Simon Breust, who murdered his friend & fellow-traveler, Fred Wm Schmidt, in a tavern at St Louis, robbed the corpse of about $1,200 in gold, & fled to Cincinnati, where he was arrested, & was hung in the former city on Friday. When on the gallows he expressed his penitence for the crime he had committed.

Warwick School for Boys, on the heights between Alexandria & Wash, will resume on Sep 19. References: Rev Drs Pinkney & Morsell, Rev W H Harris, Messrs J Earnest, Jno A Smith, & C R Maury, Mrs E L Knapp, Wash; Rev Mr Tillinghast, Dr Bohrer, W G Ridgely, Gtwn, D C.
–Rev E P Lippitt, Alexandria, Va

Miss Jennie Ross will re-open her school on Sep 10, at 402 F st, near 7th. [Ad]

Mrd: on Sep 4, by Rev Mr Aschwander, Lewis Brooks, of Gtwn, D C, to Catharine S Jones, of Phil.

Died: on Sep 4, after an illness of 38 hours, Eliz Bartholomew, consort of Wm S Morgan, in her 59th year. Her funeral will be from the residence of Mrs Morgan, 404½ 12th st, between I & K sts, on Sep 6 at 10 o'clock A M.

FRI SEP 7, 1860
Died: Sep 3, Blanche B, daughter of Benj H & M E A Ferguson, aged 10 months & 18 days.

Levi Adler, the well known proprietor of the Merchant's Hotel, lost his life by the hands of Wm H Mallory, a prominent lawyer & politician of this county. Adler was struck with a knife in his jugular vein & expired almost instantly. Mallory has been arrested & committed to jail. –Covington [Ky] Friend of Aug 30.

<u>Ladies Washington Nat'l Monument Society</u> who have received & accepted their appointments: Pres: Mrs Finlay M King, of N Y; Sec: Mrs Anna M Cosby, Wash
<u>Vice Presidents:</u>

Mrs R H Walworth, N Y	Mrs R M Henderson, Mo
Mrs Jane Van Waggoner, N J	Mrs Wm Sheets, Ind
Mrs Sara Holcomb, D C	Mrs Mary H Holbrook, Oregon
Mrs F C Cunningham, S C	Mrs Wm S Long, Calif
Mrs E R Hillyer, Miss	Mrs Gilbert C Monell, Neb
Mrs E H English, Ark	Mrs M C Brown, Fla

Toledo, Ohio, Sep 6. The lodging rooms of the Catholic Orphan Asylum here, were destroyed by fire last night. Three children & one <u>Sister of Charity</u> are missing, & it is supposed they perished in the flames. Another Sister was seriously injured by jumping from a window. The remains of one child have been found in the ruins.

SAT SEP 8, 1860

Rev Mr Bewley was hung in Texas a few days since on suspicion of abolitionism. The devoted minister of Christ, guilty of no crime, & on the merest suspicion that he cherished offensive opinions, was hung up like a murderer. –Albany Journal

Violent storm in Chas Co, Md on Friday of last week. Among the sufferers were Barnes Compton, who had a barn blown down & crop destroyed; Richd H Edelen, barn & crop destroyed; & Benton Barnes, Wm N Franklin, Jas L Brawner, E L Smoot, John W Mitchell, Dr F R Wills, J J Hughes, Judge F Digges, & Mrs Lloyd all had their crops destroyed.

Rev Alex D Moore, son of Mr Wm W Moore, of the Nat'l Intelligence, who has supplied the pulpit of Rev Mr Carother's church during his illness, has been unanimously elected Pastor of the Presbyterian Church at Dauphin, Pa, & has accepted the call, & will enter upon his duties on next Sabbath.

The three oldest pastors in Massachusetts are Rev Abraham Gushee, of Dighton, where he was settled in 1802; Rev Jos Richardson, of Hingham, settled in 1805; & Rev Dr Lowell, of the West Boston Church, settled in 1806. All are Unitarians.

In 1692 Rev Increase Mather was presented by the Corp & Overseers of Harvard College, over which he presided, with a Diploma of <u>Dr of Divinity</u>. This was the first instance in which such a degree was conferred in British America. The next was 79 years afterwards, in the case of Rev Nathl Appleton, of Cambridge.

Trustees of the Rockville Academy in Montg Co, Md, wish to employ 2 gentlemen qualified to discharge the duties of Principal & Assistant. By order of the Board. -Richd I Bowie, sec

Valuable property for sale, my farm of 120 acres, within 1 mile of the Rockville Turnpike, adjoining lands of G M Watkins & others. I will sell it as a whole for $50 per acre; & divide it, giving 55 acres, with the improvements, at $3,500; & 65 acres, without improvements, at $45 per acre. The bldg sites on both are excellent. Apply during ofc hours at 50 Winder's Bldg; at other hours at 58 First st, Gtwn, or by letter to Chas Slemmer, Gtwn, D C.

Mrd: on Sep 6, in Wash City, in the Ninth St Methodist Protestant Church, by Rev P Light Wilson, Mr Saml W Goodson, of Va, to Miss Mary W Billing, of Wash City.

Mrd: on Sep 4, in Wash City, by Rev Wm Hamilton, Mr Jerome Taylor to Miss Susan McDonald, all of Wash City.

Mrd: on Sep 4, by Rev Dr Howell, of Fairfield, near Nashville, the residence of the bride, D B De Bow, of Louisiana, to Martha E, daughter of the late John Johns, of Nashville, Tenn.

Died: on Aug 30, in Cincinnati, Mrs Lucy Bond, in her 63rd year, the excellent & beloved wife of Hon Wm Key Bond.

Montreal, Sep 7. Sir Geo Simpson, Govn'r of the Hudson's Bay Co, died at Lachine today.

MON SEP 10, 1860
Orphans Court of Wash Co, D C, Sep 8, 1860. In the case of Lucy M Johns, [late Darrell,] admx W A, of Benj E Brooke, deceased, the administratrix & Court have appointed Oct 2 next, for the final settlement of the personal estate of the said deceased, of the assets in hand. -Ed Roach, Reg/o wills

Orphans Court of Wash Co, D C. Letters of administration on the personal estate of Jas W Coombs, late of Wash Co, deceased. –Mary E Coombs, admx

Mrd: on Sep 4, at *Fort Monroe*, Va, by Rev Mr Cheevers, Lt W M Graham, U S Army, to Mary B, daughter of Capt Jas B Ricketts, U S Army.

Died: on Sep 9, after a long & painful illness, Esther Ann, eldest daughter of Robt & Sophia A Cohen. Her funeral will take place from her father's residence on Monday, at half-past 3 o'clock P M.

Chicago, Sep 8. The steamer **Lady Elgin**, in the Lake Superior line, which left here last night, was run into by the schnr **Augusta**, off Waukegan, at 2:30 this morning. Only 17 persons are known to have been saved, including the clerk, steward, & porter. From 350 to 400 persons are said to have been on board, & among them were the Black Yagers, the Green Yagers, & Rifles, & several fire companies of Milwaukee, who were on a visit to this city. Col Lumsden, of the New Orleans Picayune, & family, were on board, & are supposed to be among the lost. The steam-tug **McQueen** left this morning for the scene of the disaster. The names of the saved, as far as known, are: *H G Caryl, clerk; Fred Rice, steward; Edw Westlake, porter; Robt Gore; Thos Murphy; Thos Cummings; Michl Conner; John E Hobart, of Milwaukee; Tim O'Bryen; W A Darnes; Wildman Mills, of Ohio; Lyman Updike, of Waupan; H Ingraham, member of the Canadian Parliament. The son of the proprietor of the London News was on board, & is supposed to be lost. The books & papers of the steamer are all lost. After the collision the steamer floated south to Winetka, where she sunk. Chicago, Sep 9: *Mr H C Clavyl, was the Clerk of the lost steamer.

TUE SEP 11, 1860
Thu last Ex-Pres Pierce was thrown from his wagon in Concord, N H, his horse took fright & turned suddenly. He was stunned & bruised, but not seriously injured.

Rev W McMahon, a venerable Methodist minister, in writing reminiscences of his early life, founded the first Methodist Church in Huntsville, Ala.

Gain Robinson, a young lawyer, well known in Buffalo, N Y, a man of fine intellect, committed suicide last week, in a shocking manner, while in a state of intoxication, fell across the railroad track rails.

A beautiful daughter of Mr Asch, residing in Spruce st, & a sister of De Morris Asch, of Jefferson Medical College, died when ascending the stairs of her father's house with a pitcher of water in her hand, she tripped forward, breaking the pitcher. Fragments of the glass severed her jugular, & she died in a few minutes. She was the last born of a numerous family. –Phil Inquirer of Sep 7.

Central Coal & Wood Depot, 483 9th st, north of Pa ave. –Wm H H Barclay [Ad]

Va Military Land Warrant, No 2,538, issued to Lt Wm Broadus, of the Va State line, dated Feb 19, 1784, for 1,666 acres of land, in part consideration of his Revolutionary services for 3 years, has been lost or mislaid, & has not been satisfied in whole or in part. This is to give notice that the undersigned, atty for the heirs of said Broadus, has obtained a duplicate of said warrant from the proper authorities, & has applied to the Com'r of the Gen Land Ofc to issue scrip for the satisfaction of the same. –P Williams, atty for the heirs.

Orphans' Court of PG Co, Md. Letters testamentary on the personal estate of Richd Young, late of PG Co, deceased. –Alex McCormick, exc of Richd Young

The Elias Howe, jr, Patent for his <u>Sewing Machine</u>, which expired yesterday, was renewed by the Com'r of Patents to Sep 10, 1867. The nett profits to Mr Howe of his invention have been $468,000.

Mrd: on Monday, by Rev John C Smith, Mr Selim Slaughter to Miss Martha E Buckley, both of Va.

Died: on Sep 9, Josiah F Polk, aged 68 years, long an esteemed resident of Wash City. His funeral is this day at 12 o'clock, from Mrs Bannerman's boarding-house, on Pa ave, between 3rd & 4½ sts.

Died: on Sep 8, in Wash City, Samuel S Altemus, son of Thos & Mary Altemus, aged 7 years, 5 months & 1 day.

Cleveland, Sep 10. The monument to the memory of Cmdor Oliver Hazard Perry was inaugurated today in the presence of 30,000 persons. In the procession were 6 survivors of the battle of Lake Erie, & a large number of soldiers of the war of 1812. Hon Geo Bancroft delivered the oration. [Sep 13th newspaper: The statue was made by Mr Wm Walcott, a native of Ohio. It is 8 feet in height, & stands upon a pedestal of Rhode Island granite 17 feet in height; the statue is cut from a block of pure white marble from a Vt quarry.]

Died: on Sep 4, in Wash City, Lucy Rebecca, infant daughter of J R W & Lucy Blakistone Mankin, aged 12 months.

WED SEP 12, 1860
Effects of a Grocery Store at auction on Sep 14, at the establishment of Mr Jas Owner, on East Capitol st, between 1st & 2nd sts. -J C McGuire & Co, aucts

Wm D Totty, convicted of the murder of his sister-in-law at Richmond, Va, has been refused a new trial & sentenced to be hung on Nov 3. An appeal, however, has been taken to the Court of Appeals.

But a few weeks ago the family circle of Hon Wm H Purnell, the Comptroller of the Treasury of Md, embraced 5 interesting children. Disease recently invaded his household, & of the 5 who composed this happy family group 4 now sleep in the arms of death, & the last lies prostrate beneath the hand of affliction. Diptheria is the disease which caused the fourth death in the family, on Sep 2.

Died: on Sep 9, at Greenhill, PG Co, Md, Mary Augusta, daughter of Geo A & Sarah R Digges, aged 11 months & 27 days.

Disaster to the steamer **Lady Elgin**: Capt John Wilson was undoubtedly among the lost; the schnr **Augusta**, Capt Mallott, was on her way from St Clair river to Chicago with a cargo of lumber. Mr Michl E Smith, of Ontonagon, was saved on a float, part of the hurricane deck; Mr Smith knew two men on the raft, the capt & Mr Waldo, the clerk of the Nat'l Mine at Ontonagon. The capt called to other rafts inquiring of his Southern friends, probably Col F A Lumsden & family, of New Orleans, & Mr Garth & family, of Ky. Mr J W Eviston, of Milwaukee, was with his wife on the pilot house, & his sole care seemed to be for her. When a huge wave washed her off into the lake, her husband swam to her assistance & both were saved. Edw Spencer, a student of the Garrett Biblical Institute, tied a rope about his body & plunged into the surf, rescuing several from a watery grave. Not less than 14 persons were saved at the pier in front of Artemas Carter's house, some owing their lives to Mr Carter himself. Prominent among those from Chicago who perilled their safety in their efforts to save the unfortunates were Gurdon S Hubbard, Coroner James, & Policemen Prince, Pilgrim, Alexander, & McCauley. Special praise is due to Mr Jared Gage, of Winetka, whose efforts to succor & relieve the distressed redound to the nobleness of his heart.

Died: on Sep 10, in Wash City, Reuben Burdine, aged 64 years, for 40 years a resident of Wash. He was much distinguished in knowledge, firm in his views of God, & convinced of the truth of the Catholic religion, in which he died. His funeral is this morning at 10 o'clock, from his late residence, 358 6th st, between H & I sts.

Died: on Sep 6, at **Fort Moultrie**, near Charleston, of typhoid fever, Dr Bernard M Byrne, Surgeon in the U S Army, in his 48th year. He was a native of Ireland, & his parents emigrated to Balt, with a numerous family, while he was yet very young. He obtained a classical education in that city, & was a graduate of the Medical Dept of the Univ of Md. His connexion with the army dates almost from the beginning of the Florida or Seminole war. At the opening drama of the Mexican war we find him at Palo Alto, & on the field of battle, rendering service to the mortally wounded Ringgold. Some years since he was united in marriage to the daughter of Col Abert, Chief of Topographical Enginners, Wash, & he leaves a widow & 3 children to mourn his untimely death. –Charleston Mercury

THU SEP 13, 1860
Excellent household & kitchen furniture at auction on Sep 19, at the late residence of Hon John B Haskins, corner of I st & N J ave. -A Green, aucts

Orphans Court of Wash Co, D C. Letters of administration on the personal estate of Susan Decatur, deceased. –Lucretia Hobbs, Mary Fenwick, adms

Wm S Mitchell has association with us in the House-furnishing Dry Goods business, under the name of Wm S Mitchell & Co. –Barnes & Mitchell

Having disposed of the entire stock & fixtures of my Merchant Tailoring establishment on 7th st to Mr Jas T McIntosh, I confidently recommend him to all persons in want of good clothing as a skillful & experienced tailor.
–P J Steer Merchant Tailor, 488 7th st. –J T McIntosh

Cumberland Coal, T J & M W Galt, 282 Pa ave, between 11th & 12th sts.

Orphans Court of Wash Co, D C, Sep 11, 1860. In the case of Johana Hughes, admx with the will annexed of John Hughes, deceased, the administratrix & Court have appointed Oct 6th next, for the final settlement of the personal estate of the said deceased, of the assets in hand. -Ed Roach, Reg/o wills

Obit-died: on Sep 3, at his residence in Anne Arundel Co, Md, Mr John Linthicum, in his 45th year. He was a man of superior endowments. In the domestic relations, as a son, a father, a husband, & a brother, he was endeared by the strongest ties of affection. As a Christian, his theology was perfectly evangelical. He found this foundation able to support him amid the ravages of disease. –W H P

Died: on Sep 12, in Wash City, after a short illness, Margaret A Warder, 2nd daughter of Ann S & the late Walter Warder, in her 26th year. Her funeral will take place from the residence of her brother-in-law, Geo J Seufferie, 484 E st, between 5th & 6th sts, tomorrow afternoon at 3:30 o'clock P M.

Died: on Aug 23, in Phil, after a painful illness, Anne Harreitte, 2nd daughter of Henry T Harrison, of Leesburg, Va, aged 18 years. Asleep in Jesus.

FRI SEP 14, 1860
In Chancery, Aug 30, 1860. Tilghman Nuttle vs Hannah McCartee, wife of Jas McCartee, Levin Henry Wootters, Sarah Catharine Wootters, Jos Smith Wootters, & Chas Wootters. The object of this suit is to procure a decree for the sale of the real estate of which Levin Wootters, sen, died seized & possessed, in Caroline Co, Md, to pay off the creditors of said Levin Wootters, who remain unpaid because of the insufficiency of the personal estate of said Wootters to pay & satisfy them, the said creditors' claims. The bill states that on or about 1857, said Levin Wootters, sen, departed this life, being indebted unto Tilghman Nuttle, on two judgments obtained in the Circuit Court for Caroline Co, Md, at the Oct term of said Court, in 1856, the said judgments amounting to $400 & over; & that the said Levin Wootters, sen, was also largely indebted unto other parties besides himself; & that there has been letters of administration granted by the Orphans' Court of Caroline Co to one Sarah Wootters, who has executed the personal estate in due course of administration, & it is found to be insufficient to pay off the creditors of said Levin Wootters; & that the said Levin Wootters left as his heirs at law, Nancy Higntt, Sarah Beachamp, Cecelia Colescoth, Geo W & Wm Wootters, Francis & Wm H Wootters, Sarah Beachamp & Edw & Prath Wootters, all of the State of Md, Caroline Co, & Hannah McCartee, wife of Jas McCartee, of the State of Indiana, & Levin Henry Wootters, Sarah Catharine Wootters, Jos Smith Wootters, & Chas Wootters, all children of Jas T Wootters, who was one of the main or principal heirs of said Levin Wootters, sen, deceased, & who was also a resident of the State of Indiana, & now a resident of the State of Md. Absent dfndnts are to appear in this Court, in person or by solicitor, on or before the first Monday in Jan, 1861. –Robt J Jump, Clerk of the Circuit Court for Caroline Co.

Mr S D Huntoon, of the firm of Fellows & Huntoon, Hopkinton, N H, was horribly burnt on Thu last, when burning fluid escaped causing a barrel to explode. He lived until Sunday, in great agony, when death came to his relief.

Prof H Perobean, Organist of St Aloysius, proposes to remain in Wash 2 or 3 more days in the week, in order to accept scholars for the Piano & Organ beginners, as well as more advanced pupils. Terms: for piano $30, for organ $50 per quarter. Orders may be left at Metzerott's music store.

Died: on Sep 13, in Wash City, in his 36th year, Wm C Brent, son of the late Robt Y Brent. His funeral will take place from St Patrick's Church on Sep 15 at 10 o'clock. The remains will be carried to Carroll Chapel, Montgo Co, Md.

SAT SEP 15, 1860
Died: yesterday, suddenly, at Balt, Mrs Susan Evans, wife of Rev French S Evans, one of the proprietors of the Balt Patriot, & recently a resident of Wash City.

Texas: 1-Wm Staton, a resident of Anderson Co for many years, had been hung for inciting the slaves to insurrection & incendiarism. 2-Two men named Boardwright were hung in Robertson Co, Sunday before last, after trial before the Vigilance Cmte, & satisfactory evidence of their guilt in tampering with the slaves. 3-The notorious horse thief Robt Tucker was hung in Johnson Co on Sep 11. He had confessed his crimes just before he was hung by order of the Vigilance Cmte.

Pension Ofc: Application made under act of Jun 23, 1860, for the reissue of land warrants described herein, which are alleged to have been lost or destroyed, & new certificate or warrant of like tenor will be issued, if no valid objection should appear.
No. 12,680, for 80 acres, issued to Martha Burrow, widow of Robt Burrow, on Nov 13, 1855.
No. 14,770, for 80 acres, issued to Thos Merritt, on Dec 10, 1855.
No. 17,681, for 80 acres, issued to John McCallie, on Jan 7, 1856.
No. 19, 248, for 80 acres, issued to John Reagan, on Jan 21,1856.
No. 19, 251, for 80 acres, issued to Elijah Nelson, on Jan 21, 1856.
No. 19,253, for 80 acres, issued to John McMurray, on Jan 21, 1856.
No. 19,255, for 80 acres, issued to Robt Willox, on Jan 21, 1856.
No. 20,078, for 80 acres, issued to Moses Gamble, on Jan 19, 1856.
No. 41,266, for 120 acres, issued to Jas R Johnson, on Jan 31, 1856.
No. 46,492, for 120 acres, issued to Jesse Cashen, on Jan 29, 1856.
No. 18,194, for 160 acres, issued to Jeremiah Crowley, on Mar 13, 1856.
No. 18,483, for 160 acres, issued to John Seckell, on Mar 20, 1856.
No. 19,701, for 160 acres, issued to Danl Hewett, on Mar 31, 1856.
No. 22,604, for 160 acres, issued to Jos Robbins, on Apr 17, 1856.
No. 20,129, for 80 acres, issued to Isabella P Perry, widow of Solomon Perry, on Jan 21, 1856.
No. 37,395, for 80 acres, issued to Chas Kinsolver, on Jul 2, 1856.
No. 42,757, for 80 acres, issued to Jos Talbert, on Oct 8, 1856.
No. 49,214, for 160 acres, issued to Benj T Garnes, on Dec 3, 1856.
No. 68,656, for 160 acres, issued to Catharine D Blondel, widow of John M Blondel, on Jun 11, 1857.
No. 56,406, for 120 acres, issued to Betsey Manley, widow of Josiah B Manley, deceased, on Mar 8, 1856.
No. 50,548, for 120 acres, issued to John Bachelder, on Jan 31, 1856.
Land warrant certificate No. 80,394, for 160 acres, issued to Michl Bolley, father of Nicholas Bolley, private of Co E, 3rd Regt U S Infty, Mexican war, bearing date Mar 29, 1859. -Dec 4, 1860, Geo C Whiting, Com'r of Pensions.

Died: on Aug 28 last, at St Louis, Mo, Mrs Elvira McLean, wife of Hector D McLean, of that city; daughter of the late Chas G Wintersmith, of Harper's Ferry, Va, & niece of John S Gallaher, of Wash City; a lady of excellent qualities of head & heart.

Circuit Court of D C-in Chancery. The heirs-at-law of John Mason vs the heirs-at-law of John T Mason. The trustee reports that he has sold, in Wash City, D C, lot 24 in square 5, for $407.75, to Saml R Brick; lots 7 & 8 in square 6, for $550, to Danl McLaughlin; lot 4 in square 5, for $97, to Bernard McGee; & lot 26 in square 5, for $162.50, to W Kerr; lot 3 in square 44, to R W Barnard, for $183.67. -John Marbury, trustee

MON SEP 17, 1860
Mrs Harney, wife of Gen Harney, of the U S Army, died in Paris on Aug 27. The funeral service over her remains took place at the Church of St Philippe, Faubourg St Honore, with all the solemn & imposing ceremony of the Catholic Church, of which she was a member. Amongst those who did honor to her remains were her son, son-in-law, & nephew; Mr Faulkner, the American Minister; Mr Calhoun, a planter from Louisiana; Col Stewart, son of Com Stewart, & many others.

Chas L Newhall, of Southbridge, Mass, has been fined $20 & costs, amounting in all to $40 or $50, for sending to the Worcester Spy a false report of the death of Mr Oliver M Mason, of Southbridge. He appealed from the sentence, & gave bail in $200 to appear for trial.

Orphans Court of Wash Co, D C. Letters testamentary on the personal estate of Anna Cochran, late of Wash Co, deceased. –Eglantine Coke, excx

Mrd: on Sep 6, at Madison, Conn, by Rev W C Fowler, Rev A S Fiske, of St Paul, Minn, to Lizzie W Hand, daughter of the late Jos W Hand, of Wash City.

Died: on Sep 14, of typhoid fever, Abram Paynter, in his 39th year.

Died: on Sep 16, of water on the brain, after a very short illness, Mary Julia, aged 4 years & 3 months, daughter of Sarah S & Julius De Sauls. Her funeral will take place from the residence of her parents, at 4 o'clock, this afternoon, on 10th st, between Va ave & C st, Island.

Died: on Sep 16, at **Mount Pleasant**, near Wash, James Mason, infant son of Lt Henry B & Mary M Tyler, aged 9 months & 15 days.

I offer on Oct 10th next, on the premises, my Farm at auction: located in Fairfax Co, Va; contains 510 acres, with a new dwlg house handsomely situated, architecturally built, & conveniently arranged. –Chas S Taylor, Alexandria, Va

TUE SEP 18, 1860
Orphans Court of D C sale, on Sep 24, of household & kitchen furniture at auction at the residence of the late Lewis Carbery, on Second st. Also, negro girl Mary, 18 years of age, slave for life; & negro boy John, 16 years of age, & slave for life. –T Dowling, auct

Danl Shearin, age 3 years, was lost near Oxford, N C, last Friday. His body was found drowned in the creek a short distance away.

Orphans Court of Wash Co, D C. Letters testamentary on the personal estate of Michl R Shyne, late of Wash Co, deceased. –Catherine Shyne, excx

Mrd: on Sep 16, in Wash City, by Rev Mr Hamilton, Chas M Miller, of Shepherdstown, Jefferson Co, Va, to Miss Lavinia Flowers, of Wash City.

Died: on Sep 17, in Wash City, Mrs Mary Ashton Fitzgerald, a native of Marblehead, Mass, in her 91st year. Her funeral will be from the residence of her son, Wm A Fitzgerald, 355 F st, between 9th & 10th sts, this afternoon at 4 o'clock.

Died: on Sep 17, in Wash City, Mrs Maria Frances McCalla, consort of Gen John M McCalla. Her funeral will take place from the family residence, 9 Indiana ave, this day, at 3:30 o'clock P M.

Died: on Sep 17, in Wash City, William Lyel, 2nd & youngest son of S N & E M McIntire, aged 3 years & 3 months. His funeral will take place from the residence of his father, on E st, between 1st & 2nd sts, on Sep 19, at 3 o'clock.

Died: on Sep 15, at the residence of his grandfather, Judge Purcell, on Capitol Hill, William F Purcell, beloved son of West & Margaret Scott, aged 14 months.

WED SEP 19, 1860

Mr & Mrs Douglas visited his mother at Clifton Springs, N Y, on Sat last. The gathering there far exceeded public expectations. From there he proceeded to Syracuse where he addressed a great assemblage of people.

Don Juan Bello, the Minister from Chili to this country died on Sunday at his rooms at the Clarendon Hotel, N Y. His disease was of an asthmatic character, & his death was very unexpected to his family & friends, who are here with him. He was but 35 years of age. –N Y Post

Five persons, who were returning to Rockland, Me, in an open sail-boat, from camp-meeting at Northport, on Sep 9, were capsized when off Camden, & Mrs Dr Colby, Mrs Nancy Hopkins, & Miss Jameson, were drowned. Mr Thompson & his wife clung to the swamped boat, & were picked up by a schnr.

Circuit Court of Wash Co, D C–in Chancery. In the cause wherein Griffith & others are cmplnts, & Cooney's heirs are dfndnts, the trustee sold to Michl Cooney, square 908, in Wash City, for $994.32, & the purchaser complied with the terms of sale. -John F Ennis, trustee

Circuit Court of Wash Co, D C-in Chancery. Otis J Preston et al vs Thos Welsh. The trustee reported that on May 18, 1860, he sold the real estate mentioned to Geo A Davis for $1,255. –Davidge & Ingle, for cmplnts -Jno A Smith, clerk

Supreme Court of U S, No 151, Dec Term, 1859. Geo W Watterston, plntf in error, vs Edw Noble. In error to the Circuit Court of the U S for the eastern district of Louisiana. Mr Goold, of counsel for the dfndnt in error, having suggested the death of Geo W Watterston, the plntf in error, since the last continuance of this cause, moved the Court for an order, under the 15th rule of court, to make the proper reps parties. If the reps of the said Geo W Watterston, deceased, shall voluntarily become parties with the first 10 days of the ensuing term of this court, the dfndnt in error shall be entitled to have this writ of error dismissed. –Wm Thos Carroll, C S C U S

Orphans Court of Wash Co, D C. Letters testamentary on the personal estate of Maria J Cuvillier, late of Wash Co, deceased. –Jos Redfern, exc

Died: on Sep 17, in Wash City, in his 52nd year, Mr Geo W Moore, formerly of Balt & more recently of Charlottesville, Va.

THU SEP 20, 1860
Sale of China, Cutlery, Plated & other costly Wares, at auction, at the store of C E Green, 274 Pa av, between 11th & 12th sts, next door to the Kirkwood House, his entire stock. –Wall & Barnard, aucts

Orphans Court of Wash Co, D C. Letters testamentary on personal estate of Reuben Burdine, late of Wash Co, deceased. –Stanislaus Murray, B Johnson Hellen, excs

Died: on Sep 16, at the Hot Springs, Bath Co, Va, Mrs Catherine H, wife of Thos R Bird, in her 47th year.

Miss Arnold, 475 L st, above 11th, continues to give lessons in English Branches, Mathematics, Latin, Modern Languages, & Drawing. Refers to her present & former patrons in Wash City.

Dr Wadsworth has returned & will be pleased to see those desiring his professional services.

For sale: a fine young gray Horse; works well in harness. Apply at Fleming & Foy's Stable, C st, between 4½ & 6th sts.

FRI SEP 21, 1860
Died: on Sep 20, in Gtwn, John Connelly, in his 31st year. His funeral will be from the residence of his mother-in-law, Mrs Stanton, 33 Congress st, on Friday, at 3:30 o'clock P M.

Trustee's sale: valuable property, between 11th & 12 th sts, near Pa ave, Wash City, by deed of trust from Jos Cuvillier, dated May 13, 1854, recorded in Liber J A S No 77, filios 17 etc, of the land records of Wash Co, D C, I shall, at the request of the owner & holder of the note therein secured, on Oct 16, at public auction, sell lots 1, 2, 5, 6, 7, 8, 12 thru 18, in square 992. –Wm R Woodward, trustee -A Green, aucts

Very valuable improved property at public auction, first class residence at I & 20th sts, now occupied by S Ferguson, with a handsome 3 story brick dwlg. After the sale, I shall sell at auction the property lately occupied by Mrs Bache, 2 doors west of the above. Lot fronts on I st about 22 feet, & runs back about 135 feet. The owner is about to remove from Wash City. -Jas C McGuire & Co, aucts

Obit-died: [from the New Orleans Picayune of Sep 16.] Francis Asbury Lumsden, a native of N C; at an early age he was apprenticed to the senior Jos Gales, then editor of the Raleigh Register, in whose ofc he served his time. After spending 9 years in the Nat'l Intelligencer, at Wash City; he came to New Orleans, about 24 years ago, & in 1836 was foreman in a journal called the Standard. [Lost in the disaster of the steamer **Lady Elgin.**]

The oldest of the reigning Sovereigns in Europe, & the head of the oldest reigning family in Europe, died the other day-the Grand Duke of Mecklenburg-Strelitz. The monarch just dead was Geo Fred'k Chas Jos, born on Aug 12, 1779, so that he was over 81 years of age. He has reigned for 45 years, & is succeeded by his son, Fred'k Wm Chas Geo Ernest Adolphus Gustavus, who is married to a daughter of the late Duke of Cambridge. -Phil Bulletin

Superior Linen Goods, J W Colley & Co, 523 7th st, above Pa ave, Wash. [Ad]

SAT SEP 22, 1860
Kenmore, near Fredericksburg, was sold last week to Mrs Harrison, of Goochland Co, for $10,000. **Kenmore** was the residence of Mary, the mother of Washington, whose unfinished monument still adorns the neighboring eminence.

Mrd: on Sep 20, by Rev Mr McNally, Marian, daughter of Wm Ramsay, of the U S Navy, to Brockholdst, son of Hon R B Cutting, of N Y.

Died: on Aug 31, 1860, at Saratoga, N Y, Mrs Harriet M Garland, wife of Gen John Garland, U S Army. The funeral ceremonies of the deceased will take place at *Oakhill Cemetery*, Gtwn, at 4 o'clock P M, today, Sep 22.

MON SEP 24, 1860
Hon Jas French Strothers died at his residence in Culpeper Co, Va, on Friday. Several years since, he represented in Congress the 7th Congressional district of Va.

Presidential appointments: 1-Geo S Frost, Receiver of Public Moneys at Detroit, Mich, vice Beeson, resigned. 2-Robt W Jamison, Register of the Land Ofc at Monroe, La, vice John McEnery, removed. 3-Geo Purvis, Receiver of Public Moneys at Monroe, La, vice Chas H Dabbs, removed.

The Will Case of the late Miss Ann Reed Dermott was finally disposed of on Sat before Judge Purcell, of the Orphans Court of Wash Co, D C. The will as produced was supported by Gen Walter Jones, & fully admitted to probate. The decision is that after the payment of debts, the satisfaction of claims & payment of certain bequests to relatives & others, there will be a residuary fund to be devoted to the establishment of an asylum for destitute white female orphans, & after its successful establishment for 2 years then to the equipment & transportation of free colored emigrants to Liberia. Two of the executors name in the will, Messrs John P Ingle & Richd Smith, will probably qualify; the former has bonded already.

Died: on Sep 2, at Woodford Co, Ky, the place of his birth, Jas Railey, aged 63 years & 6 months. A noble man has fallen asleep in Jesus.

Orphans Court of Wash Co, D C. Letters testamentary on the personal estate of Thos T Houston, late of Wash Co, deceased. –Susan Houston, excx

Orphans Court of Wash Co, D C. In the case of Rebecca Connelly, admx of John Connelly, deceased, the administratrix & Court have appointed Oct 16 next, for the final settlement of the personal estate of the said deceased, of the assets in hand. -Ed Roach, Reg/o wills

Orphans Court of Wash Co, D C. In the case of John Walter, exc of Henry Carl, deceased, the executor & Court have assigned Oct 16 next, for the final settlement of the personal estate of the said deceased, of the assets in hand.
-Ed Roach, Reg/o wills

TUE SEP 25, 1860
Executor's sale, by order of the Orphans Court of Wash Co, D C, of household & kitchen furniture at auction on Sep 27, the personal effects of the late Reuben Burdine, on 6th st, between H & I sts. –Johnson Hellen, Stanislaus Murray, excs. -A Green, aucts

We the undersigned have this day entered into copartnership to transact the General Auction Commission & Furniture Business, under the name & style of Cleary & Green. –F D Cleary, J C Green, 9th st & Pa ave, Wash.

Died: on Sep 24, Hattie, wife of Geo W Boardman, of Missouri, & daughter of Robt & Mary Widdicombe, of Wash City. Her funeral is on Wed at 12 o'clock, from Trinity Church.

WED SEP 26, 1860
Capt Geo A Magruder, U S Navy, has been ordered to take charge of the Bureau of Ordnance & Hydrography of the Navy Dept, vice Ingraham, ordered to sea duty.

E Owen & Son, Merchant Tailors, 212 Pa ave, just opened their first invoice of goods for the season. [Ad]

Mr Edgar Snowden, of the Alexandria Gaz, has associated with him in the management of that paper his sons, Edgar Snowden, jr, & Harold Snowden, under the firm of Edgar Snowden & Sons.

Died: on Sep 16, at *Granville*, his residence, near Warrenton, Va, Danl Payne, in his 77th year.

Orphans Court of Wash Co, D C, Sep 22, 1860. In the case of Thos M Boyer & Hillery L Offutt, admx of Richd M Boyer, deceased, the administrators & Court have appointed Oct 16 next, for the final settlement of the personal estate of the said deceased, of the assets in hand. -Ed Roach, Reg/o wills

Orphans Court of Wash Co, D C. Letters testamentary on the personal estate of Wm Campbell, late of Wash Co, deceased. –B W Reed, exc

THU SEP 27, 1860
Sale of valuable lot by order of the Circuit Court of Wash Co, D C, by order of the Court, passed on May 6, 18_9, in the matter of the petition of the heirs of J A M Duncanson, deceased: sale on Oct 26, on the premises, east half of lot 5 in square 374, being the last of the real estate of J A M Duncanson, deceased, unsold. The lot is located on H st, between 9th & 10th sts. –Wm B Todd, Francis Mohun, Isaac Clark, Jas Towles, Com'rs -A Green, aucts

Trustee's sale of valuable Farm at auction, on Oct 9 next, by deed of trust from Thos A Mitchell, dated Nov 17, 1859, recorded in Liber J G H, No 7, folios 642 & 643, of the land records of the Circuit Court for Montg Co, Md: parcel of land in said county, near Dr Benj Duvall's land, containing 180 acres of land, more or less, being the whole of the property purchased by the said party of the first part of Jas G Jewell, with all improvements thereon. –Mahlon Ashford, trustee -A Green, aucts

Died: on Sep 26, in Wash City, in her 71st year, Mrs Ann H Scott, relict of the late Dr Thos C Scott, of Wash. Her funeral is this morning at 9 o'clock, at St Patrick's Church. The friends of the family are respectfully invited.

FRI SEP 28, 1860
Household & kitchen furniture at auction on Oct 4, at the residence of Mrs Beck, 370 6th st, near H st. -A Green, aucts

Mrs Thomas, wife of Wm H Thomas, of Fredericksburgh, Va, was seriously burnt by the explosion of a camphene lamp on Monday night.

Clark Co [Va] Conservator: on Sep 15 a young man by the name of Barr went to the house of Mr Bennett Russell at a late hour, somewhat intoxicated, & made some noise in the yard, & Mr Russell fired upon him with a shot-gun, striking him, but no serious result was apprehended until the morning of Sep 22. Barr continued to work and died on Friday, the shot penetrated the skull between the eyes, passed through the brain, & lodged against the skull in the back of the head.

The Historical Society of Va appointed Wm N McDonald, of Fred'k Co, to write the history of the late Brown Invasion.

Notice: The creditors of Patrick Calhoun, deceased, late capt in the U S Army, are to present their demands to the undersigned, administrator, by Jan 1, 1861. Sufficient evidence of indebtedness will be required. Those owing Capt Calhoun's estate will be pleased to made prompt payment.
–Edw Noble, adm, Abbeville C H, S C

Mrd: on Sep 26, at **Fountain Rock**, the residence of the bride's father, in Jefferson Co, Va, by Rev Chas W Andrews, D D, Henry A Didier, of Balt, to Angelica, 2nd daughter of Hon Alex'r R Boteler.

Mrd: on Sep 19, at **Bedford**, near Shepherdstown, Va, by Rev Chas W Andrews, D D, Col Armistead T M Rust, of Loudoun, to Miss Ida Lee, daughter of Edmund J Lee, of Jefferson Co, Va.

Died: on Sep 25, of typhoid fever, Jos P Cogswell, in his 29th year. His funeral is this afternoon at 3 o'clock, from his late residence on Mass ave, near 6th st.

Died: on Sep 21, at **Portland Manor**, Anne Arundel Co, Md, Eliel S Wilson, in his 32nd year. At an early age he graduated at Gtwn College, at the head of his class; after a course of study at Harvard he was admitted to the Bar in Balt.

Redemption of the following Va certificates. Whether surrendered or not, the interest will cease on that day. Under an act to provide for the construction of a turnpike road from Staunton to Parkersburg, passed Mar 16, 1838, as amended under the 3rd section of an act to provide for raising loans to certain railroad companies, & for other purposes, passed Mar 21, 1839:
1841: Jos Smith, of Augusta Co: $300.
1841: Thos Stevenson, of Richmond: $200.
1842: Jas Haskins, cmte of Jno Haskins, sr: $845.
1842: Saml Hannah, of Charleston, Kanawha: $600.
1843: Johanna Shaer, of Germany: $400.
1844: Norman Stewart, of Richmond: $200.
1846: Wm M Jackson, of Winchester: $200.

1847: Archibald Atkinson: $1,200.
1847: Littl'n W Tazewell, of Norfolk: $1,000.
1849: Wm Radford, exc of R Walker: $400.
1849: P St Geo Ambler, trustee for Mrs G B Brooke: $100.
1849: D H Gordon, trustee for the children of B B Gordon: $500.
1849: Eliz Bernard, of Fredericksburg: $1,000.
1851: Wm Wirt Cabell: $200.
1851: Robt King: $200.
1852: Robt King, of Orange: $600.
1853: Thos J Randolph, of Albemarle: $400.
1853: Jas M Perdue, Com'r, etc: $500.
1853: lawson Nunnally, trustee of Catharine H Friend: $500.
1853: Eliz A Fitzgerald: $300.
1854: Virginia Taylor, of Norfolk: $100.
1854: John W Toney: $1,000.
1854: R G Morriss, guardian: $300.
1854: C J Beirne: $500.
1854: Eliza A Davenport: $600.
1855: F N Watkins, for Union Theological Seminary: $800.
1856: R G Morriss, trustee under the will of C S Morriss, deceased: $2,000.
1856: Cyrus W Granby, of Norfolk: $900.
1856: Sarah C Cooke, of Norfolk: $200.
1856: Wm E Jackson, one of the surviving children: $1,900.
1857: John Stuart, trustee for Matilda Hill: $62.31.
1857: Sally B Ship: $100.
1858: L Delarue, an infant: $450.
1858: Mary & Eliz D Vass: $100.
1858: Addison A Jones: $500.
1858: Benj Waters: $100.
1859: Thos W Doswell, trustee: $180.
1859: Martin James, of Goochland: $200.
1859: G W Lewis: $300.
1859: Richd Whitfield: $400.
1860: Wm H Allison: $500.
1860: C C Armstrong, trustee of the children of W J Armstrong: $1,100.
1860: L B Conway: $750.
Under an act to increase the capital stock of the Portsmouth & Roanoke Railroad Co, passed Jan 20, 1834: 5%.
1838: Fretchville Lawson Ballantyne Dykes, of Doven Hall, Cumberland; Jas Garth Marshall, merchant of Leeds & Henry Cowper Marshall, of Leeds, merchant; trustees under the will of John Marshall, jr, deceased: $75,000.
1844: Richd Thornton, of Old Swan Wharf, upper Thames st, London: $6,000.
1849: Baroness Johanna Albertina Adelaide de Berlichingen, wife of Baron Frederic de Berlichingen, of Stuttgart: $3,000.
1850: David Barclay Chapman, of London: $20,000.

Act authorizing the Board of Public Works to subscribe, on behalf of the Commonwealth, to the stock of the Richmond, Fredericksburg, & Potomac Railroad Co, passed Jan 23, 1835.
1838: Fretchville Lawson Ballantyne Dykes, of Dovenby Hall, Cumberland, Jas Garth Marshall, merchant of Leeds & Henry Cowper Marshall, of Leeds, merchant; trustees under the will of John Marshall, jr, deceased: $35,000.
1839: Francis Marx, of Eaton Square, Middlesex, in England: $10,000.
1839: Henry Tillard, of Wiln Mills, Derbyshire, in England; Rev Geo Gotterill, of Eastham, near Norwich, & Richd Henry Tillard, of Lincoln's Inn, London, with benefit of survivorship: $5,000.
1851: Alex'r Brown & Sons, of Balt: $10,000.
1860: Henrietta Codrington, of Deane House, near Alresford, in the county of Harts, widow: $10,000.
–J M Bennett, Auditor of Public Accounts; S H Parker, Register; Geo W Munford, Sec of the Commonwealth. Com'rs of the Sinking Fund.

SAT SEP 29, 1860

Horrible tragedy in Fosterville, Rutherford Co, on Sat last. Mr Stovall, a gentleman who has heretofore been highly respected by his neighbors, killed his wife & 4 children, & afterwards killed himself by cutting his own throat & jumping into a deep cave spring, where he was found next morning. In past weeks Mr Stovall had discussed his failure of crops & financial troubles. –Nashville Gaz of Sep 25.

On Thu at Easton, Pa, Mr Castner, a farmer, & his two sons, were drowned or suffocated. It was at a cider-mill, where they have a large tank to put the cider in for fermentation. One son was suffocated, & fell to the bottom of the tank; his father tried to rescue him, & he too fell in; the other son attempted to rescue his father & brother, but fell to the botton, & all three were drowned, or suffocated by the foul air.

Mrd: on Sep 27, at Green Spring Run, Hampshire Co, Va, by Rev Mr Spear, Mr Jas Bonifant, of Montg Co, Md, to Miss L C Craigen, of Hampshire Co, Va.

Mrd: on Aug 14, in Somerset, Pa, by Rev Walter Brown, Georgia, daughter of Geo Chorpenning, of Pa, to Frank A McGee, of Wash.

Died: on Sep 22, at his residence, in King Geo Co, Va, Gustavus Brown Alexander, aged 67 years. In Alexandria & its immediate neighborhood he spent his youth & early manhood, & to the day of his death he had an affection for the old town. He was a devoted husband & father, & a Christian in profession & practice.

MON OCT 1, 1860

Orphans Court of Wash Co, D C. Letters of administration on the personal estate of John Ricks, late of Wash Co, deceased. –Augustus E Perry, adm

Mr Oliver T Beard, the Breckenridge Democratic candidate for the N Y Legislature in the 3rd Assembly District of Brooklyn, made his appearance at a Republican meeting there on Thu last, & publicly gave in his adhesion to Lincoln & Hamlin.

The wife of the Austrian General Enyatten, who committed sucide upon the discovery of his gigantic frauds during the late Italian war, was lately sentenced to 3 years' hard labor, her extravagant habit having encouraged her husband in his acts of depredation. In consideration of her children, her sentence was commuted to 3 months' imprisonment, & the giddy Baroness is now serving out the punishment meted out to her for her reckless conduct.

Dr Nathan Smith Lincoln performed the difficult & delicate operation of removing the fractured portion of the skull of Jas Moran, who was so seriously injured in the late riot near the river. The operation was performed in a very short time & without giving any pain to the patient. Dr Lincoln is a relative & was a pupil of the celebrated Prof Smith, of Balt.

Died: on Sep 24, Harriet, wife of Geo W Boardman, & daughter of Robt & Mary Widdebombe. May the memory of her life's peaceful close be to the mourning household a sacred beatitude. –W W

Died: on Sep 28, in N Y, Mrs Mary Eleanor Barney, daughter of the late Edw DeKrafft, of Wash.

Died: on Sep 30, Parker Monroe, youngest son of Alonzo R & Hannah Fowler. Her funeral is this afternoon at 3 o'clock, at 325 12th st.

TUE OCT 2, 1860

Trustee's sale of leasehold property on Nov 2, by deed of trust from Saml Kelly, dated Oct 27, 1756, recorded in Liber J A S, No 124, folios 470 etc, of the land records for Wash Co, D C: sale of the piece of ground, together with improvements, consisting of a large & well built frame bldg, known as the Washington Select School. –Nich Callan, trustee -Jas C McGuire & Co, aucts

N Y C, Sep 30, 1860. The trial of Jackalow, the Chinese, who stands charged with the murder of Capt Leete & his brother, cannot take place before Jan. The body of the murdered capt has been fully indentified by his sister, Miss Leete.

Ralph Farnham, of Acton, Maine, now in his 105th year, is the sole survivor of the Battle of Bunker Hill. He has recently been invited to visit Boston, the invitation being signed by Gov Banks & Ex-Govn'r Everett & Gardner, Mayor Lincoln, & 50 other gentlemen. He expects to be in Boston about Oct 8, & Mr Paran Stevens has tendered to him free quarters at the Revere House for himself & family during his stay in Boston. –Boston Courier

The London Times states that Rev W G Watson, chaplain of Gray's Inn, & grandson of the celebrated Bishop of Llandaff, lost his life in the Tyrol, on Aug 31. He was crossing a snow slope with another gentleman & a guide, when his footing gave way & he fell into a chasm 90 feet deep. His companion escaped. The body of Rev Watson was not recovered for several hours, when it was evident that his terrible fall had produced instant death.

The Trustees of the Male & Female Schools at Springhill, Hempstead Co, Ark, desire to establish schools at this place & are seeking a Principal, salary of $3,000 guaranteed, for the first term of 10 months. –J W Finley, Pres Board Trustees

I wish to employ in my family a Lady who had had some years' experience, & can give instruction in the higher English branches, Music & French. School to begin Oct 15. -Jas F Jones, Piedmont Station, Fauquier Co, Va

The subscriber wishes to engage the services of a competent Tutor to take charge of the education of his children. –Jas B Clay, Ashland, near Lexington, Ky

Dissolution of partnersip by mutual consent. –Geo Barber, Chas Bean

Wm R Riley & Brother are now opening one of the largest & best assorted stocks of Fall & Winter Dry Goods to be found in the District, 26 Central Stores, between 7th & 8th sts, opposite Centre Market.

Died: on Oct 1, suddenly, of paralysis, Darius Clagett, in his 69th year. His funeral will be on Wed at 2 o'clock, from his late residence, **Pomona**. Pallbearers will meet carriages at Nairn's Drug Store at 12 o'clock, corner of Pa ave & 9th st.

Died: on Oct 1, in his 51st year, of consumption, Edw W Collins, son of Rev Jos S Collins, of Balt, Md. His funeral is this afternoon at 3 o'clock, from the Methodist Protestant Church, Congress st, Gtwn, D C.

Died: on Oct 1, Robt Reeves, a native of Trowbridge, England, but for the last 21 years a resident of Wash City, aged 77 years. His funeral is tomorrow at 3:30 o'clock P M.

Died: on Sunday, in Wash City, John F Archer, of Va, in his 46th year. His funeral will take place this afternoon at 4:30 o'clock, from the residence of his brother-in-law, Gen J Morton, 288 I st.
+
The friends & acquaintances of Hon Jackson Morton, of Fla, are invited to attend the funeral of his brother-in-law, John F Archer, from the residence of the former, 288 I st, between 16th & 17th sts, on Oct 2, at half past 4 o'clock.

The funeral services of the late Mrs Mary E Barney, will take place at the residence of her cousin, J W DeKrafft, 431 11th st, this morning at 10 o'clock.

WED OCT 3, 1860
Saml Owings Hoffman, a respected citizen of Balt, & a prominent merchant there, died in that city on Friday last.

The Balt papers announce the death on Sat last of Prof __pin A Harris, a distinguished dentist, & one of the useful & laborious teachers & practioners of dentistry in the U S.

The Jamaica papers give an account of the supposed murder of Capt Burton, of the American barque **Alvarado**, at Kingston, on Sep 5. The body of the unfortunate man had been found floating in the water. When the **Alvarado** arrived at Kingston the crew was in a state of insubordination, & had demanded their discharge, which the capt refused. It is supposed he was murdered by the crew & thrown overboard.

Auction sale of stock of Dry Goods on Oct 4, the entire stock of F T Maddox, 20 Centre Market Space, between 8th & 9th sts. –Cleary & Green, aucts

Cmder Thornton A Jenkins, U S Navy, returned to his residence in Wash City yesterday, after a two year's cruise in the Gulf of Mexico, the Caribbean Sea, & the Paraguay Expedition, in command of the U S sloop of war **Preble**.

Mrs: on Oct 2, at Trinity Church, by Rev C M Butler, Julius H Berret to Alice St Clair Settle, all of Wash City.

Mrd: on Sep 25, at Wyckliff Church, Clarke Co, Va, by Rev Wm Leavel, Chas M Koones, of Wash City, to Mary E, daughter of Saml G Kneller, of Clarke Co, Va.

Died: on Oct 1, at the residence of his parents, Hattie Barker, only child of Sayles J & Mary Bowen, aged 5 years & 7 months.

Died: on Oct 2, in his 84th year, Nicholas L Queen. His funeral will take place at his late residence, near Wash, on Oct 4 at 10 o'clock A M.

Orphans Court of Wash Co, D C, Oct 2, 1860. In the case of Christopher Ingle, adm of Peter Adams, deceased, the administrator & Court have appointed Oct 27th next, for the final settlement of the personal estate of the said deceased, of the assets in hand. -Ed Roach, Reg/o wills

THU OCT 4, 1860
Excellent household & kitchen furniture at auction on Oct 8, at the residence of H W Tilley, Congress st, on the Heights of Gtwn, D C, all his effects.
-Barnard & Buckley, aucts, Gtwn, D C

Base Ball. A match game of the Potomac & Pythian Clubs is announced for tomorrow afternoon, at 2 o'clock, in the grounds south of the Pres' House.

Orphans Court of Wash Co, D C, Oct 2, 1860. In the case of Jos P Smith, adm of John W Smith, deceased, the administrator & Court have appointed Oct 27th next, for the final settlement of the personal estate of the said deceased, of the assets in hand. -Ed Roach, Reg/o wills

Mrd: on Oct 2, in Wash City, by Rev J G Butler, Mrs Chas A Yates, of Chas Co, Md, to Miss Missouri Groshon, of Wash City.

Died: on Oct 2, Geo B Lenman, in his 37th year. His funeral will leave the residence of Wm P Drury at half-past nine for the Church of St Aloysius.

FRI OCT 5, 1860
Ex-Pres Fillmore is now in N Y C, & after attending a place of public entertainment last evening, was saluted by a body of Union "Minute Men," drawn up in line to pay him respect. –N Y, Oct 3

Adm sale, by order of the Orphans Court of D C, of household & kitchen furniture, at auction on Oct 9, & the personal effects of the late Francis Holden, deceased, on 11th st, between Pa ave & E st, over the Gas Ofc. -A Green, aucts

The ship **Erie**, in charge of Lt J W Dunnington, & a prize crew, arrived at N Y on Wed from the coast of Africa. The **Erie** was captured on Aug 8 by the U S steamer **Mohican**, with 897 slaves on board. Thirty of them died on the passage from the place of capture to Monrovia, where the survivors were landed. Three prisoners, supposed to be the capt & the first & third mates of the **Erie**, were brought home in the vessel, & are held to answer for their violation of the law.

Appointments by the Pres: Consul of the U S:
Saml Clark, of Mich, consul at Aspinwall, vice C J Fox, resigned.
J J Sprenger, of Pa, consul at Venice, vice F L Sarmiento, resigned.
John A Parker, of Va, consul at Honolulu, vice A W Buel, declined.
Chas Richmond, of Mich, consul at Lahaina, vice A G Chandler, recalled.
Andrew G Carothers, of D C, consul at Turk's Island, vice J B Hayne, recalled.
Wm C Burchard, of N Y, consul at Comayaua & Tegucigalpa, in Honduras.

Phil, Oct 4. Rembrandt Peale, the eminent American painter, died here this morning, at age 82 years. [Oct 6th newspaper: Since the death of Gilbert Stuart he was the only artist who had painted a portrait of Washington from life. He retained his faculties to the last. Phil-Journal]

SAT OCT 6, 1860
Circuit Court of Wash Co, D C-in Equity, No 1, 544. Saml Cropley against Mary Ann Thecker, Jas Thecker, & Thos Knowles. Wm Redin, trustee, reported he sold part of lot 72 in old Gtwn, on Cherry alley, with 2 brick houses thereon, to Saml Cropley, for the sum of $4,575. –W Redin -John A Smith, clerk

Died: on Oct 5, in Wash City, of consumption, Sallie, second daughter of Richd R Burr, in her 23rd year. Her funeral will be from the house of her father, F & 3rd sts, tomorrow, Sunday, at 1:45 o'clock.

Trustee's sale of real estate, by decree passed on Nov 6, 1857, by the Circuit Court for PG Co, in Equity, in a cause wherein Margaret S A Cumming, next friend to Edmund B Cumming & others, is cmplnt, & Edmund B Cumming & others are dfndnts, the undersigned will offer at public sale on Oct 30: all the residue of the real estate in said county, which was conveyed to Thos W Cumming, deceased, by Martin Buel & Lucy Ann his wife, in fee simple, containing 67 acres, more or less, within 2 miles of the Soldier's Home; adjoins the estates of the late Stephen Markwood, the Messrs Wingerd, Digges, Clark, & others. –C C Magruder, trustee, Upper Marlborough, PG Co, Md.

Sale of valuable real estate, by decree of the Circuit Court for PG Co, in Equity, passed in the cause of Henry Addison, next friend of Ella Beall, vs Ella Beall, Martha E Beall, & others, the trustee, will offer at public auction, on the premises, on Oct 23, all that valuable real estate known as *Largo*, of which the late Zachariah B Beall died seized & possessed, containing 357½ acres. This property adjoins the estates of Zachariah Berry, sr, & Washington J Beall, Dr Cranford, Dr Lee, & others. -Hugh Caperton, trustee

Cincinnati, Oct 5. A private despatch from St Paul, Minn, says that Gov Willard, of Indiana, died last night of consumption.

MON OCT 8, 1860

N Y, Oct 4. Jackalow, the Chinaman, has been indicted. Five bills were found: one for the murder of Jonahtan T Leet; one for the murder of Elijah J Leet; one for the robbery of each; & one for running away with the vessel. The Court fixed the third Tue in Jan, at the city of Trenton, as the time & place of trial.

The Northern papers announce the death of H D Johnson, formerly of the State Dept, & recently appointed Consul to Constantinople. He is reported to have died in Florence.

The U S sloop-of-war **Marion**, Cmder T W Brent, arrived at Portsmouth, N H, on Oct 5, from the African Station, having been absent from the U S 30 months, within a few days. She brings 27 invalids from the squadron & the U S ship **Niagara**-among them Lt H M Garland, of the ship **Mystic**; Passed Midshipman F H Black, of the ship **Mohican**; & Sailmaker D J D Blackford, of the ship **Constellation**; & as passengers, 3rd Assist Engineers Jas Plunkett, of the **Mystic**, & Geo W Lennant, of the **Niagara**. She also has on board, to the delivered to the U S Marshal, 4 seamen from the American ship **Erie**, recently captured by the ship **Mohican**, & one seaman charged with mutinous conduct from the American barque **Cochituate**.

Summary justice, according to the code of Judge Lynch, was administered to Martin N Gilliam, a horse thief, at **Fort Smith**, Ark, on Wed, when he was hung.

Jas M Davidson, ex-member of the Tenn Legislature, was shot & killed in Fayetteville on Sat by Jas Carter. A political quarrel was the cause.
-Nashville paper

Columbian College, Wash, D C, will open Sep 26. —Geo W Samson, D D, Pres.

Orphans Court of Wash Co, D C, Oct 6, 1860. In the case of Mary A Patterson, admx of Jas Patterson, deceased, the administratrix & Court have appointed Oct 30th next, for the final settlement of the personal estate of the said deceased, of the assets in hand. -Ed Roach, Reg/o wills

Orphans Court of Wash Co, D C, Oct 6, 1860. In the case of Thos Mansfield, adm of Ann L King, deceased, the administrator & Court have appointed Oct 30th next, for the final settlement of the personal estate of the said deceased, of the assets in hand. -Ed Roach, Reg/o wills

TUE OCT 9, 1860
A case of some novelty & interest came before the Orphans Court of D C. on Sat last. It was an application for power of administration on the estate of the late Mrs Chase Barney, who died in N Y within a few days past. The application was made by Mr Edw DeKrafft, cousin of deceased, & was resisted by the friends of Mr Chas Barney, who is not in Wash, but is expected from France in a very short time. The administration was asked by Mrs Barney's cousin on the ground that the lady had been divorced, & that the law of Md of 1801 making her husband administrator did not apply. It was resisted on the ground that the divorce, procured in Iowa, on Aug 17 last, after only 3 months' residence, was null & void, being contrary to the law of that State, which requires 6 months residence; also, on the ground that there is nothing whereon to administer; &, further, that the separate estate of the lady is responsible for debts due her husband. Time was asked by Mr Barney's friends to await his arrival-this was granted. The Court postponed the case till next Sat week.

Orphans Court of Wash Co, D C, Oct 6, 1866. In the case of Eliz S Hassler & Walter D Davidge, adms of John J S Hassler, deceased, the administrators & Court have appointed Oct 30th next, for the final settlement of the personal estate of the said deceased, of the assets in hand. -Ed Roach, Reg/o wills

Died: on Oct 8, in her 28th year, Miss Mary Carver Adams, daughter of Jas Adams. Her funeral will take place from the residence of her father, 21 4½ st, tomorrow, at 3 o'clock P M.

Died: on Oct 8, in Wash City, Abner H Young, in his 58th year. His funeral will be on Wed, at 3 o'clock P M, from the Foundry Church, on 14th st.

Died: on Sep 14, 1860, at Florence, Henry D Johnson, for some years past librarian of the State Dept, & lately appointed U S Consul Gen to Constantinople. He sailed from Boston for his post, with his wife & children, in July last, but was compelled, by serious illness, to leave his ship & stop at Malta, from which place, by the advise of his physicians, he was carried to Florence. His disease proved to be beyond the reach of medical skill, & he sank quietly to his rest on Sep 14, attended & comforted by his wife, his nephew, Mr Oliver, who had sailed with him, & a brother of his wife, Capt Abert, who, being in Paris, & hearing of his illness, hastened to his bedside. Kind & constant attentions were shown him & his family by the U S Consuls at Malta & Florence & their families, & by other American citizens.

The Trustees of Allegany Co Academy, at Cumberland, Md, wish to employ a competent person as Principal of the Academy. Apply to Thos J McKaig, Pres of the Board of Trustees.

Salesman wanted at the House-Furnituer Dry Goods Store, 4 Market Space, near 9th st. –J B Dodson

WED OCT 10, 1860
Wm Auld was sentenced to 10 years in the Eastern Penitentiary, at Phil, on Sat, for arson, in firing his own house. He committed an offence that came near sending him to Court on a charge of triple murder.

On Wed last in St Louis, Wm Sullivan was convicted of the murder of Timothy Corcoran, & sentenced to the penitentiary for 25 years. On the same day H Zouresky was convicted of the murder of his wife. The brutal wretch aproached his sick & helpless wife while she lay in bed, & struck her repeatedly over the head & arms with a heavy chair, the poor woman all the while crying for help & begging for mercy. She soon died. Zouresky was sentenced to 10 years in the penitentiary, showing that in St Louis the life of a female is held at a discount of more than 60%, when compared with that of a male. –Cincinnati Times

Tuleyries for sale: having purchased the dower-right of the widow of Col Jos Tuley, deceased, I will offer at sale, on Oct 30, *Tuleyries*, the late residence of Col Jos Tuley, deceased, in Clarke Co, Va; contains 869 acres; the Mansion House is lighted with gas in every room; out-houses built of brick, large dairy, 10 pin alley 90 feet long, bath house, carriage & 2 stables, ice house, & Porter's Lodge. The property will be shown by Jos T Mitchell, Millwood, Clarke Co, Va. I will also sell a good brick house, in Wincheser, known as the residence of Judge White, with a lot of 2 acres, & a desirable residence. Also, 61 negroes; all the personal property, & 77 head of English Fallow Deer. –Jos T Mitchell, Agent & Atty in fact for the heirs. -Turk & Cushing, aucts

THU OCT 11, 1860
Excellent household & kitchen furniture at auction on Oct 13, in front of my store, furniture belonging to Lt R R Garland, U S Navy. –A Green, aucts

A young man named Richd Kobbe, of Cincinatti, who killed a man named Guelich in that city a few days since in a quarrel, has given himself up to the authorities.

The Mariana [Fla] patriot of Sep 26 says: yesterday a party in Calhoun, styling themselves Regulators, went to the house of Jesse Durden, shot him, giving him a mortal wound. They then met & shot Willis Musgrove from his horse, who died instantly; also mortally wounding Larkin C Musgrove. We were apprized that Gen Wm E Anderson had ordered out the first brigade militia.

Orphans Court of Wash Co, D C. Letters of administration on the personal estate of Abram Paynter, late of Wash Co, deceased. –Mary V Paynter, admx

Orphans Court of Wash Co, D C. Letters of administration on the personal estate of Wm H Starr, late of Wash Co, deceased. –Jane Starr, admx

Mrd: on Oct 2, in St Mary's Co, Harford Co, Md, by Rev W F Brand, Rector, Maj J G Barnard, Corps of Engineers, U S Army, to Anna E Boyd, daughter of the late Henry Hall, of Harford Co, Md.

Mrd: on Oct 10, in Trinity Church, by Rev John C Smith, Lewis Cass Forsyth to Miss Janie Barr, daughter of Benj A Janvier, all of Wash City.

FRI OCT 12, 1860
By the death of Geo B Lenman, of the firm of Lenman & Brother, it has become ncecssary to close & settle the business of the late firm. Those with claims, or indebted to the firm, are to settle the same. –Jno T Lenman, surviving partner

The new iron steamship **Connaught**, of the Galway line, running between Galway & N Y & Boston, alternately, via St John's, Newfoundland, on Sep 25 left Galway. She sprung a leak on Sat & was discovered to be on fire on Sunday, when measures were taken by Capt Leitch to insure the safety of the passengews. Including the crew there were 591 persons on board, & not a single life was lost. Discipline organized by a master mind, under the protection of Providence, saved all lives. The conduct of Capt Wilson, of the brig **Minni Schiffer**, & Mr Connanton, his first ofcr, were noble & praiseworthy. The Capt saw a ship in distress, & came to her relief. Among the passengers was Mr H Whittel, of N Y, who speaks of the highest terms of the kindness of Capt John Wilson, of the brig **Minnie Schiffer**.

For rent, the house lately occupied by Vice Pres Breckinridge, on G st, between 14th & 15th sts. –Geo C Ames, 261 G st

Mr John W Grist, of Washington, N C, a most estimable gentleman, was assaulted & killed on Thu week by two brothers, Geo A & Chas H Latham. The affair had its origin in politics. The brothers fired their revolvers in the open street on Mr Grist.

The McMinnville [Tenn] New Era announces the death on Sep 23 of Danl West, the well-known hermit of the mountains, age 78. He had lived for a number of years in the hollow of a large American poplar tree; adjoining it was a crude shed. He was born in N C, & was a soldier of the war of 1812.

Mrd: on Oct 3, in Cromwell, Conn, by Rev Jas Clarke, Rev C Collard Adams, of Providence Annual Conference Methodist Episcopal Church, [formerly of Wash City,] to Miss Eliz G Ranney, of Cromwell.

Died: on Oct 7, at the residence of Maj Geo Peter, from injuries sustained by a fall from his horse, Jas Henderson Peter, third son of the late John P C Peter, of Montg Co, Md. By this said calamity a fond mother has lost an affectinate & dutiful son, brothers & sisters a loved & loving brother. He was nearly 20 years of age, & lingered 24 hours after his fall, unconscious of the grief of friends. -N

Orphans Court of Wash Co, D C, Sep 22, 1860. In the case of Catherine Venable, excx of Geo W Venable, deceased, the executrix & Court have appointed Nov 6 next, for the final settlement of the personal estate of the said deceased, of the assets in hand. -Ed Roach, Reg/o wills

Orphans Court of Wash Co, D C. Letters of administration on the personal estate of Darius Clagett, late of Wash Co, deceased. —Wm H Clagett, adm

SAT OCT 13, 1860

Josiah F Polk, recently deceased, was the son of the late Judge Gilliss Polk, of Somerset, Md. He was educated for the profession of his father, & was engaged in its practice. He was twice elected to the Legislature of Md. Subsequently, having removed to Indiana, he filled various offices of great trust under Gov't. He was appointed to a position in the Census Bureau by Mr Van Buren, & was afterwards placed in the ofc of the 2nd Auditor, where he remained from 1831 to 1855. He has since been engaged in revising the code of laws for the District, & was a trustee of the public schools. His disease was rapid & its termination sudden & unexpected. Mr Polk's long residence in Wash gained for him many friends.

Mrd: on Oct 1, at the residence of her father, Hon R C Puryear, in Yadkin Co, N C, by Rev Mr Haughton, Miss Jennie Puryear to Lt J M Kerr, U S Army.

Died: on Oct 9, very suddenly, at *Waveland*, the residence of her husband, in Fauquier Co, Va, Eleanor Love Washington, aged 36 years, wife of John Augustus Washington, late of *Mount Vernon*.

MON OCT 15, 1860
Dr Wm Fessel, formerly a practicing physician at Hannibal, Miss, but who has recently been engaged in farming near Barclay Station, was bitten by a spider on the end of his great toe, coming down from Keokuk on Friday, from the effects of which he died on Sep 19. He leaves a wife & 3 or 4 children to mourn his untimely death.

A little son of Chas Goit, of East Lanesboro, Mass, aged 5 years, died a few days ago from the bite of a spider. He died 48 hours after he was bitten.

Wm Prescott Smith, Master of Transportation of the Balt & Ohio Railroad, who accompanied the Governors of Md & Va & Pres Garrett on their visit over the road, met with a mishap in attempting to get off the train at Harper's Ferry, Va. In jumping his foot struck the sharp rim of the car wheel cutting open the boot & injuring several of the toes so much as to require amputation at the first joint, which operation was performed at the Ferry. He returned to this city on Thu, & is now at his residence. –Balt Sun

John Swartz, a German, was instantly killed at Cincinnati by the bursting of a mill stone. [No death date given-current item.]

Fire broke out on Sat in the carpenter's shop of the Messrs Beers Brothers, on Pa ave & 1st & 2nd sts south, on Capitol Hill. The shop & contents were destroyed, as was also an adjoining frame dwlg the property of H R Maryman. The dwlg was valued at $500, & insured. The fire was, without doubt, of incendiary origin.
+
$100 reward for the arrest & conviction of the person or persons who fired the carpenter's shop of Beers & Brothers on Oct 12. There all was destroyed.
-Isaac Beers

Trustee's sale of real estate, by deed of trust, dated Oct 7, 1858, recorded in Liber C S M, No 2, folios 61, of the land records of PG Co, Md: public auction on Jan 17, 1861, all those tracts, parts of tracts, or parcels of land, in said county, except that part sold by Judson C Pumphrey to Mary Allen, lying on the south side of the Alexandria road, the same contains 5 acres, more or less, called *Poor Man's Industry*, *Edmond's Frolick*, *Slip*, & *Pumphrey's Little Addition*, containing altogether 130 acres, more or less, being the property conveyed by the said John S James & his wife, C A James, by deed bearing even date herewith, to said Horatio N Gilbert. –Horatio N Gilbert, trustee

Died: on Oct 13, in Wash City, of consumption, Silas Holman Hill, in his 53rd year. Mr Hill was a native of Portsmouth, N H, but for many years past has been one of our most respected citizens. His funeral will be from his late residence on E st, corner of 6th, on Oct 16, at 12 o'clock M

Orphans Court of Wash Co, D C. Letters testamentary on the personal estate of Abner H Young, late of Wash Co, deceased. –Mary A Young, excx

Died: on Oct 13, in Wash City, Mrs Eliz P Brown, wife of Jas A Brown, in her 30th year. Her funeral will take place from the residence of Robt Brown, on Capitol Hill, at 2 o'clock, this afternoon.

Phil, Oct 14. During a regimental muster at Van Buren, [Wash Co, Pa,] Rufus & Jackson Covington, & a son of the latter, were killed by Silas & Ben Edwards, & others were wounded. The affray was the result of an old feud between the families, the Edwards being the aggressors. They were arrested. The crowd manifested a disposition to lynch them, & it is feared they may yet succeed.

TUE OCT 16, 1860
At the late session of the French Academy the first prize of virtue was conferred on Rev John Bost, a Protestant minister of France. The prize originated with a certain M Montyon, who left a sum of money, the interest of which is every year distributed by the French Academy to such persons as are known to have performed distinguished acts of self-sacrifice & benevolence. All France is summoned to the competition. The first prize, 3,000 francs, was awarded to Jean-Mare Bost, of La Force, in Dordogne. John Bost is descended from a Hugeunot family & came to Paris in his youth. An infant, abandoned by his mother, fell under his notice, called out his charity, & in effect changed his course of life.

L S Ross, of Waco, has received orders from Govn'r Houston to raise a company of 60 mounted volunteers to proceed at once to the frontier.

Judge Silas Parson, a highly estimable & eminent citizen of Travis Co, died at Huntsville, Ala, on Sep 16.

Died: on Oct 13, in Wash City, of consumption, Silas Holman Hill, in his 53rd year. Mr Hill was a native of Portsmouth, N H, but for many years past has been one of our most respected citizens. His funeral will be from his late residence on E st, corner of 6th, on Oct 16 at 12 o'clock M.

Died: on Oct 14, in Wash City, William Irving, son of Willian H & Virginia Towers, aged 18 months. His funeral will be this morning at 11 o'clock, from the residence of his parents on M st north, between 8th & 9th sts.

Mrd: on Oct 9, at Ascension Church, N Y, by Rev Dr Tucker, of Troy, Edw H Wright, of Newark, N J, & Dora, only daughter of the late Geo Mason, of Michigan.

Mrd: on Oct 11, at Trinity Church, by Rev Jos Earnest, Wm Worthington, of PG Co, to Minnie, daughter of Gen Thos F Bowie, of Md.

Cincinnati, Oct 13. At the Breckinridge barbecue, near Winchester, Clark Co, Ky, yesterday, a young man, son of Dr West, of Bath Co, being prevented by a gentleman named Scott from rushing to the dinner table reserved for ladies, drew a pistol & fired at the latter. West missed his aim, & the shot took effect in the face of Miss Emma Hickman, inflicting a serious wound. The crowd made 3 attempts to hang him to a tree, when the sheriff of the county prevailed upon the mob to deliver the would be murderer over to the law. West was taken to Winchester Co & lodged in jail to await his trial.

Albany, Oct 13. 1-The Court of Appeals, in the case of Mrs Hartung, confined in jail so long for the murder of her husband, a new trial is granted. 2-The Manor cases of Van Rensselaer & Church against the Anit-Renters are decided in favor of the landlords, the judgments of the lower courts being revered.

WED OCT 17, 1860
Mrs Anna H Dorsey, who has contributed so largely to the Catholic literature of the country for many years past, but who has been dangerously ill for the past 6 months, is at present so much better as to have recommenced her literary labors. She is translating, as rapidly as her pulmonary affection will permit, a Life of Pius IX, M Alexandre De Saint-Aubin, a work just issued from the Paris press.

Teacher wanted to take charge of a small school in his own family for a session of 8 months, to commence Nov 1. A Southerner preferred. –Js W Foster, Plains Station, M G R Road, Fauquier Co, Va.

Orphans Court of Wash Co, D C. Letters of administration on the personal estate of Andrew J O'Bannon, late of Wash Co, deceased. –Thos H Lane, adm

Orphans Court of Wash Co, D C. Letters testamentary on the personal estate of Anne R Dermott, late of Wash Co, deceased. –John P Ingle, exc

Van Buren, Oct 15. After a regimental muster which was held here today, 3 persons, named Rugus & Jackson Conington, brothers, & Richd, a son of the latter, were killed by two brothers, Silas & Benj Edwards, & others badly cut. An old feud had existed between the parties. It is feared the prisoners will be be lynched.

THU OCT 18, 1860
Circuit Court of Wash Co, D C-in Equity. Danl Chandler, Mary Chandler, Joshua Humphreys & Margaret Ann Humphreys his wife, against Wm Chandler & Catherine his wife, Walter Hay, Benj E Gantt, Walter C Gantt, Mary S W Gantt, Ann H Gantt, Edw C Gantt, Lucy Gantt, Richd Gantt, Catherine T Gantt, Jane C Gantt, Margaret Riche Chandler, Mary J Chandler, Wm L Chandler, & John F Broome. Above parties to appear before me on Oct 27th, at my ofc in Wash, to inquire whether the premises mentioned in the bill are susceptible of partition, or not. –Walter S Cox

A terrible accident on Oct 5, on the Chesapeake & Ohio canal, caused the death of Geo Patterson, who, it appears, was filling an ethereal lamp, when it exploded, burning him most horribly, & causing his death the next day.

Orphans Court of Wash Co, D C. In the case of Wm Dixon, exc of Enos E Berkley, deceased, the executor & Court have appointed Nov 13 next, for the final settlement of the personal estate of the said deceased, of the assets in hand.
-Ed Roach, Reg/o wills

Orphans Court of Wash Co, D C. In the case of Walter Lenox, exc of Wm Stewart, deceased, the executor & Court have appointed Nov 10th next, for the final settlement of the personal estate of the said deceased, of the assets in hand.
-Ed Roach, Reg/o wills

Mrd: on Oct 16, at *Beall's Retreat*, PG Co, Md, the residence of the bride's father, Rev D Ball, Richd H Willet, of Wash, to Miss Virginia T Beall.

Mrd: on Oct 16, at the *Oaks*, Gtwn, D C, by Rev R H B Mitchel, Josiah Dent, of St Louis, to Kate, adopted daughter of E M Linthicum.

Omaha, N T, Oct 17. Gordon, the murderer, was hung at Denver on Oct 6. He fully confessed the crime of which he had been convicted.

FRI OCT 19, 1860
Cmdor Chas Wm Skinner died at *Sailor's Rest*, his residence, near Staunton, Va, on Oct 14. He was born in the then district of Maine in Apr, 1789, & entered the navy as midshipman in Jan, 1809, having previously obtained a knowledge of the practical part of his profession during several voyages in a merchant ship commanded by his father. He was acting master in the brig **Argus** in the war of 1812, & was transferred, with her cmder, other ofcrs, & crew, to Lake Ontario, where he served during the remainder of the war. The war over, Lt Skinner was selected by Cmdor Chauncy to serve with him in the flag ship **Washington, 74**, of the Mediterranean squadron. Returning from there, he was stationed at Norfolk, Va, where he married, in 1820, the estimable lady, Miss Clara Whitehead, daughter of an Episcopal clergyman, who after 40 years of happiness accorded to few, now mourns his loss. This marriage drew his affections to Va, of which State he became a citizen. He was employed against the pirates in the West Indies in 1822; the schnr **Porpoise** in 1824; promoted to Master Commandant in 1827; & in 1828 appointed to the command of the sloop-of-war **Warren**, on the Mediterranean station; in 1829 was acting capt of the frig **Java**, bearing the flag of Cmdor Biddle; returned to the U S in 1830 & was variously employed. In 1838 he was appointed to the command of the steamer **Fulton**, having been promoted to capt in 1837. In 1844 he was appointed to command the squadron on the coast of Africa, & on his return, in 1846, was assigned to the command of the navy yard at Norfolk, but was soon called to the duties of Chief of the Bureau of Construction & Equipment in the Navy Dept, until Feb 24, 1852, when at his own

request, he was relieved. He continued the light duties of Inspector of Ordnance until his discharge in 1855. He had purchased a beautiful residence near Staunton, Va, where he then returned to enjoy his family for his remaining years.

Circuit Court of Wash Co, D C-in Chancery, No 1,152. Sewell & others, creditors of John Brereton, against Eliza Ann Brereton & John Hoover, adms of said John Brereton, & Mary, Eliz, Ellen, Anne, John, & Flora Brereton, heirs at law of said John Brereton. W Redin, trustee, resported he sold the residue of the farm mentioned, 77 acres 1 rood, & 27 perches, part of *Granby*, with bldgs thereon, to Presley W Dorsey, of $6,193.50, & that he hath complied with the terms of sale. -John A Smith, clerk

SAT OCT 20, 1860
Valuable real estate for sale at public auction on Nov 19, my tract of land called *Barracks*, lying on Ivy creek, containing 597½ acres; 5 miles north of Charlottesville, & adjoins the lands of Richd Wingfield, Edw Wingfield, Jas W Garth, Garland A Garth, & Horace Goodman. Improvements: commodious brick dwlg house, brick kitchen, brick cabins, & other bldgs. Also, at the same time all the household & kitchen furniture. –Garland Garth

For sale: that splendid Farm of Dr P R Edelen, about 800 acres, on the Potomac river, in Md. Inquire of Dr P R Edelen, of Piscataway, Md, or to Wm S Holliday, 324 Pa ave, Wash City.

Mrd: on Oct 16, in Wash City, at the Church of the Epiphany, Dr Henry J Garrett, of Marion, Va, to Miss Georgie M Derrick, youngest daughter of the late W S Derrick, of Wash City. [Clergyman not given.]

Died: on Oct 18, in Gtwn, D C, Mrs Rebecca Power Tillinghast, relict of the late Hon Jos L Tillinghast, of Providence, Rhode Island. Her funeral is this afternoon at 3:30 o'clock P M, from her late residence, 54 First st, Gtwn. [Oct 23rd newspaper: She was born & reared in Rhode Island. Her loss will be mourned in South Carolina, where her early life was passed, in her native city, & in this metropolis, where, as the wife of a member of Congress, she was welcomed with a cordiality never attributed to the station of her husband.]

Mrd: on Oct 17, by Rev N P Tillinghast, of St John's Church, Gtwn, John R Offley to Eliz, daughter of the late Lt A H Marbury, U S Navy.

MON OCT 22, 1860
Mr Thos Richards, an honored merchant of Phil, died at his residence in that city on Thu last, the 50th anniversary of his wedding. He was preparing for the celebration of a golden wedding, & the marriage of a daughter to be solemnized in a few days. He was taken with a mortal illness a few minutes before the time fixed for the assembling of the company, & expired soon afterwards, in his 81st year.

The Grand Jury at Phil has found a true bill against Wm Byerly for the substitution of false election returns in the count for member of Congress in the 1st district of Pa.

Circuit Court of Wash Co, D C-in Equity. Sewell & others, creditors of John Brereton, against Eliza Ann Brereton & John Hoover, adms of said John Brereton, & Mary, Eliz, Ellen, Anne, John, & Flora Brereton, heirs at law of said John Brereton. The above cause is referred to me, as special auditor, to state the trustee's account, the balance of Brereton's indebteness & distribution of the fund among the creditors & heirs, & also the amount due to Eliza Ann Brereton, as widow of said John Brereton, for commutation of her dower in all the premises sold by the trustee in this cause. Meeting at my ofc on Nov 12 next, Wash.
–Walter S Cox

Circuit Court of D C-in Equity, No 1,666. Ann Dellaway vs Morris Adler, exc, Alex'r P Eckel, R G Lindsay, Marianna P Lindsay, Richd Rubincam, Mary Ann Rubincam, Saml Eckel, Henry Eckel, & Susan Eckel, & the other heirs of Chas E Eckel, decendants. The object of the bill filed in this cause is to obtain the appointment of a new trustee in the place of Chas E Eckel, deceased. The bill states that the said Chas E Eckel is the trustee in a certain deed made by one Wm Wilson, on Oct 14, 1848, to him of certain real property, in Wash City, upon certain uses & trusts, among others, for the sole & separate use & benefit of the cmplnt; that since the making of said deed the said Chas E Eckel has departed this life, & that it is necessary that a new trustee should be appointed; that the said dfndnts are the heirs at law of the said Chas E Eckel, except Morris Adler, who is the exec of the last will & testament of the said Chas E Eckel; & it appearing that the said Alex'r P Eckel, R G Lindsay, Marianna P Lindsay, Richd Rubincam, Mary Ann Rubincam, Saml Eckle, Henry Eckel, & Susan Eckel, & other hiers of the said Chas E Eckel, whose names & residences are unknown, although diligent inquiry hath been made therefore, reside from & without the limits of said District of Columbia. Absent dfndnts to appear on the first Monday of March next, to answer said bill. –Jno A Smith, clerk F W Jones, Solicitor for cmplnts

Orphans Court of Wash Co, D C. Letters of administration on the personal estate of John McClellan, late of the U S Army, deceased. –C Thos Bradley, adm

Mrd: on Oct 15, in Cincinnati, Ohio, by Rev B T Maltby, Wm T Riggles, of Wash City, to Mary A Wilson, of Covington, Ky.

Obit-died: on Oct 15, after a lingering illness, at his residence in PG Co, Md, Marsham Waring, aged 66 years. He was the kindest of husbands, most affectionate father, &, from the manifestation of grief by his numerous servants, the best of masters. While in the enjoyment of health he embraced the Roman Catholic faith, which was in his dying moments, the anchor of his hope for a peaceful hereafter.

Orphans Court of Wash Co, D C, Oct 20, 1860. In the case of Richd Copeland, adm of Francis Holden, deceased, the administrator & Court have appointed Nov 13 next, for the final settlement of the personal estate of the said deceased, of the assets in hand. –Ed Roach, Reg/o wills

TUE OCT 23, 1860
Signor Viscenti, assisted by his son, is restoring to the light of day the ancient part of Rome, the famous Ostia, & has already uncovered the dockyards, the marts, where still are to be seen earthen pots, with weights, a theatre, a beautiful temple, baths, gymnasium, a square, & a gate of the city. –English paper

Herbert Ingram's funeral in England was attended by 18,000 persons. He was the proprietor of the London Illustrated News, & was one of the victims of the steamer **Lady Elgin** disaster. His remains were carried to England, & the funeral services took place at Boston, where he had resided.

Superior household & kitchen furniture at auction on Oct 26, at the residence of J A Magruder; all his effects. –Barnard & Buckey, aucts

Superior Rosewood piano forte, household & kitchen furniture at auction on: Oct 29, at the residence of R J La_key , 181 G st, between 19th & 20th sts. –J C McGuire & Co, aucts

Obit-died: on Oct 7, at Portland, Maine, Mrs Maria Barrell, widow of the late Jos Moody, of Kennebunk, Maine. Born on Oct 23, 1769, she wanted but a few days of entering her 91st year. He mind was vivid & rich; she was in full communion with the Episcopal Church. –T L M

Orphans Court of Wash Co, D C. Letters of administration on the personal estate of Philip H Vanarsdale, late of Wash Co, deceased. –W J Redstrake, adm

Mrd: on Oct 16, at the Foundry Church, by Rev Mr Hamilton, Dr J Ford Thompson, of Leonardtown, Md, to Miss Marion V Greeves, of Wash City.

Mrd: on Oct 18, at the Ascension Church, in Wash City, by Rev Dr Wm Pinkney, John M Robison, jr, of N Y C, to Miss Anna Duvall, of PG Co, Md.

WED OCT 24, 1860
Railroad accident on Fri near Birmingham, some 20 miles from Detroit, killed Dexter M C Nichols, express messenger, Geo M Sines mail agent, of the passenger train, & Alex'r Wilkie, fireman of the freight train. Geo Spencer, engineer of the freight train, had an arm broken. The accident was the result of the carelessness of Mr Briscoe, the conductor of the passenger train who had received orders by telegraph to wait the eastward going freight train at Birmingham. Mr Briscoe supposed the Fentonville to be the freight train, & started his own train. The trains came together with great force.

The Santa Fe Gax of Sep 29 reports the murder of Mr Peacock & 2 other men at his ranch at Walnut Creek by the Kirwa Indians, the chief of the band pretending to be a friend of Mr Peacock.

On Sunday the corner-stone of a bldg to be used as a <u>Male Orphan Asylum</u> will be laid on the lot of ground bequeathed for that purpose by Mr Lynch, & situated a little west of St Aloysius Church, in Wash City. Rev B Maguire will deliver an address.

On Oct 14, Rev Mr McNeel, a Presbyterian minister, fell dead while preaching in the Brick church, near Mr Statenboro's, in the southern district of Dallas Co, Ala. It is supposed it was from a disease of the heart.

Extensive sale of the furniture & effects of the Casparis' Hotel, on south A st, opposite the Capitol Park, on Nov 5. -Jas C McGuire & Co, aucts

Elegant antique carved Paris cabinet furniture, gilt & bronze mantel clock, Bohemian glassware, French china, gas chandeliers, mirrors, carpeting, etc, at auction, on Nov 1, the furniture & effects of Mrs Theodosia Strother.
-Jas C McGuire & Co, aucts

Orphans Court of Wash Co, D C. In the matter of the petition of Isabella Johnston, guardian to Gabriel F, Mildred C, Eliz, & Thos J Johnston, orphans of Thos J Johnston, deceased, for sale of real estate, in Equity sitting. Isabella Johnston, the guardian, reported that on Jun 13, 1859, she sold lot 4 in square 531, to Moses Kelly, for $1,233, & he has complied with the terms of sale.
–Wm F Purcell, Judge of the Orphans Court -Ed N Roach, Register

Mrd: on Oct 16, at Balt, by Rev Mr Dunning, Geo M Bokee, of Balt, to Mrs Jennie E Campbell, formerly of St Mary's Co, Md.

Mrd: on Oct 23, in Balt, by Rev Geo D Cummins, John Keyworth to Mary A, daughter of the late John T Towers, all of Wash.

Died: on Oct 23, Alex Lammond, jr, in his 26th year. His funeral is this morning at 10 o'clock, from the residence of his father, on 3rd st, between E & F sts.

Died: on Oct 22, at the residence of her son, Rev S A H Marks, Mrs Julia A Marks, in her 75th year. For nearly 40 years she had been a member of the M E Church, East Wash station, & closed her life in great peace. Her funeral is this afternoon at 2 o'clock, from 398 G st.

Died: on Oct 23, after a protracted illness, in his 23rd year, Frederick, son of Christina & Nicholas Callan. His funeral will be at St Matthew's Church, at 9 o'clock A M, Thu.

Obit-died: on Oct 19, 1860, at Wytheville, Va, Miss Eliza Louis Matthews, in her 26th year, known in her vocation as Sister Mary Stanislaus, mother of the religious order of St Joseph at Wheeling, to which position she was appointed on Nov 16, 1858, after serving her probation, & which she filled with exemplary fidelity. She was a connexion of the Floyd family of Va, [which has furnished many members to the church,] & was the youngest of 13 children, yet the first taken from earth. The last 5 years of her life were devoted to the care of the sick, the orphan, & the widow. On the tombstone of the mother of this estimable lady is a wreath of flowers, with 13 buds & 2 full-blown roses. The roses, representing the father & mother, are separated beneath as cut off or fallen from the stem; & now the first bud is taken in all her innocence & purity. This good lady was elected to the post of Mother Superior as a tribute to her high qualifications & piety. She left the Asylum at Wheeling in July last to visit her home for the restoration of her health, impaired by constant vigils, animated with the hope of returning with renewed energy, but it was ordered otherwise by the Great Disposer of events. Mother Stanislaus died calmly, with but little suffering. Sweet angel pray for us. -G

THU OCT 25, 1860
On Oct 18, the remains of Francis Asbury Lumsden, late proprietor & editor of the New Orleans Picayune, whose untimely end was caused by the steamer **Lady Elgin** disaster, on Lake Erie, were interred with much ceremony at New Orleans. The funeral procession was very large, & comprised several Masonic, Military, & Typographical organizations. The Continental Guards fire 3 volleys over the grave.

Two boys, 16 years old, living in Quebec, engaged in a pitched battle on Friday, & continued so long, that David Colin White, died from sheer exhaustion.

From London. Cavalry, its History & Tactics, by Capt L E Nolan, [killed at Sebastopol.] New edition. –Franck Taylor

Mrd: on Oct 23, in Wash City, at Wesley Chapel, by Rev L F Morgan, Flodo W Howard to Miss Rosa Henning, all of Wash City.

Circuit Court of D C-in Equity, No 1,165. Statham, Smithson & Co, Austin Sherman, Alex M Hamilton, Wm T Dove & Coleby Young, Richd E Simms, Danl H Tibbs & Thos Tenant, cmplnts & petitioners, against John F Callan, Sarah A Callan his wife, Michl P Callan, Nicholas Callan, Mary E, Margaret A, Jas N, John, Chas C, Rosalia, Laura, Clara, & Hellen Callan, Mich A Ginsta, Mary A Nalley, Wm Robinson & Alice O his wife, Benj N Robinson, Needler R Jennings, John Brooks, Jas Jennings Brooks, Robinson Clark, & Amanda C Jennings, dfndnts. By an order of the said Court I am directed to state the account of the trustees in said cause, C Ingle & A Austin Smith, & the distribution of the fund among the creditors of said John F Callan. Parties concerned to attend in City Hall, Wash, on Nov 16 next. -W Redin, auditor

Died: on Oct 23, at the residence of Benj Ogle Tayloe, in Wash City, in her 89th year, Mrs Lydia Warren, relict of the late Hon E Warren, of Troy, N Y.

Miss Mary P Duncan can receive into her school, 21 Indiana ave, a limited number of young ladies as boarders, to be taught French & an English education.

FRI OCT 26, 1860
Naval-Paymaster Gallaher, U S Navy, reported to duty yesterday at the Naval Academy, Annapolis, to report to Paymaster Cunningham, U S Navy, who is under orders for the East Indies.

The total amount of the auction for which the objects left by the late Alex'r Von Humboldt were sold was 10,000 thalers. Humboldt's scientific instruments & large gold & silver coins of considerable value were included in the sale.
[*Possible 10,000 thalers-difficult to read.]

Excellent household & kitchen furniture at auction on Nov 1, the effects of J B Kirtland, at the Auction Rooms. –Wall & Barnard, aucts

Several weeks ago the Cathedral of Notre Dame, at Paris, was burglariously entered & robbed of valuables to the amount of 800,000 francs, [$160,000,] & thus far no discovery has been made of the burglars. This robbery has made a deep impression. The treasury of Notre Dame was sacked at the Revolution of July, & all the ecclesiastical vestments thrown into the river, where they were discovered by some fishermen several months afterwards.

The oldest Postmaster in the U S, who has never been out of office since the date of his appointment, is John Billings, at Trenton, Oneida Co, N Y. His appointment was made on Jun 19, 1805.

The subscriber, having disposed of his farm, will sell at public auction, on his premises, on the Wash & Brookeville turnpike, on Nov 1, all his household & kitchen furniture, farming implements, horses, mules, oxen, & cows.
–Richd L Ross

This morning about 4 o'clock, the little child of Mr P H Newman, living on Pa ave, near 12th st, arose from bed & tripped & fell. Mrs Newman sprang out of her bed to assist the child, & in the darkness missed the landing at the head of the stairway, & fell 14 steps, her face striking the iron lock of the door, disservering the lower part of the nose entirely from her face, tearing off all of her upper lip, cutting half an inch of her tongue, & a dreadful gash in her chin. Her delicate condition at the time of the accident renders the matter yet more serious. Drs Blanchard & Lincoln were called, & attended to her wounds, which demanded skillful action. -Star

SAT OCT 27, 1860

Hon Geo W Lay died at Batavia N Y, on Sun last. He was a member of Congress from 1833 to 1837, & subsequently charge d'affaires at Stockholm, under Pres Tyler.

Mrs Edw S Livingston died at her residence, Montgomery place, N Y, on Wed. She was in her 79th year, having been born in 1781. She was afflicted with no special disease, & expired simply of old age & debility. She was the widow of Hon Edw Livingston, formerly Sec of State of the U S & Minister to France.

Public sale of valuable Potomac bottom land & fishery, by decree of the Circuit Court of PG Co, Md, in Equity, public sale on Nov 22nd at the Bellemont House, on Broad creek, in Piscataway district, adjoining the premises, all the right, title, & interest of which the late Rozier T Daingerfield died seized to a cerrtain portion of the ***Bellemonte estate***, containing 171 acres, more or less, known as ***Indian Queen***. Also, for sale at the same time, the Fishing Landing known as the ***Sandy Bar***, adjoining the tract above described. –Wm Henry Daingerfield, trustee

Mrd: on Oct 25, in Wash City, at the Church of the Epiphany, by Rev Chas H Hall, D D, Octavius Knight, of Wash, to Mary Ellen Simpson, adopted daughter of Capt J H Simpson, of the Corps of Topographical Engineers, U S Army.

Mrd: on Oct 18, at Trinity Church, by Rev John Pilkington, of the Oneida, [N Y] Conference, Jas E Pilkington, of Balt, Md, to Annie D Adams, of Wash City.

Mrd: on Oct 18, in the Presbyterian Church, at Parkersburg, Va, by Rev Jas H Lepps, Dr Saml Q A Burche, formerly of Wash City, to Fannie M, eldest daughter of Beverly Smith, of Parkersburg.
+
Mrd: on Oct 18, in the Presbyterian Church, at Parkersburg, Va, by Rev Jas H Leppes, John O Talbott, of Waverley, Mo, to Laura V, 2nd daughter of Beverly Smith.

Mrd: on Oct 24, at Norfolk, Va, by Rev Mr Rodman, Wm J Bromwell, of Wash City, to Alice, daughter of Lt O H Berryman, U S Navy.

Obit-died: on Oct 25, at the advanced age of 88 years, Mrs Lydia Warren. This venerable lady was among the earlier residents of Troy, N Y, of which city her husband, the late Hon E Warren was one of the original founders. At an early period of her life she devoted herself to the interests of the Episcopal Church. The Charity School of St Paul's in that city, was another recipient of her bounty. Mrs Warren became a resident of Wash about 8 years ago, through the marriage of her daughter to Mr Benj Ogle Tayloe. Reduced by an unfortunate accident, at age 80, she was utterly helpless, & her daughter, unwearied & with unremitting devotion, for 8 years seldom left her side by day or night.

Positive sale of valuable farm, slaves, stock, & crops, in PG Co, Md, at public auction, on Dec 12, known as **Part of Greenwood Park Enlarged**, 3 miles from **Old Field**, upon which Danl R Wall now resides, & adjoining the farms of the late Dr David Cranfurd, Albert B Berry, & the late Zachariah B Beall, containing 212 acres; divided into 4 fields; improvements consist of a new & comfortable frame dwlg, & numerous out-bldgs. –Wall & Barnard, aucts, Pa ave & 9th st, Wash.

MON OCT 29, 1860

The Marquis of Bute, a minor nearly 13 years of age, is at present the subject of competition among his guardians as to his custody, & the occasion of some little collision between the Court of Chancery & the Court of Session in Scotland. The late Marquis of Bute died in 1848, leaving an infant son heir to his title & estate. On application of the late Lord Jas Stuart to the Court of Chancery the Marchioness was, in May, 1848, appointed the guardian of the infant heir, & from then to her death last Dec her chief residence with her charge was in Mount Stuart, in Bute Co. In her will she recommends Lady Eliz Moore, her nearest female relative to be appointed joint guardian of the Marquis with Maj Gen Stuart, one of the boy's nearest paternal relatives. The Court of Chancery, on being applied, appointed Gen Stuart & Lady Eliz Moore co-guardians, while the latter with the young Marquis was still residing in Scotland. In Mar last the Marquis was taken to England by Lady Eliz, that arrangements might be made with Gen Stuart & with the Court of Chancery for his education. On Apr 20 that Court settled a scheme for his education, but Lady Eliz Moore, who had differed from Gen Stuart on the subject, [the former desiring private tutorship & the latter proposing to prepare him for Eton or Harrow,] had 4 days earlier left for Scotland with the young Marquis in her charge. Gen Stuart proceeded to Edinburgh to ask the custody of the ward, which Lady Eliz refused to give; the Gen than applied to the Court of Chancery to remove Lady Eliz from the guardianship, & the Court granted an order accordingly. But the ward being now beyond the jurisdiction of the Court of Chancery, Gen Stuart, with the concurrence of Lady Keith Murray, aunt of the Marquis, petitioned the Court of Session to grant warrant for the removal of the ward from the custody of Lady Eliz Moore, & for his delivery to himself. Counsel were heard on Thu last upon the petition. Though the Marquis was born in Scotland, his legal domicile was a matter of question, & his estate, which exceeded L93,000 in annual value were to the extent of four-fifths in England. Mr Gordon, for Lady Eliz Moore, stated that she was the nearest unmarried cognate of the pupil in Scotland. The Marquis was born in Scotland. His father was a domicled Scotchman, & the presumption was the son was also domiciled there. After the father's death, the late Marchioness resided chiefly in Scotland. The Marquis was most desirous to remain in Scotland. The court appoints Lady Eliz Moore to answer the petition & order service upon the tutor-at-law, & also service upon the Marquis, so that he may be represented here by a tutor-ad-titem.

Norfolk, Oct 27. Cmder John L Sanders, of the Navy, died here on Friday.

Fortunate escape of Col Preston from drowning. Louisville Courier: letter from Hon Wm Preston, our Minister to Spain, who on Oct 2 sailed with his family from Marseilles in a Spanish vessel, on his route for Madrid. The vessel struck a rock; Col Preston placed his wife & 2 daughters in one boat, 3 daughters in another, & embarked himself with his son in a third. The ladies were all landed safely. The boat in which the Col & his son were in was stranded on a rocky shore, but rescued by the inhabitants who had gathered on the beach. The Col himself was drawn back 3 times by the receding waves & undertow, & though eventually saved by the desperate exertions of Maltese & Catalan boatmen, he was in an apparently lifeless condition. Restoratives were efficiently administered, & the Col & all his family were entirely recovered & had gone back to Marseilles.

Extensive sale of stock, grain, vegetables, farming implements, carriages, wagons, household & kitchen furniture at auction on Nov 16 & 17, at the farm & residence of Darius Clagett, deceased, on the 7th st turnpike, all the personal effects belonging to the said deceased. –W H Clagett, adm -Cleary & Green, aucts

The scientific world has lost a bright ornament in the decease of Geo Shroeter, which took place at his residence in Paterson, N J, on Thu morning. The immediate cause of his death was inflammation of the lungs, brought on by a severe cold. He was only in his 43rd year. His illness lasted about 8 days. Mr Shroeter was a native of Purssia, & graduated, we believe, at the universities of Konigsberg & Berlin. Like so many other disappointed lovers of liberty, Mr Shroeter decided to seek a home in the Western hemisphere, & reached this city in 1849. In 1856 he completed a map of the U S from ocean to ocean, on a canvas 30 feet by 17. The Geographical & Statistical Society last evening adopted resolutions expressing condolences to his family. We learn that the latter are placed in rather straitened circumstances. -N Y Commercial

At Norfolk, Va, on Wed, Mr Jesse T Newell, a worthy citizen & indulgent parent, found his little son playing in the yard with a pistol, not supposed to be loaded, & took it from him, & while examining it, it accidentally discharged, hitting his little daughter Laura, age 9 years, & instantly killing her. Drs Galt & Bright were called, & reached the scene, but too late.

TUE OCT 30, 1860
Cmder John L Saunders died at Norfolk on Oct 26, in his 58th year. He enters the navy in 1809. For a number of years past he has been afflicted with paralysis, for which reason he was placed on the reserved list by the action of the Naval Retiring Board.

Midshipmen promoted Masters in the line of promotion: Francis B Blake, J W Alexander, Henry D___, Jas H Pritchett, Edw Terry, Chas T___es, Francis M Bunce, Bryon Wilson, Henry B Seely, Fred'k L McNair, John W Kelly, Thos B Mills, __har R Yates, Clarke Merchant, Henry W Miller. [Side of page incomplete-best copy available.]

Handsome & superior household & kitchen furniture at auction on Nov 2, at the residence of Hon Gregory Yale, of Calif, on G st, between 14th & 15th sts. -Jas C McGuire & Co, aucts

Thousands of people will regret the death of J C Adams, better known as Old Grizzly Adams, by his numerous & perilous adventures with grizzly bears & other savage animals. He died peacefully at the home of his daughter, in Neponset, on Fri, in his 48th year. The immediate cause of his death was the open wound on his head, received in one of his encounters with a grizzly bear, & which would never heal. -Boston Herald

Died: on Oct 28, John Sam H Hammett, youngest son of Rev Jos Hammett, aged 7 years & 8 months. His funeral will be from his father's residence, College Hill, at 3:30 o'clock P M, this day.

WED OCT 31, 1860

Trustee's sale of household & kitchen furniture at auction on Nov 12, by deed of trust from Jacob Schmidt; including bar-room fixtures & liquors, being in the house on 6th st, between La ave & C st, Wash City, lately occupied by Jacob Schmidt as a Restaurant. –Thos W Berry, trustee -Cleary & Green, aucts

Hitchings, father & son, were lately arrested in S C on a charge of abolitionist conspiracy, tried & acquitted, & ordered out of the State. They were tried before a cmte of 70. The vote was 11 for hanging & 59 against it.

$5 reward for return of strayed Cow. Left from the Wash Asylum, on Oct 22. -J R Queen, Intendant

Mourning Goods, shawls & cloaks. –W M Shuster & Co, 38, opposite Centre Market, between 7th & 8th sts.

Order of distress for house rent due & in arrear from Crocker & Kugler to Stanislaus Murray, I have distrained sundry goods, 3 minieral water fountains, 1 corking machine, & a lot of marble dust; to satisfy same; sale on Nov 3, corner of B st & 2nd st. –J W Wise, Constable & Bailiff

Orphans Court of Wash Co, D C. Letters of administration on the personal estate of Jacob Schmidt, late of Wash Co, deceased. –Caroline F Schmidt, Henry Lichan, adms

Mrd: on Oct 24, at the residence of the bride's father, by Rev G W Hosmer, D D, Geo Gorham, of Canandaigua, N Y, to Miss Emily A, eldest daughter of Hon N K Hall, of Buffalo, N Y.

Died: at **Mount Air**, PG Co, Md, [the residence of his father,] Thos Edelin, in his 20th year. [No death date given-current item.]

Died: on Oct 26, at the residence of Dr Wm Selden, in Norfolk, Va, Mrs Mary Pickett, widow of the late Col Robt Pickett, of Richmond, Va, in her 56th year.

Phil, Oct 30. The jury in the case of Wm Byerly, tried on the charge of forging election returns in the first Congressional district, & thus defeating the election of Lehman, the Democratic candidate, brought in a verdict of guilty this morning. His counsel will probably carry the case to the Supreme Court.

Petersburg, Oct 30. Lt John T Barrand, of the U S Navy, died here very suddenly on Sunday. He was a native of this State, & entered the service in 1841, as a midshipman. He was stationed at the Gosport navy yard.

THU NOV 1, 1860
Brvt Brig Gen Clark, cmder of the dept of Calif, died at San Francisco on Oct 17, after an illness of 2 weeks. He has served in the U S Army since 1812, was through the war in Mexico, & was promoted to the distinguished position occupied at the time of his death for meritorious conduct at the siege of Vera Cruz.

Kingman F Page, for several years past a clerk in the Pension Ofc, has tendered his resignation to take effect the 1st proximo. He will enter upon a sphere of duty more congenial to his wishes, & promising a more lucrative pecuniary reward.

Trustee's sale of valuable improved proerty in Wash City, east of the Capitol, between 5th & 6th sts east & A & B sts north: public auction on Dec 4, by deed of trust executed by Jas Owner & Mary E Owner, his wife, dated Sep 21, 1859, recorded in Liber J A S No 183, folios 158, 159, etc, of the land records for Wash Co, D C: sale of square 839 with a brick dwlg house, stable, & other improvements; contains within a fraction of 3 acres of ground. -H Naylor, trustee -A Green, aucts

On Fri Danl Clifford was hung in the jail yard at Dubuque, Iowa, for murdering a man named Wood, whom he robbed of $27. Clifford was 22 years of age, yet the murder was so unprovoked that hardly any sympathy has been manifested for him. Although the body fell about 7 feet when the rope was cut, the wretched man died from strangulation.

Academy of Modern Language, Wash Bldg, Pa ave, 7th st. Private instruction in French & Spanish; day & evening classes, translations. A M De Monthurry, Prof of Modern Languages & Literature will resume his classes on Nov 5.

Notice: All persons indebted to the estate of my late husband, A H Young, are earnestly requested to settle their accounts as soon as possible either with Mr W Flenner, [who is authorized to make the collections,] or myself.
–M A Young, admx, I st, between 9th & 10th sts.

FRI NOV 2, 1860

The young Irish poet, Wm Allingham, is complimented by Chas Kinsgley & Robt Browning as the most gifted son of song among the rising bards. He lives in an out of the way corner of Ireland, & writes very rarely. His collected poems are soon to be published by Ticknor & Fields.

Two children of Edw Wooster, of Falls Village, Ct, were burnt to death last week, when the mother left the house for a short time, & locked in 3 children. They accidentally set the house on fire, when playing with matches. One child was found dead & the other died the same evening.

Trustee's sale of valuable real estate in Wash City, by decree of the Circuit Court of D C, passed in a cause in which Wm A Johnson is cmplnt, & Jas W Garner & others are dfndnts: sale on Nov 26 next, of parts of lots 22 & 29 in square 369, in Wash City, fronting on 9th st west, between L & M sts, with a 2 story frame dwlg-house. –C Ingle, trustee -Jas C McGuire & Co, aucts

Mrd: on Nov 1, in Wash City, in the N Y Ave Presbyterian Church, [Rev Dr Gurley's,] by Rev Dr John C Smith, Rev Alex'r D Moore, of Dauphin, Pa, [recently of Wash City,] to Maria Louisa Douglas, daughter of A O Douglas, of Wash City.

Mrd: on Oct 31, in Wash City, at the Church of the Epiphany, by Rev Chas H Hall, Mr Saml C Mills to Miss Mary A Knott, only daughter of Geo A Knott, all of Wash City.

Died: on Nov 1, in Wash City, Emilie, daughter of Wm H & Prudence E Frazure, aged 1 year & 8 months. Her funeral will be this evening at 3 o'clock, from the residence of her parents, 272 8th st, between M & N sts.

Died: at the residence of his brother-in-law, Jas Roach, in Alexandria Co, John B Carson, son of the late Dr Jas Carson, in his 45th year. His funeral will take place on Nov 3, at 10½ o'clock, from St Mary's Church, Alexandria. [No death date given.]

SAT NOV 3, 1860

Dr Wm P Johnston has removed his residence to 359 H st, between 14th & 15th sts. His ofc will be continured at his former residence, 466 7th st.

Dancing Academy, Prof R J Power, can be found at 453 9th st.

Mrd: on Nov 1, by Rev J Spencer Kennard, Jos W Colbert, of Fauquier Co, Va, to Miss Bettie A Stewart, of the same place.

Mrd: on Oct 13, by Rev J Spencer Kennard, Mr Benj T Padgett to Miss Sarah L Frink, both of Alexandria, Va.

Local Matters. Edw C Carrington has been appointed Brig Gen of the Militia of D C; he is in his 20th year, served as capt of volunteers through the whole of the Mexican war; received a military education at the Va Military Institute; commanded the Wash Light Infty, the oldest & one of the best companies of our city. He is the eldest son of Gen Edw C Carrington, deceased, late of Va, who was twice wounded in the war of 1812, & promoted for his gallantry, & esteemed by the people of Va as a scholar, a patriot, & a philanthropist. He is the grand nephew of Col Edw Carrington, of Va, who fought from the ranks in the Revolution to be second in command to Gen Green of the Southern wing of the American army, & was thrice thanked at the head of the American army for his gallantry. Gen Carrington served several terms with acceptability & efficiency in the Legislature of Va.

N Y, Nov 2. Sheridan Knowles, lost on the steamer **Arctic**, between Hull, England & Cronstadt, was not the author, but the American agent of the American Bank Note Co, charged with the performance of work for the Emperor of Russia.

New Orleans, Nov 2. The steamer **H R W Hill**, Capt T H Newell, running between this city & Memphis, exploded her boiler on Wed. She had a large number of passengers on board. Thirty persons were killed outright, & 40 to 50 more were scalded.

MON NOV 5, 1860
At Albany, N Y, on Fri, a lawyer named John Percy entered the premises kept by John Cranfield as a porter house, on Broadway, & committed a violent assault on him; Cranfield drew a revolver & shot Percy twice in the stomach. Percy cannot survive. The quarrel arose out of a suit for the possession of the premises occupied by Cranfield.

New Haven Palladium of Friday: today the boilers in the basement of Dann Brothers' carriage parts manufactory, at State & Wall sts, exploded. The second floor was occupied by Giles G Baldwin, manufacturer of clock & dental tools. He & Mr Geo De Wolf fell with the bldg, & both were severely but not dangerously scalded. John Kane was blown entirely out & received a skull fracture which will prove fatal. The Johnson boy is seriously injured. Henry Rice, a boy, was killed. Baldwin & De Wolf are very low.

Orphans Court of Wash Co, D C. Letters of administration on the personal estate of Eliz Rhoades, late of Wash Co, deceased. –Abram Rhoades, admx

Mrd: on Nov 1, at the Seventh Baptist Church, Balt, by Rev Dr Fuller, Wm R Wilson, of Wash City, to Miss Sarah E, daughter of Hiram P Evans, of the former place.

Mrd: on Oct 30, by Rev G H Norton, Mr Henry A Tayloe, of *Mount Airy*, Va, to Courtenay N, daughter of Mr B S Chinn, of Hazel Plain, Prince Wm Co, Va.

Died: on Nov 4, in Wash City, after a protracted illness, Stanislaus Murray, in his 65th year. His funeral will be from his late residence, 441 5th st, on Tue at 10 o'clock A M. The funeral service will be performed at St Patrick's Church.

Montgomery, Ala, Nov 2. The deck of the steamer **Virginia** gave way tonight, whilst Senator Douglas was addressing a few farewell remarks to the assemblage. He, with the crowd, was precipitated below, but providentially none were hurt. Mrs Douglas held to the side railing, & was rescued uninjured. Both returned to the hotel.

Montpelier, Vt, Nov 2. Hon H M Bates, late State Treasurer, is a defaulter to the State. It is asserted that $30,000 will not cover the deficit, & it may even exceed $40,000.
+
Burlington, Vt, Nov 2. Bates, the defaulting State Treasurer, absconded from Northfield last night. He has probably gone to Canada. The amount of his defalcation, so far as discovered, is $42,000.

Died: on Nov 3, in Gtwn, after a painful illness of 11 weeks' duration, C A Lavinia, wife of Wm Collins, & eldest daughter of John Clements. Her funeral will be from her late residence, 22 Prospect st, this afternoon at 3 o'clock P M.

TUE NOV 6, 1860
Chancery sale of house & lot, by decree of the Circuit Court of D C, in Chancery, dated Oct 24, 1860, passed in a cause therein depending between Ernst Loeffler, cmplnt, & Adam Raab, adm, & others, dfndnts, No 1,559; public auction on Nov 28 next, a portion of the west half of lot 1 in square 516, in Wash City, with a 2 story frame house; fronting on I st, between 4th & 5th sts. .
–Asbury Lloyd, trustee   –Wall & Barnard, aucts

Trustee's sale of valuable bldg at K & 17th sts, at auction, on Dec 7 next, by deed of trust from Edw M Thomas, dated May 15, 1856, recorded in Liber J A S, No 113, folios 464 thru 467, of the land records for Wash Co, D C; sale of lot 7 in Saml Davidson's subdivision of square 184. –Leonard Huyck, trustee
–A Green, aucts

On Oct 28, Frank M Brown, age 26 years, a native of Balt, was found dying in his house in New Orleans. Some 6 months ago he married an amiable young lady, whom he loved devotedly, & with whom & his wife's mother he lived contentedly. All were poor, he was the only stay; he lost one situation after the other; he fell to dispair. He took his life by drinking a vial of laudanum

Five young ladies took the white veil on Oct 1 at the Convent of the <u>Sisters of Notre Dame</u>, Milwaukee, Wisc, & 18 the black veil on Oct 8 in the same establishment.

Mrd: on Nov 1, at Trinity Church, by Rev C M Butler, Mr F K O'Farrell, of Cincinnati, to Lizzie, daughter of Robinson Biggs, of Ashland, Ky.

Mrd: on Oct 22, at Christ Church, Vicksburg, Miss, by the rector, Wm W Lord, D D, C Randolph Railey to Emma Laws.

Died: on Nov 3, at the **Highlands**, D C, Anthony Morris, in his 95th year.

Died: on Nov 4, Margaret Douglas, infant daughter of Francis N & Anna Brent.

WED NOV 7, 1860
The Duke of Richmond died on Oct 21, a rich man. His death will be much regretted in sporting circles, for he encouraged racing, & his house at **Goodwood** was the scene of elegant hospitality. N Y Post

At Louisville, Ky, on Sat, a wagon-load of fire-works exploded & Jos Levi was killed then he jumped over the side of the wagon & fractured his skull. A rock struck a man named McQuiddy, in the face, severely injuring him.

The late Brig Gen Newman S Clarke, colonel of the 6th infty, who died on Oct 17 at San Francisco, entered the army, as an ensign of the 11th infty, Mar 14, 1812, & served with distinction during the 2nd war with Great Britain. He performed the duties of brigade major in the campaign of 1814; for his gallantry & good conduct in the battle of Niagara he received the rank of captain by brevet. During the campaign from Vera Cruz to the Capital of Mexico he commanded a brigade, which, led by him, performed gallant & effective service in the work of the campaign. Breveted a brigadier general for his services in Mexico, Gen Clarke has since been employed upon high duties, & while commanding our whole Pacific coast, by his ability & good judgment, he concerted a plan of campaign against combined tribes of Indians in Oregon & Washington Territory, which, happily executed under his instructions, promptly reduced the enemy to submission.

We record this day the decease of one of the most gallant ofcrs of the present century, & one of the few surviving companions in arms of Lords Hardinge & Gough, & the rest of the heroes of Moodkee & Ferozeshah, in the person of Gen Sir Harry Geo Wakelyn Smith, Bart, G C B, at the age of 72. He was born in 1788 at Whittlesea, in the Isle of Ely, where his father was a local surgeon. He entered the army in 1805 as 2nd Lt in the rifle brigade, & took part in the siege, storming, & capture of Montevideo, under the late Gen Sir Saml Auchmuty, & in the attack on Buenos Ayres, under Brig Gen Crawford. He was present at the capture of Copenhagen, under the late Earl Cathcart. Extensive services are recorded to his name. The late Baronet married in 1814 a Spanish lady, the Donna Juana Maria de los Dolures de Leon, by whom he had no issue; & accordingly the baronet becomes extinct by his death. –London Times

Fatal explosion of a fluid lamp on Fri, in Second st, Phil, killed Miss Catharine Thomas, age 18 years.

THU NOV 8, 1860
The steamer **Wm L Levy**, Capt Puckett, hence for Alexandria, when opposite College Point, was hailed by the steamer **H R W Hill**, on Wed. The **Levy** ran alongside; & ascertained that the **Hill** was in distress, having exploded the 3rd boiler from the larboard side. The **Levy** returned last evening, having in tow the **Hill**, when she landed her at the foot of Girod st. Mr Lohman, cabin pasenger, had his right hand slightly wounded. The barber, G W Scurry, of Nashville, & Chas Hagger, of Nashville, jumped overboard & were drowned. Mr Glidden Marks, of New Albany, was instantly killed. Henry Foster, of Memphis, was considerably scalded, but not dangerously. The whole cabin of the **Hill** was strewn with the wounded, dead, & dying, every person on board endeavoring to help.

Mr D W Moore, special agent of the Post Ofc Dept, on Sat last, arrested John A McConnell, assist postmaster at Newry, Blair Co, Pa, on the charge of robbing the mail. Mr McConnell was committed in default of bail.

W H Wilder, who has served four out of a sentence of 10 years in the Louisiana State prison, for forging U S land warrants, has been pardoned by the Pres of the U S.

Orphans Court of Wash Co, D C. Letters of administration on the personal estate of Jas Leslie, late of Wash Co, deceased. –Wm J Belshaw, adm

Mrd: on Oct 30, at Grape Hill, in Nelson Co, Va, by Rev G W Nolan, Alpheus L Edwards, of Wash City, to Matilda C, daughter of the late Jas Smiley, of the former place.

Mrd: on Oct 17, in Cavalry Church, N Y, by Rev Dr Hawkes, Wm Speiden, of Hong Kong, China, to Marion, daughter of the late Cmdor Isaac McKeever, U S Navy.

Mrd: on Nov 7, at Wesley Chapel, by Rev Wm Krebs, Wm Coad Smith to Katharine Clay Venable, all of Wash City.

Mrd: on Nov 5, by Rev P D Gurley, at the N Y ave Church, Rev Wm Gurley, late of New Orleans, to Mary C, daughter of Rev R R Gurley, of Wash City.

FRI NOV 9, 1860
Died: on Nov 8, in Wash City, Mathew T J, infant son of Walter L & Eliz Nicholson. His funeral will be from the residence, 284 B st south, Friday at 2 o'clock P M.

harleston, Nov 8-received by telegraph. 1-Jas Conner, District Atty, has resigned; Mr Colcock, Collector of the Port, & Jacobs, Deputy Collecor, have notified the Pres of their resignation. All the Federal ofcrs intend to resign on the inauguaration of Lincoln. 2-The barque **James Gray**, owned by the Cushings, of Boston, now lying at our wharves, under the instructions of her owners, has hoisted the Palmetto flag, & is now firing a salute of 15 guns.

Household & kitchen furniture at auction on: Nov 13, at the residence of Jas Orr, 164 Pa ave, between 17th & 18th sts. –A Green, auct

London Times: The murdered person, Mary Elmsley, was a widow, about 70 years of age, of very miserly habits; lived entirely alone in the neighborhood of Mile-end, perfomring all domestic duties for herself, going out to collect her rents, for she possessed considerable property in houses. She was last seen alive on Aug 13. Mrs Elmsley was found murdered in a lumber room. A man named Emm, occasionally employed by the deceased, was accused of the murder by a man named Mullins. Mullins himself was found to be the murderer. He was by trade a plasterer, & the hammer used exactly fitted the wounds, which deprived Mrs Elmsley of her life.

The Vinginians are about to erect a monument to the memory of Peter Francisco, whose herculean hand-to-hand struggles for liberty in the Revolutionary war with British troops are common themes for fireside stories in the Old Dominion. Francisco died in 1834, previous to which event he served 3 terms as sgt-at-arms in the Va Legislature.

Mrd: on Nov 5, by Rev P D Gurley, at the N Y ave Church, Revers W Gurley, late of New Orleans, to Mary C, daughter of Rev R R Gurley, of Wash City.

Mrd: on Oct 18, at Richmond, Va, by Rev Mr Minnegerode, Mr Wm Key Howard, of Balt, to Miss Clara, daughter of the late Thos Mann Randolph, of Tuckahoe, Va.

SAT NOV 10, 1860
The following candidates passed successfully as 3rd Assist Engineers in the U S Navy: F G M Kean & John Wilson, of Balt, Md; P Voorhees, Annapolis, Md; J S Tucker, Norfolk, Va; Jas J Noble, Balt; A Murray & W S Smith, Balt; C W Jordan, Norfolk; W H Jackson, Balt. The resignation of the 3rd Assist Engineer E R Archer has been accepted by the Dept.

Mrd: on Nov 8, by Rev Mr Griffith, Wm Noble Clokey, of Wash City, to Mary H, daughter of the late Wm F King, of Howard Co, Md.

Mrd: on Nov 7, in Gtwn, by Rev Dr Woods, of Lewistown, Pa, Rev A Miller Woods, of Hartsville, Pa, to Mary D, daughter of B F Rittenhouse.

Mrd: on Nov 6, at *Clover Lea*, Hanover Co, Va, by Rev Mr Corraway, Col Lewis W Washington, of Beall Air, Jefferson Co, Va, to Ella M, daughter of Geo W Bassett In this marriage a singular coincidence occurs; the groom being the great-grandson of two brothers of Gen Washington, & the bride the great-grand-daughter of the only sister of Gen Washington, & also great-grand-daughter of the sister of Mrs Gen Washington.

Chicago, Nov 8. The propeller **Globe**, which arrived from Buffalo this morning, exploded her boiler at her dock this forenoon. The killed are Mary Ann Golden, Patrick Donohue, Jas Hobbie, Benj Wilson, 1st engineer, Forsyth, 2nd engineer, & 4 firemen. The injured are the clerk, slightly, N Luddington, & Michl Cusick, of Chicago; Peter Barnholt, of Erie; John Hayden, of Rochester; Julian Hatch & David Dana, of Chicago, & the first mate, all badly. The boat is a complete wreck.

MON NOV 12, 1860
Resignations in South Carolina: the Judge of the Court, Hon A G Magrath; & Jas Connor, the U S District Attorney.

Mr Lincoln, at home in Springfield, Ill, is continually visited by crowds of well wishers. The only letters he writes are of a private nature, & there are plently of these required.

The U S corvette **Saratoga** has been in commission at Phil, & will sail in a short time to reinforce our squadron on the coast of Africa. The sloop of war Saratoga is of 16 guns of the 2nd class, & her ofcrs are: Cmder, A Taylor; Lts, John J Guthrie, C M Hayes, J Madigan; Master, T M Ramsay; Marine Ofcr, H B Taylor; Surgeon, C W Jeffrey; Assist Surgeon, John E Lindsay; Gunner, R H Cross; Boatswain, Geo Smith; Carpenter, J W Stinson.

The Grand Jury of Lynchburg, Va, have found a true bill against Geo W Hardwicke, & ignored the bill against Wm Hardwicke, the parties engaged in the shooting of Mr Button, connected with one of the papers there.

Died: on Nov 10, after a protracted illness, Geo F Smallwood, in his 30th year. His funeral will be on Monday next, at 2 o'clock P M, from his late residence, 673 Pa ave, between 3rd & 4th sts, Capitol Hill.

Died: on Sunday, in Wash City, Jas Dodds, in his 84th year. He was a native of Northumberland Co, England, but for the last 40 years a resident of this District. His funeral is today at 3 o'clock P M, from his late residence, L st, between 9th & 10th sts.

Augusta, Nov 10. Senator Toombs, of Ga, & Senator Chesnut, of S C, have severally resigned their ofc as Senators of the U S.

Fort Kearny, Nov 10. The Rocky Mountain News reports the arrest of Judge McClure. He escaped, but was re-arrested, & placed under bail to the amount of $10,000. The charge was not specified, but, according to the News, it is a grave one.

TUE NOV 13, 1860
A week ago Geo Browne, Pres of the Buffalo & Lake Huron railway, whose residence is Goderich, visited Toronto, & stayed at Eliah's Hotel. He became ill & a telegram was sent to Mrs Browne, summoning her to Toronto. She came by the first train & finding her husband was not seriously indisposed, she caused his nephew to telegraph home to that effect, to ally the anxiety of the family. Despatch: Mr Browne is no worse; Mrs Browne will write tonight. When the despatch reached the family it said: Mr Browne is no more; Mrs Browne will write tonight. Mr R S Carter, the manager of the Buffalo & Lake Huron railway, visited the house of mourning & signified his intention of proceeding to Toronto with a special train to bring home the remains of his lamented chief. The train was got ready without delay, & Mr Carter & Mr Browne's eldest son came to this city as passengers on it. When they reached the Eliah's Hotel, they were astonished to find Mr Browne, in the public parlor, talking, laughing, & enjoying good health. Mutual explanations took place & all parties were overjoyed to find that the gentleman had only been "killed by telegraph." –Toronto Globe of 5th

R C Presley, U S Assist Treasurer, who has been absent, returned in the Savannah train. He declared he would not hold office under Lincoln under any circumstances whatever. He will resign.

Superior household & kitchen furniture at auction on Nov 15, at the residence of Col Roberts, 8th st, Heights of Gtwn, all his effects. -Barnard & Buckley, aucts, Gtwn, D C

Circuit Court of D C-in Equity, No 1,566. Thos Welsh against Edw Semmes, adm & the heirs at law of Thos Barnes. Heirs at law of said Thos Barnes are to make themselves known to me on or before Dec 5 next; creditors of said Barnes are notified to file their claims, at my ofc, City Hall, Wash. –W Redin, auditor

WED NOV 14, 1860
Geo Wm Brown, the newly elected Mayor of the City of Balt, was installed into office on Monday last.

Circuit Court-Wash, Tue. 1-Wm J Parham, having been convicted of spiriting away a witness in the Criminal Court, was deprived of his ofc of county constable.
2-Michl J McLaughlin, for contempt in disregarding a rule of the Court to appear before it, was likewise removed from the ofc of county constable.

Since the resignation of Rev Dr Hill as pastor of the First Baptist Church, the parishoners have been so fortunate as to secure the services of Rev Dr Samson, Pres of Columbia College, & Prof Shute, of the same institution. They refuse to accept any pecuniary compensation, preferring the salary to be applied to the liquidation of the Church debt.

Orphans Court of Wash Co, D C, Nov 12, 1860. In the case of Ann Shaaf, excx, of Mary Shaaf, deceased, the executrix & Court have appointed Dec 8 next, for the final settlement of the personal estate of the said deceased, of the assets in hand. -Ed Roach, Reg/o wills

Mrd: on Nov 6, by Rev Geo Woodbridge, D D, Rev Henry A Wise, Rector of the Church of Our Saviour, Phil, to Hattie, daughter of R Barton Hax_ll, of Richmond, Va.

Mrd: Oct 25th, at St Aloysius Church, by Rev B A Maguire, Wm Hamilton Williams to Mary E, only daughter of the late Geo Rufus Spalding, of Chas Co, Md.

THU NOV 15, 1860

Brvt Maj Peter G T Beauregard, capt corps of engineers, has been appointed Superintendent of the Military Academy, & will relieve the present superintendent at the close of the approaching semi-annual examination of the cadets.

Hon Judge Eccleston, of the Court of Appeals of Md, died on Monday, under circumstances peculiarly afflicting to his family. He had, with his family, on Sunday last attended divine service at a church about 6 miles from Chestertown, Kent Co, where he resided. Upon returning & when the carriage reached his dwlg, the deceased was found to be ill, helpless, & unable to alight, speechless & in a dying state. He expired on Monday. The vacancy caused by his death will be filled by the Govn'r of the State until the general election next fall. Deceased was a brother of the late Archbishop Eccleston, of Balt. -Sun

Mail from Santa Fe, New Mexico: Capt Geo McLane, of the Mounted Rifles, was killed by the Navajo Indians on Oct 13th or 18th, while on a scout with his company, about 25 miles of *Fort Defiance*. In a charge upon the Indians McLane killed 4 Indians with his pistol. Capt McLane became separated from his men & was seen to fall from his horse. His foot became entangled in his stirrup & he was dragged a considerable distance before he stopped. When the men came up they found he was dead. Capt McLane was a son of Senator McLane, of Delaware. He leaves & widow & three children, who are in Albuquerque. The Indians made their escape.

Died: Oct 14, Louisa C Lieberman, wife of Dr Chas H Lieberman. Her funeral will be from her late residence, 459 13th st, between E & F sts, on Nov 16, 3 o'clock P M.

Milledgeville, Nov 14. Georgia affairs. Speeches are made here nightly by Toombs, Thos R Cobb, & others, in favor of secession. Stephens, Johnson, & others speak in opposition to secession. Bitter feuds exist in the Legislature between the friends Iverson & Howell Cobb for the Senatorship.

Augusta, Nov 14. The popular vote in this State is nearly 2,000 majority against Breckinridge.

FRI NOV 16, 1860
Geoffrey J Lavaille, who was shot in a fight with T B Kershaw, at Petersburg, Va, died on Nov 12. The wound was inflicted on Oct 15, & the pistol was charged with aa horse-shoe nail. The nail was found in his brain, where it had been for nearly a month.

Mr Talbot, keeper of a hotel at Bardstown, Ky, was shot & killed by a young man named T Hine Slaughter, about a year ago. Slaughter got a change of venue from Nelson to Bullitt Co, & recently was admitted to bail, the jury failing to agree upon a verdict. On Sat last Mr Talbot, a son of the murdered man, shot & killed Slaughter in the streets of Bardstown as an act of revenge for the murder of his father.

Orphans Court of Wash Co, D C. Letters of administration on the personal estate of Maria Stewart, late of Wash Co, deceased. –Margaret A Supple, admx

Mrd: on Nov 14, at the residence of Mr W Roy Mason, King Geo Co, Va, W H Gibbes, U S Army, to Miss J A Mason, daughter of the late Dr A H Mason.

Mrd: on Nov 14, by Rev Dr Finckel, Mr Jos W Nairn to Miss Alice Lou Finckel, of Wash City.

The late Henry D Johnson. Letter from the American Consul at Florence, giving some account of the burial of the late Henry D Johnson, whose died at that place, while on his way to Constantinople, at which port he had been appointed U S Consul Gen, appeared in the papers. He was interred in the <u>Protestant Cemetery</u> with all the honors we could give him, Capt Abert, U S Army, Lt Macgaw, U S Navy, in full uniform, with 30 to 40 of our countrymen in attendance. [This was the first occasion on which the American flag was ever displayed by an officially recognized ofcr of the U S in Florence. Under the reign of the Grand Duke consular ofcrs were not officially recognized in that city.

Fort Kearny, Nov 13. P Sterey, a clerk in the commissary dept of the U S army, was accidentally shot & killed at Kearny City, about 2 miles west of this place, on Nov 11, by a discharged soldier, named Mount.

Circuit Court of D C-in Equity, No 1,612. Walter & Ann Butler against Amelia Butler, widow, Jane Queen, Betsy, Richd, Jane, Adaline, Edmund, James, George, & Harriet Ann Butler, heirs of Jas Butler. The parties above & Chas Walter, guardian ad litum of Amelia, are to attend at my room in City Hall, Wash, On Dec 1 next, when I shall inquire & report whether lots 3 & 4 in Davidson's subdivision of square 216, in Wash City, are susceptible of specific partition.
–W Redin, auditor

SAT NOV 17, 1860
Lady Franklin, widow of the lamented Sir John Franklin, the ill-fated Arctic Explorer, accompanied by her niece, Miss Cracroft, has arrived in this city, & is staying at the Nat'l Hotel.

McDonald, Johnson, & Small, who escaped from the District penitentiary a few weeks ago, have been arrested in Phil. Deputy Warden left to bring them back.

Danl Swearinger, a farmer, going from Tuscawara Co, Ohio, to ***Fort Dodge***, Iowa, while crossing the prairie near the latter place on Nov 2, with his wife & 4 children in a wagon, was overtaken by a prairie fire, & all except the father perished.

This morning the remains of Mrs F A Lumsden, with those of her adopted child, who perished in the steamer **Lady Elgin**, Sep 8, were deposited in the same tomb with those of her husband, a victim of the same terrible disaster. Still missing are the bodies of Frank, the only son, & of the female attendant of Mrs Lumsden.
-New Orleans Picayune, 8th

Trustees sale of house at lot at the corner of 4½ & D sts, at auction, by deed of trust from Wm Kiernan, dated Apr 24, 1858, recorded in Liber J A S, No 156, folios 177, etc, of the land records of Wash Co, D C: dated on Dec 17, public auction of lot 6 in square 536, in Wash City, with the dwlg house & other improvements thereon. –Wm R Woodward, trustee -A Green, aucts

Mrd: on Nov 7, at the residence of Francis Mallaby, U S Navy, Madison, N J, by Rev Saml Randall, Jas C McDonald, of Newark, N J, to Mary H Condit, of the former place.

Mrd: on Nov 15, at the residence of the bride's father, Col Geo West Gunnell, in Fairfax Co, Va, by Rev David Wilson, of Balt, J Owens Berry, of Gtwn, D C, to Miss Mary Josephine Gunnell.

Died: on Nov 15, at her late residence, near Trenton, N J, Mrs Jane H Welling, relict of the late Wm Welling, in her 74th year.

MON NOV 19, 1860
Richmond Whit, [Union.] The intelligence receives leaves no doubt of the election of Abraham Lincoln to the Presidency & Hannibal Hamlin to the Vice Presidency of the U S.

Alexandria [Va] Gaz, [Union.] The election of Lincoln as next President has, at least, not taken the country by surprise. The result was expected as well as dreaded.

St Louis [Mo] Evening News, {Union.] The most important contest that ever took place in the history of the Republic was fought & ended yesterday, & today Abraham Lincoln & Hannibal Hamlin are the Pres & Vice Pres elect of the U S. The 1,500,000 men who voted for Lincoln have prevailed over the 2,960,000 who voted against him; &, although it appears hard that a minority should thus triumph over a majority nearly twice as large, yet the triumph has been gained in perfect accordance with law; & if law is to prevail over passion there is nothing for us to do but acquiesce in the decision.

The U S ship **Savannah**, late flag-ship of the Home Squadron, arrived at N Y on Fri last, 28 days from Vera Cruz. She left there on Oct 19, & has been in commission since Jul 22, 1858. List of her ofcrs: Flag Ofcr Jos R Jarvis, late commanding Home Squadron; John L Worden, 1st Lt; Joel S Kennard, 2nd; Robt M McArann, 3rd; John Irwin, 4th; Thos P Pelot, 5th; Lewis W Minor, fleet surgeon; Benj J Cahoone, paymaster; Le Roy Fitch, master; Wm E Taylor, assist surgeon; Andrew J Hayes, marine ofcr; Wm C Zantzinger, flag secretary; Chas A Bragdon, boatswain; Chas Moran, gunner; Chas Bordman, carpenter; Lewis Rogers, sailmaker; Jas W Ritchie, paymaster's clerk.

Chancery sale of valuable property, by decree of the Circuit Court of D C, in chancery, dated Oct 24, 1860, passed in a certain cause there depending between Labom B Dixon, cmplnt, & John H Reiss & others dfndnts, No 1,618 chancery: public auction on Dec 2, of the following property in Wash City, D C, being 12 feet on I st of lot 14, in square 374, with improvements thereon.
–Edw C Carrington, trustee -A Green, aucts

Wm D Totty, convicted of the murder of his wife's sister because she would not run off with him, was hung at Richmond on Friday last. He was conveyed from the jail to the gallows in an open wagon, accompanied by his spiritual adviser, & upon reaching the gallows, after the religious services as usual on such an occasion, the trap was sprung & the hapless victim of retributive justice was launched into eternity. A large crowd of men, women, & children surrounded the scaffold.

The remains of Mr Carland & 2 female servants have been taken from the ruins of the Clarendon Hotel. Search for others has been discontinued as no one else is missing.

A prominent real estate broker of St Paul, Minn, named Gray, committed suicide on Sat. He was being pursued by an ofcr, regarding forged bonds, when Mr Gray jumped from a bridge into the river 100 feet below. His body has not been found. He was a native of Cape Cod, Mass.

Circuit Court of Wash Co, D C-in Equity, No 1,227. John R Woods et al vs Richd G Briscoe's heirs, Jos S Clarke et al. The trustee reported to the Court the sales made by him in the said cause: F Volk purchaser of five undivided sixth parts of lot 1 & 2 in square 356, for $369.90; John Pettibone of lot 5 in square 263, for $111.24; Wm R Riley, of part of lot 2 in square 414, for $192.86; Richd Barry, lot 15 in square 494, for $1,356.25; & Wm B Todd of the west half of lot 2 in square 633, for $1,200; & that said F Volk, Wm R Riley, Richd Barry, & Wm B Todd, & Geo E Kirk, to whom said John Pettibone assigned his said purchase, have each complied with the terms of sale. –John A Smith, clerk

Improvements within our city are the 2 new dwlgs erected the past summer in H st, between 14th & 15th sts, by our esteemed fellow-citizen, Mr Job W Angus. These houses are owned, one by Dr Johnston, of Wash City, & the other by Mr Geo D Fowle, of Alexandria. The exterior walls are of Quincey brown stone, backed by heavy & substantial brick work; each house contains 24 apartments, on the ground floor 2 kitchens & breakfast room; on the first floor double parlor & library; & the stories above contain some 18 chambers. The cost of each house & out-bldgs is $25,000. Those who assisted in their construction: stone-mason, M G Emery; brick-layer, Thos Lewis; plasterers, Messrs Allen & Jackson; painters, Messrs Parker & Spalding; iron work, Messrs F & A Snyder; carving, Messrs Hamilton & Hatton; tile-layer, Mr French; plumbers, J W Thompson & Bros.

Mrd: on Nov 13, in Wash City, by Rev J Spencer Kennard, Mr Sylvanus Meeks to Miss Sarah Hight, both of Nelson Co, Va.

Mrd: on Nov 17, in Wash City, by Rev J Spencer Kennard, Mr Robt J Mays to Miss Martha V Hagan, both of Richmond, Va.

Died: on Nov 18, Sarah, wife of Dr T C McIntire, & daughter of Col J S Williams. Her funeral will be at the Church of the Ascension, on Nov 20 at 12 o'clock M.

Died: on Nov 14, at *Spring Hill*, near Richmond, Va, very suddenly, Benj G Whitall, in his 56th year.

Died: on board the steamer **Planet**, near Vicksburg, Miss, on Oct 20, H H Rhodes, of Va, aged 58 years.

Columbia, Nov 17. Congressman Bonham resigned his seat in the House of Reps.

TUE NOV 20, 1860
Meeting of the friends of the Union was held at Lexington, Ky, on Nov 12, at which Thos H Clay, a son of Henry Clay, presided. The meeting was addressed by Gen Leslie Combs. Resolved, by the people of Fayette Co, that Ky, occupying a central position in the Confederacy, is shut out from intercourse with the world except through the surrounding States. She is dependant upon the Union for the right of exportation & importation, for the right of ingress & egress; & being exposed for 700 miles to a free State border, she is dependent upon the Union for security in the possession of her slaves & for the protection of her people from civil war. Resolved, that the elecion of Abraham Lincoln to the Presidency of the U S, as much as we shall deplore the event, affords no cause for a dissolution of the Union. Resolved, That, as far as depends upon us, we will stand by, support, & uphold the Union against all attacks from without or within, & against ultraism, whether at the North or South.

Buffalo Republic: on the morning of election at the Ninth Ward polls, Ex-Pres Fillmore, in a dignified manner, deposited his vote against sectionalism, & for the Union Electoral & State ticket.

Mr McLane, our Minister to Mexico, has resigned that post, & Ex-Govn'r Weller, of Calif, has been appointed to succeed him. -Ion

Trustee's sale of furniture & effects of the Lafayette House, on Nov 26, by 2 deeds of trust, recorded among the land records for Wash Co, the entire effects, located on F st, between 14th & 15th sts. –Chas T Griffith, trustee -Jas C McGuire & Co, aucts

Prof Chas E Dailey, of Alexandria, Va, proposes to open a Singing School for the cultivation of Sacred Music, on Nov 24, in the Lecture-Room of the N Y ave Presbyterian Church, [Dr Gurley's.] The School is under the patronage of the Church.

Com'r Barnes' Ofc, Lunenburg, Nov 15, 1860. To Henry T Roach & Linda E Roach, children of Joshua Roach, deceased. In a suit pending in the Circuit Court of Lunenburg Co, Va, between Winn, etc, against Roach, etc, a decree was rendered on Oct 12, 1860: That Com'r Barnes publish in the Nat'l Intelligencer once a week for 2 months a notice to inform Henry T Roach & Lucinda E Roach, children of Joshua Roach, deceased, who removed from Campbell Co, in this State, more than 30 years ago, that unless they or their descendants appear & claim their interest in this cause, on or before the first day of the next term of this court, then the court will then distribute their interest among their next of kin, as if they had died intestate & without issue. -E H Barnes, Com'r

Mrd: on Nov 1, at Burleigh, Hinds Co, Miss, the residence of the bride's father, by Rev Bennett Smedes, Miss Susan Dabney to Mr Lyell Smedes, of Vicksburg.

Died: on Nov 19, Jos V Willett, eldest son of Voltaire & Rachel M Willett, in his 22nd year. His funeral will take place from his father's residence, 74 Indiana ave, this afternoon, at 3 o'clock.

Died: on Nov 14, at Elkton, Ky, after a few days' illness, Wm Croghan Jesup, in his 27th year, eldest son of the late Maj Gen Jesup, U S A.

WED NOV 21, 1860
J F Suit, formerly a member of the State Senate of Indiana, committed suicide on Nov 13, by shooting himself through the head with a pistol.

Very valuable property north of Wash, on the 14th st or Piney Branch road, at public auction, on Dec 5, the *Holmead estate*, recorded as lot 3, containing 23 acres 4 perches. The owner resides in N C, & gives peremptory orders to sell. -Wall & Barnard, aucts

The curious in antiquities will be glad to learn that the sword of Tiberius is for sale at Mayence, among the collection of Jos Gold, recently deceased. It was discovered in that town, [the Moguntium of the Romans] some years since, while excavating for a new fortification. It has occupied the learned classical writers of Germany much, & they have written as many pamphlets about it as did our antiquaries about Bill Stumps's mark. -Foreign News

Orphans Court of Wash Co, D C. Letters of administration on the personal estate of Geo Johnson, late of Wash Co, deceased. -Geo W Johnson, adm

Lt Jeffers, U S Navy, & party had arrived at Aspinwall at latest dates, having just completed the hydrographic survey of the Gulf of Dulce. Lt Morton, U S Army, concerning whose safety some apprehension was felt, had found his way to Gulf Dulce, & had left there to join the Brooklyn at Boca del Toro. He had met with some hardships & was 10 days in getting from David to Gulf Dulce.

Fatal affair at Coffeeville, Miss, on Thu last, between Henry A Riddick & Adrian Snider, both prominent lawyers. The origin of the difficulty was in some remarks made by Snider in relation to a trial progressing in court. Riddick was shot in the left breast, killing him almost instantly. A brother of Riddick, Wm, seized his brother's pistol & fired at Snider, the ball passed on & entered the brain, from which he died in 3 hours afterwards.

Orphans Court of Wash Co, D C. Letters of administration on the personal estate of S Ridout Addison, late of Wash Co, deceased. -Julia H Addison, admx

Mrd: on Nov 20, at St Paul's Lutheran Church, by Rev J G Butler, Mr John H Seiffert to Miss Sarah I Patch, both of Wash City.

Died: on Nov 13, in Wash City, after a short illness, Charlie, son of Edw & Jane S Clark, in his 3rd year.

THU NOV 22, 1860
From the home of Mr Lincoln on Tue: Please excuse me on this occasion from making a speech. I thank you for the kindness & compliment of this call. I thank you, in common with all others who have thought fit by their votes to endorse the Republican cause. [Applause.] I rejoice with you in the success which has so far attended that cause. [Applause.] Yet, in all our rejoicings, let us neither express nor cherish any harsh feelings towards any citizen who, by his vote, has differed with us. [Loud cheering.] Let us at all times remember that all American citizens are brothers of a common country, & should dwell together in the bonds of fraternal feeling. [Immense applause.] Let me again beg you to accept my thanks, & to excuse me from further speaking at this time. Mr Lincoln withdrew at the close of this address amid the enthusiastic cheers of the assemblage.

Hon R W Barnwell, of S C, in a published letter, avows his wish to form a Southern Confederacy, but takes occasion to say that any policy based upon the expectation that S C, by her separate action, could force other States to join in the efforts to establish this Confederacy, would be in the highest degree mischieveus.

Superior Rosewood piano forte, household & kitchen furniture at auction on Nov 28, at the residence of K F Page, 445 C st, between 1st & 2nd sts west.
-Jas C McGuire & Co, aucts

Circuit Court of D C-in Equity, No 1,527. The Corp of Gtwn against Eliz Jewell, Thos Jewell, & others, execs, devisees, & heirs of Wm Jewell. The parties above, the trustees, & the creditors of said Wm Jewell, to attend at my room, City Hall, Wash, on Dec 11, & the distribution of the fund will be stated. –W Redin, auditor

Circuit Court of D C-in Equity, No 1,564. Murray & Semmes against Mary Ann Green & Matthew E Green, widow, admx, & heir of Owen Green. Statement of the personal estate of said Owen Green, at my room, City Hall, Wash, on Dec 14. -W Redin, auditor

Died: on Nov 18, Amanda M, only daughter of Wm & Mary A Dougherty. Her funeral will be from the residence of her father, 404 12th st, today at 2 o'clock.

FRI NOV 23, 1860
Thos Armstrong, duelist, has been convicted in Alabama of sending a challege to fight a duel. The penalty is 2 years in the penitentiary. A new trial has been granted.

Ernest Meyer, convicted in PG Co, Va, of the murder of Richd Washington, has been sentenced to 18 years in the penitentiary.

Mr Francis Bellringer, Brighton, had an unfortunate habit of sucking the pen with which he had been writing, & this, it is almost certain, was the cause of his life being so suddenly & unexpectedly brought to a close. On Oct 18, symptons of erysipelas manifested themselves. He died on Friday, his fatal malady induced by the poisonous ink. –English Journal

Circuit Court of Wash Co, D C-in Equity, No 1,527. The Mayor, Recorder, etc, of Gtwn, against Wm Jewell's devisees. The trustees reported that they have sold to Thos Jewell part of lot 12 in square 117, in Wash, for $291, & to Jas Wallace part of lot 2 of the slip, & lot 28 in Beatty & Hawkins' addition to Gtwn for $660, & the parties have complied with the terms of sale. –John A Smith, clerk

Mrd: on Nov 22, in St Alban's parish, D C, by Rev W L Childs, Thos Styles to Annie Virginia Yeabower.

Mrd: on Nov 7, at Harrisburg, Pa, by Rev J Robinson, Wm Dock, jr, to Miss Mary Rosalie, daughter of Isaac G McKinley.

Died: on Nov 21, Mr Chester Walbridge, after a protracted & suffering illness, in his 70th year. His funeral will be from his late residence at *Ingleside*, on Nov 23 at 2 o'clock P M.

SAT NOV 24, 1860
Choice assortment of fruits, preserves, pickles, candies, moulds, glass cases, & preserved meats, at public auction, on Nov 27, at the Confectionary establishment of Mr T Potentini, Pa ave, between 9th & 19th sts. -Jas C McGuire & Co, aucts

Burning of the steamer **Pacific**, at Uniontown, Ky, last Sunday. The victims were mostly boat hands & deck passengers. Capt Wm Lamb, the cmder of the steamer, lost his life. He leaves a wife & 4 children in Louisville. Mr J R Sharp saved a lady in the water. Mrs McDonald, who in company with her consumptive husband, was on the way to Cuba, clung to her feeble partner, &, aided by R H Craft, dragged him to the guards, & persisted in staying beside him until he breathed his last, when she slid down the staunchion & was received into the yawl, manifesting that pure devotion which is ever elicited from her sex in hours of trouble. There were about 150 to 180 passengers on the boat, 100 being cabin passengers.

Galt's statue of Washington: a letter from Paris states that this work of art, for the Univ of Va, was Sep 24th boxed up & put on board of ship for the U S.

Mrd: on Nov 15, at McKendree Chapel Parsonage, by Rev Wm Hamilton, Wm H Pope to Miss Eliz S Pugh, all of Wash City.

Mrd: on Nov 15, at the Church of the Ascension, by Rev Dr Pinkney, T A Jones, of Wash, N H, to Emelie M, daughter of Jas S Magee, of Wash City.

Obit-died: on Nov 22, in Wash City, Chester Walbridge, aged 70 years. For the last 15 years he was a clerk in the Genr'l Land Ofc. His first start in life was in mercantile pursuits in Vt, his native State, & then in N Y & Ohio. His high qualities were perhaps inherited from his distinguished sire, who, during our Revolutionary struggle, led the American forces at the battle of Bennington. Mr Walbridge was a devoutly pious ornament of the Presbyterian Church.

The corner-stone of the Grace Church, in Montg Co, Md, 7 miles from Wash, on the Brookville Turnpike Road, will be laid on Nov 26, at 11 o'clock A M. Rt Rev R Whittingham, Bishop of Md, will officiate.

MON NOV 26, 1860

Martin V Brantly, convicted of opening letters in the U S mail, at Savannah, Ga, has been sentenced to 10 years' imprisonment.

The tallest man in Ky, as far as the Hopkinville Press knows, is Mr John M Baker, of Burnsville, Caldwell Co, who stands 7 feet 8 inches in his boots, weighs 240 pounds, & is 23 years old. He was born & raised in Caldwell Co, & has never been 100 miles from home.

Randall Clark was fined at the late term of the circuit court of Lowndes Co, Ala, $1,000 for not feeding his slaves well.

Mrd: on Nov 22, by Rev Dr C M Butler, Chas E Gregory, of Jersey City, to Miss Alice W, daughter of the late John W Maury.

Mrd: on Nov 15, by Rev C Walker, at Selma, the residence of Hon Jas M Mason, Randolph Harrison, of Amphill, Cumberland Co, Va, to Harriet B, eldest daughter of the late Col J F Heileman, U S Army

Died: yesterday, in Wash City, Miss Mary Clay, aged about 70 years. Her funeral is today at 1 o'clock P M, from her late residence, on 4th st, near I.

Died: on Nov 16, at his residence in Louisville, Ky, of an affection of the heart, Marshall Key. The deceased was born in Fauquier Co, Va, Sep 8, 1783, & removed with his father to Mason Co, Ky, in 1795, where he continued to reside until 1857, when he removed to Louisville. The infirmities of age touched him lightly, & he died after an illness of a few hours, in full possession of his mental faculties.

TUE NOV 27, 1860

Mrd: on Nov 22, at Darkesville, Berkeley Co, Va, by Rev Mr Proctor, Thos G Foster, of Wash, to Miss Mary C Henderson, of the former place.

The steamship **Nashville**, Capt Murray, of N Y, & Charleston Steamship line, arrived at this port at 1 o'clock on Sat morning from Charleston, & brought back 47 steerage passengers, who were not permitted to land, but were sent back by order of the Mayor of Charleston. The steamship **James Adger**, of the same line, arrived from Charleston on Monday evening last, & brought back 32 steerage passengers who were sent back by the same authority. These passengers were mostly mechanics & laborers. They all came back passage free. The public works in Charleston having been suspended business of all kinds is said to be utterly prostrated there, & it is impossible for laborers to fine employment.
–N Y papers

The Govn'r has appointed Hon Brice J Goldsborough, of Dorchester Co, to the seat on the Bench of the Court of Appeals made by the death of Judge Eccleston.
-Balt American

Some 2 weeks ago, Henry O Remington, of New Bedford, accidentally drove a splinter under his thumbnail. A few days after he was attacked with lockjaw, & after suffering intense pain, died on Wed. He was an energetic man, of Indian descent, 40 years of age.

Jas McColloch, a prominent citizen of Petersburg, Va, was married on Thu in that city at 4 o'clock. The couple came over to Richmond the same evening to spend the honeymoon, & he was taken sick suddenly at the Spottswood House, & died at 11½ o'clock the same night. The papers that announce his marriage, now announce his death also.

Died: on Nov 26, in Wash City, after a lingering illness, in his 36th year, Dr Thos J Cathcart. His funeral will take place from the residence of his father-in-law, John D Barclay, on Nov 28, at 10 o'clock A M.

Died: on Nov 26, at the residence of her son-in-law, Robt H Marcellus, Mrs Mary Glover, relict of the late Richd Glover, aged 65 years. His funeral will be from 458 I st, this afternoon at 3 o'clock.

WED NOV 28, 1860
Boots & Shoes, 408 Pa ave, between 4½ & 6th sts. –H Burns [Ad]

Rich Point Farm for sale. As trustee in a deed of trust from Thos B J Frye, Annie C Frye, his wife & others, dated Jun 23, 1859, of the record in the Clerk's Ofc of Alexandria Co Court, in Liber U, No 3, folio 27, & at the instance & request of the said Annie C Frye, I will offer for sale, on Dec 28 next, the ***Rich Point Farm***, near the Little Falls. This tract will be sold in lots, viz: 30 acres, on which is a comfortable dwlg-house. –Benj A Berry, trustee

THU NOV 29, 1860
The grand-daughter of Flora Macdonald, an aged maiden lady, Miss Mary Macleod, died on Oct 29, at the village of Stein, Warnish, at Skye. She was the daughter of the late Maj Alex'r Macleod, by Ann, eldest daughter of Mrs Macdonald, of Kingsburg, better known by her maiden name of Flora Macdonald, a name celebrated in history. Maj Macleod served for some time in America, at the period of the Revolution, as an ofcr in the royalist corps; & his wife showed something of the maternal spirit in conveying intelligence to her friends during that period of trouble & danger, having on one occasion narrowly escaped while carrying a message sewed up in a button on her dress. After the hostilities had ceased Maj Macleod & his family returned to the Island Skye. They both died there, & their only daughter, Miss Macleod, continued to reside in the house at Stein till her death. She had been long in infirm health, & had nearly reached the age of 90. –London Times

The wife of Capt Wm Titus, & her sister, Mrs Durat, residing at Centreport, L I, were burnt to death a few days since. A little child of Mrs Titus had a fluid lamp in her hand, which she was directed to put upon the table. Instead of doing so she threw the lamp into her mother's lap, where it exploded. Mrs Titus, in her fright, threw the lamp from her at random, & it fell on the lap of her sister. The clothing of both women was saturatded with the inflammable fluid & set on fire; before the flames could be extinguished they were so badly burnt that they died the next day.

Orphans Court of Wash Co, D C. Letters testamentary on the personal estate of Mary A S Tate, late of Wash Co, deceased. –S C Mills, exc

In a letter from Ex-Govn'r Hammond, dated at Redcliffe on Nov 21, he says: "South Carolina will certainly secede from the Union on the 17th or 18th of Dec next."

Mrd: on Nov 27, in Annapolis, by Rev Dr Clemm, Thos J Wier, of Balt, to Miss Jane E L Bush, of Annapolis.

Died: on Nov 28, Pringle Slight, in his 70th year. His funeral is on Nov 29, from his late residence on Half st, between Va ave & G st, Island. [No time given.]

Died: on Nov 18, in PG Co, Md, near Piscataway, Ella Virginia, only daughter of Geo W & Laura V Blandford, aged 11 months.

SAT DEC 1, 1860
Household & kitchen furniture at auction on Dec 19, by deed of trust from Robt Cochran, jr, dated Mar 15, 1854, recorded in Liber J A S No 78, folios No 347 etc: public auction at the residence of the said Cochran, on B st south, between 13th & 13½ sts west, all the effects. –Andrew Wylie, trustee -A Green, aucts

Obit-died: on the 25th ult, at his residence in Bridgewater, Maws, Hon John Reed, at the ripe aged of 79 yeaars. He graduated with distinction at Brown Univ in 1803; studied law & settle in Yarmouth, Mass, where he soon attained a lucrative practice; in 1819 was elected a Rep to Congress from the district of Barnstable; in 1821 was again elected from the same district, & continued by successive re-elections until 1833; in 1844 was elected Lt-Govn'r of Mass, an ofc which he held for 7 years.

Railroad accident on Thu on the Beaver Meadow railroad, about 6 miles from Mauch Chunk, Pa, when a rail broke, the passenger car was tossed sideways into the Lehigh river, down an embankment over 15 feet high. Killed or drowned: Robt Nichols, conductor; Mrs Farrow & sister, of Beaver Meadow; Miss Smith & sister, of Mauch Chunk.

Mrd: on Nov 29, at Wesley Chapel Parsonage, by Rev Mr McCauley, Chas E Tretler to Miss Sallie V Robinson, all of Wash City.

Mrd: on Nov 27, in Wash City, by Rev Dr Gurley, Miss Maria H Wilson to Col B F Larned, U S Army.

Mrd: on Nov 29, in Gtwn, at the Church of the Most Holy Trinity, by Rev Jos Aschwanden, S J, M Williams B Peters, of Scottsburg, Oregon, to Margaret A, daughter of Mr John Major, of N Y.

Died: on Nov 29, in Wash City, suddenly, Mr Hall Neilson, formerly an eminent merchant of Richmond, Va. His funeral will take place today at 1 o'clock P M, from the residence of Dr W B H Brown, 354 N Y ave, near the corner of 10th st west.

Died: last evening, in Wash City, Miss Sophia W Smith, in her 78th year, after a very short illness. Her funeral will be from the residence of her brother, Richd Smith, on H st, between 14th & 15th sts, tomorrow at 3 o'clock P M.

MON DEC 3, 1860
Mrs Henry Miller, residing near Middleburg, Pa, a few days ago took by mistake a large dose of tincture of colchicum in place of bitters. Medical aid was procured, but it was in vain. She died in a few hours in great agony.

The Cincinnati papers record the death of Jackson Thorpe, one of the fleshiest men in the U S. He weighed at one time 410 pounds, & for 3 years past has not weighed less than 360 pounds.

During the services in the Presbyterian Church in Aisquith st, Balt, on Thu, Mrs Catharine Crawford, while in her seat in the church, singing at the time, suddenly sank back & expired. She was advanced in life, being some 50 years or more of age. Her death was due to disease of the heart. –Sun

For sale or rent, ***Morrisses' Landing***, the fishing shore formerly fished by Jas Irwin, one of the best herring fisheries on the Potomac. I have nearly all the outfit necessary, except seine & rope. –John D Freeman, Great Mill's, St Mary's Co, Md.

Died: on Friday last, in Wash City, Mrs Victoria, wife of Chas T Pope. Her funeral will be today at 11 o'clock, at 407 13th st, between G & H sts.

Died: on Nov 30, Adelaide, third daughter of the late Chas Scrivener. Her funeral will be this afternoon at 2:30 o'clock, P M, from the residence of her mother, on M st, between 6th & 7th sts.

TUE DEC 4, 1860
The venerable John Johnson, of Dayton, Ohio, being in Wash on business before Congress, called on us yesterday to pay his 60th year's subscription to the Nat'l Intelligencer. He may be found at the Clay Hotel.

Two painful accidents occurred to young gentlemen of the Ga Military Institute, now on a visit to Milledgeville, during an artillery exercise in the Capitol grounds, on Thu. The Cadets were firing rapid salutes with their brass field pieces, & Cadet D K Love, of Campbell Co, was engaged in loading one of them, when, from some defect in the rammer or gun, a premature discharge carried off his little finger, drove a portion of the wading entirely through his forearm between the bones & another part of the elbow. The wounds were very severe, & the young man seemed to suffer intensely. He was taken to the residence of Dr Hall. Some half hour later the Cadets returned to their exercise, & in firing the same gun an exactly similar explosion occurred, by which Cadet Henry G Osborn, of Richmond Co, had his forearm dreadfully laceration. He was taken to the residence of Mr Orme, his relative, & properly cared for. –Savannah Republican

A Gallant Ofce. The ofcr who so gallantly vindicated the flag of the Union from insults is Capt Chas Poor, of Wash City, whose excellent family are our next door neighbors. The Capt has, for many years, been in the naval service of his country, & as a gallant & accomplished ofcr he has no superior. With such men in command of our national vessels, we have no fear that our flag can be insulted with impunity by any foreign Powers. –States.
+
On hearing of the outrage on our flag by the revolutionary troops at Rio Hache, New Granada, the cmder of our squadron at the West Indies immediately dispatched the sloop-of-war **St Louis**, Capt Poor, with orders to demand redress. This vessel arrived at Rio Hache about Sep 1, & the cmder demanded that the flag of the Consulate should be hoisted by 2 ofcrs of the garrison, that the troops should then file under it, & afterwards salute it by 3 volleys. Although at first they endeavored to evade giving this satisfaction, they had at last to pass through the Candiac Forks by the peremptory terms in which the cmder exacted it.

Criminal Court-Wash-Monday. Grand Jury:

Wm Gunton	Wm G Freeman	Saml Lewis
Pierce Shoemaker	Thos Berry	Edw Hall
Geo A Bohrer	Jas Towles	Robt Beale
Geo S Gideon	Valentine Harbaugh	Enos Ray
Peter F Bacon	Wm J Stone, sr	Wm R Riley
Selby Scaggs	Fitzhugh Coyle	John L Kidwell
Jos N Fearson	J Brooke	Wm A Bradley
Judson Mitchell	E Lindsley	Jonah D Hoover

Petit Jury:

Thos R Brightwell	Henry G Davis	Judson C Addison
R K Nevitt	T B Entwistle	W A Wallace
D Lightfoot	John Ball	S R Sylvester
R McChesney	W H Perkins	Henry Warner
M R Coombs	Michl Nash	Edw Harbaugh
Anthony Addison	Edw Folsom	Reuben Washington
Theodore Sheckells	G W Strand	A H Paul
Henry Lyles	J R Miner	Edw Krouse
J B Holmead	Henry Thorn	F A Klopfer
Archibald White	Jas T Lloyd	Geo Taylor

F Stolp has established a Boston Brown Bread Bakery, at 281 D st, between 13 & 13½ sts, Wash.

Died: on Dec 3, George Sibley, son of Norman S & Willie I Bestor, aged 10 months. His funeral is today at 2 PM, from 482 12th st.

Obit-died: on Nov 29, 1860, suddenly, Hall Neilson, a very estimable gentleman & true Christian. He resided for a number of years in Richmond, Va, where he became a succesful merchant, & for the last 5 years has resided in Wash City. He was a devoted husband & father. His afflicted widow & children mourn his loss. -J

WED DEC 5, 1860
House of Reps: 1-Ptn of Juliana Watts & Juliana M Campbell, of Pa, only surviving heirs of Lt Col Henry Miller, of the Revolutionary army, asking that they may be placed on the same footing as was intended by the act in regard to ofcrs on service at the close of the war: referred. 2-Mr Florence asked leave to withdraw from the files of the House the ptn of Sarah K Jenks, widow of Jonathan Jenks, deceased, & the memorial of Louis G Thomas, Edw K Thomas, & Jos Shermer, guardian of the children of Saml W Thomas, deceased, legal reps of Hartshorne R Thomas, in relation to the brig **Jane**: to be referred to the Cmte of Claims.

Mrd: on Nov 22, at the Ebenezer M E Church, by Rev Dr W M D Ryan, Mr Chas F Walson, of N Y, to Miss Laura V Boteler, of Wash City.

Supreme Court of the U S, Mon, Dec 3, 1860. Present:
Hon Roger B Taney, Chief Justice
Associate Justices:
Hon John McLean
John Catron
Saml Nelson
Robt C Grier
John A Campbell
Nathan Clifford

The Putnam Phalanx has a two-fold character, military & social, their principal object being to keep alive the memory of the patriots of the Revolution. Their uniform is an exact imitation of that worn by Gen Washington during the Revolution. The organization is 3 years old, & has 240 active members, of whom the Cmder is Mr Horace Goodwin, aged 76 years, & standing 6 feet 6 inches high. All the members of this corps are direct descendants of Revolutionary partiots. It is stated that the Phalanx represents an amount of wealth exceeding eight millions of dollars. The ofcrs of the Phalanx are: Maj, Horace Goodwin. First Co: Capt Allyn S Stillman; 1st Lt, Timothy M Allyn; 2nd Lt, Jas B Shuttas; Ensign, Allyn Godwin. Second Co: Capt, Alex'r M Gordon; 1st Lt, Oliver D Seymour; 2nd Lt, Jas H Ashmead; Ensign, Wm J Denslow. Staff-Adj, Jos D Williams; Quartermaster, E B Strong; Paymaster, Jas B Crosby; Commissary, Henry C Deming; Assist Commissary, Alonzo W Birge; Judge Advocate, Isaac W Stuart; Chaplain, Rev Asher Moore; Surgeon, Dr Thos Miner; Sgt Maj, Wm Isham; Quartermaster Sgt, Oliver Ellsworth.

Criminal Court-Wash-Monday. 1-Thos J Johnston, Thos Jefferson Page, & Wm F Mattingly, were admitted to practice at the bar of this Court. 2-Lawrence Dent, colored, was convicted of stealing a watch & other property belonging to Mr Geo M Miller. He was found guilty & sentenced to 18 months in the penitentiary.

Mrd: on Nov 29, by Rev John McNally, Mich B Larkin, of Kilkenny, Ireland, to Mary Virginia Hilbus, daughter of Jacob Hilbus, of Wash City.

Died: on Dec 4, in Wash City, Danl W Hall, aged 75 years. His funeral is on Thu at 1 o'clock P M, from his late residence, 401 C st. On Friday morning his remains will be taken to Balt for interment.

THU DEC 6, 1860
On Sat, John Murray, a young married man, residing at Newark, N J, while cleaning a gun he had taken the stock, put the muzzle in his mouth, & holding the barrel so that the nipple was near a burning candle, tried to see if he could agitate the flame by blowing through it, thus testing whether it contained a load. By the unsteadiness of his hands, it is supposed the nipple came in contact with the flame & the barrel was discharged, blowing the poor fellow's head into a hundered fragments, &, rebounding with tremendous force, struck his mother-in-law, who sat directly opposite him, & penetrated her right breast just below the collar bone, a depth of 6 inches. The young wife found the dead body of her husband, & her mother lies in critical condition.

Stock & fixtures of a retail grocery at auction, on Dec 10, at the store of Messrs Ritter's at Wash st & Canal, Gtwn, all their stock & fixtures. Also, the house & lot occupied by the Messrs Ritter. -Barnard & Buckley, aucts, Gtwn, D C

Borromeo College, at Pikesville, near Balt, is now in operation under the superintendence of Rev E Q S Waldron, [Catholic Priest,] aided by Prof S S Haldeman, from Pa, & other teachers.

Criminal Court-Wash-Wed. 1-Several youths, John McCann, Patrick McCann, Chas Finley, Joshua Scribner, & Patrick Cassidy, were found guilty of an affray, in Gtwn, & each fined $5 & costs. 2-Wm Rawlings, charged with assault & battery, submitted his case, & was sentenced to pay a fine of $8. 3-On motion of W J Stone, jr, Mr Saml L Phillips was admitted to practice at the bar of this Court.

Died: on Dec 2, at *Fort Monroe*, Va, of typhoid fever, 1st Lt David Bell, of the 1st regt of U S Cavalry.

Died: on Dec 4, in Gtwn, Mary Farrell, aged 80 years. Her funeral will be from the residence of Saml McKenney, Dunbarton st, today at 12 o'clock M.

FRI DEC 7, 1860
Fire yesterday in the carpenter's shop of Mr Henry Parker, on G st, near 17th, & the shop itself was consumed, & fire caught to the adjoining brick house, one of a row, the property of Mr Francis Lutz, & tenanted by Mr Milton Garret. Mr Lutz lived in the next house to Mr Garrett, & suffered also to some extent in his own furniture, but not so as to necessitate moving. The fire is believed to have been an incendiary one. Mr Parker was not insured, & will lose everything. Mr Lutz was partially insured.

Died: on Dec 6, in Wash City, Col Michl Nourse, in his 83rd year. His funeral will be from his late residence, 461 13th st, Sat at 1 o'clock P M.

Died: on Dec 6, John Randolph Harbaugh, in his 52nd year. His funeral will be from his late residence, 6th st, between E & F sts, Sat at 3 o'clock P M.

Died: on Nov 28, at *Seclusaville*, Halifax Co, N C, the residence of his stepfather, Col Hunter, Charlie, in his 12th year, of the diptheria, only surviving child of the late Lemuel C Wheat, formerly of Wash City.

Managers of the Society for the Poor:
Mrs E B Mills	Mrs Capt Powell	Mrs Danl Ratcliffe
Mrs Stephen P Hill	Mrs Harkness	Mrs Rev Mason
Mrs M A Cox	Mrs John Houston	Noble
Mrs Rev Wm McLain	Mrs Dr Noble Young	Mrs Rev Meador
Mrs Maria Gillis	Mrs Enoch Tucker	

The Methodist church bldg at **Long Old Field**, PG Co, Md, was destroyed by fire on Sunday last, from a stove pipe, & broke out during service. The bldg was entirely destroyed, nothing being saved. It was rebuilt but a few years since.

SAT DEC 8, 1860
Lt John M Brooke having arrived on Aug 13, 1859, at Kanagawa Bay, off Yokahama, in the island of Japan, was interrupted in the further prosecution of the survey of the route between San Francisco & China. On Aug 23 occurred a severe cyclone, which caused the ship **Fenimore Cooper** to drag her anchors & strike repeatedly, so that, to avoid the loss & save the lives of her crew, Lt Brooke was obliged to run her ashore. Every assistance was afforded by Cmdor Popoff, of the Russian squadron, to repair & refit her.

The late Hon Geo Washington Lay was the 4th son of John Lay, & was born at Catskill, Greene Co, N Y, on Dec 26, 1798; graduated at Hamilton College, N Y, in 1817, & came that year to Batavia, Genesee Co, & studied law in the ofc of Hon Phineas L Tracy; entered into partnership with Mr Tracy, & engaged in a large & lucrative practive. In 1832 he succeeded Mr Tracy to the House of Reps of the 23rd & 24th Congress, from 1832 to 1836. In 1840 he represented Genesee Co in the Assembly of N Y; in 1842 was appointed Charge d'Affaires to the Court of Sweden & Norway, of which Marshal Bernadotte was King, being the only monarch created by the influence of Napoleon who retained his crown upon his head. In 1848 Mr Lay was stricken with paralysis, which nearly prostrated his locomotive powers, without impairing his brilliant mind or tenacious memory. He died on Oct 21, 1860, in the communion of the Protestant Episcopal Church, leaving in his immediate family a widow & 3 sons to honor his memory. -T

Notice is given that 2 pieces of Revolutionary Bounty Land Scrip, No 10,961 for 80 acres, & No 10,962 for 10,110,147 acres, issued to Wm Blackwell, one of the heirs of Jos Blackwell, deceased, a Brig Quartermaster in the Continental line, & duly assigned to the undersigned by the heirs of the late Wm Blackwell, whose names are, Jas G Blackwell, Wm Blackwell, Harriet E Blackwell, Lucy H Payne, & Sarah H Keith, were lost ot stolen in their transmission per mail to Sweeny, Rittenhouse, Fant, & Co, in Wash City; & that application will be made to the Com'r of the Gen Land Ofc, at Wash City, for the issuance of duplicates of said pieces of scrip. –A J Parr, Assignee of Wm Blackwell's heirs.

Died: on Dec 7, Andrew Schiebler, in his 58th year, formerly of Balt, Md, but for the last 10 years a resident of Wash City. His funeral will be on Sunday next, at 2 o'clock, from his late residence, 273 D st, between 13th & 13½ sts.

Died: on Sep 20 last, on board the U S storeship **Relief**, at sea, Lt Miles King Warrington, U S Navy, in his 36th year.

The Board of Ofcrs of the Wash City Bible Society are requested to attend the funeral of Col M Nourse, for more than 30 years Treasurer of the Society, from his late residence, 461 13th st, this afternoon, at 1 o'clock.

Criminal Court-Wash-Thu. 1-John Urle was convicted of stealing a gold eagle coin from John F Collins: sentenced to 1 year in the penitentiary. 2-Jos Robbins, alias Dolly Dobbins, was found guilty of stealing a quantity of lead from Mr H L Offut, of Gtwn: sentenced to 18 months in the penitentiary. 3-Chas C Newman, a professional burglar, found guilty of stealing clothing & jewelry from Lewis Kurtz: sentenced to 3 years in the penitentiary. Chas C Newman was again put to trial for stealing jewelry & money from Mary Platz; verdict guilty; sentenced to 3 years in the penitentiary, to commence after the expiration of the other sentence. 4-Peter West Scott was found guilty of assault & battery on Bertrand Hays: jury recommended him to the mercy of the Court. 5-Geo Sayles, a U S Marine, was found guilty of a very violent & unprovoked assault & battery on Mr Richd Hanson, on Capitol Hill. The same dfndnt was also convicted of a very aggravated case of assault & battery on Mr Jas T Ball, on the same evening.

MON DEC 10, 1860
According to the report of the Com'r of Pensions but 87 soldiers of the Revolution yet survive, out of 165 who on Jun 30, 1859, were on the pension rolls. Pensions are allowed to 66 widows of Revolutionary soldiers, making the number now on the rolls, 3,204.

At Ridge, N H, on Thanksgiving Day, two sons of Mr A A Bradford, aged 11 & 14 years, with permission from their parents to skate round the edge of the pond, were both drowned. The eldest ventured out too far, & broke through the ice, & his little brother tried to rescue him.

At Troy, recently, two sons of Stephen B Farrar, 10 & 12 years of age, drowned when they broke through the ice while skating

The case of the will of Mrs Mary Ann Jones, of Dinwiddie Co, Va, in which $30,000 worth of slaves were set free, was decided in the circuit court at Petersburg on Tue, in favor of the slaves, who will now have to leave for the North.

Criminal Court-Wash-Sat. 1-Levi Barrett, colored, convicted of stealing about $10 from Jas F Gordon: sentenced to 12 months in the penitentiary. 2-John Pesps, alias Rentzell, convicted of stealing a silver coin, in value $6.40, from S A Schloss: sentenced to 15 months in the penitentiary. 3-Chas Vancey convicted of stealing 2 hams from Benj I Baden: sentenced to 6 months in jail. 4-Robt McCluskey was found guilty of stealing cigars, valued at $3, from Henry Lehne: motion for a new trial entered. 5-Geo Sales, convicted on Friday in 2 cases of assault & battery, sentenced to 2 months in jail in each case.

Dedication of the Four-and-a half st Presbyterian Church took place yesterday, sermon preached by Rev Dr Gardiner Spring, of N Y. Drs McLain & Sunderland assisted in the ceremony of dedication.

Circuit Court of Wash Co, D C-in Equity, No 1,517. Edwin Wheeler & John A Baldwin et al vs Eliz M Garner & Thos M Garner, heirs of McConchie. The trustee reported he sold lot 19 in square 117 to B H Clements, for $214.75; lot 20 in square 117, to Wm Walker, for $810; lots 21 & 22 in square 117 to Uzziel Nalley, for $626.66; & purchasers have complied with the terms of sale.
–Walter S Cox, Edwin C Morgan, trustees

The service at the Capitol yesterday by Rev Dr Thos H Stockton was attended by great numbers of persons of both sexes, filling the seats on the floor & all the galleries.

Mrd: on Nov 29, in St John's Church, St Louis, Mo, by Rev John Coleman, D D, [rector] A Dupont Davis, of Wash City, to Miss Mattie G McCook, daughter of Danl McCook, of Illinois.

Died: on Dec 9, of consumption, Mrs Jane Ellis, in her 39th year. Her funeral will take place from the residence of her husband, Jonas B Ellis, 117 B st [Island,] on Tue afternoon, at 2 o'clock.

Died: on Dec 5, in Piscataway, PG Co, Md, Robert Ignatius, 2nd son of Dr John I & Eliza F Dyer, aged 22 months & 20 days.

TUE DEC 11, 1860
Senate: 1-Memorial from Thaddeus Hyatt, asking the enactment of a law for the relief of the destitute & suffering citizens in the Territory of Kansas.

Hon Howell Cobb yesterday resigned the ofc of Sec of Treasury.

A man named Kanary, with his 2 sons, one about 4 & the other about 6 years of age, were drowned a few days ago at Milwaukee, Wisc, while attempting to cross the river upon the ice.

Hon Wm A Palmer died a few days since at Danville, Vt, at an advanced age. From 1818 to 1825 he was a U S Senator. In 1831 he was elected Govn'r of Vt, & continued to occupy the Executive chair until 1845.

Maj Gen Duncan McDonald died on Nov 25, at Edenton, N C, of which town he was the oldest citizen. He had command of the N C forces at *Fort Norfolk*, in Va, during the late war with England, & acquitted himself with commendable zeal & ability. He had filled the station of Maj Gen of the 1st division of N C militia during the last 40 years.

The Pittsburgh papers announce the death of the venerable Dr Francis Herron, for many years the pastor of the First Presbyterian Church of that city. He was among the earliest ministers of the Gospel west of the mountains, & at his death was the oldest. He was born in Shippenburg, Cumberland Co, Pa, Jun 28, 1774, & graduated at Dickinson College in 1794.

N Y, Dec 10. 1-A young man, giving the name of Alfred Buchanan, has been arrest for the murder of Mrs Shanks. He has confessed the act. 2-Fred'k, the first mate of the slaver **Cora**, has escaped.

Criminal Court-Wash. 1-Thos Curry was put to trial for assaulting Mary Curry, his wife; but a nolle prosequi was entered, as the principal witness appeared unwilling or unable to testify. 2-Geo Davis was convicted of stealing clothing: sentenced to 1 year in the penitentiary. 3-Henry Taylor, colored, was found guilty of grand larceny in stealing a gold watch & chain valued at $125 of Mr Jesse B Haw: sentenced to 18 months in the penitentiary.

Died: on Dec 10, at Harrisburg, Pa, Isaac G McKinley, formerly of Wash City.

Died: on Nov 17, at Geneva, Switzerland, where she has resided for the last 5 years, after a long & painful illness, Emilie Laurencine, wife of Aaron Vail, aged 43 years.

Milledgeville, Ga, Dec 9. Govn'r Brown is out in a long letter favoring immediate secession.

N Y, Dec 9. 1-Cmder Page & the ofcrs of the La Plata Exploring Expedition arrived here today. 2-<u>Buenos Ayres</u> has been annexed to the Argentine Confederation.
3-The U S brig **Dolphin** sailed from Buenos Ayres Oct 21st for N Y.

WED DEC 12, 1860
A man named Connelly, one of the oldest & most relable members of the St Louis police, was attacked with heart disease while in the Recorder's court-room, in that city, on Wed last, & expired almost immediately.

Senator Bright, of Indiana, is confined to his house & bed by a severe attack of inflammatory rheumatism, & is unable to discharge his duties in the Senate.
-Constitution

Auction sale of horses, mules, wagons, farming utensils; the undersigned having sold his Farm near Bladensburg depot: public auction on Dec 17 next.
--H C Matthews -Thos Dowling, auct

Died: on Dec 10, in Wash City, Mrs Matilda H Beard, relict of the late Capt Wm C Beard, U S Army, in her 67th year. Her funeral is this afternoon at half-past 2 o'clock, from her late residence, 400 9th st.

Senate: 1-Memorial from Lt Geo L Hartsuff, of the U S Navy, asking to be reimbursed for the loss of public property, while in his charge, by the wreck of the steamer **Lady Elgin**, on Lake Michigan: referred. 2-Ptn from John Duvalt, asking an increase in pension: referred. 3-Bill for the relief of Wm H Linn's estate: referred to the Cmte on the Judiciary.

THU DEC 13, 1860
Chas F Engleman, who for 43 years has furnished the principal calculations for the almanacs, died on Friday last at Reading, Pa, at age 79 years. Mr Engleman emigrated to this country in 1803; was an honorary member of the New England Society of Mathematics; & became an early settler of Berks Co, Pa.

On Dec 5, Mrs Buer died a short time after a lamp exploded, severely burning her. She was alone with her child in an upper room of the house.
–Rochester Express, Dec 6

Found trespassing on my premises, adjoining the farm of the late Jos Gales, on Dec 7, two white hogs. Owner is to come forward, prove property, pay charges, & take them away, or I shall dispose of them according to law. –John W Conner

Obit-died: on Dec 6, Col Michl Nourse; born at Charlestown, Va, on Sep 1, 1778; his parents emigrated from England in 1764, & both died at Annapolis, Md, in 1784, leaving him, at age 6, to be cared for by his elder brother, Jos Nourse, who, for the first 40 years of the Gov't, was Register of the Treasury. Col Nourse entered that ofc in 1796, & remained there until 1853, a period of 57 years, as a Clerk, Chief Clerk, & occasionally as Register. He was the last survivor of those who founded the F st Church, & aided in inducing the late Dr Laurie to preside over it. In 1814, when the war brought the enemy to Wash City, he was appointed a lt colonel, & perilled his life in its defence. He was connected by marriage with the celebrated astronomer, Rittenhouse, & in his old age was surrounded by numerous descendants, who are among our most esteemed citizens. After a well-spent life he was gathered to his fathers, in his 83rd year, enjoying to the last a confident hope in the Redeemer. The life of such a man lights the path of duty to the citizen & the way of the Christian to the gate of Heaven. –R H G

Orphans Court of Wash Co, D C. Letters of administration on the personal estate of Hall Neilson, late of Wash Co, deceased. –Mary A Neilson, admx

FRI DEC 14, 1860
Senate: 1-Cmte on the Judiciary: bill for the relief of Wm H Linn: passed.

The co-partnership in the practice of the law, conducted by the undersigned, was dissolved by mutual consent on Oct 12th last. All persons indebted are to call & settle with R H Clarke, who will hereafter conduct the business, at the same ofc, corner of 6th st & Louisiana ave. –Richd H Clarke, A Austin Smith

Orphans Court of Wash Co, D C. Letters of administration on the personal estate of Sylvanus E Benson, late of Wash Co, deceased. –Chas I Queen, adm

Died: on Dec 13, Mrs Eliza Hamilton, relict of the late Dr Chas B Hamilton, of Wash City. Her funeral will take place from her late residence on 2nd st east, Capitol Hill, at 1 o'clock P M on Dec 15th.

Died: Dec 11, in Wash City, Freddy E, son of Fred'k & Mary L Depro, in his 6th year.

SAT DEC 15, 1860
Jas Hurley, convicted of murder in the 2nd degree in killing police Ofcr Loughrey at Cambridge, Mass, & Bryant Moore, convicted of killing his wife, were both sentenced on Tuesday to imprisonment for life.

Indicted for obstructing the fugitive slave law. Rev Geo Gordon, Jas Hammond, Asbury Parker, Calvin Rowland, Jos T Baldwin, E D Asbury, & Jonathan, indicted by the grand jury of the U S Circuit Court of Northern Ohio, for obstructing the U S Marshal & his deputies, at Iberia, Monroe Co, on Sep 20th last, in their efforts to secure, by legal process, a fugitive slave. The same parties are also indicted for assaulting the owners of the negro & their assistants, with a view to prevent the reclamation of the slave under the fugitive slave law.

Mrd: on Dec 13, at Trinity Church, by Rev T Addison, of Balt, Clement L West to Sallie C, daughter of Anthony Addison.

Mrd: on Dec 13, at Grace Church, by Rev Mr Holmead, Thos C Weisiger, of N C, to Miss Sue B Suttle, daughter of T T O'Dell, of Wash City.

Mrd: on Dec 12, by Rev J Spencer Kennard, Mr John T Hicks to Miss Margaret F Bibb, daughter of Walter T Bibb, of Richmond, Va.

Died: on Dec 14, Jane Eliza Mary Shyne, daughter of the late Michl Shyne, aged 20 years. Her funeral is tomorrow, Sunday, at 2 o'clock, from her late residence, 341 F st north, between 9th & 10th sts.

Died: on Dec 14, in Wash City, at the residence of his father, [E L Childs,] Rev Wentworth L Childs, Rector of St Alban's Church, D C, aged 33 years. His funeral will take place from St John's Church on Dec 17, at 2 o'clock P M.

Criminal Court-Wash-Fri. 1-Henry Wilson, alias T M Marsh, not guilty of stealing 2 hams of Thos Williams, livery stable keeper in Wash City. 2-Jas Boyle was convicted of stealing 3 prayer books from St Matthew's Church: sentenced to 6 months in the county jail. 3-Geo Rawlings was found not guilty on a charge of stealing horseshoes from John Duval. 4-Michl Lenhady was tried in connexion with the foregoing prisoner for the same offence: found guilty & sentenced to 10 months in jail.

MON DEC 17, 1860

Boston, Nov 22, 1860. The Earl of Spencer has kindly sent to me precise copies of the two Memorial Stones of the English family of Geo Washington. They will give you an exact idea of these most interesting memorials in the Parish Church at Brington, near Althrop, in Northampshire. The largest is of Lawrence Washington, the father of John Washington, who emigrated to America. Here is the inscription:

HERE LIETH THE BODI OF LAVRENCE
WASHINGTON SONNE AND HEIRE OF
ROBERT WASHINGTON OF SOVLGRAVE
IN THE COUNTIE OF NORTHAMTON
ESQUIER WHO MARRIED MARGARET
THE ELDEST DAUGHTER OF WILLIAM
BUTLER OF TEES IN THE COUNTIE
OF SUSSEXE ESQUIER, WHO HAD ISSU
BY HER 8 SONNS AND 9 DAUGHTERS
WHICH LAVRENCE DECESSED THE 13
OF DECEMBER A. DNI 1616.

THOSE THAT BY CHANCE OR CHOICE
OF THIS LAST SIGHT
KNOW LIFE TO DEATH RESIGNES
AS DAYE TO NIGHT;
BUT AS THE SUNNS RETORNE
REVIVES THE DAY
SO CHRIST SHALL US
THOUGH TURNDE TO DUST & CLAY

Above the inscription, carved in stone, are the arms of the Washingtons, with an additional quartering of another family.

The other is of Eliz Washington, daughter of Lawrence Washington, & sister of the emigrant. This is a slab of the same sandstone. The inscription is on a small brass plate set into the stone, & is as follows:

HERE LIES INTERRED YE BODIES OF ELIZAB. WASHING-
TON WIDDOWE WHO CHANGED THIS LIFE FOR IMMOR-
TALITIE YE 19H OF MARCH 1622. AS ALSO YE BODY OF ROBERT
WASHINGTON GENT. HER LATE HUSBAND SE-
COND SONNE OF ROBERT WASHINGTON OF SOLGRAVE IN
YE COUNTY OF NORTH. ESQR. WHO DEPTED THIS LIFE

YE 10TH OF MARCH 1622. AFTER THEY LIVED LOVINGLY TOGETHER MANY YEARS IN THIS PARISH.
The slab which covers Lawrence Washington is in the chancel of the church, by the side of the monuments of the Spencer family. The other slab, covering Elizabeth, the sister of the emigrant, is in one of the aisles of the nave, where it is scrapped by the feet of all who pass. The Register of the Parish, which is still preserved, commences
in 1560. From this it appears that Wm Proctor was the rector from 1601 to 1627, covering the period of the last of the Washingtons there. Other entries:
1616: Mr Lawrence Washington was buried XVth day of December.
1620: Mr Philip Curtis & Mis Amy Washington were married August 8.
1622: Mr Robert Washington was buried March ye 11th.
____ Mrs Elizabeth Washington, widow, was buried March ye 20th.

Died: on Dec 15, Mr Chas L Coltman, in his 60th year. His funeral is on Monday next at 2 o'clock P M, from his late residence, 420 M st, between 13th & 14th sts.

The funeral of Rev W L Childs will take place this afternoon at 2 o'clock, St John's Church.

Springfield, Dec 15. Hon Edw Bates, of Missouri, had a long interview with Mr Lincoln today, & it is said he was formally tendered the Secretaryship of the Dept of the Interior. Mr Bates is strongly against secession. He says that secession is treason, & must be put down, & the authority of the Gov't maintained at all hazards.

TUE DEC 18, 1860
House of Reps: 1-Bill for the relief of Wm Riggs: referred to the Cmte on the Judiciary. 2-Bill for the benefit of G J Johnson.

For rent: spacious Mansion formerly occupied by the late Mr Silas H Hill, on E st, corner of 6th, with furniture; possession in March next, or sooner if desired. Apply to Jas F Wollard, 371 D st, between 7th & 8th sts.

Chancery sale of valuable property on the Island; by decree of the Circuit Court of D C, in Chancery, dated May 30, 1860, passed in cause therein depending between D W Moore & Co, cmplnts, & Geo E Kirk & others, dfndnts, No 1,563 Chancery: public auction on Jan 3, 1861, of lot 78 in square 465, & parts of lots 7 & 9 in square 437, in Wash City, with a good frame house & parts of vacant lots. -Edw C Carrington, trustee -A Green, aucts

Orphans Court of Wash Co, D C. Letters testamentary on the personal estate of Sophia W Smith, late of Wash Co, deceased. –Rd Smith, exc

Orphans Court of Wash Co, D C. Letters of administration on the personal estate of Danl W Hall, late of Wash Co, deceased. –Stewart Hastings, Sarah Ann Hall, excs

Senate: 1-Ptn from M C Mordecai & others, owners of the steamship **Isabel**, asking compensation for mail services between the cities of Charleston & Havana: referred. 2-Ptn from Mrs Jane Gantt, asking indemnity for losses sustained by her husband, Dr Jos Gantt, by the invasion of Florida by the troops of the U S: referred. 3-Bill for the relief of E P Hunt: referred. 4-Joint resolution to repeal the joint resolution approved Jun 15, 1860, for the relief of Wm H DeGroot: referred.

Orphans Court of Wash Co, D C, Dec 15, 1860. In the case of Asbury Lloyd, adm of Eliz Ford, deceased, the administrator & Court have appointed Jan 9th next, for the final settlement of the personal estate of the said deceased, of the assets in hand. -Ed Roach, Reg/o wills

Mrd: on Dec 13, in Wash City, by Rev Mr McCauley, Chas E Conrad to Miss Rebecca W Parker, daughter of M T Parker, all of Wash City.

Mrd: on Dec 6, by Rev D P Bestor, Mr John T Bestor, of Mobile, to Miss Tide Barnett, daughter of Col Nat Barnett, of Jasper Co, Miss.

Mrd: on Dec 13, in Boston, by Rev Dr Orville Dewey, Edw Clark, of Wash City, to Miss Eveline F Freeman, daughter of Watson Freeman, U S Marshal for Mass District.

Died: on Dec 16, Miss Thomason Wilkinson. Her funeral will take place from the residence of Mrs Ditty, 311 Pa ave, today at 2 o'clock.

Criminal Court-Wash-Mon: 1-Julia Newton, colored, was convicted of stealing a book & bedspread, the property of Mr Wm Ellis: sentenced to 6 months in jail. 2-Chas Cassidey was acquitted on a charge of assault on Michl Ash. 3-Abraham Johnston, colored, charged with stealing some pots of plants, was convicted: sentenced to 6 months in jail. 4-Anna Bogle was convicted of stealing 2 cloaks, a skirt, wrapper, bedspread, tablecloth, & China vases, in all worth about $56, from Mr Chas McNamee: sentenced to 1 year in the penitentiary. 5-Wesley Mahoney was found guilty of stealing chickens, a pot, basket, etc, from Emily Staples: sentenced to 6 months in jail. 6-Ellen Lewis was put on trial on a charge of stealing from John Burns a shawl & a pair of flat-irons.

WED DEC 19, 1860
The nomination of Hon Jeremiah S Black to the ofc of Sec of State, in the place of Gen Cass, resigned, was confirmed by the Senate on Monday.

Henry Walter Ovenden, British Consul for the State of Md, died at Balt on Monday, in his 31st year.

Mississippi Item: Josiah Winchester & Alex K Farrar, have been nominated in Adams Co, Miss, as delegates to the State Convention. Both are opposed to separate State secession & in favor of waithing Southern co-operation. The ultra secessionists have nominated Saml A Boyd & Geo A Marshall.

Senate: 1-Ptn from Lydia Lord, widow of a soldier of the war of 1812, asking a pension: referred. 2-Ptn from Geo Briggs & Cornelius Vanderbilt, asking that the amount recovered from them as sureties of David A Bokee may be refunded: referred. 3-Court of Claims: adverse opinions on the claims of Saml Norris, R R Ward & other, assignees of Jacob Barker, John P Baldwin, Richd Irwin, trustee of the Pres & Dirs & Co of the Mechanics' Bank of N Y, Jaques Charlant, Chas J Jenkins, & Wm McMann, assignees of John McKenne, Elias Brevort, Joab Houghton, Jas W Knaggs, adm with the will annexed of Whitmore Knaggs; Nathl P Causin, adm of John K Stone; & the claim of Richd S Coxe, adm of Ann Gibson: all of which were referred to the Cmte of Claims. 4-Court of Claims: reports in favor of Theodore Adams, of Lydia Cruger, excx of Moses Sheppard, Selmar Seibert, Jos San Roman, & Wm Armstrong, adm of Jas B Armstong; & Gilbert Cameron.

Late European advices announce the decease, at Bonn, Germany, of the eminent scholar & diplomatist, Chevalier Bunsen. Christiau Karl Josias Bunsen was born in Aug, 1791, at Corbach, in the German principality of Waldeck. He was educated principally at Gottingen, where he comenced his career in 1811 as a teacher in a gymnasium. In 1816 he visited Paris, & soon after went to Rome, where he married the daughter of an English clergyman, & became private secretary to Niebuhr, who was then Russian Minister to the Papal Court. Such is the brief outline of the history of one of the most learned men of the present century, statesman, philosopher, theologian, & traveller. –N Y Evening Post

The death of the Duke of Norfolk is announced by the last foreign arrival. The deceased nobleman was the 14th Duke of Norfolk, & was born in 1815, & had succeeded to the dukedom only 4 years ago. He was a son-in-law of Lord Lyons. His son & heir, the Earl of Arundel & Surrey, is a boy only 13 years old.

Rev Dr Croly, the well-known author & preacher, fell dead in the street, in London, on Nov 24. For 25 years previous he had been rector of St Stephen's, Walbrook, London.

Orphans Court of Wash Co, D C. Letters of administration on the personal estate of August Ebert, late of Wash Co, deceased. –H Rockaway, adm

Mrd: on Dec 13, by Rev Fr Boyle, Mr George Washington Morley, of Laytonsville, Montg Co, Md, to Miss Eliz Cornelia Ayton, of Wash.

Died: on Dec 6, suddenly, of heart disease, at the residence of his son-in-law, M T Goldsborough, of Talbot Co, Md, Edw Tilghman, in his 75th year.

Died: on Dec 17, at the residence of Jas E Harvey, Kate Hort, only daughter of the late Dr Wm P Hort, of New Orleans. Her funeral is today at 12 o'clock, at the Church of the Epiphany.

THU DEC 20, 1860
The Pres yesterday nominated to the Senate Edw M Stanton, as Atty Genr'l of the U S.

Saml Hartt, Naval Constructor, & formerly Chief of the Bureau of Construction, Equipment, & Repairs of the Navy Dept, died at Scituate, Mass, on Tue night.

Adms sale of the personal effects of Sylvanus E Bruson, deceased, in front of the auction rooms, by order of the Orphans Court of Wash Co, D C.
-Chas A Queen, adm   -Wall & Barnard, aucts

Senate: 1-Ptn from Amos Kyle & other invalid pensions residing in Androscoggin Co, Maine, asking that the decision of the Court of Claims granting pay from the time of disability may be carried into effect: referred. 2-Cmte on Military Affairs: discharged from further consideration of the memorial of Thos H Burley, asking that the right to use a machine for dove-tailing wood, patented by him, may be purchased by the U S. Same cmte: adverse report on the House bill for the relief of Julius Martin.

Marine disaster on Tue, in the Chesapeake Bay, off Five Fatham Bank. The ship **Noonday** was lying loaded with guano, & the schnr **Richmond**, of Balt, was engaged in lightening the ship, to enable her to get up to the city. On Monday the **Richmond**, Capt Chiveral, commenced loading & moved out, when she sprung a lead, & sunk in less then 5 minutes. Eight persons, among whom was Capt Chiveral, were drowned. Mr Geo Melville, pilot, found safety in the rigging, where he remained for 4 hours, when he was rescued by Capt League, of the steam-tug **Lioness**. -Exchange

Orphans Court of Wash Co, D C. Letters testamentary on the personal estate of Pringle Slight, late of Wash Co, deceased. –Catherine Slight, excx

A drover, named Carden, who arrived at the Clarendon House, from Grafton, Va, on Monday, with a large sum of money in his possession, when retiring to bed, for safety's sake, locked his door & subsequently blew out the gas, but without stopping it off. The next morning the escaping gas was noticed about the house & led to the room of the drover. He was found to be quite senseless & Dr Crow succeeded in bring him him back from the very jaws of the grave. He will recover.

Mrd: on Dec 18, in Gtwn, at the Methodist Protestant Church, by Rev W Robey, Jos Libbey, jr, to Mary R, 2nd daughter of the late Jeremiah Orme, all of Gtwn.

Died: on Dec 19, suddenly, Janet P Lynch, in her 10th year, oldest child of Jas & Jane Lynch. Her funeral will be from the residence of her parents, on Friday next, at 2 o'clock P M.

FRI DEC 21, 1860
Fasting & Prayers. Govn'r Thos H Hicks, of Md, has promptly responded to the recommendation of the President of the U S for the observance of the first Friday in the coming month as a day of national humiliation & prayer.

Com Chas T Plait, aged 65 years, died suddenly at Newburgh, N Y, on Dec 12. He was an ofcr in the U S Navy, & was wounded at the battle of Lake Champlain. He was also at the battle of Lake Erie. He entered the naval service of his country in 1812, & continued in it till the day of his death, a period of nearly 48 years.

Senate: 1-Ptn from Mrs J A Constant, heir & for the co-heirs of John Sinclair, asking indemnity for French spoliations prior to 1800: laid on the table. 2-Ptn from John S Livermore, an invalid pensioner, asking that he may be paid from the time of his disability: referred. 3-Ptn from Wm R Combs, asking a pension from his country on account of his services during the war of the Revolution & in the war of 1812: referred. 4-Cmte on Military Affairs: bill for the relief of Lt Geo L Hartsuff, asking compensation for property destroyed by the loss of the steamer **Lady Elgin.**

Indian massacres in Texas, from letter dated Jacksboro, Nov 26, says that mangled corpses were found at the houses of Mrs Gage, Mr Landman, & Mr Hays, near Briscoe's. One account states that 4 of the children of Mrs Gage were dangerously, if not mortally, wounded, & Mrs Saunders, the mother of Mrs Gage, killed & her body horribly mangled. A daughter of Mr Landman, aged 12 years, was mortally wounded, & his wife & 2 children massacred. Miss Matilda Gage & Miss Landman were made prisoners, but, after being stripped of their clothing, & ill-treated, were released & returned to their desolated homes. A man named Sherman, missing his wife, went in search of her, & found her lying near a creek with an arow in her side & her scalp taken. All the houses of the murdered were plundered of every thing they contained.

Fire on Sunday at Marietta, Pa, in a 2 story frame house occupied by a colored man, John Walker, 3 children of Mr Walker, & one other child of his sister-in-law, perished in the flames.

Mrd: on Dec 18, at *Cottage View*, the residence of the bride's father, by Rev Mr Kershaw, Benton Tolson to Pattie M, only daughter of Frank Bowie, all of PG Co, Md.

Wash Corp, Dec 17, 1860. 1-Ptns of John Walsh; of W H Dice; & of Geo Savage, for the remission of fines: referred to the Cmte of Claims. 2-Ptn of Geo McNaughton, praying to have refunded to him a certain amount of money on account of an unexpired license: referred to the Cmte on Finance. 3-Bill for the relief of John H McCutchen: passed.

Ex-Govn'r McDonald of Georgia, died at his residence in Marietta on Monday.

Mrd: on Dec 18, by Rev Dr Morsell, Edw D R Bean, of Bryantown, Md, to Miss S Rebecca Turner, of Wash City.

Died: on Dec 20, in Gtwn, in her 56th year, Mrs Frances H P, widow of the late Col Wm Robinson. Her funeral will take place from her late residence on the Heights of Gtwn, on Sat, at 3 o'clock P M.

SAT DEC 22, 1860
The Govn'r of Alabama has appointed the following gentlemen as Commissioners to confer with the following States: I W Garrott, N C; E W Pettus, Miss; J A Elmore, S C; A F Hopkins, Md; Frank Gilmer, Va; L Pope Walker, Tenn; Stephen F Hale, Ky; John Anthony Winston, Ark. There are others to be appointed.

Senate: 1-Ptn from Wm Wheeler Hubbell, of Pa, urging protection of rights in slave property in S C, & the adoption of measures suggested for the peace & stability of the Union; which was referred to the select Cmte of Thirteen. 2-Ptn from Peter Quinn, asking to be indemnified for a horse lost in the public service, under command of Maj J C Pemberton, U S Army: referred. 3-Ptn from H T Bacon, owner of the Canadian schnr **Perseverance**, asking that a register may be granted for said vessel: referred. 4-Ptn from Jno Breeson, asking that immediate attention may be given to the report of the Com'r of Indian Affairs; that in consequence of the drought last summer, & consequent failure of crops, many Indians must perish unless aided by Gov't: referred. 5-Ptn from Wm L S Dearing, asking to be paid for furnishing horses & equipage for a company of Tenn volunteers in the Florida war of 1837: referred. 6-Mr Latham moved to reconsider House bill, on which was an adverse report at the last session, for the relief of D F D Fairbanks, Fred Dodge, & the Pacific Mail Steamship Co: which was agreed to.

Obit-died: on Dec 20, in Gtwn, at the residence of her late husband, Col Wm Robinson, Mrs Frances H P Robinson, in her 56th year. She has been afflicted but a few months previously to her disease with symptoms of heart disease. She was a lady of great worth, & was a devoted wife & mother. She died in the communion of the Protestant Episcopal Church, & sweet is the consolation to those she leaves behind that a life so well spent on earth will meet a sure reward in Heaven. -C

MON DEC 24, 1860

On Tue last at the residence of Mr S Morgan Ramsey, in Phil, his son Norton, age 11 years, playfully shot at his sister Kate Ella, aged 9 years, not knowing the gun was loaded. She was a corpse in a few minutes.

On Wednesday week Miss Martha Rivins, daughter of Roland Rivins, of Bibb Co, Ga, was accidentally shot by a pistol in the hands of a lady of the family. The pistol exploded while she was handling it. The wound terminated fatally 3 days after the accident.

Resignation of Cmdor Kearny. Published in the N Y papers:
Perth Amboy, N J, Dec 21, 1860. To Hon Jas Buchanan, Pres of the U S: Sir: It is with deep regret that I find myself so siutated professionally as to request to be placed upon the reserved list of the navy, or otherwise to tender my resignation of the commission I hold as Captain. I am, very respectfully, sir, your obedient servant, Lawrence Kearny

Mrd: on Dec 20, by Rev Mr Casady, Mr Chas H Hays to Miss Margaret E Brown, both of Wash.

Died: on Dec 22, in Wash City, John T Killmon, in his 37th year. His funeral will take place at his late residence, corner of 2nd & D sts, this day, at 2 o'clock.

New Haven, Dec 21. A tenement house, occupied by 26 families, was burnt here this morning. The entire family of Michl Colbert, his wife & 4 children, perished in the flames.

TUE DEC 25, 1860

Trustee's sale of fine groceries, wines, liquors, & cigars, on Dec 27, at the store of S T Drury, 14th & Pa ave; the entire stock. –Wall & Barnard, aucts

House of Reps: 1-Cmte on Revolutionary Claims: reported favorably on a bill for the relief of Mary Beroult, admx of Jos Wheaton, of Rhode Island: referred. Same cmte: bill for the relief of the legal reps of Capt Chas Ferier, deceased: referred. Same cmte: bill to refund to the State of Georgia certain moneys paid by the said State to Peter Tuzvant, the legal rep of Robt Farquhar: referred. 2-Cmte on Private Land Claims: bill for the benefit of Gabrial J Johnston: referred. 3-Cmte on Military Affairs: bill for the relief of Lt L Harstoff, U S Army: passed. 4-Cmte on Invalid Pensions: bill to provide a pension to Eliza Reeves: passed. Same cmte: bill for the relief of Thos Chittenden: referred. Same cmte: bill granting a pension to Susan McGaulick: referred. Same cmte: bill for the relief of Peter Josephs: referred. 5-Cmte on Revolutionary Claims: reported adversely on Senate bill for the relief of Fred'k Vincent. Same cmte: adversely on a bill for the relief of Stephen C Graham. Same cmte: reportedly adversely on a bill for the relief of H S Carson.

Circuit Court of Wash Co, D C-in Chancery. Edw Chapman vs Saml L Harris, Curtis B Graham. The bill of cmplnt states that Edw Chapman was appointed Trustee by a decree of the Circuit Court of D C, rendered in a cause therein depending, in which Edw Chapman & others were cmplnts, & Henry H Dodge & other dfndnts, & authorized & directed to sell the real estate in D C of which Margaret Davidson died seized; that in pursuance of the requisitions of the said decree he offered a portion of said estate at public auction on Apr 24, 1851, & at such sale Saml L Harris purchased Lot 9 in square 372, in Wash City, for $1,121.33; that the said Saml L Harris complied with the terms of sale, by paying one-fourth of the purchase money in cash on the day of sale, & giving his 3 bonds for the deferred payments, each bearing date the day of sale, each for the sum of $280.33, & payable respectively in 8, 16, & 24 months after date; & that the said sale was reported to & ratified by said Court. The bill further charges that Saml L Harris, in making this purchase, acted as agent for Curtis B Graham; & that said Curtis B Graham in fact made the cash payment, & also paid the first bond that became due. The bill further charges that neither of the two bonds payable respectively in 16 & 24 months, nor any interest on either, has yet been paid. The object of the said bill of cmplnt is to obtain a decree of said Court for a sale of the said lot, & the application of the proceeds of such sale to the satisfaction of the two bonds, principal & interest. It appears to Hon Jas S Morsell, one of the Judges of said Court, that said Saml L Harris has left D C, & is now in some place unknown to cmplnt. Said Saml L Harris is to appear in said Court, either in person or by atty, on or before the 5th Monday of April next. –Jno A Smith, clerk

Circuit Court of Wash Co, D C-in Chancery. Edw Chapman vs Saml L Harris & Curtis B Graham. The bill of cmplnt in the above cause states that Edw Chapman was appointed trustee, by a decree of the Circuit Court of Wash Co, D C, rendered in a cause therein depending, in which Edw Chapman & others were cmplnts & Henry H Dodge & others dfndnts, & directed & authorized to sell the real estate in D C of which Eliz A Chapman died seized; that, in pursuance of the requisitions of said decree, he offered a portion of said estate for sale at public auction on Apr 5, 1854, & at the sale Saml H Harris became the purchaser of lot 10 in square 372, in Wash City, for $1,268.57; that the said Saml L Harris complied with the terms of sale by paying one-fourth of the purchase money in cash on the day of sale, & giving his 3 bonds for the deferred payments, each bearing date the day of sale, each for the sum of $292.14, & payable separately to the order of said Chapman, in 6, 12, & 18 months after sale; & the sale was reported & ratified by said Court. The bill further states that after the day of sale, said Saml L Harris transferred all his right, title, & estate in said lot to Curtis B Graham, who paid the first bond that fell due. The bill further charges that neither of the 2 bonds payable respectively in 12 & 18 months, nor any interest on either, has yet been paid. The object of the said bill of cmplnt is to obtain a decree of said Court for a sale of the said lot, & the application of the proceeds of such sale to the satisfaction of the two bonds, principal & interest. It appears to Hon Jas S Morsell, one of the Judges of said Court, that said Saml L Harris has left D C, &

is now in some place unknown to cmplnt. Said Saml L Harris is to appear in said Court, either in person or by atty, on or before the 5th Monday of April next.
—Jno A Smith, clerk

Orphans Court of Wash Co, D C, Dec 18, 1860. In the case of Richd Smith, adm of Geo P Tolson, deceased, the administrator & Court have appointed Feb 12 next, for the final settlement of the personal estate of the said deceased, of the assets in hand. -Ed Roach, Reg/o wills

Mr Steen de Bille, formerly for many years Minister of Denmark to the U S, & highly esteemed for his amiable character, died at Brussels Nov 28, in his 80th year.

State of Md, Calvert Co Orphans' Court, Dec 11, 1860: Ordered by the Court that Washington Jones, adm of Mathew Byrne, late of Calvert Co, deceased, advertise, for at least 12 months, making inquiries for Lawrence Byrne, [or his rep,] one of the legal reps of the aforesaid Mathew Byrne, deceased. —Wm A Parran, Register of Wills for Calvert Co.
+
Prince Fred'k, Calvert Co, Md. I hereby give notice to the said Lawrence Byrne, if living, or his legal reps, if dead, to come forward in person or by atty, with the proper vouchers, & prove their interest in the estate of the said Mathew Byrne. —Washington James, Adm of Mathew Byrne, deceased.

Senate: 1-Bill for the relief of Lt Geo L Hartsuff, U S Army: passed. 2-Bill for the relief of Maj Benj Alvord: passed. 3-Bill for the relief of Mrs Eliza A Merchant, widow of the late Brvt Capt Chas G Merchant, of the U S Army: pension increased from $15 to $25 per month: passed.

THU DEC 27, 1860
Rev J H Ingraham, of Holly Springs, Miss, who has lain in critical condition for some time past due to an accidental wound by a pistol shot, died on Dec 18. He was born in Portland, Maine, in 1809; briefly in the mercantile business, & became a teacher in Wash College, near Natchez, & in 1836 published his first work, The Southwest, by a Yankee. He acquired an extensive popularity with the general reading public.

Criminal Court-Wash-Wed. 1-Wm Brown found guilty for an assault & battery on John P Dennis. 2-John Cullinane acquitted of an assault & battery on Ellen McLaughlin. 3-Mary Hogan, convicted for assault & battery on Mary Donahue, & fined $12.

Mrd: on Wed, in Wash City, by Rev John C Smith, D D, Jas Metzger to Miss Mary Louisa, daughter of Gen Geo W Bowman, all of Wash City.

Circuit Court of D C-in Equity, No 1,658. Isaac Beers, Benj F Beers, Isaac Beers, jr, Wallace Kirby, & Virginia Kirby, cmplnts, against Chas E Walker, Albert C Floyd, & Gertrude Floyd, dfndnts. The bill states that on Sep 29, 1854, a certain deed was executed between Chas E Walker & wife, Milly Ann Beers, the wife of Isaac Beers, & John B Floyd, reciting that the said Milly Ann Beers had purchased the parcel of ground hereinafter mentioned, from the said Chas E Walker, & had not fully paid for the same, & conveying to the said John B Floyd, his heirs & assigns, all that part of lot 9 in square 532, being the eastern 20 feet of the said lot, & running back with that width 75 feet, the depth of said lot, together with the right to tap the sewer running through said lot, upon trust, to secure the payment of the said unpaid purchase money, & then afterwards, upon the further trust for the separate use of the said Milly Ann Beers, & to permit her to receive & take the rents & profits of the same or her own use, free from the control of her husband, the said Isaac Beers, & from any liability for his debts, with power to appoint the fee simple of the said parcel of ground by deed or by last will & testament, & in default of such appointment, in trust for the heirs of the said Milly Ann Beers at her death; that on Mar 22, 1860, the said Milly Ann Beers, by her last will & testament, did, in pursuance of the said power appoint & devise the said parcel of ground to the said Isaac Beers, Benj F Beers, Isaac Beers, the younger, & Virginia Kirby, the wife of Wallace Kirby, as tenants in common, the said share of the said Virginia Kirby to be conveyed to the said Isaac Beers, for the sole & separate use of the said Virginia, free from the control of her said husband; that afterwards the said Milly Ann Beers departed this life without revoking the said devise & appointment; that, after the execution of the deed aforesaid, the said trustee, John B Floyd, departed this life, leaving as his heirs at law 2 children, Albert C Floyd & Gertrude Floyd, who are infants of tender years; that the said parcel of ground cannot be divided, & that the said devisees have agreed to sell the same & divide the proceeds of such sale, but that such sale cannot be made with advantage whilst the legal title of the said parcel of ground is outstanding in the said infant heirs of the said John B Floyd. The bill avers that the whole of the said unpaid purchase money hath been fully paid & satisfied, & prays the said Court to decree a sale of the said parcel of ground, & to appoint some suitable person in the room of the said John B Floyd to convey the legal title of the same. It appears that the dfndnts, Albert C Floyd & Gertrude Floyd, are non-residents, living beyong the jurisdiction of this Court. Said non-residents to appear & answer to the said bill, on or before the first Monday in May, 1861.
—Wm M Merrick, A J -Carlisle & Maury -Jno A Smith, clerk

Died: on Dec 17, at Burleigh, in Hinds Co, Miss, Mrs Sophia Dabney, wife of Col Thos S Dabney, in her 51st year.

Died: on Dec 20, in Wash City, at his residence, Mr Rezin Wilburn, in his 86th year. He was a native of Md, but for the last 40 years a resident of Wash City.

Great Falls, N H, Dec 26. Ralph Farnham, the last survivor of the battle of Bunker Hill, died this morning at Acton, Maine, aged 104 years.

Phil, Dec 26. Hon Henry M Fuller, ex-member of Congress from the Honesdale district, died this morning, in this city, of typhus fever, aged 40 years. He was the defeated candidate in the second district last October.

FRI DEC 28, 1860
Senate: 1-Ptn from Dexter R Crocker, asking compensation for transporting the mail from Canyonville, Oregon, to Yreka, Calif: referred. 2-Ptn from John W Mason, of N Y, asking compensation for services performed by the ship **Lucy Thompson**, in rescuing & transporting to N Y 100 ofcrs & soldiers of the U S Army: referred. 3-Bill for the relief of Eliza Reeves: passed. 4-Bill for the relief of Thos Chittenden: passed.

The U S brig-of-war **Dolphin** arrived at Norfolk on Sunday from the coast of Brazil. The **Dolphin** is the last vessel of the Paraguay Expedition to go out of commission. She left Norfolk in the winter of 1858, & in a week after joined Cmdor Shubrick's fleet in La Plata, where she has spent the greater part of her cruise. She is the smallest vessel in the regular navy, being only 224 tons burden, & carrying 4 guns. Her ofcrs are: Cmder, C H Stedman; Lts, L Paulding, E P Williams, & C W Fluper; Passed Assist Surgeon, John Y Taylor.

House of Reps: 1-Memorial of Dr Isaac J Hayes, praying Congress to pass a law to change the name of the schnr **Spring Hill** now on a voyage of discovery in the Arctic Sea, to the schnr **United States**: referred. 2-Memorial of Capt Saml Beaston, master of the schnr **George Harris**, praying to be reimbursed for a fine paid by him to the U S: referred. 3-Memorial of Eliz Mills, widow of John Mills, praying Congress for an increase of pension: referred.

Hon Henry M Fuller died this Wed morning at his residence in Phil, aged 40 years. His disease was typhoid fever, & he had been ill for about 2 weeks. He was educated at Princeton College, & afterwards studied law in Wilkesbarre; he was elected to Congress in 1850 as a Whig, & again in 1858 as a member of the American party. After his last term in Congress Mr Fuller made Phil his place of residence. He leaves a deeply afflicted widow & a family of 7 children. -Bulletin

Among the latest English intelligence is the death of the Earl of Aberdeen, an eminent diplomatist & statesman. He was born in 1784; in 1813 Ambassador from England to Austria; & in 1828 he was Minister of Foreign Affairs.
[No death date given-current item.]

Died: on Dec 26, at Eastport, Maine, J H Kilby, at the age of 31 years.

Mrd: on Dec 27, by Rev Smith Pyne, Maj Henry J Hunt, U S Army, to Mary Bethune, 2nd daughter of Col H K Craig, U S Army.

Mrd: on Dec 27, at St John's Church, by Rev Dr Pyne, M J Cookman Adams to Miss M Virginia Harkness, both of Wash City.

99,289 29-100 acres of land for sale in New Mexico. Under the 5th section of an Act of Congress, approved Jul 21, 1850, confirming private land claims in New Mexico, I have a FLOAT for sale for the above number of acres. The float can be located in a square body on any vacant land, not mineral, in New Mexico or Arizona. Lands are not taxed in <u>New Mexico</u>. Address John S Watts, Wash, D C

Charleston, Dec 27. *Fort Moultrie* was evacuated last night. The guns were spiked, & the carriages were demolished by fire. Only 4 soldiers were left in charge of the fort. The troops were all conveyed to *Fort Sumter*. The excitement in the city is intense. It is believed that the Convention is now taking action upon the resolution in relation to taking the forts. [Capt Foster, with a small force, still occupied *Fort Moultrie*.]

SAT DEC 29, 1860
Danl Devlin has been appointed City Chamberlain of N Y in place of Mr Platt, removed by acting Mayor Peck in the absence of Mayor Wood, who is on a bridal trip. The office is the most responsible one in the city.

Mrd: on Dec 20, by Rev John Martin, Jas L Addison to Mrs Betty Tolson, daughter of the late Wm Bayne, both of PG Co, Md.

Died: on Dec 27, at Winchester, after several months' severe illness, Jacob Senseney, aged about 66 years. He was a proment citizen & merchant; filled the ofc of magistrate of Fred'k Co; a gentleman of fine qualities of heart & mind. His numerous friends will long cherish his memory.

Charleston, Dec 28. *Fort Moultrie* & *Castle Pinckney* were both taken possession of by the Carolinians last night. They were taken possession of under the instructions of Govn'r Pickens.

MON DEC 31, 1860
Mrd: on Nov 21, at the residence of the bride's father, San Jose, Calif, by Rev Fr Briglione, Sallie, youngest daughter of Hon P H Burnett, late Govn'r of Calif, to Francis Poe, of San Francisco.

Circuit Court of Wash Co, D C-in Equity, No 1,492: Oct Term. Henry K Randall & Emily M Randall, cmplnts, vs Columbus Munroe, Seaton Munroe, Thos Franck Munroe, Richd Smith, & Francis M Ramsay, dfndnts. The return & report of the Com'rs containing the partition & allotment made by them of the estate of Thos Munroe, deceased, in Wash City, D C, among the persons entitled to portions thereof, having been by the Court here seen & duly considered, it is by the Court, this 17th day of Nov, 1860, ordered & adjudged that the proceedings of the said com'rs & the said partition & allotment made by them shall be ratified, confirmed, & recorded, to remain & be binding according to the act of Assembly in such cases made & provided. –John A Smith, clerk

Criminal Court-Wash-Sat. 1-Chas F Lausman convicted of larceny: sentenced to 3 years in the penitentiary.

State of Ohio, Cuyahoga Co, in the Court of Common Pleas. Madison Miller, plntf, vs Wm Richards & Sarah A Richards his wife, Thos N Murphy, John N Murphy, Mrs Pearson, Mrs McGuire, Mr Rogers, all of whom but said William devisees of Fannie G Cox, deceased, dfndnts. In pursuance of an order of said Court of Common Pleas, the said dfndnts are notified that said plntf has commenced a suit in said Court setting forth in substance that said Wm & Sarah A, by their mortgage deed dated Mar 23, 1858, conveyed to said plntfs one half in common of lots 907 thru 919, lots 928 thru 940, 1017 & 1918, 1022 thru 1041, 1045, in S S Stone's subdivision, called *College Tract*, in original lot 87, in Brooklyn, in said county, subject to a condition of defeasance in the payment of their 2 promissory notes of same date given for the payment of $316.50 each, & payable in one year, & the other in 2 years from date, with interest; that said notes were given towards the purchase money of said lots, & that no part, either of principal or interest, has been paid thereon; that said mortgage was left for record Apr 8, 1858, & recorded in Volume 96 & 73; that said Wm & Sarah, by their deed dated Nov 1, 1854, mortgaged the same lots to Fannie G Cox, deceased, to secure the payment of $3,000; that said mortgage was given before said Wm or Sarah had any title to said lots, that plntf's lien therein is entitled to preference over the lien of said mortgage; that said Fannie G died leaving all said dfndnts, except said William, her devisees, who are supposed to reside in Va, but whose names plntf cannot give anymore fully; & praying that said one half in common of said lots may be sold & the proceeds applied in payment of the costs of the suit, the amount due & to become due to the plntfs, & the surplus, if any, be brought into Court. Dfndnts are required to answer on or before Feb 25, 1861, or the petition will be taken as confessed. –Williamson & Riddle, Attys for Plntf.
–Cleveland, Dec 24, 1860.

Hon Wm Wilkins, of Pittsburg, Pa, former Senator in Congress, member of the Cabinet, Minister to Russia, etc, has written a letter in which he takes decided ground against secession. He is over 85 years of age, & still wields an immense influence in Western Pa. He is an old Jackson man, & takes the Jackson ground that secession must end in coercion, & that disunion will produce civil war.

We learn from the Mobile Register, that Col Rudler, the second in command of Walker's expedition, has been pardoned by the authorities of Honduras. The intelligence is conveyed in a letter from Col Rudler himself.

Mrs M M Reily, wife of Dr Reily, of New Albany, Indiana, was burnt so badly at that place on Dec 24, that she died in a few hours afterwards. Her dress had taken fire from the grate. She was an intelligent & estimable lady.

Hon John B Floyd resigned the ofc of Sec of War on Saturday last, & his resignation was accepted by the Pres.

Defection of a Revenue Ofcr. The Charleston Courier of Friday very coolly states that Capt N L Coste, late of the U S revenue service, in command of the cutter **William Aiken**, has given official notification of his resignation, & has discharged his crew. The crew, on being notified of the position of Capt Coste under the late ordinance concerning the customs, promptly volunteered to remain under his command as an ofcr of South Carolina under that ordinance. We infer from this statement that the Gov't has lost one of its revenue cutters, as well as her ofcrs & crew. What next?

The family of Maj Anderson, consisting of his wife & 3 children & servant, are stopping at the Brevoort House, in Fifth ave, N Y, where they have spent several winters.

The Charleston papers of Friday bring us the particulars of the occupation of ***Fort Sumter*** by Maj Anderson, of the U S Army, & of the subsequent seizure by the militia of S C of ***Castle Pinckney & Fort Moultrie***. The two ofcrs & 4 men left behind at ***Fort Moultrie*** were ordered to hold themselves in readiness, with knapsacks packed; they were ordered to 2 schnrs, lying in the vicinity, where they embarked, taking with them all the necessaries, & stores, requisite in their evacuation.

A

Abbot, 102
Abbott, 19, 62, 128
Abert, 56, 257, 275, 302
Abrams, 203
Acheson, 230
Achin, 164
Acker, 39, 109
Adam, 142
Adams, 8, 34, 39, 75, 76, 85, 96, 111, 118, 119, 129, 131, 144, 165, 166, 173, 176, 183, 190, 194, 207, 217, 244, 271, 274, 277, 288, 291, 327, 335
Adams' mill, 249
Adamson, 62
Addison, 27, 30, 61, 130, 172, 191, 250, 273, 307, 315, 323, 336
Adger, 245
Adler, 252, 283
Agassiz, 206, 249
Aguello, 169
Ailer, 249
Ailworth, 242
Airley, 221
Albertson, 93, 141
Alexander, 30, 39, 73, 80, 81, 83, 90, 100, 145, 147, 148, 160, 186, 192, 256, 268, 290
Alexandre, 280
Alison, 139
Allen, 5, 10, 21, 35, 39, 56, 96, 109, 118, 119, 130, 173, 278, 305
Allendale, 154
Allens, 136
Allibone, 89
Allingham, 293
Allison, 267
Allman, 192
Allyn, 316
Alma, 26
Alsten, 190
Altemus, 255
Alvord, 114, 116, 333

Ambler, 20, 267
Amendariz, 204
Ames, 127, 186, 276
Amman, 80
Analostan Island, 154
Anchison, 100
Anderson, 39, 49, 87, 102, 109, 134, 138, 141, 187, 207, 276, 338
Andrews, 206, 250, 266
Andrus, 39
Angus, 5, 58, 90, 119, 125, 151, 163, 194, 238, 305
Anhaeuser, 234
Ankenny, 109
Ansart, 160
Anthony, 20, 132
Appleby, 39
Applegarth, 158
Appleton, 2, 3, 13, 28, 100, 113, 160, 177, 180, 253
Archer, 15, 64, 126, 270, 298
Arden, 39
Arfroedson, 100
Arguello, 34, 109, 194, 235
Arliffe, 4
Armant, 208
Armistead, 8, 39
Armitage, 39
Arms, 53, 135
Armstrong, 16, 78, 107, 112, 132, 267, 308, 327
army chaplains, 245
Arnold, 58, 189, 262
Arsington, 169
Asbury, 323
Asch, 255
Aschwanden, 313
Aschwander, 252
Ash, 58, 326
Ashby, 81
Ashford, 39, 265
Ashley, 66, 100
Ashmead, 316
Ashton, 39, 261
Aspinwall, 217

Athey, 39
Atkins, 52, 141, 184, 188, 194
Atkinson, 36, 52, 71, 76, 81, 93, 109, 180, 184, 267
Atlantic cable, 91
AtLee, 72
Atocha, 29
Atwell, 188
Atwill, 100
Aubert, 204
Auchmuty, 296
Augus, 76
Auld, 275
Austin, 157
Averill, 11
Avery, 39, 81
Ayliffe, 194, 238
Aymar, 184
Ayott, 76
Ayres, 61
Ayton, 122, 327

B

Babcock, 121
Baby, 207
Bache, 206, 263
Bachelder, 259
Bacon, 12, 75, 100, 125, 136, 156, 193, 236, 315, 330
Baden, 319
Bagby, 86
Bagman, 40
Bailey, 43, 59, 122, 130, 137, 179, 206
Bailou, 77
Baily, 137, 209
Baird, 102, 170, 184
Baker, 39, 40, 93, 100, 101, 151, 160, 162, 173, 310
Balcolm, 182
Baldwin, 40, 64, 90, 95, 157, 163, 166, 186, 194, 244, 251, 294, 320, 323, 327
Balek, 184
Balfe, 134
Balhuff, 63

Ball, 3, 6, 40, 67, 135, 163, 281, 315, 319
Ballenger, 39
Ballinger, 215
Balmer, 96
Bancroft, 116, 255
Bangs, 61
Bankhead, 125
Banks, 206, 217, 269
Banner, 15
Bannerman, 255
Banon, 197
Barbee, 117
Barber, 270
Barbot, 126
Barbour, 212
Barca, 21
Barclay, 14, 255, 311
Bargy, 71, 163
Barker, 8, 40, 72, 94, 271, 327
Barnard, 3, 4, 24, 50, 74, 79, 137, 148, 157, 207, 220, 260, 276
Barnes, 8, 39, 40, 63, 104, 114, 149, 166, 253, 300, 306
Barnett, 326
Barney, 72, 112, 269, 270, 274
Barnholt, 299
Barnsley, 21, 69
Barnt, 100
Barnum, 23
Barnwell, 308
barque **Alvarado**, 271
barque **Cochituate**, 273
barque **Helen Blood**, 38
barque **James Gray**, 298
barque **Orion**, 114
barque **Resolute**, 239
barque **Saladin**, 173
barque **Sarah Bond**, 38
barque **Smyrniote**, 53
Barr, 40, 85, 119, 169, 266, 276
Barracks, 282
Barrand, 292
Barrell, 284
Barret, 63, 96
Barrett, 15, 34, 39, 40, 319

Barron, 39, 44, 78, 81, 90, 151, 170
Barrow, 91
Barry, 8, 14, 22, 39, 40, 56, 63, 81, 96, 131, 170, 206, 305
Bart, 42
Bartholomew, 171, 252
Bartless, 194
Bartlett, 37, 96, 121, 142, 151, 176, 235
Barton, 19, 109, 186, 239, 301
Base Ball, 271
Bass, 5, 211, 212
Bassett, 299
Bateman, 39
Batemen, 212
Bates, 40, 55, 116, 141, 160, 179, 295, 325
Battell, 35
Batti, 192
Baumgarten, 217
Bawtree, 207
Bayard, 53
Baylis, 39
Baylor, 127
Bayly, 55, 113, 115, 187, 191
Bayne, 40, 113, 336
Beach, 53, 88, 89, 136, 228
Beacham, 207
Beachamp, 76, 258
Beale, 39, 60, 161, 187, 215, 237, 315
Beall, 39, 40, 45, 78, 187, 227, 273, 281, 289
Beall's Retreat, 281
Bean, 6, 57, 82, 270, 330
Bear, 84, 142
Beard, 160, 269, 322
Beardsley, 146
Beaseley, 39
Beasoleil, 223
Beaston, 335
Beatie, 121
Beatles, 119
Beatley, 40
Beatty, 21, 35
Beauregard, 301

Beband, 223
Bechtel, 138
Beck, 39, 203, 265
Becker, 63, 226
Beckert, 22
Beckstein, 216
Beckwith's Lodge, 50
Bedford, 266
Bedinger, 156
Beer, 57
Beers, 278, 334
Beeson, 264
Beirne, 267
Beizell, 58
Belden, 212
Bell, 26, 39, 40, 65, 81, 118, 119, 141, 154, 158, 173, 182, 317
Bellemonte estate, 288
Bellenger, 212
Bello, 261
Bellringer, 309
Belshaw, 297
Belt, 20
Beman, 109
Ben Lomond, 8
Benedict, 72
Benefield, 102
Benham, 116
Bennett, 39, 50, 94, 156, 268
Benson, 101, 323
Benton, 40, 231
Berault, 127
Beresford, 204
Berkley, 281
Bernadotte, 318
Bernard, 130, 191, 267
Berne, 150
Beroult, 331
Berret, 18, 55, 271
Berrett, 37
Berrian, 136
Berry, 38, 39, 64, 78, 84, 100, 160, 161, 173, 174, 189, 208, 226, 227, 273, 289, 291, 303, 311, 315
Berryman, 66, 118, 141, 288
Berwin, 85

Besant, 31
Bester, 187
Bestor, 315, 326
Bethune, 227, 335
Bevans, 163
Beverly Manor House, 244
Bewley, 253
Bibb, 323
Bibby, 88, 151
Bibeand, 223
Bickley, 120
Bicksler, 40
Biddle, 165, 281
Biddleman, 39
Bigby, 67
Bigelow, 5, 147, 207, 217
Biggs, 63, 124, 296
Bigler, 200
Bigsby, 174
Bilansky, 108
Billing, 253
Billings, 287
Bindon, 130
Bingham, 52, 100, 155, 172, 203
Binns, 190
Birch, 40
Bircle, 112
Bird, 40, 53, 56, 90, 100, 141, 247, 262
Birdsong, 24
Birge, 316
Bishop, 135, 148, 245
Bispham, 129
Bissell, 98
Bittinger, 5, 39, 123
Black, 24, 27, 37, 273, 326
Black Yagers, 254
Blackford, 1, 2, 273
Blackhurst, 220
Blackman, 119, 144
Blackwell, 94, 147, 156, 180, 318
Blagden, 165
Blair, 26, 228, 231
Blake, 63, 240, 290
Blakely, 63
Blakemore, 39

Blakistone, 50, 256
Blanchard, 39, 40, 287
Blandford, 312
Blantyre, 174
Bledsoe, 170
Bligh, 10, 33
Blocker, 30, 109, 160
Blodgett, 16, 130
Blondel, 259
Bloomfield, 49
Blow, 242
Bluckman, 76
Blunt, 87, 187
Boardman, 264, 269
Boardwright, 259
Boarman, 189
boat **Lake Erie**, 197
Boatswain, 130
Bochman, 244
Bogan, 73
Bogart, 159
Boggs, 9, 28, 52, 74, 180
Bogle, 326
Bogus, 114
Bohlayer, 4, 8, 39
Bohrer, 57, 78, 252, 315
Boies, 86
Boisseau, 56
Bokee, 91, 285, 327
Boker, 143
Bolivar, 101
Bolley, 259
Bomford, 25, 39
Bonaparte, 204
Bond, 39, 187, 254
Boneviento, 192
Bonham, 306
Bonifant, 268
Bonini, 39
Bonney, 100, 156, 163
Bonnin, 112
Boone, 14, 40, 246
Boorn, 226
Bootes, 8, 55
Booth, 107, 126, 226
Boothe, 81

Booze, 68
Bordman, 304
Borland, 39, 217
Borreman, 88
Borromeo College, 317
Boschke, 61, 175
Boscoe, 81
Bosley, 116
Boss, 39
Bosse, 40
Bossier, 207
Bost, 279
Boteler, 120, 139, 151, 249, 266, 315
Botts, 144, 153, 182
Boucher, 78, 212, 221
Bouligny, 142
Boultenhouse, 96
Boulterhouse, 70
Boulton, 96
Bounin, 86
Bourke, 40
Bouton, 139
Bowden, 100
Bowen, 17, 40, 46, 51, 142, 192, 271
Bowers, 101, 119
Bowhay, 118, 160, 194, 234
Bowie, 119, 198, 253, 279, 329
Bowkay, 34, 116
Bowler, 119
Bowles, 238
Bowley, 100
Bowling, 149
Bowman, 71, 86, 116, 126, 145, 194, 333
Bowtray, 130
Bowyer, 22
Boyce, 206
Boyd, 26, 35, 101, 109, 187, 208, 276, 327
Boyden, 1
Boyer, 265
Boyle, 10, 17, 33, 35, 39, 118, 233, 249, 324, 327
Braden, 106
Bradford, 119, 319

Bradley, 40, 113, 154, 210, 211, 226, 283, 315
Brady, 39, 40, 167
Bragdon, 304
Bragg, 93, 141, 166, 193
Braiden, 162
Brand, 276
Brandt, 15, 56, 151
Brannan, 63, 65, 89, 149, 184, 194, 237
Branson, 40
Brantly, 310
Brashear, 119
brass cannon, 220
Brawner, 253
Bray, 190, 195
Brayley, 139
Brazier, 94
Bread, 192
Breckenridge, 20, 269
Breckinridge, 276, 280, 302
Breeson, 330
Brent, 28, 40, 141, 146, 168, 242, 258, 273, 296
Brereton, 39, 40, 95, 282, 283
Brett, 82
Breust, 252
Brevort, 327
Brewer, 27, 37, 63, 109
Brewster, 100
Briant, 204
Brick, 260
Brickley, 39
Bridges, 15
Bridget, 40, 63, 78, 227, 232
Brien, 184
Brierly, 100, 197
brig **Argus**, 281
brig **Atlanta**, 82
brig **Dolphin**, 321
brig **Gen Armstrong**, 110
brig **Good Hope**, 236
brig **Jane**, 315
brig **Jessie**, 120, 176, 193, 237
brig **Minni Schiffer**, 276
brig of war **Mondeigo**, 101

343

brig **Porpoise**, 239
Briggs, 33, 71, 327
Bright, 290, 321
Brightwell, 315
Briglione, 336
brig-of-war **Dolphin**, 335
brig-of-war **Mondiego**, 232
Brinide, 240
Brink, 162
Brintnall, 31
Brisband, 251
Briscoe, 40, 110, 115, 172, 233, 284, 305
Brisk, 63
Brister, 149
Broach, 124
Broadhead, 78
Broadus, 255
Brockholst, 18, 124
Broderick, 7, 24, 74, 123, 137, 175
Brody, 128
Bromwell, 288
Bronaugh, 40
Bronsen, 154
Bronson, 9
bronze doors, 168
Brook, 51, 68
Brooke, 8, 39, 128, 133, 187, 241, 254, 267, 315, 318
Brookes, 246
Brooks, 39, 40, 58, 64, 78, 93, 123, 142, 149, 150, 169, 176, 194, 217, 252, 286
Broome, 164, 280
Brorick, 64
Brose, 119
Brosnahan, 40
Brothers' Fifth Part, 81, 219
Brott, 76, 100, 156, 193
Brown, 7, 8, 9, 13, 21, 25, 26, 30, 39, 40, 49, 52, 55, 56, 61, 63, 69, 71, 73, 74, 77, 84, 86, 87, 89, 92, 94, 95, 100, 102, 118, 138, 154, 155, 161, 162, 183, 185, 186, 191, 192, 197, 204, 206, 207, 210, 221, 242, 243, 252, 268, 279, 295, 300, 313, 321, 331, 333
Brown Invasion, 266
Browne, 12, 105, 117, 143, 175, 206, 300
Browning, 40, 79, 133, 293
Brownlow, 128
Broyles, 240
Brubaker, 159
Bruin, 88
Brundell, 178
Brunett, 117, 229
Brunner, 215
Bruson, 328
Bryan, 47, 81, 244
Bryant, 39, 112, 115, 130, 138, 160, 235, 246
Buard, 207
Buchanan, 14, 75, 101, 321, 331
Buchly, 7
Buckey, 4
Buckingham, 108, 187
Buckley, 6, 64, 255
Bucklin, 144, 147
Buckly, 40
Buel, 272, 273
Buenos Ayres, 321
Buer, 322
Buke, 76
Bukey, 80, 126
Bull, 216
Bulley, 7
Bullock, 100, 109
Bunce, 290
Bunker Hill, 334
Bunnel, 121
Bunnell, 93, 109
Bunsen, 327
Burbank, 205
Burch, 56, 64, 190, 193, 227
Burchard, 272
Burche, 39, 40, 48, 288
Burchell, 78, 245
Burckhardt, 137
Burdine, 40, 63, 198, 256, 262, 264
Burford, 26

Burgess, 210, 214
Burhman, 84
Burk, 88
Burke, 64, 119, 132, 154, 193, 245
Burkhead, 230
Burkley, 124
Burley, 19, 40, 167, 328
Burlingame, 217
Burlingham, 156
Burnett, 107, 121, 336
Burnham, 93, 142
Burns, 40, 100, 193, 311, 326
Burnt Mill Road, 1
Burr, 19, 106, 173, 273
Burroughs, 169
Burrow, 259
Burrows, 4, 96
Burt, 107
Burton, 34, 50, 125, 199, 271
Bury, 251
Busby, 208
Busey, 34, 148
Bush, 7, 39, 40, 210, 211, 212, 230, 312
Buskirk, 182
Butcher, 40, 70
Buthman, 11
Butler, 24, 39, 51, 54, 55, 73, 119, 125, 126, 130, 139, 142, 182, 184, 187, 200, 221, 271, 272, 296, 303, 308, 310
BUTLER, 324
Butt, 69
Butterfield, 66, 124, 207
Butterworth, 75, 155
Button, 193, 299
Butts, 211
Byerly, 283, 292
Byington, 40
Byrd, 143
Byrne, 40, 147, 257, 333
Byron, 130, 166

C

Cabell, 106, 135, 267
Cable, 135
Cabot, 163
Caddis, 94, 156, 183
Caden, 198, 243
Cady, 137
Cahal, 150
Cahill, 63
Cahoone, 304
Cain, 49
Calderon, 21
Caldwell, 243
Calhoun, 260, 266
Call, 109, 161, 177
Callan, 40, 41, 56, 115, 178, 180, 225, 233, 269, 285, 286
Calloway, 32, 55, 73, 100, 148, 176, 194
Calvert, 40, 81, 162
Cameron, 90, 96, 151, 162, 327
Cammack, 28, 106
Camp, 109
Campan, 125
Campbell, 7, 8, 10, 41, 121, 153, 175, 210, 227, 249, 265, 285, 315, 316
Canady, 127
Canfield, 130
Cannon, 21, 27, 62, 118, 155, 184, 212, 214
Cantwill, 138
Caperton, 147, 164, 174, 273
Carbery, 41, 139, 152, 192, 202, 260
Carden, 328
Carew, 129
Carey, 199, 231
Carhart, 30
Carl, 264
Carland, 305
Carlisle, 17, 40, 55, 334
Carlisle White Sulphur Springs, 191
Carlos, 109
Carlyle, 240
Carney, 188
Carother, 253
Carothers, 6, 195, 202, 272
Carow, 117
Carpenter, 62, 94, 134, 177

Carr, 101, 204
Carrico, 41, 227
Carrington, 141, 175, 294, 304, 325
Carroll, 15, 22, 23, 40, 204
Carrolls, 140
Carrow, 112
Carson, 62, 84, 118, 169, 183, 293, 331
Carstang, 191
Carter, 2, 40, 58, 65, 66, 99, 116, 118, 132, 134, 145, 148, 251, 256, 274, 300
Caruthers, 198, 219
Caryl, 254
Carztang, 88
Casady, 331
Casanave, 111
Casey, 186
Cash, 230
Cashen, 259
Casparis, 40, 285
Cass, 19, 326
Cassaday, 84
Cassady, 64
Cassel, 56
Cassell, 178
Cassels, 136
Cassidey, 326
Cassin, 41, 244
Castle Pinckney, 336, 338
Castleman, 78, 241
Castner, 268
Castor, 79, 90, 194
Cater, 247
Cathcart, 134, 296, 311
Catlett, 221
Catron, 316
Causin, 201, 327
Causten, 117, 155
Cavanah, 154
Cavard, 155
Cavis, 247
Cazanove, 218
Cazeau, 5
Cazenove, 40, 81
Cedar Grove, 24

Cesalto, 7
Chadwick, 211, 212
Chafee, 41
Chalfield, 126
Chalmers, 215, 216
Chamberlain, 114
Chambers, 40
Champ, 102
Champe, 80
Champion, 93, 102, 155, 248
Champlain, 126
Chandler, 41, 111, 164, 250, 272, 280
Chandonet, 76, 109
Chapin, 151, 160
Chaplain, 241
Chaplin, 21, 125
Chapman, 40, 62, 78, 212, 267, 332
Charlant, 327
Chase, 41, 72, 112, 212
Chatfield, 80
Chaudenet, 156
Chaudonet, 101
Chauncy, 281
Cheever, 64
Cheevers, 245, 254
Chenery, 17, 75
Cheney, 11, 100, 125
Cherry, 128
Cheshire, 40
Chesley, 18
Chesnut, 299
Chichester, 133
Child, 96
Childress, 112
Childs, 28, 41, 96, 99, 126, 309, 323, 325
Chillon Castle Manor, 110
Chilton, 41, 69
Chinn, 294
Chipchase, 20
Chipley, 58
Chism, 40
Chittenden, 40, 331, 335
Chiveral, 328
Choice, 207

Choppin, 41
Chorpenning, 268
Christian, 73, 208
Chubb, 40
Chunk, 313
Church, 40, 71, 166, 228, 280
Cis, 212
Cissel, 195
Clagett, 29, 71, 88, 153, 154, 198, 203, 207, 248, 270, 277, 290
Claggett, 31
Clampitt, 90
Clapp, 112
<u>Clarendon Hotel</u>, 305
Clark, 3, 4, 40, 57, 58, 78, 93, 102, 103, 104, 107, 110, 119, 131, 156, 169, 178, 184, 191, 194, 195, 202, 211, 212, 222, 223, 224, 265, 272, 273, 286, 292, 308, 310, 326
Clarke, 26, 40, 41, 53, 55, 56, 90, 97, 113, 115, 118, 172, 216, 237, 247, 277, 296, 305, 323
Clarkson, 100, 160, 173
Clavyl, 254
Clay, 76, 101, 125, 130, 157, 191, 194, 238, 246, 270, 306, 310
Cleary, 55, 187, 207, 211, 264, 271, 290
Cleave, 132
Clemens, 63, 211
Clements, 21, 24, 41, 64, 75, 207, 211, 295, 320
Clementson, 150
Clemm, 312
Clemmens, 73, 75
Cleveland, 207, 213
Cliffburne, 212
Clifford, 292, 316
Clokey, 105, 298
Clopton, 98, 108
Close, 94
Closkey, 41
Clough, 146
Clover Lea, 299
Cloyes, 131
Clubb, 169

Cluskey, 41
Clymer, 181
Coakley, 5, 41
Coale, 169
Cobb, 1, 100, 151, 160, 183, 205, 302, 320
Cochran, 41, 139, 260, 312
Cochrane, 20, 223
Cocke, 3, 17, 19, 75, 83, 109, 194
Cockerill, 82
Cockerille, 55
Cockerville, 51
Cocking, 41
Cocock, 123
Coddington, 40
Codrington, 268
Coe, 69, 84
Cogswell, 206, 266
Cohen, 224, 254
Cois, 100
Coke, 260
Colbert, 293, 331
Colburn, 26
Colby, 261
Colclaser, 72, 140
Colclazer, 233
Colcock, 298
Cole, 56, 57, 87, 119, 126, 127, 160, 205, 239
Cole Brook, 27
Coleby, 286
Colegate, 204
Coleman, 40, 63, 320
Colescoth, 258
Colescott, 76
Colineau, 2
College Tract, 337
Colley, 117, 263
Collins, 7, 41, 58, 63, 64, 145, 270, 295, 319
Colman, 81
Colmesnil, 100
Colquhoun, 184
Colt, 110, 142
Coltman, 78, 325
<u>Columbian College</u>, 274

Columbus, 63, 123
Colvesville, 1
Colvin, 52, 55
Colwell, 108
Combs, 21, 306, 329
Compton, 58, 119, 253
Comstock, 27
Conaway, 63
Condict, 148
Condit, 303
Cones, 138
Conger, 220
Congressional Burial Ground, 121
Congressional burying ground, 183
Congressional Burying Ground, 219
Conine, 176
Conington, 280
Connanton, 276
Connel, 63
Connell, 62, 182
Connelly, 41, 107, 262, 264, 321
Conner, 80, 151, 192, 194, 198, 234, 254, 298, 322
Connody, 63
Connolly, 66, 183
Connor, 63, 64, 140, 149, 160, 184, 187, 188, 200, 299
Conrad, 212, 326
Conray, 40
Conroy, 40, 96
Constant, 329
Contee, 139
Convent of the Visitation, 198
conveyed, 278
Conway, 84, 166, 192, 267
Cook, 41, 104, 144, 155, 174, 210, 212
Cooke, 51, 90, 199, 267
Cookendorfer, 241
Cooley, 149
Coolidge, 135
Coombe, 40
Coombs, 40, 41, 63, 120, 250, 254, 315
Cooms, 84

Cooney, 218, 261
Cooper, 9, 57, 222, 250
Copeland, 284
Corbett, 139
Corbin, 34, 124, 239
Corby, 243
Corcoran, 41, 196, 231, 275
Corey, 154
Cornelius, 84
Corraway, 299
Correll, 118, 155
Cortin, 96
Corum, 132
corvette **Saratoga**, 299
Cosby, 252
Cosgrove, 54
Coste, 338
Costello, 200
Coster, 56
Costigan, 40, 95, 123
Cottage View, 329
Coulter, 6, 103
Coumbe, 40
Covington, 279
Coward, 119
Cowing, 125
Cowling, 111
Cox, 2, 41, 85, 94, 101, 110, 115, 130, 162, 164, 242, 280, 283, 317, 320, 337
Coxe, 11, 17, 33, 41, 138, 158, 166, 187, 327
Coyle, 41, 65, 88, 96, 152, 156, 315
Cozzens, 125
Cozzey, 192
Crabbe, 9
Cracroft, 303
Cradlebaugh, 72, 129
Craft, 309
Cragg, 40
Cragin, 41
Craig, 90, 120, 138, 210, 211, 237, 335
Craige, 83
Craigen, 268
Crain, 50

Crampton, 134
Cranch, 41, 53, 167
Crane, 23, 205
Cranfield, 294
Cranford, 273
Cranfurd, 289
Cranshaw, 70
Cravan, 76
Craven, 39, 41, 140, 158
Crawford, 41, 53, 78, 97, 100, 198, 248, 296, 313
Crawley, 180
Crealock, 209
Crenshaw, 91, 170
Cripps, 41
Crittendens, 136
Crocker, 96, 167, 291, 335
Crockett, 92
Crofts, 208
Croggon, 27, 79
Croly, 327
Crombies, 174
Cronans, 110
Cronkright, 103
Crooks, 13
Cropley, 251, 272
Crosby, 62, 118, 145, 160, 316
Cross, 22, 98, 113, 170, 299
Cross Roads, 1
Crossfield, 12
Crossman, 141
Croukright, 157
Crow, 328
Crowe, 22, 192
Crowley, 78, 108, 218, 259
Crown, 21, 40, 62, 91
Crozier, 191
Cruger, 327
Cruit, 22, 60
Crum, 83, 144, 176
Crump, 161, 171, 186, 194, 237
Crutchet, 40
Cudmore, 40
Cull, 41, 57
Cull, 123
Cullen, 147

Cullinane, 333
Culpeper, 73
Culver, 102
Culver's Chance, 1
Cumberland, 57
Cummin, 126
Cumming, 273
Cummings, 111, 254
Cummins, 133, 285
Cunningham, 14, 53, 63, 100, 108, 143, 252, 287
Curlee, 205
Curran, 206
Curry, 321
Curtis, 26, 135, 325
Cushing, 275
Cushings, 298
Cushley, 40
Cusick, 299
Cutter, 100
cutter **Daring**, 70
cutter **William Aiken**, 338
Cutting, 263
Cuvillier, 262, 263

D

d'Antrive, 119
D'Ouville, 230
Dabbs, 264
Dabney, 135, 307, 334
Daggey, 44
Dailey, 27, 173, 306
Dainese, 25, 41, 99, 194, 237, 240
Daingerfield, 111, 200, 288
Dale, 57
Daley, 41
Dallas, 206, 207
Dalno, 65
Dalton, 27, 41
Daly, 51, 96, 155
Damon, 141
Damrell, 25, 155
Dana, 90, 133, 299
Dangerfield, 218
Daniel, 167
Daniels, 226

Dann, 294
Dant, 41, 63
Dardenne, 3, 25, 99, 119
Darnes, 254
Darrell, 195, 254
Darsman, 155
Dart, 67, 109, 118, 121, 175, 194, 237
Dashiells, 230
Dashu, 182
Davenport, 30, 146, 267
David, 123
Davidge, 40, 233, 262, 274
Davidson, 2, 37, 41, 63, 153, 172, 184, 274, 295, 332
Davis, 5, 11, 22, 30, 41, 56, 57, 79, 81, 84, 87, 99, 109, 115, 119, 123, 127, 141, 151, 160, 175, 184, 201, 212, 226, 231, 249, 262, 315, 320, 321
Davison, 2
Daw, 57
Dawes, 2, 3, 53, 167
Dawson, 94, 138, 223
Day, 51, 93, 94, 120, 154, 176, 193, 216, 237
Dayton, 41
de Arguello, 194, 235
de Berlichingen, 267
de Bille, 333
De Bodisco, 165
de Bonne, 19, 99, 194
De Bow, 253
De Boye, 250
De Coursey, 63
De Groot, 34, 93, 159, 176, 194, 235
De Grost, 156
De Haven, 178
de Klyn, 100
de Leon, 296
de Llorente, 21
de Luchet, 72
De May, 109, 161, 181
De Monthurry, 292
De Nemegyei, 248
de Prilly, 32

de Quincey, 21
de Repentigny, 19, 99, 194
De Sauls, 260
De Treville, 100
de Villamont, 109
de Visser, 4, 75, 125
de Waldegg, 188
De Wolf, 294
Deal, 63
Deale, 66
Dearing, 9, 330
Dearman, 141
Deasey, 41
Deatherage, 31, 118, 160
DeCamp, 221
Decatur, 41, 218, 257
Deeth, 37, 97, 155
DeForest, 200
DeGriffin, 173
DeGroot, 326
Deitrich, 49
DeKrafft, 269, 270, 274
Delafield, 186
Delaney, 96
Delany, 60
Delarue, 267
Delaus, 96
Delaway, 4
Delk, 157
Dellaway, 283
Dellett, 215
Delmas, 155
Delvigne, 111
Demidoff, 205
Deming, 316
Denham, 42, 151
Denhan, 240
Dennier, 19
Dennis, 333
Denny, 109
Denslow, 316
Dent, 14, 281, 316
Depau, 55
Depro, 323
Derby, 16
Dermott, 244, 264, 280

Derrick, 62, 118, 282
Derringer, 142
Dersus, 169
DeSelding, 41
Deter, 41
Devere, 106
Devereux, 101, 174
Devers, 42
Devillers, 41
Devine, 21, 56
Devlin, 336
Devroux, 64
Dewall, 199
Dewees, 42
Dewey, 41, 243, 326
Dewitt, 154
Dewlin, 51
Dice, 330
Dick, 41
Dickens, 34, 118
Dickins, 184
Dickinson, 97, 212
Dickson, 84
Didier, 266
Diehl, 11, 119
Dietz, 218
Digges, 90, 131, 140, 253, 256, 273
Diliard, 141
Dillard, 144
Diller, 87
Dillingham, 9
Dillon, 191, 212
Dimmick, 155
Dimock, 66
Dimon, 143
Dinsmoor, 73
Dinwiddie, 34
Disharoon, 82, 160
Ditrez, 185
Ditty, 326
Divine, 91, 127
Dixon, 41, 76, 100, 109, 156, 163, 176, 193, 281, 304
Dobbin, 26, 63, 80, 153
Dobbins, 90, 319
Dobson, 41, 65

Dochterman, 221
Dock, 309
Dodd, 155
Dodds, 299
Dodge, 41, 112, 175, 330, 332
Dodson, 230, 275
Doebler, 76, 119, 176, 194
Doebles, 134
Dolan, 68
Doland, 119
Dole, 79
Dolet, 134, 140
Dolley, 84
Domas, 204
Domber, 81
Domingues, 204
Donahue, 333
Donaldson, 58, 228
Donalson, 63
Donegan, 204
Donelan, 42
Donelly, 201
Doniphan, 41, 42
Donn, 41, 44, 57, 78, 131, 143, 220
Donoghue, 34, 137, 214, 249
Donogue, 29
Donoho, 41, 55, 58, 151, 163
Donohoo, 55, 63, 136
Donohue, 299
Donovan, 224
Dooley, 63, 207
Doolittle, 177
Dorland, 142
Dorman, 95
Dornin, 186
Dorr, 52, 89, 123, 248
Dorsey, 6, 81, 148, 241, 280, 282
Doswell, 267
Doty, 170, 174
Doug, 130
Dougherty, 92, 104, 207, 221, 308
Douglas, 20, 41, 140, 172, 217, 226, 242, 261, 293, 295, 296
Douglass, 57, 109, 132, 141, 230
Dousman, 110, 162
Dove, 41, 55, 63, 286

Dowling, 35, 39, 41, 56, 123, 128, 151, 164, 174, 186, 203, 249, 260, 321
Downes, 96
Downey, 74, 140
Downing, 12, 41, 65, 197
Downs, 41, 233
Dozier, 95
Dr of Divinity, 253
Draper, 36, 100
Drew, 138
Driehaus, 116
Driggs, 138
Driscoll, 137, 192
Drose, 22
Drury, 41, 57, 78, 187, 272, 331
Druses, 213
Du Closel, 76
Dubois, 6, 72
Duddy, 18
Dudley, 16, 65, 140, 148, 155
Dufair, 51
Duffield, 95, 227
Duffy, 240
Dufour, 55
Duhamel, 56
Duke of Norfolk, 327
Duke of Richmond, 296
Dulaney, 41
Duley, 21, 69, 198
Dulin, 12
Dumbarton, 117
Dumm, 101
Dummer, 232, 240
Dunbar, 15
Duncan, 37, 54, 129, 207, 287
Duncanson, 178, 202, 265
Dunham, 23, 109
Dunivan, 221
Dunlop, 34, 71
Dunn, 29, 34
Dunnawin, 56
Dunning, 100, 114, 160, 183, 285
Dunnington, 55, 272
Dunton, 65
Durant, 155

Durat, 312
Durden, 276
Durham, 91, 128, 175
Durkee, 107, 127
Durr, 41
Dutton, 41, 65
Duval, 324
Duvall, 31, 34, 41, 92, 109, 151, 192, 265, 284
Duvalt, 322
Dwight, 172
Dwyer, 63, 64, 98, 230
Dye, 140
Dyer, 11, 41, 68, 74, 105, 108, 140, 151, 170, 187, 320
Dykes, 267, 268
Dyneley, 215
Dyser, 8

E

Earhart, 167
Earl, 64
Earl of Aberdeen, 335
Earl of Arundel & Surrey, 327
Earl of Spencer, 324
Earl of Stafford, 215
Early, 18, 211, 233
Earnest, 252, 279
Easby, 42, 90, 113, 189, 190, 210, 212
Eastlack, 81
Eastman, 70, 99
Easton, 103
Eaton, 54, 76, 93, 112, 141, 143, 158
Eavitt, 154
Eberling, 92, 139
Ebert, 327
Eccleston, 301, 311
Eckel, 283
Eckerson, 54
Eckington, 217, 219
Ecklof, 42
Eckloff, 18, 58
Eddy, 72, 100, 160, 173, 247
Edelen, 32, 51, 247, 253, 282
Edelin, 34, 42, 58, 68, 291

Edes, 42, 92, 177
Edmesnil, 28
Edmond's Frolick, 278
Edmonston, 56, 241
Edward VI, 60
Edwards, 3, 6, 8, 13, 31, 42, 58, 62, 66, 67, 74, 84, 93, 109, 118, 122, 123, 135, 140, 147, 149, 152, 155, 172, 191, 193, 210, 229, 235, 279, 280, 297
Effinger, 84, 163
Egan, 203
egg-nogg, 4
Egleston, 35
Ehle, 126
Ehrmantrout, 174
Einolf, 7
Ela, 152
Elder, 73
Elfe, 141
Elgin, 209
Eliason, 221
Eliot, 217
Elisha, 5, 74, 126, 193
Ellicott's Mills, 15
Elliot, 158
Elliott, 42, 109, 119, 141, 155, 157, 160, 169, 193, 234
Ellis, 24, 82, 108, 139, 159, 320, 326
Ellsworth, 316
Elmore, 19, 330
Elms, 226
Elmsley, 298
Elvans, 42
Elwood, 63
Ely, 54, 128, 238
Emerson, 100, 151
Emery, 305
Emm, 298
Emmerson, 42, 59
Emmert, 33
Emnson, 126
Emory, 146
Encyclopedia Britannica, 229
England, 250
Engleman, 322

Englesby, 51
English, 31, 78, 244, 252
English Nobility, 225
Englison, 192
Ennis, 8, 42, 151, 261
Enos, 130
Entwisle, 13, 90
Entwistle, 315
Enyatten, 269
Erickson, 141
Ericsson, 34
Erskine, 139
Escobar, 207
Esputa, 113
Espy, 23, 26, 64, 187
Essex, 13
Estes, 130
Estrange, 206
Etchison, 84
Etting, 19, 75, 93, 155
Euston, 106
Evan, 96
Evans, 13, 36, 42, 64, 65, 100, 109, 118, 125, 155, 165, 207, 227, 240, 249, 258, 294
Everett, 206, 207, 269
Everetts, 21
Eviston, 256
Ewell, 42
Ewer, 97
Exchange, 1

F

Faber, 42
Fagan, 42
Faherty, 57
Fairbanks, 112, 175, 330
Fairfax, 196, 229
Fairfield, 118, 121
family of Geo Washington, 324
Fanning, 58
Fant, 140, 151, 156, 194, 318
Farley Vale, 239
Farlock, 94
Farmer, 51
Farnham, 269, 334

Farnum, 148
Farquhar, 42, 71, 331
Farragut, 87, 149
Farrar, 94, 319, 327
Farrell, 42, 296, 317
Farren, 23, 192
Farrow, 150, 188, 197, 313
Father of his Country, 181
Faulkner, 28, 260
Fauquier White Sulphur Springs, 149
Favier, 33
Fearson, 8, 42, 315
Featherson, 9
Featherston, 70, 140
Febrey, 3
Federal Orrery, 249
Fedler, 100
Fellius, 227
Fellows, 258
Felsom, 42
Felton, 206, 217
Fendall, 49, 137, 144
Fenelow, 149
Fenno, 42
Fenwick, 111, 257
Ferguson, 42, 64, 94, 100, 126, 179, 252, 263
Ferier, 331
Ferrel, 8
Ferrell, 230
Ferry, 93, 215
Fessel, 278
Fetter, 102
Field, 20, 81
Fields, 53, 293
Figaro, 58
Files, 94
Filius, 201
Fillebrown, 35, 93, 118, 120, 194, 235
Fillmore, 244, 246, 272, 306
Finch, 42, 148
Finckel, 87, 302
Findlay, 215
Finkel, 153

Finley, 270, 317
Fischer, 42, 85
Fish, 245
Fisher, 21, 42, 55, 68, 78, 81, 91, 99, 110, 125, 139, 194, 203, 219
Fiske, 260
Fitch, 304
Fitzgerald, 33, 35, 42, 59, 83, 152, 155, 261, 267
Fitzpatrick, 34, 118, 130
flag ship **Washington, 74**, 281
Flaherty, 63, 181, 224
Flanagan, 115
Flat Grounds, 219
Fleet, 139
Fleischell, 151
Fleming, 64, 262
Flemming, 79, 82, 100
Flenner, 292
Fletcher, 42, 60, 136, 196, 215
Fleury, 189
Flint, 68
Flood, 78, 151, 163, 187
Florence, 53, 315
Flowers, 185, 261
Floyd, 54, 59, 93, 182, 286, 334, 337
Fluper, 335
Flynn, 229
Foley, 42, 222
Follanabee, 44
Follen, 32
Foller, 85
Follett, 228
Folsom, 315
Folson, 160
Foot, 93, 98, 99
Foote, 102
Force, 18, 57, 214, 243
Ford, 56, 81, 94, 326
Foreman, 73, 129
Forrest, 42, 64, 99, 162, 173, 228, 233
Forrest Hall, 145
Forrester, 93
Forsyth, 55, 114, 211, 276, 299
Fort, 57, 167

Fort Chadbourne, 245
Fort Columbus, 245
Fort Defiance, 301
Fort Dodge, 303
Fort Erie, 239
Fort Fillmore, 245
Fort Kearny, 300, 303
Fort Laramie, 238, 245
Fort Leavenworth, 245
Fort Mackinac, 245
Fort McHenry, 97
Fort Monroe, 245, 254, 317
Fort Moultrie, 257, 336, 338
Fort Mountrie, 245
Fort Niagara, 227
Fort Norfolk, 320
Fort Ridgely, 23, 245
Fort Ripley, 245
Fort Smith, 77, 111, 215, 236, 274
Fort Steilacoom, 245
Fort Sumter, 336, 338
Fort Union, 245
Fort Vancouver, 245
Fort Washita, 236, 245
Foster, 12, 126, 280, 297, 310, 336
Foulkes, 107
Fountain Rock, 266
Fournet, 204
Fowke, 42
Fowle, 10, 13, 88, 305
Fowler, 24, 42, 63, 123, 152, 233, 260, 269
Fox, 14, 100, 127, 160, 272
Foxwell, 50
Foy, 42, 262
Frame, 59
Francisco, 298
Franklin, 118, 124, 188, 253, 303
Frantz, 2
Franzonie, 42
Fraser, 42, 125
Frazee, 73, 100, 119, 236
Frazer, 13, 66, 247
Frazier, 42
Frazure, 293
Free Mason, 217

Freeman, 42, 153, 186, 189, 204, 208, 314, 315, 326
Fremont, 7, 54, 231
French, 42, 49, 104, 151, 176, 181, 206, 236, 245, 249, 305
Frere, 10, 42, 131, 220
Fricker, 73
Fridler, 35
Fridley, 63, 125, 141, 157, 194, 234
Friend, 46, 267
Friendship, 96
Frierick, 33, 66
frig **Congress**, 234
frig **Java**, 281
frig **Philadelphia**, 109
frig **Princeton**, 127
frig **Savannah**, 158
Frincks, 200
Frink, 170, 293
Frisbee, 100
Frisby, 97
Frishie, 93
Frizzel, 133
Frost, 18, 75, 93, 239, 264
Fry, 42
Frye, 44, 311
Fryer, 134
Fugett, 165
Fugitt, 42, 191, 212, 228
Fuller, 93, 156, 162, 194, 294, 335
Fulmer, 24, 42, 63
Fulsom, 100
Fuss, 42

G

Gaddis, 151
Gadsby, 42, 45, 69, 165
Gage, 54, 256, 329
Gaines, 77
Gaither estate, 1
Galbraith, 23, 186, 251
Gale, 100, 159
Gales, 67, 162, 217, 219, 243, 263, 322
Gallaher, 35, 259, 287
Gallant, 42, 43, 57, 227

Gallaudet, 135
Gallaway, 121
Galligan, 32, 42, 79
Galloway, 13, 235
Galt, 142, 187, 257, 290, 309
Gamble, 259
Gants, 212
Gantt, 248, 280, 326
Gardener, 163
Gardiner, 4, 56, 78, 227, 240
Gardner, 42, 84, 100, 269
Garland, 195, 242, 263, 273, 276
Garmbo, 169
Garner, 42, 85, 98, 114, 130, 163, 293, 320
Garnes, 259
Garnett, 131, 224
Garret, 317
Garretson, 123
Garrett, 42, 278, 282
Garrison, 138, 166, 205
Garrott, 330
Garth, 256, 282
Gartland, 227
Gartrell, 197
Garvey, 168
Gas Light Co in D C, 109
Gates, 11, 38, 56, 57, 102, 158, 182
Gaughran, 63
Gaylord, 62
Gear, 245
Geary, 14
Geddes, 57
Gedney, 13, 42, 66, 118
Gee, 184
Geiger, 13, 18, 73, 100, 119, 236
Geisinger, 82
Gelston, 42
Genand, 149
Genevre, 35
Gerecke, 42, 219, 242, 244, 247
Gerecks, 42
Gerrard, 9
Gettings' Cross Roads, 1
Ghee, 184
Gholson, 237

Gibbes, 302
Gibbons, 42, 167
Gibbs, 93, 130
Gibson, 8, 11, 42, 48, 93, 141, 166, 187, 193, 197, 235, 327
Giddings, 196
Gideon, 40, 72, 203, 315
Giesborough Manor, 50
Gilbert, 84, 278
Gilkeson, 106
Gill, 58, 64
Gillett, 186
Gilliam, 274
Gillis, 42, 127, 150, 153, 317
Gilliss, 77, 138
Gillium, 94
Gilmer, 330
Gilmore, 171
Gilpin, 28, 30, 36
Ginnaty, 58, 88
Ginsta, 286
Gittings, 151
Given, 56
Gladman, 42
Glascow, 183
Glasgow, 53, 100, 160
Glass, 184
Glavesveck, 119
Glawecke, 34
Glaze, 209
Gleason, 63
Glen May, 159
Glendy, 161
Glenville, 131
Glover, 61, 65, 69, 107, 311
Glynn, 105, 182
Gobright, 72, 80
Goddard, 18, 43, 57, 63, 210
Godfrey, 42
Godwin, 316
Godwyn, 60
Goff, 29, 118, 130, 154, 178, 193, 194
Goggin, 65
Goheens, 42
Goit, 278

Gold, 307
gold vein, 17
Golden, 299
Golder, 174
Goldsborough, 44, 111, 180, 311, 328
Goldsmith, 18, 78, 82
Gonor, 122
Gonzaga College, 223, 247
Gooch, 42
Goodale, 53
Goodell, 247
Goodman, 282
Goodnow, 54
Goodrich, 71, 93, 151, 174
Goods, 230
Goodsell, 103, 152
Goodson, 253
Goodspeed, 109
Goodwin, 316
Goodwood, 296
Goodyear, 202
Goold, 262
Gordon, 42, 67, 109, 111, 138, 197, 267, 281, 289, 316, 319, 323
Gore, 254
Gorham, 291
Gorin, 212
Gorman, 72, 138, 140, 166
Gormley, 6, 7, 211
Gormly, 58
Goss, 53, 91
Gosselin, 76
Gotterill, 268
Gouge, 214
Gough, 246, 296
Gouldin, 7
Gouverneur, 14, 88, 151
Gower, 160
Gowland, 25, 73
Grace Church, 310
Graham, 11, 29, 60, 93, 94, 106, 117, 147, 148, 154, 218, 227, 247, 254, 331, 332
Grainger, 209
Grammer, 13, 42, 156

Grampp, 169
Granberry, 222
Granby, 95, 161, 175, 193, 267, 282
Grandin, 84
Granger, 132, 134, 192
Grant, 35, 63, 107, 123, 124, 137, 233
Granville, 265
Graves, 42, 173
Gray, 20, 31, 42, 99, 148, 156, 176, 187, 191, 194, 305
Grayson, 27
Green, 12, 42, 52, 109, 115, 119, 154, 171, 174, 214, 219, 232, 262, 264, 294, 308
Green Yagers, 254
Greenan, 42
Greenbarth, 55
Greene, 79, 123, 154
Greenhow, 120
Greenland, 148
Greenleaf, 42, 124
Greenough, 249
Greentrup, 150, 165
Greenway, 101
Greenway Court, 196
Greenwell, 43
Greenwood, 14, 214, 217, 219, 230
Greenwood Park Enlarged, 50
Greeves, 42, 284
Gregg, 73
Gregory, 128, 228, 310
Greitzner, 130
Gresk, 178
Grier, 251, 316
Griffin, 50, 64, 146, 221, 232
Griffith, 261, 298, 306
Grignon, 112, 169, 180, 193
Grimshaw, 233
Grinnell, 207
Grist, 277
Griswold, 68
Gritzner, 75, 89, 121, 170, 194, 234
Groenvelt, 42
Groff, 42
Gros, 209

Groshon, 272
Gross, 229
Grubb, 62, 63, 118
Gruner, 243
Grymes, 42, 57
Gtwn College, 216
Guelich, 276
Guest, 42
Guild, 16
Guillory, 76, 119, 134, 176, 193
Gulls, 14
Gunnell, 42, 43, 66, 114, 118, 130, 141, 303
Gunsally, 3, 35, 118, 155
Gunton, 42, 43, 206, 315
Gurley, 30, 109, 123, 160, 293, 297, 298, 306, 313
Gushee, 253
Guthrie, 35, 140, 195, 212, 299
Guy, 246
Guy's Monument House, 246
Gwinn, 55

H

Habersham, 157
Hacatts, 145
Haddock, 61, 160
Haden, 161, 183
Hagan, 305
Hager, 43, 62
Hagerty, 62, 63, 139
Hagger, 297
Haggerty, 43
Hagie, 11, 146
Hagner, 127
Hail, 192
Haldeman, 317
Hale, 58, 330
Haliday, 39, 55
Hall, 13, 25, 36, 43, 76, 78, 93, 94, 100, 102, 109, 114, 119, 126, 128, 137, 148, 149, 171, 173, 185, 187, 191, 205, 227, 232, 249, 276, 288, 291, 293, 314, 315, 316, 326
Halleck, 246
Hallett, 172, 176

Halley, 157
Hallock, 29
Hallowell, 81, 250
Hamilton, 43, 49, 50, 83, 84, 100, 114, 117, 137, 160, 183, 195, 214, 247, 253, 261, 284, 286, 305, 309, 323
Hamlin, 240, 246, 247, 269, 304
Hammack, 153
Hammett, 291
Hammond, 21, 45, 312, 323
Hamtramck, 30
Hancock, 147
Hand, 260
Handy, 43, 124
Haney, 43
Hanna, 43, 66
Hannah, 266
Hannah More Academy, 233
Hannan, 251
Hannay, 43
Hansbrough, 150, 188, 197
Hanscomb, 67, 76, 109, 156, 194
Hansell, 67, 76, 119, 127, 176, 194, 237
Hanson, 43, 63, 77, 94, 156, 248, 319
Happy Home, 208
Harbaugh, 56, 189, 208, 315, 317
Harbin, 168
Harbison, 73
Harburger, 206
Hardeman, 211
Harden, 97, 142, 199, 204, 219
Hardenbergh, 136
Hardesty, 20, 119
Hardin, 158
Hardinge, 296
Hardwicke, 193, 299
Hardwickes, 193
Hare, 89, 115, 151, 155, 161
Harkins, 160
Harkness, 60, 317, 335
Harman, 244
Harmon, 138
Harney, 260

358

Harper, 43, 73, 81, 98, 101, 119
Harper's Ferry, 19, 21, 53, 89, 101, 259, 278
Harpers Ferry, 78
Harrell, 92
Harrington, 89, 126, 186
Harriot, 104
Harris, 22, 26, 31, 75, 87, 93, 126, 139, 149, 154, 155, 157, 194, 213, 217, 245, 252, 271, 332
Harrison, 34, 38, 43, 67, 71, 79, 109, 141, 186, 197, 258, 263, 310
Harrold, 248
Harrover, 58, 63, 244
Harry, 95, 101
Harstoff, 331
Hart, 50
Harten, 201
Hartnell, 91
Hartstene, 35, 58, 100, 194, 239
Hartsuff, 322, 329, 333
Hartt, 328
Hartung, 280
Harvey, 31, 64, 157, 215, 328
Haskell, 58
Haskin, 182
Haskins, 257, 266
Haslup, 43
Hass, 88
Hassan, 9
Hassler, 9, 41, 82, 212, 274
Hastings, 28, 99, 184, 326
Hatch, 299
Hatcher, 221
Hatfield, 178
Hatton, 43, 305
Hatwood, 97
Haughton, 208, 277
Haun, 201, 205
Havenner, 43, 60, 232
Haw, 6, 43, 52, 321
Hawke, 35, 43
Hawkes, 76, 119, 121, 193, 297
Hawkins, 21, 69, 169
Hawks, 61, 87
Hax_ll, 301

Hay, 280
Hayden, 100, 109, 242, 299
Hayes, 61, 93, 119, 161, 175, 193, 206, 299, 304, 335
Hayman, 2
Hayne, 24, 272
Haynes, 173
Haynie, 160
Hays, 109, 163, 183, 319, 329, 331
Hazard, 162, 220, 221
Hazel, 226
Hazlehurst, 15
Hazlett, 53, 184
Hazlitt, 92
Hazzard, 141
Health report, 214
Health Report, 18
Heanna, 155
Heap, 37
Heard, 50, 126
Hearmand, 32
Heath, 135
Heaton, 123
Hebb, 242
Heebner, 102
Heffern, 108
Heileman, 90, 310
Heimler, 207
Heine, 43
Heineman, 24
Heiner, 145
Heintzleman, 94
Heisinger, 188
Heiskell, 43
Heiss, 63
Heitmiller, 139, 224
Hellen, 262, 264
Helmer, 126
Hemmerdinger, 66
Henderson, 43, 55, 81, 90, 99, 100, 104, 117, 131, 156, 157, 165, 175, 220, 252, 310
Henkle, 101
Henley, 162
Henning, 43, 47, 286
Henry, 43, 55, 68, 83, 129, 161, 184

Henry II, 130
Henry VIII, 60
Hensley, 29, 79, 115, 122, 170, 194, 195, 235
Hepburn, 137
Herbert, 43, 78
Herity, 43
Herney, 199
Herrell, 43
Herrick, 53, 194
Herring, 84
Herron, 210, 212, 321
Herskell, 39
Hertnee, 178
Hetzel, 43
Heudebert, 72
Hewett, 259
Hewson, 6
Hezekiah, 43
Hibbs, 36
Hickey, 43, 243
Hickman, 92, 160, 203, 280
Hicks, 6, 43, 119, 158, 170, 173, 184, 185, 203, 211, 323, 329
Higbee, 43
Higdon, 30, 227
Higgins, 126, 140, 176, 193, 209
Highlands, 296
Hight, 305
Higntt, 258
Hignutt, 76
Hilbus, 63, 316
Hildreth, 160
Hill, 10, 32, 43, 50, 71, 100, 108, 112, 130, 147, 176, 207, 267, 278, 279, 301, 317, 325
Hill View, 242
Hillery, 245
Hillyard, 63
Hillyer, 252
Hilton, 55, 100, 121
Hinds, 221
Hines, 43, 212, 220
Hinton, 43, 77, 151
Historical Society of New Mexico, 27

Historical Society of Va, 266
Hitchcock, 119
Hitchings, 291
Hite, 51
Hittmann, 75
Hitz, 8, 57
Hoard, 144
Hoban, 43, 207
Hobart, 254
Hobbie, 43, 212, 299
Hobbs, 11, 160, 257
Hocaday, 126
Hockaday, 109, 172, 194
Hockey, 234
Hockie, 119
Hodesty, 126
Hodge, 155
Hodges, 9, 80, 130, 217
Hodgson, 63
Hodson, 105
Hoffman, 43, 224, 271
Hogan, 43, 138, 333
Hoge, 186, 242
Holbrook, 252
Holcomb, 9, 80, 252
Holden, 4, 272, 284
Holgate, 66
Holland, 43, 73, 151, 187
Holliday, 51, 68, 180, 247, 282
Hollidge, 43
Hollingshead, 43, 187
Hollohan, 43, 72
Holmead, 182, 185, 315, 323
Holmead estate, 307
Holmes, 170, 175, 188, 238
Holston, 73
Holston Springs, 179
Holt, 111, 239
Holtzman, 62
Homan, 29
Homes, 100
Honeyville, 158
Hood, 91
Hooe, 158
Hoofnagle, 63
Hook, 65, 70, 127, 149, 224

Hoole, 186
Hooper, 107
Hooten, 93, 141
Hooter, 182
Hoover, 27, 37, 136, 282, 283, 315
Hope, 151, 160, 161
Hopkins, 7, 10, 43, 242, 261, 330
Hopper, 93, 112, 126, 141, 169
Horner, 93
Horr, 112
Horseman, 43
Hort, 328
Horton, 217
Hortz, 94
Horwitz, 207
Hosmer, 291
Hough, 63
Houghton, 327
Hougland, 73
Houmas, 102
House, 75, 93, 193
Houston, 26, 178, 215, 251, 264, 279, 317
Houzam, 43
Howard, 9, 18, 27, 43, 49, 67, 81, 107, 116, 118, 126, 155, 175, 216, 286, 298
Howe, 43, 53, 93, 141, 242, 255
Howell, 3, 145, 253
Howle, 104
Howlett, 233
Hoxie, 170
Hoyle, 29
Hoyt, 100, 160, 183, 207
Hubbard, 109, 256
Hubbell, 174, 330
Hudgin, 149
Hudry, 9, 149
Hudson, 91, 166, 192, 194, 195
Huertes, 53
Hugeunot, 279
Huggeford, 155
Huggins, 145
Hughes, 5, 21, 30, 43, 62, 95, 118, 155, 189, 200, 210, 253, 257
Hull, 120, 125, 177

Humber, 23, 71, 140, 184
Hume, 208
Humes, 43, 140
Humphrey, 115, 119
Humphreys, 71, 109, 139, 241, 280
Humphries, 43
Hungerford, 123, 134, 171
Hunt, 23, 43, 72, 83, 110, 119, 130, 193, 194, 326, 335
Hunter, 144, 163, 194, 240, 317
Huntington, 251
Huntley, 126
Hunton, 157, 166
Huntoon, 258
Hurdle, 78, 211
Hurlehy, 63
Hurley, 323
Hurtt, 216
Hussey, 19, 228
Hutchins, 75, 100, 168, 173, 193
Hutchinson, 43, 64, 93, 142, 147, 151, 160, 161
Huter, 112
Hutman, 120
Huttman, 17, 170, 194
Huttmann, 38, 93, 118
Huyck, 295
Hyam, 9, 12
Hyams, 189
Hyatt, 171, 320
Hyde, 43, 137, 178, 190
Hygeia Hotel, 164

I

Iardella, 43
Ihrie, 65, 89
Indermauer, 43
Indian Queen, 288
Indian tribes, 16
Ingersoll, 37, 38, 78, 246
Ingle, 33, 43, 56, 78, 110, 131, 178, 233, 262, 264, 271, 280, 286, 293
Ingleside, 309
Inglis, 21
Ingraham, 254, 265, 333
Ingram, 66, 284

Irby, 70
Ironside, 57
Irving, 1, 117, 211
Irwin, 4, 304, 314, 327
Isaacs, 43
Isham, 316
Isherwood, 21, 69
Israel, 1
Ittig, 112
Iverson, 75, 302
Izard, 176, 183

J

Jack, 175
Jackalow, 269, 273
Jackson, 3, 12, 24, 43, 55, 56, 66, 71, 73, 77, 78, 80, 138, 155, 159, 161, 166, 183, 187, 190, 266, 267, 298, 305, 337
Jacobi, 43
Jacobs, 231, 298
Jader, 169
Jaloson, 81
James, 59, 195, 198, 212, 256, 267, 333
Jameson, 119, 227, 261
Jamison, 60, 208, 264
Janney, 107, 230
Jansoleil, 223
January, 119
Janvier, 276
Jardin, 33
Jarvis, 93, 158, 304
Javins, 81
Jay, 38
Jefferds, 201
Jefferies, 130
Jeffers, 307
Jefferson, 16
Jeffords, 201, 202, 217
Jeffrey, 299
Jellison, 184
Jenes, 43
Jenifer, 24
Jenkins, 43, 145, 158, 271, 327
Jenks, 315

Jennings, 82, 174, 286
Jernigan, 167
Jesup, 177, 182, 183, 200, 307
Jeter, 208
Jewell, 2, 22, 43, 164, 265, 308, 309
Jewett, 76, 228
Jillard, 78, 151
Joachim, 153
Joan of Arc, 214
John, 87
Johns, 133, 195, 253, 254
Johnson, 4, 18, 20, 34, 43, 51, 56, 66, 85, 93, 106, 108, 109, 111, 112, 118, 119, 128, 134, 136, 137, 141, 152, 154, 155, 158, 159, 169, 171, 173, 176, 177, 188, 192, 193, 194, 205, 217, 221, 226, 235, 238, 247, 259, 273, 275, 293, 294, 302, 303, 307, 314, 325
Johnston, 43, 76, 90, 137, 180, 194, 200, 285, 293, 305, 316, 326, 331
Johnstone, 76
Jolley, 100
Jonathan, 323
Jones, 7, 10, 21, 33, 43, 54, 56, 62, 66, 71, 84, 92, 93, 94, 98, 103, 105, 118, 125, 130, 136, 154, 155, 156, 160, 162, 165, 169, 170, 179, 187, 194, 212, 231, 238, 252, 264, 267, 270, 283, 310, 319, 333
Jordan, 43, 62, 94, 112, 173, 180, 298
Joseph, 16, 52
Josepha, 251
Josephs, 331
Joslyn, 126
Jost, 150, 162
Joyce, 155, 187
Judson, 38, 43, 62, 118, 160
Jullian, 99
Jump, 76, 258
Junot, 116

K

Kahelrt, 66
Kaighn, 24

Kalorama, 244
Kanary, 320
Kane, 44, 178, 186, 225, 294
Kaufman, 8, 78, 82, 153
Kay, 44
Kean, 298
Kearen, 44
Kearny, 331
Keating, 8, 44, 139
Kedglie, 44
Keech, 158
Keefe, 44
Keeley, 63
Keenan, 10, 92, 126
Kehrmann, 20
Keilholtz, 56
Keiser, 44
Keith, 83, 87, 212, 318
Keitt, 68, 79
Keleher, 145, 227
Kellar, 44
Keller, 65, 95
Kelley, 80
Kellogg, 195
Kelly, 44, 63, 64, 93, 145, 151, 211, 269, 285, 290
Kemp, 153
Kendall, 8, 44, 81, 127, 151, 186
Kendrick, 14
Kenmore, 263
Kennard, 64, 189, 200, 205, 293, 304, 305, 323
Kennedy, 15, 44, 51, 56, 60, 65, 109, 123, 150, 155, 200, 211
Kenny, 207
Kent, 17, 75, 100, 156, 194, 237
Kenyon, 140
Kephart, 209
Kepley, 96
Kerley, 96
Kerlin, 215
Kern, 23, 72
Kerr, 44, 100, 246, 260, 277
Kershaw, 302, 329
Kerwin, 28
Ketchum, 224

Key, 44, 108, 117, 310
Keys, 63, 86
Keyser, 234
Keyworth, 285
Kibbey, 44, 113, 176
Kicker, 155
Kidder, 190
Kidinski, 110
Kidwell, 39, 44, 64, 92, 187, 207, 212, 315
Kiernan, 44, 303
Kilby, 335
killed by telegraph, 300
Killmon, 331
Kimball, 174
Kimmel, 10
Kimmell, 94
Kincaid, 93
Kincheloe, 88
King, 10, 44, 58, 78, 95, 100, 112, 132, 137, 141, 161, 187, 189, 190, 200, 207, 252, 267, 274, 298
Kingman, 44
Kingsford, 239
Kinkead, 16
Kinny, 44
Kinsgley, 293
Kinsolver, 259
Kinsolving, 61, 200
Kinzer, 81, 158
Kirby, 102, 106, 334
Kirk, 24, 104, 134, 231, 305, 325
Kirkman, 79
Kirkpatrick, 128
Kirkwood, 212, 262
Kirtland, 287
Kirwin, 9
Kisselstein, 210, 212
Kissick, 67, 79, 127
Kleiber, 55
Klein, 133
Klier, 133
Klingaman, 154
Kloman, 110
Klopfer, 44, 55, 148, 315
Klopper, 86

Klotz, 224
Knaggs, 327
Knap, 53, 100, 125, 194
Knapp, 44, 47, 73, 105, 252
Kneller, 271
Knife, 144
Knight, 151, 160, 207, 242, 288
Knighthood, 232
Knights of Golden Circle, 120
Knott, 122, 293
Knowles, 44, 69, 71, 272, 294
Knox, 44
Kobbe, 276
Konig, 63
Koones, 44, 159, 271
Kozel, 44
Kraft, 63
Kraitsir, 151
Kramer, 84
Krebs, 87, 297
Kreemer, 64
Krouse, 228, 315
Kuezorwitch, 169
Kugler, 218, 291
Kunkle, 61
Kurtz, 2, 44, 243, 319
Kyle, 221, 328

L

La Grange, 226
La Reintrie, 61
La Vega, 155, 156
la Venture, 35
La_key, 284
Labaree, 205
Labarre, 80
Laborite, 76
Lacey, 32, 119, 127
Lacy, 76, 176, 194
Ladd, 44
Ladies Washington Nat'l Monument Society, 252
Laeffler, 165
Lafayette, 11, 146
Lafontaine, 44
Lakeman, 62

Lakemeyer, 167
Lamar, 1, 148
Lamb, 78, 130, 309
Lambell, 125
Lambert, 71, 207
Lammond, 159, 285
Lamson, 151
Lanahan, 84
Land, 115
Lander, 118
Landers, 152
Landes, 89
Landie, 63
Landman, 329
Landry, 76, 120, 134, 207
Landsdale, 9, 44
Landstreet, 84
Lane, 44, 210, 280
Laneghan, 240
Langdon, 67, 83, 94, 156, 195
Lanman, 93, 141, 154, 176, 193
Lansdale, 44, 80, 127
Larcombe, 63
Largo, 273
Larkin, 316
Larned, 100, 132, 313
Larner, 92, 187
Laskey, 55, 85, 209
Latham, 8, 56, 151, 277, 330
Lathrop, 98, 175
Latimer, 73
Latshaw, 184
Lauck, 123, 127
Laurenson, 25
Laurie, 322
Lausman, 337
Lavaille, 302
Lavalette, 154, 161
Lavender, 137
Laventure, 180
Laverty, 135
Lavonture, 112, 169, 193
Law, 44, 203
law of Scotland, 134
Lawman, 235
Lawrence, 65, 73, 207

Lawrenson, 59
Laws, 296
Lay, 38, 288, 318
Le Caze, 87, 187
Le Comte, 212
Le Roy, 114
Lea, 78
Leach, 32, 65, 84, 195
Leacock, 241
League, 328
Leak, 12, 93, 141, 193
Leaman, 133
Lear, 125
Learned, 102, 150
Leary, 10
Leavel, 271
Leavenworth, 14
Lee, 1, 26, 63, 72, 94, 106, 109, 116, 136, 161, 169, 185, 200, 228, 231, 266, 273
Leeds, 153
Leet, 273
Leete, 269
Leggett, 158, 242
Legrand, 145
Lehman, 292
Lehne, 319
Leipziger, 85
Leishear, 86
Leitch, 276
Lemon, 44, 84
Lenegham, 34
Lenhady, 324
Lenman, 44, 272, 276
Lennant, 273
Lennoy, 55
Lenox, 281
Leonard, 71
Leopole, 100
Leppes, 288
Lepps, 288
Leslie, 96, 105, 134, 297
Leuber, 211
Levi, 160, 202, 296
Levin, 89, 90, 105
Levy, 23, 62, 121

Lewis, 8, 17, 27, 44, 73, 78, 90, 151, 159, 168, 182, 187, 220, 267, 305, 315, 326
Lews, 27
Libbey, 5, 172, 329
Lichan, 291
Lieberman, 302
Liggit, 126, 172, 194
Lighter, 18
Lightfoot, 78, 315
Lilly, 170, 183
Lincoln, 44, 73, 176, 206, 240, 246, 269, 287, 298, 299, 300, 304, 306, 308, 325
Lindsay, 44, 59, 79, 154, 283, 299
Lindsey, 58, 159, 222
Lindsley, 44, 86, 148, 315
Lindsly, 78
Linkins, 44
Linn, 165, 170, 193, 194, 322
Linscott, 66
Linthicum, 2, 84, 257, 281
Linton, 128
Lints, 70, 140
Lippett, 73
Lipphardt, 234
Lippitt, 252
Little, 44, 121, 123
Littleton, 94
Livermore, 3, 28, 130, 217, 329
Livingston, 16, 18, 93, 100, 124, 141, 181, 186, 194, 205, 288
Livingstone, 20, 126
Lloyd, 1, 44, 58, 81, 85, 131, 141, 175, 227, 253, 295, 315, 326
Loch, 209
Locke, 55, 56
Lockwood, 44, 155
Loeffler, 295
Logan, 15, 157, 166, 221
Lohman, 297
Lomax, 44, 64, 221
Lombardi, 225
London Morning Chronicle, 206
Loney, 157
Long, 63, 168, 201, 212, 220, 252

Long Old Field, 318
Long Old Fields, 25, 32, 247
Longwood, 173
Lookingdill, 55
Loomis, 83, 112, 232
Lopez, 157, 166
Lord, 34, 70, 107, 109, 155, 296, 327
Loretto Springs, 167
Loughborough, 44, 115
Loughrey, 323
Louisette, 39
Love, 314
Lovejoy, 44, 57, 76
Lovelace, 166
Lovell, 178
Lovett, 161
Loving, 130
Lowe, 37, 187, 215, 225
Lowell, 249, 253
Lower, 44
Lowrie, 222
Lowry, 44
Loyd, 72
Lucas, 70, 120
Luce, 23, 44
Lucus, 119
Lucy, 96
Luddington, 299
Luggett, 109
Lumley, 139
Lumpkin, 44
Lumsden, 254, 256, 263, 286, 303
Luney, 63
Lunt, 44
Lutz, 317
Lycett, 44
Lyle, 167
Lyles, 315
Lyman, 3, 207
Lynch, 6, 12, 41, 44, 103, 133, 274, 285, 329
Lyon, 32, 100, 106, 156, 182
Lyons, 56, 57, 162, 197, 248, 327
Lysle, 100

M

Macalester, 36
Macaulay, 17
Maccaboy, 11, 62, 118
Macdonald, 312
Macgaw, 302
MacGowan, 112
Machen, 45
Macintosh, 169
Mack, 108
Mackall, 15, 80, 157
Mackle, 1
Mackubin, 185
Macleod, 312
Macnamara, 45
Macomb, 16, 44, 69, 83, 193
Macon, 227
MacPherson, 28
Macrae, 111
Macready, 135
Macy, 158
Madden, 76, 93, 96, 119
Maddin, 91, 161, 182
Maddox, 50, 53, 163, 193, 271
Maddux, 156
Mades, 150, 177
Madigan, 45, 299
Madison, 51, 83, 100, 107, 137
Magee, 4, 45, 310
Maggill, 14
Magill, 45
Magrath, 299
Magruder, 55, 61, 69, 84, 118, 140, 148, 164, 214, 265, 273, 284
Maguire, 54, 174, 227, 301
Mahan, 19
Maher, 68, 82, 92
Mahon, 230
Mahoney, 7, 326
Maid of Orleans, 214
Mailliard, 223
Maine, 174
Major, 102, 211, 313
Malbon, 210, 211
Malihan, 22
Malin, 155

Mallaby, 303
Mallet, 87, 187
Mallory, 103, 135, 252
Mallott, 256
Malone, 173, 225
Maltby, 12, 38, 102, 283
Malvin, 144
Manahan, 146
Mandeville, 155
Maniz, 44
Mankin, 45, 256
Manley, 186, 259
Mann, 65, 92, 151, 241, 249
Manning, 65, 163, 220, 229
Mansfield, 64, 274
Marble, 104, 141
Marbury, 2, 3, 132, 145, 148, 208, 217, 260, 282
Marcellus, 311
Marche, 8
Marion, 207
Marix, 243
Markell, 45
Markland, 44
Markle, 81
Marks, 285, 297
Markwood, 273
Marlow, 45, 164
Marmaduke, 126
Marnay, 76
Maron, 186
Marquis of Bute, 289
Marr, 45
marriages in the District of Columbia, 52
Marryman, 45
Marselis, 158
Marsh, 16, 119, 170, 175, 194, 237, 247, 324
Marshall, 21, 45, 69, 83, 120, 127, 174, 176, 193, 197, 208, 267, 268, 327
Marshall's Pavilion, 174
Marston, 61
Marten, 53

Martin, 4, 14, 40, 45, 56, 57, 64, 67, 76, 82, 96, 109, 112, 125, 140, 141, 143, 156, 160, 161, 168, 190, 193, 197, 212, 224, 241, 328, 336
Martindale, 136
Marx, 268
Maryman, 278
Masi, 9, 12, 184, 198
Masoletti, 45
Mason, 45, 53, 69, 71, 73, 93, 123, 138, 163, 174, 179, 191, 194, 198, 232, 238, 260, 279, 302, 310, 335
Massacre of Christians, 213
Massey, 81
Massie, 222, 246
Mather, 253
Mathews, 201, 204
Mathieson, 97
Mathiot, 47
Matlock, 99
Matthews, 93, 107, 231, 286, 321
Matthieson, 99
Mattingly, 34, 46, 187, 316
Maud, 45
Maude, 14, 226
Maughlin, 45
Maulden, 86
Maulsby, 103
Maultby, 154
Maury, 50, 60, 97, 117, 252, 310, 334
Maxcy, 45
Maxwell, 45, 90
May, 63, 115, 155, 156, 212, 228
Maynadier, 127
Maynard, 45
Mayo, 65, 73, 119, 135, 175, 188
Mays, 305
Mazeen, 43
McAleer, 24
McArann, 304
McBee, 45, 120, 164
McBlair, 69, 165
McCabe, 19
McCaffrey, 96
McCafray, 63

McCain, 64
McCalla, 45, 261
McCallie, 259
McCann, 317
McCartee, 76, 227, 258
McCarthy, 26, 44
McCarty, 45, 63, 245
McCathran, 245
McCauley, 84, 182, 256, 313, 326
McChesney, 315
McClellan, 283
McClelland, 108, 235
McClery, 15, 37, 59
McClintock, 94
McCloskey, 63
McClosky, 23
McCluney, 158
McClung, 150, 218
McClure, 9, 300
McCluskey, 319
McColgan, 187
McColloch, 311
McComb, 35, 75
McComber, 174
McConchie, 320
McConnel, 198
McConnell, 297
McCook, 320
McCord, 206
McCorkle, 44, 103
McCormick, 4, 45, 67, 81, 100, 102, 119, 171, 255
McCowns, 145
McCoy, 56, 129
McCrabb, 13, 75, 93, 161, 193, 234
McCraven, 75
McCuen, 63
McCullough, 12, 75, 100, 156, 193, 207
McCully, 126
McCune, 243
McCutchen, 330
McDaniel, 84, 126, 155
McDermott, 8, 57, 85, 96
McDonald, 44, 45, 152, 253, 266, 303, 309, 320, 330

McDowell, 45, 76, 119, 153
McElderry, 125
McEldery, 60
McEmmett, 174
McEndree, 197
McEnery, 264
McFarland, 5, 74, 140
McFerran, 93, 169, 182
McGagen, 145
McGarvey, 130
McGaulick, 331
McGee, 29, 192, 200, 260, 268
McGhan, 108
McGil_on, 40
McGill, 45, 202
McGinnis, 45, 58
McGlue, 131, 141, 220
McGowan, 130, 194
McGrann, 45, 63, 127
McGraw, 45
McGregor, 50, 98, 187, 188
McGuerin, 96
McGuire, 45, 63, 65, 171, 175, 208, 337
McGunnigle, 100
McHenry, 57, 111, 167
McIntire, 25, 33, 44, 88, 261, 305
McIntosh, 250, 257
McIntyre, 80, 126
McKaig, 275
McKee, 155
McKeever, 297
McKelden, 60, 84, 87, 88, 151
McKenna, 57
McKenne, 327
McKenney, 317
McKenny, 45
McKenzie, 81
McKim, 146
McKinley, 309, 321
McKissock, 146
McKnew, 57, 106
McKnight, 31, 45, 81, 109, 119, 194, 219, 239
McLain, 317, 320
McLane, 50, 101, 301, 306

McLaughlin, 15, 18, 88, 193, 207, 210, 211, 260, 300, 333
McLean, 26, 88, 227, 242, 259, 316
McLeod, 44, 53, 79, 145, 169, 207
McLeod, Alex'r, 44
McMahon, 83, 125, 254
McMann, 327
McMenany, 199
McMicken, 185
McMillan, 100, 160
McMullen, 202
McMurray, 259
McNair, 186, 221, 290
McNally, 263, 316
McNamara, 44, 58, 63, 163
McNamee, 131, 326
McNancy, 45
McNaughton, 169, 218, 224, 330
McNeal, 249
McNeel, 285
McNemar, 84
McNerhany, 55, 167
McNulty, 79
McPherson, 92, 99, 249
McPiers, 45
McQuiddy, 296
McRae, 63, 157, 163
McRay, 188
McRee, 108, 207
McRoberts, 189
McVeigh, 81, 138, 206
McVerry, 64
McVicker, 245
McWilliams, 45, 64, 211
Mead, 106
Meade, 12, 45, 75, 93, 110, 143, 188, 193, 236
Meador, 317
Meadow Grove, 153
Means, 109, 160, 181
Mebek, 80
Mechlin, 49, 149
Mecker, 93
Medley, 50
Meeker, 141
Meeks, 305

Meekum, 63
Mehrling, 225
Meigs, 61
Melville, 328
Melvin, 45, 232
Menzies, 112
Mercer, 198
Merchant, 100, 156, 180, 290, 333
Meredith, 45, 55, 169
Meridian Hill, 242
Merman, 45
Merriam, 49
Merrick, 10, 67, 122, 126, 179, 216, 231, 334
Merrill, 4, 21, 72, 86, 91, 118
Merritt, 259
Merriwether, 62
Merryman, 119, 198
Mersereau, 155
Merville, 109
Messiner, 187
Metzerott, 258
Metzger, 333
Meyer, 35, 309
Michel, 184, 204
Michie, 244
Mickum, 44, 45
Middleton, 44, 45, 78, 127, 148, 165, 187, 198, 225
Mignault, 76
Milam, 171
Milburn, 44, 45, 78, 151, 241
Miler, 9, 92
Miles, 13, 63, 70, 78, 168, 218
Millan, 175
Miller, 5, 44, 45, 48, 55, 57, 63, 66, 69, 76, 77, 78, 97, 100, 109, 112, 114, 119, 128, 154, 157, 162, 169, 187, 192, 206, 223, 232, 242, 247, 261, 290, 313, 315, 316, 337
Miller's Spring, 223
Millington, 70
Mills, 45, 66, 142, 144, 170, 254, 290, 293, 312, 317, 335
Miner, 86, 240, 315, 316
Minnegerode, 298

Minor, 187, 304
Mitchel, 28, 133, 281
Mitchell, 2, 11, 23, 29, 33, 44, 45, 52, 53, 103, 118, 141, 146, 177, 194, 228, 229, 236, 245, 248, 253, 257, 265, 275, 315
Mix, 14
Mohler, 45, 141
Mohoney, 6
Mohun, 45, 56, 78, 80, 178, 201, 202, 265
Moise, 99
Monell, 252
Money, 53, 118, 154
Monks, 74
Monroe, 68, 88, 107, 118, 141, 228, 269
Montford, 154
Montgomery, 71, 119, 125, 127, 140, 146, 170, 176, 191, 193, 211
Montgomey, 19
Montrose, 60
Monty, 119
Montyon, 279
Moody, 284
Moor, 4, 137
Moore, 14, 30, 44, 50, 55, 63, 100, 102, 119, 128, 130, 137, 160, 169, 174, 187, 211, 218, 227, 253, 262, 289, 293, 297, 316, 323, 325
Moors, 17, 19, 75, 112
Moran, 14, 45, 62, 212, 269, 304
Mordecai, 186, 326
Moreland, 133, 139
Morfit, 26, 135
Morgan, 14, 45, 55, 56, 58, 63, 70, 84, 85, 86, 101, 112, 114, 120, 130, 135, 168, 172, 176, 182, 187, 189, 221, 227, 244, 252, 286, 320
Morin, 70
Morley, 327
Morrill, 6
Morris, 64, 76, 100, 104, 107, 115, 123, 144, 193, 201, 219, 296
Morrison, 96, 213
Morriss, 267

Morrisses' Landing, 314
Morse, 15, 61, 106, 109, 119
Morsell, 2, 3, 138, 252, 330, 332
Morss, 77
Mortimer, 201
Morton, 45, 168, 219, 239, 270, 307
Moseley, 18, 75
Mosher, 45
Moshier, 93
Moss, 120, 174
Moss Neck, 239
Mother Abbess, 5
Mother Stanislaus, 286
Motley, 98, 211, 248
Mott, 138, 160, 166
Motzen, 123
Mount, 45, 303
Mount Air, 34, 291
Mount Airy, 294
Mount Hope lunatic asylum, 89
Mount Olivet Cemetery, 31, 133, 167, 171, 198
Mount Pleasant, 153, 154, 260
Mount Prospect, 5
Mount Vernon, 277
Mourks, 188
Mowatt, 121
Moxley, 44, 187, 212
Moylan, 127
Mudd, 30
Mullen, 63, 228
Muller, 63
Mulley, 56
Mullikin, 60
Mullin, 44
Mullins, 298
Mulloy, 45
Munck, 44
Mundy, 161
Munford, 268
Munroe, 336
Muntz, 200
Murdoch, 9
Murdock, 96
Mure, 133, 137
Murphey, 63

Murphy, 16, 45, 119, 153, 156, 248, 254, 337
Murray, 101, 114, 133, 170, 187, 227, 262, 264, 289, 291, 295, 298, 308, 311, 316
Muse, 168
Musgrave, 251
Musgrove, 276
Muster, 123
Myer, 31, 85, 120
Myerle, 34, 93, 109, 125, 154, 194, 237
Myers, 2, 10, 44, 61, 62, 108, 180

N

Nadal, 29
Nailor, 45
Nairn, 81, 270, 302
Nalley, 49, 126, 286, 320
Nally, 64
Napier, 74, 77
Napoleon, 111, 204, 318
Napoleon III, 62
Nash, 13, 62, 75, 93, 96, 315
Nason, 34, 70, 107, 109, 155
Nathensham, 5
Naudain, 164
Navarre, 115, 119
Naylor, 41, 45, 60, 79, 125, 292
Neagle, 65
Neal, 154, 157
Neale, 179, 207
Needwood, 151
Neill, 229
Neilson, 109, 313, 315, 322
Nelson, 20, 45, 103, 178, 191, 194, 259, 316
Nesbitt, 103
Netita, 85
Nettles, 145
Neumann, 6
Neville, 197
Nevin, 133
Nevitt, 315
Nevius, 1
New Mexico, 336

Newbold, 14
Newcomb, 14
Newell, 23, 45, 87, 217, 290, 294
Newhall, 260
Newman, 63, 132, 287, 319
Newstead Abbey, 130
Newton, 27, 42, 45, 171, 187, 200, 229, 326
Nicely, 230
Nicholls, 7
Nichols, 213, 284, 313
Nicholson, 45, 90, 210, 211, 226, 297
Niebuhr, 327
Nightingale, 119
Niles, 19, 74
Nippes, 138
Nixon, 22, 84, 218, 232
Noble, 76, 100, 118, 119, 141, 236, 262, 266, 298, 317
Noel, 166
Nolan, 286, 297
Noland, 63
Nolti, 188
Nooe, 206
Noonan, 24
Norment, 247
Norris, 45, 128, 207, 327
Northway, 174
Norton, 64, 85, 138, 147, 294
Norwood, 165
Nott, 119
Nourse, 34, 53, 112, 115, 118, 141, 229, 230, 248, 251, 317, 319, 322
Novell, 96
Noyes, 45
Nugent, 179
Nunnally, 267
Nuttle, 76, 258
Nye, 163
Nyer, 126

O

O'Bannon, 240, 280
O'Brien, 4, 7, 17, 26, 82, 85, 109, 145, 177, 194, 234, 245

O'Bryen, 254
O'Callaghan, 63
O'Callahan, 63
O'Connor, 10
O'Conor, 5
O'Day, 199
O'Dell, 323
O'Donnell, 46, 56
O'Donnoghue, 35, 45, 220
O'Hara, 64
O'Neal, 118, 221
O'Neale, 34, 212
O'Neill, 32
O'Reily, 233
O'Rourke, 45
O'Toole, 1, 150, 200
Oak Hill, 133
Oak Hill Cemetery, 8, 161, 201, 214
Oakes, 145
Oakhill Cemetery, 263
Oaks, 281
Oakville, 192
Ober, 56, 151
Odenheimer, 224
Offley, 282
Offut, 319
Offutt, 201, 212, 265
Ogden, 38, 71, 98, 116, 121, 140, 241, 248
Ogle, 47, 287, 288
Old Field, 289
Old Long Fields, 50
Oldfield, 28
Oldham, 116
Oliver, 275
Omohundro, 155
Oppenheimer, 110
Ord, 100
Order of Mercy, 5
order of St Joseph, 286
Organist of St Aloysius, 258
Orme, 56, 187, 207, 314, 329
Ormond, 134
Ormsby, 169
Orr, 298
Orsini, 62

Ortega, 142
Osborn, 314
Osborne, 45
Osgood, 90, 217
Osmun, 73
Ostia, 284
Ott, 148, 229
Ould, 4
Oussler, 209
Ovenden, 327
Owen, 84, 151, 265
Owens, 36, 56, 92, 105, 139, 147, 169, 185, 212, 216
Owner, 45, 256, 292
Oyster, 45

P

Packwood, 93
Paddock, 186
Padgett, 200, 293
Page, 7, 46, 65, 111, 131, 144, 157, 158, 159, 217, 245, 292, 308, 316, 321
Paine, 168, 175
Pairo, 46
Palfrey, 249
Palmer, 13, 15, 28, 46, 56, 63, 81, 98, 100, 124, 130, 173, 180, 210, 320
Pankey, 154
Parham, 300
Parke, 46, 128, 176
Parker, 6, 46, 56, 92, 109, 129, 142, 198, 207, 217, 240, 268, 272, 305, 317, 323, 326
Parkhurst, 126
Parkison, 84
Parks, 160
Parley, 151
Parr, 318
Parran, 333
Parratt, 249
Parris, 4
Parrott, 107
Parry, 46
Parson, 279

Parsons, 130, 187, 217
Part of Greenwood Park Enlarged, 289
Partridge, 52
Pascall, 201
Passey, 211
Patapso City, 15
Patch, 308
Pattee, 80, 112, 155
Patten, 135, 243
Patterson, 14, 42, 78, 165, 171, 192, 204, 211, 274, 281
Patti, 53, 109, 161
Paul, 315
Paulding, 80, 82, 93, 117, 335
Paulin, 134
Paxon, 67
Payne, 212, 221, 265, 318
Paynter, 260, 276
Peabody, 79, 163, 217
Peacock, 285
Peake, 46
Peale, 62, 118, 130, 272
Pearce, 55, 64
Pearl, 46
Pearson, 55, 75, 87, 112, 122, 169, 194, 235, 337
Peay, 194, 238
Peck, 6, 22, 85, 336
Peddecord, 242
Peden, 9
Pedrick, 100, 170, 188
Peebles, 34
Pegg, 46, 52, 118, 141
Peifer, 221
Pelot, 304
Pelrick, 238
Pelton, 16
Pemberton, 330
Pendell, 63
Pendergast, 11, 21, 38, 91, 118, 155, 161, 193, 234
Pendergrast, 12, 75, 100, 156, 193
Pendleton, 51, 182
Penniston, 155
Penny, 221

Pension Ofc, 259
Pensions, 319
Pepe, 200
Pepperell, 214
Percy, 294
Perdue, 267
Perez, 100
Perkins, 83, 95, 109, 125, 138, 151, 166, 315
Perobean, 258
Perrie, 67
Perrigo, 130
Perry, 22, 23, 70, 119, 130, 168, 171, 244, 255, 259, 268
Persifer, 21
Persse, 14
Pesps, 319
Pesy, 4
Petchaka, 82
Peter, 46, 277
Peter's Mill Seat, 209
Peters, 46, 48, 313
Peters' Mill Seat, 117
Peterson, 9
Petit, 46, 187, 212
Pettet, 64
Pettibone, 305
Pettigrew, 73
Pettis, 225
Pettit, 242
Pettus, 330
Pettz, 1
Peugh, 46, 120, 244
Peyton, 162
Pfeifer, 7
Pfeiffer, 24, 29
Pfhegee, 211
Pfleuger, 240
Phelan, 93, 120, 154, 176, 193, 237
Phelps, 9, 46, 53, 77, 112, 118, 160, 169
Philip, 46
Philips, 64, 154
Phillips, 46, 61, 118, 172, 225, 317
Philp, 65, 110, 115, 152
Pichard, 184

Pickens, 177, 336
Pickett, 21, 185, 292
Pickrell, 2, 172, 187
Pierce, 1, 12, 13, 46, 55, 78, 103, 112, 127, 254
Pierey, 100
Piggott, 62
Pike, 104, 130, 174
Pilcher, 133
Pilgrim, 256
Pilgrims, 195
Pilkington, 288
Pinckney, 65
Piney Branch Trotting Course, 209
Pinkney, 214, 252, 284, 310
Piper, 94
Pipes, 183
Pitachaca, 79
Pitcher, 46
Pitzer, 84
Pius IX, 280
Pius VII, 204
Place, 63, 130
Plait, 329
Plant, 46
Platt, 46, 336
Platz, 319
Plauche, 12
Playfair, 161
Pleasant Plains, 210
Pleasanton, 157
Pleasonton, 46
Plume, 116
Plummer, 217
Plumsell, 46
Plumsill, 123
Plunkett, 273
Plympton, 176, 180
Poe, 217, 336
Poiret, 122
Polishly, 201
Polk, 46, 108, 231, 255, 277
Polkinhorn, 13, 191
Pollard, 36, 46, 206, 251
Polly, 112
Pomona, 270

Pond, 147
Pool, 112, 128
Poole, 89
Poor, 314
Poor Man's Industry, 278
Pope, 10, 99, 181, 201, 221, 309, 314
Poplar Hill, 219
Popoff, 318
Porsser, 81
Port, 138
Porte, 93
Porter, 12, 75, 91, 93, 140, 146, 154, 159, 170, 192, 193, 236
Porterfield, 65, 76, 101, 109, 118, 193, 244
Portland Manor, 266
Portman, 119, 161, 172, 186, 194, 238
Posey, 46
Post, 16, 17, 130, 167
Potentini, 309
Pott, 150
Potter, 113
Potts, 20, 46, 64, 155
Powell, 46, 56, 165, 317
Power, 46, 293
Powers, 25
Prather, 46
Pratt, 130
Pratte, 121
Prescott, 65, 98
Presley, 300
Preston, 33, 46, 93, 94, 110, 129, 159, 161, 184, 191, 194, 262, 290
Prettyman, 84, 142, 233
Prevention Enlarged, 50
Price, 46, 55, 81, 102, 161, 192
Priestley, 123
Priman, 223
Primeau, 223
Prince, 256
Pritchard, 186
Pritchett, 23, 128, 290
Proctor, 46, 310, 325
propeller **Globe**, 299
propeller **Kenosha**, 199

Prospect Hill, 34, 136
Prospect Hill Cemetery, 128
Protestant Cemetery, 302
Prout, 46, 78
Provest, 22, 129
Puckett, 119, 297
Pugh, 309
Pulizzi, 54
Pumphrey, 46, 278
Pumphrey's Little Addition, 278
Purcell, 46, 60, 88, 112, 227, 234, 261, 264, 285
Purchase, 119
Purdy, 46, 187
Purfield, 22
Purnell, 256
Pursell, 192
Purvis, 264
Puryear, 277
Putnam, 126, 246
Putnam Phalanx, 316
Pyne, 189, 335

Q

Queen, 46, 71, 126, 227, 271, 291, 303, 323, 328
Queen Mary, 60
Queen Victoria, 94, 207
Queener, 8
Quiggle, 14
Quigley, 105, 161
Quigly, 109
Quinlan, 135
Quinn, 46, 330
Quinter, 242
Quirke, 46
Quitman, 26

R

Raab, 150, 165, 295
Raborg, 13
Radcliff, 122
Radford, 267
Rady, 10
Ragan, 46
Railey, 46, 264, 296
Rainals, 89
Rainey, 212
Ramsay, 263, 299, 336
Ramsey, 73, 331
Rand, 37
Randall, 94, 119, 132, 156, 162, 187, 191, 193, 194, 196, 303, 336
Randolph, 26, 57, 108, 185, 200, 242, 267, 298
Rannahan, 46
Ranney, 277
Rapley, 46
Ratcliffe, 214, 317
Rathbone, 155
Ratley, 141
Ratz, 240
Rawcliffe, 192
Rawlings, 56, 317, 324
Rawlinson, 139
Ray, 46, 315
Rea, 99
Read, 94, 146, 186, 189
Reading, 37
Ready, 46, 63
Reagan, 120, 259
Realf, 21
Reardon, 46, 64
Reaver, 136
Rebee, 191
Redfern, 47, 262
Redin, 69, 162, 251, 272, 282
Redinger, 96
Redmond, 3, 63
Redstrake, 284
Ree, 46
Reed, 46, 78, 93, 118, 165, 184, 264, 265, 313
Rees, 29
Reese, 46, 74, 80, 101, 128, 146, 223
Reeside, 46
Reeves, 9, 11, 70, 100, 104, 119, 270, 331, 335
Regester, 108
Register, 84
Reichter, 63
Reid, 52, 84

Reidy, 46
Reigart, 133
Reille, 111
Reilly, 46, 145, 193
Reily, 337
Reiss, 304
Relch, 38
Remick, 126
Remington, 311
Renard, 160
Rendig, 245
Renk, 209
Renniff, 112
Renshaw, 176
Rent, 121
Rentzell, 319
Revolutionary soldiers, 319
Reynolds, 9, 63, 130, 155, 165, 227
Rham, 216
Rhea, 4, 205
Rheem, 74
Rhett, 230
Rheves, 140
Rhind, 93, 166
Rhoades, 294
Rhoads, 95
Rhodes, 49, 305
Rhodier, 212
Ricar, 46
Rice, 102, 115, 163, 169, 180, 187, 217, 254, 294
Ricers, 251
Rich, 19, 109, 161, 180
Rich Point Farm, 311
Richards, 46, 116, 126, 130, 194, 239, 282, 337
Richardson, 70, 96, 100, 116, 175, 199, 253
Richbourg, 145
Riche, 280
Richey, 57
Richlands, 24
Richmond, 183, 272
Ricker, 46, 52, 118
Ricketts, 84, 204, 254
Ricks, 268

Ridaway, 10
Riddick, 307
Riddle, 337
Ridenour, 227
Rider, 230
Ridgeley, 46, 56
Ridgely, 9, 33, 80, 252
Ridgway, 47
Ridley, 60
Ridout, 118, 222, 307
Rigby, 184
Riggles, 57, 283
Riggs, 46, 231, 325
Riley, 28, 46, 73, 75, 83, 98, 130, 198, 225, 270, 305, 315
Rin, 47
Rind, 79
Ringgold, 72, 90, 257
Ringold, 47
Ripley, 76, 101, 109, 161
Ritchie, 37, 46, 121, 135, 155, 202, 304
Rittenhouse, 79, 89, 140, 156, 165, 194, 231, 298, 318, 322
Ritter, 317
Rives, 46, 106, 207
Rivins, 331
Roach, 7, 8, 136, 293, 306
Roane, 138
Robaldo, 161
Robb, 31, 34, 118
Robbins, 107, 259, 319
Robbinson, 107
Roberts, 46, 47, 57, 100, 113, 155, 156, 160, 226, 300
Robertson, 126, 147, 154, 176, 194
Robey, 63, 329
Robideau, 119
Robidoux, 141
Robinson, 8, 32, 36, 46, 63, 89, 104, 118, 136, 145, 156, 186, 196, 199, 219, 224, 242, 255, 286, 296, 309, 313, 330
Robison, 284
Roby, 101
Rockaway, 327

Rockwell, 119, 176, 194, 237
Rodbird, 197
Rodger, 168
Rodgers, 18, 46, 227
Rodier, 46
Rodman, 59, 127, 288
Rodrigue, 126
Rogers, 30, 33, 60, 61, 84, 87, 107, 109, 130, 145, 158, 169, 172, 200, 304, 337
Rogerson, 93, 120, 176, 193, 237
Rolfe, 148
Rollin, 47
Rollins, 184
Roman, 327
Rooker, 11, 62
Rookwell, 127
Root, 134
Roscoe, 60
Rose, 37, 47, 69, 159, 166, 168
Rosebrugh, 174
Ross, 1, 46, 58, 212, 252, 279, 287
Rosslyn, 136
Rost, 207
Roszel, 84
Roth, 63
Rothwell, 113, 151
Rotteris, 52
Rountree, 54, 171
Rous, 63
Roux, 229
Rowan, 101
Rowland, 73, 119, 151, 323
Rowles, 75
Roy, 29
Rozer, 181, 228
Rubincam, 283
Rudio, 62
Rudler, 337
Ruggles, 47
Rumery, 109
Runnells, 14
Rupert, 162
Rupp, 63
Ruppart, 26
Rush, 46

Rusk, 26
Russell, 17, 56, 60, 67, 85, 86, 109, 141, 174, 176, 201, 216, 247, 266
Rust, 266
Ruter, 55
Rutherford, 245
Ryan, 84, 315
Ryder, 14, 18, 46
Rye, 11, 28
Ryland, 84
Ryland Chapel, 106
Ryon, 25, 211, 229, 248

S

Sabal, 160
Sacia, 158
Sackett, 174
Saeger, 47
Sage, 250
Sagozaimon, 203
Sailor's Rest, 281
Sales, 319
Salsman, 226
Saminego, 96
Sample, 166
Sampson, 155, 182
Samson, 73, 228, 274, 301
Samuel, 132
Sanborn, 125
Sandermeister, 243
Sanders, 166, 289
Sanderson, 109, 161, 184
Sandles, 83
Sands, 47, 194
Sandy Bar, 288
Sandy Hill, 136
Sanford, 8, 100, 102, 119, 156, 171
Sangeter, 138
Sardo, 125
Sargent, 52
Sarmiento, 272
Satey, 125
Satterlee, 119
Saturday Chance, 50
Saunders, 47, 290, 329
Sauter, 63, 251

Savage, 126, 187, 330
Savarnway, 93
Savory, 191
Sawyer, 11, 54, 59, 119, 170
Saxton, 93
Sayers, 55, 85
Sayles, 319
Sayre, 125, 126, 184, 194, 238
Scaggs, 18, 185, 229, 315
Scaife, 34, 76, 100, 118, 119, 236
Scalla, 47
Scanlin, 221
Scanlon, 88
Scarf, 4
Scarsdale, 166
Schad, 150, 177
Schaef, 80
Schaffer, 63, 105
Schandler, 76, 193
Schaum, 130
Schealled, 169
Schee, 164
Scheener, 147
Scheere, 193
Scheerer, 116, 130, 175, 176
Schele, 106
Schell, 1
Schiebler, 318
Schirmer, 199
Schlander, 176
Schley, 122, 186
Schloss, 7, 319
Schlosser, 50
Schmidt, 252, 291
Schneider, 108
Schnell, 157
schnr **Alice Rogers**, 139
schnr **Andrew Stewart**, 203
schnr **Augusta**, 254, 256
schnr **Commonwealth**, 236
schnr **Coquette**, 100
schnr **Delta**, 236
schnr **Emma**, 89, 115
schnr **Five Sisters**, 236
schnr **George Harris**, 335
schnr **Helen Blood**, 73

schnr **Jasper**, 236
schnr **Mary Elizabeth**, 155
schnr **Metamora**, 100
schnr **Perserverance**, 330
schnr **Porpoise**, 281
schnr **R G Johnson**, 195
schnr **Richmond**, 328
schnr **Sarah Bond**, 73
schnr **Sardine**, 236
schnr **Spring Hill**, 335
schnr **Two Brothers**, 236
schnr **United States**, 335
Scholfield, 47
Schoolcraft, 107
Schooley, 80
Schoonover, 14
Schosser, 5
Schott, 92
Schroeder-Devrient, 62
Schuermann, 27
Schureman, 47
Schussler, 47
Schwagge, 209
Schwartz, 47, 71, 190
Schwinghamer, 47
Scott, 12, 17, 19, 27, 47, 59, 64, 75, 83, 87, 93, 94, 96, 100, 110, 135, 143, 153, 156, 162, 165, 170, 174, 183, 193, 218, 227, 232, 261, 265, 280, 319
Scribner, 317
Scripture, 209
Scrivener, 187, 314
Scrivner, 214
Scurry, 297
Seaman, 88, 188
Searles, 113
Sears, 100, 224
Seaton, 67, 219
Seckell, 259
Seclusaville, 317
Sedgwick, 178
Seely, 290
Segar, 164
Seger, 192
Seibert, 224, 327

Seiffert, 308
Seitz, 47, 249
Selden, 13, 15, 47, 174, 292
Selhausen, 177
Selser, 173
Semmes, 34, 47, 204, 207, 300, 308
Sener, 87
Sengstack, 47, 225
Senny, 209
Senseney, 227, 336
Sents, 160
Sergeant, 79, 145
Serrin, 47, 58
Serrurier, 62
Sessford, 63
Settle, 151, 271
Seufferie, 257
Seufferle, 18
Sewall, 47, 212
Seward, 75, 131
Sewell, 95, 100, 156, 180, 282, 283
Sewing Machine, 255
Seyfert, 210, 211
Seymour, 112, 135, 210, 211, 212, 316
Shaaf, 89, 301
Shackelford, 24, 81
Shackleford, 63
Shaer, 266
Shaffer, 63
Shanahan, 63
Shanchesney, 47
Shank, 96
Shankland, 144
Shanks, 78, 321
Shannon, 77
Sharp, 80, 142, 309
Sharretts, 47
Shaughnessy, 5
Shaw, 19, 88, 191, 225
Shea, 58, 163, 198, 200
Shearin, 261
Shearman, 140
Sheath, 167
Sheckells, 315
Sheckels, 56, 78

Sheckles, 224
Shed, 86
Shedd, 151
Sheehan, 96
Sheets, 252
Sheffey, 232, 244
Shekell, 47, 71
Shellhausen, 150
Shepard, 199
Shepherd, 23, 26, 144
Sheppard, 29, 47, 327
Sheriff, 90, 138
Sherlock, 194
Sherman, 22, 47, 77, 178, 233, 286, 329
Shermer, 101, 315
Sherrard, 251
Sherrod, 129
Shields, 94
Shinn, 81
Shinnors, 47
Ship, 267
ship **Antartic**, 121
ship **Arabella**, 225
ship **Arabia**, 246
ship **Cahawha**, 176
ship **Constellation**, 273
ship **Constitution**, 59
ship **Corinthian**, 11, 74
ship **Cyane**, 59
ship **Dacotah**, 158
ship **Erie**, 272, 273
ship **Fenimore Cooper**, 318
ship **Flora Temple**, 20
ship **Great Eastern**, 38
ship **Growler** or **Eagle**, 59
ship **Hungarian**, 77
ship **Iroquois**, 215
ship **Levant**, 59
ship **Lucy Thompson**, 335
ship **Massachusetts**, 184
ship **Mayflower**, 195
ship **Mohican**, 273
ship **Mystic**, 273
ship **Niagara**, 91, 273
ship **Noonday**, 328

ship **Northumberland**, 237
ship **Norway**, 102
ship **Pawnee**, 158
ship **Pluto**, 114
ship **Princeton**, 67
ship **Rockville**, 184
ship **San Francisco**, 121
ship **San Jacinto**, 99
ship **Savannah**, 304
ship **Seminole**, 158
ship **St Louis**, 158
ship **Uriel**, 101, 232
ship **Wasp**, 82
ships **Constitution** & the **Marion**, 114
Shircliff, 100, 160
Shirecliff, 181
Shirley, 194
Shockley, 67, 94
Shoemaker, 3, 47, 130, 315
Short, 47
Shorter, 47
Shotard, 24
show-boat **Banjo**, 173
Shreeve, 47, 101
Shreve, 63, 110
Shroeter, 290
Shryock, 230
Shubrick, 34, 35, 58, 93, 116, 160, 181, 192, 194, 335
Shucking, 47
Shull, 235
Shurtleff, 217
Shuster, 29, 103, 291
Shute, 301
Shuttas, 316
Shyne, 250, 261, 323
Sibley, 16, 25, 99, 315
Sickels, 114
Sickles, 170
Sievers, 20
Sileming, 169
Silvey, 90
Simmons, 63, 64, 130
Simms, 47, 85, 148, 286
Simonds, 133

Simons, 105, 126
Simpson, 38, 78, 81, 114, 116, 254, 288
Sims, 47
Sinclair, 4, 63, 329
Sines, 284
Sinnot, 248
Sipes, 84
Sister Mary Louise, 198
Sister Mary Stanislaus, 286
Sister of Charity, 252
Sisters of Charity, 247
Sisters of Notre Dame, 295
Sitgreaves, 200
Skerrett, 230
Skinner, 100, 174, 281
Slade, 47, 73
Slater, 47, 95, 120, 172, 244
Slatford, 63
Slaughter, 52, 255, 302
slaver **Cora**, 321
Slemmer, 253
Slevin, 150
Slight, 312, 328
Slip, 278
Sloan, 27
Slocomb, 146
Slocum, 224
sloop **E A Johnson**, 158, 173
sloop **Harvard**, 141
sloop of war **Preble**, 271
sloop-of-war **Marion**, 273
sloop-of-war **Portsmouth**, 12, 75, 100, 156, 193, 236
sloop-of-war **Richmond**, 158
sloop-of-war **Savannah**, 158
sloop-of-war **St Louis**, 314
sloop-of-war **Vandalia**, 4
sloop-of-war **Vincennes**, 114
sloop-of-war **Warren**, 281
Smack, 218
Small, 303
Smallwood, 47, 56, 299
Smead, 98
Smedes, 307
Smedley, 64

Smiley, 297
Smith, 1, 2, 4, 7, 10, 14, 17, 21, 35, 36, 47, 49, 55, 56, 58, 63, 73, 75, 76, 77, 78, 80, 81, 83, 85, 94, 98, 100, 101, 105, 106, 109, 112, 118, 127, 141, 152, 155, 156, 161, 166, 169, 170, 172, 176, 178, 180, 182, 184, 186, 187, 189, 190, 192, 193, 198, 199, 210, 211, 212, 218, 220, 233, 239, 249, 251, 252, 255, 256, 258, 264, 266, 269, 272, 276, 278, 282, 286, 288, 293, 296, 297, 298, 299, 313, 323, 325, 333, 336
Smith's Row, 97
Smithson, 131, 178, 220, 233, 286
Smitson, 47
Smoot, 2, 37, 81, 82, 133, 155, 253
Snelling, 125
Snider, 307
Snow, 155
Snowden, 5, 36, 81, 169, 265
Snyder, 47, 108, 119, 211, 305
Soldiers of the War of 1812, 59
Soloman, 83
Solomon, 51, 110
Solomons, 115
Sommer, 47
Sommerville, 4
Sorsby, 138
Sothoron, 81, 227
Soulard, 135, 210, 211
South Carolina, 312
Southerland, 101
Southwell, 145
Sovereigns in Europe, 263
Spadding, 62
Spalding, 4, 56, 301, 305
Spangler, 146
Spaulding, 78
Speake, 47
Spear, 35, 118, 155, 229, 268
Spearing, 98
Speddin, 47
Speer, 169
Speiden, 297
Spence, 68, 82

Spencer, 12, 56, 109, 135, 225, 256, 284
Sperry, 203
Spooner, 169
Sprenger, 272
Spring, 320
Spring Hill, 305
Spring Vale, 208
Springer, 14
Springman, 47
Spruance, 183
Spry, 29
Squier, 194, 239
Squires, 191
St John, 124
Stabler, 146, 242
Stacey, 47
Stafford, 64, 129, 160
Stake, 212
Stalker, 34, 76, 100, 118, 119, 236
Stanfill, 155
Stanford, 224
Stanhope, 189
Stanley, 63, 185
Stanmore School, 247
Stanton, 262, 328
Stanwood, 52, 184
Staples, 326
Starr, 126, 246, 276
Starrs, 5
Start, 84
Statenboro, 285
Statham, 178, 233, 286
Staton, 259
Stealey, 16, 75, 93, 141, 193, 236
steamboat **Antelope**, 122
steamboat **Fox**, 94
steamboat **James Adams**, 236
steamer **A T Lacey**, 139
steamer **Africa**, 77
steamer **Arabia**, 247
steamer **Arctic**, 294
steamer **Ben Lewis**, 197
steamer **Edinburgh**, 247
steamer **Edward Walsh**, 154
steamer **Etna**, 247

steamer **Fulton**, 281
steamer **H R W Hill**, 294, 297
steamer **Homer**, 157
steamer **Hungarian**, 70, 96
steamer **J M Manning**, 92
steamer **Judge Porter**, 94
steamer **Kate McLaurin**, 165
steamer **Kennebec**, 195
steamer **Lady Elgin**, 254, 256, 263, 284, 286, 303, 322, 329
steamer **Lexington**, 32
steamer **Malabar**, 209
steamer **Mohawk**, 158
steamer **Mohican**, 272
steamer **Niagara**, 245
steamer **Northerner**, 49, 116
steamer **Pacific**, 309
steamer **Pennsylvania**, 218
steamer **Pensacola**, 31
steamer **Planet**, 305
steamer **R F Lass**, 157
steamer **R F Sass**, 154
steamer **San Francisco**, 11, 102, 124
steamer **Sunnyside**, 197
steamer **Virginia**, 295
steamer **Walker**, 192, 195
steamer **Wm L Levy**, 297
steamers **Mystic & Sumter**, 114
steamship **Connaught**, 276
steamship **Delaware**, 192
steamship **Empire City**, 64
steamship **Illinois**, 64
steamship **Isabel**, 326
steamship **James Adger**, 311
steamship **Marion**, 28, 33
steamship **Moses Taylor**, 64
steamship **Nashville**, 311
steamship **Niagara**, 166
steamship **Northerner**, 114
steamship **Philadelphia**, 64
steamship **Princeton**, 79
steamship **Star of the West**, 64
steamship **Susquehannah**, 165
steam-tug **Lioness**, 328
steam-tug **McQueen**, 254
Stearne, 73, 157

Stedman, 335
Steele, 74, 105, 119, 127, 172, 176, 193, 219, 224
Steenrod, 250
Steer, 257
Steers, 47
Stelle, 47
Stephens, 32, 76, 119, 148, 302
Sterey, 303
Sterling, 139
Sterrett, 37
Sterritt, 37
Stettinius, 47
Steuart, 251
Stevens, 51, 53, 61, 92, 107, 119, 178, 215, 224, 269
Stevenson, 266
Stewart, 47, 56, 84, 151, 152, 163, 168, 201, 222, 260, 266, 281, 293, 302
Stier, 6
Stiger, 47
Stiles, 148
Stillman, 76, 119, 316
Stillmore, 168
Stimpson, 73, 102
Stinson, 299
Stinzing, 47
Stires, 199
Stirling, 250
Stocker, 126
Stockton, 80, 155, 320
Stoddard, 245
Stokely, 76
Stoll, 123
Stolp, 315
Stone, 56, 78, 116, 148, 181, 203, 245, 315, 317, 327
Stoneman, 94
Stonestreet, 47, 49, 223
Stoops, 32
storeship **Relief**, 318
Stouffer, 121, 124
Stoughten, 47
Stoughton, 57
Stout, 29, 80, 121

Stovall, 268
Stoveall, 242
Stover, 108
Stovin, 221
Strand, 315
Stratton, 149, 160
Straub, 63
Strayer, 101
Street, 27
Strider, 241
Strong, 110, 119, 161, 207, 316
Strother, 7, 47, 285
Strothers, 263
Strothier, 182
Stuart, 96, 139, 162, 242, 244, 267, 272, 289, 316
Stumps, 307
Sturgeon, 73
Stuyvesant, 186
Styles, 309
Sublette Cut-off, 169
Sugrue, 47
Suit, 58, 307
Sullivan, 47, 63, 72, 82, 168, 275
Sully, 133
Summons, 93
Sumner, 89
Sunby, 47
Sunderland, 36, 178, 191, 320
Supple, 302
Surratt, 47, 227
Suter, 47
Sutherland, 47
Suttle, 323
Sutton, 31, 34, 130, 192
Swan, 47
Swann, 14, 47, 120, 139, 186, 192, 207
Swart, 160
Swartz, 278
Swayze, 97
Swearinger, 303
Sweeney, 8, 15, 35
Sweeny, 140, 187, 194, 201, 318
Sweester, 52
Sweet, 99, 245
Sweetman, 155
Sweetser, 71
Sweetzer, 47, 141, 194
Sweigart, 8
Swentzell, 101
Swift, 29, 108, 109
Swilling, 76
Swope, 84
Sylvester, 47, 78, 108, 315
Syme, 73

T

Tabb, 145
Tabler, 31, 187
Tagg, 96
Taggart, 48
Tait, 8
Talbert, 111, 259
Talbot, 14, 302
Talbott, 160, 288
Taliaferro, 170, 205, 240
Talman, 73
Taney, 14, 147, 316
Tansell, 103
Tappan, 171
Tark, 119
Tate, 142, 312
Tayloe, 3, 43, 48, 78, 186, 287, 288, 294
Taylor, 17, 19, 21, 31, 33, 48, 54, 56, 63, 64, 78, 79, 80, 91, 92, 93, 97, 107, 109, 110, 111, 117, 119, 124, 125, 130, 139, 140, 144, 149, 157, 161, 165, 168, 177, 192, 193, 194, 202, 210, 229, 231, 238, 253, 260, 267, 286, 299, 304, 315, 321, 335
Tazewell, 145, 267
Teal, 218
Tebbs, 109
Teel, 5
Teleford, 213
Telegraph Co, 81
Temple, 61
Templeman, 37
Templeton, 100, 160, 175
Ten Eyck, 69

Tenant, 286
Terret, 102
Terry, 7, 290
Thecker, 75, 201, 246, 251, 272
Thielecke, 229
Thom, 231
Thoma, 26
Thomas, 47, 48, 51, 57, 84, 92, 94, 108, 141, 183, 187, 221, 266, 295, 297, 315
Thompson, 8, 42, 43, 47, 48, 53, 57, 58, 59, 62, 63, 64, 76, 101, 118, 119, 128, 141, 170, 172, 194, 223, 230, 235, 251, 261, 284, 305
Thorn, 31, 48, 66, 315
Thornley, 78
Thornton, 2, 267
Thorpe, 313
Thread, 171
Threlkeld, 125
Throop, 202
Tibbs, 286
Tiberius, 307
Ticknor, 53, 293
Tilghman, 17, 47, 75, 93, 120, 194, 236, 258, 328
Tillard, 268
Tilley, 132, 271
Tillinghast, 55, 252, 282
Timms, 48
Tindall, 60
Tinkler, 62, 63
Tippett, 3, 30, 62, 103, 124, 168
Tipton, 107
Tircuit, 204
Titus, 312
Toadvine, 230
Tobin, 10, 48
Todd, 48, 78, 114, 178, 202, 265, 305
Todsen, 48
Tohuler, 85
Toll, 48
Tollman, 212
Tolson, 329, 333, 336
Tomkpins, 67

Tompkins, 27, 48
Toner, 57
Toney, 267
Toombs, 184, 188, 299, 302
Toomey, 63
Topping, 243
Torbert, 162
Torre, 175
Torrence, 97, 115
Totten, 114, 213
Totty, 256, 304
Tough, 48
Towers, 48, 151, 173, 180, 279, 285
Towles, 181, 202, 265, 315
Towson, 48, 107, 156
Tracy, 100, 318
Traphagen, 113
Trauter, 142
Travers, 48
Traverse, 76
Travis, 147
Tree, 56, 202
Treichel, 235
Treikel, 19
Trescot, 177
Tretler, 48, 313
Trevitt, 112
Trewendt, 241
Trewitt, 117, 129
Trezvant, 71
Triche, 126
Trimble, 34
Trook, 48
Troup, 97
Trout, 126, 193
Trowbridge, 141
Trunnell, 212
Truxton, 215
Tschiffely, 11, 123
Tucker, 48, 52, 64, 119, 121, 151, 259, 279, 298, 317
Tudor, 84
Tuel, 56
Tuell, 56
Tuley, 189, 196, 275
Tuleyries, 275

Tull, 47
Turk, 275
Turly, 53
Turner, 13, 47, 48, 89, 146, 182, 183, 191, 196, 330
Turton, 48, 56, 101, 187
Tustin, 8
Tuttle, 20
Tuzvant, 331
Tyler, 13, 260, 288
Tyson, 100, 251

U

Underhill, 28, 62, 118, 126
Underwood, 119, 127, 176, 194, 237
Updike, 254
Upshaw, 48
Upshur, 72, 195
Urle, 319
Urquiza, 35, 58
Usher, 48
Utermehle, 120, 164
Utermuehle, 210
Uttermehle, 46

V

Vail, 321
Valentine, 63
Valette, 235
Vallego, 236
Vallejo, 13, 73, 100, 119
Valleor, 185
Vallot, 185
Valuable Relic, 214
Van Buren, 28, 277, 279, 280
Van Buskirk, 23, 31, 87, 101, 129, 176, 193, 237
Van Congdon, 73
Van Cortlandt, 48
Van Cott, 155
Van Ness, 48, 202
Van Patten, 48
Van Pelt, 119
Van Rensselaer, 160, 222, 280
Van Reswick, 56, 78, 122
Van Verst, 160

Van Waggoner, 252
Van Wert, 80
Van Wyck, 113
Vanarsdale, 284
Vance, 93
Vancey, 319
Vanderbilt, 327
Van-Deusen, 79
Vandeventer, 28
Varden, 101
Varn, 87
Varnell, 48
Vass, 48, 267
Vaux, 245
Vega, 155, 156
Veirs, 138
Vemeyer, 63
Venable, 48, 109, 277, 297
Venale, 151
Verbiski, 17, 52
Verettad, 229
Verison, 100
Vernon, 48
Vesey, 83, 158
Vespre, 21
vessel **Curtis Peck**, 218
vessel **Dolphin**, 159
vessel **Spring Hill**, 206
vessel **United States**, 206
Vickers, 68
Villarubia, 4, 75, 126
Vincent, 87, 187, 331
Vinson, 25, 160
Viscenti, 284
Vischer, 191
Volk, 63, 305
Von Buskirk, 76
Von Humboldt, 287
Von Schmidt, 29, 55
Vondersmith, 93
Voorhees, 146, 298
Voss, 48, 63, 179

W

Waddel, 30
Wade, 82

Wadeworth, 229
Wadsworth, 5, 48, 134, 154, 184, 194, 241, 262
Wagner, 49, 155
Wail, 48
Wailes, 8, 151
Wait, 145
Waite, 157
Walbach, 28, 112, 120, 121
Walbridge, 309, 310
Walcomb, 62
Walcott, 255
Waldo, 114, 172, 191, 238, 256
Waldron, 317
Wales, 52, 184
Walker, 8, 36, 48, 49, 56, 63, 74, 82, 98, 101, 106, 109, 182, 186, 195, 207, 210, 211, 231, 232, 267, 310, 320, 329, 330, 334, 337
Wall, 50, 79, 187, 289
Wallace, 35, 56, 118, 155, 203, 309, 315
Wallace's, 222
Wallach, 48, 70, 101, 113, 173, 177
Waller, 7, 102
Walling, 63
Wallingsford, 48
Wallis, 88, 240
Walmsly, 34
Walnut Hill, 241
Walsh, 56, 57, 88, 131, 212, 227, 330
Walson, 315
Walter, 7, 49, 58, 105, 131, 141, 145, 220, 234, 244, 264
Walters, 48, 52, 80
Walton, 119, 141, 193, 201, 202, 217
Walworth, 233, 252
Wandell, 114
Wantland, 49
war of 1812, 3, 9, 11, 12, 15, 16, 19, 21, 23, 25, 28, 30, 31, 34, 35, 53, 54, 62, 66, 72, 80, 82, 86, 87, 93, 95, 100, 103, 105, 107, 109, 118, 121, 123, 124, 125, 127, 129, 152, 156, 157, 159, 160, 163, 169, 171,
176, 183, 198, 255, 277, 281, 294, 327, 329
war of 1812., 3, 62, 79, 157, 255
Ward, 15, 35, 48, 49, 55, 62, 82, 100, 101, 177, 198, 201, 210, 327
Warden, 303
Warder, 257
Ware, 119, 147, 194, 239
Warfield, 204
Waring, 48, 185, 212, 227, 233, 283
Warley, 116
Warner, 141, 155, 315
Warren, 32, 63, 108, 116, 136, 210, 211, 287, 288
Warring, 83
Warrington, 318
Washburn, 27, 137
Washington, 59, 62, 66, 83, 168, 181, 227, 263, 272, 277, 299, 309, 315, 316, 324
Water Board of Gtwn, 61
Waterford, 91
Waterman, 196
Waters, 7, 31, 48, 49, 56, 71, 116, 208, 212, 267
Waterson, 67
Waterston, 48
Watkins, 44, 48, 172, 253, 267
Watson, 38, 48, 58, 64, 158, 186, 270
Watterston, 61, 262
Watts, 130, 173, 201, 315, 336
Waugh, 84, 187
Waveland, 277
Way, 52, 184
Wayne, 49
Weary, 132
Weasner, 136
Weaver, 48, 49, 80, 107
Webb, 14, 18, 36, 49, 67, 108, 113, 208
Webber, 72, 114, 128
Webster, 98, 146, 166, 246
Weed, 48, 100, 112
Weeden, 64
Weeks, 49, 100, 144, 156

Wegener, 134
Wehrheim, 71, 112, 169, 194
Weisiger, 323
Welby, 73
Welch, 18, 33
Welding, 119
Weller, 63, 306
Welling, 304
Wells, 14, 64, 72, 85, 100, 105, 160, 180, 226
Welsh, 49, 110, 140, 262, 300
Wendell, 105
Wentworth, 166
West, 12, 38, 48, 49, 52, 63, 75, 86, 100, 138, 146, 156, 193, 277, 280, 323
Western, 62
Westlake, 254
Weston, 162, 241
Westwood, 84, 221
Wetherell, 25, 99
Wetonsaw, 80, 140, 160, 194, 234
Weverton Mfgr Co, 103
Weyman, 143
Whalan, 64
Whalen, 48, 64, 210, 211
Wharton, 186
Wheat, 209, 317
Wheaton, 127, 331
Wheeler, 11, 27, 37, 48, 87, 107, 130, 138, 141, 320
Whelan, 48
Whicker, 183
Whipple, 109, 137, 199
Whitacre, 60
Whitall, 305
Whitcomb, 62
White, 16, 48, 49, 63, 78, 83, 116, 140, 141, 155, 159, 205, 217, 224, 275, 286, 315
white glass coffin, 214
Whitehall, 231
Whitehead, 109, 119, 144, 186, 194, 281
Whiteley, 230
Whiteman, 144

Whitfield, 267
Whiting, 27, 93, 107, 142, 152, 175, 259
Whitlock, 49
Whitman, 126
Whitmore, 49
Whitney, 110, 155, 229, 241
Whittaker, 232, 240
Whittel, 276
Whittier, 154
Whittingham, 310
Whittington, 81
Whittlesey, 146, 178
Whitwell, 171
Whyte, 57
Wickham, 60
Wickizer, 3, 65, 100
Wickliffe, 239
Widdebombe, 269
Widdicombe, 264
Wier, 312
Wigg, 130, 153, 157
Wightman, 5
Wilbur, 119
Wilburn, 334
Wilder, 297
Wildman, 130
Wiley, 31, 62
Wilke, 161
Wilkes, 48
Wilkey, 105
Wilkie, 112, 123, 284
Wilkins, 16, 25, 99, 109, 337
Wilkinson, 326
Willard, 59, 100, 141, 164, 197, 273
Willet, 281
Willett, 57, 307
Williams, 13, 22, 48, 49, 52, 55, 57, 60, 63, 65, 76, 80, 84, 90, 92, 93, 111, 124, 137, 138, 148, 155, 159, 184, 202, 212, 240, 249, 255, 301, 305, 316, 324, 335
Williamson, 49, 58, 64, 90, 337
Willing, 66
Willis, 49, 125, 144, 209
Williss, 182

Willox, 259
Wills, 253
Willson, 184
Wilson, 10, 31, 32, 48, 49, 57, 63, 78, 96, 97, 101, 118, 139, 154, 155, 160, 182, 184, 189, 192, 202, 207, 217, 245, 253, 256, 266, 276, 283, 290, 294, 298, 299, 303, 313, 324
Wiltberger, 48, 187
Wimsatt, 57
Winchester, 327
Winder, 48, 76, 119, 132, 176, 191, 193, 194, 253
Windsor, 203, 220
Windsor Place, 133
Wingerd, 273
Wingfield, 282
Wingot, 173
Winn, 222, 306
Winslow, 119, 124
Winston, 14, 330
Winter, 22, 94, 129
Wintersmith, 259
Winthrop, 207, 225
Wirt, 161, 196, 267
Wise, 13, 48, 131, 134, 242, 291, 301
Witcher, 73, 75
Witham, 86
Witherell, 16
Witherow, 106, 202
Withers, 48, 149, 155
Woehler, 75
Wolf, 33, 141, 294
Wolfe, 52, 184, 189
Wollard, 325
Wonderlick, 48
Wood, 16, 48, 60, 83, 97, 98, 100, 108, 109, 120, 141, 166, 174, 176, 180, 184, 187, 188, 193, 197, 243, 292
Wood Cot, 200
Wood's Barn, 165
Woodbridge, 301
Woodbury, 242

Woodcock, 116
Woodley, 108
Woodruff, 53, 176
Woods, 96, 103, 110, 115, 118, 172, 176, 194, 298, 305
Woodson, 109
Woodward, 48, 58, 172, 263, 303
Woody, 48
Wool, 59, 183, 210
Woolard, 212
Wooster, 91, 125, 293
Wooters, 76
Wootters, 258
Worcester, 217
Worden, 3, 304
Wordsworth, 21
Wormley, 49
Worrell, 49
Worster, 72, 79, 124, 214, 233
Worth, 59, 122
Worthington, 48, 49, 222, 279
Wren, 95
Wright, 14, 38, 76, 78, 94, 96, 142, 174, 194, 212, 279
Wrightson, 73
Wroe, 48, 49, 135
Wyatt, 96
Wylie, 48, 207, 312
Wyman, 112, 193
Wynn, 98
Wynne, 205
Wyse, 6, 91

Y

yacht **Wanderer**, 148
yacht **Zinga**, 224
Yale, 291
Yale College, 243
Yancey, 160
Yanner, 116
Yates, 49, 76, 109, 157, 161, 168, 272, 290
Yauger, 63
Yeabower, 309
Yeatman, 58
Yeaton, 49

Yerger, 141
Yerkes, 186
Yonnells, 80
Yooward, 174
York, 55, 100
Yorke, 72
Young, 29, 38, 49, 78, 81, 84, 88, 89, 94, 98, 114, 119, 130, 136, 145, 155, 157, 171, 175, 176, 189, 205, 211, 216, 218, 220, 223, 247, 248, 255, 274, 279, 292, 317
Yulee, 82, 140, 184

Z

Zabriskie, 240
Zacharie, 98
Zane, 207
Zantzinger, 304
Zappone, 79
Zimerman, 188
Zimmerman, 84
Zindorf, 5
Zouresky, 275

Other Heritage Books by Joan M. Dixon:

National Intelligencer *Newspaper Abstracts*
Special Edition: The Civil War Years
Volume 1: January 1, 1861-June 30, 1863
National Intelligencer *Newspaper Abstracts*
Special Edition: The Civil War Years
Volume 2: July 1, 1863-December 31, 1865

National Intelligencer *Newspaper Abstracts*
Volume 1840 - Volume 1860
National Intelligencer *Newspaper Abstracts, 1838-1839*
National Intelligencer *Newspaper Abstracts, 1836-1837*
National Intelligencer *Newspaper Abstracts, 1834-1835*
National Intelligencer *Newspaper Abstracts, 1832-1833*
National Intelligencer *Newspaper Abstracts, 1830-1831*
National Intelligencer *Newspaper Abstracts, 1827-1829*
National Intelligencer *Newspaper Abstracts, 1824-1826*
National Intelligencer *Newspaper Abstracts, 1821-1823*
National Intelligencer *Newspaper Abstracts, 1818-1820*
National Intelligencer *Newspaper Abstracts, 1814-1817*
National Intelligencer *Newspaper Abstracts, 1811-1813*
National Intelligencer *Newspaper Abstracts, 1806-1810*
National Intelligencer *Newspaper Abstracts, 1800-1805*

www.ingramcontent.com/pod-product-compliance
Lightning Source LLC
Chambersburg PA
CBHW051624230426
43669CB00013B/2175